'Teeth and Talons Whetted for Slaughter'

Studies in the History of Church and Theology

Edited by
Andreas J. Beck. Leuven

In cooperation with
Ulrich L. Lehner, Milwaukee
Kenneth P. Minkema. New Haven
Richard A. Muller, Grand Rapids
Peter Opitz, Zurich
Ulrike Treusch, Giessen

Volume 5

1. Pieter L. Rouwendal, *Predestination and Preaching in Genevan Theology from Calvin to Pictet.*
2. Antonie Vos, *John Duns Scotus. A Life.*
3. Willem J. op 't Hof, *The Ice Broken. Puritan Influences on the Netherlands in the Seventeenth Century*, Volume 1.
4. Willem J. op 't Hof, *The Ice Broken. Puritan Influences on the Netherlands in the Seventeenth Century,* Volume 2.

Piet Slootweg

'Teeth and Talons Whetted for Slaughter'

Divine Attributes and Suffering Animals
in Historical Perspective (1600-1961)

Summum

Cover design: Brainstorm
Typesetting: Gewoon Geertje

ISBN 9789492701367 (hardcover)
ISBN 9789492701411 (paperback)
ISBN 9789492701428 (e-book))

© 2022 Summum Academic Publications, Kampen, The Netherlands.
All rights reserved. No part of this publication may be reproduced, translated, stored in a retrieval system, or transmitted in any form by any means, electronic, mechanical, photocopying, recording or otherwise, without prior written permission from the publisher.

'For let us pause for one moment to think of what suffering in nature means. Some hundreds of millions of years ago some millions of millions of animals must be supposed to have been sentient. (…) Looking to at the outcome, we find (…) teeth and talons whetted for slaughter, hooks and suckers moulded for torment—everywhere a reign of terror, hunger, and sickness, with oozing blood and quivering limbs, with gasping breath and eyes of innocence that dimly close in deaths of brutal torture!'

George Romanes, *A Candid Examination of Theism* (London: Trübner & Co., 1878), 171.

Preface

This book is the slightly modified version of a dissertation that I defended in November 2021 to obtain the degree of doctor of philosophy at the Vrije Universiteit in Amsterdam. A work like this would not have been possible without the help of others. In the first place, I would like to thank here my supervisor Prof. Gijsbert van den Brink. Thanks to his guidance, I was able to study in a scientifically sound way a subject that had occupied me for many years. I also mention my co-supervisors Dr. Ab Flipse and Dr. Bethany Sollereder. Dr. Flipse ensured that I could place my work in the required historical context, and Dr. Sollederer guarded me from gaps and omissions in my discussion of contemporary theological views on animal suffering. I have also benefited greatly from discussions with friends who share my interest in this topic. Of these, I mention Dr. Johan Hegeman, Dr. Jan Poortman, and Prof. Mart-Jan Paul. My special thanks also go to Dr. John van Eck for his help in interpreting the Latin texts and alerting me to sources that would certainly have escaped my attention without his directions. Last but not least, I thank my wife Hankie. Not only was she willing to accept that after finishing a time-consuming career in medicine I was embarking on a path that again left little time for domestic duties, but her down-to-earth look also helped me translate complex reasoning into clear language.

In my journey through time, I have met many authors who have struggled with the question of how an animal world in which violent death is the rule rather than the exception can be reconciled with the belief that everything was created by someone of whom the psalmist tells us that 'his compassion is over all that he has made' (Psalm 145:9, NRSV). What struck me most was that all these authors held fast to the belief in a God who intends good for all his creatures. Their attempts to reconcile this belief with a reality that often suggests the opposite may sometimes appear somewhat contrived or implausible, but that does not diminish the sincerity of their desire to honor God as the Creator of all that lives. In this sense they served as examples for me to follow. To what extent I have succeeded in this, I leave to the reader to judge. For what serves God's glory I am grateful and for what does not reach that goal I ask for forgiveness.

Bennekom, March 2022.

Contents

CHAPTER 1
Introduction: Reconciling Animal Suffering with Divine Goodness and Justice — 17
1.1. Background — 17
1.2. The Main Research Question — 19
1.3. Relevance of the Subject — 20
1.4. Method — 21
1.5. Content of the Chapters — 27

CHAPTER 2
Only for Our Use. Animals and Divine Attributes from Irenaeus to Calvin (200–1600) — 27
2.1. Introduction — 27
2.2. Method — 29
2.3. The Literary Sources — 30
  2.3.1. The Patristic Period — 30
    2.3.1.1 Irenaeus (c.140–c.202) — 30
    2.3.1.2. Theophilus of Antioch († c.183) — 32
    2.3.1.3. Origen (184/185–253/254) — 34
    2.3.1.4. Lactantius (c.250–320) — 34
    2.3.1.5. Athanasius (c.296–373) — 35
    2.3.1.6. Cyril (c.313–386?) — 36
    2.3.1.7. Arnobius († c.330) — 36
    2.3.1.8. Basil the Great (c.330–379) — 39
    2.3.1.9. Gregory of Nyssa (c.335–c.395) — 41
    2.3.1.10. Ambrose (339–397) — 42
    2.3.1.11. John Chrysostom (c.349–407) — 43
    2.3.1.12. Augustine (354–430) — 44
    2.3.1.13. Common Trends in the Patristic Age — 50
  2.3.2. The Medieval Period — 53
    2.3.2.1. Hugh of St. Victor (c.1096–1141) — 52
    2.3.2.2. Thomas Aquinas (1225–1274) — 54
    2.3.2.3. Bestiaria — 56
  2.3.3. The Period of the Reformations — 59
    2.3.3.1. Martin Luther (1483–1546) — 59
    2.3.3.2. John Calvin (1509–1564) — 63

2.4. Discussion 67
   2.4.1. Do Animals Suffer? 68
   2.4.2. Did Predation Occur in the Uncorrupted Creation? 69
   2.4.3. Humanity Lost Dominion Over the Animals 70
   2.4.4. Animal Natures Changed for the Worse 70
2.5. Conclusion 73

CHAPTER 3
Eclipse of Eden. Animals and Divine Attributes in Early Modernity (1600–1709)   75

3.1. Introduction 75
3.2. Poetic Reflections 76
3.3. The Book of Scripture Revised 78
3.4. The Book of Nature Revised 80
3.5. Political and Religious Background 81
3.6. Early-Modern Science 83
3.7. Method 86
3.8. The Literary Sources 88
   3.8.1. Edward Topsell (c.1572–1625) 88
   3.8.2. Nicholas Gibbons (c.1600) 90
   3.8.3. Andrew Willet (1562–1621) 92
   3.8.4. Thomas Draxe (†1618) 94
   3.8.5. Godfrey Goodman (1583–1656) 95
   3.8.6. Edward Elton (1569–1624) 98
   3.8.7. George Hakewill (1578–1649) 99
   3.8.8. George Walker (1581–1651) 101
   3.8.9. Thomas Browne (1605–1682) 104
   3.8.10. Kenelm Digby (1603–1665) 106
   3.8.11. John Waite (c.1666) 107
   3.8.12. Henry More (1614–1687) 109
   3.8.13. John Wilkins (1614–1672) 113
   3.8.14. Richard Baxter (1615–1691) 115
   3.8.15. Samuel Gott (1614–1671) 116
   3.8.16. Thomas Hodges (1600–1672) 118
   3.8.17. Ralph Cudworth (1617–1688) 119
   3.8.18. Stephen Charnock (1628–1680) 121
   3.8.19. Richard Franck (1624?–1708) 124
   3.8.20. Robert Boyle (1627–1691) 125
   3.8.21. John Ray (1627–1705) 127
   3.8.22. John Edwards (1637–1716) 128
   3.8.23. Thomas Emes (†1707) 131

3.8.24.	John Norris (1657–1712)	132
3.8.25.	John Witty (c.1682–1712)	134
3.8.26.	Thomas Robinson (†1719)	135
3.9. Discussion		136
3.9.1.	Animal Death and Predation	136
3.9.2.	Suffering Animals and Divine Benevolence	140
	3.9.2.1. Adam Guilty	141
	3.9.2.2. Are Animals Able to Suffer?	142
	3.9.2.3. The Joys Outweigh the Sufferings	147
	3.9.2.4. The Argument from Design	147
	3.9.2.5. Serving a Greater Good	148
	3.9.2.6. A Blissful Future Awaits.	148
3.9.3.	Conformists and Dissenters	149
3.10. Conclusion		151

CHAPTER 4
Links in a Chain. Concerns with Animals in the Age of Enlightenment (1710–1799) — **153**

4.1. Introduction		152
4.2. Attitude to Animals		154
4.3. The Argument from Design		158
4.4. New Views on the Living World		162
4.5. Method		165
4.6. The Literary Sources		166
4.6.1.	William Derham (1657–1735)	166
4.6.2.	Bernard Nieuwentijt (1654–1718)	167
4.6.3.	Bernard Mandeville (1670–1733)	169
4.6.4.	William King (1650–1729)	171
4.6.5.	Guillaume-Hyacinthe Bougeant (1690–1743)	173
4.6.6.	John Hildrop (1682–1756)	175
4.6.7.	Isaac Watts (1674–1748)	178
4.6.8.	David Hartley (1705–1757)	181
4.6.9.	John Hill (1706/1714/1716?–1775)	184
4.6.10.	Soame Jenyns (1704–1787)	186
4.6.11.	John Wesley (1703–1791)	192
4.6.12.	Thomas Amory (1691?–1788)	201
4.6.13.	Capel Berrow (1716–1782)	202
4.6.14.	Richard Dean (fl. 1768)	204
4.6.15.	James Rothwell (fl. 1769)	207
4.6.16.	John Bruckner (1726–1804)	209
4.6.17.	Humphry Primatt (1735–1776/7)	211

	4.6.18. Joseph Priestly (1733–1804)	213
	4.6.19. Thomas Balguy (1716–1785)	215
	4.6.20. William Smellie (1740–1795)	216
4.7.	Discussion	220
	4.7.1. Animals Suffer Because Adam Sinned	221
	4.7.2. Animals Will Be Compensated in a Blessed Afterlife	223
	4.7.3. Animals Suffer as Punishment	223
	4.7.4. Animals Suffer for the Goodness of the Whole	224
	4.7.5. Preliminary Summary	226
	4.7.6. Dissenting Voices	226
4.8.	Conclusion	227

CHAPTER 5
A Tale of Two Darwins. Concerns with Animals in the First Half of the Nineteenth Century (1800–1859) — 229

5.1.	Introduction	229
5.2.	Natural Theology and Geology	233
	5.2.1. The Waning Tide of Natural Theology	233
	5.2.2. Geology Enters the Scene	237
5.3.	Method	245
5.4.	The Literary Sources	246
	5.4.1. Erasmus Darwin (1731–1802)	246
	5.4.2. William Paley (1743–1805)	249
	5.4.3. Thomas Gisborne (1758–1846)	253
	5.4.4. Alexander Crombie (1760–1842)	254
	5.4.5. Thomas Chalmers (1780–1847)	256
	5.4.6. William Buckland (1784–1856)	259
	5.4.7. Charles Bell (1774–1842)	262
	5.4.8. Peter Mark Roget (1779–1869)	263
	5.4.9. William Prout (1785 1850)	264
	5.4.10. William Kirby (1759–1850)	265
	5.4.11. The 'Scriptural Geologists'	269
	5.4.12. John Pye Smith (1774–1851)	276
	5.4.13. Hugh Miller (1802–1856)	280
	5.4.14. John Anderson (1796–1864)	281
	5.4.15. Paton James Gloag (1823–1906)	282
	5.4.16. New Ideas from the New World	285
	5.4.17. Flies in the Ointment	299
	5.4.18. Charles Darwin (1809–1882)	293

5.5. Discussion		299
5.5.1.	Adam Is to Blame	300
5.5.2.	For the Goodness of the Whole	300
5.5.3.	Beyond Our Understanding	302
5.5.4.	Just a Stick to Beat the Dog?	302
5.6. Conclusion		304

CHAPTER 6
After Darwin. The Divine Attributes at Stake (1860–1961) 307

6.1. Introduction		307
6.2. Background		311
6.3. Whatever Is Is Right		315
6.3.1.	Christian Anti-Darwinians About Animal Suffering and Divine Benevolence	316
6.3.2.	Christian Darwinists About Animal Suffering and Divine Benevolence	320
6.4. Behind the Veil		336
6.5. God and Nature at Strife		343
6.6. Discussion		350
6.7. Conclusion		353

CHAPTER 7
Epilogue. A Comparison of Past and Present Arguments 355

7.1. Introduction		355
7.2. Past and Present Views Compared		358
7.2.1.	Animals Do Not Suffer at All	358
7.2.2.	Animal Suffering Does Not Count as Evil	362
7.2.3	Animals Have Deserved Their Sufferings	365
7.2.4.	Adam Is to Blame	373
7.2.5.	Evil Spirits Are to Blame	376
7.2.6.	Biology Is a 'Package Deal'	378
7.2.7.	Animal Suffering Is a Necessary Condition for Securing Greater Goods	381
7.2.8.	Animals Receive After-life Compensation	387
7.3. New Wine in Old Wineskins?		390
7.4. Brief Theological Postscript		395
7.5. Conclusion		397

Summary	399
Bibliography	411

Index of Names 483
ndex of Terms 491
Index of Holy Scripture 494

General notes

1. The use of symbols and italics in the quotations conforms to the original text unless otherwise indicated.
2. The text in the quotes between square brackets has been added to clarify the quote without compromising the content or for typographical reasons.
3. All quotations from the Bible are taken from the New Revised Standard Version (NRSV) unless, for historical accuracy, quoting from the King James Version (KJV) was considered to be more appropriate.

Chapter 1

Introduction: Reconciling Animal Suffering with Divine Goodness and Justice

1.1. Background

In 2013, a Dutch minister wrote a book in which one of the topics concerns the question why God could permit so much human and animal misery. Why did God create the world through an evolutionary process which involves the death and extinction of huge numbers of animals and animal species over millions of years? For this writer, a negative outcome of his ponderings was inevitable. Nature is full of death and grief, and therefore, the time-honored concept of a personal God who is benevolent towards all of his creatures has to be rejected:

I not only have no answer to the indescribable suffering that is connected with evolution – I neither detect any sense, purpose or direction in this entire process. I do not recognize the hand of God in it.[1]

Indeed, we may ask whether a life cycle that depends on eating or being eaten is compatible with a creation in which 'the heavens are telling the glory of God; and the firmament proclaims His handiwork'.[2] Are animal death and extinction manifestations of a good God's majesty and power? When creating the world, did God use animal death and extinction as a means to realize his intentions? These ideas may at first sight be difficult to reconcile with the image of a good God who cares for each of his creatures. Charles Darwin's concerns in this regard as expressed in one of his letters are well known:

With respect to the theological view of the question; this is always painful to me.—I am bewildered.—I had no intention to write atheistically. But I own that I cannot see, as plainly as others do, & as I sh'd wish to do, evidence of design & beneficence on all sides of us. There seems to me too much misery in the world. I cannot persuade myself that a beneficent & omnipotent God would have designedly created the Ichneumonidæ with

---

[1] Linden, C. ter. 2013. *Wat doe ik hier in GODSNAAM. Een Zoektocht* [What Do I Do Here for God's Sake? A Quest]. Uitgeverij De Arbeiderspers, Utrecht: 85. 'Ik heb niet alleen geen antwoord op het onbeschrijfelijke lijden dat met het evolutieproces gegeven is—ik bespeur ook geen enkele zin, doel, of richting in dit hele proces. Ik herken er de hand van God niet in.'

[2] Psalm 19:1. (NRSV)

whence his frame had been taken.'[14] Adam lost his immortality, but the Church father is silent about whether the same fate befell the animals. He may have thought this to be unimportant given his premise that '[a]ll things have been created for the service of man'.[15] Moreover, the fact that Irenaeus made immortality dependent on the breath of life that God breathed into Adam makes it unlikely that he would attribute this quality to the animals as well. This action of God is, after all, exclusively linked to the creation of humankind.[16]

Animals matter because of their usefulness to humans. This usefulness will be fully restored in the future, as on the new earth the animals will be again 'in subjection to man'.[17] Possibly, Irenaeus interpreted the return to the original plant-based diet not so much as something beneficial to the animals, but as a sign of the reinstatement of humanity's rule over them. The well-being of the animals themselves seems no matter of concern, given his silence on this.

2.3.1.2. Theophilus of Antioch († c.183)

In the same way as Irenaeus, Theophilus[18] assumed a relationship between animal behavior and human sin. In his apology to Autolycus, he is clear about this:

> They [the animals] were not created evil or poisonous, for nothing was originally created evil by God; everything was good and *very good*. The sin of man made them evil, for when man transgressed they transgressed

---

14 Irenaeus. 'Proof of the Apostolic Preaching': 56. Cf. Hiestand, G. 2018. 'A More Modest Adam: an Exploration of Irenaeus' Anthropology in Light of the Darwinian Account of Pre-Fall Death' in: *Bulletin of Ecclesial Theology* 5 (1): 55-72.

15 Irenaeus 'Against Heresies': 1372 (V.29.1). See for Irenaeus' anthropocentricity also Steenberg, *Irenaeus on Creation*: 145-150.

16 For Irenaeus' thoughts about the first humans's immortality, their maturation to perfection, the thwarting of that maturation by Adam's transgression, and the restoration by Christ, see Brown, R.F. 1975. 'On the Necessary Imperfection of Creation: Irenaeus' *Adversus Haereses IV, 38*' in: *Scottish Journal of Theology* 28 (1): 17-25; Steenberg, *Irenaeus on Creation*: 120-138, 191-192.

17 The fact that Irenaeus assigns animals a place in the new creation should not be understood in the sense that they are resurrected animals entitled to a place in the new creation as compensation for the suffering they endured in the old one. The idea that God should compensate animals for undeserved suffering in this way did not arise until the eighteenth century, well over a millennium and a half after Irenaeus. I will return to this in Chapter 4.

18 Grant, R.M. 1947. 'Theophilus of Antioch to Autolycus' in: *The Harvard Theological Review* 40 (4): 227-256; Bouteneff, *Beginnings*: 68-73. For Theophilus' influence on Irenaeus, see Steenberg, *Irenaeus on Creation*: 88-92.

with him. If the master of a house does well, his servants necessarily live properly; if the master sins, his slaves sin with him. Just so, it turned out that man, the master sinned and the slaves sinned with him. Whenever man again returns to his natural state and so no longer does evil, they too will be restored to their original tameness.[19]

It should be noticed that Theophilus used the qualifications *evil* and *venomous,* in this way restricting animal attributes we dislike to properties that adversely influence human well-being. He was not so much concerned with the way the animals interact with each other but with their submission to humans. The proper relationship between the human race and the animals is lost through the fall, but will be restored in due time. Elsewhere, however, Theophilus gave the animals a more independent role. 'But also the great fish and the carnivorous birds are in the likeness of greedy men and transgressors. For as marine animals and birds are of one nature, and some remain in their natural state, not harming those weaker than themselves but keeping the law of God and eating seeds from the earth, but some of them transgress the law of God, eating flesh and harming those weaker than themselves'.[20] Interestingly, predation appears to be not a consequence of Adam's transgression here, but the result of a deliberate decision of the animals themselves to violate a divine law. Apparently, they are not only innocent victims but also active perpetrators.[21]

Predation would thus be the result of animals' disobedience, but I doubt that Theophilus would also believe that sin—either human or animal—had changed the animals from immortal to mortal. Immortality was a privilege not even granted to Adam. 'God (…) made him neither immortal nor mortal but (…) capable of both. If he were to turn to the life of immortality by keeping the commandment of God, he would win immortality as a reward from him and would become a god; but if he turned to deeds of death, disobeying God, he would be responsible for his

---

19 Theophilus. 1970. *Theophilus of Antioch ad Autolycum. Text and Translation by Robert M. Grant.* Clarendon Press, Oxford: 55 (II.17).
20 Theophilus, *Ad Autolycum*: 53, 55 (II.16).
21 See for an active role for the animals in transgressing divine rules also Evans, J.M. 1968. *Paradise Lost and the Genesis Tradition.* Clarendon Press, Oxford: 84. 'As the Rabbis had noticed, the terms of this curse seem to imply that the other animals were included in it. Their consequent assumption that Eve must have distributed the forbidden fruit to all the beasts of the field was perhaps in Theophilus' mind.' The idea that animals may consciously violate divine laws reappears with some twenty-first-century theologians. I will return to this in Chapter 7.

own death.'²² In short, the disobedience of humans and animals has corrupted creation; God is not to blame.

2.3.1.3. Origen (184/185–253/254)

Origen²³ wrote extensively on creation, not so much in terms of animal suffering but emphasizing the dominant role in the creation assigned to humans: 'The Creator, then, has made everything to serve the rational being and his natural intelligence.'²⁴ The animals serve to meet humanity's physical needs. The animal world has no value in itself, as is clear from a metaphor Origen derived from midwifery: as the role of the placenta and the membranes is to feed and protect the fetus in the womb, in that same way, the role of animals is to meet the needs of men.²⁵ These needs are also spiritual. Origen, in his pioneering work on the allegorical reading of Scripture, pointed out that the animal world reflects our inner self and that the command given to Adam to rule over the animals is in fact an urge to control our emotions. Not the animals in the outside world but the beasts within matter.²⁶

2.3.1.4. Lactantius (c.250–320)

Lactantius, an early Christian author who also was a tutor of a son of Constantine, the first Christian Roman emperor, wrote his *Divine Institutes* to defend the Christian faith against the criticisms of pagan Rome.²⁷ In these writings, several text fragments are devoted to animals and their attributes.

It is a foregone conclusion for Lactantius that animals are 'completely mortal'²⁸ as 'they are earthly, and they do not get immortality which is of

---

22 Theophilus, *Ad Autolycum*: 71 (II.27).
23 Bouteneff, *Beginnings*: 94-119; Scott, M.S.M. 2012. *Journey Back to God. Origen on the Problem of Evil*. Oxford University Press, Oxford.
24 Origen. 1965. *Contra Celsum. Translated with an Introduction & Notes by Henry Chadwick*. Cambridge University Press, Cambridge: 246 (IV.78).
25 Origen, *Contra Celsum*: 243 (IV.74).
26 Harrison, P. 1999. 'Subduing the Earth: Genesis 1, Early Modern Science, and the Exploitation of Nature' in: *The Journal of Religion* 79: 86-109; Steiner, *Anthropocentrism and Its Discontents*: 119-122; Benjamins, 'The Analogy between Creation and the Biblical Text in Origen of Alexandria' in: Vanderjagt & van Berkel, *The Book of Nature in Antiquity and the Middle Ages*: 13-20.
27 Lane Fox, R. 1986. *Pagans and Christians*. Viking, Harmondsworth: 604-605. Cf. Lactantius. 'The Divine Institutes. Books I-VII. Translated by Mary Francis McDonald' in: Dressler, H. et al. (eds.) 1964. *The Fathers of the Church. A New Translation Volume 49*. The Catholic University of America Press, Washington, D.C.: ix-xiii.
28 Lactantius, *Divine Institutes*: 138 (II.9).

heaven'.²⁹ Furthermore, whereas mankind has been given wisdom, such 'wisdom was not given to the other animals, they were endowed and fortified with natural protections'.³⁰ Animals apparently needed attributes for defense, from which it follows that they were not created to live together peacefully. And in contrast to Irenaeus' exegesis of Isaiah's visions as discussed above, Lactantius emphasized that a blessed future should not be conflated with a presumably lost Edenic past. Isaiah's vision does not depict a lost original state to be restored in the future because 'the prophets generally give out and pronounce the happenings of the future as though they were already finished'.³¹

To summarize Lactantius' ideas on the topic of animal life: Animals are created as mortal beings with instruments to defend themselves. Apparently, their death is of no concern, and neither is the possibility considered that they could suffer. It is all included in the creation as intended by the Creator who made anything—also the animals—for the benefit of humanity. This even applies to the animals that we consider harmful. When the Roman philosopher *Cicero* asked why 'since god made all things for our sake, did he put such great power in serpents and vipers? Why did he spread so many destruction-bearing animals over land and sea?', Lactantius had the answer ready: '(…) reason itself and necessity demand that both goods and evils be set before him; goods which he may use, evils *which he may* shun and avoid'.³²

2.3.1.5. Athanasius (c.296–373)

The Alexandrian bishop *Athanasius*³³, well known from his efforts in defending the divine nature of Christ against the Arian heresy, confined the consequences of the curse evoked by Adam's transgression to humanity only. 'Now, nothing in creation had gone astray with regard to their notions of God, save man only. Why, neither sun, nor moon, nor heaven, nor the stars, nor water, nor air had swerved from their order; but knowing their Artificer and Sovereign, the Word, they remain as they were made.'³⁴ To be sure, Athanasius does not explicitly address the animals here as he only mentions the heavenly bodies and two of the four natural elements as remaining in the state in which they were created.

---

29 Lactantius, *Divine Institutes*: 486 (VII.5).
30 Lactantius, *Divine Institutes*: 482 (VII.4).
31 Lactantius, *Divine Institutes*: 532 (VII.24).
32 Lactantius, *Divine Institutes*: 482 (VII.4).
33 Bouteneff, *Beginnings*: 122-123.
34 Athanasius. 'On the Incarnation of the Word' in: Schaff, Ph. (ed.). 1891. *Nicene and Post-Nicene Fathers Series II, Volume 4. Athanasius.* T&T Clark, Edinburgh. Republished by Wm. B. Eerdmans, Grand Rapids: 249-333 (315, § 43.3).

Therefore, one may object that this author cannot serve to support the conviction that, after the fall, animals, kept the state in which they were created. Yet, the phrase 'nothing in creation ... save man only' is quite comprehensive and seems to encompass animals next to the entities that are explicitly mentioned.

2.3.1.6. Cyril (c.313–386?)

Cyril,[35] archbishop of Jerusalem, suffering from ongoing conflicts with the Arians in the same way as Athanasius,[36] had no problems with the way of life of the animals either.

> The command of God (…) said, *Let the earth bring forth wild beasts and cattle and creeping things after their kinds*; and distinct natures sprung from one voice at one command,—the gentle sheep, and the carnivorous lion. (…) Is not the Artificer then rather worthy to be glorified? For what if thou know not the nature of every thing? Are the things therefore, which He has made, without their use? For canst thou know the efficacy of all herbs? or canst thou learn all the advantage which comes of every animal? Even from poisonous adders have come antidotes for the preservation of men. (…) Thus from this varied workmanship, think of the Artificer's power.[37]

First, on divine command, the earth brought forth both carnivorous as well as herbivorous beasts. Apparently, the existence of predation was God's intention and not a sign of postlapsarian corruption. Next, we have to admit our ignorance when we tend to doubt the usefulness of some animals. And finally, everything created is reason for praising the Creator. Animals find their purpose in their usefulness to humanity; any harm they could cause to humanity does not outweigh this aim. That they could suffer, is not addressed.

2.3.1.7. Arnobius († c.330)

During the reing of the Roman emperor Diocletian (284–305), the charge that 'from the time when the Christian people began to exist in the world the universe has gone to ruin, (…) the human race has been visited with

---

35 Bouteneff, *Beginnings*: 122.
36 For biographical details, see Britannica, The Editors of Encyclopaedia. "Saint Cyril of Jerusalem". *Encyclopedia Britannica*, 30 March 2020, https://www.britannica.com/biography/Saint-Cyril-of-Jerusalem. Accessed on 13 December 2021.
37 Cyril. 1839. 'The Catechetical Lectures of S. Cyril, Archbishop of Jerusalem…' in: *A Library of Fathers of the Holy Catholic Church, Anterior to the Division of the East and West…Volume II*. John Henry Parker, Oxford: 95-96.

ills of many kinds' was used to justify the persecution of Christians. This charge prompted *Arnobius*, an early Christian defender of the Christian faith, to write the apology known as the seven books *Adversus Gentes* ('against the Pagans').[38] In this work Arnobius first refuted this allegation by showing that similar calamities such as now afflicting humankind also occurred earlier, so that attributing them to the abandonment of the ancient gods is nonsense.[39] Thereafter, he elaborated on what evil actually is and how God relates to it. In this connection, he also referred to animals, which justifies his place in my survey.

Interestingly, according to Arnobius not everything that gets in our way should be called evil. 'Would you venture to say that, in this universe, this thing or the other thing is an evil, whose origin and cause you are unable to explain and to analyze? And because it interferes with your lawful, perhaps even your unlawful pleasures, would you say that it is pernicious and adverse?' That would be very presumptuous. 'Hellebore is poison to men; should it therefore not grow? The wolf lies in wait by the sheepfolds; is nature at all in fault, because she has produced a beast most dangerous to sheep?'[40] Things we consider evil may 'have regard to the interest of the whole'.[41] In a way that sounds remarkably modern, Arnobius criticizes a common anthropocentric view of nature in such sentences.

Putting things into perspective in this way does not mean that Arnobius denied that evil exists. It is there, but God has nothing to do with it. 'This we are assured of, this we know, on this one truth of knowledge and science we take our stand,—that nothing is made by him except that which is for the well-being of all, which is agreeable, which is very full of love and joy and gladness, which has unbounded and imperishable pleasures'.[42] Hence, Arnobius denied that 'flies, beetles, and bugs, dormice, weevils, and moths, are made by the Almighty King' and anticipates the obvious question who is responsible for them by noting that 'we should not be required in consequence to say who made and formed them'. We can be sure that the 'Supreme Diety' did not create animals 'so useless, so needless, so purposeless, nay more, at times even

---

38 The Seven Books of Arnobius Adversus Gentes, Translated by Archd. Hamilton Bryce and Hugh Campbell, in: Roberts, A., Donaldson, J. (eds). 1871. *Ante-Nicene Christian Library. Translations of the Writings of the Fathers Down to A.D. 325. Volume XIX.* T&T Clark, Edinburgh: 12. For biographical details of Arnobius, see pp. ix-xix. Arnobius' quoted motivation for writing these books is on p. 4.
39 Arnobius, 'Adversus Gentes': 4-14.
40 Arnobius, 'Adversus Gentes': 12.
41 Arnobius, 'Adversus Gentes': 13.
42 Arnobius, 'Adversus Gentes': 123.

hurtful, and causing unavoidable injuries'.⁴³ That we don't know where harmful and dangerous animals come from doesn't matter; there are so many things we don't know.

> For what purpose have so infinite and innumerable kinds of monsters and serpents been either formed or brought forth? what purpose do owls serve in the world,—falcons, hawks? what other birds and winged creatures? what the [different] kinds of ants and worms springing up to be a bane and pest in various ways? what fleas, obtrusive flies, spiders, shrew, and other mice, leeches, water-spinners?⁴⁴

We should '[l]eave these things to God, and allow him to know what is, wherefore, or whence; whether it must have been or not; whether something always existed, or whether it was produced at the first; whether it should be annihilated or preserved, consumed, destroyed, or restored in fresh vigour'.⁴⁵

Like Irenaeus and Theophilus, and in spite of his wider considerations quoted above, Arnobius largely viewed animals from the perspective of humankind's interests. But he differs from his peers in that he did not associate the troubles humans encounter through nasty or dangerous animals with human sin. Adam is not mentioned at all. Arnobius was sure that God has made nothing but what is beneficial for the good of all, and where the things that harm us come from, '(…) we neither strive to know, nor care to inquire or examine'.⁴⁶ He did not worry about animal suffering and death; for him the threat and danger they impose on humans counted as problematic as this was difficult to reconcile with a benevolent Creator. Instead of proposing a solution, he just held that God cannot be responsible for the creation of harmful animals. An inclination towards Gnosticism might be suspected here, since God is disconnected from parts of the material world.⁴⁷

---

43 Arnobius, 'Adversus Gentes': 115.
44 Arnobius, 'Adversus Gentes': 128.
45 Arnobius, 'Adversus Gentes': 129.
46 Arnobius, 'Adversus Gentes': 123.
47 Whether Arnobius indeed is influenced by Gnosticism would be interesting to explore but lies beyond my scope. His ideas about the origin and the attributes of the human soul at least suggest the assumption of other gods. See 'Adversus Gentes': 131. Cf. Simmons, M.B. 1995. *Arnobius of Sicca. Religious Conflict and Competition in the Age of Diocletian*. Clarendon Press, Oxford.

2.3.1.8. Basil the Great (c.330–379)
In the view of *Basil the Great*,[48] creation serves to guide our hearts to our Creator, for 'as the apostle said; "things invisible will be seen and known from the creation of the world by the creatures within it."'[49] Basil proceeded by expounding his thoughts on animals, starting with reflections on their inner life. It is true that they are devoid of reason 'but they possess sensations through their souls. For they are happy in their joy and they suffer in their anxiety'.[50]

Basil did not, however, elaborate on his views on the mental qualities of the animals. Apparently, the relationship between animals and humans is more important than what goes on in the mind of the animals themselves; whales, for example, 'were created for our terror and fright'.[51] And in the same vein, Basil wrote elsewhere: 'So let no one blame the Creator for making with us in the world dangerous animals and harmful snakes, and setting our lives in fear of them. That would be as if one were to find fault with his tutor, for he is his instructor and director to virtue through harshness'.[52] Apparently, the existence of dangerous animals is explicitly intended by God.

Another issue is animal mortality: 'they [the animals] adhere to their forms until their final end is determined for them. (…) The species of each one of the animals and birds are constituted by birth from them, proceeding in the permanence in which they are set until the end of everything occurs.'[53] The animal species is kept intact—Basil apparently did not see any extinction—but its individual members are replaced in a cycle of being born, flourishing, and perishing.[54] For that purpose, all animals are provided with an anatomy fitted for taking the food allotted to them: 'In the animals which regularly only eat flesh he set sharp teeth. These are necessary for them so that they can have flesh as food.' (…) The bear and the lion and the tiger (…) are carnivorous and their nourishment comes from hunting animals.'[55] And this applies not only to the mammals but to the birds as well: 'Their claws are strong and firm, and the beak of

---

48 Bouteneff, *Beginnings*: 125-140.
49 Basil. 1995. *The Syriac Version of the Hexaemeron by Basil of Caesarea. Translated by Robert W. Thomson*. Peeters, Leuven: 8 (1.6).
50 Basil, *Hexaemeron*: 108 (VIII.1).
51 Basil, *Hexaemeron*: 105 (VII.6).
52 Basil, *Hexaemeron*: 134 (IX.5).
53 Basil, *Hexaemeron*: 126 (IX.2).
54 This conviction that God preserves and protects the species from extinction would persist into the nineteenth century when the discovery of the fossils refuted this view. Giving up the idea was, however, not without pain as I will show in Chapters 4 and 5.
55 Basil, *Hexaemeron*: 132-133 (IX.5).

their mouth is curved and sharp and hard, and their wings are rapid for easy hunting' which makes it 'easy for them to tear the food which falls into their grasp'.[56]

The preliminary conclusion is that Basil considered animal mortality and the presence of carnivorous animals with their outfit designed to kill as belonging to the uncorrupted creation. This does not mean that he denied that the fall had consequences for the natural world. But in reflecting on these consequences, he did not go beyond paraphrasing Genesis 3:18. Initially, 'the rose was still without thorns before the curse in the first time; but later that bane was coupled to the beauty of its flower' to remind us of our sin 'through which the earth brought forth thorns and tares'.[57] The idea that Adam's transgression could also have consequences for the animals was not discussed, at least not in his *Hexaemeron*, the series of homilies devoted to the creation.

Surprisingly, however, an opposite view is found in another writing attributed to Basil. The relevant passage deserves to be quoted full length:

> For doubtless indeed vultures did not look around the earth when living things came to birth. For nothing died of these things given meaning or brought into existence by God, so that vultures might eat it. Nature was not divided, for it was in its prime; (…) nor did wild beasts claw prey, for they were not carnivores. And it is customary for vultures to feed on corpses, but since there were not yet corpses, not yet their stench, so there was not yet such food for vultures. But all followed the diet of swans and all grazed the meadows.[58]

In this text, Basil agrees with Irenaeus but unlike that author, he did not attribute the occurrence of predation to the fall of Adam but related it to God's permission to eat animals given to mankind after the flood.[59] 'By this concession the rest of living beings also received the freedom to eat them. For this cause the lion is a carnivore, for this cause also vultures await carcasses.'[60] There is only an indirect connection with the fall of Adam, since predation did not occur until long after that catastrophic event.

---

56 Basil, *Hexaemeron*: 112 (VIII.3).
57 Basil, *Hexaemeron*: 62 (V.6).
58 Basil. 2005. *St. Basil the Great. On the Human Condition. Translation and Introduction by Nonna Verna Harrison*. St. Vladimir's Seminary Press, New York: 53. For the original Greek text, see Smets, A, Esbroeck, M. van. 1970. *Basile de Césarée. Sur l'Origine de l'Homme. (Hom. X et XI de l'Hexaémeron)*. Introduction, Texte Critique, Traduction et Notes (Sources Chrétiennes 160). Les Éditions du Cerf, Paris: 242.
59 Cf. Genesis 9:3. 'Every moving thing that lives shall be food for you; and just as I gave you the green plants, I give you everything.' (NRSV)
60 Basil, *On the Human Condition*: 53.

It is difficult to reconcile Basil's conflicting views on this point; on the one hand he states that predators belong to God's good creation, but on the other hand he denies this with just as many words. In view of this discrepancy, it is of interest to notice that scholars disagree as to whether this text comes from Basil himself or from his younger brother Gregory of Nyssa, the author to be discussed next.[61]

2.3.1.9. Gregory of Nyssa (c.335–c.395)

If we assume that *Gregory of Nyssa*[62] is indeed the author of the text attributed to Basil and quoted above, it is clear that Gregory holds the view that animal death and predation date from after the fall. Like Irenaeus before him, Gregory believed that the current situation is not as God had intended and that, in the future, animals now devouring each other will return to eating only vegetables. In view of this, it is surprising to read that Gregory elsewhere describes how 'the lion, the boar, the tiger, the leopard, and all the like have natural power sufficient for their safety (…) and generally in all there is some protective power implanted by nature'.[63] Noting that the Creator provides animals with what is needed for protection begs the question of what they must protect themselves against in a creation that—as Gregory pointed out—is free from danger.

A contradiction between Gregory's texts is also apparent in his discussion of the consequences of the fall for the first human couple. The garments God made for Adam and Eve to replace the loincloths that they had made for themselves not only served to cover their nudity but also made them share in the nature of the skins' previous owners: '(…) sexual intercourse, conception, parturition, impurities, suckling, feeding, evacuation, gradual growth to full size, prime of life, old age, disease, and death'.[64] Here, too, Gregory gave a picture of animal life that differs from what we usually imagine of paradise.

---

61 Harrison, N.V. in: Basil, *On the Human Condition*: 14-16. Cf. Smets & Esbroeck, *Basile de Césarée*: 13-26; Amand, D. 1971. 'Alexis Smets, S.J. et Michel van Esbroeck, S.J., *Basile de Césarée. Sur l'Origine de l'Homme*. (Homélies X et XI de l'Hexaéméron). Introduction, Texte Critique, Traduction et Notes [compte-rendu]' in: *L'Antiquité Classique* 40 (1): 295-297. Given this uncertainty, I will regard both Basil and Gregory as authors of the text under discussion.
62 Bouteneff, *Beginnings*: 152-166.
63 Gregory of Nyssa. 'On the Making of Man. VII. Why Man Is Destitute of Natural Weapons and Covering' in: Schaff, Ph. (ed.). 1892. *Nicene and Post-Nicene Fathers Series II, Volume 5. Gregory of Nyssa*. T&T Clark, Edinburgh. Republished by Wm. B. Eerdmans, Grand Rapids: 725-726 (725, VII.1).
64 Gregory of Nyssa. 'On the Soul and the Resurrection' in: Schaff, *Nicene and Post-Nicene Fathers II.5*: 799-870 (863). Cf. Ladner, G.B. 1958. 'The Philosophical Anthropology of Saint Gregory of Nyssa' in: *Dumbarton Oaks Papers* 12: 59-94.

And with regard to the mental properties of the animals, we see in Gregory the same thoughts that we already encountered in Basil: '(...) they [the animals] are not only the subjects of nourishment and growth, but also have the activity of sense and perception.'[65] But, again like Basil, he did not attach consequences to this view that could call into question the divine attributes. That 'sense and perception' can lead to suffering was apparently not considered by the two Cappadocians, let alone that this would be something for which God should be accountable.

2.3.1.10. Ambrose (339–397)

Ambrose, the well-known bishop of Milan and teacher of Augustine[66] paid attention to the creation and the role of the animals therein in his *Hexameron*.[67] According to Ambrose, animals are not created immortal. '[A]s God had ordained, all kinds of living creatures were quickly produced from the earth. In compliance with a fixed law they all succeed each other from age to age according to their aspect and kind. (...) The original species of living creatures is reproduced for future ages by successive generations of its kind.'[68] Obviously, Ambrose agreed with Basil that God takes care to preserve the species but does not care for the individual. In a distant future, an English author would put this thought into poetry: 'So careful of the type she seems / So careless of the single life.'[69]

With such a premise, it is not necessary to associate the presence of carnivorous animals with a creation that has lost its original unspoiled state. Ambrose noted how they, as all other animals, are witnesses of the Creator's craftsmanship who provided the carnivores with the equipment fitted 'for waylaying a deer or for dismembering an ox or a sheep'.[70]

That Ambrose accepted animal death can also be inferred from his thoughts about emotions in animals. Referring to the enmity between wolves and sheep or chickens and hawks, he wrote that '[t]here is an

---

65 Gregory of Nyssa, 'On the Making of Man. VIII. Why Man's Form Is Upright; and That Hands Were Given Him Because of Reason; Wherein Also Is a Speculation on the Difference of Souls' in: Schaff, *Nicene and Post-Nicene Fathers II.5*: 727-730 (728, VIII.4).
66 For biographical details, see Brown, P.R.L. "St. Ambrose". *Encyclopedia Britannica*, 1 January 2021, https://www.britannica.com/biography/Saint-Ambrose. Accessed on 14 December 2021.
67 Ambrose. 'Saint Ambrose, Hexameron, Paradise, and Cain and Abel' in: Deferrari, R.J. et al. (eds). 1961. *The Fathers of the Church. A New Translation. Volume 42*. Fathers of the Church, New York.
68 Ambrose, *Hexameron*: 232.
69 See Chapter 5, § 5.2.2.
70 Ambrose, *Hexameron*: 246.

instinct innate in all living creatures which impels them to dread even what they have not yet experienced as harmful. (...) In irrational animals there is a certain innate fear of creatures of a different species to the extent that, even though these animals are irrational, they have a feeling that death is something to be shunned.'[71] In a creation without animal death and predation, such an instinct would be superfluous, because in that situation, there is nothing to fear. In none of these texts did Ambrose refer to anything like a cosmic fall as the cause for animal death and predation, let alone suffering. Out of all animals, only the serpent was cursed.[72] Animal life as observed nowadays is as it was in the beginning.

2.3.1.11. John Chrysostom (c.349–407)

In *John Chrysostom*'s opinion, everything in creation has its own purpose, but what this purpose encompasses may not always be grasped by the human mind. '[T]here is nothing which has been created without some reason, even if human nature is incapable of knowing precisely the reason for them all.'[73] That Adam's fall had any consequences for animal behavior in terms of violence and predation seems unlikely in view of Chrysostom's writing that God deems a creation to which belong 'wild and unclean [birds like] hawks and vultures' as well as 'snakes, vipers, serpents, lions and leopards' to be good, yes even 'very good'.[74] Clearly, Chrysostom considered harmful animals to belong to the original creation. For him, the problem is not that God created carnivorous animals but that these animals are a threat to humans. The authority over the animals has changed due to Adam's sin, animals now becoming terrifying instead of obeying their masters.

> The fact that now we have fear and dread of the wild animals and have lost control of them, I personally don't dispute; but this doesn't betray a false promise on God's part. From the beginning, you see, things weren't like this; instead, the wild beasts were in fear and trembling, and responded to direction. But when through disobedience human beings forfeited their position of trust, their control was also lost.[75]

---

71 Ambrose, *Hexameron*: 307.
72 Ambrose, *Hexameron*: 355.
73 Chrysostom. 1986. 'Homily 7' in: *Saint John Chrysostom. Homilies on Genesis 1–17. Translated by Robert C. Hill. The Catholic University of America Press. Washington D.C.*: 89-104 (100).
74 Chrysostom, 'Homily 10' in: *Homilies on Genesis*: 127-142 (136-137).
75 Chrysostom, 'Homily 9' in: *Homilies on Genesis*: 115-126 (121-122).

From this, it is evident that Chrysostom characterized the prelapsarian human relationship with the animals not as a friendly and peaceful paradisiacal stewardship because that is difficult to reconcile with the description of animals as being 'in fear and trembling'. This exegesis of Genesis 1: 28 –'(…) fill earth and subdue it; and have dominion'— evidently differs from the common picture which assumes that the uncorrupted creation was a place without any fear or threat. This suggests that apart from their relevance for men's well-being, the fate and behavior of animals did not raise any problems worthwhile thinking about for this Father of the Church, his main concern being the loss of humanity's dominion over the beasts. The Lord created everything for our use; due to Adam's fall, this usefulness now is less than it was in the past.[76]

2.3.1.12. Augustine (354–430)

Whereas Irenaeus' thoughts were shaped by his struggle with Gnosticism, *Augustine* faced a similar enemy despising creation: Manichaeism with its dualist cosmology, according to which the cosmos is a battlefield between the forces of good and evil.[77] Recognizing this as a serious danger for the Old Testament account of creation, Augustine felt obliged to defend the Genesis text which was challenged by this Manichaean doctrine.[78] In his *Refutation of the Manichees* as well as in *The Unfinished Literal Commentary on Genesis*, Augustine paid attention to the animals, not only discussing why they were created but also considering their lives. Concerning their relationship with humans, they may be useful,

---

76 Prof. dr. Wim van Vlastuin drew my attention to Chrysostom's sermons on Romans 8 in which he described the creation in which we now live as corrupted and pointed to its groaning and looking forward to its promised redemption. What this present corruption consists of and what it entails for the animals, however, is not further specified by Chrysostom. See Chrysostom. 'Homily XIV' in: Schaff, Ph. (ed.). 1889. *A Select Library of the Nicene and Post-Nicene Fathers of the Christian Church. Series I, Volume 11. Saint Chrysostom: Homilies on the Acts of the Apostles and the Epistle to the Romans*. T&T Clark, Edinburgh. Republished by Wm. B. Eerdmans, Grand Rapids: 784-804.
77 Fergusson, *Creation*: 21-24.
78 See for more details on Augustine's debate with the Manichaeans: Clarke, T.E. 1958. 'St. Augustine and Cosmic Redemption' in: *Theological Studies* 19 (2): 133-164; Hill, E. 'Introduction' in: Rotelle, J.E. (ed.). 2017. *The Works of Saint Augustine. A Translation for the 21st Century. On Genesis I/13…4th printing*. New City Press, New York.: 3-14; Fergusson, *Creation*: 21-24; Miller, 'Cosmos and Exegesis in Late Antiquity' in: Vanderjagt & van Berkel, *The Book of Nature in Antiquity and the Middle Ages*: 57-69. For Augustine's thoughts about the status of animals in general, see Huff, P. 1992. 'From Dragons to Worms: Animals and the Subversion of Hierarchy in Augustine's Theology' in: *Melita Theologica* 43 (2): 27-43; Sorabji, *Animal Minds and Human Morals*: 195-198.

pernicious, or superfluous.[79] But due to sin, the dominion over animals by God assigned to the human race has partly been taken away.[80]

Regarding the food that animals are permitted to eat, his thoughts are a little bit ambiguous. In the *Refutation of the Manichees* Augustine suggested that the text in Genesis 1:30 according to which all animals feed on green grass should not be taken literally. He refers to birds of prey that feed on flesh in this connection.[81] In a later text, however, he wrote that from the current presence of carnivorous animals, '(…) it does not follow that we can only take in an allegorical sense what the book of Genesis says about the green grass and fruit trees being given for food to wild animals of every kind and to all birds and all snakes'.[82]

In the *Literal Meaning of Genesis,* Augustine expounded his views in a more extensive and unequivocal way. Several issues are discussed in this text. For our purpose, the issue of dangerous animals is relevant. On this theme, Augustine wrote as follows:

> The question is also commonly asked about various poisonous and dangerous animals: whether they were created after the sin of man as a punishment or rather had already been created as harmless and only began after that to do sinners harm. (…) [I]t would have been quite possible for these creatures to do no harm when they were created, if no occasion had arisen for punishing vices and frightening people off them or for testing virtue and making people perfect.[83]

Augustine evidently supposed that animals were created as harmless to human beings, a condition that changed after the fall. Being harmless for humans, however, does not imply being harmless for other animals, as can be inferred from the following text in which he seeks an explanation for the evil that afflicts the animals. The way he does this justifies that this text is quoted at some length:

---

79 Augustine, 'A Refutation of the Manichees' in: Rotelle, *The Works of Saint Augustine*: 39-40 (I.16.25).
80 Augustine, 'A Refutation of the Manichees' in: Rotelle, *The Works of Saint Augustine*: 43 (I.18.29).
81 Augustine, 'A Refutation of the Manichees' in: Rotelle, *The Works of Saint Augustine*: 45 (I.20.31).
82 Augustine, 'Extract from Revisions' in: Rotelle, *The Works of Saint Augustine*: 18 (I.10.3).
83 Augustine, 'The Literal Meaning of Genesis' in: Rotelle, *The Works of Saint Augustine*: 246 (III.15.24).

> Someone is going to say: "Then why do beasts injure one another, though they neither have any sins, so that this kind of thing could be called punishment, nor by such trials do they gain at all in virtue?" For the simple reason, of course, that some are the proper diet of others. Nor can we have any right to say, "There shouldn't be some on which others feed." (…) So, all things, properly considered, are worthy of acclaim; nor is it without some contribution in its own way to the temporal beauty of the world that they undergo change by passing from one thing into another. (…) And certainly all such goings-on in the animal world provide us human beings with plenty of salutary admonitions; thus we should observe what trouble we ought to take over our spiritual, everlasting health and welfare by which we so surpass all non-rational animals when we see them (…). None of this would be evident unless there were some beasts that prey on the bodies of others for the sustenance of their own bodies, while the others look after themselves either by their ability to fight back or by their speed in taking flight, or by taking refuge in their hiding holes. And after all, even bodily pain in any animate creature is itself a great and wonderful power of the soul, which is quickening the entire organism and holding it together by being mixed in with it in a manner beyond words, and giving it a certain unity in its own small measure (…).[84]

In writing this, Augustine left little doubt that animals preying or being preyed upon are as God intended them to be in his original creation. Predation is no punishment for sin, as in animals there is no misbehavior for which they deserve to be punished. Augustine then adopts the traditional thought that animal behavior—including predation and its consequences—is intended by God to teach us humans important spiritual lessons. In some phrases, however, Augustine sounds strikingly modern. This is the case when he describes how animals under attack show either fight, flight, or hiding. In doing so, they are guided by a *soul* that strives to maintain unity. In modern biology this phenomenon is known as homeostasis: 'the ability, present in all living organisms, to continuously and automatically maintain their functional operations (…) within a range of values compatible with survival'.[85]

---

84 Augustine, 'The Literal Meaning of Genesis' in: Rotelle, *The Works of Saint Augustine*: 246 -247 (III.16.25).
85 Damasio, A. 2018. 'Why Your Biology Runs on Feelings'. In: Biology – Neuroscience. http://nautil.us/issue/56/perspective/why-your-biology-runs-on-feelings. Accessed on 13 December 2021.

Furthermore, Augustine apparently subscribed to the view, more extensively elaborated (and confirmed) in recent discussions, that to enable animals to avoid physical damage or even death, the ability to experience pain is indispensable.[86] '[T]he pain suffered by animals enables us to see a power in the souls of beasts, which is in its way wonderful and admirable. It shows us how their souls strive for unity in governing and animating their bodies.'[87] Therefore, God provided them with tools and instincts that they need to preserve and defend their life, which would be unnecessary when animals were created immortal. That is not the case—animals 'running their course through every age until old age and death'.[88] And by the way, pain in animals is not something that concerns us for 'we see and hear by their cries that animals die with pain, although man disregards this in a beast, with which, as not having a rational soul, we have no community of rights'.[89] Augustine, therefore, had little appreciation for those who disrupt the faith of the simpler Christians by asking what makes animals suffer.[90]

Also his exegesis of Genesis 3 illustrates Augustine's thoughts about the quality of prelapsarian animal life and behavior: 'When they [Adam and Eve], forfeited this condition, then, their bodies contracted that liability to disease and death which is present in the flesh of animals.'[91] It is evident that Augustine considered that the fall took away the differences between the animal and human condition as far as they concern the status of the body; the postlapsarian human condition became the same as the condition the animals already had from the beginning, subjected to

---

86 About the life-saving effects of pain, see a.o. Murray, M.J. 2008. *Nature Red in Tooth and Claw: Theism and the Problem of Animal Suffering*. Oxford University Press, Oxford: 112-121.

87 Augustine. 'St. Augustine. The Problem of Free Choice. Translated and Annotated by Dom Mark Pontifex' in: Quasten, J., Plumpe, J.C. (eds). 1955. *Ancient Christian Writers. The Works of the Fathers in Translation No. 22*. The Newman Press, Westminster: 211 (III.23.69).

88 Augustine, 'The Literal Meaning of Genesis' in: Rotelle, *The Works of Saint Augustine*: 319 (V.11.27).

89 Augustine. 'On the Morals of the Manichaeans' in: Schaff, Ph. (ed.). 1887. *A Select Library of the Nicene and Post-Nicene Fathers of the Christian Church. Volume IV. St. Augustin: the Writings against the Manichaeans and against the Donatists*. T&T Clark, Edinburgh. Republished by Wm. B. Eerdmans, Grand Rapids: 112-156 (17.59); quote on p. 147. In recognizing that animals can suffer, Augustine was definitely not a Cartesian *avant la lettre*. Yet, as is clear from the quote, he denied that animal suffering is morally relevant.

90 Augustine, 'The Problem of Free Choice' in: Quasten & Plumpe, *Ancient Christian Writers*: 210 (III.23.69).

91 Augustine, 'The Literal Meaning of Genesis' in: Rotelle, *The Works of Saint Augustine*: 518 (XI.32.42).

disease and death. With this view, Augustine concurred with the aforementioned theologian Gregory of Nyssa, who also believed that, after the fall, human nature became liable to weaknesses that until then only animals had to deal with.[92]

Clearly, the idea of a prelapsarian paradisiacal animal life free from ailments is alien to Augustine. There are no big differences between animal life in the uncorrupted and the corrupted creation, animal death and predation being features of both. Only the relationship between humans and animals has changed; at first, all creatures were harmless for mankind, but now, some of them have become dangerous and threaten human well-being or even life. In spite of this, however, anything in creation is as it should be and is put in the appropriate order:

> On the other hand, in the case of cattle, trees and the other changeable and perishable things that lack understanding or sensation or life altogether, it is absurd to think that the defects by which their perishable nature is sullied are subject to adverse judgement. It is absurd because these created things by decree of their creator have been endowed with a pattern whereby, coming and going one after another, they produce a beauty of the lowest order, namely, that of the seasons, such as harmonizes on its own level with the parts of this world. For while it would not have been right to put earthly things on an equality with heavenly things, neither was there any need to omit them from the universe just because heavenly things are higher. Accordingly, when in the region where this sort of thing might fittingly have a place it happens that some things arise as others pass away, the less succumbs to the greater, and the characteristics of the conqueror are assumed by the conquered, here we have an order which is that of transitory phenomena.[93]

---

92 It is unknown to what extent Augustine was aware of Gregory's ideas. Rotelle makes no mention of Gregory in his enumeration of the authors who might have influenced Augustine's thinking about creation. See Rotelle, *The Works of Saint Augustine*: xix-xxii. For more general information on Augustine's knowledge of the texts written by Gregory, see Bartelink, G.J.M. 'Die Beeinflussung Augustins durch die Griechischen Patres' in: Boeft J. den, Oort, J. van. 1987. *Augustiniana Traiectina. Communications Présentées au Colloque International d'Utrecht, 13-14 Novembre 1986*. Études Augustiniennes, Paris: 9-24.

93 Augustine. 1966. *The City of God Against the Pagans. Books XII-XV. With an English Translation by Philip Levine*. Harvard University Press, Cambridge (MA): 17, 19 (XII.4). See for a detailed analysis of Augustine's ideas about animal life as expounded in the *City of God* Huff, 'From Dragons to Worms'.

In this quote from the *City of God,* Augustine explicitly states that birth and death of animals are part and parcel of the creation as intended by the Creator and, to add, that this is not penal. On the contrary, '(...) although the flesh of dead animals be devoured by other animals, no matter (...) what transformation or permutation it undergoes, it still finds itself among the same laws that are everywhere diffused for the preservation of every mortal species, and act as peacemakers in that they match the parts that belong together'.[94] The cycle of life as reigning in the animal kingdom is no punishment connected with the curse that Adam had to face after his transgression. Rather, the death of the one serves to make room for the other, and in his remark that 'the less succumbs to the greater' Augustine, who obviously was a very keen observer of nature, even seems to allude to something Charles Darwin in a distant future would formulate as the 'survival of the fittest'.

Throughout the next centuries, the concept of death as indispensable for the development of life on earth would remain a powerful argument for vindicating the divine attributes. Things we may perceive as faults may on closer examination illustrate the craftsmanship of the Creator just as 'a beautiful picture is improved by dark colours if they are fitly placed'.[95] Preying and being preyed upon are part of God's good creation. And those who complain about it,

> (...) do not take note how vigorous such agents are in their natural character and proper situation, in what a beautiful scale of being they are distributed, how much they contribute, in proportion to their share of beauty, to the universe as if to their common polity, or how they serve our needs as well, if we employ them with a knowledge of their appropriate uses. Thus even poisons, which are deadly if we use them in the wrong way, are turned into wholesome remedies when suitably applied.[96]

All these apparent evils are worthwhile, not only for meeting men's physical needs but also because of the moral lessons offered by them. Indeed, animal behavior is a mirror of the passions of the mind that should be kept under control: 'Restrain yourselves from the grotesque passion of pride; from idle longing for self-indulgence; and from what is

---

94 Augustine. 1960. *The City of God Against the Pagans. Books XVII.36-XX. With an English Translation by William Chase Greene.* Harvard University Press, Cambridge (MA): 173 (XIX.12).
95 Augustine. 1968. *The City of God Against the Pagans. Books VIII-XI. With an English Translation by David S. Wiesen.* Harvard University Press, Cambridge (MA): 517 (XI.23).
96 Augustine, *City of God VIII-XI*: 509, 511 (XI.22).

misleadingly termed "knowledge": then wild animals will be gentled, and livestock brought under control, and snakes rendered harmless.'[97]

To summarize: in Augustine's opinion, God's curse upon the earth as punishment for Adam's transgression spoiled the relationship between humans and the animal kingdom, some animals now turning from harmless to us into harmful. Animals themselves were created mortal and intended to provide food for each other in a cycle of life and death all along. In this regard, there are no differences between the corrupted and the uncorrupted creation.[98] That animals could be liable to suffering can be disregarded as 'we have no community of rights'. Animals are for the physical and spiritual benefits of human beings.[99] Christopher Roedell depicts Augustine as propagating the idea that the fall was not merely a moral but also a physical catastrophe, in which living beings were altered for the worse.[100] This misinterprets, however, the more nuanced conviction Augustine expounded in his writings.[101] Animals did not change for the worse—their relationship with humankind did. Calling this a physical catastrophe betrays an anthropocentrically oriented frame of mind.

2.3.1.13. Common Trends in the Patristic Age

Our survey of the opinions of the Early Church theologians concerning the questions put in § 2.2 is summarized in Table 2.1. None of them explicitly held that the animals were created immortal, and only Irenaeus and Theophilus saw a connection between the fall and predation.[102] Most

---

97 Augustine. 2016. *Confessions. Books 9-13.* Edited and Translated by Carolyn J.-B. Hammond. Harvard University Press, Cambridge (MA): 387 (XIII.30). Cf. Augustine, 'On Genesis: A Refutation of the Manichees' in: Rotelle, *The Works of Saint Augustine*: 44-45 (I.20.31).

98 Cf. Clarke, 'St. Augustine and Cosmic Redemption': 150. 'In his [Augustine's] view, the material world lies under no curse, is afflicted with no stain, no subjection to Satan, is not alienated from God, because of man's sin.'

99 Cf. Clark, G. 'The Fathers and the Animals: The Rule of Reason?' in: Linzey, A., Yamamoto, D. (eds). 1998. *Animals on the Agenda. Questions about Animals for Theology and Ethics*. University of Illinois Press, Urbana: 67-79; Hick, J. 1968 [1966]. *Evil and the God of Love*. Collins, London: 92-93; Steiner, *Anthropocentrism and Its Discontents*: 116-119.

100 Roedell C.A. 2005. *The Beasts that Perish: the Problem of Evil and the Contemplation of the Animal Kingdom in English Thought, c.1660–1839*. PhD Thesis, Georgetown University, Washington D.C.: 29.

101 Cf. Rosenberg, S.P. 'Can Nature Be "Red in Tooth and Claw" in the Thought of Augustine' in: Rosenberg, S.P. (ed.). 2018. *Finding Ourselves After Darwin. Conversations on the Image of God, Original Sin, and the Problem of Evil*. Baker Academic, Grand Rapids: 226-243.

102 It is remarkable that we do not find the thoughts of Irenaeus or Theophilus on this subject with any of the other Church Fathers, nor with the medieval theologians, as

authors limited the consequences of the fall to a corruption of the relationship between humanity and the animals, especially as a result of the loss of authority of the former over the latter.[103] That animals might be liable to suffering is recognized by a few, but no one brings it up as an issue damaging God's goodness and benevolence. In this respect, the outcome of my research does not differ from the findings of others who have investigated the way Christian authors in the first centuries interpreted the relationship between animal suffering and divine attributes.[104] Apparently, the view that death and violence in the animal kingdom would result from the fall of Adam was not as widespread in the Early Church as is claimed by some present-day theologians.[105]

---

we shall see below. The cause of this could be that Irenaeus contended that the restoration of the creation to its former pristine state will precede the renewal of earth and heaven—a view condemned as heretic by later theologians. This may also explain why in many Latin texts of Irenaeus' *Adversus Haereses* the last five chapters of the fifth book, the chapters in which this matter is discussed, are missing, possibly deliberately omitted in order to save the image of Irenaeus as a martyred saint. See Hiestand, '"And Behold It Was Very Good": 18-24. For the question of whether Irenaeus indeed harbored chiliastic ideas, see Smith, C.R. 1994. 'Chiliasm and Recapitulation in the Theology of Ireneus' in: *Vigiliae Christianae* 48 (4): 313-331; Steenberg, *Irenaeus on Creation*: 49-60.

103 The belief that animals rebelled following the fall is also conveyed in Late Antique Jewish sources. In the pseudepigraphal story of Adam and Eve, a serpent attacks Seth and when Eve asks the animal how it dares to attack the image of God, the animal replies that she must blame herself for it. 'It is not our concern, Eve, thy greed and thy wailing, but thine own; for [it is] from thee that the rule of the beasts hath arisen.' See Wells, L.S.A. 'The Books of Adam and Eve' in: Charles, R.H. (ed.). 1913. *The Apocrypha and Pseudepigrapha of the Old Testament in English with Introductions and Critical and Explanatory Notes to the Several Books. Volume II. Pseudepigrapha*. Clarendon Press, Oxford: 123-154 (143).

104 Garvey, *God's Good Earth*: 73-86.

105 Murray, *Nature Red in Tooth and Claw*: 73-80; Schneider, J.R. 2020. *Animal Suffering and the Darwinian Problem of Evil*. Cambridge University Press, Cambridge: 80. Cf. Ladouceur, P. 2013. 'Evolution and Genesis 2-3: The Decline and Fall of Adam and Eve' in: *St. Vladimir's Theological Quarterly* 57 (1): 135-176. 'Paradise, Adam and Eve in the Garden of Eden, the existence of prior state of perfection, the Fall and the expulsion of Adam and Eve from Paradise (…) were not the subject of dogmatic pronouncements in ancient times' (172-173).

Table 2.1. Early Church Theologians on Human Sin and Animal Life*

Author	Animal death before the fall	Predation before the fall	Fall spoiled men's authority
Irenaeus	Silent	No	Yes
Theophilus	Silent	No	Yes
Lactantius	Yes	Yes	Silent
Athanasius#	Silent	Silent	Silent
Cyril	Yes	Yes	Silent
Basil	Ambiguous	Ambiguous	Ambiguous
Gregory	Ambiguous	Ambiguous	Ambiguous
Ambrose	Yes	Yes	Silent
Chrysostom	Yes	Yes	Yes
Augustine	Yes	Yes	Yes

* Authors who did not address the items listed in the table are not included.
# Included because he restricts the consequences of the fall to humanity.

This rather limited interpretation of the curse evoked by the fall also appeared in non-theological writings. In a poem on the *Creation and the Fall* from the Christian poetess *Faltonia Betitia Proba* (c.306/315–c.353/366), one reads: 'On the fourth [sic] day the earth brings forth monstrous wild beasts of all kinds and every species of cattle, without any keeper, in the fields, suddenly from the woods, a wondrous sight. Then the lion begins to fight, then the most deadly tigress, the scaly serpent, and the tawny-necked lioness begin to rage and huge wolves to howl.'[106]

The message is clear and unequivocal: fierce and ferocious behavior as displayed by beasts of prey belongs to the uncorrupted creation. One may conclude that such convictions were shared by a wider circle. Nowhere in Christian circles any concern with the fate of animals was shown. Such a lack of concern, however, was common at the time. The multitude of animals sacrificed in the Roman arenas is just one illustration of this neglect of animals' interests.[107]

---

106 Proba. '*Cento Vergilianus de Laudibus Christi*. Quoted in Latin and Translated in English' in: Evans, J.M. 1968. *Paradise Lost and the Genesis Tradition*. Clarendon Press, Oxford: 116-118.
107 Shelton, J.A. 'Beastly Spectacles in the Ancient Mediterranean World' in: Kalof, A *Cultural History of Animals in Antiquity*: 97-126.

2.3.2. The Medieval Period

As addressed in detail by historian Peter Harrison, the advent of the second millennium witnessed an increased interest for the physical world. Nature no longer only reflected spiritual and allegorical truths, but came to be seen as invested with its own patterns of order worthwhile to be investigated.[108] As a result, the book of nature gained new significance. Nature did not merely prompt to meditation and spiritual growth by inspiring fabulous stories about real and imaginary animals and their wondrous ways of life, but came to be seen as reflecting the power and skills of its Creator. This change of mind was in part fueled by the translation of the biological works of Aristotle into Latin.[109] A Creator-centered view of nature partly replaced an anthropocentrically oriented view. The question 'What does creation teach us about human nature?' turned into 'What does creation teach us about God?', at least in part. Authors representative for this period are Hugh of St. Victor and Thomas Aquinas, the first for his ideas about the book of nature, the second for the detailed way in which he addressed evil in the animal kingdom.

2.3.2.1. Hugh of St. Victor (c.1096–1141)

Hugh of St. Victor eloquently wrote on the wisdom of God as exemplified by his creation: 'By contemplating what God has made, we realize what we ourselves ought to do. Every nature tells of God, every nature teaches men; every nature reproduces its essential form, and nothing in the universe is infecund.'[110] But recognizing and acknowledging the real purposes of God with each of these natures requires a prepared mind. Without this, we are like 'an unlettered person [who] sees an open book and notices the shapes but does not recognize the letters.'[111]

Animals are created because of their utility. This utility encompasses four elements: the necessary, the beneficial, the fitting, and the pleasing:

---

108 Harrison, *The Bible*: 34-63; Harrison, P. 2015. *The Territories of Science and Religion.* The University of Chicago Press, Chicago: 67-71.

109 Harrison, *Subduing the Earth*. For the different opinions on 'the two books metaphor' in the Patristic and Medieval Age, see Tanzella-Nitti, G. 2005. 'The Two Books Prior to the Scientific Revolution' in: *Perspectives on Science and Christian Faith* 57 (3): 235-248; Williams, G.H. 2015 (original edition 1970). *Christian Attitudes toward Nature.* Wipf & Stock, Eugene: 36-43.

110 St. Victor, H. 1991. *The Didascalicon of Hugh of Saint Victor. A Medieval Guide to the Arts. Translated From the Latin with an Introduction and Notes by J. Taylor.* Columbia University Press, New York: 145. By 'every nature' here is meant every created entity, both alive and lifeless.

111 St. Victor, H. 'On the Three Days'. Introduction and Translation by H. Feiss, in: Coolman, B.T., Coulter, D.M. (eds). 2013. *Trinity and Creation. A Selection of Works of Hugh, Richard, and Adam of St Victor.* New City Press, New York: 49-102 (63).

some animals provide items needed, others make our lives more comfortable, and still others are only delightful to look at. God created all of these to display his goodness to human beings:

> God created all other things for human beings. (…) If He created only what was necessary that would be goodness but not richness. So when God also joined the beneficial to the necessary He showed the riches of His goodness. When, however, the beneficial are augmented by the fitting, that manifests the abundance of the riches of His goodness. Then, when to the fitting the pleasing are also added, what does that tell other than how superabundant are the riches of His goodness.[112]

About animal behavior, let alone animal suffering, this medieval scholar remained silent. Apparently, these were not issues that could blemish a good creation or a benevolent Creator who created everything to serve humanity, not only taking care of their daily sustenance but also satisfying their less urgent needs. The immensity of creatures manifests power, elegance manifests wisdom, and usefulness manifests goodness. The anthropocentric view on the non-human creation is evident, leaving little or no room for concerns about animal life proper. 'Hugh considers the visible world and its symbolic value to be important only as far as they are able to guide human beings to the love and praise of the Creator of the universe.'[113] That animal life might contain elements that could blemish the image of this Creator does not enter his mind.

2.3.2.2. Thomas Aquinas (1225–1274)

As compared to Hugh of St Victor, *Thomas Aquinas* was more precise about the concerns raised by apparently evil things in a creation deemed to be good, including animal death: '(…) the whole itself (…) is all the better and more perfect if some things in it can fail in goodness. (…) Hence many good things would be taken away if God permitted no evil to exist; for fire would not be generated if air was not corrupted, nor would the life of a lion be preserved unless the ass were killed.'[114]

---

112 St. Victor, 'On the Three Days': 74.
113 Palmén, R. 2016. 'The Experience of Beauty: Hugh and Richard of St. Victor on Natural Theology' in: *Journal of Analytic Theology* 4: 234-253 (247). Cf. Cizewski, W. 1987. 'Reading the World as Scripture: Hugh of St. Victor's De Tribus Diebus' in: *Florilegium* 9 (1): 65–88.
114 Aquinas. 'Question 48. The Distinction of Things in Particular. Article 2. Whether Evil is Found in Things? Reply to Objection 3' in: Aquinas, T. 2020 [1920]. *The Summa Theologiae of St. Thomas Aquinas. Literally Translated by Fathers of the English Dominican Province. First Part*. The Collected Works of St. Thomas Aquinas. Electronic Edition. http://www.newadvent.org/summa/

Some evils are needed to ensure a greater good. The nature of beasts of prey belong to this category. Aquinas observed that according to some, animals that are now ferocious and kill others had been tame before the fall—not only with respect to humans, but also with respect to each other. He disagreed, however: 'But this is quite unreasonable. For the nature of animals was not changed by man's sin, as if those whose nature now it is to devour the flesh of others, would then have lived on herbs, as the lion and falcon.'[115] It is only humanity that suffers. '[F]or his disobedience to God, man was punished by the disobedience of those creatures which should be subject to him.'[116] Nor did God have immortality in mind for the animals when he created them. They had been denied that quality from the beginning—'animals necessarily become weaker and finally die.'[117]

For Aquinas, anything created serves the goodness of the whole. As is clear from the first quote given above, even things that we consider to be less perfect or evil are indispensable to obtain the outcome intended by the Creator—including animals preying and being preyed upon. In this approach, a new element is introduced in the discussion; the animals are not only there to serve men's physical needs or to represent a source for spiritual or allegorical reflections. They also form an indispensable link in the *Great Chain of Being*: nature's scale that encompasses anything in the creation from the tiny grain of sand to God standing at the top.[118]

Creatures now are assigned a new significance which arises out of their relatedness to each other; the meaning of each animal only emerges as the whole is known.[119] The value of an animal may be restricted to serve as food for a fellow creature—but seen from the whole this *is* a value. The decay of some things is necessary to the flourishing of others.[120] According to Aquinas, everything created not only 'exists for its own

---

115 Aquinas. 'Question 96. Of the Mastership Belonging to Man in the State of Innocence. Article 1. Whether Adam in the State of Innocence Had Mastership over the Animals? Reply to Objection 2' in: *Summa Theologiae. First Part*.
116 Aquinas. 'Question 96. Article 1' in: *Summa Theologiae. First Part*.
117 Aquinas. 'Question 5: On the Punishment of Original Sin. Article 5. Whether Death and Other Such Defects Are Natural to Man?' in: Aquinas, T. 2003. *On Evil*. Translated by Richard Regan. Edited with an Introduction and Notes by Brian Davies. Oxford University Press, Oxford: 250.
118 Lovejoy, *Chain of Being*: 55-66, 73-86; Berkman, J.R. 'Towards a Thomistic Theology of Animality' in: Deane-Drummond, C., Clough, D. (eds). 2009. *Creaturely Theology: on God, Humans and Other Animals*. SCM Press, London: 21-40; Garvey, *God's Good Earth*: 88-90.
119 Harrison, *The Bible*: 42.
120 Aquinas. 'Question 48. Article 2. Reply to Objection 3' in: *Summa Theologiae. First Part*. Cf. Fergusson, *Creation*: 24-30.

proper act and perfection' but 'all parts [also] are for the perfection of the whole'.[121]

Aquinas's worldview displayed a static society in which everybody and everything finds its allotted place and the way of life that is suitable for that position. The whole is more than the sum of the parts, even if this implies that some members merely serve as food for others. This leaves little room for any concerns about animal feelings, let alone their sufferings. Aquinas nevertheless showed such a concern when warning against treating animals cruelly; he did so, however, not out of compassion with the animals but because the 'Lord wished to withdraw them [= us, humans] from cruelty even in regard to irrational animals, so as to be less inclined to be cruel to other men, through being used to be kind to beasts'.[122] And elsewhere: '(…) for since the passion of pity is caused by the afflictions of others; and since it happens that even irrational animals are sensible to pain, it is possible for the affection of pity to arise in a man with regard to the sufferings of animals. Now it is evident that if a man practice a pitiful affection for animals, he is all the more disposed to take pity on his fellow-men.'[123] In brief, animal suffering was definitely acknowledged by Thomas, who considered it not as something blaming the Lord but as a divine means to make us 'better members of the human community'.[124]

2.3.2.3. Bestiaria

Other medieval texts that serve to illustrate the relationship between humans and the animal world are the so-called *Bestiaria*, lavishly illustrated books that contain descriptions of beasts and other products of creation, such as trees and gems. While the allegorical significance of animal life was well covered in the writings of the Church Fathers, these *Bestiaria* disclosed the moral meanings which can be inferred from the created world. The oldest example of these books is the so-called

---

121 Aquinas. 'Question 65. The Work of Creation of Corporeal Creatures. Article 2. Whether Corporeal Things Were Made on Account of God's Goodness?' in: *Summa Theologiae First Part*. Cf. Yamamoto, D. 'Aquinas and Animals: Patrolling the Boundary' in: Linzey & Yamamoto, *Animals on the Agenda*: 80-89.
122 Aquinas. 'Question 102. Of the Causes of the Ceremonial Precepts. Article 6. Whether There Was Any Reasonable Cause for the Ceremonial Observances? Reply to Objection 1' in: *Summa Theologiae. First Part of the Second Part*.
123 Aquinas. 'Question 102. Article 6. Reply to Objection 8' in: *Summa Theologiae. First Part of the Second Part*.
124 Steiner, *Anthropocentrism and Its Discontents*: 131; for Steiner's discussion of Aquinas: 126-131.

Chapter 2: Only for our use - 57

Fig. 2.1. Details of the left panel of Hieronymus Bosch's *The Garden of Earthly Delights* (1490-1510). On the left we see a cat with a mouse, on the right a bear eating an antelope. Museo del Prado, Madrid.

Fig. 2.2. Illustration depicting the fifth day of creation. Note the owl devouring one of his fellow creatures. From Hartman Schedel. 1493. *Schedelsche Weltchronik*. Anton Koberger, Nürnberg.

Physiologus, written by an anonymous author and probably dating as far back as the first quarter of the second century.[125] Many others were added over the years that would follow, the genre obtaining its most widespread distribution from the twelfth to the fifteenth centuries.[126]

The basic assumption advertised in these books was the idea that animals and their way of life illustrate virtues to pursue and vices to avoid. The reason for this assumption is found in Scripture (Romans 1:20), where Paul writes that 'the invisible things are understood by the things that are made'. Real and imaginary qualities of animals were interpreted as means to illustrate Christian virtues and theological truths.[127] Anatomical as well as behavioral features of the animals were presented for pedagogical as well as moral purposes.[128] Even traits that represented moral vices were seen as part of God's good creation—and therefore considered to be good as well.[129] A medieval Dutch manuscript provides a nice summary. 'No creature is so insignificant that it is without any use: it is after all unthinkable that the all-wise God should have created something without reason.'[130]

From this, it may be inferred that all animals—regardless of their nature—are part and parcel of a good creation. Animals preying upon each other are an image of the devil devouring sinners: the fox seizing birds is an image of the devil who may hold sinners within his gullet.[131] The fox itself is not declared guilty, nor is its maker for creating such a bloodthirsty animal. Hieronymus Bosch's famous painting, *The Garden of Earthly Delights* figures as a pictorial representation of that conviction: the Garden of Eden showing a cat devouring a mouse and a bear tearing an antelope in pieces (Fig. 2.1); other contemporary sources showed a similar lack of concern about predation in the good creation (Fig. 2.2).

---

125 Curley, M.J. 2009. *Physiologus. A Medieval Book of Nature Lore.* The University of Chicago Press, Chicago: xviii.
126 Barber, R. 1992. *Bestiary Being an English Version of the Bodleian Library.* The Boydell Press, Woodbridge.
127 Harrison, *The Bible*: 21-27.
128 E.g., it is said of the beaver that if it is chased by hunters, it will bite off its testicles and thus ceases to be worthwhile to the hunters. Thus, anyone who wants to live holy must kill his lust and thereby resist the devil. Paraphrased from Barber, *Bestiary*: 43-44.
129 Harrison, 'Subduing the Earth': 90-96.
130 Maerlant, J. van. 1952. *Het Boek der Natuur. Samenstelling en Vertaling door P. Burger.* Querido, Amsterdam: 8. Quote in main text translated, text in original: 'Geen schepsel is zo onaanzienlijk of het is wel van enig nut: het is immers ondenkbaar dat de alwijze God iets zou hebben geschapen zonder reden.'
131 *Physiologus*: 27.

2.3.3. *The Period of the Reformations*

The magisterial Reformers considered the plain text of Scripture to be more important than the allegorical meanings held in such a high esteem by the aforementioned authors. Even though, as we will see, they did not avoid allegorical interpretations as consistently as they suggested, more literal approaches to the texts came to prevail.[132] Thus, it is not surprising that their ideas about animal life and creation are mainly presented in their commentaries on the biblical text. Leaving aside many other representatives who could be scanned on their views on animals and animal suffering, for the sake of brevity I focus here on Martin Luther and John Calvin, both of whom wrote extensively about various aspects of animal life.

2.3.3.1. *Martin Luther (1483–1546)*

In contrast to previous scholars who wrote on creation, *Martin Luther* read the Bible first and foremost as history, postponing any of the allegorical interpretation so important in the past until he had determined the historical sense of the Scriptures. In this approach of the biblical text, Luther showed the consequences of his Reformation theology and his humanistic scholarship, as emphasized by a modern editor of Luther's works, Jaroslav Pelikan.[133]

---

[132] Harrison, *The Bible*: 107-112; Harrison, 'Subduing the Earth': 96-102; Yarchin, W. 2004. *History of Biblical Interpretation. A Reader*. Hendrickson Publishers, Peabody: xxiii-xxvi and 184-185; Harrison, *The Territories of Science and Religion*: 74-78. The view that it was mainly the literal reading of the Bible that caused a change in the opinion about the animals is disputed by Jon Garvey, who contends that the cause must be sought in the more optimistic view of humankind and its faculties that arose with the transition from the Middle Ages to the Modern Period. To counterbalance this human pride, the Reformers would have felt compelled to emphasize the spoilage of creation due to human sin. In support of this hypothesis, Garvey refers to the increasing appeal at the time of the Greek myth of Prometheus, the Titan who rose up against the Olympic gods and was punished for his hubris. However, the fact that this story was also widely known before, makes this assumption less likely. See Garvey, *God's Good Earth*: 103-115. Cf. Raggio, O. 1958. 'The Myth of Prometheus: Its Survival and Metamorphoses up to the Eighteenth Century' in: *Journal of the Warburg and Courtauld Institutes* 21 (1/2): 44-62. In my opinion, the (revival of the) theory of a cosmic fall attributable to Adam has its origin in the Reformers' wish to emphasize, over against 'softer' Roman Catholic notions of sin, the total depravity of man (and thus the impossibility of meritorious good works as a contribution to salvation).

[133] Pelikan, J. 1961. 'Cosmos and Creation: Science and Theology in Reformation Thought' in: *Proceedings of the American Philosophical Society* 105: 464-469.

One of the examples of Luther taking the Genesis text literally are his thoughts on the subject of animal food: 'I think that in the beginning all trees were good and productive and that the beasts of the field (...) lived on rye, wheat, and other higher products of nature.'[134] Apparently, in his view, animals in the uncorrupted creation were vegetarians. But why are some animals troubling and even threatening to humans? As with their food, Luther left no room for doubt, writing that 'troublesome and harmful creatures were not yet in existence but were brought into being later on out of the cursed earth as a punishment for sin.'[135] When discussing what kind of changes in the non-human creation were evoked by Adam's fall, Luther went into great detail. Some kinds of animals probably did not exist in the uncorrupted creation: 'It is likely that only then [after the fall] were the accursed and pernicious insects produced out of the earth, which was cursed because of man's sin.'[136] Other kinds became nasty or harmful by changing their habits: '(...) if Adam had not fallen into sin, wolves, lions, and bears would not have acquired their well-known savage disposition (...). There were neither thorns nor thistles, neither serpents nor toads; and if there were any, they were neither venomous nor vicious.'[137]

Thus, wolves, lions, and bears changed their habits for the worse and became a danger to humans. And regarding other animals that Luther labelled as pestiferous: either they did not exist from the beginning, or if they did, they didn't do any harm. Because of these changes, mankind should humiliate itself and repent. '[W]hat of thorns, thistles, water, fire, caterpillars, flies, fleas, and bedbugs? Collectively and individually, are not all of them messengers who preach to us concerning sin and God's wrath, since they did not exist before sin or at least were not harmful and troublesome?'[138] In this way, Luther adopts (and adapts) the tradition of interpreting animal behavior as providing moral and spiritual lessons for humans.

---

134 Luther, M. in: Pelikan, J. (ed.). 1958. *Luther's Works. Volume 1. Lectures on Genesis. Chapters 1-5*. Concordia Publishing House, St. Louis: 38.
135 Luther in: Pelikan, *Lectures on Genesis*: 54.
136 Luther in: Pelikan, *Lectures on Genesis*: 72. The postlapsarian appearance of a second set of animals should not be taken as a second creation; rather, it is the product of decomposing corpses. In this respect, Luther goes back to Augustine, who had also already suggested that insects could originate from the decaying bodies of dead animals. Augustine, however, did not attribute this phenomenon to the fall. For Luther it was a result of man's sin. Cf. Augustine, *On Genesis*: 244-245 (III.14.22-23). As such, the idea that insects came from rotting meat was not weird. People started to doubt this only in the course of the seventeenth century, and it was not until the nineteenth century that science would definitively refer it to the realm of fiction.
137 Luther in: Pelikan, *Lectures on Genesis*: 76-77.
138 Luther in: Pelikan, *Lectures on Genesis*: 208.

The changes brought about by fall and curse in the animal kingdom, however, did not mean that animals turned from being immortal into mortal. Here, Luther made a clear distinction: '(…) man was created not for this physical life only, like the other animals, but for eternal life.'[139] This difference between human and non-human creatures is also evident at other places: '(…) although according to his animal life man is similar to the remaining living brutes, he has the hope of immortality, which the remaining living things do not have.'[140] Unlike prelapsarian humans, '(…) the bodies of the remaining living things (…) become feeble and die'.[141]

For other texts from Scripture that are often taken into account when discussing past, present, and future animal behavior, Luther favored an allegorical reading. For example, in his exegesis of the prophesies of Isaiah (11:6-8 and 65:25) about the wolf and the lamb dwelling peacefully together, the Reformer simply wrote that these 'are allegories', the prophet foreseeing that 'the tyrants who formerly preened themselves with their power, wisdom, and wealth will shed their feathers and tufts and with bowed neck confess themselves to be sinners, and they will be harmless.'[142]

A similar allegorical interpretation was given to Psalm 104, where young lions roar after their prey (vs. 21). According to Luther this is to be 'understood as referring to the leaders of the Jews and of the heretics whom Scripture calls lions in many places'.[143] And also Romans 8:19-22—often quoted within the context of animal suffering[144]—should not be interpreted literally; rather, it is a call to turn away from studying creation and to be satisfied with God alone. 'The creation becomes vain, evil, and harmful from outside itself, and not by its own fault, namely, because it is perverted and regarded as better than it really is by the

---

139 Luther in: Pelikan, *Lectures on Genesis*: 81.
140 Luther in: Pelikan, *Lectures on Genesis*: 87.
141 Luther in: Pelikan, *Lectures on Genesis*: 92.
142 Luther, M. in: Pelikan, J., Oswald, H.C. (eds). 1969. *Luther's Works. Volume 16. Lectures on Isaiah. Chapters 1-39.* Concordia Publishing House, St. Louis: 122-123; Luther, M. in: Oswald, H.C. (ed.). 1969. *Luther's Works. Volume 17. Lectures on Isaiah 40-66.* Concordia Publishing House, St. Louis: 393-394.
143 Luther, M. 'Psalm 104' in: Oswald, H.C. (ed.). 1976. *Luther's Works. Volume 11. First Lectures on the Psalms II. Psalms 76-126.* Concordia Publishing House, St. Louis: 316-344 (340). The attentive reader will have noticed the anti-Semitic tendency of this text. In various places in his commentary on this Psalm, Luther makes a disdainful reference to the Jews. For example, he compares the forest from which the wild animals appear at the beginning of darkness with the synagogue, the animals themselves being the Jews that 'became beasts because of their cruelty' (339).
144 See e.g. Southgate, C. 2008. *The Groaning of Creation. God, Evolution, and the Problem of Evil.* Westminster John Knox Press, Louisville, 92-96.

erroneous thinking and estimation or love and enjoyment of man.'[145] Creation does not suffer from the consequences of an event in the past—Adam's fall—but from human behavior in the present: a too high esteem of it which amounts to idolatry. Humankind gives creation the honor which is due only to God. In this way, creation becomes 'vain, evil, and harmful'—not in itself but in its consequences, distracting humanity from worshipping the true and only God. Creation also groans because humans abuse it to sin, so that the purpose for which it was created, the glory of God, is not achieved.[146]

Luther's opinion on animals and their lives before and after the fall thus encompasses several topics. First, there was no predation between animals in the uncorrupted creation; second, after the fall, some animals changed their behavior from peaceful to ferocious, thus becoming harmful to humanity; third, some nasty animals probably were absent in the uncorrupted creation;[147] and fourth, there was animal death before the fall but—in the absence of predation—due to feebleness.

Whether Luther thought that animals (like humans) could suffer as a consequence of sin is not clear, but his plea for a gentle treatment of animals, at least those who are entrusted to our care like livestock or pets, suggests that he did acknowledge that animals might suffer from human misconduct,[148] thus exemplifying the contemporary emergence of some sensitivity towards the animals' interest.[149] But whether this means that predation also implies suffering remains a question not addressed by the

---

145 Luther, M. in: Oswald, H.C. (ed.). 1972 [1540]. *Luther's Works. Volume 25. Lectures on Romans. Glosses and Scholia.* Concordia Publishing House, St. Louis: 360-363 (362-363).

146 Luther, M. 1535. *Ein Christlicher Schöner Trost inn Allerley Leiden und Trübsal / Aus dem Achten Cap. Zun Römern / Sampt der Auslegung des Euangelion Auff den Vierden Sontag nach Trinitatis / Gepredigt durch D. Mart. Luth.* Georg Rhau, Wittemberg. This final line of thought will recur in the Puritans (cf. § 3.9.3). The knowledge that this groaning will come to an end is comforting to persecuted Christians, but it is doubtful whether Luther also includes animals in the deliverance of creation from the futility to which it is subjected given his contradictory writings on the subject, cf. Clough, D. 'The Anxiety of the Human Animal: Martin Luther on Non-human Animals and Human Animality' in: Deane-Drummond & Clough, *Creaturely Theology*: 41-60.

147 Which might imply a second creative act. See for this contested issue Pelikan, 'Cosmos and Creation: Science and Theology in Reformation Thought': 467.

148 Ickert, S. 'Luther and Animals: Subject to Adam's Fall?' in: Linzey & Yamamoto, *Animals on the Agenda*: 90-99, 269n5; Clough, 'The Anxiety of the Human Animal: Martin Luther on Non-human Animals and Human Animality' in: Deane-Drummond & Clough, *Creaturely Theology*: 41-60.

149 Boehrer, B. 'The Animal Renaissance, Introduction' in: Boehrer, B. (ed.). 2007. *A Cultural History of Animals in the Renaissance.* Berg, Oxford: 1-26.

Reformer. As was the case with Aquinas, his warnings against cruelty towards animals might reflect a concern with proper human behavior rather than with the well-being of animals.

2.3.3.2. John Calvin (1509-1564)
John Calvin's ideas about animals can be derived from his *Commentaries* on Genesis, the Psalms, Isaiah, and Romans as well as from the *Institutes*. Also his sermons on Job and on Genesis serve to demonstrate his opinion about animal life and behavior.

On animal predation, Calvin is clear. In his commentary on the Genesis text, he writes that at the time of creation, all beasts fed on herbage; meat did not belong to their daily sustenance.[150] Furthermore, noxious animals like insects entered the world after men's sin, indicating creation's degeneration from a previous better state: '(…) respecting the existence of fleas, caterpillars, and other noxious insects. In all these, I say, there is some deformity of the world, which (…) proceeds rather from the sin of man than from the hand of God. Truly these things were created by God, but by God as an avenger.'[151]

Also, the dominion of humanity over animals changed for the worse: 'This gentleness [of the animals] towards man would have remained also in wild beasts, if Adam, by his defection from God, had not lost the authority he had before received.'[152] Similar thoughts are conveyed in Calvin's commentary on the prophet Hosea. The animals 'were all created, we know, for this end,—to be subject to men. Since, then, they were destined for our benefit, they ought, according to their nature, to be in subjection to us: and we know that Adam caused this,—that wild beasts rise up so rebelliously against us; for otherwise they would have willingly and gently obeyed us.'[153]

Calvin's conviction that, in the uncorrupted creation, we lived in harmony with the entire non-human creation and that all animals prospered

---

150 Calvin, J. n.d. *Commentaries on the First Book of Moses Called Genesis by John Calvin. Translated from the Original Latin, and Compared with the French Edition by John King. Volume First.* Christian Classics Ethereal Library. Grand Rapids: 50. Comment on Genesis 1:24-30.
151 Calvin, *Genesis*: 62-63. Comment on Genesis 2:2. In which way noxious animals entered the creation, by animals changing their habits or by a second act of creation, remains ambiguous in Calvin's writings (just as in Luther's).
152 Calvin. *Genesis*: 82. Comment on Genesis 2:19. In this comment, Calvin agrees with the common feeling of the Church Fathers.
153 Calvin, J. n.d. *Commentaries on the Twelve Minor Prophets by John Calvin. Now First Translated from the Original Latin by John Owen. Volume First. Hosea.* Christian Classics Ethereal Library. Grand Rapids: 95. Comment on Hosea 2:18. Cf. Calvin's comment on Genesis 9:2 in Calvin, *Genesis*: 211-212.

on herbs in the absence of carnivorous behavior, was also expounded in his commentary on the prophesies of Isaiah 11 and 65. In his notes on Isaiah 11, the point was made clear.

> Whence comes the cruelty of brutes, which prompts the stronger to seize and rend and devour with dreadful violence the weaker animals? There would certainly have been no discord among the creatures of God, if they had remained in their first and original condition. When they exercise cruelty towards each other, and the weak need to be protected against the strong, it is an evidence of the disorder which has sprung from the sinfulness of man.[154]

And in the same vein ran Calvin's commentary on Isaiah 65. When wild animals hurt humankind and its livestock, (…) 'this ought to be imputed to his sin, because his disobedience overthrew the order of things'.[155] In these commentaries on Isaiah 11 and Isaiah 65, Calvin made clear that he takes both scriptural fragments as evidence that a blissful past without animals threatening and devouring each other has changed for the worse because of humanity's sin.

Romans 8, where Paul describes the groaning creation, was another source to illustrate the big gap between the uncorrupted creation and the current situation: '(…) all created things in themselves blameless, both on earth and in the visible heaven, undergo punishment for our sins; for it has not happened through their own fault, that they are liable to corruption.'[156]

Next, Calvin's thoughts about animal life can be deduced from his sermons on Job. In Chapters 38–41, the Lord replies to Job's complaints by referring to his power and majesty in creation through pointing to examples of animal behavior. This led Calvin to a new insight, *viz.* that even the corrupted creation shows God's majesty and power: '(…) they [the animals] ceasse not to be as beutifyings of this world, to the end that men might behold the maiestie of God in them.'[157]

---

154 Calvin, J. n.d. *Commentary on the Book of the Prophet Isaiah by John Calvin. Translated from the Original Latin by William Pringle. Volume First.* Christian Classics Ethereal Library. Grand Rapids: 296. Comment on Isaiah 11:6.
155 Calvin, J. n.d. *Commentary on the Book of the Prophet Isaiah by John Calvin. Translated from the Original Latin by William Pringle. Volume Fourth.* Christian Classics Ethereal Library. Grand Rapids: 322. Comment on Isaiah 65:25. It is not predation among animals but the threat to livestock that counts.
156 Calvin, J. n.d. *Commentaries on the Epistle of Paul the Apostle to the Romans by John Calvin. Translated and Edited by John Owen.* Christian Classics Ethereal Library. Grand Rapids: 264. Comment on Romans 8:21.
157 Calvin, J. 1574. 'The clij [=152] Sermon, Which is the Second Vpon the xxxix

Adam may have lost his rule over the animals, they still serve to adorn the creation by reflecting the fingerprints of the Creator, even in their dumbness: '(...) ought not wee to glorifie God's goodnesse towards vs? For who had giuen vs more understanding than the Estridges haue?'[158] Lessons may be drawn from the birds of prey as well:

> (...) looke mee then vpon the Eagles that are bredde to the pray: yea euen from the shell they haue the propertie of sucking blood: and it is a straunge thing that a bird should so feede and nurrish itself with bloud. Behold what a crueltie is put into them, needes therefore must they haue that nature giuen them of another. And whence commeth the diuersitie that is betweene the birdes that live by pray, and the other foules? Must not that difference bee of Gods putting (...) for if all beasts where of one nature and inclination: Gods prouidence should bee more darkesome than it is.[159]

The life of the birds illustrates the diversity in God's creation. To the birds of prey, God gave the need for blood as nourishment and even attributes labelled by Calvin as cruel. In the different natures of the animals, God's working shines more brightly, for if all beasts had the same nature and behavior, God's providence would be less conspicuous. At the end of these sermons on the book of Job, Calvin concluded: 'VVherfore are all things created, but only for our vse?'[160]

Apparently, in Calvin's opinion, everything in the creation serves men and women, if not in a literal way by providing food or labor then at least in an allegorical way by offering moral lessons, and in all instances showing the majesty and power of the Lord, even in the current corrupted stage.[161]

The text Calvin devoted to creation in his *Institutes* reflects the same admiration of God and his works: 'There are innumerable evidences both in heaven and on earth that declare his wonderful wisdom (...) which thrust themselves upon the sight of even the most untutored and ignorant persons, so that they cannot open their eyes without being compelled to

---

Chapter' in: *Sermons of Master Iohn Caluin, vpon the Booke of IOB. Translated out of French by Arthur Golding.* Lucas Harison and George Byshop, n.p.: 713-717 (715).
158 Calvin, 'The clij Sermon': 716.
159 Calvin, 'The cliij Sermon': 718-722 (719-720).
160 Calvin, 'The clv Sermon': 727-731 (731).
161 Huff, P.A. 1999. 'Calvin and the Beasts: Animals in John Calvin's Theological Discourse' in: *Journal of the Evangelical Theological Society* 42 (1): 67-75. The author of this article also discusses Calvin's use of images from the animal kingdom to reinforce his polemic, designating opponents as 'blinder than moles,' 'horses turned into asses,' or 'strutting peacocks' to name only a few of his colorful metaphors.

witness them.'¹⁶² Although God Himself dwells in a light which no human being can approach, his works bear sufficient testimony of his existence and his attributes. There are no excuses for ignoring him or not paying him due honor, even though 'there is no doubt that they [all creatures] are bearing part of the punishment deserved by man, for whose use they were created'.¹⁶³

To conclude this overview of Calvin's writings on the subject, it can be said that this author considered the current state of the creation to be different from the past. Animals—at least some of them—do not feed on herbs anymore as was the case in their original state but now are threatening to humans and their livestock; and noxious insects have entered the creation to be also a nuisance to them. We have lost the authority over the beasts, and life is only possible because God in his mercy restrains the consequences of this disturbed relationship. Nevertheless, in spite of this corrupted state, creation is still a theatre displaying God's majesty and power, clearly visible to anybody, even the dullest.¹⁶⁴ And within this theatre, the animals offer us lessons that should not be neglected, either to urge us to glorify the Creator for divine benefactions or to keep us on the right track.

Clearly, it was inconceivable to Calvin that God could have intended that animals should prey upon each other when he created them. This cruel¹⁶⁵ behavior is humanity's fault and not something jeopardizing any of God's attributes, not even God's justice which apparently tolerates that innocent victims are condemned to a miserable life or even to death as a result of sinful deeds of others. 'It would be greatly presumptuous of us to

---

162 Calvin, J. 1960 [1559]. *Calvin: Institutes of the Christian Religion. In Two Volumes.* Edited by John T. McNeill. Translated and Indexed by Ford Lewis Battles. The Westminster Press, Philadelphia: 53 (I.v.2). Cf. Fergusson, *Creation*: 31-33; Young, D.A. 2007. *John Calvin and the Natural World*. University Press of America, Lanham: 101-137.
163 Calvin, *Institutes*: 246 (II.i.5).
164 This clearly diverges from Hugh of St. Victor who stated that recognizing the meanings of the creation requires a prepared mind. This shift in opinion may be connected with the decline in allegorical interpretation of nature, nature as empirically observed gaining importance.
165 Whether Calvin means cruel behavior experienced as such by the animals or merely being our subjective interpretation, cannot be inferred with certainty from the sources. I consider, however, the latter possibility the most likely because in another text, Calvin denies the animals the capacity to experience feelings: '(...) non quòd praeditæ sint aliquo sensu'. Cf. Calvin, J. 1559. *Institvtio Christianæ Religionis...* Oliua Roberti Stephani, Geneva: 361 (III.xxv.2). Since the details matter here, I have quoted the original Latin text. In Calvin, *Institutes* this text is translated as: 'Not that they [the animals] are endowed with any perception (...)' (989).

raise our voice against God for perpetrating such harsh rigor on the animals, for everything is in His hands.'[166] And in the same vein elsewhere: '(…) if we find it strange that He punishes the animals, which are not guilty in our way of thinking, let us realize that it is not our role to oversee His judgments, which surpass all human understanding.'[167]

2.4. Discussion

The above summarizes how, in the period from the Early Church to the era of the Reformations, authors explained those aspects of animal life that seemingly contradicted the goodness of the Creator. Will these raw data allow the recognition of a common opinion on this subject for this period?

To answer this question, two different issues have to be considered. First: did these authors show any concern about animal life, and especially about predation and animal suffering? And second: if animal suffering and predation were mentioned, did these phenomena raise questions about the goodness or power of the Creator? This distinction is important because, in contrast to assumptions made by others,[168] predation cannot be considered to be synonymous with suffering. The former may be the cause of the latter, but causes of animal suffering other than a violent death in the maw of a predator are also conceivable. Nor does predation always have to be accompanied by suffering when death is sudden and rapid. The one cannot be taken to imply the other, and therefore, suffering and predation have to be discussed separately (§ 2.4.1 and § 2.4.2).

---

166 Calvin, J. 2009. 'Sermon 38' in: *Sermons on Genesis. Chapters 1:1-11:4. Forty-Nine Sermons Delivered in Geneva between 4 September 1559 and 23 January 1560. Translated Into English by Rob Roy McGregor*. The Banner of Truth Trust, Edinburgh: 653. Original quote: Calvin, J. 2000. *Sermons sur la Genèse Chapitres 1,1–20,7*, Supplementa Calviniana 11/1–2, ed. M. Engammare, Neukirchen-Vluyn, Volume 11/1, 429, ll. 8-10: 'Car de disputer icy contre Dieu, de ce qu'il a exercé une telle rigueur et si aspre sur les bestes, ce seroit une trop grande presumption à nous, car tout est en sa main.'

167 Calvin, 'Sermon 43' in: *Sermons on Genesis*: 736. Apparently, Calvin feels an obligation to defend the Creator against his own convictions about justice and injustice. May be the former lawyer shimmers through? Original quote: Calvin, J. 2000. *Sermons sur la Genèse Chapitres 1,1–20,7*, Supplementa Calviniana 11/1–2, ed. M. Engammare, Neukirchen-Vluyn, Volume 11/1, 479, ll. 21-23: 'Et si nous trouvons estrange qu'il punisse les bestes, qui ne sont point coulpables comme nostre opinion le porte, cognoissons que ce n'est point à nous de contreroller ses jugemens qui surmontent tout sens humain.'

168 Cf. Roedell, *The Beasts that Perish*: 6. '(…) predation and suffering, though they are indeed logically separable, were often linked, explicitly or otherwise'.

2.4.1. Do Animals Suffer?

For the period examined, animal suffering appears to be an almost completely neglected theme. Five authors mentioned the subject, all of them just in passing. Basil the Great and Gregory of Nyssa both referred to animals as having an inner life—which may include the ability to suffer—but did not elaborate on this belief when they focussed on predation and animal death. Augustine described animals as being capable of feeling pain, but for him, this attribute serves to preserve life and hence is beneficial. In his thoughts about animal life, Augustine roughly corresponded with Aristotle.[169] The latter was convinced the body of an animal must be capable of sensing by touch [which implies sensation of pain as well] if the animal is to save itself.[170] It is not inconceivable that Augustine may have borrowed his positive interpretation of the meaning of pain from Aristotle. And that sensitivity to pain is something that should be gratefully acknowledged is also Aquinas' view—according to him, however, mainly because of its pedagogical role. Seeing animals in pain will deter us from treating them cruelly; this is beneficial because tormenting animals dulls the sense of compassion so that those who misbehave in this way will more easily treat their fellow humans cruelly as well.

The fifth author is John Calvin, who briefly referred to 'brutes devouring with dreadful violence the weaker animals' in his commentaries on Isaiah and spoke about cruelty shown by birds of prey in one of his sermons on the book of Job. Perhaps in these texts we see the first glimpses of a new attitude toward animals. But this does not alter the fact that the predominant view was that the animals have to meet the needs of humanity; they are created for providing food, garments, or muscle strength, and no one is concerned about what this means for the animals themselves.[171] In brief: yes, animals did suffer, at least according to some—but their sufferings were considered morally irrelevant by all.

---

169 Cf. Byers, S. 'Augustine and the Philosophers' in: Vessey, M. (ed.). 2012. *A Companion to Augustine*. Blackwell, Chichester: 175-187, in particular pp. 176-180. 'Augustine clearly thinks of the soul as the form that accounts for the actual existence of the bodily organism, as Aristotle did' (178).

170 Apostle, H.G. 2021 [1981]. *Aristotle's on the Soul. Translated with Commentaries and Glossary*. Thomas More College Press, Merrimack: 23-24 (B.3), 58-61 (Γ.12,13). Quote on p. 59-61.

171 Cohen, E. 'Animals in Medieval Perceptions. The Image of the Ubiquitous Other' in: Manning, A., Serpell, J. (eds). 1994. *Animals and Human Society: Changing Perspectives*. Routledge, London: 59-80. Cf. Duncan, I.J.H. 2006. 'The Changing Concept of Animal Sentience' in: *Applied Animal Behaviour Science* 100: 11-19; Proctor, H. 2012. 'Animal Sentience: Where Are We and Where Are We Heading?' in: *Animals* 2: 628-639.

2.4.2. Did Predation Occur in the Uncorrupted Creation?

Given the fact that animal suffering was outside the general purview, one would expect that animal predation would not be an issue of major concern either. After all, animals were considered to reflect God's majesty and power as well as to serve as an inexhaustible source for allegorical and moral reflections, irrespective of their behavior. Nevertheless, animal predation turned out to be a topic discussed extensively by Christian authors throughout the centuries as shown in the preceding text. This concern with animal predation clearly arose from the need to explain types of animal behavior that were nasty or even dangerous towards humankind. How could it be that, in a world designed to serve humanity, animals may threaten and even kill those who were appointed as their masters? Only gradually an additional concern about inter-animal predation emerged.

Apart from Arnobius, who could not accept that God created dangerous animals and preferred to leave the problem of their origin unsolved, the opinions on animal behavior vis-à-vis humans were rather straightforward and unanimous. First, God had given the apparently less useful or even harmful animals the role of embodying spiritual or allegorical truths. Through this interpretation, the less pleasant aspects of animal behavior acquired a moral or figurative meaning, thus contributing to the goal that God wants to achieve with his creation. After all, the natural world was not only ordered in such a way as to meet man's physical requirements but also as a repository of eternal spiritual truths. Not only the theological texts but also the *Bestiaria* give ample testimony of this widespread conviction.[172]

Second, an explanation for the existence of less useful or even noxious creatures was provided by Adam's fall. Regarding this event, two lines of thought about the implications of God's curse can be discerned. The first emphasizes Adam's loss of dominion over the animals but does not assume that the nature of the animals themselves changed, which implies—either tacitly admitted or explicitly stated—that the uncorrupted creation already knew predation and animal death. In the second line of thought, Adam's fall not only had consequences for the relationship between the animals and human beings but also changed the nature of the animals themselves. In the next two sections, I will examine how the collected texts and comments above fit into either of these categories.

---

172 Harrison, *The Bible*: 20-21; Harrison, *The Territories of Science and Religion*: 57-67.

2.4.3. Humanity Lost Dominion Over the Animals

Already in Irenaeus, we found the idea emerging that humanity's authority over the animals had been disrupted by Adam's fall. This could be deduced from his belief that on the new earth the animals will obey the resurrected righteous, just as they had obeyed Adam in the uncorrupted creation. Such a return to an earlier state would not have been necessary if sin had left the relationship between humanity and animal untouched. Also, Theophilus and John Chrysostom were convinced that the authority over the animals was diminished as a result of human's disobedience, and Augustine agreed with this when pointing out that we cannot equate the current relationship between humans and animals with the situation before the fall.[173]

Luther and Calvin addressed this issue in the same way as was done by these Early Church theologians, and it would remain so in the generations after them.[174] *Zacharias Ursinus*, one of the authors of the canonical *Heidelberg Catechism*, epitomized this belief when writing that 'the beasts which at first kept a low profile towards humans, now insidiously oppose and injure him'.[175] Whether authors also believed that the fall of Adam changed the nature of animals for the worse, either by depriving them of an immortality originally assigned to them or by turning some of them into predators, is the subject of the next paragraph.

2.4.4. Animal Natures Changed for the Worse

How the Church Fathers felt about the relationship between the fall of Adam and any related change in the nature of the animals is sometimes difficult to follow because their statements about this subject are not always consistent with each other. This is especially true of the Cappadocians Basil the Great and Gregory of Nyssa, who, on the one hand, denied that in the uncorrupted creation the animals would die, but, on the other, spoke of animals that are adequately equipped for the

---

173   Augustine, 'A Refutation of the Manichees' in: Rotelle, *The Works of Saint Augustine*: 43 (I.18.29).
174   A useful historical overview of the opinions on whether or not nature suffered in a more general sense from Adam's fall is given by Williams, *Christian Attitudes toward Nature*: 7-16.
175   Ursinus, Z. 1598. *Explicationvm Catecheticarvm D. Zachariae Vrsini Silesii Absolvtvm Opvs*...Widow of Matthäus Harnisch, Neustadt. English translation from the original Latin from pp. 41-42. 'Namquae bestiae prius metuebant hominem, nunc ei repugnant, insidianter, ac nocent' [translation with kind help from dr. John van Eck]. For an English translation of this book and a biography of Ursinus, see Ursinus, Z. 1888. *The Commentary of Dr. Zacharias Ursinus, on the Heidelberg Catechism. Translated from the Original Latin, by the Rev. G.W. Williard. Fourth American Edition*. Elm Street Printing Company, Cincinnati.

struggle for life including tools for predation or armor so as not to become prey.

Others are less equivocal about this subject, as I have shown above and will summarize briefly here. Lactantius, Cyril, Ambrose, John Chrysostome, Augustine, and Thomas Aquinas all held that predation and animal death belong to the uncorrupted creation. Lactantius claimed that animals are created mortal and equipped with the weapons to defend themselves against threats. Cyril wrote that the 'Artificer' is 'worthy to be glorified' for creating 'the carnivorous lion'. Ambrose pointed to animal anatomy specifically created for predation and John Chrysostom emphasized how God deems a creation to which belong 'hawks and vultures' as well as 'snakes, vipers, serpents, lions and leopards' to be good, even 'very good'. Augustine didn't see it as a problem either that 'one animal is the nourishment of another', and Aquinas wrote that animal predation is not something that could be traced back to Adam's fall. Other late antique and medieval texts, such as Proba's poem and the *Bestiaria*, expounded a similar view.

Only a few claimed that Adam's disobedience also affected non-human creation, but not in the sense that the animals lost a supposed immortality. A change of animals' nature affecting both humanity as well as themselves was assumed by Theophilus. Some animals became 'evil and poisonous', thus afflicting humankind; others harm each other because they 'transgress the law of God, eating flesh'. Irenaeus contended the same. Now the animals devour each other, but one day that will end.[176]

Luther and Calvin also assumed that the nature of the animals had changed for the worse. The literal approach to Scripture as advocated by both led them to consider animals preying upon each other as one of the effects of the curse that followed Adam's fall.[177] However, neither Luther nor Calvin taught that animals were created with the intention to live forever. Luther even explicitly denied that animals have immortality and

---

176 Interestingly, when restricted to animal life, it seems that the thoughts of Augustine better fit within an evolutionary framework then those of Irenaeus, Augustine leaving room for animal death unrelated to Adam's fall whereas Irenaeus explicitly restricts carnivorousness to a fallen creation now being cursed and in need of restoration. This conclusion is remarkable since Irenaeus is often invoked over Augustine as the one whose ideas are more malleable to contemporary evolutionary thought patterns. See Hick, *Evil and the God of Love*: 217-221, 262-266; Emberger, G. 1994. 'Theological and Scientific Explanations for the Origin and Purpose of Evil' in *Perspectives on Science and Christian Faith* 46: 150-158.
177 Young, *John Calvin and the Natural World*: 127-129; Garvey, *God's Good Earth*: 91-95.

Calvin remained silent on this topic.[178] Therefore, Ury's statement: 'Thus as with Luther, the key to Calvin's theodicy is the idea that *all* natural evils are all the result of sin'[179] is correct as far as predation is concerned. But it is going too far to attribute to these Reformers the view that the death of animals *as such* is also a consequence of sin. That animals had to die at some point of time was God's intention from the beginning.

It is, on the other hand, not only young-earth creationists who go astray when exploiting Calvin to support their opinion. John Collins makes a similar mistake when claiming that Calvin 'was not troubled by the possibility of meat-eating [by the animals] before the fall'[180] and thus left room for the view that animals were carnivorous even before the fall of Adam. What Calvin was not 'troubled by', however, was whether humans ate meat already before the flood or whether this was the case only afterwards. 'Some infer, from this [sic] passages that (…) [only] after the deluge, he [God] expressly grants them the use of flesh. These reasons, however are not sufficiently strong: for (…) the first men offered sacrifices from their flocks. This, moreover, is the law of sacrificing rightly, not to offer unto God anything except what he has granted to our use. Lastly men were clothed in skins; therefore it was lawful for them to kill animals. For these reasons, I think it will be better for us to assert nothing concerning this matter.'[181] In his commentary on Genesis 9:3, Calvin returned to this theme in similar terms. 'For since they had before [the flood] offered sacrifices to God, and were also permitted to kill wild beasts, from the hides and skins of which they might make for themselves

---

178 In his *Institutes* Calvin wrote that God gave animals the ability to procreate in order to prevent the extinction of animal species. This could indicate that Calvin presupposed animal death before the fall, as claimed by John Munday; see Munday Jr, J.C. 1992. 'Creature Mortality: from Creation of the Fall?' in: *Journal of the Evangelical Theological Society* 35 (1): 51-68. The relevant passage is from Calvin, *Institutes*: 180 (I.xiv.20): '(…) that, although all were subject to corruption, he [God] nevertheless provided for the preservation of each species until the Last Day. We shall likewise learn that he nourishes some in secret ways, and, as it were, from time to time instills new vigor into them; on others he has conferred the power of propagating, lest by their death the entire species perish'. However, it seems more likely that Calvin wrote this to praise God for the providential care with which God upholds creation as it presents itself to us today, rather than to describe the pre-fall situation. Therefore, in my opinion this text by Calvin cannot serve as conclusive evidence for the view that he accepted animal death before the fall.
179 Ury, T.H. 'Luther, Calvin, and Wesley on the Genesis of Natural Evil: Recovering Lost Rubrics for Defending a *Very Good* Creation' in: Mortenson & Ury, *Coming to Grips with Genesis*: 399-423 (408).
180 Collins, C.J. 2006. *Genesis 1-4. A Linguistic, Literary, and Theological Commentary*. P&R Publishing Company, Phillipsburg: 165n45.
181 Calvin, *Genesis*: 56. Comment on Genesis 1:28-30.

garments and tents, I do not see what obligation should prevent them from the eating of flesh [before the flood].'¹⁸² Application of these texts to animal behavior in the pre-fall situation misses the point. Calvin speaks about the relationship between humankind and animals here and not about the interaction between the animals.

In sum, in the large period stretching from the first centuries to early modernity the relationship between humankind and the animal kingdom was more important than the question why a good God permitted animals to suffer. This is evident from the fact that the various authors we examined were clearly concerned with finding a conclusive explanation for the harmfulness of animals to humanity, but much less so with the violent behavior of the animals towards each other.

2.5. Conclusion

Throughout the period I examined in this chapter, the fact that animals eat each other did not detract from the goodness or justice of God. Both those who believed that predation existed already in the uncorrupted creation and those who saw it as one of the consequences of the curse that followed Adam's fall agreed on this. No one unequivocally held that God had created the animals immortal. Animals were created to meet men's physical needs; furthermore, they offered moral and other allegorical truths.

At the doorstep of the Early Modern Period, no one who we surveyed cared about the fact that animals might suffer, even though we found a fledgling awareness of the reality of such suffering. The thoughts of the triumvirate Aristotle, Augustine, and Aquinas were pivotal, as Linzey wryly noted.[183] Their conviction that animals should be excluded from proper moral consideration ruled unopposed for almost two millennia. This is not surprising as both the Hellenistic as well as the Christian worldview are marked by a profound anthropocentrism, that left little room for the minority traditions that deviated from this 'Greco-Christian arrogance'.[184]

The notion of humanity as created in the image of God in fact served as the Christian variant of Aristotle's conviction that reason separates humanity from the non-human animal kingdom. Similarly, the Stoic thought that the world exists for the sake of human beings dovetailed

---

182 Calvin, *Genesis*: 212. Comment on Genesis 9:3.
183 Linzey, A. 'Is Christianity Irredeemably Speciesist?' in: Linzey & Yamamoto, *Animals on the Agenda*: xi-xx.
184 Attfield, R. 1983. 'Christian Attitudes to Nature' in: *Journal of the History of Ideas* 44 (3): 369-386 (371). This author emphasizes that from the beginning of Christianity, there have also been people who advocated stewardship instead of exploitation.

closely with the notion from the creation story that humanity is destined to subdue the earth.[185] There was no need for Christian thinkers to develop an alternative view on the relationship between humanity and its fellow creatures as 'the New Testament reflects the influence of Stoic thought, which denies intellect to animals and argues that animals were created for the sake of human beings'.[186] Hellenistic anthropocentrism was adopted and baptized by the Christians and largely determined the thoughts of the authors analyzed in this chapter. The current emphasis on animal welfare may reveal a sense of guilt for the long-held belief that humans were uniquely made in the image of God and hence object of his special concern.[187]

---

185 Sorabji, *Animal Minds and Human Morals*: 195-203; Steiner, *Anthropocentrism and Its Discontents*: 53-92, 112-131; Clough, D.L. 2012. *On Animals. Volume 1. Systematic Theology*. T&T Clark International, London: 3-15; Williams, *Christian Attitudes toward Nature*: 21-27.
186 Steiner, *Anthropocentrism and Its Discontents*: 116. Cf. Wennberg, R.N. 2003. *God, Humans, and Animals. An Invitation to Enlarge Our Moral Universe*. Wm. B. Eerdmans, Grand Rapids: 302-307.
187 Tallis, R. 2011. *Aping Mankind. Neuromania, Darwinitis and the Misrepresentation of Humanity*. Acumen, Durham: 148.

Chapter 3: Eclipse of Eden

Animals and Divine Attributes in Early Modernity (1600–1709)

Abstract
In order to trace the history of the shift in opinion from the past view that nature is a manifestation of God's power and glory to today's common belief that nature is a slaughterhouse in which animal life is short and miserable, in this chapter, texts by British authors from the Early Modern Period (1600–1709) are examined to determine whether at that time people already had problems seeing violence and death in an animal world. It turns out that animal suffering had not yet become an issue that could harm the belief in a good and benevolent Creator. The few who did not rule out the possibility that animals might suffer indeed condoned this by (1) taking advantage of Descartes's *beast-machine* doctrine that animals lack the mental properties required for suffering, (2) considering suffering of animals to be outweighed by their joyful experiences, or (3) regarding animals' mishaps serving the greater good of a well-designed universe. Some vindicated God by blaming Adam for the suffering of the animals, but the consequences of the fall were more often limited to a disturbance of the relationship between humanity and its fellow creatures and only rarely associated with the way the animals interact with each other. That the justice of God would require animals to be entitled to compensation for any suffering did not come into view either; if animals were already part of the new earth, it was only to contribute to the bliss of the redeemed sinners. One could conclude that the human-centered thinking that had characterized Christianity from the beginning still prevailed, but that is not the full story as a few came to believe that God had created animals as goals in themselves, not exclusively for the good of mankind. This heralds the arrival of an era of greater attention to animals, regardless of their usefulness to humans.

3.1. Introduction
The advent of the Modern Period saw allegorical interpretations of Scripture declining in favor of the literal meaning of the biblical text, a development especially prominent in Protestantism because Roman

Catholic circles remained tied to canonical exegetical traditions.[1] Before, there had already been some voices advocating that a literal reading of the Bible should not be neglected in favor of allegory, but it was only now that the tables turned definitely.[2] The biblical text was no longer mainly a treasury of eternal and spiritual truths but gained independent value in describing past events and making reliable predictions about things to come. In this context, Isaiah's prophetic visions of the wolf dwelling with the lamb did not depict a human mind at rest but described a real peaceful cohabitation of animals to be expected in the future; in the same way, the Garden of Eden and the events occurring therein gained a new significance.

In this chapter, I will analyze whether the new view of Scripture led to a change in view on the relationship between animals and their Creator, in particular regarding animal suffering and death; three poems presented in § 3.2 will serve to illustrate this evolution. Then, I will outline some developments in the interpretation of the books of Scripture and nature in § 3.3 and § 3.4, respectively, followed by a brief discussion—as far as relevant to my subject—of the contemporary situation in church and society in § 3.5, and of the state of affairs in the contemporary study of nature in § 3.6. In § 3.7, I account for the methodology used, and in § 3.8, the texts of the authors who meet my inclusion criteria are examined. Data thus collected are discussed in § 3.9 and summarized in § 3.10.

3.2. Poetic Reflections
On the doorstep of the seventeenth century, the allegorical significance of animals had not yet waned as can be deduced from *John Donne*'s (1572–1631) verse entitled *To Sir Edward Herbert, at Julyers*:

> Man is a lumpe, where all beasts kneaded bee,
> Wisdome makes him an Arke where all agree;
> The foole, in whom these beasts do live at jarre,
> Is sport to others, and a Theater;
> Nor scapes hee so, but is himselfe their prey:
> All which was man in him, is eate away,
> And now his beasts on one another feed,
> Yet couple in anger, and new monsters breed.

---

[1] Harrison, P. 1998. *The Bible, Protestantism, and the Rise of Natural Science*. Cambridge University Press, Cambridge: 108-114, 121-138, 205-206; Almond, P.C. 1999. *Adam and Eve in Seventeenth-Century Thought*. Cambridge University Press, Cambridge: 65-66; Yarchin, W. 2004. *History of Biblical Interpretation. A Reader*. Hendrickson Publishers, Peabody: 184-185.

[2] Harrison, *The Bible*: 109-110.

> How happy'is he, which hath due place assign'd
> To'his beasts; and disaforested his minde?
> Empal'd himselfe to keepe them out, not in;
> Can sow, and dares trust corne, where they have bin;
> Can use his horse, goate, wolfe, and every beast,
> And is not Asse himselfe to all the rest.[3]

Man is but an earthen vessel containing a large variety of animals that symbolize his passions. In a fool, they rule unconstrained whereas the wise man knows how to handle them, using each passion to his profit. Creation mirroring the human mind as contemplated in Late Antique and Medieval times is expressed poetically here.

This idea about the significance of the animal world would not last. Halfway through the century, *John Milton* (1608–1674) published his famous and proverbial *Paradise Lost*:

> (…) Thus began
> Outrage from liveless things; but Discord first
> Daughter of Sin, among th' irrational,
> Death introduc'd through fierce antipathie:
> Beast now with Beast gan war, & Fowle with Fowle,
> And Fish with Fish; to graze the Herb all leaving,
> Devourd each other; nor stood much in awe
> Of Man, but fled him, or with count'nance grim
> Glar'd on him passing: (…)[4]

The allegorical reading of the Genesis text has disappeared. Milton paraphrased Scripture in a poetical way but nevertheless took the message literally. Due to Adam's sin, animals start devouring each other, and humankind's authority over them is lost. But whereas the allegorical reading did not last, neither would the literal be durable. In fact, after

---

3 Donne, J. 1639 [1610]. 'To Sr. Edward Herbert, Now Lord Herbert of Cherbury, Being at the Siege of Iulyers' in: *Poems, by J.D. With Elegies on the Authors Death*. John Marriot, London: 165. Edward Herbert was an English army officer who had committed himself to the cause of the Low Countries in their fight against the Spanish domination. The siege of Juliers was part of this conflict. For more details see Sellin, P.R. '"Souldiers of One Army". John Donne and the Army of the States General as an International Protestant Crossroads, 1595–1625' in: Papazian, M.A. (ed.). 2003. *John Donne and the Protestant Reformation, New Perspectives*. Wayne State University Press, Detroit: 143-192.
4 Milton, J. 1667. *Paradise Lost. A Poem Written in Ten Books*. Peter Parker, London. Book IX: 706-714. For the development of the *Paradise Lost* tradition from its source in Genesis through subsequent writings on the fall from early Jewish and Christian texts till Milton's own time, see Evans, J.M. 1968. *Paradise Lost and the Genesis Tradition*. Clarendon Press, Oxford.

Milton's *magnum opus*, no major literary work on this subject came from the press, *Paradise Lost* thus being both the culmination as well as the end of the 'literary development of the Edenic myth'.[5] Only a few years later, John Flavel (c.1627–1691) offered a much less gloomy view on animal life.

> Yea, birds and beasts, as well as men, enjoy
> Their innocent delights: these chirp and play ;
> The cheerful birds among the branches sing,
> And make the neighboring groves with music ring:
> With various warbling notes they all invite
> Our ravished ears with pleasure and delight.
> The new-fall'n lambs, will in a sun-shine day,
> About their feeding dams jump up and play
> Are cisterns sweet ? and is the fountain bitter ?
> Or can the sun be dark when glow-worms glitter ?
> Have instruments their sweet, melodious airs ?
> All creatures their delights; (…)[6]

Now nature is described as full of joy, bearing testimony of a benevolent Creator. Birds, beasts, and humans enjoy their 'innocent delights'. Apparently, bright colors have replaced the dark tones of a sad memory to a Paradise now lost forever. These three fragments reflect the changed role of Scripture for interpreting nature that took place during the seventeenth century. Next, more details will be given on the decline and fall of the 'Mosaick' history.

3.3. The Book of Scripture Revised

As mentioned before, the literal approach to the biblical text became increasingly dominant in the sixteenth century.[7] The Bible was thought not to convey merely theological and moral truths but to provide knowledge relating to history and nature as well. Whereas in the past historical and geographical information in Scripture had been accepted and taken for granted without further pondering any significance it could have for contemporary observations of nature or for mankind's history, now it was considered to provide information relevant for the geographical

---

[5] Almond, *Adam and Eve*: 210. Cf. Greenblatt, S. 2017. *The Rise and Fall of Adam and Eve*. W.W. Norton & Company, New York; Flasch, K. 2004. *Eva und Adam. Wandlungen eines Mythos*. Verlag C.H. Beck, München.

[6] Flavel, J. 1824 [1674]. *Husbandry Spiritualized; or the Heavenly Use of Earthly Things, in Which Hushbandmen Are Directed to an Excellent Improvement of their Common Employments*…J.A. Boswell, Middletown: 63.

[7] Harrison, *The Bible*: 107-120, 205-222.

location of the Garden of Eden as well as for guiding enquiries about the deluge and Noah's ark.[8] In the same way, the story of the fall became to be understood in a literal way, Genesis 1–3 recording real historical events with consequences still to be felt in the present.[9]

Parallel to the line of authors adhering to the literal meaning of Scripture, another line arose in which the reliability of Scripture regarding nature and history itself was questioned.[10] Doubts came from two sources: discrepancies between the biblical text and astronomical data showing a heliocentric replacing a geocentric cosmos[11] and problems identified in the record itself. 'For it were a strange interpretation to say Moses spake of his own sepulchre (…) that it was not found to that day wherein he was yet living. (…) It is therefore sufficiently evident that the five Books of Moses were written after his time, though how long after it be not so manifest.'[12]

Thus, on one side, there was a growing interest in biblical information that came to be seen as an independent source of knowledge about nature and history. On the other side, concerns arose about the reliability of the text itself, especially when this text collided with data empirically

---

8 Pelikan, J. 1961. 'Cosmos and Creation: Science and Theology in Reformation Thought' in: *Proceedings of the American Philosophical Society* 105: 464-469; Harrison, *The Bible*: 126.

9 Almond, *Adam and Eve*: 173-209.

10 For the changing attitude towards the biblical text that arose in the seventeenth century, see Mandelbrote, S. 'Isaac Newton and Thomas Burnet: Biblical Criticism and the Crisis of late Seventeenth-Century England' in: Force J.E., Popkin R.H. (eds). 1994. *The Books of Nature and Scripture. Recent Essays on Natural Philosophy, Theology, and Biblical Criticism in the Netherlands of Spinoza's Time and the British Isles of Newton's Time*. Kluwer Academic Publishers, Dordrecht: 149-178; Popkin, R.H. 'Spinoza and Bible Scholarship' in: Force & Popkin, *Books of Nature and Scripture*: 1-20; Israel, J.I. 2001. *Radical Enlightenment. Philosophy and the Making of Modernity 1650-1750*. Oxford University Press, Oxford: 447-456.

11 McColley, G. 1938. 'The Ross-Wilkins Controversy' in: *Annals of Science* 3 (2): 153-189; Brooke, J.H. 1991. *Science and Religion. Some Historical Perspectives*. Cambridge University Press, Cambridge: 83-99; Taylor, Ch. 2018 [2007]. *A Secular Age*. Harvard University Press, Cambridge (MA): 271, 327-331.

12 Hobbes, T. 1651. *Leviathan or the Matter, Forme, & Power of a Common-wealth Ecclesiasticall and Civill*. Andrew Crooke, London: 233. Similar thoughts were advocated by the French Calvinist Isaac La Peyrère in his *Men before Adam*, see Popkin, R.H. 1987. *Isaac la Peyrère (1596-1676). His Life, Work and Influence*. E.J. Brill, Leiden: 42-59. It is not known whether both authors were aware of each other's work. In the original text of la Peyrère, one reads 'Hoe kond Moses na zijn doot schrijven' in: [Peyrère, I. la]. 1661. *Praeadamieten of Oefening over het 12, 13, en 14. Vers des Vijfden Capittels van den Brief des Apostels Pauli tot den Romeynen, waer door Geleert Wort: Datter Menschen voor Adam Geweest Zijn*. [Johannes Janssonius, Amsterdam]: 332. [How was it possible for Moses to write after his death.]

obtained.[13] As a consequence, 'Biblically grounded Mosaick philosophy' indeed 'hardly outlasted the seventeenth century'.[14] Gradually, the conviction that information about the way God did create had been adapted to the comprehension of the contemporary hearers—'rude, and newly taken from making Bricks for *Pharaoh* in *Aegypt*'[15]—gained acceptance. These developments influenced the thoughts about the goodness of the Creator and the life of his creatures; results yielded by the study of nature and changes in convictions about politics and religion, subjects also asking for attention, had their impact as well.

3.4. The Book of Nature Revised

Natural theology—the discipline that assumes that knowledge of God can be obtained from other sources than divine revelation—has ancient roots.[16] The idea that God makes himself knowable not only from Scripture but also from nature as well goes back to antiquity. Scripture itself supports this conviction at many places, in particular in the Psalms.[17] Similar to the book of Scripture, the book of nature bears testimony of divine attributes that cannot be ignored except at our peril.[18]

But as the interpretation of the book of Scripture changed in the seventeenth century, so did the interpretation of the book of nature. In the past, as was addressed in the previous chapter, nature had been seen either as mirroring the human mind, animals reflecting human passions or as offering allegorical lessons and moral truths, and thus, its value was

---

13 Harrison, P. '"The Book of Nature" and Early Modern Science' in: Berkel, K. van, Vanderjagt, A., (eds). 2006. *The Book of Nature in Early Modern and Modern History*. Peeters, Leuven: 1-26.

14 Harrison, P. 2007. *The Fall of Man and the Foundations of Science*. Cambridge University Press, Cambridge: 137.

15 More, H. 1653. *Conjectura Cabbalistica or, a Conjectural Essay of Interpreting the Minde of Moses, According to a Threefold Cabbala: viz. Literal, Philosophical, Mystical, or, Divinely Moral*. William Morden, Cambridge: 131.

16 McGrath, A.E. 2011. *Darwinism and the Divine. Evolutionary Thought and Natural Theology. The 2009 Hulsean Lectures. University of Cambridge*. Wiley-Blackwell, Chichester: 11-26; Holder, R.D. 2016. *Natural Theology. Faraday Paper 19*. The Faraday Institute for Science and Religion, Cambridge. For an overview about the several branches of natural theology, see Manning R.R. 'Introduction' in: Manning, R.R., (ed.). 2013. *The Oxford Handbook of Natural Theology*. Oxford University Press, Oxford: 1-5; McGrath, A.E. 2017. *Re-Imagining Nature. The Promise of a Christian Natural Theology*. Wiley Blackwell, Chichester: 18-22.

17 Psalm 8:3. 'When I look at your heavens, the work of your fingers, the moon and the stars that you have established'. (NRSV)

18 Romans 1:20. 'Ever since the creation of the world his eternal power and divine nature, invisible though they are, have been understood and seen through the things he has made. So they are without excuse'. (NRSV)

mainly in supplementing the content of Scripture. 'Once one understood God's wisdom, love, and power, then one could see these attributes declared in nature.'[19] In this century, however, the book of nature gained an independent value unconnected with scriptural revelation; observation of nature led to the unavoidable conclusion that it must have been designed and created by somebody. Nature points to a creator that, however, is not necessarily the God that Christians worship but at least a metaphysical reality although at that time, such an alternative was not considered a real option. Furthermore, the idea arose that not only the existence of God can be deduced from nature but also his intentions.[20] Physico-theology with its emphasis on goal-oriented design was born. The observation that 'order implies an orderer' was supplemented by the conviction that 'there is no purpose without a purposer'.[21] It is to be expected that both arguments would play a role in shaping the contemporary ideas about the relationship between animal life and divine attributes. To what extent will be addressed when examining the authors from this period. But first I will give a brief overview of the political and ecclesiastical situation and describe how the study of nature underwent drastic changes and became a significant factor in this period.

3.5. Political and Religious Background

The history of seventeenth-century England was determined by ongoing conflicts between groups with opposing religious convictions, for the purpose of brevity to be summarized as Anglican at one side and non-Anglican at the other, within the latter, the Puritans being the most influential and vociferous.[22] The conflict already dated back to the middle

---

19 Gillespie, N.C. 1987. 'Natural History, Natural Theology, and Social Order: John Ray and the "Newtonian Ideology"' in: *Journal of the History of Biology* 20 (1): 1-49 (11).
20 Brooke, *Science and Religion*: 192-203; Harrison, 'The Book of Nature and Early Modern Science' in: van Berkel & Vanderjagt, *The Book of Nature in Early Modern and Modern History*: 1-26; Harrison, P. 'The Cultural Authority of Natural History in Early Modern Europe' in: Alexander, D.R., Numbers, R.L. (eds). 2010. *Biology and Ideology. From Descartes to Dawkins*. The University of Chicago Press, Chicago: 11-35; Mandelbrote, S. 'Early Modern Natural Theologies' in: Manning, *Oxford Handbook of Natural Theology*: 75-99.
21 McGrath, *Darwinism and the Divine*: 52-53, 63-71 (53). Cf. Harrison, P. 2015. *The Territories of Science and Religion*. The University of Chicago Press, Chicago: 109-115; McGrath, *Re-Imagining Nature*: 19.
22 For the anachronistic but nevertheless justifiable use of 'Anglican' for the Church in England already for that period, see Strong, R. 'Series Introduction' in: Milton, A. (ed.). 2017. *The Oxford History of Anglicanism. Volume I. Reformation and Identity, c.1520-1662.* Oxford University Press, Oxford: xvii-xxvi. For the complicated history of Anglicanism and its relationship with dissenting convictions inside and outside its

of the sixteenth century when differences about worship and liturgy divided the congregations of English Protestants who had fled for Queen Mary's terror and now lived in exile on the Continent.[23] The divisiveness subsequently continued to smoulder until its outbreak in open violence in the midst of the seventeenth century, resulting in Civil War followed by Commonwealth and Protectorate.[24] Full description of the controversies between both religious camps and how the Anglicans ultimately won victory would be far beyond the scope of this study, but some notes on the different attitudes of Anglicans versus Puritans regarding society, natural world, and human abilities are needed for interpreting their writings on the subject of animal fates properly.

The Anglicans stood for an authoritarian position and appealed to the teachings of Bible, creeds, and church. They saw the church as the repository of and guarantee for true doctrine. The Bible was the possession of the church and could be properly understood only through the exposition of the authorities of that church.[25] This conviction was supported by the Anglican view that society and the position of the church therein were the outcome of benevolent divine providence, defending the established church as a divinely ordained institution. For the Puritans, the connection between the established order and the will of God was less close; their conviction allowed or even could require active intervention or resistance when deemed necessary on scriptural grounds or because of natural events with assumed theological significance.[26]

---

ranks in the seventeenth century see Milton, 'Reformation, Identity, and 'Anglicanism'' in: Milton, *Oxford History of Anglicanism*: 1-25; Milton, 'Unsettled Reformations, 1603–1662' in: Milton, *Oxford History of Anglicanism*: 63-83; Lake, P. ''Puritans and 'Anglicans' in the History of the Post-Reformation English Church' in: Milton, *Oxford History of Anglicanism*: 352-379; Fincham, K., Taylor, S. 'Episcopalian Identity, 1640–1662' in: Milton, *Oxford History of Anglicanism*: 455-482.

23 VanderMolen, R.J. 1973. 'Anglican against Puritan: Ideological Origins During the Marian Exile' in: *Church History* 42 (1): 45-57.

24 The Commonwealth and Protectorate (1649–1660) refer to the republican governments of England, Scotland and Ireland during the Interregnum between the reigns of the Stuart King Charles I (1625–1649) and his son King Charles II (1660–1685). For a concise and adequate overview of the troubled political and social situation of that period, see Kishlansky, M. 1997. *A Monarchy Transformed. Britain 1603-1714*. Penguin Books, London.

25 Lamprecht, S.P. 1926. 'Innate Ideas in the Cambridge Platonists' in: *The Philosophical Review* 35 (6): 553-573; MacKenzie, I.M. 2002. *God's Order and Natural Law. The Works of the Laudian Divines*. Ashgate, Aldershot.

26 VanderMolen, R.J. 1978. 'Providence as Mystery, Providence as Revelation: Puritan and Anglican Modifications of John Calvin's Doctrine of Providence' in: *Church History* 47 (1): 27-47; Mandelbrote, S. 2007. 'The Uses of Natural Theology in Seventeenth-Century England' in: *Science in Context* 20 (3): 451-480; Fergusson, D.

It is obvious that this latter conviction was fiercely contested by the Anglicans because of its threat to established political and ecclesiastical order. Looking back onto decades of violence and disorder, culminating in the beheading of King Charles I, the Anglican divine *Joseph Glanvill* wrote in 1676 that 'so possest they [the Puritans] were with the conceit of the divineness and necessity of their *Fancies* and *Models*, that they despised and vilified the *Ecclesiastical* Government' and 'broke out (…) into down-right *Rebellion*' whereas the 'Pious Prince was depos'd and murder'd'.[27]

Anglicans and Puritans also had different opinions about the value and place of reason. Whereas the former emphasized reason to be the 'Candle of the Lord', the Puritans were convinced that reason is an unreliable guide. As summarized by the historian Peter Harrison, '[t]he claim that design is evident in the world assumes both the intelligibility of nature and our mind's capacity to detect that intelligibility. Both sit uneasily with a strong view of the Fall and its noetic consequences.'[28] Reason can tell us something about God's creative power but for knowledge about other divine attributes like goodness, we have to consult Scripture and pray for the Holy Spirit to enlighten our minds and hearts.[29] For the Anglicans, knowledge about divine attributes could be obtained by studying the creation but not so for the Puritans.

In view of these different opinions, it is likely that Anglicans go to greater lengths than Puritans to reconcile the divine attributes with animal suffering. After all, for the former, nature illustrates not only divine power but goodness and benevolence as well. Whereas for the latter, nature merely illustrates divine power, Scripture being the only reliable source for speculating about other divine attributes. Therefore, the Puritans are *a priori* discharged from any troubles with contradictions between divine attributes and animal miseries, a way out not available for the Anglicans.

3.6. Early-Modern Science
When addressing ideas about the relationship between divine attributes and animal suffering, not only interpretation of Scripture or politics and

---

2018. *The Providence of God. A Polyphonic Approach.* Cambridge University Press, Cambridge: 103-108.
27 Glanvill, J. 1676. 'Essay VII. The Summe of my Lord Bacon's New Atlantis' in: *Essays on Several Important Subjects in Philosophy and Religion.* John Baker, London: 5.
28 Harrison, *The Fall*: 241. Cf. Lamprecht, 'Innate Ideas': 556; Morgan, J. 'The Puritan Thesis Revisited' in: Livingstone, D.N., Hart, D.G., Noll, M.A. (eds) 1999. *Evangelicals and Science in Historical Perspective.* Oxford University Press, New York: 43-74.
29 Morgan, J. 1979. 'Puritanism and Science: a Reinterpretation' in: *The Historical Journal* 22 (3): 535-560.

religion deserve our attention, but also some aspects of the drastic changes in the study of nature in the seventeenth century. A new 'experimental' natural philosophy emerged, which can be seen as the first step towards modern science.[30] The pivotal place of this period in the history of knowledge, the so-called scientific revolution, is generally acknowledged. It was the age of *Galileo Galilei* (1564–1642), who got in trouble because he robbed the earth of its central place in the universe; *René Descartes* (1596–1650), whose 'cogito ergo sum' became proverbial; and *Isaac Newton* (1642–1727), whose innovations in mathematics, theory of universal gravitation, and experimental works in optics, can be seen as the culmination of all these developments. It was the period in which the belief arose that the universe is governed by laws issued by the Creator.[31] It is not the properties residing in matter itself that determine what happens in nature, but the forces acting on matter from the outside, a

---

30 The appropriateness of the term 'science' to denote the activity of the seventeenth-century scholars who studied nature is a topic of discussion among historians of science. Nowadays, science is understood as an activity that encompasses the collection of knowledge by observation or experimentation with the aim to identify natural laws and to make predictions. The seventeenth-century scholars practiced science to deepen their knowledge of God and his acts and purposes, seeing nature as God's creation and witnessing his design. They called themselves not 'scientists' but 'natural philosophers' and their activity 'natural philosophy' and not 'science'. Currently, the term 'philosophy' is generally taken for abstract reasoning and not connected with activities aimed at increasing extant knowledge. Therefore, I have chosen to use the term 'science' also for this period because, in my opinion, for the contemporary reader it better represents what these scholars really did than is indicated by the term 'natural philosophy'. For more information on this discussion, see Cunningham, A. 1988. 'Getting the Game Right: Some Plain Words on the Identity and Invention of Science' in: *Studies in History and Philosophy of Science Part A* (3): 365-389; Cunningham, A. 1991. 'How the *Principia* Got Its Name' in: *History of Science* (4): 377-392; Cunningham, A., Williams, P. 1993. 'De-Centring the 'Big Picture': "The Origins of Modern Science" and the Modern Origins of Science' in: *The British Journal for the History of Science* 26 (4): 407-432; Grant, E. 2000. 'God and Natural Philosophy: the Late Middle Ages and Sir Isaac Newton' in: *Early Science and Medicine* 5 (3): 279-298; Cunningham, A. 2000. 'The Identity of Natural Philosophy. A Response to Edward Grant' in: *Early Science and Medicine* 5 (3): 259-278; Flipse, A. 2014. *Christelijke Wetenschap. Nederlandse Rooms-Katholieken en Gereformeerden over de Natuurwetenschap, 1880–1940*. PhD Thesis, Vrije Universiteit, Amsterdam: 13-20; Harrison, *The Territories of Science and Religion*: 1-19, 145-170; Wootton, D. 2015. *The Invention of Science. A New History of the Scientific Revolution*. HarperCollins, New York: 22-32, 573-575.
31 Brooke, *Science and Religion*: 117-151; Jones, R.H. 2012. *For the Glory of God. The Role of Christianity in the Rise and Development of Modern Science. Volume II. The History of Christian Ideas and Control Beliefs in Science*. University Press of America, Lanham: 1-40; Fergusson, *The Providence of God*: 111; Wootton, *The Invention of Science*: 6-14, 318-379, 431-448.

belief that encourages the study of nature through observation of the activity of these forces and their manipulation through experiments. Mechanical philosophy replaced Aristotelean teleology.[32]

This development also implied that animals no longer served as mirrors of the human passions or a source for allegorical speculations but—as matter also governed by external forces—became objects for study and experimentation.[33] Anatomical dissection revealed pages of the book of nature not seen before. Discoveries thus made added to the glory of the Creator[34] but also raised concerns about the relationship between humanity and the non-human animal kingdom.[35] The close similarity between human and animal brains suggested similarity in function as well and therefore threatened to erase the distinction between humans and animals.[36] Needless to say, this created big problems: What did it mean that God created humankind in his image? Mental functions were assigned to the brain but also conceived as attributes of the immortal soul. Denying animals a soul implied that one accepted the possibility of living sensitive matter with mental functions, which opened the gateway to denying the existence of a soul for humans as well, but the opposite, safeguarding the distinct immaterial human soul by accepting that animals had souls as well, was no less problematic in view of the specific position that God has assigned to humanity.[37]

---

32 Deason, G.B. 'Reformation Theology and the Mechanistic Conception of Nature' in: Lindberg D.C., Numbers, R.L. (eds). 1986. *God & Nature. Historical Essays on the Encounter between Christianity and Science*. University of California Press, Berkeley: 167-191; Ashworth Jr, W.B. 'Christianity and the Mechanistic Universe' in: Lindberg, D.C., Numbers, R.L. (eds). 2003. *When Science & Christianity Meet*. The University of Chicago Press, Chicago: 61-84.
33 Guerrini, A. 'Natural History, Natural Philosophy, and Animals, 1600–1800' in: Senior, M. (ed.). 2007. *A Cultural History of Animals in the Age of Enlightenment*. Berg, Oxford: 121-144.
34 Harrison, 'The Book of Nature and Early Modern Science' in: van Berkel & Vanderjagt, *The Book of Nature in Early Modern and Modern History*: 1-26.
35 Zimmer, C. 2004. *Soul Made Flesh. The Discovery of the Brain—and How It Changed the World*. Free Press, New York: 209-235.
36 Bynum, W.F. 1973. 'The Anatomical Method, Natural Theology, and the Functions of the Brain' in: *Isis* 64 (4): 444-468.
37 Harrison, P. 1993. 'Animal Souls, Metempsychosis, and Theodicy in Seventeenth-Century English Thought' in: *Journal of the History of Philosophy* 31: 519-544; Thomson, A. 2010. 'Animals, Humans, Machines and Thinking Matter, 1690–1707' in: *Early Science and Medicine* 15 (1/2): 3-37; Clough, D.L. 2012. *On Animals. Volume 1. Systematic Theology*. T&T Clark, London: 137-144.

A way out of this dilemma was the uncoupling of life and sensitivity as done by Descartes in his doctrine of the *beast-machine*.[38] His influence was far-reaching and would determine the discussion on the mental properties of animals for the time to come.[39] Especially in France, the discussion focused on the relationship between Descartes's thoughts and divine attributes and the thoughts advocated are briefly presented in Box 3.1.[40] How this came out for the British authors will be examined in the paragraph devoted to the literary sources (cf. § 3.8) and in the discussion (cf. § 3.9).

3.7. Method

Authors to be discussed in this chapter have been selected from recent secondary sources that addressed the problem of harmful animals in a good creation.[41] These secondary publications served as a point of departure for any additional enquiries. In order to be relevant for the topic, authors needed to address the question if and how animal behavior

---

38 Descartes, R. 2008. *A Discourse on the Method. A New Translation by Ian Maclean.* Oxford University Press, Oxford.

39 Cottingham J. 1978. ''A Brute to the Brutes?': Descartes' Treatment of Animals' in: *Philosophy* 53 (206): 551-559; Thomas, K. 1983. *Man and the Natural World. Changing Attitudes in England 1500–1800.* Penguin Books, Harmondsworth: 33-35; Brooke, *Science and Religion*: 127-130; Harrison, P. 1992. 'Descartes on Animals' in: *The Philosophical Quarterly* 42 (167): 219-227; Maehle, A.H. 'Cruelty and Kindness to the 'Brute Creation'. Stability and Change in the Ethics of the Man-Animal Relationship, 1600-1850' in: Manning, A., Serpell, J. (eds). 1994. *Animals and Human Society: Changing Perspectives.* Routledge, London: 86-87; Harrison, P. 1998. 'The Virtues of Animals in Seventeenth-Century Thought' in: *Journal of the History of Ideas* 59 (3): 463-484; Steiner, G. 2005. *Anthropocentrism and Its Discontents. The Moral Status of Animals in the History of Western Philosophy.* University of Pittsburgh Press, Pittsburgh: 132-152; Senior, M. 'The Souls of Men and Beasts, 1630-1764' in: Senior, *A Cultural History of Animals in the Age of Enlightenment*: 23-45; Harrison, 'The Cultural Authority of Natural History in Early Modern Europe' in: Alexander & Numbers, *Biology and Ideology*: 11-35.

40 Adapted from Strickland, L. 2013. 'God's Creatures? Divine Nature and the Status of Animals in the Early Modern Beast-Machine Controversy' in: *International Journal of Philosophy and Theology* 74 (4): 291-309.

41 Lovejoy, A.O. 1936. *The Great Chain of Being. A Study of the History of an Idea. The William James Lectures Delivered at Harvard University, 1933.* Harvard University Press, Cambridge (MA); Thomas, *Man and the Natural World*; Brooke, *Science and Religion*; Manning & Serpell, *Animals and Human Society: Changing Perspectives*; Harrison, *The Bible*; Almond, *Adam and Eve*; Roedell, C.A. 2005. *The Beasts that Perish: the Problem of Evil and the Contemplation of the Animal Kingdom in English Thought, c.1660–1839.* PhD Thesis, Georgetown University, Washington, D.C; Harrison, *The Fall*; Jorink, E. 2010. *Reading the Book of Nature in the Dutch Golden Age 1575–1715.* Brill, Leiden; McGrath, *Darwinism and the Divine*.

including aggression and predation reveals or refutes the hand of a benevolent Creator. This implies that they should address how to relate *animal death and predation with the attributes of God*.

The thoughts of the various authors will be demonstrated by quoting fragments of their texts that serve to illustrate their convictions, followed by summarizing their position on the issues at stake: Do their writings express any concern about animal death, predation and suffering, and if so, how are these reconciled with the image of God as a benevolent

---

Box 3.1. Plausibility of Descartes's beast-machine doctrine viewed from the attributes of God.*

Arguments pro
1. Divine justice
   If animals have souls, they can also suffer pain. But pain is a punishment for sin. Animals don't sin, so they don't deserve punishment. Therefore, a just God cannot make animals suffer.
2. Divine providence
   Animals seem to show intelligent behavior. That could result from an intrinsic ability of the animal itself or from a guiding principle from outside. The first does not make sense because then even the most primitive animal would have intelligence, since every animal, even the smallest, shows purposeful behavior. The principle that directs behavior therefore lies outside the animal. God has arranged this in his providence in such a way that behavior does not require a (passible) soul that governs behavior in the animal itself.
3. Divine economy
   God can make a body that behaves like an ingenious mechanism; therefore assigning a soul to animals would mean that God would do something that was unnecessary.
4. Divine glory
   Creating a beast-machine that demonstrates behavior required to stay alive without a guiding principle like a soul, is more difficult than creating an animal which, because it possesses a soul, can independently take care of the preservation of life.
5. Divine wisdom
   This argument presupposes that when animals have souls, the soul is annihilated by God when the animal dies. Thus, the nobler substance, the soul, is annihilated, whereas the inferior animal bodies are not; they decompose but are not annihilated. It is implausible that the inferior will remain and the nobler annihilated. Hence it is against God's wisdom to assign to the animal a soul.

Arguments contra
1. Nothing created in vain
   God has given animals and humans the same senses; but if the animals would not feel anything, God has made something that does not function. God does not do anything without reason, however; it follows that he allotted them the capacity of sensation as well. Therefore animals cannot be purely machines.
2. God is no deceiver
   God is perfect, even in his reliability, and that means he is not fooling us. Yet, he would be doing so if animals showed patterns of behavior that suggest they are in pain whereas in fact they are not.

*Cf. Strickland, L. 2013. 'God's Creatures? Divine Nature and the Status of Animals in the Early Modern Beast-Machine Controversy' in: International Journal of Philosophy and Theology 74 (4): 291-309.

Creator? Thereafter, I will discuss the results obtained in this way and look for commonly held convictions. Finally, some concluding remarks will be made. I again apologize for the high number of quotes and their length, but their inclusion is justified by the need to present the various authors' opinions in their own words rather than paraphrasing their texts to avoid loss of style and content. It is evident that authors relevant for the subject have been overlooked, but their absence in secondary sources might indicate that they were either less influential or considered not to have contributed something that wasn't covered already by others writing on the subject of animal death and suffering. With this *caveat* in mind, I am rather sure that all major lines of thinking are represented by the sources analyzed below.

3.8. The Literary Sources
3.8.1. *Edward Topsell (c.1572-1625)*
The Puritan cleric *Edward Topsell*[42] is best remembered for his posthumously published major opus *The History of Four-Footed Beasts, Serpents and Insects*.[43] But for my subject he is especially important because of a different writing: the sermons on the Old Testament book of the prophet Joel.[44] The prophet chastised an unfaithful Judah, who was punished by the Lord with locusts and drought. Not only humans but also animals suffered; the latter groan and cry because the watercourses are dried up.[45] Topsell—'seeing there is too pleasant an harmony in the sinnes of *Iudah* and *England*'[46]—employed these texts as well as others to digress about the miserable fate of animals and the spiritual lessons this offers for the present as well as to provide instructions how people should care for their animals.

Topsell wondered why the animals mourn. 'For it cannot be that beastes shoulde be faultie or sinfull before the Lorde, why then (although guiltles) are they thus tormented?' The answer is obvious: '(...) the beastes

---

42 Topsell is listed as 'a cleric of distinctly puritan stripe'. Cf. Tyacke, N. 'Puritan Politicians and King James VI and I, 1587-1604.' in: Cogswell, T., Cust, R., Lake, P. (eds). 2002. *Politics, Religion and Popularity in Early Stuart Britain. Essays in Honour of Conrad Russell.* Cambridge University Press, Cambridge: 21-44 (24).

43 Topsell, E. 1658 [1607]. *The History of Foure-Footed Beasts and Serpents...* G. Sawbridge et al., London.

44 Topsell, E. 1599. *Times Lamentation; or, An Exposition of the Prophet Ioel, in Sundry Sermons and Meditations.* George Potter, London.

45 'How do the beasts groan! the herds of cattle are perplexed, because they have no pasture; yea, the flocks of sheep are made desolate.' Joel 1:18; 'The beasts of the field cry also unto thee: for the rivers of waters are dried up, and the fire hath devoured the pastures of the wilderness.' Joel 1:20. (KJV)

46 Topsell, *Lamentation*: 1.

are punished for mans cause.' Man's transgression 'may shew vnto vs, the verie originall of the rebellion of some beastes. For there was not alway eminitie betwixt man[,] serpents, and lyons and beares, and wolfes and tygers, and such like'.[47] But not only the relationship between mankind and the animals has been spoiled; between the animals themselves things have changed for the worse as well:

> The great birdes are enimies to the small, the great fishes to the little, the great beastes to the inferiour; (...) the oxe cannot abide the lyon; the sheepe cannot endure the woolfe; the foxe will not tarrie with the goate; the horse will not dwell with the Beare; the Hart will not attende the hounde; and many moe [sic] liue in hatred one with another, but most of them al are enimies to man. The reasons are these; First, as man destroyed his owne nature, (...) so God destroieth or rather altereth the nature of all other things.[48]

Sin 'made the angels damnable, it made the world abhominable, it maketh the beastes corruptible, and it maketh men miserable'.[49] Topsell continued by pointing out that we should repent when realizing that our sins make the animals cry to God 'for vengeance against man'.[50] Therefore, we should not aggravate our sins by handling them harshly and cruelly.[51] Topsell urged us to refrain from adding miseries to the animals under our custody by handling them cruelly, lest abusing them for our pleasure in detestable spectacles like bull or bear baiting at the expense of multiplying our sins. 'The righteous know the needs of their animals.'[52] He had an open mind and eye for the miseries of animal life, both the wild ones in their harsh daily life or the tame ones inappropriately handled by their masters. His commitment to the animals is also evident in his conviction that they, at least some of them, will join mankind in the liberation from bondage as

---

47 Topsell, *Lamentation*: 194.
48 Topsell, *Lamentation*: 235.
49 Topsell, *Lamentation*: 76.
50 Topsell, *Lamentation*: 195.
51 Topsell, *Lamentation*: 196.
52 Proverbs 12:10. (NRSV) On the issue of inappropriate handling of animals in sports, see also William Perkins: '*We may not make recreations of Gods iudgements, or of the punishments of sinne.* (...) Againe, the Bayting of the Beare, and Cockefights, are no meete recreations (...) And the Antipathie and crueltie, which one beast sheweth to another, is the fruit of our rebellion against God, and should rather mooue vs to mourne, then to reioyce.' In: Perkins, W. 1606. *The Whole Treatise of the Cases of Conscience Distinguished into Three Bookes*...Printed by John Legat, Printer to the University of Cambridge, [Cambridge]: 588-589.

described by the apostle in Romans 8:20,[53] a belief that had gained influence among the English clergy since the beginning of the Early Modern Period[54] and that we will come across several other authors below.

In *The History of Foure-Footed Beasts, Serpents and Insects,* Topsell used the format of the medieval *Bestiaria,* extended by new information and insights but without making any distinction between real and imaginary details of animal life when referring to spiritual truths they embody. His aim with this book is clear—to provide the reader with edifying literature appropriate for a Sunday afternoon but of course only after attending public worship beforehand.[55] In this text, he put more emphasis on the beauty of creation than on the corruption caused by sin. The more we know about the animals, the more we will realize that 'that every Beast is a natural Vision, which we ought to see and understand, for the more clear apprehension of the invisible Majesty of God'.[56]

In his concerns about animal suffering, the Puritan Topsell added a new thought not heard thus far, providing support for the idea that Puritanism played an important role in arousing sensitivity to the suffering of non-human creatures.[57] But as responsibility for animal suffering can be ascribed exclusively to humankind, either indirectly through the curse evoked by Adam's sin or directly when we mistreat our fellow creatures, it nowhere does blemish the divine image, Topsell thus following Calvin's interpretation.

3.8.2. Nicholas Gibbons (c.1600)
Almost simultaneously with Topsell, *Nicholas Gibbons* (or *Gibbens*), calling himself 'Minister and Preacher of the Word of God', published a heavy tome devoted to the first fourteen chapters of Genesis with the aim

---

53 Topsell, *Lamentation*: 194-195.
54 Bradford, J. [1555]. 'The Restoration of All Things' in: Townsend, A. (ed.). 1848. *The Writings of John Bradford, Containing Sermons, Meditations, Examinations, &c.* Cambridge University Press: 350-364. Cf. Rudrum, A. 1989. 'Henry Vaughan, the Liberation of the Creatures, and Seventeenth-Century English Calvinism' in: *The Seventeenth Century* 4: 33-54; Roedell, *The Beasts that Perish*: 191-226; Tyra, S.W. 2019. 'Christ Has Come to Gather Together All the Creatures' in: *Journal of Theological Interpretation* 13 (1): 53-75. For the history of this view since antiquity, see Williams, G.H. 2015. *Christian Attitudes toward Nature.* Wipf & Stock, Eugene: 46-48.
55 Topsell, *Foure Footed Beasts, Epistle Dedicatory*: page not numbered.
56 Topsell, *Foure Footed Beasts, Epistle Dedicatory*: page not numbered.
57 Lane, B.C. 2011. *Ravished by Beauty. The Surprising Legacy of Reformed Spirituality.* Oxford University Press, New York: 32-33, 120-121, 223; Watson, R.N. 2014. 'Protestant Animals: Puritan Sects and English Animal-Protection Sentiment, 1550–1650' in: *English Literary History* 81 (4): 1111-1148.

to provide 'briefe, faithfull and sound expositions *of the most difficult and hardest places*: Approved by the testimony of the Scriptures themselues (…) Wherein also the euerlasting truth of the word of God, *is freed from the errors and slaunders of Atheists, Papists, Philosophers, and all Heretikes*'.[58] The Genesis text should be taken literally. Before the fall, animals 'did [not] hurt or molest another', but 'so soon as man had rebelled against the Lord', they 'began to oppresse and deuoure one another, as they shooke off the yoke of obedience vnto man their gouernour'.[59] The behavior of the animals was changed because of the sin of man.[60] Predation was ascribed to animal disobedience 'unto man', which could mean that before, it had been merely men's dominion over the animals that prevented them from internecine behavior.

Men's authority being lost, or at least diminished, by the fall, animals were not kept under adequate control anymore and developed carnivorous habits. In this view, predation is not due to a divine curse causing animals' nature changing for the worse but the manifestation of an aptitude possibly already present before but now set free because of loss of men's control. The preliminary conclusion may be drawn that for Gibbons, it was mainly the disturbed relationship between mankind and creation that counts as also can be inferred from his thoughts written elsewhere:

> It is rightlie supposed there were thornes before, and thistles, and venomous herbes, and Serpents; but they were not noisome, nor had power to hurt: they were for the full perfection of the creature, not as sores and blemishes therein: they were *rare* and *scarce*, as serving but to shew the wisedome of God in the diversitie of his works, and more fruitfull plants were then more plentiful. But when the curse was powred forth for sinne, thornes and thistles and such like fruits of barrenness increase euerie where and choked them of better fruit, which of themselues were readie to decay.[61]

Thorns and thistles as well as venomous herbs and serpents already occurred in the uncorrupted creation, being manifestations of God's creative power. After God's curse upon the earth, however, these became

---

58 Gibbons, N. 1601. *Questions and Disputations Concerning the Holy Scripture… Approued by the Testimony of the Scriptures Themselues…The First Part of the First Tome*. Felix Kyngston, London: title page. For the biographical details of this author, see Bayne, R. 'Gibbon, Nicholas (fl. 1600)' in: *Dictionary of National Biography, 1885-1900, Volume 21*.
59 Gibbons, *Questions*: 41.
60 Gibbons, *Questions*: 44.
61 Gibbons, *Questions*: 162-163.

more common, and hence noxious. The corruption appears to imply mainly a quantitative and not so much a qualitative change. Whether the animal was mortal before Adam fell is not explicitly addressed, but the fact that Gibbons made the immortality of Adam dependent on access to the tree of life makes it plausible that, in his view, the animals, to whom this privilege was not granted, were already subject to death from the beginning.[62] The animals did not change their nature but only their habits; they cast off the authority of mankind whereby they deranged human life.

The cause for the change in animal behavior is clear. 'Such was the fiercenesse of the wrath of God against the sinnes of that wicked world, as that the Lord, when hee was constrained to take vengeance of their vngodliness, could not in iustice but punish the vnreasonable creatures for their sakes, which were created for their vse, as though they had beene partakers of their offences.'[63] When the master is punished, his servants are punished with him. That this punishment might imply suffering of creatures innocent in themselves, and hence jeopardize divine justice, was not noticed.

3.8.3. Andrew Willet (1562-1621)

The next author is the clergyman *Andrew Willet*, 'minister of the 'gospell of Iesus Christ.' In the year 1605, he published the *Hexapla in Genesin & Exodum*[64] with the promise to explain difficult questions and 'doubtfull' places; some of these concern the creation and the role of the animals therein. Willet held that 'God is the principall end of all things' and added that 'man is the secondary end, for whose use all things were created'.[65] However, since '*Adams* fall, (...) preeminence and dominion of man over the beasts is greatly diminished and impaired, that as he first disobeied his Creator, so they also have cast off mans yoake' although 'his Lordship and authority remaineth still' as 'there remaineth yet a naturall instinct of obedience in those creatures which are for mans use, as in the oxe, asse, horse, wherein Gods mercy appeareth'.[66] Thus, Adam's fall results in a disturbed relationship between humanity and the non-human living

---

62 Gibbons, *Questions*: 69-70.
63 Gibbons, *Questions*: 268.
64 Willet, A. 1633 [1605]. *Hexapla in Genesin & Exodum: that Is, a Sixfold Commentary upon the Tvvo First Bookes of Moses, Being Genesis and Exodus.... Now the Fourth Time Imprinted, with the Authors Corrections before His Death* ... Iohn Grismond, London. Willet's ranking with the Puritans is contested, this author being strongly opposed to all 'separatists,' whether on the Roman or Free-Church side. See Wilkinson, J.F. 'Willet, Andrew' in: *Dictionary of National Biography, 1885-1900, Volume 61*.
65 Willet, *Hexapla in Genesin*: 12.
66 Willet, *Hexapla in Genesin*: 13.

creation but men's authority is—thanks to God's mercy—not completely lost.

Willet obviously rejected Aquinas's view that animals did not change their nature due to Adam's fall. Referring to Romans 8:22, Willet was convinced that 'killing of beasts, upon what occasion soever, whether for food, for knowledge or pleasure, belongeth unto the bondage of corruption, which by sin was brought into the world'.[67] Death due to sin includes not only mankind but animals as well. But that the animals share humanity's bondage and corruption, however, does not imply that they also participate in the liberation from bondage. In his commentary on Romans 8, Willet wrote also that 'the bruit creatures which now onely serue for our necessarie vse, shall not be partakers of the glorie of the Sonnes of God, there shall then be no vse of them (…), it is probable, that they shall be abolished'.[68]

Elsewhere, not just animal death but more specifically predation was addressed. Before Adam fell, there was no predation for two reasons. The first is that there was no death yet, the other was that the authority of mankind restrained the animals from predation. Both fell away when the first human couple broke God's commandment.[69] Apparently, Willet propagated—as Gibbons did—that men's unbroken dominion over the animals acted as a barrier to predation.

But linking predation to the fall does not go without difficulties. 'What became of Lions and Beares, that lived of flesh, all this while of *Adams* being in Paradise? they could not fast so long, and flesh they did not eat, because there was no death before mans fall: and they did not feed on grasse: for then their nature should not so soone have beene changed to devoure flesh.' To prevent the starvation to death of these meat-eating animals, Willet offered an elegant solution. Only a very short period of time elapsed between their creation and the transgression of Adam: 'It was the coole of the day, about the Eventide, when sentence was given against *Adam*: so that in the space of eight or nine houre from his creation to his fall, all these matters might easily be done.'[70] The lions and bears only had to wait a few hours before they were allowed to take their first meal.

---

67 Willet, *Hexapla in Genesin*: 14. It is interesting to read that Willet also took issue with vivisection in seeing the need to kill animals for obtaining knowledge also as a consequence of the fall.
68 Willet, A. 1620 [1611]. *Hexapla: That Is, A Six-fold Commentarie vpon the Most Diuine Epistle of the Holy Apostle S. Paul to the Romanes…The First Booke.* Cantrell Legge, Cambridge: 367.
69 Willet, *Hexapla in Genesin*: 15.
70 Willet, *Hexapla in Genesin*: 45.

Willet acknowledged the presence of animal death and predation but since that is a result of Adam's sin, the goodness and benevolence of the Creator are not in danger. In this way, Willet did not leave the old path. But in trying to reconcile the Genesis story with the biological problems that arise when assuming that animals now carnivorous had been herbivorous before, he recognized a potential conflict between the results obtained by the study of nature and the scriptural record that had so far not received attention but would gradually become more important. Attempts to adapt scientific findings to biblical information or *vice versa* have not ceased since then.

3.8.4. Thomas Draxe (†1618)

When contemplating the moral implications of animal life, looking forward to future blessings may be as helpful as looking back to past disasters. In a sermon on Romans 8:22-23, delivered in 1612, the Anglican divine *Thomas Draxe* propagated the conviction that the animals will 'bee repaired and renewed',[71] which implies that their current situation qualifies for such a recovery. That recovery is not unlimited. First, the fish are excepted for obvious reasons. Second, the animals conceived through a God-forbidden intercourse of different animal species, for example the mule, are excluded from this new world. And, third, the animals that 'have their beginning from, and are bred of corruption and putrefaction, as frogs, flies, worms, mouldes, mise, crickets, bats, barnacles, have no part in this restitution'. And, fourth, '(…) all those (or such) plants, beasts, fowls, that either are already dead and dissolved, or, that afterwards, and at Christ his second coming shall be found deed and without life, are to be deducted out of this number'.[72] But for what remains after this dropout

---

71 Draxe, T. 1613. *The Earnest of Our Inheritance: together with a Description of the New Heaven and the New Earth, and a Demonstration of the Glorious Resurrection of the Bodie in the Same Substance. Preached at Pauls Crosse the Second Day of August. 1612*. George Norton, London: 4. For biographical details, see https://en.wikipedia.org/wiki/Thomas_Draxe. Accessed on 13 December 2021. Affinity with Puritanism may be assumed as Draxe translated the works of the Puritan divine William Perkins (1558-1602) into Latin.

72 Draxe, *Inheritance*: 5-6. In his comments about animals bred of corruption and putrefaction, Draxe harked back to the thoughts of Luther who advocated the postlapsarian emergence of nasty insects out of decomposing bodies, see § 2.3.3.1. In the course of the seventeenth century, this idea would become increasingly incredible, see Bentley, R. 1699 [1692]. *The Folly and Unreasonableness of Atheism Demonstrated from the Advantage and Pleasure of a Religious Life…The Fourth Edition Corrected*. H. Mortlock, London: 121-131. 'But (…) we affirm, That no Insect or Animal did ever proceed equivocally from Putrefaction, unless in miraculous Cases, as in Ægypt by the Divine Judgments' (121).

race a joyful future beckons. 'The creatures vanity and bondage hath not beene alwaies, neither shall it so continue: For when mans sinne that caused and occasioned it, shall be (at the last day) wholly blotted out and abolished, then of necessity must the creatures bondage of *corruption and abuse* which is the effect of it, cease.'[73]

Draxe acknowledged that now we live in a groaning corrupted creation, but because this is a result of man's, the misery of animals does not raise concerns about the divine attributes. It is true that, in the future, some animals will join mankind in a renewed creation, but it is clear that this does not compensate for the suffering in the present, given the limitations in number and species mentioned: '(…) they shall serue to set forth Gods *power, wisedome, mercy, goodnes*, and shall serue for the Saints *delight* & *contemplation*, and not otherwise.'[74] Just as in the first creation everything was for the glory of God and the welfare of man, so will it be in the renewed one.

Apparently, Draxe did not conceive that participation of the animals in the renewed creation could also serve to compensate for suffering endured in the present one from which can be deduced that, in Draxe's view, animal suffering is not something for which God is accountable. That did not mean, however, that he was blind to animal suffering as such. '[I]f the poor dumbe Creature, (bird or beast) bee in any paine and miserie, let vs not ioy, nor sport our selues in it paines and torments, but rather be sorry for it, and be greeued for our owne sinnes, which the silly and sinlesse creature smarteth for.'[75] Not God but we ourselves are to blame and the awareness of this guilt should keep us from deliberately aggravating the animals' miseries. The aforementioned author Topsell had said the same.

3.8.5. Godfrey Goodman (1583–1656)
For the Anglican bishop *Godfrey Goodman*, all evils that occur in this corrupted creation are the outcome of man having lost his authority. In his book—written to assist the reader in daily meditations of God's eternal providence—Goodman contended that because mankind lost its authority over creation, everything had fallen into disorder; 'if the Captaine and guide first breake the ranke, no maruell if the souldiers fall to confusion.'[76] As a consequence, nature now 'being defectiue, and not

---

73 Draxe, *Inheritance*: 13.
74 Draxe, 'The Epistle Dedicatorie' in: *Inheritance*: page not numbered.
75 Draxe, *Inheritance*: 26-27.
76 Goodman, G. 1616. *The Fall of Man, or the Corrvption of Natvre, Proved by the Light of Our Naturall Reason*…Felix Kyngston, London: 17. For biographical details, see Lee, S. 'Goodman, Godfrey' in: *Dictionary of National Biography, 1885-1900, Volume 22*.

able to produce couragious Lions, braue Vnicornes, fierce Tigers, stout Elephants, shee [nature] makes it her taske and imployment to be the mother, and mid-wife of wormes, of gnats, and of butterflies'.[77]

Apparently, carnivorous animals like lions and tigers belong to the uncorrupted creation but nasty insects—which according to Goodman surprisingly also includes the butterflies—and other invertebrates are species that were not previously encountered. Whether this implies that Goodman put predation before the fall remains conjectural as there are no further elaborations on this issue in his writings. However, it is clear that, in Goodman's opinion, animals have no value in themselves and that animals' suffering is only important as a means of reminding humanity of its sinfulness. '[N]either was this world intended for dumbe beasts, but onely for man; and therefore as their slaughter is ordained for man, so if their punishment might serue for mans admonition, and bee a remembrancer of his sinne, this were sufficient for the exercise of Gods iustice, and to excuse his works of imperfection.'[78]

Animals are created for man's use only, and because of human transgression, they now have a role as divine instruments for punishment; their suffering plays only a subordinate role.[79] But these gloomy tones do not detract from the fact that Goodman also had more positive thoughts about the fate of the animals. Since our fall they groan and toil under the effects of sin like we do, then it is just that they will also participate in the renewal of creation, either 'in their owne first elements and principles, or as they haue now entred into mans body, and are become parts of mans flesh'.[80]

Like Topsell and Draxe, Goodman was convinced that animals will join humans in the new creation either in their original uncorrupted state ('first elements and principles') or because they became part of the human body after having served as our food.[81] This conviction, however was

---

His involvement with Catholicism made him trouble and even took him to jail for some months. For an extensive description of Goodman's gloomy views put in context, see Jones, R.F. 1961. *Ancients and Moderns. A Study of the Rise of the Scientific Movement in Seventeenth-Century England. Second Edition with an Index, New Preface, and Minor Revisions*. Washington University Studies, St. Louis: 25-29.

77 Goodman, *Fall*: 19.
78 Goodman, *Fall*: 217-218.
79 Goodman, *Fall*: 262-263.
80 Goodman, G. 1622. *The Creatvres Praysing God: or, the Religion of Dumbe Creatures. An Example and Argument, for the Stirring vp of Our Deuotion, and for the Confusion of Atheisme...*Felik Kingston, London: 29.
81 It is doubtful to what extent the prospect of being part of a renewed creation only by being part of the glorified human body would comfort animals.

not universally shared. The Puritan *Thomas Edwards* (1599–1647)[82] repudiated the belief that '[t]here shall be in the last day a resurrection from the dead of all the bruit creatures, all beasts and birds that ever lived upon the earth, every individuall of every kinde of them that died shall rise again (…) and all these creatures shall live for ever upon the earth'.[83] Another divine, *John Swan* (†1671) of Trinity College, Cambridge did not reject the idea outright but still had reservations; a resurrection of the animals that serve our daily needs is, after all, not necessary because in a renewed creation, such needs no longer exist.[84] Any reticence, on the other hand, was foreign to the Leveller *Richard Overton* (c.1609–c.1668).[85] Commenting on 1 Corinthians 15:22[86] and Romans 6:23,[87] he wrote that if the animals would not rise from the dead, the promise that all will be made alive in Christ would not be fulfilled.[88] It appears that the issue of animals partaking in the resurrection—and if so, in what way—was a hot topic at that time. I will return to this shortly.

---

82 For biographical details, see Vian, A.R. 'Edwards, Thomas (1599-1647)' in: *Dictionary of National Biography, 1885-1900, Volume 17*.

83 Edwards, T. 1646. *The First and Second Part of Gangræna: or a Catalogue and Discovery of Many of the Errors, Heresies, Blasphemies and Pernicious Practices of the Sectaries of this Time, Vented and Acted in England in these Four Last Yeers*. Ralph Smit, London: 27. The quoted statement is the 90th of the 176 *Errours, Heresies, [and] Blasphemies* as listed by this author.

84 Swan, J. 1643. *Specvlvm Mundi. Or a Glasse Representing the Face of the World…The Second Edition Enlarged*. Roger Daniel, Cambridge: 6-7. For details on John Swan, see MacKenzie, *God's Order and Natural Law*: 184-188. John Swan belonged to a group of theologians known as the Laudian Divines for which order in creation and society was a guiding principle. Cf. Gillett, E.H. 1874. *God in Human Thought; or, Natural Theology Traced in Literature…from Spenser to Butler. In Two Volumes. Volume II*. Scribner, Armstrong & Co., New York: 487-488.

85 Overton, R. 1655. *Man Wholly Mortal; or, a Treatise wherein 'T is Proved, both Theologically and Philosophically, that as Whole Man Sinned, so Whole Man Died…The Second Edition, by the Author Corrected and Enlarged*. n.p., London. Richard Overton was a Leveller, member of a political movement advocating a return to a flat society with the monarchy abolished, as well as a mortalist, holding that, in the Bible, soul was simply synonymous for life, and that there was no conscious existence after death until the resurrection, when the human race would be raised together with the entire animal creation. Cf. Zimmer, *Soul Made Flesh*: 77-79; McDowell, N. 2005. 'Ideas of Creation in the Writings of Richard Overton the Leveller and "Paradise Lost"' in: *Journal of the History of Ideas* 66 (1): 59-78; Marshall, W.W. 2016. *Puritanism and Natural Theology*. Pickwick Publications, Oregon: 23.

86 'For as in Adam all die, even so in Christ shall all be made alive.' (KJV)

87 'For the wages of sin is death; but the gift of God is eternal life through Jesus Christ our Lord.' (KJV)

88 Overton, *Man Wholly Mortal*: 111, 114.

3.8.6. Edward Elton (1569-1624)

The Puritan pastor *Edward Elton*[89] had no doubt that the evils we have to face are all due to Adam's fall. In his sermons on Romans 8:19–22,[90] he explained what it means that the creation has lost its original goodness, is subjected to vanity, and longs to be delivered from the bondage of decay. The creatures are no longer able to achieve the intended purpose for which they were called into existence. 'That is the curse of God upon the visible creatures, that be under the highest heavens, that they are weak and unable to attain the end for which they were created, that they now serve not for the good of man, that in the good use of them the goodnesse of God might by man be acknowledged.'[91]

Some may ask how 'it stand with the justice of God that the poor creatures that sinned not should be subject to vanity, and brought under the curse for the sin of man?' The answer is that 'it is just with the Lord not onely to punish man in his own person, but in the things belonging to him, in the things that should serve for his use and for his comfort, even to make them weak and unable to do that service to man'. In this way, we can understand that 'the vanity and curse that the poor creatures now lye under is not properly the punishment of the creatures themselves, but is part of mans punishment for his sin'.[92]

The fact that animals derive their value only from the significance they have for humans also explains why Elton recoiled from a too generous admission of the animals into the new creation. For him, only those animals that were created at the sixth day will be restored to their original immortal state and join mankind in the world to come. At that place, they can resume the task for which they were originally created and which they could no longer perform properly after the fall.[93]

The fact that Elton saw animals primarily as a means of inducing us to recognize and honor God as our Creator does not mean, however, that he completely neglected their interests. On the contrary: '(…) is it so that the creature is under the curse for the sin of man? Surely then we must learn to be mercifull to the poor creatures standing in need of our mercy.'[94] In this urge to treat the animals gently, Elton joined the aforementioned Puritan author Topsell and the Anglican divine Draxe.

---

89 For concise biographical information, see Lane, *Ravished by Beauty*: 289n18.
90 Elton, E. 1653 [1618]. *Three Excellent and Pious Treatises…in Sundry Sermons upon the Whole Seventh, Eight, and Ninth Chapters of the Epistle to the Romans*. Christopher Meredith, London: 232-259.
91 Elton, *Three Excellent and Pious Treatises*: 242 [erroneously printed as 142].
92 Elton, *Three Excellent and Pious Treatises*: 245.
93 Elton, *Three Excellent and Pious Treatises*: 248-249.
94 Elton, *Three Excellent and Pious Treatises*: 247.

3.8.7. George Hakewill (1578–1649)

In 1627, *George Hakewill*, fellow and later rector of Oxford's Exeter College and strong defender of the Calvinist position in the Anglican Church,[95] published the first edition of his *Apologie*.[96] A slightly expanded edition followed by in 1630 and a greatly expanded one in 1635.[97] The 1635 edition will be analyzed as, in this text, Hakewill explicitly addressed the gloomy thoughts expressed by the aforementioned author Godfrey Goodman, which offers insight not only into the opinion of the author himself but also into the way he conducted a debate on a controversial issue.[98] Invoking Augustine as witness and with support from other authors, Hakewill concluded that

> God ceasing from the works of the Creation upon the seventh day in regard of the production of any new species, and having created all the severall kind of vegetables upon the third day should not afterwards create new kind of plants, as thornes and thistles & poyson-some herbs, & the like (…). Neither is it more inconvenient that before the fall we should admit of such kind of plants, then of *Wolves* or *Beares*, or *Crocodills*, or *Serpents*, or *Tygers*, or *Lyons*, or *Scorpions*, or *Dragons*, or such like noysome animals.[99]

Apparently, Hakewill denied that the curse upon the earth evoked by Adam's fall had consequences for the natural world. 'No part of the materiall world (man onely excepted) is tainted with sinne, nor subject

---

95 The Calvinist conviction of Hakewill is beyond doubt. 'While a student, he had travelled abroad to receive theological instruction at Heidelberg from the prominent Calvinists David Pareus and Abraham Scultetus (…) and in 1618 there were rumours that Hakewill was to be sent as one of the English delegates to the Synod of Dort.' In: Poole, W. 2010. 'The Evolution of George Hakewill's Apologie or Declaration of the Power and Providence of God, 1627–1637: Academic Contexts, and Some New Angles from Manuscripts' in: *Electronic British Library Journal* 7:1-32 (2).
96 Hakewill, G. 1627. *An Apologie of the Povver and Prouidence of God in the Gouernment of the World…Diuided into Fovre Books*. Iohn Lichfield and William Turner, Oxford.
97 Hakewill, G. 1635. *An Apologie or Declaration of the Povver and Providence of God in the Government of the World… Divided into Six Bookes. The Third Edition Revised…* William Turner, Oxford. For notes on the several editions of the *Apologie*, see Poole, 'Evolution'
98 Williamson, G. 1935. 'Mutability, Decay, and Seventeenth-Century Melancholy' in: *English Literary History* 2(2): 121-150; Williams, *Christian Attitudes toward Nature*: 13-15. For more details on Hakewill and his conflict with Goodman, see Jones, *Ancients and Moderns*: 29-40.
99 Hakewill, *Apologie* II: 153.

either to a curse or vanity, but in relation to sinfull man.'[100] Animals did not change their nature for the worse, and thorns and thistles also occurred in the uncorrupted creation. As God declared his work in creating to be finished and took rest at the seventh day, there is no room for a new creation as source for anything now considered threatening or noisome. A more recent scholar traces Hakewill's deeper motivation. '[To] believe in a Cosmic Fall and subsequent degeneration saps energy, hope and virtue.'[101]

In reply to Godfrey Goodman who stated that *'But by the sinne of Adam as there was a propagation in respect of his posterity, so was here a contagion in respect of all the Creatures'*,[102] Hakewill pointed to the incongruities arising from this view. Since the objections arise from the pen of an unadulterated Calvinist—from whom one would not expect a compromise on the literal content of the Bible—they are quoted here in full.

> That by the fall of man the whole world became infected with sinne, may not bee yielded; where is no act of reason nor free choyce of the will, there can be no actuall sinne, nor originall, but by propagation; so as unlesse wee shall say, that the dumbe Creatures are propagated from *Adam*, or have in themselves an exercise of reason and freedome of will, they can in no sort bee capable either of actuall or originall sinne, and consequently not infected with sinne at all. That the world since the Creation is changed in state and condition in regard of mans use I grant, that proving discord and opposition to him, which unlesse hee had fallen had not beene so; but in respect of it selfe the sinne of man could not alter the worke of God, or marre that sweet harmony which hee had set in it (…) much lesse did it put an enmity betwixt God and the Creatures, neither doe they revenge upon each other the injuries done unto God, these are meere fictions and fancies of your [Goodman's] owne braine without any sufficient warrant. The Creatures as being the workemanship of his owne hands, and constantly persevering in their obedience, are as deare unto their maker as ever, and he as bountifull unto them, they never were in any point injurious to him by sinning against him, but hee [Goodman] rather seemes to bee injurious both to him [God] and them [the animals], who taxeth them with disobedience, and him with injustice, in punishing them for disobedience, and both undeservedly: If this be not to wound

---

100 Hakewill, *Apologie* V: 145.
101 Hepburn, R.W. 1955. 'George Hakewill: the Virility of Nature' in: *Journal of the History of Ideas* 16 (2): 135-150 (150). Cf. VanderMolen, 'Providence as Mystery': 33-47.
102 Hakewill, *Apologie* V: 142.

him in his justice, and them in their innocency, through the sides of I know not what imaginerie corrupt nature, I know not what it is.¹⁰³

It is obvious that Hakewill took a firm stand against the idea of a cosmic fall. Nature became hostile to humanity, but the non-human animal kingdom itself was not subjected to any curse. This would be against God's justice, for without sin there is no reason for punishment. Centuries before, Augustine had already written similar notes. Those who ask 'why do beasts injure one another, though they neither have any sins, so that this kind of thing could be called punishment?' are told that this is just the way nature works. It is '[f]or the simple reason (…) that some are the proper diet of others'.¹⁰⁴ Animal life and behavior before and after the fall are the same as 'the sinne of man could not alter the worke of God'. In this latter statement, the Calvinist agreed with the Roman Catholic scholar Aquinas: 'For the nature of animals was not changed by man's sin.'¹⁰⁵

We may assume that the Calvinistic theologian Hakewill would endorse the conviction that Scripture should be taken literally, but that does not come true.¹⁰⁶ For Hakewill, animal death and predation belong to the uncorrupted creation. In no way does this blemish the attributes of the Creator. On the contrary, animals changing their nature for the worse as punishment for Adam's transgression, while being innocent themselves, would raise doubts about God's attributes. But that these doubts also could arise when questioning how animal death and predation in an uncorrupted creation square with divine goodness and benevolence was for Hakewill yet out of sight. Within a few decades, this latter point would become a big issue.

3.8.8. George Walker (1581-1651)

In his sermons devoted to the importance of a proper observation of the Lord's Day, the Puritan theologian *George Walker*¹⁰⁷ paid attention to the

---

103 Hakewill, *Apologie* V: 143.
104 Augustine. 'The Literal Meaning of Genesis' in: Rotelle, J.E. (ed.). 2017. *The Works of Saint Augustine. A Translation for the 21st Century. On Genesis I/13…4th printing.* New City Press, New York: 246 (III,16,25). Cf. § 2.3.1.12.
105 Aquinas. 'Question 96. Of the Mastership Belonging to Man in the State of Innocence. Article 1. Whether Adam in the State of Innocence Had Mastership over the Animals? Reply to Objection 2' in: Aquinas, T. 2020 [1920]. *The Summa Theologiae of St. Thomas Aquinas. Literally Translated by Fathers of the English Dominican Province. First Part.* The Collected Works of St. Thomas Aquinas. Electronic Edition. http://www.newadvent.org/summa/
106 See for Calvin's thoughts on this Chapter 2, § 2.3.3.2.
107 For biographical details, see http://www.apuritansmind.com/puritan-favorites/george-walker-1581-1651/. Accessed on 13 December 2021. His clerical superiors

creation as described in Scripture as well. '[T]he world was created for us, & for our use, not for any need which God had of it.'[108] We, however, have spoiled this precious gift and therefore, we, '(…) so often as wee see or remember the unprofitablenesse, loathsomnesse and poison which is in some creatures, bee stirred up to repent of our sinnes which have brought them under this corruption for a scourge of our dis-obedience.'[109] If an animal behaves hostile to us, it is no reason to complain; because we have transgressed, the animals that were created for our benefit 'are become our enemies; and they by our transgression are made subject to vanity and corruption, under which they groane together with us.'[110]

Realizing that our guilt and sin lay behind our troublesome relationship with the animals as well as behind the troubles of the animals themselves should make us careful in our dealings with them. Although we may kill 'hurtfull beasts and noysome creatures', we should not do it 'with cruelty, and with pleasure, delight, and rejoycing in their destruction' as that would be 'a kind of scorne and contempt of the workmanship of God our Creatour and of the worke of his hands'.[111] Apparently, Walker advocated a gentle handling of the animals because God made them. Also, he was concerned about the feelings of the animals themselves that suffer as 'they groane together with us'. In this compassion with the animals, the Puritan Walker joined his fellow Puritans Topsell and Elton, thus providing additional evidence for the important role Puritanism played an in arousing sensitivity to the suffering of non-human creatures.[112]

Walker also paid attention to another issue commonly addressed by authors writing on the problem of noxious animals. Did they form part of the uncorrupted prelapsarian animal world but became noxious only afterwards, or were they newly created after the fall? On this point, he noted that 'it is cleare, that the creatures which are now most hurtfull and venomous; and curses, plagues, and cruell instruments, to punish men, were created harmelesse and serviceable to man at the first, and by the Divell, and mans sin are become hurtfull and hatefull enemies'.[113] Walker

---

disliked his insistence on respecting the Sunday as a day for worship and put him in jail for several weeks on accusation of being a 'Preacher of factious and seditious Doctrine, and (…) the great troubler of the City of *London*'. In: Walker, G. 1641. *The History of the Creation as It Is Written by Moses in the First and Second Chapters of Genesis*…John Bartlet, London: A3.
108 Walker, G. 1641. *God Made Visible in His Workes*…John Bartlet, London: 25.
109 Walker, *Workes*: 152.
110 Walker, *Workes*: 160.
111 Walker, *Workes*: 160.
112 Watson, 'Protestant Animals': 1141-1142.
113 Walker, *Workes*: 163.

evidently excluded a postlapsarian new creative act of God as well as their postlapsarian emergence from decaying dead bodies as contemplated by Luther and Draxe. Animals changed their nature for the worse. Both devil and humankind are the evildoers. Due to humanity's sin, 'death came upon *all*'[114] and 'by mans fall, many beasts are become ravenous, and devour other living creatures, and feed upon their flesh; as Lyons, Bears, and such like: Yet in the creation and state of innocency, they did like oxen feed on green grasse.'[115] Animal death and a carnivorous diet did not belong to the uncorrupted creation but are the outcome of the curse upon the earth that was evoked by Adam's disobedience, a disobedience which has not only led to the murderous behavior of the animals among themselves, but has also profoundly changed our own relationship with the animals.

> So often as wee see (…) living creatures killed, and their flesh eaten for necessity of mans nourishment, let it put us in minde, and remembrance of our sin and fall in our first Parents (…). Let the groanes of beasts slaine for us, and their bloud shed and poured out with strugling, and with cryes and sighes (…) smite us with the sight of our naturall corruption, and make us loath our sinnes, and sigh and groane under the burden of them, and labour to subdue corruptions, and put away our sinnes by repentance.[116]

These considerations should motivate us even more to 'hate, feare, shunne and abhorre sin, which was and is the cause of all' where we can comfort ourselves with the knowledge that, in the future, '(…) all poison and enmity should cease to bee in the creatures; they should bee at peace with us, and should be restored to the *liberty of the Sons of God*'.[117]

His concern with animal well-being prompted him also to warn against enjoying animal sports: '(…) all enmity, which is among the creatures, vexing and destroying one another, came in by sin; and all the pleasure which men take therein, is corrupt, sinfull, and against pure nature'.[118] In this, the Puritan George Walker agreed with other Puritan theologians like Topsell and Perkins as mentioned above. It is difficult to disentangle whether their aversion to animal sports came from theological considerations or from a more mundane Puritan aversion to any idleness.

---

114 Walker, *Workes*: 233.
115 Walker, *Workes*: 168.
116 Walker, *Workes*: 234-235.
117 Walker, *Workes*: 166. Walker here casually alludes to the fact that humans and animals will both share in the bliss of the renewed creation, but he doesn't elaborate on this.
118 Walker, *Workes*: 26.

Thomas Macaulay's famous assertion that 'the Puritan hated bear-baiting, not because it gave pain to the bear, but because it gave pleasure to the spectators',[119] at least suggests the latter possibility.

3.8.9. Thomas Browne (1605-1682)

In his *Religio Medici*,[120] Thomas Browne, a physician welcoming the Restoration of the Stuart monarchy after the intermezzo of Commonwealth and Protectorate, and throughout those turbulent years remaining a staunch Royalist,[121] unfolded his thoughts about the relationship between Scripture and nature. For him, '(...) there are two books from whence I collect my divinity; besides that written one of God, another of his servant nature, that universal and publick manuscript, that lies expansed unto the eyes of all'.[122] The book of nature should be read because the 'wisdom of God receives small honour from those vulgar heads that rudely stare about' whereas only 'those highly magnify him, whose judicious inquiry into his acts, and deliberate research into his creatures, return the duty of a devout and learned admiration'.[123]

The book of nature reflects the craftsmanship of the Creator. Browne—agreeing with Hakewill—rejected the thought that Adam's sin had corrupted nature. 'Now this course of nature God seldom alters or perverts, but, like an excellent artist, hath so contrived his work, that with the self same instrument, without a new creation, he may effect his obscurest designs.'[124] People who think otherwise because of the text as recorded in Genesis were rebuked by Browne: '(...) though divines have, to the power of human reason, endeavoured to make all go in a literal meaning, yet those allegorical interpretations are also probable, and perhaps the mystical method of Moses, bred up in the hieroglyphical schools of the Egyptians.'[125] Scripture should be read for its message, not for its literal content.[126]

This did not mean that a literal interpretation of Scripture should always be rejected. Browne exploited this for broaching the difficult point that whereas the Bible says that the animals have been given the green

---

119 Macaulay, T.B. 1849. *The History of England from the Accession of James the Second*. Vol. I. Bernhard Tauchnitz, Leipzig: 159.
120 Browne, T. 1898 [1642]. *Religio Medici*. George Bell and Sons, London.
121 Breathnach, C.S. 2005. 'Sir Thomas Browne' in: *Journal of the Royal Society of Medicine* 98: 33-36.
122 Browne, *Religio*: 28.
123 Browne, *Religio*: 25.
124 Browne, *Religio*: 29
125 Browne, *Religio*: 62
126 Browne, *Religio*: 81.

herb for food,[127] there, nevertheless, are also carnivorous animals. Taking into account that all flesh is like grass,[128] we should acknowledge that 'all those creatures we behold are but the herbs of the field, digested into flesh in them, or more remotely carnified in our selves'.[129] All food can be traced back to grass, grass being transformed to flesh in all living beings, both human and non-human. Hence, eating meat or eating grass is morally equal.

Browne also expressed doubts on the Genesis text on creation and curse in his *Pseudodoxia Epidemica*, a book he wrote to unmask vulgar errors as well as time-honored superstitions. One of the targets under fire is again the view that 'carnivorous animals now, were not flesh devourers then', an assumption based on 'very grave conjectures'.[130]

This did not mean that Browne jettisoned the entire contents of the first three chapters of Genesis, but he mainly focused on the relationship between humans and animals. Speaking of the meeting between the woman and the serpent, he explained why this meeting did not frighten Eve as 'in that place as most determine, no creature was hurtful or terrible unto man'. The special situation of Paradise also explains that the gathering of all kinds of animals there to receive their names from Adam did not end in tearing each other in pieces, let alone devouring the name giver himself. For that occasion, God had temporarily suspended the ferocious nature of carnivorous animals: '(…) as they peaceably received their names, so they friendly possessed their natures'. Therefore, '(…) they could not at that time destroy either man or themselves; for this had frustrated the command of multiplication, destroyed a species, and imperfected the Creation'.[131] It was only after their expulsion from Paradise that Adam and Eve were confronted with an animal world that was hostile to them, a situation they had never encountered before.

Browne's view on animal life and behavior was mainly determined by empirics and less by Scripture. In case of conflict, Scripture should be

---

127 Genesis 1:30. 'And to every beast of the earth, and to every fowl of the air, and to every thing that creepeth upon the earth, wherein there is life, I have given every green herb for meat: and it was so.' (KJV)
128 'For all flesh is as grass, and all the glory of man as the flower of grass.' 1 Peter 1:24. (KJV)
129 Browne, *Religio*: 67.
130 Browne, T. 1658. *Pseudodoxia Epidemica: or, Enquiries into Very Many Received Tenents and Commonly Presumed Truths. The Fourth Edition…and a Table Alphabetical*. Edward Dod, London: 210.
131 Browne, *Pseudodoxia Epidemica*: 290. The argument that God protects every animal species from extinction to preserve the perfection of his creation came to play a significant role over time. It also comes up in Browne's younger contemporaries Wilkins and Ray, authors to whom I will return shortly.

taken in an allegorical sense. Here, he disagreed with his contemporary scholar *John Johnston* (1603-1675) who almost at the same time wrote that 'by faith we understand, that the world was Made. The History is in the Scripture, but the perfect description in *Moses*'s Works, *Gen.* 1. (…) The dictates of the Holy Ghost cannot be false, the knowledge of God is free from errour',[132] this author thus emphasizing the value of Scripture above empirics.

In Browne's view, animals behave as they were created; only their relationship to humanity changed for the worse due to sin. Furthermore, animal behavior was taken for granted; it is as it is, and it does not threaten the divine attributes. Knowledge provided by nature is meant to worship God, not to ask questions about him.

3.8.10. Kenelm Digby (1603–1665)
For the philosopher and diplomat *Kenelm Digby*, who converted from Anglicanism to Catholicism and had been imprisoned by Parliament for his Royalist sympathies,[133] animal suffering was not a matter of concern either. With him, we encounter, for the first time, the metaphor of animals behaving like automata that Digby indicates to have borrowed from Descartes. 'This then is the summe of Monsieur des Cartes his opinion, which he hath very finely expressed, with all the advantages that opposite examples, significant words, and cleare method can give unto a witty discourse.'[134] Animals are testimony of the craftsmanship of he who made them, and we should 'looke with reverence and duty upon the immensity of that provident Architect, out of whose hands these masterpieces issue'.[135] If we attribute a mental life to the animals, we fall into the trap of anthropocentrism. This occurs when we 'will have beasts rationate and

---

132 Johnston, J. 1657. *An History of the Wonderful Things of Nature: Set Forth…Written by Johannes Jonstonus. And now Rendred into English by a Person of Quality*. John Streater, London: 1-2.
133 Miles, W. 1949. 'Sir Kenelm Digby, Alchemist, Scholar, Courtier, and Man of Adventure' in: *Chymia* 2: 119-128; Porter, R. 2003. *Flesh in the Age of Reason. How the Enlightenment Transformed the Way We See Our Bodies and Souls*. Penguin Books, London: 69-70. Digby also wrote a criticism on Browne's *Religio Medici*, see Wise, J.N. 1973. *Sir Thomas Browne's Religio Medici and Two Seventeenth-Century Critics*. University of Missouri Press, Columbia: 57-121. For the text of Digby's criticism, see Digby, K. 'Observations upon Religio Medici Occasionally Written by Sir Kenelm Digby' in: Browne, *Religio*: 143-187. In this criticism, no attention is paid to the subject of animal suffering.
134 Digby, K. 1645. *Two Treatises: In the One of Which, the Nature of Bodies; in the Other, the Nature of Mans Soule; Is Looked into: In Way of Discovery, of the Immortality of Reasonable Soules*. Iohn Williams, London: 335.
135 Digby, *Two Treatises*: 400.

understand, upon their observing some orderly actions performed by them, which in men would proceed from discourse and reason'.[136]

Animals behave as ordered to them by their maker, 'without the need of a soul and its attendant psychological life'.[137] Possibly, Digby assumed that lack of reason and understanding means lack of the capacity to suffer as well. Notions that human sin and divine curse might be relevant for animal miseries as observed nowadays are lacking in his writings.

3.8.11. John Waite (c.1666)

As mentioned above, in this period the idea emerged that there will be animals on the renewed earth. This topic has been widely elaborated by *John Waite*[138] who unfolded his thoughts on this subject through the text about the liberation of the creature from the bondage of corruption as found in Romans 8.[139] First, the reason for creation's bondage was discussed. This reason is evident; the bondage of the creation is God's punishment which involves the non-human creation as well. That the latter is innocent does not collide with God's justice because the animals are men's possession, and their change for the worse is part of mankind's punishment.[140]

The reason for the bondage of creation thus established, Waite continued by asking: '(…) after what manner the Creature shall be delivered, and what Creatures they are that shall be delivered?' There are two options. Their deliverance can be a total annihilation, or a return to the state as it was before the fall.[141] Waite chose to agree with 'those learned men that have given their judgments for a liberation of the Creature by mutation and repurgation, rather then by totall abolition of the materiall or visible Creature'.[142]

After the question of what the deliverance from the bondage entails, the question arises as to which animals will be delivered. Also here, there are several possibilities. It could be the animals that lived in the time of

---

136 Digby, *Two Treatises*: 419.
137 Strickland, 'God's Creatures': 295.
138 For this author, no other details are available than his academic qualification, Bachelor of Divine. Some speculations about his identity and background are mentioned in Rudrum, 'Henry Vaughan, the Liberation of the Creatures'. This author provisionally identifies him as a Cambridge raised divine who sided with the rebels which may indicate Puritan sympathies.
139 Waite, J. 1650. *Of the Creatures Liberation from the Bondage of Corruption…*Tho. Broad, York.
140 Waite, *Of the Creatures Liberation*: 89-91, 100.
141 Waite, *Of the Creatures Liberation*: 145.
142 Waite, *Of the Creatures Liberation*: 172.

Adam, or all the animals that ever lived on earth, or the animals that lived in the time of the second coming of Christ. The first option was dropped because these animals cannot be said to 'travell in pain together, (…) even untill now'. The second option is less likely for practical reasons for 'Who can conceive that the Earth should contain them?'[143]

Waite favored the third option: only animals alive at the Day of Judgment will be liberated from bondage and restored, but then the question remains whether it will concern every animal species still occurring or each individual animal still alive. This 'God hath not clearly revealed unto us'.[144] This perceived lack of scriptural information did, however, not preclude Waite from writing: 'I conceive, that all Creatures may be said to be renewed, when their several sorts; or species shall be renewed.'[145] But 'how many Individualls God shall renew of every sort, that is left to his wisdom, and good pleasure, as it was when he preserved the severall species at the time of the Flood'.[146]

After having established the reason for the bondage of the creatures, the way they will be liberated from that bondage, and which creatures will enjoy that liberation, Waite continued by considering the usefulness of that liberation. Why will non-human animals inhabit the renewed earth? We will not be in need of them for feeding, clothing, or other benefits. But then we need to recall that although the animals will no longer be there to fulfill a necessary task as before, they will nevertheless continue to be of use as signs of God's multifaceted wisdom.[147] And besides illustrating divine attributes, they also have another role to play. It will delight the saved sinners 'that they see the poor Creatures, their old, and *quondam* servants freed from vanity, slavery, and misery, and now restored to liberty, and from that corruption they fell under, by reason of their former disobedience, and impiety'.[148] The earth may be renewed but the purpose for which the animals were created has not changed. They still play a subservient role as it is not the animal that benefits from the blessed afterlife but the 'saved sinner' for whom the consequences of Adam's disobedience now are blotted out—mankind safeguarded from any confrontation with groaning animals reminding it of its wickedness.

Those who expected that the creation's liberation from bondage would imply a personal remuneration for each individual animal as compensation for past miseries will be disappointed by the outcome of Waite's

---

143 Waite, *Of the Creatures Liberation*: 248.
144 Waite, *Of the Creatures Liberation*: 249.
145 Waite, *Of the Creatures Liberation*: 260.
146 Waite, *Of the Creatures Liberation*: 330.
147 Waite, *Of the Creatures Liberation*: 332.
148 Waite, *Of the Creatures Liberation*: 335.

considerations. The liberation is restricted to only a small number; so the vicissitudes of the overwhelming majority of animals was taken for granted. 'The sovereign Lord (…) can be touched with no injustice',[149] a statement not surprising when the assumption that Waite subscribed to Puritanism is correct. We learn about God's righteousness from Scripture, not from nature. This makes a big difference with the author to be discussed next.

3.8.12. Henry More (1614-1687)

For *Henry More*, one of the Cambridge Platonists,[150] the several aspects of animals represented 'an Argument of divine Providence'.[151] The life of animals is at the service of humans if only that 'their life is but for Salt to keep them sweet till we shall have need to eat them'.[152] And also, in other things they are for our benefit because some of them are also useful 'in removing those Evils we are pester'd with by reason of the abundance of some other hurtful Animals, such as are *Mice* and *Rats*, and the like; and to this end the *Cat* is very serviceable'.[153] Animal predation appears to be a behavior that serves us very well, nothing to be concerned about.

---

149 Waite, *Of the Creatures Liberation*: 91.
150 The Cambridge Platonists wanted to remove the tension between religion and the new science and to combine faith with rationality. In human reason they saw a reflection of God's reason and therefore they rejected the Calvinist conviction that God's sovereign action is beyond our standards of reasonableness. They may be considered the first representatives of those Anglicans known as 'Latitudinarians', divines who had managed to survive Cromwell's Interregnum, now taking prestigious positions to the dismay of other Anglican divines who had suffered for their Church convictions. They agreed with Descartes in their distrust of empiricism but did not subscribe to his belief that natural processes have no (divine) purpose. Adapted from Britannica, The Editors of Encyclopaedia. "Cambridge Platonists". *Encyclopedia Britannica*, 2 Januari 2020, https://www.britannica.com/topic/Cambridge-Platonists. Accessed on 14 December 2021. Cf. Lamprecht, 'Innate Ideas': 553-554; Spurr, J. 1988. "Latitudinarianism' and the Restoration Church' in: *The Historical Journal* 31 (1): 61-82; Porter, *Flesh*: 80-93; Calloway, K. 2010. *God's Scientists: the Renovation of Natural Theology in England, 1653-1692*. PhD Thesis, University of British Columbia, Vancouver: 40-71.
151 More, H. 1655. *An Antidote against Atheism or, an Appeal to the Naturall Faculties of the Minde of Man, whether there Be Not a God. The Second Edition Corrected and Enlarged: with an Appendix thereunto Annexed*. William Morden, Cambridge: 112-141 (112). For the role, More assigned to divine providence, see Mandelbrote, 'The Uses of Natural Theology in Seventeenth-Century England'.
152 More, *Antidote*: 116. That animal life merely serves as preserving salt is a thought already found by Chrysippus the Stoic (279-206 B.C.), see Newmyer, S.T. 1999. 'Speaking of Beasts: the Stoics and Plutarch on Animal Reason and the Modern Case against Animals' in: *Quaderni Urbinati di Cultura Classica, New Series* 63 (3): 99-110 (105).
153 More, *Antidote*: 119.

Furthermore, '(...) to expect and wish that there were nothing but such dull *tame* things in the world that will neither bite nor scratch is as groundless and childish, as to wish there were no *choler* in the body, nor *fire* in the universal compass of Nature'.[154] Even those animals we dislike are of value as 'though some of them be of an *hateful* aspect, as the *Toad*, the *Swine* and the *Rat*, yet these are but like discords in Musick, to make the succeeding chord go off more pleasantly'.[155] However, the importance that animals have for humans does not exclude other aspects.

> [S]urely a good God is bountiful and benign, and takes pleasure that all his Creatures enjoy themselves that have life and sense, and are capable of any enjoyment. So that the swarms of little *Vermine*, and of *Flyes*, and innumerable such like diminutive Creatures, we should rather congratulate their coming into Being, then murmure sullenly and scornfully against their Existence; for they find nourishment in the world, which would be lost if they were not, and are again convenient nourishment themselves to others that prey upon them.[156]

God aims for a joyful existence for all his creatures; this joy may be felt by the hunter who succeeds in capturing his prey as well as by the prey who manages to escape. To those who raise that animals preying one upon each other is inconsistent with that '*Eternal Goodness* that we profess to have created and ordered all things', More replied that the interest of the whole prevails over the interest of the individual what entails that 'some particular Creatures [are loaded] with greater inconveniency then the rest'.[157]

Predation increases the amount of joy. 'Wherefore what can be more grateful to a terrestrial Animal, then to hunt his prey and to obtain it?' And others 'not only enjoy themselves, but occasionally afford game and food to other Creatures. In which notwithstanding the *wisdome* of God as well as his *goodness* is manifest.'[158]

That More was convinced that predation already existed in the uncorrupted creation is evident elsewhere also. In his *Divine Dialogues,* More addressed the topic of animal life as related to divine attributes in the form of a discussion between imaginary participants identified as the 'zealous, but airy minded, Platonist or Cartesian' *Cuphophron*, the 'young,

---

154 More, *Antidote*: 118.
155 More, *Antidote*: 120.
156 More, *Antidote*: 124
157 More, *Antidote*: 368-369.
158 More, *Antidote*: 369-370.

witty and well moralized Materiallist' *Hylobares*, and *Philotheus*, 'a zealous and sincere lover of God and *Christ*, and of the whole Creation'.[159]

Hylobares raised that 'nothing does so harshly grate against [God showing his footsteps in creation] as that law of *cruelty* and *rapine*, which God himself seems to have implanted in nature amongst ravenous birds and beasts',[160] but *Philotheus* told him that he should note that

> divine Providence in the generations of fishes, birds and beasts, cast up in her account the supernumeraries that were to be meat for the rest (…). But to complain that some certain numbers are to be lopp'd off, which notwithstanding must at last die, and if they lived and propagated without any such curb, would be a burthen to the earth and to themselves for want of food, it is but the cavil of our own *softness* and *ignorant effeminacy*, no just charge against God or nature.[161]

God is not to blame for the presence of predation, and neither are we. The problem is our 'softness and ignorant effeminacy'. The possibility that animals might suffer from predation is outweighed by the joy they experience when alive. In contrast with some contemporary theologians discussed above, there are no allusions to predation in relationship with human sin.[162]

Details that may be difficult to digest contribute to a greater good, '(…) as the art of painting requires dark colours as well as those more bright and florid in well-drawn pictures'.[163] More joined Aquinas in emphasizing that the interests of the whole prevail above those of the parts and is echoing the Late Antique Neoplatonist philosopher *Plotinus* (204/5–270), who already used a similar metaphor when writing that complaining about the works of the Creator makes us 'like people ignorant of painting who complain that the colours are not beautiful

---

159 See for this description More, *Dialogues*: page after xi. I suppose Philotheus to be More's *alter ego*.
160 More, H. 1743 [1668]. *Divine Dialogues, Containing Disquisitions Concerning the Attributes and Providence of God. In Three Volumes*. Robert Foulis, Glasgow: 187.
161 More, *Dialogues*: 190-191.
162 More leaves no doubt about his reservations regarding the literacy of Scripture. '[T]he urging of the bare literal sense [of Scripture], has either made or confirmed many an Atheist.' In: More, *Conjectura Cabbalistica*: preface, page not numbered. For more details on More's attitude towards Scripture see also Hutton, S. 'More, Newton, and the Language of Biblical Prophecy' in: Force & Popkin, *Books of Nature and Scripture*: 39-53; Iliffe, R. ' "Making a Shew": Apocalyptic Hermeneutics and the Sociology of Christian Idolatry in the Work of Isaac Newton and Henry More' in: Force & Popkin, *Books of Nature and Scripture*: 55-88.
163 More, *Dialogues*: 194.

everywhere in the picture'.[164] The Cambridge Platonist More followed in the footsteps of his predecessor.

Furthermore, we have seen that More assigned the non-human animal creation also its own meaning. Despite his comments that their lives only serve to keep them fresh until we are ready to eat them, he nevertheless believed that the animals are not only made for men's use only but also to enjoy themselves. By ascribing the sense of joy to animals, More refuted Descartes *beast-machine* doctrine,[165] again employing the format of the discussion between the aforementioned participants.

For *Cuphophron*, the advantage of the Cartesian stand is obvious as it 'takes away all that conceived hardship and misery that brute creatures undergo (…) by their fierce cruelty one upon another', but *Philotheus* disagrees:

> the *Cartesian* hypothesis (…) is so far from helping out any difficulty in divine Providence, that it were the greatest demonstration in the world against the goodness thereof, if it were true; namely, that such an infinite number of animals, as we call them, capable of being so truly, and of enjoying a vital happiness, should be made but mere senseless puppets, and devoid of all the joys and pleasure of life.[166]

In one of his letters to Descartes, More also was quite clear on this issue; his doctrine would metamorphose all animals into 'marble statues and machines'.[167] Denying animals sense might save them from sufferings but also bereaves them from delights. And with that suffering, it is not so bad, 'there not being that Reflexiveness nor so comprehensive and presagient an Anxiety or present deep Resentment in Brutes in their suffering as in rational Creatures'.[168]

---

164 Plotinus. 1956. *The Enneads*. Translated by Stephen MacKenna, Second Edition Revised by B.S. Page…Faber and Faber, London: 170.
165 For More's initial acceptance but subsequent rejection of Cartesianism see Webster, C. 1969. 'Henry More and Descartes: Some New Sources' in: *The British Journal for the History of Science* 4 (4): 359-377; Harrison, *The Fall*: 122n132.
166 More, *Dialogues*: 187-189.
167 More to Descartes, December 11, 1648. Quoted in: Cohen, L.D. M.A. 1936. 'Descartes and Henry More on the Beast-Machine—A Translation of Their Correspondence Pertaining to Animal Automatism' in: *Annals of Science* 1 (1) 48-61 (50). Cf. Muratori, C. 2012. 'Henry More on Human Passions and Animal Souls' in: Ebbersmeyer, S. (ed.). 2012. *Emotional Minds*. De Gruyter, Berlin: 207-224; Muratori, C. 2017. "In Human Shape to Become the Very Beast!' – Henry More on Animals' in: *British Journal for the History of Philosophy* 25 (5): 897-915.
168 More, *Dialogues*: 188. Statement by *Hylobares* that *Philotheus* endorsed.

In summary: More considered animal death and predation to be necessary for the greater good of a well-designed creation; there is no reference to any change for the worse due to men's sin. And we should not fall into the mousetrap of the pathetic fallacy, reading our own emotions into animals. More after all endorsed a mitigated Cartesianism, not completely denying animals sensibility but also not allotting them the mind required for suffering in the same way as humans do. Herein, he followed in the footsteps of the French philosopher *Pierre Charron* (1541-1603) who also wrote that the animal does not worry about the future and is not tormented by what has passed.[169]

The ability of the animals to consciously experience both pain and joy does not mean, however, that they also have immortal souls and consequently would have access to a blissful afterlife. 'For we conceive that the Soul of a Brute may be of that nature as to be vitally affected only in a Terrestrial Body, and that out of it may have neither sense nor perception of any thing; so as to it self it utterly perishes.'[170] An afterlife for the animals is an utopia. More obviously disagreed with some of his aforementioned contemporaries who kept this possibility open, albeit only for a privileged minority.

3.8.13. *John Wilkins (1614-1672)*

John Wilkins, broad-minded Puritan advocating the middle road in promoting 'an ethical, plain, practical version of Christianity in the course of refuting enthusiasm and infidelity' and hence ranked among the Latitudinarians as well,[171] was one of the founders of the Royal Society.[172] He shared Browne's reluctance to take Scripture literally when the scientific study of nature suggested otherwise and was more inclined to 'revise concepts of biblical authority in order to make room for scientific propositions that seemed at odds with the plain meaning of Scripture.'[173]

---

169 Charron, P. 1707 [1601]. *Of Wisdom. Three Books. Written Originally in French by the Sieur de Charron. With an Account of the Author. Made English by George Stanhope. The Second Edition, Corrected.* R. Bonwick et al., London: 255-256. This opinion has its roots in Late Antique Stoicism. Cf. Sorabji, R. 1993. *Animal Minds and Human Morals. The Origins of the Western Debate.* Cornell University Press, Ithaca: 52.
170 More, *Antidote*: 354.
171 Zimmer, *Soul Made Flesh*: 131. Quote from Spurr, 'Latitudinarianism': 72.
172 For the contribution of Wilkins to the scientific debate and the way he managed to find a middle road between Anglicans and Puritans, see Brooke, *Science and Religion*: 57, 99-108, 115; Zimmer, *Soul Made Flesh*: 92-94; Calloway, *God's Scientists*: 104-134.
173 Brooke, *Science and Religion*: 54. Cf. McColley, 'The Ross-Wilkins Controversy'.

An example of Wilkins's attitude to Scripture is found in his *Essay Towards a Real Character, and a Philosophical Language*.[174]

> Tho it seem most probable, that before the *Flood*, both Men, Beasts and Birds did feed only upon Vegetables, this proof [from Genesis 1: 29,30] is not so very cogent to convince a captious Adversary, but that he may still be apt to question, whether the Rapacious kinds of Beasts and Birds, who in the natural frame of their parts are peculiarly fitted for the catching and devouring of their prey, did ever feed upon herbs and fruits. Therefore to prevent such Cavils, I shall be content to suppose that those *Animals* which are now *Praedatory* were so from the beginning.[175]

Apparently, Wilkins found it difficult to accept that Adam's fall should have profound consequences for animal behavior taking in view the intimate correspondence between feeding habits and 'the natural frame of their parts'. As anatomy cannot be changed overnight, neither can processing of ingested food. Hence, the literal meaning of the Genesis text is difficult to reconcile with the available scientific results. This led Wilkins to conclude that beasts of prey 'were so from the beginning', a conclusion that implies that predation and animal death belong to a good creation; they are no threats for divine goodness and benevolence. In contrast, that some animals are 'fitted for the catching and devouring of their prey' bears testimony of divine craftsmanship.

In interpreting animal anatomy in terms of final causes—what purposes are intended—Wilkins opened the door to physico-theology,[176] the branch of natural theology that looks for final causes as proof of divine contrivance. That theme was emphasized in his posthumously published *Of the Principles and Duties of Natural Religion*.[177] In this text, Wilkins grew eloquent about the

> excellent *Contrivance* which there is in all natural things. Both with respect to that Elegance and Beauty which they have in themselves separately considered, and that regular Order and Subserviency wherein they stand towards one another; together with the exact fitness and propriety, for the several purposes for which they are designed. From all

---

174 Wilkins, J. 1668. *An Essay towards a Real Character, and a Philosophical Language*. Sa. Gellibrand and John Martyn, London.
175 Wilkins, *Essay*: 165.
176 McGrath, *Darwinism and the Divine*: 64-65; Mandelbrote, 'The Uses of Natural Theology in Seventeenth-Century England'.
177 Wilkins, J. 1710. *Of the Principles and Duties of Natural Religion: Two Books. The Sixth Edition*. R. Chiswell et al., London.

which it may be inferred, that these are the productions of some Wise Agent. The most sagacious man is not able to find out any blot or error in this great volume of the world, as if any thing in it had been an imperfect Essay at the first, such as afterwards stood in need of mending: But *all things continue as they were from the beginning of the Creation*.[178]

Wilkins discovered 'Contrivance' both in the individual as well as in the order 'wherein they stand to each other', and since the time of creation, no changes were made nor needed as creation was 'without blot or error'. That included even the most insignificant creatures as there is 'Order and Symetry in the Frame of the most minute Creatures, a *Lowse* or a *Mite*'.[179] Nature testifies to the Creator's power. Whether it testifies to God's benevolence as well was not mentioned but neither is the opposite. Wilkins's writings nowhere reflected any compassion for animals themselves and their fate, which may explain the absence of any concern about the divine attributes in view of animal death and predation. These are things that 'continue as they were from the beginning of the Creation', and, since they 'are the productions of some Wise Agent', they cannot threat the attributes of this 'Wise Agent' in any way, at least not in Wilkins's view.[180]

3.8.14. Richard Baxter (1615–1691)

The Puritan minister *Richard Baxter*, known for his books about how to live a holy life as well as for his attempts to mediate in the conflict between the Puritans and the Anglican episcopate[181] had an open eye for the value of the book of nature as well. The smallest bird testifies to the Creator's wisdom. Anyone who doubts that is even worse than insane. 'We should think Bedlam too honourable a place for that man.'[182] In addition, we should also be grateful, because anything created is for our use. We are 'LORD among them in the World'.[183]

---

178 Wilkins, *Principles and Duties*: 78. May be Wilkins quoted 2 Peter 3:4. '[a]ll things continue as they were from the beginning of the creation.' (KJV) In his book, Wilkins did not refer to this text.
179 Wilkins, *Principles and Duties*: 80.
180 That the discovery of the fossils would become a problem for the conviction that everything remains as it was created, was not yet an issue during the life of Wilkins. In Chapters 4 and 5 I will return to this theme.
181 For biographical details, see Calloway, *God's Scientists*: 72-103.
182 Baxter, R. 1667. *The Reasons of the Christian Religion… Answering the Objections of Unbelievers*. Fran. Titon, London: 23. Bedlam was a notorious hospital dedicated to the care for the insane, see Andrews, J. et al. 1997. *The History of Bethlem*. Routledge, London.
183 Baxter, *The Reasons of the Christian Religion*: 5.

To explain ostensible imperfections, Baxter resorted to an image we have encountered before. 'Those things which in particulars we call Bad, are Good as they are parts of the Universal frame; as many darknings and shadowings in a Picture may conduce to make it beautiful.'[184] Moreover, it is not for us to submit God to our judgment. 'The complacency of his Will then is the ultimate end of all his works, as the Glory of his own Power, Wisdom and Goodness shineth in them.'[185]

God has no obligations to the animals to be judged in terms of right or wrong, nor do these criteria apply to the behavior of the animals.[186] It is therefore not necessary to compensate them for anything, either in the present or in the afterlife. 'A Beast hath no knowledge that there is a God, no thoughts of a Life to come, no desire to know God, or love him, or enjoy him; no obligation to take care for another life, nor to provide for it, nor once to consider whether there be any such or not: Because he is not made for any life but this.'[187]

For Baxter, the animals were created to illustrate the attributes of God and to serve his purposes; discussions about whether they can feel and suffer were dismissed as meaningless. Referring to Descartes and his opponents, Baxter warned that those who indulge in this will find that 'by study and learning they learn to know less than they did before, and do but study to corrupt their understandings, and obliterate things that are commonly known'.[188] That human sin may be the cause of animal misery was not contemplated; nor was attention paid to that misery itself. The 'Measure of God's Goodness is not to be taken from the Creatures interest'.[189] It is our depraved spirit that can see something good only in senseless pleasure: but true reason recognizes that God has a higher purpose for his creation.[190]

3.8.15. Samuel Gott (1614–1671)

The low-profile politician *Samuel Gott* who served both the Parliamentary as well as the Royalist's cause,[191] wrote his *Divine History of the Genesis of the World*, because 'Men in these latter Ages seem to forget the Original

---

184 Baxter, *The Reasons of the Christian Religion*: 99.
185 Baxter, *The Reasons of the Christian Religion*: 26.
186 Baxter, *The Reasons of the Christian Religion*: 125.
187 Baxter, *The Reasons of the Christian Religion*: 141-142.
188 Baxter, *The Reasons of the Christian Religion*: 523.
189 Baxter, *The Reasons of the Christian Religion*: 97.
190 Baxter, *The Reasons of the Christian Religion*: 98.
191 For biographical details, see Henning, B.D. (ed.). 1983. 'Gott, Samuel (1614-71)' in: *The History of Parliament: the House of Commons*. Boydell and Brewer, Martlesham.

Creation'.[192] He was convinced that the 'End of all Created Nature is the Divine Glory of the Creator, which the whole World as a Mirror was made to Represent to us Naturaly (...) being taught by God, the Author both of Scripture and Nature'.[193]

But Gott also acknowledged the consequences of Adam's fall; animals were 'not Ravenous, or Rebellious so as certeinly none were Created before the Fall and Curs. (...) [N]one of them were Carnivorous at first, nor did devour one another; for both they and man had then another Diet appointed for them by God, that is Vegetative.'[194] Sharing the same vegetarian diet, however, does not imply that initially there were also no differences in the animal kingdom regarding qualities and behavior. On the contrary:

> I doubt not, but that some Beasts were Created farr more strong then others, as they still are; and that some were Venaturient as they now are, and had the same Specifike Sagacity, as well as Noses; and so might hunt others with a great Natural Delight (...) which appears, not only by their Indefatigable Industry, but also by their very great Exultation, and Cry; yet I conceiv; that then they had no Cruentous our Murdrous Appetite; as now a Lion doth not usually prey when he is full; and Cats first play with a Mous, and then kill it; but then they did only play, and not Kill, when they could not Eat therof; which is the chief End of Killing.[195]

But absence of predation before the fall does not mean that there was no death anyhow. '[I]f there be no such Violence offered unto it, then the Sensitive *Animal* doth continue from the Birth untill the Death (...) in sound and perfect Health.'[196] Animals were mortal already in their prelapsarian state but passed away by a natural, non-violent death.

Gott also exemplified that, in the course of the seventeenth century, some of the authors who wanted to hold on to the belief that predator behavior arose as a result of the curse that followed Adam's transgression began to have difficulty to reconcile this belief with emerging science, in this case, a sudden change in feeding habits. The aforementioned author Willet had tried to solve this problem by supposing that some animals were created as carnivorous from the beginning but had to fast till Adam fell, thus avoiding the need of a change at all. Gott conjectured that

---

192 Gott, S. 1670. *The Divine History of the Genesis of the World Explicated & Illustrated.* Henry Eversden, London: 1.
193 Gott, *Divine History*: 13.
194 Gott, *Divine History*: 417.
195 Gott, *Divine History*: 418-419.
196 Gott, *Divine History*: 356.

animals that would turn into beasts of prey after the fall already possessed all qualities they would need in their postlapsarian future; in that way, the change that the animals underwent could remain more limited, and therefore more plausible.[197] About the moral implications of predation itself Gott is silent. He just mentioned it as curse-related but without pointing to any threat to the divine attributes. Maintaining the biblical text against scientific objections was his aim.

3.8.16. Thomas Hodges (1600-1672)

Thomas Hodges, Anglican cleric[198] and honored as a forgotten pioneer in asking attention for a proper attitude towards animals,[199] delivered two sermons that were published posthumously in 1675.[200] He felt compelled to speak these sermons because '*it hath often grieved my Soul, to see how the poor bruit Beasts have been used, or abused rather, by their inhumane, merciless, absurd, & unreasonable cruel Masters*'.[201]

In the first sermon—on Genesis 1:31[202]—Hodges described how God gives each animal its appropriate food. 'The sheep doth not feed on flesh; nor doth the Horse take pleasure to gnaw the bones like the Dog.'[203] It is evident that the existence of predation does not blemish the attributes of the Creator. After all, the 'Swallow and the Bat (…) purge the Air of Flyes. (…) The crows pick up the Worms after the plough (…). Some Birds are meat for the rest.'[204]

---

197 It is fascinating to see how as early as the mid-seventeenth century authors interpreted data provided by the study of nature in such a way that they could not threaten the literal reading of the biblical creation story and it's instructive to see that it wasn't such a success back then either. The ideas of Willet and Gott illustrate that proposals to smooth things out this way are not only artificial but also do not really settle the problem. In their case, the question remains whether a creation in which the animals are already equipped for predation and it only takes a provocative moment to put this behavior into practice, so much differs from a creation in which animals devouring each other has become reality.

198 As Hodges dedicates his work to a person characterized as a 'loyal Subject to his Majesty', the author may be reckoned among the Anglicans welcoming the monarchy's restoration after the turmoil in the decades before.

199 Morillo, J. *The Rise of Animals and Descent of Man, 1660-1800. Toward Posthumanism in British Literature between Descartes and Darwin*. University of Delaware Press, Lanham: 72-79.

200 Hodges, T. 1675. *The Creatures Goodness, as They Came out of God's Hands, and the Good Mans Mercy to the Brute Creatures, Which God Hath Put under His Feet…* Tho. Parkhurst, London.

201 Hodges, *Creatures Goodness*: A2.

202 'God saw everything that he had made, and, behold, it was very good.' (KJV)

203 Hodges, *Creatures Goodness*: 8.

204 Hodges, *Creatures Goodness*: 12.

Hodges made no connection between the observation that some animals live at the expense of others and the fall; for him, predation apparently was part of the prelapsarian creation. This did not mean, however, that he completely ignored the fall, but he restricted its consequences. 'If there be any Creatures which are evil and pernicious to Man, he must blame the evil of sin for that; that is the fly in this Box of Ointment.'[205] Men's transgression of the divine command corrupted the relationship between humanity and the non-human animals. 'So that now, they are not generally so pleasant, so useful, so serviceable, and obedient to us, as they would have been if we had not sinned.'[206]

In his second sermon—on Proverbs 12:10[207]—Hodges emphasized how and why the righteous man has to regard the life of his beast. We should not increase the curse of the disturbed relationship between men and beasts by deliberately mistreating or neglecting them. Our plights to the animals under our care are obvious.

> Let us consider, these Creatures were partakers of the curse of Mans Sin; by reason of this *they groan and travail in pain*; their yoke is harder and their burden heavier: We should look on their sorrows and sufferings as occasioned, as merited by us, by our disobedience to our sovereign Lord. (…) They suffer for us; We eat the sour Grapes; and their Teeth are set on edge (…) let them never suffer unnecessarily from us.[208]

The suffering of our livestock should remind us to our sins, and we should not increase our guilt by mistreating them. We have our responsibilities towards the beings entrusted to us. In this view, the Anglican divine Hodges agreed with the Puritans Topsell, Elton, and Walker as well as with his Anglican fellow brother Draxe, who all had the same opinion as I have already mentioned above. Commitment to animal welfare apparently exceeds ecclesiastical boundaries.

3.8.17. Ralph Cudworth (1617-1688)
Ralph Cudworth, theologian and philosopher and, as More, belonging to the Cambridge Platonists, wrote his *True Intellectual System of the Universe* to confute the reason and the philosophy of atheism.[209] For our study, two topics from his work are relevant, the first being his conviction

---

205 Hodges, *Creatures Goodness*: 14.
206 Hodges, *Creatures Goodness*: 15.
207 'A righteous man regardeth the life of his beast'. (KJV)
208 Hodges, *Creatures Goodness*: 37-38.
209 Cudworth, R.C. 1845 [1678]. *The True Intellectual System of the Universe…In Three Volumes*. Thomas Tegg, London.

that animals are not merely automata, thus contesting the ideas of Descartes, and the other, the way he addresses the atheist's argument that evil refutes a benevolent Creator.

Regarding the first point, Cudworth stated that it is evident that animals have sense: '(…) brutes are not mere senseless machines or automata, and only like clocks or watches'.[210] Plain common sense tells us that animals have feelings which for Cudworth meant that they have sensitive souls.[211] The worries of Descartes that ascribing to animals a soul implies their immortality as well does not hold true because 'there is no absolute necessity that these souls of brutes, because substantial, should therefore have a permanent subsistence after death to all eternity; because though it be true that no substance once created by God will of itself ever vanish into nothing, yet is it true also, that whatsoever was created by God out of nothing, may possibly by him be annihilated and reduced to nothing again'.[212]

The soul of man must be immortal; 'they having both morality and liberty of will, and thereby being capable of rewards and punishments, and consequently fit objects for the divine justice to display itself upon', but 'the case may be otherwise as to the souls of brute animals'. Animals are 'devoid both of morality and liberty of will, and therefore uncapable of reward and punishment'. After having had 'some enjoyment of themselves for a time', they are 'annihilated in their deaths and corruptions; and if this be absolutely the best, then doubtless is it so'.[213]

This mortality of the soul, as advocated by Cudworth, should not, however, be construed too narrowly. His belief that the animal soul will eventually be annihilated did not prevent Cudworth from considering that one and the same soul could animate successive bodies over time as advocated by the Greek philosopher Pythagoras. Nature itself provides evidence for this. 'But as for that supposed possibility of their [the souls] awakening again afterwards in some other terrestrial bodies, this seemeth to be no more than what is found by daily experience in the course of nature, when the silkworm and other worms, dying, are transformed into butterflies.' After all, '(…) there is little reason to doubt but that the same soul which before acted the body of the silkworm, doth afterward act that of the butterfly'.[214]

---

210 Cudworth, *True Intellectual System* III: 441-453 (441).
211 Cf. Sailor, D.B. 1962. 'Cudworth and Descartes' in: *Journal of the History of Ideas* 23 (1): 133-140; Kaldas, S. 2015. 'Descartes versus Cudworth on the Moral Worth of Animals' in: *Philosophy Now. A Magazine of Ideas* 108: 28-31.
212 Cudworth, *True Intellectual System* III: 451-452.
213 Cudworth, *True Intellectual System* III: 452.
214 Cudworth, *True Intellectual System* III: 451. The Pythagorean conviction that one

In the second place, Cudworth disagreed that the world, with everything on it, was only created for the benefit of mankind. '[F]leas and lice, had they understanding, might conclude the bodies of other greater animals, and men also, to have been made only for them.' We should refrain from unwarranted anthropocentricity; it is more 'reasonable to think that even the lower animals likewise, and whatsoever hath conscious life, was made partly also to enjoy itself'.[215]

Neither is there reason to blame the Creator for anything we encounter in his creation. Evils are 'like discords in music, to contribute to the harmony of the whole'.[216] The whole prevails above the details. '[I]n judging of the works of God, we ought not to consider the parts of the world alone by themselves; and then, because we could fancy much finer things, thereupon blame the Maker of the whole'.[217] We should realize that 'we are like unskillful spectators of a picture, who condemn the limner, because he hath not put bright colours everywhere; whereas he had suited his colours to every part respectively, giving to each such as belonged to it'.[218] Similar as with More, the other Cambridge Platonist, the Plotinian line of thought is easily discerned.

For Cudworth, this world refutes atheism and details that worry us should not distract from admiring the Creator of the whole. Creation not only glorifies divine power but also reflects divine goodness and benevolence as well. Animals have their own enjoyments. Animal suffering remains out of sight.

3.8.18. Stephen Charnock (1628–1680)
That God reveals himself from nature is also a foregone conclusion for the Puritan divine *Stephen Charnock*.[219] If we do not observe the wisdom of God in the creatures, we are like 'Asaph, a foolish and *ignorant beast before God*'.[220] Both sources, Scripture as well as nature convey messages

---

and the same soul could successively animate different earthly bodies would lead several authors in the eighteenth century to believe that suffering endured in one life could be compensated for in another existence or also to explain animal suffering as punishment for wrongdoing in an earlier life. This is not yet the case with Cudworth. I will return to this in more detail in Chapter 4 (cf. § 4.6.5).
215 Cudworth, *True Intellectual System* III: 466-467.
216 Cudworth, *True Intellectual System* III: 468.
217 Cudworth, *True Intellectual System* III: 478.
218 Cudworth, *True Intellectual System* III: 479.
219 For biographical details, see Beeke, J., Pederson, R.J. 2006. 'Stephen Charnock' in: *Meet the Puritans. With a Guide to Modern Reprints*. Reformation Heritage Books, Grand Rapids: 142-146.
220 Charnock, S. 1815 [1682]. *The Works of the Late Rev. Stephen Charnock, B.D. In Nine Volumes. With a Prefatory Dedication and Memoir by Edward Parsons*. Baynes et al.,

to be taken at heart. 'Though the appearance of God in the one be clearer than in the other, yet neither is to be neglected: The scripture directs us to nature to view God (...). Nature is not contrary to scripture, nor scripture to nature; unless we should think God contrary to himself, who is the author of both.'[221]

However, this positive view did not alter the fact that Charnock, as befits a Puritan, also had an eye for the fact that we live in a corrupted world that—because of the sin of man—'hath borne thorns and thistles, and venomous beasts'.[222] It goes without saying that the fall of Adam has wide consequences. 'The treasons of man against God brought misery upon that which was framed for the use of man: as when the majesty of a prince is violated by the treason and rebellion of his subjects, all that which belongs to them, and was, before the free gift of the prince to them, is forfeit.'[223] Everything was created for the glory of God and for mankind to use it in honor of the Creator. But when Adam lost his integrity, the animals were humiliated to obey an unfaithful rebel, now serving his vices instead of supporting his virtues. But, happily, that will not last forever.

A future will come in which the corrupted creation will be restored—a restoration that will be all-encompassing. Then, the animals will 'receive a new glory suited to their nature, and answerable to the design of God'.[224] The disturbed relationship between humanity and the non-human animal kingdom will also come to an end. Nowadays, the animals suffer because they are 'tyrannized over by man, contrary to the end of its creation',[225] but then, it will be 'the joy of God to see all his works in their due order; every one pointing to their true end; marching together in their excellency, according to his first intendment in their creation'.[226]

Charnock's thoughts on the suffering of the animals focused on the fact that today they are unable to properly fulfill their assigned role in creation. That role was a subservient one as they were 'not made for themselves, but for the service of the Creator, and the service of man'.[227] In

---

London: II: 308. In mentioning Asaph, Charnock refers to Psalm 73:22. Here, the poet confesses that 'So foolish was I, and ignorant: I was as a beast before thee.' (KJV)
221 Charnock, *Works* I: 99.
222 Charnock, S. 1853 [1682]. *Discourses upon the Existence and Attributes of God. With His Life and Character, by William Symington. In Two Volumes.* Robert Carter & Brothers, New York: I: 314.
223 Charnock, *Discourses* II: 250.
224 Charnock, *Discourses* I: 314.
225 Charnock, *Discourses* I: 314.
226 Charnock, *Discourses* I: 315.
227 Charnock, *Discourses* I: 596.

the world to come, that order will be restored as the 'disorder and unruliness of the creature, arising from the venom of man's transgression, all the fierceness of one creature against another shall vanish'.[228]

It is unclear how Charnock imagined the relationship between the animals restored to its former state; it could be an abolishment of predation but that is not explicitly stated. What, on the other hand, is entirely clear is that Charnock saw the consequences of the fall mainly in a disturbed relationship between humans and the non-human animal world and the redemption from vanity as a return to the world as it was in the prelapsarian state. Herein, Charnock followed in the footsteps of the theologians of the Early Church; they, too, limited the consequences of the fall mainly to a change in the relationship between mankind and the non-human animals.

Charnock still left open whether the 'fierce of one creature against another' that becomes manifest after the fall must be attributed to a change in the nature of the animals or to man's diminished authority. More clarity about this was provided by the Puritan judge and jurist *Matthew Hale* (1609–1676).[229] 'Among Animals some are fierce, strong, and untameable, as Lions, Tigers, Wolves, Foxes, Dragons, Serpents; and these stand in need of some coercive power over them, that they destroy not the *Species* of more profitable, and yet weaker Animals.'[230] Therefore, 'Man was invested with power, authority, right, dominion, trust, and care, to correct and abridge the excesses and cruelties of the fiercer Animals, to give protection and defence to the mansuete [= gentle, tame] and useful' and although 'after the Fall of Man this difficulty of this Employment was greater, by reason of the Curse that thereby befell the Earth, yet even before the Fall the nature of his Employment was the same.'[231] The animals' behavior towards each other did not change because of a change in their nature but because of an 'impair of that Sovereignty and Dominion over the Creatures, who rebelled against Man as soon as he forlook his Maker'.[232] As a result, predation became associated with 'excesses and cruelties', traits that Adam and his descendants should have inhibited.

---

228 Charnock, *Discourses* II: 294.
229 For biographical details, see Yale, D.E.C. "Sir Matthew Hale". *Encyclopedia Britannica*, 28 October 2021, https://www.britannica.com/biography/Matthew-Hale. Accessed on 14 December 2021.
230 Hale, M. 1677. *The Primitive Origination of Mankind, Considered and Examined According to the Light of Nature*. William Shrowsbery, London: 369.
231 Hale, *The Primitive Origination of Mankind*: 370.
232 Hale, *The Primitive Origination of Mankind*: 318.

3.8.19. Richard Franck (1624?-1708)

Close to the end of the seventeenth century, *Richard Franck*, officer in the Parliamentary army and thus siding with Cromwell which may imply Puritan sympathies,[233] wrote *A Philosophical Treatise of the Original and Production of Things*.[234] The reason for writing this book is made clear; studying creation is one of our daily duties as God makes himself knowable in the book of nature. For Franck, it was evident that '*every Creature God has made, as Animals, and Inanimates to replenish the Earth; was made to explain the excellency of him (...)*'. Therefore, '*to contemplate (...) this imbellished Creation, is to study the tracts and the high way to heaven*'.[235]

Franck, however, paid due honors to the contents of the book of Scripture as well. In the beginning, '(...) the Creation was unacquainted with fear, whiles our Ancestor stood in a state of Innocency; and had for ever so remain'd without contradiction (by authority of the Text) had not Sin struck out the Character of simplicity'.[236] Next to this note, Franck described in detail the delightfulness of this blessed past, surprisingly taking arguments from the mediaeval *Bestiaria*: the pelican not yet ripping her breast to feed her young, the swan not singing a song in preparation for her funeral, and the crocodile without the need to shed tears about the loss of relatives that had passed away.[237] Franck here rekindled ideas from a past age, stories already considered to be fabrications in his own time but that did not seem to hinder him from using them as examples when indicating the changes for the worse that the fall has brought about.[238]

The delights of the uncorrupted creation were manifold as 'Fear was a thing altogether unexperimented, and Death and the Grave such eminent strangers'.[239] Furthermore, '*Alegators* in the beginning were not devourers;

---

233 For biographical details, see Watkins, M.G. 'Franck, Richard' in: *Dictionary of National Biography, 1885-1900, Volume 20.*
234 Franck, R. 1687. *A Philosophical Treatise of the Original and Production of Things...* John Gain, London.
235 Franck, 'The Epistle to the Reader' in: *Philosophical Treatise*: pages not numbered.
236 Franck, *Philosophical Treatise*: 123.
237 Franck, *Philosophical Treatise*: 123-124. It is interesting to see that Franck's examples still live on in current parlance, the pelican exemplifying sacrificial maternal love, the swan song indicating imminent death, and the shedding of crocodile tears as feigned sorrow.
238 See Harrison, *The Bible*, about the decline of the magical and mythological interpretation of the book of nature in the seventeenth century, in particular pages 107-120, 269. For a then-contemporary critic, see Browne, *Pseudodoxia Epidemica*: 37-38.
239 Franck, *Philosophical Treatise*: 156.

nor were there known any Birds of Prey. The *Vulture*, and the *Tigre* liv'd not then upon Vermine, for *Morts* were altogether unknown.'[240] These notes are clear; there are no animals that feed on the flesh of their fellow creatures. Curiously, that does not apply to humans 'for all the Beasts on the Earth, with the Fowl of the Air, and the Fish in the Sea, were given him [Adam] for Food, by a Royal Grant from Heaven, to eat of (…)'.[241] Apparently, the paradox of an uncorrupted creation without animal death and predation as opposed to Adam feeding on the meat of the animals eluded this author.

That Franck—apart from his notes on Adam's diet—largely conformed to the established tradition is evident not only from the fact that the presence of carnivorous animals was attributed to the sin of the first human couple but also from his comments about the relationship between humans and animals. The fall not only has corrupted the peaceful coexistence of the animals but also damaged man's dominion over the animals. But Franck chose a path different from the traditional one to explain how this loss of dominion came about. 'Sin had so strangely disfigured and disguised him [Adam], that none of his Subjects could remember to know him, or think, or believe him their natural Prince.'[242] It was the change of Adam's nature—not that of the animal—that made the animals no longer submit to the rule of man.

Franck deviated from his contemporaries in his choice of examples to illustrate the consequences of the fall and in his explanation how the loss of dominion over the animals came about. But that did not alter his conviction that all violence among animals is due to man's sin. It is not God's fault that the animals now live in fear of each other.

3.8.20. Robert Boyle (1627-1691)

In his writings on animal life and behavior, *Robert Boyle*'s interpreted the natural world as providing proof of God's design. Both atheism as well as Cartesianism err: the first because it rejects the existence of a designer, the latter because it denies the existence of final causes.[243] The animals are equipped for the purpose for which they are created. Some of them feature 'Arms, as Horns, Hoofs, Scales, Tusks, Poysons, Stings, *&c.* to

---

240 Franck, *Philosophical Treatise*: 160.
241 Franck, *Philosophical Treatise*: 153.
242 Franck, *Philosophical Treatise*: 161.
243 Robert Boyle, suffering from being mistrusted by Royalists as well as Puritans, was a natural philosopher (famous until today) and one of the founding members of the Royal Society. Cf. Gillespie, 'Natural History, Natural Theology, and Social Order'; Brooks, *Science and Religion*: 130-135; Zimmer, *Soul Made Flesh*: 134-135; Wootton, *The Invention of Science*: 446.

Defend themselves, and Offend their Enemies; *some* with Wings or swiftness to fly from Dangers.'[244] It is clear that such a design is not tailored to a peaceful dwelling together of wolf and lamb as was allegedly the case in a paradise past.

Elsewhere, the same conviction was uttered. 'The Provident Maker of the World hath so wisely contrived the Fabrick of the Parts, as to make them fit for the uses they were designed for (…) And the Camelion hath a Tongue disproportioned in length and Shape to the rest of his Body, to enable him to catch his Prey by shuteing it out of his Mouth (…) and Birds of Prey, as Hawks, *&c.* have crooked Bills to tear their food.'[245] Specific anatomic details were mentioned that are needed for animals' specific way of feeding, even if this means catching and devouring fellow creatures.

To convince those who are in doubt about the intentions of the Creator, Boyle emphasized that 'the Welfare of particular Animals is [not] further designed than consists with the Cosmical Ends of the Universe, and the Course of God's General Providence, to which his special Providence in respect of particular Animals is but Subordinate'.[246] This explains 'why Vegetables were not the Food of all Animals, some feeding on Flesh, and furnished with Appetites and Organs to devour others, and live upon the Destruction of the Weaker'.[247]

Animals are not created merely for their own sakes but to be parts of a universe, and by their specific properties, they contribute to the wellbeing of the whole. This implies that the 'destruction of the weaker' is just a matter of fact. Nowhere did Boyle make mention of an uncorrupted creation without beasts or birds of prey. In contrast, beasts of prey are proof of divine contrivance, Boyle thus following Wilkins who explained animal anatomy and behavior in a similar way. And in his emphasis on the 'Cosmical Ends of the Universe' above the 'Welfare of particular animals', he joined the Cambridge Platonists More and Cudworth.

From other sources, it is known that Boyle believed that animals had sensation and, in particular, that they could experience pain. 'Yet euident it is, that a Feeling they haue of Paine; which causelesly to make them endure, is a thing manifestly contrary to humanity: & always detested by those whom all men confesse the best Natures: as being indeed but a Delight to make those Creatures Miserable, whom God takes Pleasure to

---

244 Boyle, R. 1690. *The Christian Virtuoso… The First Part.* John Taylor, London: 28.
245 Boyle, R. 1715. *The Theological Works of the Honourable Robert Boyle, Epitomized by Richard Boulton. Vol. II.* W. Taylor, London: 227.
246 Boyle, *Theological Works*: 272.
247 Boyle, *Theological Works*: 273.

see happy.'[248] Knowing this should make us careful in dealing with them, but there is no reason for asking why God had made them so.

3.8.21. John Ray (1627–1705)

John Ray wrote 'to contemplate the Works of God, and give him the Glory of his Wisdom, Power and Goodness, manifested in the Creation of them'.[249] In discussing the properties of animals, this scholar whose academic career ended because he refused to comply with the governmental rules imposed during the Restoration[250] explicitly opposed Descartes. The idea that animals cannot suffer is 'contrary to the common Sense of Mankind, all Men naturally pitying them, as apprehending them to have such a Sense and Feeling of Pain and Misery as themselves have; whereas no Man is troubled to see a Plant torn, or cut, or stampt, or mangled'.[251] And anyone who believes that if animals can suffer, they should therefore have an immortal soul, is mistaken. '[T]here is no Necessity they should be immortal, because it is possible they may be destroy'd or annihilated.'[252]

In his description of the animals and their behavior, Ray showed striking similarities to the ideas of Robert Boyle. Like him, he wrote that some animals are strong and equipped to fight, while others are weak and 'able to save themselves by Flight'.[253] In an uncorrupted creation, weapons to fight or swiftness to escape would be of no use. It is obvious that for Ray, predation does not threaten the divine attributes, in which he agreed

---

248 Oster, M.R. 1989. 'The 'Beame of Diuinity': Animal Suffering in the Early Thought of Robert Boyle' in: *The British Journal for the History of Science* 22 (73): 151-179 (174). Cf. MacIntosh, J.J. 1996. 'Animals, Morality and Robert Boyle' in: *Dialogue* 35 (3): 435-472; Guerrini, A. 1989. 'The Ethics of Animal Experimentation in Seventeenth-Century England' in: *Journal of the History of Ideas* 50 (3): 391-407 for information on how Boyle experimented with animals and how he justified it.
249 Ray, J. 1722 [1691]. *The Wisdom of God Manifested in the Works of the Creation. In Two Parts…The Eight Edition, Corrected.* William and John Innys, London: 170.
250 Ray refused to take the oath that was prescribed by the Act of Uniformity, legislation for the organization of liturgical affairs in the Church of England. Submission was required in order to hold any office in government or church. However, whether Ray took this decision because of Puritan sympathies or for other reasons has been questioned. See McMahon, S. 2000. 'John Ray (1627–1705) and the Act of Uniformity 1662' in: *Notes and Records of the Royal Society of London* 54 (2): 153-178. For more general information about Ray and his thoughts, see Gillespie, 'Natural History, Natural Theology, and Social Order'; Thomson, K. 2005. *Before Darwin. Reconciling God and Nature.* Yale University Press, New Haven: 59-82; Calloway, *God's Scientists*: 135-171.
251 Ray, *Wisdom*: 55-56.
252 Ray, *Wisdom*: 56-57.
253 Ray, *Wisdom*: 126.

with other physico-theologians like Wilkins and Boyle. And Ray agreed with More and Cudworth that the animals were not created just to serve humanity. '*God is Bountiful and Benign, and takes Pleasure that all his Creatures enjoy themselves that have Life and Sense, and are capable of Enjoyment.* (…) For my Part, I cannot believe that all the Things in the World were so made for Man, that they have no other Use.'[254]

With Ray, we encounter the same differentiated view on animals and their mental properties as shown by the Cambridge Platonists. Animals are not only created for human benefit but also to enjoy themselves and they can suffer as well because they share with us the same 'sense and feelings'. No concerns, however, were uttered about predation as a cause of suffering; neither were there any doubts about the goodness of the Creator, though he made both fierce and timorous animals. In contrast, God created them as they are now as his works are 'by Him conserv'd to this Day in the same State and Condition in which they were at first made'.[255]

Ray's emphasis on the immutability and preservation of the species should not go unnoticed. His conviction that there is no difference between the animal world before and after the fall is not surprising; other authors had the same opinion. His view that God protects any animal species from extinction deserves more attention. In the near future, this thought—which had also been put forward by Basil centuries earlier (cf. § 2.3.1.8) and by Ray's older contemporaries Browne and Wilkins—would have to face the discovery of the fossils as will be discussed in Chapter 4 (cf. § 4.4).

Finally, looking back at what Ray brought up about the animals and their fate, I conclude that it is indeed unlikely that he refused to subscribe to the Act of Uniformity because of Puritan sympathies since in his silence about any consequences of the fall for animal life as perceived nowadays, he is clearly more in line with the Latitudinarian Anglicans than with the Puritans.[256]

3.8.22. John Edwards (1637-1716)
John Edwards, who had to resign his fellowship of St. John's College in Cambridge because of his Calvinistic views,[257] wrote two texts that are

---

254 Ray, *Wisdom*: 176. Cf. Brooke, J.H. 2000. "Wise Men nowadays Think Otherwise': John Ray, Natural Theology and the Meanings of Anthropocentrism' in: *Notes and Records of the Royal Society of London* 54 (2): 199-213.
255 Ray, *Wisdom*: preface, page not numbered.
256 McMahon, 'Ray and the Act of Uniformity': 169-170.
257 For biographical details, see Robinson, C.J. 'Edwards, John (1637-1716)' in: *Dictionary of National Biography, 1885-1900, Volume 17.*

relevant for my analysis—one encompassing three volumes in which he defended the authority of Scripture,[258] the other to demonstrate the fingerprints of God in his creation.[259]

Second thoughts about the literal meaning of Scripture, especially regarding Genesis had become common as can be deduced from the publications of Hakewill, Browne, More, and Wilkins. Edwards, on the other hand, held the belief that the *'first Chapter of Genesis is a real History, and records Matter of fact'*.[260] The first chapters of Genesis are pivotal for the Christian faith, and if taken allegorically, the whole building collapses. When 'in a literal and historical Sense there was no such thing as that *first Disobedience* of Adam (…) then *Christ's* Coming in the Flesh was in vain'.[261]

This text sounds strikingly similar to modern discussions on the relationship between Scripture and science: no first Adam who fell, no need for a second Adam as savior. It is evident that Edwards stuck to a literal reading of the Genesis text for otherwise, any foundation for the Christian faith crumbles away. It goes beyond all limits that some people are convinced that:

> [A]ll the Account given by *Moses*, not only of the *Origine* and *Creation of the World*, but of *Adam*, and the *first Transgression*, and the *Serpent*, and the *cursing of the Earth*, and other Matters relating to the Fall, is not true in it self, but only spoken popularly, to comply with the dull Israelites, lately slavish Brickmakers, and smelling strong of the Garlick and Onions of *Egypt*. To humour these ignorant Blockheads that were newly broke loose from the Egyptian Taskmasters, and had no Sense nor Reason in their thick Sculls, *Moses* talks after this rate; but not a Syllable of Truth is in all that he saith.[262]

---

258 Edwards, J. 1693. *A Discourse Concerning the Authority, Stile, and Perfection of the Books of the Old and New-Testament*…Richard Wilkin, London; Edwards, J. 1694. *A Discourse…Vol. II. Wherein the Author's Former Undertaking Is further Prosecuted…* Jonathan Robinson and John Wyat, London; Edwards, J. 1695. *A Discourse…Volume III…Wherein Are Also Several Remarkable Texts Interpreted According to the Author's Particular Judgment.* Jonathan Robinson et al., London.
259 Edwards, J. 1696. *A Demonstration of the Existence and Providence of God, from the Contemplation of the Visible Structure of the Greater and Lesser World*…Jonathan Robinson et al., London.
260 Edwards, *Discourse* III: 45.
261 Edwards, *Discourse* II: 36. Cf. Almond, *Adam and Eve*: 211-214; Mandelbrote, 'Isaac Newton and Thomas Burnet' in: Force & Popkin, *Books of Nature and Scripture*: 149-178.
262 Edwards, *Discourse* II: 35. Edwards here paraphrasingly quotes from [Burnet, T.] 1692. *Archaeologiae Philosophicae: Sive Doctrina Antiqua de Rerum Originibus. Libri*

With this in mind, it is worthwhile to look at Edward's second text that was written with the aim to demonstrate the existence and providence of God. To what extent did Edward's conviction that the Bible should be taken literally influence his handling of this theme?

For Edwards, all kind of animals are examples of the goodness of God; 'the Indulgent Creator would have all the various Species of Brutes enjoy their Essence in the way which is most agreeable to them'.[263] Apparently, men's sin has not changed their nature for the worse. '*The young Lions roar after their Prey, and seek their Meat from God*; they seek it and procure it in this notable way, which is by the singular Providence of God. This their natural way of getting their Food is call'd *seeking it from God*, because he hath given them this particular Instinct and Sagacity.'[264] Predation reflects divine design.

That does not mean that there are no questions left such as why God created nasty animals like rats or mice or wasps and hornets, to name only a few. 'Doth not the Troublesome Existence of these Creatures prove rather a Carelessness in the Divine Management than a Provident Care of the World?'[265] That, however, was not a problem either. Also for these unpleasant animals applies that 'God made these Creatures (...) to enjoy their Essence and Life, and therein to be partakers of his Bounty and Munificence' and therefore, '*God's Goodness* is seen even in those Animals which on some account are not good'.[266] Moreover, we must realize that the fact that there are animals that we experience as troublesome at all is the result of the sin of Adam and the curse that followed.

> [W]hatever noxious Qualities are now discern'd in any of the Creatures, they proceed not from God, but the Sin of Man, whereby they are

---

duo. Gualterus Kettilby, London: 320. In Burnet's own text: '[N]eque enim hi laterum coctores, spirantes adhuc porrum et coepe Aegyptiacum: Qui vitulum fusilem à Deo, Optimo Maximo, discernere non poterant, potuissent unquam, prima Dei opera, rerum principia, leges & motus naturae, recognoscere, & ad veritatis normam exigere.' Almost three decades later, the text became available to the public in translation: 'Nor could these Makers of Bricks, whose Breath then smelt strong of the Leeks and Onions of *Egypt*, and could not discern a Molten Calf from the supreme God, ever be able curiously to examine these first Works of the Creator, the Principles of Things, and the Laws and Motions of Nature, and compare them with the Rule of Truth,' in: Burnet, T. 1729. *Archaeologiae Philosophicae...Faithfully Translated into English, with Remarks thereon by Mr. Foxton. Part I. Being a Critique on the Mosaic Creation*. E. Curll, London: 55.

263 Edwards, *Demonstration*: 188.
264 Edwards, *Demonstration*: 224.
265 Edwards, *Demonstration*: 230.
266 Edwards, *Demonstration*: 241.

corrupted. *We* have changed the Nature of them, we made them hurtful, and therefore we have no reason to complain. But it is our Duty to accept of the Penalty of our Delinquencies, and to make it useful (...) to Repentance, and our Turning unto God.[267]

Edwards was convinced that 'if we survey the World and All the Works of the Creation, we shall find that they were made for excellent Ends'.[268] These ends may relate to the life of the animal itself, and—for those animals that are at first sight hurtful or noxious—to a usefulness as tools in a divine pedagogy. But Edward's belief that the 'Mosaick history' is a record of real historical events, as he so eloquently explained elsewhere, apparently did not hold true for Genesis 1:30.[269] 'If God makes one Creature to be Meat for another, it is so far Beneficial.'[270]

Edwards limited the consequences of the fall to a change in the animals' attitude toward humanity; they become hurtful and this allows God to use the animals to correct a wicked humanity. Animal death and predation on their own belong to the uncorrupted creation. In stating that all 'were made for excellent Ends', Edward's thoughts did not differ from those expounded by Wilkins, Boyle, and Ray. And in allotting them enjoyments, he followed the Cambridge Platonists More and Cudworth and agreed with Ray again.

3.8.23. *Thomas Emes (†1707)*

During the seventeenth century, some English scholars paid attention to the ideas of Descartes that animals are senseless automata,[271] but mainly to refute them as I already mentioned above. This is, however, not true for *Thomas Emes*, medical doctor and millenarian, but best known for the strange events around his funeral.[272] In his *Vindiciae Mentis. An Essay of the Being and Nature of Mind*[273] he wrote that animals 'are curious Engines,

---

267 Edwards, *Demonstration*: 243.
268 Edwards, *Demonstration*: 245.
269 'And to every beast of the earth, and to every fowl of the air, and to every thing that creepeth upon the earth, wherein there is life, I have given every green herb for meat: and it was so.' (KJV)
270 Edwards, *Demonstration*: 234.
271 Descartes, *A Discourse on the Method.*
272 Close to the end of his life, Emes was a member of a community known as the French Prophets. After his death in December 1707, his fellow prophets predicted that he would be raised from the dead on May 25, 1708. A large crowd gathered on the appointed day, but the prophecy did not come true. Adapted from https://www.findagrave.com/memorial/64533929/thomas-emes. Accessed on 14 December 2021.
273 Emes, T. 1702. *Vindiciae Mentis. An Essay of the Being and Nature of Mind:...In a New Method, by a Gentleman.* H. Walwyn, London.

such as may become the Almighty, and Al-Wise Author of Nature to make'.[274] We should admire the divine Creator for having designed such wonderful objects.

But if we attribute to them the property of sense, we run into great difficulties. First, it has consequences for the relationship between humankind and the non-human animal kingdom: it would be cruel to kill animals. Next, imagine the guilt felt by beasts of prey that are forced to kill their fellow creatures for their sustenance. Invoking Adams sin does not solve the problem as this runs counter to God's justice.[275] Therefore, we should not admire the animals for their seemingly intelligent behavior but instead adore the Creator for making so well-adapted machines. And for those who fear that this belief makes us hard and cruel to the animals, Emes has an original solution. What sense does it make to beat a machine? After all, 'does any Man fight his Watch or beat his Windmill?'[276]

When animals are able to suffer, the benevolence of the Creator is at stake. The theological advantages of the Cartesian hypothesis are obvious. Animal death and predation are signs of God's wisdom and power and are no reason to doubt his goodness. Neither is there any human responsibility for animal death and predation. Emes explicitly recognized that animal suffering might jeopardize God's righteousness and that led him to reject the possibility; as no injustice is found in God, it is impossible to accept that animals might suffer.

3.8.24. John Norris (1657–1712)

The second proponent of Cartesianism was *John Norris*, an Anglican clergyman.[277] Accepting that animals have sense erases the distinction between humans and the non-human creation for 'if we ascribe Thought, or Perception to brutes in any degree, tho' it be only in that of *Sensation*, where shall we stop, or what shall we deny them? If they are allow'd to have it in the degree of Sensation, why may they not be capable of it in the

---

274 Emes, *Vindiciae*: 83.
275 Emes, *Vindiciae*: 141.
276 Emes, *Vindiciae*: 142.
277 Norris tried to integrate the thoughts of Descartes, Malebranche, Augustine, Aquinas and Plato, with his concept of the Christian God who is 'truth, love and the aim of all religious and practical life.' Adapted from Yang, J. '"John Norris"' in: Zalta, E.N. (ed.). 2014. *The Stanford Encyclopedia of Philosophy* (Spring 2014 Edition). https://plato.stanford.edu/entries/john-norris/. Accessed on 07 February 2022; Harrison, 'Animal Souls, Metempsychosis, and Theodicy in Seventeenth-Century English Thought': 526.

degree of *Reason?*²⁷⁸ And 'if we allow any degree of it [thought] to Brute Creatures, so neither shall we know where to stop as to *Brutes*. (…) If you will suppose a Horse to think, or a Dog, or a Bird, then why not a Fly, or a Louse, or a Worm, or a Snail, or even an Oyster?'²⁷⁹ But not only men's specific position as being created in the image of God is at stake when allowing animals the ability of sensation. Even the doctrine of original sin is jeopardized.

> St. *Austin* [Augustine] (…) lays down this Principle, That under a just God no Innocent can be miserable. (…) And then from the Miseries and Afflictions of Infants concludes upon that Principle, that they can't be innocent. But now if this be a good consequence, Infants are miserable; therefore they are not innocent, because the justice of God will not permit that Innocence should be afflicted; then it seems a reasonable Question to demand why the consequence on the other side should not be full as good: Brutes are innocent, therefore they are not miserable, since 'tis plain that in both Arguments the consequence proceeds upon the same common Principle. But then they must have no Sense or Perception, since if they have, 'tis plain that they are often miserable or in pain.²⁸⁰

In place of attributing to animals the properties of thought and sensation, we should accept that 'those Actions or Movements which are observ'd in Brutes to resemble such as we do by Thought, may in them be the result of pure Mechanism'.²⁸¹ The theological consequences of ascribing thought and sensation to animals force us to assume that they lack them, but we can sense Norris's reluctance to accept the consequences of this conviction when reading that, '(…) on the contrary, I would have them used and treated with us [sic] much tenderness and pitiful regard, as if they had all Sense and Perception, which is commonly (tho' I think without sufficient Reason) attributed to them'.²⁸²

---

278 Norris, J. 1704. *An Essay towards the Theory of the Ideal or Intelligible World…Part II.* S. Manship, London: 63.
279 Norris, *Essay*: 66.
280 Norris, *Essay*: 75-76. See for the relevant text of Augustine himself 'Saint Augustine against Julian, Translated by M.A. Schumacher' in: Deferrari, R.J. et al. (eds). 1957. *The Fathers of the Church. A New Translation. Volume 35*. Fathers of the Church, New York: 113; Augustine. 'The Catholic Faith Concerning Infants' in: Schaff, Ph. (ed.). 1887. *A Select Library of the Nicene and Post-Nicene Fathers of the Christian Church. Volume V. St. Augustin: Anti-Pelagian Writings*. T&T Clark, Edinburgh. Republished by Wm. B. Eerdmans, Grand Rapids: 1093 (II.8). 'Whence, then, in infants, is so wretched a penalty as that [death], if there is no original fault?'
281 Norris, *Essay*: 92.
282 Norris, *Essay*: 100. For more details on Norris's role in the debate over the nature of

It is striking to see how on one side, Norris emphasized that both the justice of God as well as the boundary between immortal humans and mortal beasts are threatened when allowing animals mental properties whereas on the other side, he advocated a gentle and compassionate handling of them. The Cartesian approach seems not emotionally convincing in explaining animal suffering away, gut feelings interfering with cool and abstract reasoning. *In dubio, abstine.*

About predation and animal death, no explicit statements were made by Norris, but from the content of his writings, it may be deduced that he did not see any problems. Animal behavior, be it mechanical or conscious, is as God intended when creating, and no reference was made to fall and sin.

3.8.25. John Witty (c.1682–1712)

John Witty introduced himself as affiliated with St. John's College in Cambridge on the title page of his book entitled *An Essay towards a Vindication of the Vulgar Exposition of the Mosaic History of the Creation*....[283] He is included, not because of his writings about animal life in a pre- and postlapsarian creation but because of the response he elicited with concerns about the declining acceptance of the literal truth of the Genesis text.

> If Moses's *History of the* Creation is *not to be literally interpreted, then neither is that of the* Fall; *and if the* Fall *is a piece of Mythology, then so is the* Redemption; *and if the* Redemption *is a Fable, then welcome* Deism, and *farewell reveal'd Religion. This method of Argumentation very many think conclusive; and some from hence venture to guess at the design of those who deny the first of* Genesis *a literal construction: They look upon it as their end, in such conduct, in one considerable part of it, to undermine the whole Bible; in the first of* Genesis *to invalidate the authority from end to end of both the Old and New Testament.*[284]

When doubt is raised about the first chapters of Genesis, the whole building collapses. Elsewhere in his booklet, the spoke in the same vein:

---

the animal and his reluctance to take a position on it, see Boddice, R. 2008. *A History of Attitudes and Behaviours toward Animals in Eighteenth- and Nineteenth-Century Britain. Anthropocentrism and the Emergence of Animals*. Edwin Mellen Press, Lewiston: 60-63, 66-67.

283 Witty, J. 1705. *An Essay towards a Vindication of the Vulgar Exposition of the Mosaic History of the Creation of the World, and of the Fall of Adam. In Two Parts*. John Wyat, London.

284 Witty, 'Preface' in: *Essay*: A3.

'I have made it appear, that none is so really advancing of Piety as *the most vulgar Exposition*. If these things will establish it, *Moses's* History must in all reason be literally interpreted (…) in matter of History, the literal has most right to be look'd upon as the true Explication.'[285] The idea that Scripture should not be taken literally in any detail had gained influence since the first allusions in this direction had been made by George Hakewill. To this idea, Witty took issue, but without acknowledging the consequences of this conviction for animal life and behavior. Those consequences were drawn for him by the author to be addressed next.

3.8.26. *Thomas Robinson (†1719)*
Witty's conviction that Scripture should be taken literally, also when it comes to reporting past events, was contested by *Thomas Robinson*, rector of Ousby—an author better known for his encouragement of village sports and his collection of data on mining, minerals and the natural history of the countryside that was his home than for his theological achievements.[286]

Robinson accused Witty—whom he denoted as an 'Ingenious young Divine'—of ignoring the fact that 'much of the Majesty of the Scripture-Style, which distinguishes it from all Humane Authority, consists in the *Metaphor* and *Figure*'.[287] It must be admitted that God ordered the fruits of the earth as food for the animals but we 'cannot possibly understand this in a Literal Sense, being that a full third part both of Beasts and Fowl are Carnivorous, and feed altogether upon Flesh, unless he will take advantage of the Metaphor, *That all Flesh is Graß*'.[288]

'*Worms* are, by God's Providence, ordained for the Food of the *Vernal Birds*.' It prompts to adoration to see how 'the *Birds* do Hatch their young ones and *Nature* hath provided these *Worms* (…) for their first Food and Nourishment.'[289] Predation among animals not only supplies food but is also for our benefit because to arrange 'that the Number of these [animals hurtful to mankind such as rats, mice and the like] might not increase so as to be offensive to *Man*, God hath ordained the *Cat*, the *Weesel* and the *Owl* to destroy them.'[290]

---

285 Witty, *Essay*: 146.
286 For biographical details, see Nicholson, A. 'Robinson, Thomas' in: *Dictionary of National Biography, 1885-1900, Volume 49*.
287 Robinson, T. 1709. *An Essay…To Which Is Annexed, a Vindication of the Philosophical and Theological Paraphrase of the Mosaick System of the Creation, &c.* W. Freeman, London: 1-2.
288 Robinson, *Vindication*: 36.
289 Robinson, *Vindication*: 69-70.
290 Robinson, *Vindication*: 72.

Admittedly, Robinson seemed to recognize that sometimes, animals are 'torn in pieces by such cruel Masters, as the *Lyon*, the *Bear*, or *Tiger*; who would not give them time to die, but even eat their Flesh from their Bones alive'.[291] An atheist could use this as an argument to deny the existence of God.[292] This, however, makes no sense as 'to expect, or wish, that there should be nothing in the World, but such *Dull* and *Tame Animals* as can neither *Bite* nor *Scratch*, is as groundless and childish as if there should neither be Choler in the Body, nor Fire in the Universe'.[293] When making up the balance, predation is as God intended. 'Every Animal is perfect in its own Class or Order.'[294] In his emphasis on purpose-oriented design, Robinson joined the ranks of Wilkins, Boyle, and Ray. Many would follow suit as will be seen in the next chapter.

3.9. Discussion

The above collected information gives us insight into the ideas and thoughts about animal death and suffering as expressed by theologians, philosophers and others in the period lasting from the dawn of the seventeenth century to the end of the first decade of the eighteenth century. When analyzing these thoughts, the same issues as mentioned in Chapter 2 have to be considered. First: Do authors show any concern about animal death and predation? And second: If animal death and predation are mentioned, does this imply suffering that could raise doubts about God's wisdom and benevolence, let alone his existence? For the sake of convenience, opinions of authors discussed are listed in Table 3.1.

3.9.1. Animal Death and Predation

When making up the balance, it can be noted that only a few scholars attributed animal death to the curse evoked by Adam's fall or claimed that animals initially fed on herbs to become carnivores only after the transgression of the first human couple. Most authors assumed that animals feeding on their fellow creatures were already present in the original creation—acknowledging that feeding habits are related with anatomical and physiological properties that cannot be changed overnight. The influence of natural philosophy, the 'scientific' study of nature, on the interpretation of the Bible is beginning to assert itself.

---

291 Robinson, *Vindication*: 77.
292 Robinson, *Vindication*: 78.
293 Robinson, *Vindication*: 78. Literally quoted from More, *Antidote*: 117-118.
294 Robinson, *Vindication*: 115.

Chapter 3: Eclipse of Eden - 137

Table 3.1. List showing the respective views with the authors in chronological order. Only authors with an opinion on at least one of the mentioned issues are included.

Year	Author	Animal death in the uncorrupted creation	Predation in the uncorrupted creation	Suffering of animals*	Afterlife of animals	Disturbed relationship with mankind	Created exclusively for humanity's benefit
1599	Topsell	Ambiguous	No	Yes	Yes	Yes	
1601	Gibbons	Ambiguous	No			Yes	Yes
1605	Willet	No	No		No	Yes	Yes
1613	Draxe	Ambiguous	Ambiguous	Yes	Yes	Yes	Yes
1616	Goodman	Ambiguous	Ambiguous	Ambiguous	Yes	Yes	Yes
1623	Elton	Ambiguous	Ambiguous	Yes	Yes	Yes	Yes
1635	Hakewill	Yes	Yes			Yes	
1641	Walker	No	No	Yes	Yes	Yes	Yes
1643	Browne	Yes	Yes			Yes	
1645	Digby			No			
1645	Waite	Ambiguous	Ambiguous	Yes	Yes	Yes	Yes
1650	More	Yes	Yes	Yes	No		No
1655	Overton	No	No		Yes		
1655	Wilkins	Yes	Yes				
1667	Baxter			Irrelevant	No		
1668	Gott	Yes	No			Yes	
1675	Hodges	Yes	Yes	Yes		Yes	
1678	Cudworth				No		No
1682	Charnock		Ambiguous	Ambiguous	Yes	Yes	Yes
1687	Franck	No	No	Ambiguous		Yes	
1690	Boyle	Yes	Yes	Yes			No
1691	Ray	Yes	Yes	Yes			No
1693	Edwards	Yes	Yes			Yes	No
1702	Emes			No	No		
1704	Norris			No	No		

* Suffering means that an author described animals as 'suffering' or 'groaning'. Attributing animals merely sense does not qualify as suffering.

Various authors attempted to bridge the gap between the Genesis text and the results of science by adapting ideas about nature to the contents of Scripture. Willet proposed that animals were created carnivorous but had to postpone their first meal till after Adam's fall, whereas Gott thought that some animals were created already as hunters in catching prey but not yet eating it. In general, however, authors chose other options, questioning the reliability of the Genesis account on the subject of the animals' diet.

Hakewill was the first of those who disputed that Adam's fall had drastic consequences for the natural world and a row of other authors would follow suit. This negligence or reinterpretation of Scripture evoked only weak and ineffective opposition; an ultimate attempt of Witty halfway through the first decade of the eighteenth century was harshly rebutted by Robinson as I addressed above. In addition, the absence of any reference to Scripture in the writings of others, already from the

Fig. 3.1. In the opinion of Bochart, God temporarily suspended the nature of the animals, thus allowing a peaceful being together of both predator and prey during Adam's name-giving session. ©Adam Naming the Animals & the Appearance of Eve. http://RosemarieAdcock.com. With permission.

sixties of the seventeenth century onwards, illustrates the declining authority of the literal interpretation of the 'Mosaick History' as I sketched in the Introduction. After all, it seems safe to conclude that Adam being guilty for animals preying upon each other was an idea supported by few if any at the end of the seventeenth century. Most of them saw the consequences of humankind's transgression being restricted to a disturbed relationship, animals created to serve humanity becoming threatening or at least nasty.

In this mitigation of the consequences of Adam's transgression, British scholars were not unique. Similar thoughts can be found in the writings of the French Protestant theologian *Samuel Bochart* (1599–1667).[295] This author also restricted the consequences of the fall to a loss of men's authority over the beasts:

> But by the sin of the man thrown down from this height, we hold the reins of former dominion only with difficulty, and the animals stand up against us as we did against God. With that, they avenge the wrong done to their Creator. And not only attack us the wild animals, and the snakes threaten us with their poisoned bite, but also the smallest creatures, such as fleas, wall- and other lice, bite and expel sleep.[296]

This rebellion of the animals against their masters did, however, not change the relationships the animals had among themselves. That Bochart thought this way is clear from his assumption that God had to take special measures to enable Adam to give the names to the animals (Fig. 3.1) in an orderly manner:

---

295 For biographical details, see https://en.wikipedia.org/wiki/Samuel_Bochart. Accessed on 14 December 2021. For the reception of Bochart by Dutch reformed theologians, see Asselt, W.J. van. 'De Neus van de Bruid. De 'Profetische' en Zinnebeeldige' Godgeleerdheid van Henricus Groenewegen en Johannes d'Outrein' in: Broeyer, F.G.M., Honée, E.M.V.M. (eds). 1997. *Profetie en Godsspraak in de Geschiedenis van het Christendom. Studies over de Historische Ontwikkeling van een Opvallend Verschijnsel*. Boekencentrum, Zoetermeer: 163-184.

296 Bochart, S. 1712 [1663]. *Samuelis Bocharti Opera Omnia...Editio Quarta*. Cornelius Boutesteyn et al., Leiden. Lib. I: 58. 'Sed, per peccatum primi hominis hoc culmine dejecti, prioris imperii habenas nonnisi aegre retinemus, & bruta in nos insurgunt, quomodo nos in Deum, injuriam creatori suo factam sic ulciscentes. Nec solum ferae nos invadunt, & venenato morsu angues appetunt; sed minima quaeque animalcula, ut pulices, cimices, & pediculi, pungunt, & somnos avertunt.' With thanks to dr. John van Eck for his assistance with this text. Bochart's Latin text has never been translated. Therefore the original is quoted here whereas the translation is in the main text.

It did not happen without God that here as well as in the Ark the wolf behaved peacefully with the lamb, the dog with the hare, the cat with the mouse, and the hawk with the dove, while the Creator temporarily suppressed the ferocity of the one and the fear, and the flight of the other, in order that gathering of animals so different would not be disturbed by untidy quarrels.[297]

Bochart evidently presupposed a temporary peace among the animals when they convened to be named by Adam, which implies that before and after, no such peace existed. Similar thoughts we saw with the aforementioned author Thomas Browne.

3.9.2. Suffering Animals and Divine Benevolence

Because of the declining relevance of Scripture, the persuasiveness of Adam's sin as explanation for offending aspects of animal life lost its power as well. When, after all, Adam cannot be charged with the guilt for the miseries of animal life, other arguments to save the goodness of the Creator are required to clarify those aspects of animal life that may hurt us physically or psychologically.

Furthermore, scholars had to cope with a new attitude towards animals. Through the writings of the Frenchman *Michel de Montaigne* (1533–1592), denying the animals mental life became less self-evident than it had been before, when a Christianized Stoicism with its inherent anthropocentrism was the prevailing conviction as shown in Chapter 2. 'How knoweth he by the vertue of his understanding the inward and secret motions of the beasts?'[298] Both those who stuck to the old belief about the significance of Adam's fall as well as those who accepted a less literal interpretation of Scripture had to cope with this changing balance between human and animal interests.[299]

---

297 Bochart, *Samuelis Bocharti Opera Omnia* I: 56: 'Non sine Deo factum est, quod tam hic, quam in arca, lupus cum ove, canis cum lepore, felis cum mure, accipiter cum columba, simul pacate degebant; creatore illorum rabiem, & horum trepidationem, & fugam, ad tempus reprimente, ne intemptestivis tam diversae naturae animalium dissidiis conventus turbaretur.' Quoted from the original with the translation in the main text.

298 Montaigne, M. 1885 [1580, 1603]. *The Essayes of Michael Lord of Montaigne Translated by John Florio. Edited with an Introduction and a Glossary by Henry Morley*. George Routledge and Sons, London: 226.

299 For reviews on the changing attitudes towards animals in this period, see Thomas, *Man and the Natural World*: 33-35, 165-172; Harrison, 'Animal Souls, Metempsychosis, and Theodicy in Seventeenth-Century English Thought'; Maehle, 'Cruelty and Kindness' in: Manning & Serpell: *Animals and Human Society: Changing Perspectives*: 81-105; Harrison, 'The Virtues of Animals in Seventeenth-Century Thought';

To comply with this new situation, several roads were taken. First, there were those who clung to the literacy of Scripture. Others still denied animals the capacity to suffer or assumed that their joys outweigh their sufferings. Finally, there were those who argued that the goodness of the Creator pertains to the creation as a whole and not to every single member of it.

The question is how the writings of the authors collected and examined above reflect these changes in perspective on animals and their abilities? Did they attribute to animals a mind capable of suffering, and if so, what about the attributes of the Creator? Can any changes be identified in relationship with the development in thinking about animals as sketched above?

3.9.2.1. Adam Guilty
Authors may acknowledge the relationship between Adam's fall and animal death and predation, but most of them did not report that this may also involve animal suffering. The main exceptions were Topsell and Draxe, the former in particular being very eloquent in describing the manifold miseries of our fellow creatures. Adam's sin changed the nature of the animals for the worse. Now they rebel against our authority, are subjected to death, and suffer from their own internecine behavior and also from humans who treat them cruelly. However, nowhere was this suffering considered to blemish the goodness of the Creator. Apparently, Topsell did not feel the urge to explain why innocent beings are punished for men's transgression. In this, he deviated from authors writing a few decades later such as Gibbons, Goodman, Elton, Waite, and Charnock; they justified the Creator for his deeds by assuring us that there is no injustice in punishing the servants (i.e., the animals, together with the master).

We may not find the way these authors saved God from wrongdoing towards animals very convincing, but that does not alter the fact that now people felt the need to do so. This had never been the case before, and it announced a concern about animal welfare that has hitherto been absent.

Guerrini, A. 2003. *Experimenting with Humans and Animals. From Galen to Animal Rights*. The Johns Hopkins University Press, Baltimore: 23-47; Roedell, *The Beasts that Perish*: 100-157; Duncan, I.J.H. 2006. 'The Changing Concept of Animal Sentience' in: *Applied Animal Behaviour Science* 100:11-19; Kalof, L. 2007. *Looking at Animals in Human History*. Reaktion Books, London: 97-99; Senior, 'The Souls of Men and Beasts, 1630-1764' in: Senior, *A Cultural History of Animals in the Age of Enlightenment*: 23-45; Steiner, *Anthropocentrism and Its Discontents*: 112-171; Wiertel, D.J. 2017. 'Classical Theism and the Problem of Animal Suffering' in: *Theological Studies* 78: 659-695; Morillo, *Rise of Animals and Descent of Man*: 69-111.

Apparently, the influence of Montaigne seeped through. And this increased importance of animal welfare was also reflected in the exhortations to handle animals with care as found in the writings of Topsell, Draxe, Walker, and Elton, and proclaimed from the pulpit by Hodges. When we see their miseries and realize that they suffer because of our sins, we should repent rather than increase our guilt by treating them inappropriately or cruelly.

3.9.2.2. Are Animals Able to Suffer?
The question of whether animals are able to suffer is closely connected with the mental properties we attribute to them. Two opposing views on this determined the debate. On one side, there was *Pierre de Charron* (1541–1603) who, following Montaigne, was convinced that animal behavior akin to human behavior reflects an animal mental state similar to a human. The extent to which animals are able to feel pain will remain controversial,[300] but assuming that their behavior is purely instinctive 'is so far from Truth, that one would wonder, how it could ever enter into any Man's Head'.[301]

On the other side, there was the philosophy of Descartes whose 'doctrine of the beast machine' is 'the most remarkable early modern theory about animals'.[302] His influence on the thoughts about animals was far-reaching as I have already mentioned above (cf. § 3.6).

Other foreign authors with much influence on the British scholars writing on the subject—and hence to be included in the discussion—are *Pierre Bayle* (1647–1706) and *Nicolas Malebranche* (1638–1715). Both emphasized that animal suffering might raise concern about the goodness of the Creator. Bayle wrote, 'It is pity that the opinion of Des Cartes should be so hard to maintain, and so improbable; for it is otherwise very advantageous to religion.'[303] Why it is so advantageous to religion Bayle explained as follows in text that deserves to be quoted full length.

> [F]or all the proofs of original sin, drawn from sicknesses and death, which children are subject to, fall to the ground, if you suppose that beasts have sensation, they are subject to pain and death, and yet they never sinned. And therefore you argue wrong, when you say, *little children*

---

300 Charron, *Wisdom*: 249.
301 Charron, *Wisdom*: 252.
302 Harrison, 'The Cultural Authority of Natural History in Early Modern Europe' in: Alexander & Numbers, *Biology and Ideology*: 11-35.
303 Bayle, P. 1737 [1697]. 'Rorarius' in: *The Dictionary Historical and Critical of Mr Peter Bayle. The Second Edition...Volume The Fourth. M—R.* D. Midwinter et al., London: 900-916 (901).

> *suffer, and die, therefore they are guilty*; for you suppose a false principle which is contradicted by the condition of beasts, *viz. That a creature, which never sinned can never suffer.* This is nevertheless a most evident principle, which flows necessarily from the ideas we have of the justice and goodness of God. (...) The souls of beasts confound this order, and overthrow those distinct ideas: it must therefore be granted, that the *automata* of Des Cartes very much favour the principles by which we judge of the infinite Being, and by which we maintain Orthodoxy. (...) *That GOD being just, misery is a necessary proof of sin*; from whence it follows, That beast not having sinned are not subject to misery: but they would be subjected to it, if they were endowed with sense; therefore they have none.[304]

Here we encounter the problem that plagues Christians even today—how to reconcile the suffering of innocent beings with a benevolent God? The theological implications were clearly stated. If animals have sense, they suffer innocently. And whereas Bayle put the problem clearly but preferred to remain agnostic on this issue in writing that '[t]he Actions of Brutes are, perhaps, one of the most profound Mysteries, on which our Reason can be exercised',[305] Malebranche was less cautious, overtly subscribing to the Cartesian dogma and demonstrating the theological difficulties that arise when accepting that animals might suffer. His text will also be quoted full length.

> [T]hey [the animals] never sinn'd; or made an ill use of their Libirty, since they have none: Therefore God [would be] *Unjust* in Punishing them and making them Miserable (...). Moreover there is this difference between the condition of Men and Beasts, that Men after Death may receive an Happiness which may countervail the Pains endur'd in Life. But Beasts at Death lose all; they have been miserable, and innocent, and have no Future Retribution. Therefore, though God be Just, yet Man may suffer in Order to Merit; but if a Beast suffers, God is not Just. It may be said, perhaps, that God may do with the Beast as he thinks fit, provided he observes the Rules of Justice, with respect to Man. But if an Angel should think in like manner, that God could not punish him without some Demerits; and that he was not oblig'd to do justice unto Man, should we like that thought? Certainly God renders Justice to all his Creatures; and

---

304 Bayle, 'Rorarius' in: *The Dictionary* 4: 902.
305 Bayle, P. 1734 [1697]. 'Barbara' in: *The Dictionary Historical and Critical of Mr Peter Bayle. The Second Edition...Volume The First. A—Bi.* J.J. and P. Knapton et al., London: 638-641 (641).

if the meanest of them are liable to Misery, they must needs be capable of being Criminal.[306]

For Malebranche, God's righteousness was at stake when animals are able to suffer. This risk outweighs observations suggesting that animals have sense and hence could suffer. Because God is righteous, animals cannot have feelings; otherwise they would suffer unjustly.[307]

Not everyone saw the problem. The Anglican divine *Richard Bentley* (1662–1742),[308] at least, didn't care, as can be inferred from the content of his sermon on the faculties of the soul, the second of the eight that together formed the first series of the *Boyle Lectures*. 'If Brutes be said to have Sense and Immaterial Souls; what need we be concern'd, whether those Souls shall be immortal, or annihilated at the time of Death. (…) He [God] will do all things for the wisest and best ends. Or if Brutes be supposed to be bare Engins and Machins; I admire and adore the divine Artifice and Skill in such a wonderful contrivance.'[309] What was certainly beyond doubt is that the ability to feel pain is linked to an immaterial soul. If animals feel pain, they must have one, but that does not necessarily mean that they are also immortal. God can both create and destroy, and the decision on the fate of such an immaterial soul after the animal's death is up to him.

Most authors refused to accept a philosophy—regardless of the theological advantages if offered—that was neither confirmed from daily experience, nor from the scientific study of nature.[310] Only Digby—and at a later time Emes and Norris—subscribed to Descartes's thoughts. In his

---

306 Malebranche, N. de. 1700. *Father Malebranche His Treatise Concerning the Search after Truth…The Second Edition, Corrected with Great Exactness…* Thomas Bennet et al., London. 2: 185.

307 Descartes himself seems more concerned about human dietary needs than about divine attributes. In one of his letters to Henry More he wrote: 'And thus my opinion is not so much cruel to wild beasts as favourable to men, whom it absolves (…) of any suspicion of crime, however often they may eat or kill animals.' in: Descartes to More, February 5, 1649. Quoted in Cohen, 'Descartes and Henry More on the Beast-Machine': 53.

308 For biographical details, see Calloway, *God's Scientists*: 172-204.

309 Bentley, *The Folly and Unreasonableness of Atheism Demonstrated…*: 59-60. Robert Boyle had left a sum of money for the purpose of providing an annual salary to a preacher, who undertakes to give 'Eight sermons in the year, for proving the Christian religion against notorious infidels, atheists, deists, Gentiles, Jews and Mahometans, and does not descend to some controversy among Christians' (preface, page not numbered).

310 For the futile attempts to demonstrate anatomical differences between humans and the non-human animals that could support the beast-machine doctrine, see Bynum, 'The Anatomical Method'.

classical treatise on human understanding, *John Locke* wrote that those who deny animals mental capacities must have a lot of insight if they consider themselves able to judge that 'dogs or elephants do not think, when they give all the demonstration of it imaginable, except only telling us that they do so'.[311] Others were less polite, even making the theory an object for mockery:

> Before my Conversion to *Cartesianism*, I was so pitiful and Tenderhearted, that I could not so much as see a Chicken kill'd: But since I was once persuaded that Beasts were destitute both of Knowledg and Sense, scarce a Dog in all the Town, wherein I was, could escape me, for the making [of] *Anatomical* Dissections, wherein I my self was *Operator*, without the least inkling of Compassion or Remorse.[312]

A refusal, however, to subscribe to genuine Cartesianism did not imply that authors attributed to animals the same mental qualities as mankind has. Although they might suffer, these sufferings are less because in 'Animals, the Sense and the Apprehension of Evil have both the same Date; till it comes, they know nothing of it; and when it hath done, they have done with it; and from the moment of its Cessation, are in perfect Ease, and Tranquillity'.[313] This of course makes their sufferings incomparable with those of humans. This consideration also prompted to warnings against falling into the trap of the pathetic fallacy, reading our mental states into animals; on this point, Cartesians and non-Cartesians agree.

Whether animals have the capability to suffer was also hotly debated outside of academic and clerical circles. Periodicals had their share in this; an exchange of thoughts in the weekly *Athenian Gazette* (1693) illustrated how the problem was perceived by the general public. The discussion started with repeating the timeworn objections: (1) that attributing animals the ability to feel pain would make God unjust because animals have done nothing for which they should be punished, (2) that allowing animals a sensitivity to pain would erase the distinction between men and beast, and (3) that brutes, unlike humans, have no access to a blessed hereafter, where they can receive compensation for undeserved suffering.[314]

---

311 Locke J. 1836 [1689]. *An Essay Concerning Human Understanding. Twenty-Seventh Edition, with the Author's Last Additions and Corrections...* T. Tegg and Son, London: 59.
312 Daniel, G. 1694. *A Voyage to the World of Cartesius. Written Originally in French... The Second Edition.* Thomas Bennet, London: 240-241.
313 Charron, *Wisdom*: 255-256. Cf. Steiner, *Anthropocentrism and Its Discontents*: 79.
314 [T.B., R.S.] 1728 [1693]. 'That Brutes Have No Souls but Are Pure Machines, or a Sort of Clockwork, Devoid of Any Sense of Pain, Pleasure, Desire, Hope, Fear, &c.' in:

The answer given extended over many pages. First, the accusation of God being unjust was answered. God is not unjust because the animals are included in the curse of Adam, similar as children suffer for their parents' sins, God '*visiting the Sins of Parents upon the Children*, unto the third and fourth generation'. Regarding the difference between humanity and the non-human animal kingdom, we should realize that only man '*was made after the Image of God*, which beasts are not'. And as for the soul of the animals, there are several options: annihilation, transmigration or 'partakers of the same happiness and vigour that they had before *Adam* fell; [which will] be a recompence for their sufferings now'.[315] At the end of his rebuttal of the Cartesian *beast-machine* doctrine, the respondent appealed to common sense.

> What makes the Fox use such stratagems and cunning to escape the hounds, or to seek his prey, nothing but memory, judgment, imagination, reflection, compounding, dividing, and making intelligent conclusions from true or very propable [sic] premises, as these instances all abound with: Nothing, I say, can thus actuate or influence brutes but a thinking rational spirit within 'em, which exerts it self after such different modifications.[316]

Most contemporary secular writers rejected the doctrine of the *beast-machine* in the same way as the respondent in the *Athenian Gazette* did.[317] In the belletristic literature, it was even mocked or ridiculed:

> The brute creation here below,
> It seems, is Nature's puppet-show;
> But clock-work all, and mere machine,
> What can these idle gimcracks mean?[318]

All these critical notes, however, did not alter that the Cartesian approach absolved God from any incrimination of injustice by punishing innocent

---

Athenian Oracle...The Third Edition. Vol. I. J. and J. Knapton et al., London: 504-512 (504). Initially published in the *Athenian Gazette* of February 11, 1693 as indicated by Shugg, W. 1968. 'The Cartesian Beast-Machine in English Literature (1663–1750)' in: *Journal of the History of Ideas* 29 (2): 279-292.

315 [T.B., R.S.] 'That Brutes Have No Souls': 504-512. Transmigration means that one soul successively inhabits different bodies. That can be both human and animal. For more background information, see Chapter 4, § 4.6.5.
316 [T.B., R.S.] 'That Brutes Have No Souls': 510.
317 Shugg, 'The Cartesian Beast-Machine in English Literature'.
318 Sommerville, W. 'The Officious Messenger' in: Anderson, R. (ed.). 1794. *The Works of the British Poets...Volume Eight*. John & Arthur Arch, London: 529-531 (529).

living beings with death and sufferings. If they would save divine benevolence, the non-Cartesians had to look for other arguments.

3.9.2.3. The Joys Outweigh the Sufferings
For those who rejected the transgression of Adam or the *beast-machine* doctrine as arguments to save the Creator from being unjust against innocent creatures, the assumption that the sufferings served a greater good offered a way out, an approach nowadays known as the *good-harm analysis*.[319] If animals are able to suffer, they should also be able to have positive feelings (i.e., to enjoy themselves and the good of positive feelings might compensate for the sufferings experienced).

Authors who invoked the good-harm analysis to justify animal suffering without incriminating the Creator for unjust practices mainly come from the latter decades of the seventeenth century, the first of them being More, followed by Cudworth and Ray. Also, John Edwards joined these ranks, surprisingly because of his philippics against those who contested the literal interpretation of Scripture. For these authors, the possibility to experience joy outweighs the disadvantage of suffering, and in this way, the Creator pours out his goodness over all his creatures. A brief moment of pain is more than offset by the blessings of a joyous life.

3.9.2.4. The Argument from Design
Whereas the British authors in general rejected Cartesianism, the statement that animals resembled machines was nevertheless a useful concept. After all, a machine has a designer, and the step from acknowledging the complexity of animals to admiring the Maker was easily made. This 'argument from design' served as proof for the existence of God, most welcome in a period in which Scripture suffered from decreased authority and the Christian faith came under attacks from atheists.[320] However, evidence for design could also raise doubts by wondering whether God had contrived some animals as murderous machines, and so, the argument from design could be used to demonstrate the existence of a Creator and his craftsmanship, but not his goodness and benevolence.

---

319 Southgate, C., Robinson, A. 'Varieties of Theodicy: an Exploration of Responses to the Problem of Evil Based on a Typology of Good-Harm Analysis' in: Murphy, N., Russell, R.J. Stoeger, W.R. (eds). 2007. *Physics and Cosmology: Scientific Perspectives on the Problem of Natural Evil*. Vatican Observatory and Center for Theology and the Natural Sciences, Vatican City and Berkeley: 67-90.
320 Thomas, *Man and the Natural World*: 19-21, 166-172; Brooke, *Science and Religion*: 56-57, 133-134; Israel, *Radical Enlightenment*: 456-464; Harrison, 'The Cultural Authority of Natural History in Early Modern Europe' in: Alexander & Numbers, *Biology and Ideology*: 11-35; McGrath, *Darwinism and the Divine*: 49-84.

For this latter point, authors had to extend the argument from design from the individual to a wider area, even to the entire universe.

3.9.2.5. Serving a Greater Good

The idea that individual suffering may serve a greater good was not new; already in the Late Antique Period, Augustine had adopted the Plotinian thought that the beauty of the painting is enhanced by the contrast between dark and bright colors (cf. § 2.3.1.12). The metaphysical concept of the *Great Chain of Being*—the hierarchical arrangement of anything created and ascending from the finest grain of sand below to God at the top[321]— now acquired a new significance, not being an abstract idea anymore but instead a frame for interpreting and evaluating observations in nature.

More and Baxter echoed Plotinus and Augustine by also employing the metaphor of the painting, whereas Cudworth referred to discords in music required for the harmony of the whole. Animal suffering is interpreted as necessary for the greater good intended by the divine Providence; it nowhere threatens the Creator's image. On the contrary, the well-designed universe illustrates his power and majesty. It is interesting to note that similar thoughts can be found with continental Reformed theologians. 'For the providence whereby God governs things is similar to the providence whereby the head of the household governs the home, and the king his state, for whom the common good takes priority over an individual one.'[322]

3.9.2.6. A Blissful Future Awaits.

For those who subscribe to the view that animals have immortal souls, compensation for earthly sufferings in a blessed afterlife can be another option helpful in saving the benevolence as well as the justice of the Creator. The Pauline text from Romans 8:18–21[323] gave cause for this, in spite of the reluctance of Calvin who wrote that it is true that 'God will restore to a perfect state the world, now fallen, together with mankind'

---

321 Lovejoy, *Chain of Being*: 58-66. Cf. Plotinus, *Enneads*: 170; Mahoney, E.P. 1987. 'Lovejoy and the Hierarchy of Being' in: *Journal of the History of Ideas* 48 (2): 211-230.
322 Velde, D. te (ed.). 2015. *Synopsis Purioris Theologiae. Synopsis of a Purer Theology. Latin Text and English Translation. Volume 1*. Brill, Leiden: 275. Disputation 11:18.
323 'For I reckon that the sufferings of this present time are not worthy to be compared with the glory which shall be revealed in us. [19] For the earnest expectation of the creature waiteth for the manifestation of the sons of God. [20] For the creature was made subject to vanity, not willingly, but by reason of him who hath subjected the same in hope, [21] Because the creature itself also shall be delivered from the bondage of corruption into the glorious liberty of the children of God.' (KJV)

but 'what that perfection will be, as to beasts as well as plants and metals, it is not meet nor right in us to inquire more curiously'.[324]

Later Protestant theologians went further than the Reformer thought appropriate. Topsell, Draxe, Elton, Walker, and Charnock were convinced that some animals will join mankind in the liberation from bondage, as I have shown above. Overton was less parsimonious; not limiting this grace to some animals but including the entire commonwealth of living beings. The subject was most extensively handled by Waite, who, however, ended with the sobering conclusion that probably only species as a type might be preserved and not any particular individual.

With Overton as the only exception, the thoughts of the above authors give little reason to suppose that a participation of the animals in the renewed creation was to compensate them for suffering in the present. It was to serve a different purpose: to reflect God's power and majesty and to contribute to the happiness of the redeemed sinners. The basic attitude from which the Pauline text was interpreted is anthropocentrism. Goodman even suggested that animals join us in the liberated creation as parts of our bodies—made our flesh by having served as our food—which also illustrates the central place still allotted to humanity. The idea that an afterlife can also serve to compensate animals for current suffering had not yet occurred to anyone. In that sense, nothing has changed since Irenaeus (cf. § 2.3.1.1). Only in the next century would a more favorable interpretation for the animals emerge.

3.9.3. Conformists and Dissenters

The final question to be answered is how far ecclesiastical issues were reflected in thoughts about creation and divine attributes. In the midst of the period that is analyzed in this chapter, colliding views on the role of Church and Creed (cf. § 3.5) had escalated into the turmoil of Civil War, Interregnum, and Restoration, and it can be assumed that such matters also left their mark here.

When looking at the authors examined, the assumption that the Puritans neglected the study of the book of nature does not hold true. As already mentioned, the Puritan Topsell wrote his *History* to promote 'heavenly meditations upon earthly creatures'[325] and the aforementioned authors Baxter and Charnock had agreed, calling people who ignore the book of Nature lunatics and lesser than the beasts.

---

324 Calvin, J. n.d. *Commentaries on the Epistle of Paul the Apostle to the Romans by John Calvin. Translated and Edited by John Owen.* Christian Classics Ethereal Library. Grand Rapids: 265. Comment on Romans 8:21.
325 Topsell, 'Epistle Dedicatory' in: *Foure Footed Beasts*: page not numbered.

In this emphasis on the plight to adore God in his works, there are no differences between the Puritans and the Latitudinarian Anglican writers, the Cambridge Platonists included. All were convinced that creation mirrors divine power and glory. A tension between Puritanism and natural theology appears to be less evident than sometimes assumed.[326] Neither are differences observed in concerns with humanity's plight to promote animal well-being, an issue addressed by respectively the Anglicans Draxe and Hodges; the Puritans Topsell, Elton, and Walker; the Cartesian-minded Anglican cleric Norris; and the physico-theologian Boyle. Puritan writers have indeed contributed to a sensitivity for animal suffering but considering Puritanism to be the main player in this field seems to be an overstatement.[327]

Also in the conviction that animals will share a blessed afterlife with humans, no sharp line can be drawn between the several denominations as can be noted from the writings of the Puritans Topsell, Elton, Waite, Draxe, and Charnock, the Anglican converted to Catholicism Goodman, and the Leveller Overton. Surprisingly, the Puritans Thomas Edwards and Baxter disagreed on this point.

The most conspicuous difference between the Puritans on one side and the Anglican Latitudinarians on the other side is the interpretation of animal death and predation in relationship to divine attributes. It was mostly the Puritans who attributed this to Adam's sin. In their view, Genesis contains a reliable and accurate account of events that explains death and predation among animals as a result of the loss of humanity's authority over the non-human animal creation, animals changing their feeding habits because of improper behavior of those appointed as their masters.

Another aspect in which the Puritans and the other denominations disagreed was their interpretation of the Pauline text in Romans 8 about the groaning of creation. Generally, this was related to the suffering of the animals as I have shown above, but the Puritans added another aspect. The creation groans because it is—due to Adam's fall—no longer able to glorify God in the way it should. That which mankind has retained of its authority over animals after its expulsion from Eden's garden, it abuses for its own fame instead of honoring its Creator. In this view, they agreed with Martin Luther, who in the previous century had put forward similar thoughts—creation groaning because humanity deals with it in the wrong way (cf. § 2.3.3.1).[328]

---

326 For contrasting opinions on this, see Harrison, *The Fall*: 241 versus Marshall, *Puritanism and Natural Theology*: 17-31.
327 Watson, 'Protestant Animals': 1141-1142.
328 Obviously, the idea that the groaning of the creation is the result of human abuse is

Those who were less convinced that Scripture should be taken literally and disagreed that animals were only created for human use and interests looked for alternative explanations for animal death and predation. The Cambridge Platonists subscribed to the Plotinian view that the whole is more important than the composing parts, a beautiful painting requiring both bright and dark colors. Benevolent divine providence is reflected in an order perceived and to be respected in society as well as in nature. Neither was animal death and predation an issue of concern for the physico-theologians. Beasts of prey are wonders of divine contrivance, fit for the purpose the Creator had in mind.

It appears that different convictions about ecclesiastical issues had little impact on the way animal life was reconciled with divine attributes and that these themselves were not yet questioned. Nature glorifies the Lord; every Christian, of whatever denomination, agreed on that.[329]

3.10. Conclusion

It may be concluded that throughout the period examined in this chapter, animal suffering was not understood as something that could damage the attributes of a good and benevolent Creator. If the possibility that animals might suffer had already been considered, then it was condoned (1) by assuming that animals lacked the mental properties required for suffering, (2) by considering suffering of animals to be outweighed by their joyful experiences or (3) by regarding animals' mishaps serving the greater good of a well-designed universe. In the book of nature, all pages 'are telling the glory of God'.[330] Even pages at first sight deemed black proclaim the Creator's benevolence and craftsmanship. If any significance was given to the fall of Adam, it was confined to a disruption of the relationship between mankind and the non-human animals, making the animals' contribution to the welfare of humanity less than it could have been. Seeing the fall only from the drawbacks it has brought to mankind and only giving animals access to a blessed afterlife for contributing to the happiness of saved sinners make evident that anthropocentrism had not

---

not a '20th and 21st century aberration' as claimed by young-earth creationist Henry Smith. Luther and the Puritans already felt that way. See Smith Jr, H.B. 2007. 'Cosmic and Universal Death from Adam's Fall: an Exegesis of Romans 8:19–23a' in: *Journal of Creation* 21 (1): 75-85 (85n64).

329 Webster, C. 'Puritanism, Separatism, and Science' in: Lindberg & Numbers, *God & Nature*: 192-217, in particular pp. 200-203.

330 Psalm 19:1. (NRSV)

yet lost its power. Blount's lamentation: '(…) if Sickeness and Afflictions are sent us because of our Sins, what makes Brutes subject to the same?'[331] had evoked little response thus far.

---

331 Blount, C. 1695 [1679]. 'Anima Mundi; or an Historical Narration of the Opinions of the Ancients Concerning Man's Soul after this Life: According to Unenlightened Nature' in: *The Miscellaneous Works of Charles Blount…With the Contents of the Whole Volume*. n.p., n.p.: 11-133 (120). Charles Blount was a notorious freethinker. For a nuanced view on his life and works, see Redwood, J.A. 1974. 'Charles Blount (1654–93), Deism, and English Free Thought' in: *Journal of the History of Ideas* 35 (3): 490-498.

Chapter 4: Links in a Chain

Concerns with Animals in the Age of Enlightenment (1710–1799)

Abstract

To explore how the shift of opinion from the past view that nature witnesses God's glory to today's common belief that nature is a battlefield where everything and everyone is at odds with each other and the weakest loses out, in this chapter, texts of British authors published throughout most of the eighteenth century (1710–1799) are explored, focusing on how they linked the death and predation of animals with divine benevolence and providential care. It turns out that throughout this time span, animal sufferings did not in general pose any threat to divine goodness, wisdom, and benevolence. That animals could suffer was widely accepted, in contrast with the previous period in which it was largely ignored, but their sufferings could be made acceptable by assuming that (1) it came from Adam's sin but that they would be rewarded for their undeserved miseries in a blessed hereafter, (2) suffering did not afflict the animals themselves but wretched souls that were imprisoned in animal bodies, (3) happiness in animal life predominated above their miseries which went hand in hand with allotting them limited mental abilities, and (4) animals suffered for the greater good of the whole, especially in preserving any species from going extinct. Although the validity of these considerations as support for divine benevolence and other attributes was doubted by a few, none of these dissenters invoked animal suffering as evidence against God's existence. They only rejected that nature could reflect divine properties.

4.1. Introduction

As addressed in the previous chapter, the end of the seventeenth century witnessed the loss of Scripture as a source for reliable data concerning cosmography and the origin of the earth. The fall could not be invoked anymore to reconcile animal mishaps with divine goodness and benevolence. Nor did the solution based on the Cartesian *beast-machine* doctrine outlive the first decades of the eighteenth century; it crumbled away as did Cartesianism itself.[1] At the same time, developments already seen in the seventeenth century became more important, such as an increased sensitivity for animal well-being,[2] utilitarianism replacing religion as a foundation for morality,[3] and the significance of the argument from design,[4] pertaining to both the individual creature and the whole creation, the latter interpreted as a well-designed edifice with anything in its proper place and contrived to meet the requirements for that particular place.[5]

In this chapter, I will examine how in this new intellectual climate, the potential conflict between animal suffering and a benevolent Creator was addressed. Before, in § 4.2, I will pay attention to the attitude towards the animal as it manifested itself during this period, followed by some notes on the importance of looking for design in § 4.3. In § 4.4, I will sketch developments in the study of nature relevant for the subject. Thereafter, in § 4.5, I will account for the followed methodology. Texts by the authors who focused on the relationship between animal suffering and divine attributes are discussed in § 4.6, and data thus collected will be analyzed in § 4.7. At the end, in § 4.8, I will formulate some concluding remarks.

4.2. Attitude to Animals
It is generally assumed that the daily contact with household pets played an important role in changing the human attitude towards animals from at best indifferent to respecting them as living beings with their own interests. Pet owners were at the forefront in rejecting the Cartesian *beast-machine* theory by offering a never-ending flow of stories about the behavior of their darlings from which far-reaching conclusions about animal intelligence and character were drawn.[6]

---

1 Israel, J.I. 2001. *Radical Enlightenment. Philosophy and the Making of Modernity 1650–1750*. Oxford University Press, Oxford: 475-501; Wolloch, N. 2019. *The Enlightenment's Animals. Changing Conceptions of Animals in the Long Eighteenth Century*. Amsterdam University Press, Amsterdam: 49-61.
2 Thomas, K. 1983. *Man and the Natural World. Changing Attitudes in England 1500–1800*. Penguin Books, Harmondsworth: 121-136, 150-181; Preece, R. 2002. *Awe for the Tiger, Love for the Lamb: a Chronicle of Sensibility to Animals*. Routledge, London: 231-327.
3 Steiner, G. 2005. *Anthropocentrism and Its Discontents. The Moral Status of Animals in the History of Western Philosophy*. University of Pittsburgh Press, Pittsburgh: 153-166.
4 Israel, *Radical Enlightenment*: 456-464.
5 Lovejoy, A.O. 1936. *The Great Chain of Being. A Study of the History of an Idea. The William James Lectures Delivered at Harvard University, 1933*. Harvard University Press, Cambridge (MA): 181-226.
6 Turner, J. 1980. *Reckoning with the Beast. Animals, Pain, and Humanity in the Victorian Mind*. The Johns Hopkins University Press, Baltimore: 1-14; Thomas, *Man and the Natural World*: 121-136; Ritvo, H. 1987. *The Animal Estate. The English and Other*

Another illustration of this changed climate is the appearance of epitaphs and elegies devoted to the demise of pets that became an established genre in the course of the eighteenth century.[7] The sad story of the widowed blackbird is an appropriate example. The poem starts with the description of a lovely honeymoon:

> He [the male blackbird] led her to the nuptial bow'r,
> And nestled closely by her side,
> The happiest bridegroom in that hour,
> And she the most enamour'd bride.

But the happiness would not last as

> [a]t him the gunner took his aim :
> The aim he took was much too true ;
> O! had he chose some other game,
> Or shot as he had us'd to do!
>
> Divided pair! forgive the wrong,
> While I, with tears, your fate rehearse ;
> I'll join the widow's plaintive song,
> And save the lover in my verse.[8]

Because the gap between humans and animals narrowed, the conviction that animals lacked an immortal soul lost persuasion.[9] And even those who clung to the anthropocentric tradition in which animals were denied immortality realized that the conviction that the beasts had been created

---

Creatures in the Victorian Age. Harvard University Press, Cambridge (MA): 1-42; Raber, K. 'From Sheep to Meat, from Pets to People. Animal Domestication 1600–1800' in: Senior, M. (ed.). 2007. *A Cultural History of Animals in the Age of Enlightenment.* Berg, Oxford: 73-99.

7 Tague, I.H. 2008. 'Dead Pets: Satire and Sentiment in British Elegies and Epitaphs for Animals' in: *Eighteenth-Century Studies* 41 (3): 289-306.

8 Jago, R. 'An Elegy on a Blackbird' in: Fisher, A. (ed.). 1807. *The Pleasing Instructor…to Which Are Prefixed New Thoughts on Education.* J. Brambles et al., London: 321-323. The 'nuptial bow'r' conjures up associations with John Milton's poetic representation of the meeting between Adam and Eve: 'To the Nuptial Bowre / I led her blushing like the Morn'. In: Milton, J. 1667. *Paradise Lost. A Poem Written in Ten Books.* Peter Parker, London: 156. (Book VII, lines 147-148).

9 Turner, *Reckoning with the Beast*: 4, 8; Thomas, *Man and the Natural World*: 137-142; Roedell, C.A. 2005. *The Beasts that Perish: the Problem of Evil and the Contemplation of the Animal Kingdom in English Thought, c.1660–1839.* PhD Thesis, Georgetown University, Washington, D.C.: 100-157, 191-226.

for humans' sakes was no license for ill-treating them unnecessarily.[10] People should refrain from treating animals cruelly, not only because this makes them cruel to each other as was already observed in the past but also for the interest of the animals themselves.[11] 'The more entirely the inferior creation is submitted to our power, the more answerable we should seem for our mismanagement of it; and the rather, as the very condition of nature renders these creatures incapable of receiving any recompence in another life for their ill treatment in this.'[12]

Also in other fields, the significance of animal interests was emphasized. Texts were published with the aim to teach children about showing kindness to the brute creation,[13] and from the pulpits clergy delivered sermons in which people were urged to show clemency and respect for animals.[14] Furthermore, animal experiments including vivisection raised second thoughts.[15] The easy way out offered by the Cartesian doctrine was blocked, and other justifications for experiments on living animals had to be sought, either by defending vivisection and other experiments on animals on the theological grounds of gaining knowledge about God's creation[16] or by the utilitarian argument that the inflicted suffering of animals could be justified by the aims pursued, in this case, the benefit for humans.[17] It was not clear to everyone that this aim could justify the

---

10 Thomas, *Man and the Natural World*: 165.
11 Thomas, *Man and the Natural World*: 150.
12 Pope, A. 1713. 'On Cruelty to the Brute Creation' in: *The Guardian*, Tuesday May 21: 90. For more details on Pope's attitude toward animals, see Boddice, R. 2008. *A History of Attitudes and Behaviours toward Animals in Eighteenth- and Nineteenth-Century Britain. Anthropocentrism and the Emergence of Animals*. Edwin Mellen Press, Lewiston: 91-96.
13 Turner, *Reckoning with the Beast*: 5-7, 9-12; Morillo, J. 2018. *The Rise of Animals and Descent of Man, 1660-1800. Toward Posthumanism in British Literature between Descartes and Darwin*. University of Delaware Press, Lanham: 23-68.
14 Morillo, *Rise of Animals and Descent of Man*: 69-112.
15 Turner, *Reckoning with the Beast*: 96-121; Ritvo, *Animal Estate*: 157-166; Guerrini, A. 1989. 'The Ethics of Animal Experimentation in Seventeenth-Century England' in: *Journal of the History of Ideas* 50 (3): 391-407; Maehle, A.H. 'Cruelty and Kindness to the 'Brute Creation'. Stability and Change in the Ethics of the Man-Animal Relationship, 1600-1850' in: Manning, A., Serpell, J. (eds). 1994. *Animals and Human Society: Changing Perspectives*. Routledge, London: 81-105; Guerrini, A. 2007. 'Natural History, Natural Philosophy, and Animals, 1600-1800' in: Senior, *A Cultural History of Animals in the Age of Enlightenment*: 121-144; Franco, N.H. 2013. 'Animal Experiments in Biomedical Research: a Historical Perspective' in: *Animals* 3: 238-273; Wolloch, *The Enlightenment's Animals*: 27-46, 71-111.
16 Guerrini, 'Ethics of Animal Experimentation'.
17 Bentham, J. 1789. *An Introduction to the Principles of Morals and Legislation. Printed in the Year 1780, and now First Published*. T. Payne, and Son, London: 308n-309n;

means employed, as can be inferred by the varying reactions of those who attended the spectacle of the bird subjected to an experiment with Boyle's air pump (Fig. 4.1). Then as now, people disagree on the usefulness of vivisection, an everlasting bone of contention.[18]

Fig. 4.1. An Experiment on a Bird in the Air Pump. Joseph Wright of Derby, 1768. National Gallery, London. A scientist shows how the bird he upholds in the bowl, a white cockatoo, will suffocate when all air is withdrawn.

Also the influence of a changing theological climate has to be acknowledged. As summarized by Turner,[19] Puritanism with its emphasis on God's justice came to be replaced by a more latitudinarian view of the divine attributes in which benevolence and goodness prevailed. Mankind should reflect these attributes in showing benevolence as well, not only towards other people but also to non-human fellow creatures. '[I]t was the fervent hope of the "Latitude-men" that they might succeed in freeing the religion of the English people from those errors concerning the nature

---

Franco, 'Animal Experiments in Biomedical Research'; Steiner, *Anthropocentrism and Its Discontents*: 162-165.
18 Franco, 'Animal Experiments in Biomedical Research'; Bates, A.W.H. 2017. *Anti-Vivisection and the Profession of Medicine in Britain. A Social History.* Palgrave MacMillan, London. I will return to this theme in Chapter 5.
19 Turner, *Reckoning with the Beast*: 5-6.

of God and the value of human works which had been spread by the Puritans.'[20]

Thomas gives a succinct summary of the reasons for the changed attitude to animals: 'It [the campaign against unnecessary cruelty to animals] grew out of the (minority) Christian tradition that man should take care of God's creation. It was enhanced by the collapse of the old view that the world existed exclusively for humanity; and it was consolidated by a new emphasis on sensation and feeling as the true basis for a claim to moral consideration.'[21] And for those stubborn people, especially in the lower classes, who refused to change their minds and habits, Hogarth's *Four Stages of Cruelty* (Fig. 4.2) served as a warning not to be misunderstood; boys torturing cats will end at the anatomist's dissecting table after being hanged by neck until death for murder.[22]

It is to be expected that this increased sensitivity for the animals' interests had its influence on the ideas about animal life and divine attributes since questions about the relationship between a benevolent Creator and animal miseries will not be made when nobody worries about the latter. However, when animal suffering becomes a matter of concern, questions about the attributes of the God who made them thus may become a matter of concern as well.

4.3. The Argument from Design

Because of changes in the interpretation of the book of Scripture, God's existence had to be supported by evidence from other sources. Natural theology, the discipline that 'is concerned with what we can know about God purely by being human and thinking about the world—apart from any special revelation'[23]—offered opportunities. The time-honored conviction that the beauty and orderliness of nature pointed to the

---

20 Crane, R.S. 1934. 'Suggestions toward a Genealogy of the "Man of Feeling" ' in: *Journal of English Literary History* 1 (3): 205-230 (208).
21 Thomas, *Man and the Natural World*: 180.
22 Steintrager, J.A. 2001. 'Monstrous Appearances: Hogarth's "Four Stages of Cruelty" and the Paradox of Inhumanity' in: *The Eighteenth Century* 42 (1): 59-82; Boddice, *A History of Attitudes and Behaviours toward Animals*: 96-101; Beirne, P. 2013. 'Hogarth's Animals' in: *Journal of Animal Ethics*, 3 (2): 133-162.
23 Holder, R.D. 2016. *Natural Theology*. Faraday Paper 19. The Faraday Institute for Science and Religion, Cambridge. Cf. Brooke, J.H. 1991. *Science and Religion. Some Historical Perspectives*. Cambridge University Press, Cambridge: 192-225; Mandelbrote, S. 'Early Modern Natural Theologies' in: Manning, R.R. (ed.). 2013. *The Oxford Handbook of Natural Theology*. Oxford University Press, Oxford: 75-99; Ruse, M. 'Natural Theology: The Biological Sciences' in: Manning, *Oxford Handbook of Natural Theology*: 397-417.

Chapter 4: Links in a Chain - 159

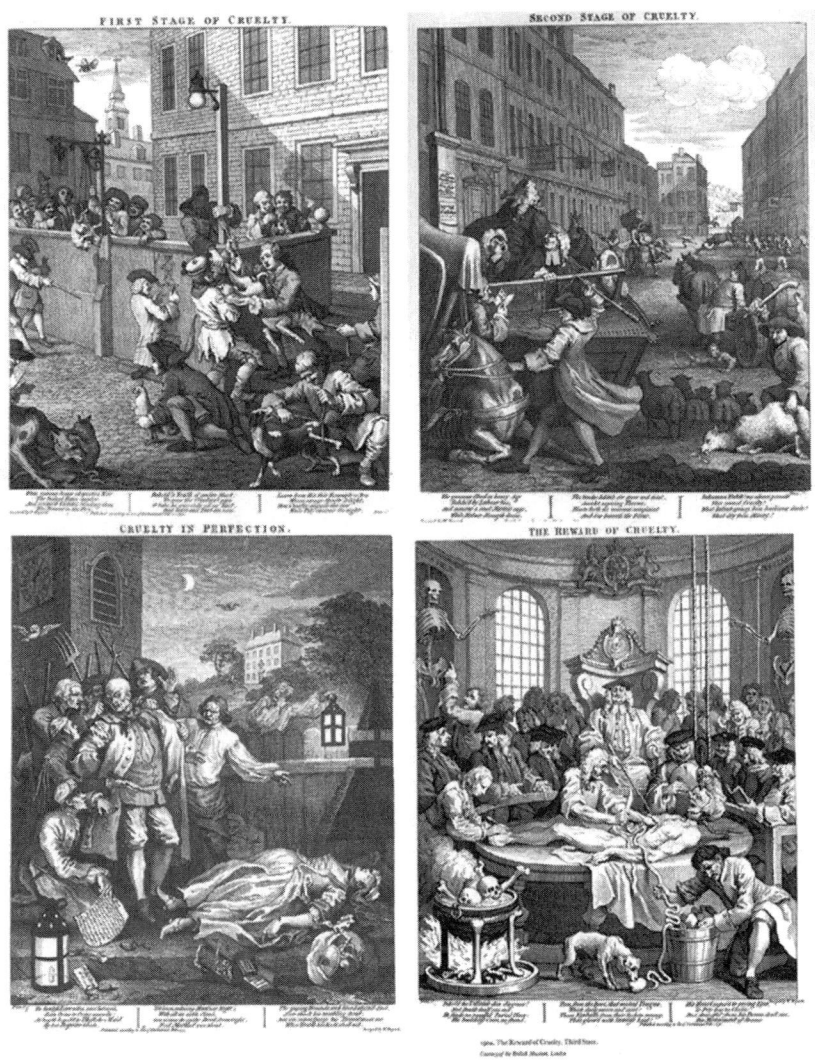

Fig. 4.2. Four Stages of Cruelty. William Hogarth, 1751. The series of prints tells the life of Tom Nero, a child from the slums. What begins with abusing dogs, continues with beating horses and murdering his pregnant lover. The story ends on the dissection table in an anatomical theatre.

existence of God now became an apologetic strategy, natural theology taking advantage of natural history.[24]

To explain the elevated status of natural theology in this particular period, the theologian and scientist Alister McGrath mentions three factors that played a role. They are (1) the growing influence of biblical criticism that damaged the reputation of Scripture and sparked interest in nature as an alternative source of knowledge, (2) the desire for a source of knowledge that was not under ecclesiastical control, and (3) an aversion to church organizations and doctrines which caused 'many to search for a simpler "religion of nature" in which nature was valued as a source of revelation'.[25] Furthermore, at the end of a century tormented by the vicissitudes of Civil War, Commonwealth and Protectorate,

Restoration, and Glorious Revolution, the British felt that a stable social and political situation was desperately needed.[26] Natural theology served this aim well by advising contemplation of nature reflecting order. Religious disputes fed by divergent opinions on Scripture from which tensions and warfare easily arose and that had been so devastating in the recent past, should be avoided.[27]

Also, physico-theology—the specific branch of natural theology already introduced in the previous chapter (cf. § 3.4)—gained in importance. Hitherto, natural evil had been condoned by stating that it contributed to the beauty of the whole as is the case with dark colors in a painting or discords in a melody. Now, people became more and more convinced that nature not only reflected God's majesty and power, but also showed purpose and therefore pointed to a God who had actively designed and built the world.[28] The insight that animal species balance each other through predation made this behavior of the animals understandable; it served a laudable aim. The belief that God created

---

24 Gillespie, N.C. 1987. 'Natural History, Natural Theology, and Social Order: John Ray and the "Newtonian Ideology"' in: *Journal of the History of Biology* 20 (1): 1-49; Brooke, J., Cantor, G. 1998. *Reconstructing Nature. The Engagement of Science and Religion. Glasgow Gifford Lectures.* Oxford University Press, New York: 148-153; Israel, *Radical Enlightenment*: 456-464; Harrison, P. 'The Cultural Authority of Natural History in Early Modern Europe' in: Alexander, D.R., Numbers, R.L. (eds). 2010. *Biology and Ideology. From Descartes to Dawkins.* The University of Chicago Press, Chicago: 11-35; McGrath, A.E. 2011. *Darwinism and the Divine. Evolutionary Thought and Natural Theology. The 2009 Hulsean Lectures. University of Cambridge.* Wiley-Blackwell, Chichester: 49-84.
25 McGrath, *Darwinism and the Divine*: 51.
26 Kishlansky, M. 1997. *A Monarchy Transformed. Britain 1603–1714.* Penguin Books, London.
27 McGrath, *Darwinism and the Divine*: 50-51.
28 McGrath, *Darwinism and the Divine*: 53, 66.

anything with a foreordained aim in his mind served as a scientific paradigm, fruitful in guiding scientific research and yielding additional support to the Creator's craftsmanship.

Order and design were the pillars for the concept of the *Great Chain of Being*.[29] Plenitude, continuity and gradation were the underlying ideas. Plenitude implies that the universe contains all possible forms of existence; all conceptual possibilities must be realized in actuality. Continuity means that if, theoretically, there was an intermediate type between two natural species, that type must be realized, for otherwise, there would be gaps in the universe which implied a lack of fullness and an inadmissible inadequacy of the Good or Absolute. Gradation means all created things arranged in a single *scala naturae*, according to degree of perfection, and ranging from the inanimate to the animate with imperceptible transitions,[30] the range occasionally extended to include spiritual beings like angels as well.[31] 'The whole chasm in nature, from a plant to a man, is filled up with diverse kinds of creatures, rising one over another, by such a gentle and easie ascent, that the little transitions and deviations from one species to another, are almost insensible.'[32]

Similar thoughts are found with Locke, who wrote that 'when we consider the infinite power and wisdom of the Maker, we have reason to think, that it is suitable to the magnificent harmony of the universe, and the great design and infinite goodness of the architect, that the species of creatures should also, by gentle degrees, ascend upward from us, toward his infinite perfection, as we see they gradually descend from us downwards.'[33] And also Robinson—an author we already encountered in the previous chapter—employed the metaphor, when writing that 'Life is a Chain, by which we may ascend from the meanest *Insect*, Link by Link, (…) till we ascend to the *Supream Being*, the Fountain of Life and Perfection' thus even including the Creator himself as link and—in passing—adding that 'every animal is perfect in its own Class or Order.'[34]

---

29 Lovejoy, *Chain of Being*: 183-226.
30 Lovejoy, *Chain of Being*: 56.
31 Preece, R., Fraser, D. 2000. 'The Status of Animals in Biblical and Christian Thought: a Study in Colliding Values' in: *Society & Animals* 8 (3): 245-263.
32 Addison, J. 1730. *The Evidences of the Christian Religion:…With a Preface, Containing the Sentiments of Mr. Boyle, Mr. Lock, and Sir Isaac Newton, Concerning the Gospel-Revelation.* J. Tonson, London: 121-122.
33 Locke J. 1836 [1689]. *An Essay Concerning Human Understanding. Twenty-Seventh Edition, with the Author's Last Additions and Corrections…* T. Tegg and Son, London: 326-327.
34 Robinson, T. 1709. *An Essay…To Which Is Annexed, a Vindication of the Philosophical and Theological Paraphrase of the Mosaick System of the Creation, &c.* W. Freeman, London: 35 [erroneously numbered as 19], 115.

The metaphor of the chain of life not only found its way in scientific and theological texts but also inspired poets as well, such as *Alexander Pope* (1688-1744) who wrote:

> Vast chain of being! which from God began,
> Natures aethereal, human, angel, man,
> Beast, bird, fish, insect, what no eye can see,
> No glass can reach; from infinite to thee,
> From thee to nothing.[35]

I suppose that because of its pervasive influence the argument from design—design being manifest both at the level of the individual organism and in the way each individual had its place in the chain of life—played a major role in the contemplations about the relationship between divine attributes and animal misery. Whether that is really the case will be discussed below in § 4.7.

4.4. New Views on the Living World

Another issue influencing the way people looked at the non-human animal creation were the scientific developments that took place during the course of the eighteenth century. The gap between humanity and the non-human animal kingdom narrowed with the discovery of the African and Asian great apes with their close anatomical similarity to humans.[36] This posed a problem for the determination of the position of humans as opposite to animals, but left the subject of animal death and predation in relationship to the goodness of the Creator untouched. Developments relevant to this theme were in other areas.

First, the discoveries made by the microscope revealed a world unsuspected before: a universe of tiny animals in which death and

---

35 Pope, A. 1881 [1734]. *Essay on Man. Edited by Mark Pattison. Sixth Edition.* Clarendon Press, Oxford: 35. Epistle I, lines 237-241.
36 Greene J.C. 1961. *The Death of Adam. Evolution and Its Impact on Western Thought.* The New American Library, New York: 177-202; Bynum, W.F. 1973. 'The Anatomical Method, Natural Theology, and the Functions of the Brain' in: *Isis* 64 (4): 444-468; Turner, *Reckoning with the Beast*: 7-8; Niekerk, C.H. 2004. 'Man and Orangutan in Eighteenth-Century Thinking: Retracing the Early History of Dutch and German Anthropology' in: *Monatshefte* 96 (4): 477-502; Roedell, *The Beasts that Perish*: 129-139; Blancke, S. 'Lord Monboddo's *Ourang-Outang* and the Origin and Progress of Language' in: Pina, M., Gontier, N. (eds). 2014. *The Evolution of Social Communication in Primates. A Multidisciplinary Approach.* Springer International Publishing, Switzerland; Sebastiani, S. 2019. 'A 'Monster with Human Visage': the Orangutan, Savagery, and the Borders of Humanity in the Global Enlightenment' in: *History of the Human Sciences* 32 (4): 80-99.

predation rule at an unimaginable scale.[37] The *Great Chain of Being* appeared to contain many more links than previously thought and extended into the realm of the invisible. Life seemed to be ubiquitous. 'Every part of matter is peopled; Every green leaf swarms with Inhabitants.'[38] But these observations also created problems unknown thus far; when realizing that each droplet of water contains myriads of minute living beings, the distinction between animals feeding on herbs and those being carnivorous becomes difficult to maintain. A cow slobbering water from a pool unintentionally kills countless numbers of fellow creatures enjoying their own lives.

Second, a reason for concern came from observations made during geological explorations. It turned out that the crust of the earth contained structures that had to be interpreted as the remains of real creatures, fossils.[39] The problems these findings raised for time-honored convictions about the creation and the Creator can be sensed from the writings of contemporary scholars. '[By] the Works of the Creation (...) I mean the Works created by God at first, and by Him conserv'd to this Day in the same State and Condition in which they were at first made'[40], thus wrote John Ray—already introduced in the previous chapter—shortly before the turn of the eighteenth century.

Only three years later, *Robert Hooke* (1635–1703) told the members of the Royal Society that '[c]ertainly there are many *Species* of Nature that we have never seen, and there may have been also many such *Species* in former Ages of the World that may not be in being at present and many variations of those *Species* now, which may not have had a Being in former Times.'[41]

Ray knew what Hooke was referring to. He was also aware of the threat posed by these findings to the belief that creation had not changed since

---

37 Hill, J. 1752. *Essays in Natural History and Philosophy Containing a Series of Discoveries, by the Assistance of Microscopes*. J. Whiston et al., London; Lovejoy, *Chain of Being*: 239.
38 Addison, *The Evidences of the Christian Religion*: 118.
39 Greene, *The Death of Adam*: 96-133; Thomson, K. 2005. *Before Darwin. Reconciling God and Nature*. Yale University Press, New Haven: 111-137; Rudwick, M.J.S. 2005. *Bursting the Limits of Time. The Reconstruction of Geohistory in the Age of Revolution*. The University of Chicago Press, Chicago: 194-203, 239-287, 639-644.
40 Ray, J. 1722 [1691]. *The Wisdom of God Manifested in the Works of the Creation. In Two Parts...The Eight Edition, Corrected*. William and John Innys, London: preface, page not numbered. The principle of plenitude did not permit any loss nor novelty. Cf. Lovejoy, *Chain of Being*: 242-244.
41 Hooke, R. 1705. *The Posthumous Works of Robert Hooke Containing His Cutlerian Lectures and Other Discourses, Read at the Meetings of the Illustrious Royal Society...* Richard Waller, London: 450. Read in the Royal Society July the 25th, 1694.

the beginning. 'What can we say to this?'[42] Perhaps animal species that appear to be extinct may still exist in remote areas of the Earth. 'For though they may have perished, or by some Accident been destroyed out of our Seas, yet the Race of them may be preserved and continued still in others.'[43] In speculating that fossilized animals were not really extinct but still might exist in unexplored parts of the earth, Ray was no exception; after all, large parts of the earth, let alone the sea, had not yet been mapped out, and the assumption that apparently extinct species of animals could still be found somewhere was not far-fetched.[44] Moreover, this explanation also fitted better with the static world view that was still prevailing at that time. The belief that the earth had undergone no substantial changes since its inception would only gradually give way to the idea that other worlds had preceded the present and only at the turn of the nineteenth century, authors would become less reluctant to accept the fact that animal species that had previously populated the earth no longer existed.[45]

James Parkinson (1755–1824),[46] the physician better known for the description of the neurological disorder that bears his name than for his accomplishments in geology and paleontology, illustrated this changing view of the fact that animal species could become extinct.

> [Although] some very good and learned men have regarded the loss of a single link, in the chain of creation, as inadmissible; it implying, they say, such a deviation from the first plan of creation, as might be attributed to a failure in the original design. But such an inference does by no means follow; since that plan, which prevents the failure of a genus, or species from disturbing the general arrangement, and economy, of the system, must manifest as great a display of wisdom and power, as could any

---

42 Ray, J. 1713. *Three Physico-Theological Discourses...The Third Edition...*William Innys, London: 150. One of the alternative explanations considered but rejected by Ray was the assumption '*That the Monkeys and Apes, at the Cape of Good Hope, are almost continually carrying Shells and other Marine Bodies from the Sea-Side up to the Mountains*' (148).

43 Ray, *Three Discourses*: 173

44 See for the competing hypotheses brought up to explain differences between fossils and extant fauna Rudwick, *Bursting the Limits of Time*: 242-246, 639-644. The differences between the fossils and the current animal species could be explained by the assumption of disappearance due to extinction, replacement by migration, or transmutation in which one animal species evolves into another. Current theories of evolution are a combination of all three elements. During the eighteenth century, migration was the preferred solution.

45 Bowler, P.J. 1974. 'Evolutionism in the Enlightenment' in: *History of Science* 12 (2): 159-183.

46 Rudwick, *Bursting the Limits of Time*: 432-434, 496-498, 512-514.

fancied chain of beings, in which the loss of a single link would prove the destruction of the whole.⁴⁷

For Parkinson, a design that can endure the loss of some components without any problems was much more excellent that one that is so vulnerable that it cannot afford the loss of the least of them. '[C]hanges cannot furnish sufficient grounds, for doubting of the wisdom or power of God: not even [when] several worlds had existed before the present.'⁴⁸

Divine design even allows the entire replacement of one world by another; why then whine about the loss of some species of shell-fish? 'Does it not appear [Parkinson asks] from this repeated occurrence of new beings, from the late appearance of the remains of land animals, and from the total absence of the fossil remains of man, that the creative power, as far as respects this planet, has been exercised, continually, or at distant periods, and with increasing excellence, in its objects, to a comparatively late period: the last and highest work appearing to be *man*, whose remains have not yet been numbered among the subjects of the mineral kingdom[?]'⁴⁹

Whereas Ray hoped that the offspring of animal species that seemed extinct would have survived in some remote place, thus saving the perfection of the original creation, Parkinson, in contrast, viewed the appearance, flourishing, and perishing of animals as well as animal species as a testimony of the Creator's power working to greater perfection by replacing new for old. Between these two extremes, scholars had to find their place in acknowledging that not only the death of individual animals but also the extinction of entire species had to be reconciled with divine goodness and wisdom, and furthermore, they had to envisage that, in the animal creation, death and predation were far more widespread than thus far assumed. It can hardly be otherwise than that this had an influence on the thinking about the relationship between animal suffering and divine qualities, but research of the sources must reveal whether my assumption comes true.

4.5. Method

Authors to be discussed in this chapter have been selected from recent secondary sources that address the problem of suffering animals in a

---

47 Parkinson, J. 1820. *Organic Remains of a Former World...In Three Volumes.* Sherwood et al., London: I: 459-460.
48 Parkinson, *Organic Remains* I: 457-458.
49 Parkinson, *Organic Remains* III: 455.

creation proclaimed to be good.[50] These secondary publications served as point of departure for any additional enquiries. In order to be relevant for the topic, authors should address the question if and how animal behavior including aggression and predation reveals or refutes the hand of a benevolent Creator. This implies that they should discuss how to relate *animal death and predation with the attributes of God.*

The thoughts of the various authors will be demonstrated in chronological order, followed by summarizing their position on the issues at stake. Do their writings express any concern about animal death, predation, and suffering, and if so, how are these reconciled with the image of God as a benevolent Creator? Thereafter, the results obtained in this way will be discussed searching for commonly held convictions. Finally, some concluding remarks will be made. I cannot rule out the possibility that relevant authors can be missed with this way of working but their absence in secondary sources might indicate that they were either less influential or did not write something that had not already been covered sufficiently by others.

4.6. The Literary Sources
4.6.1. William Derham (1657–1735)
Within the ranks of eighteenth-century scholars who took efforts to prove the existence and benevolence of God from his works in creation, a prominent place was occupied by *William Derham*, a Church of England clergyman and natural philosopher.[51] In 1713, he published his *Physico-theology or a Demonstration of the Being and Attributes of God from his Works of Creation,* a work that would see many editions throughout the eighteenth century. The twelfth edition, printed in 1754, is taken as the source for the analysis of Derham's thoughts.[52]

The wisdom of the Creator manifests itself in the huge variety of living beings. Some may ask why there are 'so many Insects, so many Plants,

---

50 Lovejoy, *Chain of Being*; Greene, *The Death of Adam*; Thomas, *Men and the Natural World*; Manning & Serpell, *Animals and Human Society: Changing Perspectives*; Roedell, *The Beasts that Perish*; Steiner, *Anthropocentrism and Its Discontents*; Thomson, *Before Darwin*; Duncan, I.J.H. 2006. 'The Changing Concept of Animal Sentience' in: *Applied Animal Behaviour Science* 100:11-19; Senior, M. 'The Souls of Men and Beasts, 1630-1764' in: Senior, *A Cultural History of Animals in the Age of Enlightenment*: 23-45; McGrath, *Darwinism and the Divine*; Morillo, *Rise of Animals and Descent of Man*.
51 For biographical details, see The Galileo Project (rice.edu). Accessed on 14 December 2021.
52 Derham, W. 1754 [1713]. *Demonstration of the Being and Attributes of God from His Works of Creation…The Twelfth Edition*. W. Innys and J. Richardson, London.

and so many other Things?' That question is all the more pressing when we realize that 'some of them, that are so far from being useful, that they are very noxious'. For these skeptics, Derham had his answer ready. 'That in greater Variety, the greater Art is seen.'[53] And animals that are of no use to us, such as, by example, insects 'are Food to Birds, Fishes, Reptiles, Insects themselves, and other Creatures (...), for whose happy and comfortable Subsistance, I have said the bountiful Creator hath liberally provided.'[54]

Animal death and predation were no issues to be concerned about, as the various ways animals feed themselves are the means to keep an ecologically sound balance, showing the wisdom of the Creator. '[T]hat (...) sufficient Food should be afforded to (...) so great Variety of Beasts, Birds, Fishes, and Insects; is owing to that Being, who hath as wisely adapted their Bodies to their Place and Food, as well as carefully provided Food for their Subsistence there.'[55] All animals bear testimony of the Creator's craftsmanship and contribute to the well-being of others. 'Even those Animalcules in the Waters, discoverable only with good Microscopes, are a Repast to others there, as I have often with no less Admiration then Pleasure seen.'[56]

For Derham, the non-human animal kingdom runs like a well-designed machine in which every individual has its own place, contributing to the preservation of the whole. Animal death is required to prevent destruction of one animal species by overgrowth of another, and predation is one of the means to reach that aim. That this could imply suffering of individuals and that this suffering might raise concerns about divine justice or benevolence was not addressed. Admiration for divine wisdom and craftsmanship prevailed.

4.6.2. Bernard Nieuwentijt (1654–1718)

The Dutch physician and philosopher *Bernard Nieuwentijt* can be seen as representative of those scholars who heavily relied on the argument from design in contesting atheism. His book *The Religious Philosopher, or the Right Use of Contemplating the Works of the Creator*—initially written in Dutch and published in 1715[57]—had a profound influence on the contemporary discussion about natural theology and physico-theology in England; hence, inclusion of this author from abroad who intended to

---

53 Derham, *Demonstration*: 55.
54 Derham, *Demonstration*: 59.
55 Derham, *Demonstration*: 181.
56 Derham, *Demonstration*: 187.
57 Nieuwentijt, B. 1715. *Het Regt Gebruik der Wereltbeschouwingen ter Overtuiginge van Ongodisten en Ongelovigen Aangetoont...*Weduwe J. Wolters en J. Pauli, Amsterdam.

make science acceptable within the circles of orthodox believers,[58] is justified.

For Nieuwentijt, the earth is created for mankind's well-being. Because we cannot live off grass, there are 'Oxen, Sheep and all other Creatures, that are taken by Men for Food, as so many living and walking Kitchens; in which is prepared the otherwise unprofitable Grass, and becomes good, wholsome and palatable Food'.[59] Animals serving for food is no issue to be concerned about; it demonstrates divine wisdom. Neither did Nieuwentijt have any worries about death. It is part of the well-designed cycle of birth and death in which the wisdom of the Creator is reflected; the earth is the workshop in which the Lord keeps this cycle running, using anything that has died as material for new life.

> Can it be then thought that such ingeniously contrived Bodies of Men, of Beasts, and of Plants, proceed all from the Earth, without the Concurrence of a great Director? and having appeared in such Forms after a little while are turned to Earth again, which brings forth more that are likewise to undergo the same Fate. And can an Atheist be so void of all Reason, as to conceive, that such a wonderful Circulation and Revolution of Things, during so many Ages, can come to pass without a wise Direction?[60]

These observations should convert even the stubbornest atheist into a pious Christian, at least in Nieuwentijt's view. It is interesting to note the new element now introduced; animal death plays an important role in maintaining or restoring the earth's fertility. Death is not something that questions divine benevolence but rather supports this. Similar thoughts inspired Alexander Pope to write:

> See dying vegetables life sustain,
> See life dissolving vegetate again:
> All forms that perish other forms supply,
> (By turns we catch the vital breath, and die)
> Like bubbles on the sea of matter born,
> They rise, they break, and to that sea return,

---

58 Vermij, R.H. 'Nature in Defense of Scripture. Physico-Theology and Experimental Philosophy in the Work of Bernard Nieuwentijt' in: Berkel, K. van, Vanderjagt, A. (eds). 2006. *The Book of Nature in Early Modern and Modern History*. Peeters, Leuven: 83-96; McGrath, *Darwinism and the Divine*: 88-89.
59 Nieuwentyt. B. 1719. *The Religious Philosopher...Designed for the Conviction of Atheists and Infidels...Vol. II...Translated from the Original by John Chamberlayne*. J. Senex and W. Taylor, London: 547.
60 Nieuwentyt, *The Religious Philosopher* II: 556.

Nothing is foreign; parts relate to whole;
One all-extending, all-preserving soul
Connects each being, greatest with the least;
Made beast in aid of man, and man of beast ;
All served, all serving: nothing stands alone;
The chain holds on, and where it ends, unknown.[61]

Theologically, Nieuwentijt differed slightly from the British physico-theologians, not so much emphasizing design in nature as evidence for the existence of God but rather seeking support for Scripture from nature.[62] But this different intention does not imply that he has any troubles with animal death.

4.6.3. Bernard Mandeville (1670-1733)
Bernard Mandeville, Dutch by birth, spent most of his life in the United Kingdom where he became notorious for his 'vision of man as driven by egotistical impulses, always seeking his own individual preservation and advancement', thus eliminating 'all Bible-based and religion-based morality'.[63] In his satire, the *Fable of the Bees: or, Private Vices, Publick Benefits,*[64] Mandeville considered the effects of these 'egotistical impulses' to be beneficial; without private vices, common benefit exists neither. Even our positive feelings are nothing else than disguised vices. 'Love enters into the Compound of *Jealousy,* and is the Effect as well as happy Disguise of that Passion that prompts us to labour for the Preservation of our Species. (…) Could we undress Nature, and pry into her deepest Recesses, we should discover the Seeds of this Passion before it exerts it self, as plainly as we see the Teeth in an Embryo, before the Gums are form'd.'[65] For my purpose, his ideas about animal life and creation as forwarded in this publication require attention.

First, he chastised Descartes for his *beast-machine* doctrine. '[I]n such perfect Animals as Sheep and Oxen, in whom the Heart, the Brain and Nerves differ so little from ours, and in whom the (…) Organs of Sense, and consequently Feeling itself, are the same as they are in Human

---

61 Pope, *Essay on Man*: 48. Epistle III, lines 15-26.
62 Vermij, 'Nature in Defense of Scripture' in: van Berkel & Vanderjagt. *The Book of Nature in Early Modern and Modern History*: 83-96.
63 Israel, *Radical Enlightenment*: 623-627 (625).
64 Mandeville, B. 1924 [1729, 1732]. *The Fable of the Bees: or, Private Vices, Publick Benefits. With a Commentary Critical, Historical, and Explanatory by F.B. Kaye.* Clarendon Press, Oxford. Cf. Harth, P. 1969. 'The Satiric Purpose of The Fable of the Bees' in: *Eighteenth-Century Studies* 2 (4): 321-340.
65 Mandeville, *Fable of the Bees* 1: 142-143.

Creatures; I can't imagine how a Man not hardened in Blood and Massacre is able to see a violent Death, and the Pangs of it, without Concern.'[66]

Second, the relationship between animal behavior and divine design was discussed; this was the subject of one of Mandeville's *Dialogues*.[67] Partners in this dialogue were *Cleomenes*, who speaks for Mandeville, and *Horatio*, the imaginary opponent who believes in 'the ultimate goodness of the universe'.[68] *Cleomenes* questions the literal interpretation of Scripture. 'The History which he [Moses] has given us of those Times is extremely succinct, and ought not to be charged with any thing, contain'd in the Glosses and Paraphrases, that have been made upon it by others.'[69] An Edenic past as depicted in Milton's *Paradise Lost* is unlikely as 'nothing is more common to Nature, or more agreeable to her ordinary Course, than that Creatures should live upon one another'.[70]

Horatio hesitates. 'Has Religion nothing to do with it, that you make God the Author of so much Cruelty and Malice?' To this, *Cleomenes* replies that 'nothing can be call'd cruel, or malicious, in regard to him who did it, unless his Thoughts and Designs were such in doing it'.[71] In *Cleomenes's* view, we should not judge God's intentions from what happens in nature. *Horatio*, however, persists that if the animal behavior reflects the 'Purposes wild Beasts were designed for', these purposes in that case are 'clashing with our Idea of the Divine Goodness'. On this, *Cleomenes* emphasizes again that God's actions are beyond our understanding: 'So will every thing seem to do which we call Natural Evil; if you ascribe human Passions to the Deity and measure infinite Wisdom by the Standard of our most shallow Capacity.'[72]

---

66 Mandeville, *Fable of the Bees* 1: 173.
67 Mandeville, *Fable of the Bees* 2: 218-265.
68 See Mandeville, *Fable of the Bees* 2: 7-24. Mandeville explains why he employed the style of a dialogue to explain his thoughts, this being '*the easiest way*' to '*illustrate and explain several Things*'. (7) Cleomenes is introduced as Mandeville's friend '*who speaks my* [Mandeville's] *sentiments*' (21) and Horatio is a person '*who had found great Delight in my Lord* Shaftsbury' (20) whose view that nature and society everywhere speak of harmony was heavily contested by the skeptic Mandeville. Cf. Porter, R., 2003. *Flesh in the Age of Reason. How the Enlightenment Transformed the Way We See Our Bodies and Souls*. Penguin Books, London: 130-147. Quote from Primer, I. 'Introduction' in: Mandeville, B. 1962 [1795] *The Fable of the Bees or Private Vices, Publick Benefits. Newly Edited, with an Introduction by Irwin Primer*. Capricorn Books, New York: 1 -17 (16).
69 Mandeville, *Fable of the Bees* 2: 234-235.
70 Mandeville, *Fable of the Bees* 2: 247.
71 Mandeville, *Fable of the Bees* 2: 251.
72 Mandeville, *Fable of the Bees* 2: 261.

Mandeville shared the feelings prevailing in this century that the Bible has no decisive authority in matters of science. Second, his views on animal life and suffering and his rejection of the ideas of Descartes also complied with the majority view. What is different, however, is his reluctance to see divine goodness and wisdom in the animal kingdom. 'I would not make God the Author of Evil (…) but I am likewise persuaded, that (…) all the Calamities we can suffer (…) are under a wise Direction that is unfathomable.'[73] God is justified in his works, not because these works glorify him but because they surpass the understanding of humble earthlings.

If there is any argument from design, it argues for divine power but nowhere for goodness and benevolence. About the latter, the book of nature is silent. Elsewhere, Mandeville even wrote—again employing *Cleomenes* as his mouthpiece—that 'the rude and ignorant of our Species are always more apt to suspect, that this invisible Cause is their Enemy, than they are to think it to be their Friend, and will sooner believe it to be an evil and malicious, than a good beneficent Being'.[74] Apparently, revelation is needed to correct the information provided by the book of nature; when this is missing, this book only gives birth to fear.[75]

4.6.4. William King (1650–1729)

William King was an Anglican divine in the Church of Ireland and Archbishop of Dublin; in philosophy, he strongly opposed atheistic materialism.[76] In 1702, he wrote *De Origine Mali,* translated into English and supplemented with extensive notes by Edmund Law in 1731 and published under the title *An Essay on the Origin of Evil.*[77] This latter text is my source for examining the thoughts of this author.

In his approach to the subject of animal death and predation, King followed a thoroughly Plotinian approach. It is not the individual that counts, but the whole. The goodness of the latter requires contributions of varying perfection.[78]

---

73 Mandeville, *Fable of the Bees* 2: 261-262.
74 Mandeville, B. 1732. *An Enquiry into the Origin of Honour, and the Usefulness of Christianity in War.* John Brotherton, London: 113.
75 Shagan, E.H. 2018. *The Birth of Modern Belief. Faith and Judgment from the Middle Ages to the Enlightenment.* Princeton University Press, Princeton: 272.
76 For biographical details, see http://www.informationphilosopher.com/solutions/philosophers/king/. Accessed on 14 December 2021.
77 King, W. 1731. *An Essay on the Origin of Evil. Translated from the Latin…With Some Account of the Origin of the Passions and Affections.* W. Thurlbourn, London.
78 Plotinus. 1956. *The Enneads. Translated by Stephen MacKenna, Second Edition Revised by B.S. Page…*Faber and Faber, London: 170-173. King's writings on animal life were

> [F]rom hence we may affirm, that God, tho' infinitely good and powerful, could not separate things from the concomitant Evils of Imperfection, and did not esteem it unbecoming himself to create the Good, tho' that brought some Evils along with it, so long as these Evils are less than the Good with which they are connected. Nor can the Creature justly complain of its Condition, if it have not all, or equal Perfection, with some others; since 'twas necessary that it should fill the Station wherein it was placed, or none at all.[79]

Building on these premises, King drew his conclusions. 'Animals (...) have solid Bodies, are by Nature Mortal, and cannot last for ever, without violence done to the Laws of Nature, of Matter, and Motion. There must then have been either none at all created, or such as are naturally Mortal. (...) for an Animal subject to Death is better than none at all.'[80] The animals enjoy their lives without fear of the future or agonizing memories from the past, and in case of illness or old age, predation guarantees a quick release from suffering. 'Let us not be surpris'd then at the Universal War as it were among Animals; or that the Stronger devour the Weaker, for these are made on purpose to afford Aliment to the others.'[81]

Pain is indispensable because '[a]n Animal in the present State of things, must therefore either, be obnoxious to these [pain] or quickly perish'. Things could have been otherwise but 'how dangerous this would be to Animals, any one may understand, who recollects how very short their Lives must be, if they died with the same Pleasure as that they eat or drink or propagate their Species'.[82] And to those who insist that animal death and predation are consequences of the curse evoked by Adam's transgression, King had his arguments as well. 'Scripture no where teaches that there would have been no manner of natural Evil, if Man had not sinned.'[83]

Only some kinds of evils have to be attributed to Adam's transgression. King listed them consecutively: (1) the mortality of humanity, (2) the barrenness of the earth and growth of harmful plants, (3) hard labor to

---

also approved by Leibniz, who discussed the original Latin text in an appendix to his *Theodicy*. In: Leibniz, G.W. 1951 [1710]. 'Observations on the Book Concerning 'the Origin of Evil'' Published recently in London' in: *Theodicy: Essays on the Goodness of God, the Freedom of Man, and the Origin of Evil*...Routledge & Kegan Paul, London: 405-442.

79 King, *Essay*: 96.
80 King, *Essay*: 110-111.
81 King, *Essay*: 119.
82 King, *Essay*: 115.
83 King, *Essay*: 146.

cultivate the earth, (4) 'that *impotent Affection* and Necessity of Obedience whereby *Women* are made subject to *Men*', (5) the difficulties of pregnancy and childbirth, (6) the enmity towards the snake, and (6) the expulsion from Paradise.[84] The consequences of the fall cannot be extended to the animal kingdom. Animal death and predation belong to the creation as God intended. Only humanity suffers from the consequences of Adam's transgression.

4.6.5. Guillaume-Hyacinthe Bougeant (1690–1743)

Guillaume-Hyacinthe Bougeant, better known *as Père Bougeant* was a French Jesuit.[85] His *Amusement Philosophique sur le Language des Bêtes*, published in 1737, was translated into English, Italian, and German. The English edition[86] evoked a lot of discussion among contemporary scholars on the British Isles, and hence, this author is included.

Whereas Descartes was convinced that animals were mere machines devoid of any conscious experiences, Bougeant, figuring as an imaginary author,[87] disagreed. 'Persuaded as we are that Beasts have Intelligence, have we not all of us a thousand times pitied them for the excessive Evils, which the Majority of them are exposed to, and in reality suffer?' Why they so suffer is a riddle: 'If Men are subject to a multitude of Miseries that overwhelm them, Religion acquaints us with the Reason of it, *viz.* their being born Sinners. But what Crimes can Beasts have committed, by birth to be subjected to Evils so very cruel?' Divine justice requires that without sin there can be no punishment. 'What are we then to think of the horrid Excesses of Misery undergone by Beasts: Miseries indeed far greater than those of Men?'[88]

Possibly, animals are not as innocent as they seem to be at a first glance. 'Beasts by nature are extremely vicious. (…) The voracious Beasts and Birds of Prey are cruel. Many Insects of one and the same Species devour each other. *Cats* are perfidious and ungrateful. *Monkeys* are mischievous. *Dogs* are envious.' Thus raising doubts that animals are indeed blameless, Bougeant supposed 'that the Nature of Beasts has, like that of Man, been corrupted'. They are corrupted because '[t]he Souls of Beasts are refractory Spirits [fallen angels turned into devils], which have

---

84 King, *Essay*: 146.
85 Randall, C. 2014. *The Wisdom of the Animals: Creatureliness in Early Modern French Spirituality*. University of Notre Dame Press, Notre Dame: 93-124.
86 Bougeant, G.H. 1740. *A Philosophical Amusement upon the Language of Beasts and Birds, Written Originally in French…The Second Edition Corrected*. T. Cooper, London.
87 Why Bougeant delivered his opinion in this way is not clear. See for this point Morillo, *Rise of Animals and Descent of Man*: 91; Randall, *The Wisdom of the Animals*: 104.
88 Bougeant, *Amusement*: 18-19.

made themselves guilty towards God. (...) Let us then be contented with saying, that, as Man is a Soul and an organized Body united, so is each Beast a Devil united to a Body organized.' Each animal is animated by its own private evil spirit because 'as Man has not two Souls, Beasts likewise have each but one Devil. This is so very true, that *Jesus Christ* having one day driven out many Devils, and these having asked his leave to enter into a Herd of *Swine* that fed near the Sea, he permitted it, and they entered into the *Swine* accordingly. But what happened? Each *Swine* having his own Devil already, there was a Battle, and the whole Herd threw themselves headlong into the Sea.'[89]

The animals are merely the outward manifestations of the evil spirits that animate them. So, any utterance of suffering reflects the suffering of the embodied devil. Their suffering never ends.

> The Devils, by God appointed to be Beasts, necessarily out-live their Bodies, and would cease to answer their Destination, if at the Moment of the Destruction of their first Body they passed not immediately into another, to begin to live a-new under another Form. Thus such or such a Devil, after having been a Cat or a Goat, is forced to pass into the Embryo of a Bird, a Fish, or a Butter-Fly, to animate them. Happy those who light upon a good Lodging, as many Birds, Horses, and Dogs do; and woe to such as become Beasts of Burden, or the Hunter's Game. It is a kind of Lottery, in which the Devils very likely have not themselves the Choice of their Lots.[90]

---

89 Bougeant, *Amusement*: 19-22. In this passage, Bougeant refers to the story described in Matthew 8:28-34, Mark 5:1-20, and Luke 8:26-39.

90 Bougeant, *Amusement*: 24-25. Bougeant consciously modified the Pythagorean idea of Metempsychosis. In its original form, this doctrine holds that the same soul successively animates the bodies of different beings, both humans and animals (its basic idea comes close to that of reincarnation). For Bougeant, only devilish spirits inhabit animal bodies in succession. Cf. Long, H.S. 1948. 'Plato's Doctrine of Metempsychosis and Its Source' in: *The Classical Weekly* 41 (10): 149-155; Harrison, P. 1993. 'Animal Souls, Metempsychosis, and Theodicy in Seventeenth-Century English Thought' in: *Journal of the History of Philosophy* 31: 519-544; Osborne, C. 2007. 'On the Transmigration of Souls: Reincarnation into Animal Bodies in Pythagoras, Empedocles, and Plato' in: *Dumb Beasts and Dead Philosophers: Humanity and the Humane in Ancient Philosophy and Literature*. Chapter 3. Published to Oxford Scholarship Online: May 2008. Pages not numbered; Wiertel, D.J. 2017. 'Classical Theism and the Problem of Animal Suffering' in: *Theological Studies* 78: 659-695.

Eight years later, the Scottish-born writer *Andrew Michael Ramsay* (1686–1743)[91]—commonly called the *Chevalier Ramsay*—wrote similar notes, ascribing animal miseries to inhabiting fallen 'angelical spirits' that are 'imprisoned in brutal machines' where each 'perhaps animates successively many brutal forms of different kinds; and (…) passes gradually from insects to reptiles, from reptiles to quadrupeds, and thence to birds according to the different degrees of its devolopement'. For him, animal bodies are nothing else than vehicles whereas the spirits 'imprisoned in brutal forms have no other ideas, sentiments, nor desires, but what are necessary to the conservation of the machines, which they animate'.[92]

In general, interpreting animal miseries as punishments for imprisoned evil spirits gained little support as it was considered to be incompatible with Christian doctrines. Bougeant was reprimanded by the censors, not surprisingly when we note that, at the same time, his fellow Jesuits struggled with doctrines about transmigration of souls they encountered during their missionary activities in the Far East.[93] His idea of migrating souls, however, did not die a quiet death as I will show shortly.

4.6.6. John Hildrop (1682–1756)

The unconventional thoughts of Bougeant prompted the Anglican cleric *John Hildrop* to a rebuttal.[94] First, Hildrop ridiculed the idea by his tongue-in-cheek description of the embarrassment that arose in an unprepared audience when they were told 'that *all the Animal Functions and Operations of the Brute-Creation (…) were entirely owing to the Operation of evil Spirits*, who are the moving Principle in every one of them'.[95] Thus summarized, Bougeant's views raised a lot of confusion.

---

91 For biographical details, see https://en.wikipedia.org/wiki/Andrew_Michael_Ramsay. Accessed on 14 December 2021. There are no indications that Ramsay was inspired by Bougeant as nowhere in his writings, he mentioned him.

92 Ramsay, Chevalier, A.M. 1748. *The Philosophical Principles of Natural and Revealed Religion. Unfolded in a Geometrical Order.* Robert Foulis, Glasgow: 385, 488; 1749; *Idem, Part Second.* Robert and Andrew Foulis, Glasgow: 321.

93 Colas, G., Colas-Chauhan U. 2017. 'An 18th Century Jesuit "Refutation of Metempsychosis" in Sanskrit' in: *Religions* 8: 192, subsequent pages not numbered.

94 Hildrop, J. 1742. *Free Thoughts upon the Brute-Creation: or, an Examination of Father Bougeant's Philosophical Amusement, &c. In Two Letters to a Lady.* R. Minors, London. For biographical details, see https://peoplepill.com/people/john-hildrop. Accessed on 14 December 2021. This book was highly acclaimed by John Wesley who republished its contents in an abridged form in the 1783 Volume of the *Arminian Magazine* (cf. § 4.6.11).

95 Hildrop, *Free Thoughts* I: 1-2. For details on Hildrop versus Bougeant, see Morillo, *Rise of Animals and Descent of Man*: 90-93.

> I [Hildrop] shall never forget the puzzled afflicted Face of the honest Justice, who (...) had spent so many Years in following a *Pack of Devils*, which he had innocently mistaken for a Pack of harmless Beagles.—But the whimsical Distresses of the poor Ladies, gave me no small Diversion. Sweet Miss *Jenny* who has lavish'd away more Kisses upon her favourite Cat, than she would bestow upon the best Man in the Parish, felt some compunction within herself, that she had been wantonly, and almost maliciously, throwing away those Caresses upon an evil Spirit, which many a good Christian would have been glad of. Dear Miss *Harriot* had the same regret for her beloved Monkey, and poor *Dolly* for her Parrot; and resolved, one-and-all, never to hold commerce or correspondence with evil Spirits for the future, in whatever amiable Shape or Figure they might appear; which, I apprehended, could end in nothing less than an intire destruction of all the favourite Domesticks of the Family.[96]

One can imagine the convincing power of this mockery when realizing that eighteenth-century England saw a tremendous increase in pet holding as already mentioned (cf. § 4.2). After showing the absurdities of Bougeant's philosophy, Hildrop continued to develop his own views on the subject of the mental life of animals. Not only Bougeant but also Descartes were under attack. Considering animals to be merely automata verges on blasphemy. 'Is not this offering Violence to Reason; Nature, and common Sense? Is it not making a Mock of God's Creatures?'[97]

The suffering of animals worried Hildrop because he recognized that this creates a threat for the divine attributes such as goodness and justice. 'They are not properly moral Agents, no Command or Prohibition had ever been given them; and, where there was no Law, there could be no Transgression; and where there was no Transgression, one would naturally imagine there would be no Punishment.'[98] Furthermore, the suffering of the animals puzzled Hildrop also because it collides with Scripture where we are told 'that God pronounced them all to be *good*, yea *very good*: Endued with every Perfection, that their Nature and Rank in the Scale of Beings required'. Thus, the question emerged where this 'unhappy Subversion of their primitive State' comes from, a question to which Hildrop replied that the 'present lamentable Condition' of the animals is the fault of man'.[99] As 'Man was by his Transgression devoted to Darkness and Death, so were all the Brute-Creation, who were his Domesticks and

---

96 Hildrop, *Free Thoughts* I: 2-3.
97 Hildrop, *Free Thoughts* I: 7.
98 Hildrop, *Free Thoughts* II: 9.
99 Hildrop, *Free Thoughts* II: 10.

Dependants. (...) They were by his Transgression made subject to Vanity, Misery, and Death. (...) guiltless Sufferers for our Transgressions.'[100] It is all due to human sin. Animals had been created immortal, just like mankind. 'Could any Creature be mortal before Death entered into the World? And was not Death the immediate, the necessary Consequence of Sin?'[101] Those who tell that animals have been created mortal from the beginning because they had 'to make room for their Successors in the same Circle of Vanity and Corruption' err.[102]

But if animals share in the punishment of the human race, they have to share in its salvation as well. After all, '(...) what difficulty is there in comprehending, or what possible Danger in asserting, that all the inferiour Creation, that fell with and in our first Parent, and suffer for our Transgression, shall at last be restored to their primitive Happiness.'[103] This prospect caused Hildrop to burst out into awe.

> If infinite Wisdom and Goodness saw fit to produce such numberless Ranks and Orders of Creatures, to compleat the Harmony of the universal System, and to share with Man in the Blessings and Glories of Paradise, before Sin and Death entered into the World, is it not highly reasonable to imagine, that they are preserved by the same infinite Wisdom and Goodness to be Sharers in the Happiness and Glory of the new World, when Sin and Sorrow shall cease, when Corruption and Mortality shall be no more, and *Death itself shall be swallowed up in Victory*?[104]

Hildrop saved the divine goodness and justice by trusting that the innocent animals will get recompense for their sufferings in a blessed afterlife. Another author wrote in the same vein: 'God (...) in his Wisdom, and tender Mercies, which are over all his Works, has reserved for them [the animals] a future Deliverance from their Bondage of Corruption, which will sufficiently compensate them for their present Sufferings.'[105]

---

100 Hildrop, *Free Thoughts* II: 12-14.
101 Hildrop, *Free Thoughts* II: 40.
102 Hildrop, *Free Thoughts* II: 44. Hildrop does not mention authors by name but in referring to a cycle of vanity and corruption, he probably attacks Derham, Nieuwentijt, and King who all interpreted a cycle of life and death as an illustration of the wisdom of the Creator.
103 Hildrop, *Free Thoughts* II: 76.
104 Hildrop, *Free Thoughts* II: 82. Hildrop quotes 1 Corinthians 15:54.
105 P[arker], B. [1745?]. *An Essay Proving the Immateriality and Immortality of the Spirits of the Whole Animal Creation, both from Scripture and Reason...The Second Edition*. Printed for the Author, London: 31-32. Biographical details of this author are limited. The publication itself lacks a year of publication and the author is only denoted by his initials: B.P. Support for Benjamin Parker as author and for 1745 as the year of

And this author argued that also Scripture itself tells us so, paraphrasing to that end 1 Corinthians 15:22 in such a way that it also seems to apply to animals: 'So as by *Adam's* Transgression all Flesh, in which is Life, shall die, *so in Christ shall all be made alive.*'[106]

4.6.7. Isaac Watts (1674-1748)

The nonconformist Congregational minister *Isaac Watts* is mainly known as the writer of numerous popular hymns, many of them remaining in use today.[107] Watts was deeply convinced that the current world is a corrupted one. All miseries of humankind can be ascribed to the transgression of Adam.[108] But how to explain the sufferings of the non-human animal creation? 'Do not all brute Creatures, the Beasts and Birds, and the Insects of the Earth, lie continually subject to the same Pains, Calamities, Accidents, Diseases and Death, which attend upon Mankind? And did their Progenitors sin and offend God, or have they themselves offended him?' After putting this question, Watts addressed the miserable conditions animals have to face. 'Do not the Cow and the Hind, and most of the four-footed Mothers bring forth their Young with extreme Pain?'[109]—an astute observation in view of scriptural notes in which painful childbirth is a curse onto female humans only and does not include the non-human female animals. Watts described animal suffering in colorful terms which can only be valued if fully quoted.

> Again, are not the feebler Creatures, both wild and tame, subject to the cruel and perpetual Ravage of Birds and Beasts of Prey? Do not these

---

publication comes from a text that is indisputably from the hand of Benjamin Parker in which this author also propagates that animals will join humanity in 'the glorious Liberty of the Children of God' with the announcement that this will be more fully treated in another tract, see Parker, B. 1745. *A Survey of the Six Days Works of The Creation: Philosophically Proving the Truth of the Account Thereof, as Deliver'd by Moses in the First Chapter of Genesis*. Printed for the Author, London: 195. In another text, Parker also addressed this subject, noting that 'tho' the Innocent are hereby [by mankind's transgression] made subject to the Punishment of the Guilty, there is a Hope of Deliverance reserved for them', see Parker, B. 1734. *Philosophical Meditations with Divine Inferences*. Printed for the Author, London: 39.

106 P[arker], *Essay*: 49. The original text paraphrased by Parker reads: 'For as in Adam all die, even so in Christ shall all be made alive.' (KJV)
107 For biographical details, see Britannica, The Editors of Encyclopaedia. "Isaac Watts". *Encyclopedia Britannica*, 6 December 2021, https://www.britannica.com/biography/Isaac-Watts. Accessed on 14 December 2021.
108 Watts, I. 1740. *The Ruin and Recovery of Mankind: or, an Attempt to Vindicate the Scriptural Account of these Great Events upon the Plain Principles of Reason…*R. Hett and J. Brackstone, London: 136-161.
109 Watts, *Ruin and Recovery*: 354-355.

Animals live by devouring one another and tearing their Flesh from their Bones, ere they are quite dead, and this according to the very Constitution of their Natures? And even the milder Fowls, who seem so innocent and harmless, the Partridge and the Redbreast, and the Chicken, do they not devour Millions of Insects, as their constant and appointed Food? Are not the mangled Bodies and Limbs of the Hare and the Sheep, the Dove and the Thrush, subject to extreme Pain, when they are torn and bruised, and half eaten by the Tyger and the Wolf, the Eagle and the Hawk? And do not all those milder and gentler Creatures occasion Millions of painful Sensations to the living Insects which they prey upon, (*viz.*) the Ants, and the Flies, and the Worms? And have any of these sinned against their Maker, or degenerated from the first Laws of their Creation? (…) A Horse stalking over an Ant-hill shall crush a hundred of the busy Inhabitants with his broad and heavy foot, (…) and leave Multitudes of their little Members bruised and broken, and the tiny Creatures expiring in Anguish? And if their Organs were strong enough to form a Sound which could reach our Ears, what shrill Outcries and Screams, what dying Groans, what innumerable Accents of Misery would arise from this little mangled Nation, and pierce the Heart of a compassionate Traveller on every such Accident? And let me ask how, Did these diminutive Animals, these tiny Atoms of Being ever offend the hand that formed them?[110]

Why are all these living beings subjected to such a terrible life, whereas no sin has been committed by them that justifies Providence acting in such a way? In his efforts to answer this question, Watts proposed several solutions. First, he addressed the view that 'these Varieties of Wretchedness came upon the brutal Creation, as a general Curse for the Sin of Man'. Watts disagreed. 'I must confess I never well approved of this Solution of the Difficulty; (…) I can hardly persuade myself that God made so many Millions of sensible Creatures so miserable, or would permit them to be so, who are in themselves perfectly sinless and innocent.'[111] Therefore, we 'may infer *Guilt* from the endless Pains, Calamities, and Death of Men, because Scripture reveals it, as the original Cause; but we cannot infer the same from the Sickness, Wounds, and Deaths of Brute-Creatures.'[112]

Watts rejected the view that animal suffering and death are connected with the human fall and the divine curse. Hence, animal sufferings had to be explained in some other way. First, Watts considered these to be unavoidable. 'Brutes are appointed for Food for each other, as flying

---

110 Watts, *Ruin and Recovery*: 356-357.
111 Watts, *Ruin and Recovery*: 359-360.
112 Watts, *Ruin and Recovery*: 361.

Insects for the Spider, small Birds for the Hawk, and Sheep for Wolves and Lions', which 'cannot be without Wounds and Bruises, and mortal Convulsions and Death.'[113]

Second, Watts supposed that animals probably 'have no proper Sensations of Pleasure or Pain; or at least that all their Sensations of Pain are but feeble and dull, and very imperfect'.[114] By this, Watts took recourse to considerations heard before. Animal sensations and experiences are not at the same level as ours. Furthermore, it may well be that, in spite of having pain, the pleasures are more. When 'their pleasing Sensations exceed the painful; then they are happy; for Misery is only found where the Pain exceeds the Pleasure in Degree, or Duration, or both'.[115]

In considering that the joys may outweigh the sufferings, Watts agreed with earlier authors like Henry More, Ralph Cudworth, and John Ray, who had a similar opinion as discussed in the previous chapter. And finally, Watts urged us to 'remember also that Brutes have no proper Reflection on things past, but only a Sensation of the present' without any 'Retrospects nor Foresights to torment them'.[116]

Thus having unfolded his views, Watts summarized that 'whatsoever Calamities and Death attend Brutes, these, for wise Purposes, are appointed by the God of Nature, tho' they are without Sin while the Calamities and Death of Mankind are expressly attributed to Sin in the Word of God'.[117] Watts rejected the option that animals suffer from the curse. The old but still prevailing Stoic thought that animals only live in the present, and hence are less liable to suffering, was more acceptable.[118] As long as pleasures outweigh pains, life is worthwhile. Although Watts struggled with finding a satisfying solution for the problem that animals suffer, he nevertheless remained convinced that God has 'wise Purposes'.

Two decades later, an anonymous author disagreed. After an extensive description of miseries that afflict both humankind as well as brutes, he concluded that 'it may perhaps be allowed, that there is a greater share of

---

113 Watts, *Ruin and Recovery*: 361.
114 Watts, *Ruin and Recovery*: 362.
115 Watts, *Ruin and Recovery*: 364.
116 Watts, *Ruin and Recovery*: 365.
117 Watts, *Ruin and Recovery*: 367.
118 Sorabji, R. 1993. *Animal Minds and Human Morals. The Origins of the Western Debate*. Cornell University Press, Ithaca: 52. The author quotes the Stoic philosopher Seneca. 'The dumb animal grasps what is present by its senses. It is reminded of the past when it encounters something that alerts it senses. Thus the horse is reminded of the road when it is brought to where it starts. But in its stable it has no memory of it, however often it has been trodden. As for the third time, the future, that does not concern dumb animals.'

happiness than misery, and that, upon the whole, good is prepollent; but is there such a prepollency of good as seems suitable to infinite wisdom, goodness, and power? (…) Nature is inveloped in obscurity. Clouds and darkness surround the throne of God.'[119] In this article, that appeared in a magazine devoted to the instruction and entertainment of an educated readership[120], the author raises doubts not only about divine wisdom and goodness but about power as well. Nature is shrouded in darkness and does not show the fingerprints of a Creator with 'infinite wisdom, goodness, and power'.

4.6.8. David Hartley (1705–1757)
David Hartley, English philosopher and physician, is mainly known for his pioneering thoughts about the way our mental faculties are dependent on the brain. Originally preparing for the ministry, he shifted to medicine because of some concerns with Anglican doctrine, considering that 'the great differences of opinion and contentions which happen on religious matters are plainly owing to the violence of man's passions more than to any other cause'.[121] His principal work *Observations on Man, his Frame, his Duty, and his Expectations* was published in 1749.[122] Although the title would not suggest that, the author paid a lot of attention to the animals as well.

As all contemporary British authors, Hartley disagreed with Descartes about animals' mental capacities, considering that 'Brutes have more Reason than they can shew, from their Want of Words, from our

---

119 Anonymous. 1760. 'A View of the Distresses of Mankind, and of the Brute Animals' in: *The Universal Magazine of Knowledge and Pleasure* 27: 231-233 (233).
120 The *Universal Magazine of Knowledge and Pleasure* was a periodical published in London in the period 1747–1814. It dealt with "Letters, Debates, Essays, Tales, Poetry, History, Biography, Antiquities, Voyages, Travels, Astronomy, Geography, Mathematics, Mechanics, Architecture, Philosophy, Medicine, Chemistry, Husbandry, Gardening and other Arts and Sciences; which may render it Instructive and Entertaining…". Adapted from https://en.wikipedia.org/wiki/The_Universal_Magazine_of_Knowledge_and_Pleasure. Accessed on 14 December 2021.
121 Langdon-Brown, W. 1941. 'David Hartley: Physician and Philosopher (1705–1757)' in: *Proceedings of the Royal Society of Medicine* 34 (5): 233-239 (234). Cf. Thomson, A. 2008. *Bodies of Thought, Science, Religion, and the Soul in the Early Enlightenment*. Oxford University Press, New York: 204-209.
122 Hartley, D. 1749. *Observations on Man, His Frame, His Duty, And His Expectations. In Two Parts*. James Leake and Wm. Frederick, London. Republished in 1966 with an Introduction by Theodore L. Huguelet. Scholars' Facsimiles & Reprints, Gainesville. For biographical details of Hartley, see Britannica, The Editors of Encyclopaedia. "David Hartley". *Encyclopedia Britannica*, 24 August 2021, https://www.britannica.com/biography/David-Hartley. Accessed on 14 December 2021.

Inattention, and from our Ignorance of the Import of those Symbols, which they do use in giving Intimations to one another, and to us'.[123]

In a preface preceding the second part of his book, Hartley admitted that 'there are Difficulties both in the Word of God, and in his Works; and these Difficulties are sometimes so magnified, as to lead to Skepticism, Infidelity, or Atheism'.[124] This can be avoided if we realize that the Bible also contains passages that are not intended to be taken literally.[125] Difficult passages in the book of Scripture thus are no reason for atheism; neither are the pages of the book of nature. And when having doubts about the divine attributes when looking at 'his Works', we should understand that the miseries that animals have to endure do not annihilate the evidences of the divine benevolence derived from happiness unless we suppose that misery equals or even surpasses happiness.[126] However, to assume the latter is without foundation; although 'Disorder, Pain, and Death, do very much abound every-where in the World, yet Beauty, Order, Pleasure, Life, and Happiness, seem to superabound'.[127]

Second thoughts about the attributes of the Creator are out of the question because 'the Origin of Evil may be made consistent with the Benevolence of God, by supposing that every Creature has a Balance of Happiness'.[128] For mankind, such a positive outcome necessitates, however, a future state because it happens 'seldom, that a good Man is rewarded here in any exact Proportion to his Merit, or a vicious Man punished exactly according to his Demerit'.[129] Therefore there has to be a *post mortem* adjusting of this balance.

The question is whether there is such a remuneration for the animals as well. Hartley did not know. It is better to be concerned about one's own future state than to speculate about an afterlife for animals.[130] Nevertheless, Hartley hoped the best for them as can be inferred from his consideration that 'there is Mercy in Store for them also, more than we may expect, to be revealed in due time'.[131] And although the future status of the animals may remain hidden for us, the idea itself that they 'should be Partakers of the same Redemption as well as of our Fall, and be Members of the same

---

123 Hartley, *Observations* I : 414-415.
124 Hartley, *Observations* II: iii.
125 Hartley, *Observations* II: 105.
126 Hartley, *Observations* II: 13.
127 Hartley, *Observations* II: 15.
128 Hartley, *Observations* II: 63.
129 Hartley, *Observations* II: 388. Apparently, divine grace to blot out human sins is out of sight.
130 Hartley, *Observations* II: 391.
131 Hartley, *Observations* II: 436.

mystical Body', should increase our concerns with their well-being.[132]

From calling animals 'partakers of mankind's Fall', one could deduce that Hartley saw a connection between the fall and the current condition of the animals. Another text in his *Observations* supports this assumption; there we read about 'evil mutual Influences in Animals' that are 'Marks and Evidences of a fallen and degenerate State' as well as 'Evidences also of the Truth of the Scriptures, which not only declare this our Degeneracy but also 'give a general Idea of the Means by which it was introduced'.[133] Whether Hartley here meant that animal suffering is also related to the fall or just explains why animals can display mischievous behavior is not clear; neither did Hartley comment on whether or not this detracts from divine benevolence. What is clear, however, is that Hartley reconciled animal suffering with divine benevolence by the positive outcome of the balance of happiness versus miseries for each of the animals individually. Whether this included correcting any deficit in this balance in an afterlife was left open, although hoped for.

Finally, Hartley considered that it is unavoidable that one animal has to be food for another, especially when considering data recently provided by the study of nature. Newly discovered living beings revealed through the microscope blurred the distinction between animals feeding on herbs and those that prey upon others, thus making an uncorrupted creation wherein each species of animals had only grass as their food even more unlikely than it already was. 'Philosophy has of late discovered such numberless Orders of small Animals in Parts of Diet formerly esteemed to be void of Life, and such an Extension of Life into the Vegetable Kingdom, that we seem under the perpetual Necessity, either of destroying the Lives of some of the Creatures, or of perishing ourselves, and suffering many others to perish.'[134]

When summarizing Hartley's views on animal death and predation as related to divine attributes like goodness and benevolence, it appears that he resorted to a happiness-versus-misery balance to justify animal suffering, happiness outweighing misery for each animal separately. The Plotinian assumption that the happiness-versus-misery balance applies to the whole and not to the individual parts was rejected because this collides with divine justice. For humans, any imbalance will be corrected in the hereafter; whether this will apply to animals as well is uncertain, but hopefully, God will also be merciful to them.

---

132 Hartley, *Observations* II: 223.
133 Hartley, *Observations* II: 226-227.
134 Hartley, *Observations* II: 223.

Scriptural data on the creation are difficult to understand and therefore, not each detail should be interpreted in a literal sense. Furthermore, the extension of the chain of living beings into a microscopic world makes a strict vegetarian diet in an uncorrupted creation unlikely. And in his concerns about a gentle handling of animals, Hartley reflected the contemporary sensitivity towards the suffering of domestic animals and pets that gained influence in the course of the eighteenth century as addressed above (cf. § 4.2).

4.6.9. John Hill (1706/1714/1716(?)–1775)

John Hill started his career as an apothecary but today, he is mainly known as one of the pioneers of the science of botany in England.[135] For the purpose of our investigation, his accomplishments in the use of the microscope for the study of the animal kingdom require attention.[136] As already mentioned in § 4.4, the use of the microscope extended the realm of life into areas thus far unseen and unsuspected. These new observations raised new questions. First, they made Hill doubt the cherished idea that all creation is made for humanity's use. Mankind is not the Lord of the creation but 'only one Species of Being, formed by the Hand that has made Millions of others'.[137]

The application of the principles of the *Great Chain of Being*—plenitude, continuity, and gradation—is as evident as is the Plotinian flavor by seeing Hill stating that it is 'our Ignorance only, that leads us to censure the Disposition of the Parts; and a more perfect Knowledge will as surely lead us to reverence and adore their Author in one as in the other'.[138] The end of the creation is not the benefit of humanity but the enjoyments of each individual creature, a note in which Hill joined aforementioned authors like his contemporaries King, Watts, and Hartley, and the seventeenth-century Cambridge Platonist Henry More.

Second, the microscope revealed a world of predation at least similar to or even surpassing the mutual internecine animal behavior observed in the visible part of the non-human animal kingdom. However, this does not have to worry us if we pay attention to the goal. 'Nature, wherever she has implanted the Means of such Destruction, has provided a Supply

---

135 For biographical details, see Fraser, K.J. 1994. 'John Hill and the Royal Society in the Eighteenth Century' in: *Notes and Records of the Royal Society of London* 48 (1): 43-67; Morris, A.D. 1959. '"Sir" John Hill, M.A., M.D. (1706–1775). Apothecary, Botanist, Playwright, Actor, Novelist, Journalist' in: *Proceedings of the Royal Society of Medicine* 53: 55-60.
136 Hill, *Essays in Natural History and Philosophy*.
137 Hill, *Essays*: 21.
138 Hill, *Essays*: 41.

necessary to the preserving the Species beside answering all its Calls.'[139] Great losses are compensated by great fecundity, and thus, no link in the *Great Chain of Being* will be lost. Apparently, Hill subscribed to the view that no species has gone, or will go, extinct in spite of concerns about this possibility by others in this same period as addressed above (cf. § 4.4).

Although it is interesting to note how Hill extended the principle of plenitude to include the microscopic world, far more interesting is his colorful description of the propagation of the ichneumon fly—the proverbial example of cruelty among animals that led Charles Darwin to abandon any thoughts on divine benevolence in creation.[140] Because of its canonical status, I will reproduce this story here full length in Hill's own words.

> As I [Hill] was one Afternoon watching their [caterpillars'] Manner of feeding, I was Witness to an Assault made upon one of the Family of a very extraordinary Kind, and by an Insect very inconsiderable in Appearance in proportion to it. (…) The caterpillar was rolling its large Form about upon the upper Side of a Leaf and seeming to bask in the Sun when the Enemy approached. This was no more than a little Fly, of that Kind called (…) the Ichneumon. (…) It made a little Buzzing with its Wings as it approached and I could perceive the Caterpillar twist and roll its hinder Part about the Sound, as if sensible of some approaching Danger. Many Efforts were made to prevent it, but at length after having pitched upon the proper Place, the Fly alighted on the Body of the Caterpillar, and immediately raising its hinder-part aloft, and pointing downward the Extremity of it, which was armed with something resembling a Sting, it darted it with Violence against the Back of the Caterpillar. I could distinguish that the sharp Body was plunged to its Base into the Flesh of the Creature. (…) I saw this repeated more than fifty Times, and a new Place chosen for every Wound: At length the Fly clapped its Wings together several Times as if in Triumph, and made off unhurt. If the Caterpillar had shewed Terror on the Approach of the Enemy, the Anguish it expressed at the repeated Wounds seemed intolerable; at every Stroke it wreathed and twisted its whole Frame about. (…) It was all in vain, the little, tho' cruel Tormentor kept its Place, and seemed to defy all the Attempts of the unweildy Enemy to dislodge or hurt it.

---

139 Hill, *Essays*: 53.
140 Darwin to Gray. 22 May 1860. *Darwin Correspondence Project*, "Letter no. 2814," accessed on 14 December 2021, https://www.darwinproject.ac.uk/letter/?docId =letters/DCP-LETT-2814.xml

Hill confessed to be 'shocked', but also to be 'surprised at the Sight', telling that he 'could conceive no Reason, no End in in [sic] the Cruelty', because he knew 'the brute Creation never destroy or hurt one another, unless some Benefit to themselves give the Temptation'. So there had to be some reason for the fly to attack the caterpillar in this way. And so it was because after catching and dissecting some of the flies, Hill noted that

> what had appeared at first an Act of wanton Cruelty in the Fly, now presented itself in a new Light: The Cruelty indeed did not appear any less, but the Intent of the Action was evident: It was plain that the Wounds were not given in Sport, but that they were the Means of laying the Eggs; and nothing could be more evident than that an Egg had been left in every Wound.

This conclusion made Hill sigh that '[t]here appeared a strange Cruelty in the Disposition of nature, that the Eggs of one Animal were to be hatched in the very Flesh of another'. But the story did not end here.

> [T]he Ease in which she [the caterpillar] passed the two first Days after the Wounds from the Fly did not last over the third. She was (…) in the most violent Agitations: A thousand Contortions of Body in a Moment shewed her Uneasiness and Anguish, and on examining her nicely with magnifying Glasses, I could (…) distinguish the Motion of living Animals under her Skin. (…) Upon the Evening of the fifth and Morning of the sixth Day (…) a number of the Creatures hatched from the Fly's Eggs, and which had hitherto lived in the Body of the Caterpillar, made their Way out by a yet more painful Operation than that by which they were let in. They gnawed their own Passage thro' several parts of the Back and Sides of the Creature, and often made Wounds much larger than were necessary for their Exclusion. Soon after the Death of the unhappy Creature the rest all made their Way out in the same Manner.[141]

The propagation of the ichneumon fly at the expense of the caterpillar thus being described, Hill commented that it is 'a very surprising Thing in this Instance of the Provision for an Animal by the Means of another, that the Worms, tho' they evidently feed on the Juices drawn by the Caterpillar from its Food, yet never erode the vital Parts of that Animal, but feed in so careful a Manner as not to destroy the Creature at whose Expence they are supported'.[142]

---

141 Hill, *Essays*: 75-80.
142 Hill, *Essays*: 90.

It is not surprising that these findings have shocked many sensitive minds ever since. Hill himself did not provide any note about the moral implications of his observations. Elsewhere, he commented on predation in more general terms.

> The several Ranks of living Creatures seem in a continual and even natural State of Depredation one upon another. We see it in the larger more conspicuously; but it is most abundantly shewn in the more minute, when we have the Curiosity and the Opportunities for examining them. The Wolf feeds on the Sheep, the Lyon on the Wolf; the Wren feeds on the Worm, and is itself eaten by the Hawk: and so on through the whole Race of the carnivorous Animals, whether they be of the quadrupede or winged Tribes. But this is little in Comparison to what the least Drop of standing Water shews to the inquisitive Examiner, in Myriads of different Creatures roving in it as a Sea, and feeding in their several Degrees on one another.[143]

Because Hill nowhere explicitly related predation to divine benevolence, it might be reasonable to suppose that for him it was not an issue of concern because of the limited scope of animal (self)consciousness that he took for granted, at least for that part of the animal kingdom that he investigated. When commenting on the behavior of some tiny animals seen through the microscope, he wrote about them that predation 'might appear a very hard Lot; but the utter Insensibility of the Creature itself to it, takes off the whole Severity. There does not seem an Animal in the whole Creation that enjoys its Period, short as it is, with more Jollity than this; Life is one continued Dance and Sport, and at its Termination it sinks in a Moment into that Nothing out of which it knows not how it arose.'[144] And elsewhere, 'Nature, having ordained them [the tiny animals microscopy reveals] as the Food to one another, has given them no Sense of Danger, nor any Inclination to escape it'.[145]

Apparently, Hill considered a positive outcome of the balance between happiness and misery sufficient to justify the Creator's actions. How this balance functions in the caterpillar-ichneumon interaction was left unaddressed. Maybe, Hill would contemplate that a design, in which the death of one implies that many may have life, also reflects divine wisdom, bearing in mind the words of the Jewish high priest Caiaphas.[146]

---

143   Hill, *Essays*: 251.
144   Hill, *Essays*: 258.
145   Hill, *Essays*: 314.
146   John 11:49–52. '49. But one of them, Caiaphas, who was high priest that year, said to them, "You know nothing at all! 50. You do not understand that it is better for you to have one man die for the people than to have the whole nation destroyed." 51. He did

4.6.10. Soame Jenyns (1704–1787)

Soame Jenyns—an English writer and politician and according to his biographer 'ever professing the greatest veneration for the Church of England and its government, (…) holding her liturgy as the purest and most perfect form of public worship in any established Church in Christendom'[147]—contributed to the topic under discussion in various ways.

His first work that is relevant for my purpose is a letter published anonymously in 1753.[148] Here, the author invoked the benefits of the doctrine of the transmigration of souls in explaining human and animal miseries. Jenyns started with a short summary of this concept—the so-called metempsychosis—that I already brought up when discussing Père Bougeant. When the soul leaves the physical body—that can be human or animal—at the time of death, it thereafter migrates into another, again either human or animal, to begin a new life that may be happier or more miserable, according to the soul's behavior in the previous existence.[149]

Jenyns considered this thought that comes from the Greek philosopher Pythagoras very useful. 'First, from its justice, secondly from its utility, and lastly, from the difficulty we lie under to account for the sufferings of many innocent creatures without it.' Misbehavior in one life gets its appropriate punishment thereafter as people 'may suffer in one life the very same injuries which they have inflicted in another; and that too in the very same persons, by a change only of situation'. Apparently, Jenyns had bad experiences with medical doctors as one of his examples concerns 'the physician, who in one life has taken exorbitant fees, may be obliged to take physic in another'.[150]

The transmigration may even cross borders of species. Therefore, all 'those who (…) have entertained themselves with the miseries and

---

not say this on his own, but being high priest that year he prophesied that Jesus was about to die for the nation, 52 and not for the nation only, but to gather into one the dispersed children of God.' (NRSV)

147 For biographical details, see the 'Sketches, &c.' in: Cole, C.N. (ed.). 1791. *The Works of Soame Jenyns, Esq. In Two Volumes. Including Several Pieces never before Published…* Vol. I. P. Wogan et al., Dublin: xii-xxxiv (xix).

148 [Jenyns, S.] 1756. Untitled Letter in: *The Gentleman's Magazine, and Historical Chronicle. Volume XXVI. For the Year M.DCC.LVI*: 65-67. This letter was reprinted in: Cole, *The Works of Soame Jenyns*: 285-291. At p. vii, Cole writes that all literary papers included in this work were bequeathed to him by Jenyns with the desire that he should superintend their publication. Thus, Jenyns's authorship of the letter initially published anonymously is confirmed by Jenyns himself.

149 [Jenyns], Untitled Letter: 65.

150 [Jenyns], Untitled Letter: 65.

destruction of innocent animals, may be terrified and murthered in the shapes of hares, partridges, and woodcocks; and all those who (…) have delighted in the devastation of their own species, may be massacred by each other in the forms of game cocks and pertinacious bull-dogs'.[151] The doctrine even helps to overcome resistance to some dishes.

> Never can the delicious repast of roasted lobsters excite my appetite, whilst the ideas of the tortures in which those innocent creatures have expired, present themselves to my imagination. But when I consider, that they must have once probably been *Spaniards* at *Mexico*, or *Dutchmen* at *Amboyna*, I fall to, both with a good stomach and a good conscience.[152]

Jenyns was well aware that his ideas would meet unbelief, but he strongly defended his views—unmasking the implicit anthropocentrism that often lurks behind comments like 'ludicrous' or 'the productions of an exuberant imagination'.[153] The advantages of the doctrine of transmigration are too obvious; the miseries of animals being the well-deserved punishments for misbehaviors the animating soul committed in an earlier life.

A few years later, Jenyns again paid attention to the subject of animal miseries, this time in a series of letters published openly under his own name, but now, also, other strings were touched. 'Evils (…) owe their existence, not to any voluntary admission of a benevolent Creator, but to the necessity of their own natures, that is, to the impossibility of excluding them from any system of created beings whatever'. This led Jenyns to discuss how his views relate to the Christian religion, since 'in order to make room for this necessity of Evil, the real existence of a paradisiacal state is represented as impossible at all times; and consequently, the Mosaick account of that state is utterly exploded, on which the whole fabric of the Christian Religion is erected'. But that did not matter because '[h]ow far the literal belief of that account is essential to the true faith of a Christian, need not be here decided'.[154] In any case, Adam's fall did not play a role in explaining natural evil because other causes are more obvious. It was evident that 'the good order of the whole, and the

---

151 [Jenyns], Untitled Letter: 65.
152 [Jenyns], Untitled Letter: 66. The reference to the Dutchmen in this context is, of course, humbling to the present writer and his fellow countrymen.
153 [Jenyns], Untitled Letter: 66.
154 [Jenyns, S.] 1761. *A Free Inquiry into the Nature and Origin of Evil. In Six Letters to—. The Fourth Edition. With an Additional Preface, and Some Explanatory Notes*. R. and J. Dodsley, London: iii-iv. For evidence of Jenyns as the author of this treatise, see Cole, *The Works of Soame Jenyns*: xxx.

happiness it receives from a proper subordination, will sufficiently account for the sufferings of individuals'.[155]

Thereafter, Jenyns again emphasized the usefulness of the transmigration of souls, now, however, not in terms of punishment but as something that ensures that the imperfections experienced in one life are compensated in another. The rotation of the souls guarantees that every living being can contribute to both the most preferable and the most despicable duties 'subservient towards carrying on the Business of the Universe and thus at the same time answer the purposes both of justice and utility'.[156] By going through successive lives, each soul gets its share of the pleasant as well as the unpleasant things that life entails. In another life the fox may become a hare and *vice versa*.

Thus, the suffering of animals was not only explained as punishment for incarcerated human souls. It was also necessary for the 'Business of the Universe'. The transmigration of souls serves both aims because deserved punishment is indeed inflicted and undeserved suffering is adequately compensated. It will be clear that these purposes require a cross-species transmigration of souls from animals into humans and *vice versa*, and therefore, it is no wonder Jenyns is advocating this. Herein he differed from Bougeant who excluded humankind explicitly from this rotation because it is 'unwarrantable with regard to Men, and is besides proscribed by Religion',[157] as well as from Ramsay who wrote that his theory of transmigration 'from one brutal form to another has nothing in common with the senseless doctrine of the Pagan metempsychosis, by which the souls of beasts pass into the bodies of men, and the souls of men into the bodies of beasts'.[158]

The relationship between the vicissitudes of the individual and the conditions required for a properly designed 'Whole' were addressed in detail in a third publication from Jenyns's hand, a collection of essays published in 1782. 'In order to diffuse all possible happiness, God has been pleased to fill this earth with innumerable orders of Beings, superior

---

155 [Jenyns], *A Free Inquiry*: 101.
156 [Jenyns], *A Free Inquiry*: 104.
157 Bougeant, *Amusement*: 24. Randall misses this point when writing that Bougeant includes human souls in this transmigration, cf. Randall, *The Wisdom of the Animals*: 110-111.
158 Ramsay, *Philosophical Principles*: 385. Whether oriental philosophy played a role in the concept of metempsychosis as interpreted by Jenyns is a contested issue. For a detailed discussion of the roots of this doctrine and its influence on eighteenth century English authors, see Yang, C. 'Gross Metempsychosis and Eastern Soul' in: Palmeri, F. (ed.). 2006. *Humans and Other Animals in Eighteenth-Century British Culture. Representation, Hybridity, Ethics*. Ashgate, Aldershot: 13-30.

to each other in proportion to the qualities, and faculties which he has thought proper to bestow upon them.'[159] After this summary that served as preface to the text that followed, Jenyns described the order he perceives in creation in detail in words that deserve to be quoted in full:

> Thus is this wonderful chain extended from the lowest to the highest order of terrestrial Beings, by links so nicely fitted, that the beginning and end of each is invisible to the most inquisitive eye, and yet they all together compose one vast and beautiful system of subordination. (…) He [God] constantly unites the highest degree of the qualities of each inferior order to the lowest degree of the same qualities, belonging to the order next above it; by which means, like the colours of a skilful painter, they are so blended together, and shaded off into each other, that no line of distinction is any where to be seen. (…) [A]nimal life rises from this low beginning in the shell-fish, thro' innumerable species' of insects, fishes, birds, and beasts to the confines of reason, where, in the dog, the monkey, and chimpanzè, it unites so closely with the lowest degree of that quality in man, that they cannot easily be distinguished from each other. From this lowest degree in the brutal Hottentot, reason, with the assistance of learning and science, advances, thro' the various stages of human understanding, which rise above each other, 'till in a Bacon, or a Newton it attains the summit.[160]

Within the chain of life, anything is connected to anything and transitions between several kinds of creatures, even the mental properties of dogs, monkeys and apes at one side and those of the 'brutal Hottentots' at the other are imperceptible. To maintain the order thus described, sufferings of sensitive beings could not be avoided. Furthermore, so added Jenyns, we should realize that 'Brutes are exempted from numberless anxieties, by that happy want of reflection on past, and apprehension of future sufferings, which are annexed to their inferiority'[161], thus echoing the Stoic thoughts about the inner life of the animals prevailing since antiquity.

Summarizing Jenyns's thoughts about natural evils including the suffering of animals, I conclude that he combined several approaches, taking recourse in the Pythagorean concept of metempsychosis, the Stoic

---

159 Jenyns, S. 1782. *Disquisitions on Several Subjects*. J. Dodsley, London: 3.
160 Jenyns, *Disquisitions*: 7-10. Putting the dog at the same level as the primates illustrates the high status assigned to dogs in eighteenth century Britain; for more on this subject, see Ritvo, *Animal Estate*: 82-115.
161 [Jenyns], *A Free Inquiry*: 66.

thoughts about the limited mental properties of animals, and the Plotinian view that the whole is more than the parts. In this way, divine justice as well as wisdom were vindicated: justice in the punishment of evildoers imprisoned in animal bodies and wisdom in the creation of a well-designed universe with everything in its proper place and with its proper function.

Finally, as with other authors, theorizing about animals' perceptions and sensations did not prevent Jenyns from asking for compassion with those animals which are entrusted to our care. 'We are unable to give life, and therefore ought not want only to take it away from the meanest insect, without sufficient reason; they all receive it from the same benevolent hand as ourselves, and have therefore an equal right to enjoy it.'[162] A 'benevolent hand' was assumed to care for all that lives. So, divine benevolence was vindicated as well. But whether a rejection of the literal interpretation of the Genesis text on Adam's fall and an acceptance of the pagan doctrine of metempsychosis befit someone characterized as a devout Anglican is, to say the least, questionable.

4.6.11. *John Wesley (1703–1791)*

John Wesley, one of the leaders of the early Methodist movement, did not only write on spiritual issues but on more mundane subjects as well.[163] In 1763, he published his *Survey of the Wisdom of God in the Creation,* a work that went through a lot of editions over the years thereafter. I will use both the first edition[164] as well as the fourth edition[165]—the last one published under Wesley's own direction—as points of reference. Comparing these two editions will tell us whether there were any changes in Wesley's opinion about the creation and its inhabitants.[166] In the preface to both editions, Wesley explained why he felt compelled to write this book, in spite of the availability of other works on the same subject, with

---

162 Jenyns, *Disquisitions*: 18.
163 For biographical details, see Britannica, The Editors of Encyclopaedia. "John Wesley". *Encyclopedia Britannica*, 14 July 2021, https://www.britannica.com/biography/John-Wesley. Accessed on 22 December 2021.
164 Wesley, J. 1763. *A Survey of the Wisdom of God in the Creation: or a Compendium of Natural Philosophy. In Two Volumes.* William Pine, Bristol.
165 Wesley, J. 1784. *A Survey of the Wisdom of God in the Creation: or, a Compendium of Natural Philosophy. In Five Volumes.* The Fourth Edition. J. Paramore, London.
166 The 1784 edition is the last one published under Wesley's own supervision and thus may be considered to contain his final thoughts. See for a cautionary note on the editions published posthumously Felleman, L.B. 2006. 'John Wesley's Survey of the Wisdom of God in Creation: a Methodological Inquiry' in: *Perspectives on Science and Christian Faith* 58 (1): 68-73. This cautionary note however especially applies to editions published from 1836 onwards.

the aim '*to display the amazing Power, Wisdom, and Goodness of the great Creator*'.[167] Because Wesley is ambiguous in his ideas on the subject of animal suffering and divine attributes, I will quote him more extensively to allow my readers to draw their own conclusions.

In his *Survey of the Wisdom*, Wesley followed the well-trodden paths taken by previous authors, first in rejecting the Cartesian *beast-machine* doctrine, because this is not only contrary 'to the doleful significations they [animals] give, when beaten or tormented' but also contrary to Scripture. '*A righteous man regardeth the life of his beast: but the tender mercies of the wicked are cruel*, Prov. xii. 10. (…) Cruelty then may be exercised toward beasts. But this could not be, were they mere machines.'[168]

Wesley realized that rejecting Descartes's theory has consequences that should not be overlooked. After all, '(…) if they [the animals] are not mere machines (…) then they are not mere matter; they have in them an immaterial principle. But of what kind? Will it die with the body, or not? Is it mortal or immortal? Here again we are got into an unknown path. We cannot order our speech, by reason of darkness.'[169] In his sermons to be discussed below, Wesley would strike an entirely different chord about the soul of the animal and its fate after death, free of any uncertainty about it. But for now, Wesley praised animal mortality as something God ordered to keep nature in balance. The limited life span of each animal testifies to a well-designed creation.

> To keep the balance even, the great Author of nature has determined the life of all creatures to such a length, and their increase to such a number, proportioned to their Use in the World. (…) And whatever death seems to destroy, it destroys no part of that primitive life, which is diffused through all organized beings. Instead of injuring nature, it only causes it to shine with the greater lustre. If death is permitted to cut down individuals, it is only, in order to make of the universe, by the reproduction of beings, a theatre ever crouded, a spectacle ever new. But it is never permitted to destroy the most inconsiderable species. That beings may succeed each other, it is necessary that there be a destruction among them.[170]

In writing that nature 'is never permitted to destroy the most inconsiderable species', Wesley took the same position as Ray and Hill had done: divine benevolence does not allow the loss of any animal species

---

167 Wesley, 1763. *Survey of the Wisdom* I: vi; 1784. I: viii.
168 Wesley, 1763. *Survey of the Wisdom* I: 220; 1784. II: 139-140.
169 Wesley, 1763. *Survey of the Wisdom* II: 253-254; 1784. V: 251-252.
170 Wesley, 1763. *Survey of the Wisdom* I: 224-226; 1784. II: 145-147.

once these have been created. He seems to conclude this from the fact that even species that are the 'most inconsiderable' continue to survive.

There is no ground to suppose that animal *death* troubled Wesley. On the contrary, on many pages, Wesley illustrated the divine attributes by referring to things connected with death and predation. 'The various Form of the *Teeth* in various creatures, is another instance of the Divine Wisdom. How curiously are they adapted to the peculiar food and occasion of each species! Thus in the Rapacious, they are fitted to catch and hold their prey'.[171] That predation may imply suffering was not addressed; apparently, this was not recognized by Wesley as a problem that might blemish the divine attributes. It is surprising to see that even the way the ichneumon wasp propagates, so colorfully described by John Hill as an example of animal cruelty, did not shock Wesley.

> Consider this caterpillar thick-set with hair: the birds dare not touch it: notwithstanding which, it serves them for food: by what means? a fly pierces the living caterpillar; she lays her eggs in his body. The caterpillar remains alive. The eggs hatch. The young ones grow at the expence of the caterpillar, and are afterwards changed into flies which serve for sustenance to the birds. There are continual wars betwixt animals, but things are so wisely combined, that the destruction of some of them occasions the preservation of others, and the fecundity of the species is always proportionable to the dangers that threaten individuals.[172]

In the next century, Darwin thought otherwise when writing: 'I cannot persuade myself that a beneficent & omnipotent God would have

---

171 Wesley, 1763. *Survey of the Wisdom* I: 105; 1784. I: 200-201.
172 Wesley, 1784. *Survey of the Wisdom* IV: 129-130. This text is quoted *verbatim* from Charles Bonnet's *La Contemplation de la Nature*, a text that Wesley included in an abridged form first in the third edition of his *Survey* that was published in 1777. For the original text, see Bonnet, C. 1764. *Contemplation de la Nature. Tome Premier*. Marc-Michel Rey, Amsterdam: 122. 'Considérez cette Chenille hérissée de poils; les Oiseaux n'oseroient y toucher; elle sert pourtant à leur nourriture: comment cela? Une Mouche pique la Chenille vivante. Elle dépose ses Oeufs dans son Corps. La Chenille continue de vivre. Les Oeufs éclosent. Les Petits croîssent aux dépends de la Chenille, & se changent ensuite en Mouches, qui servent de pâture aux Oiseaux. Il est entre les Animaux des guerres éternelles, mais les choses ont été combinées si sagement, que la destruction des uns fait la conservation des autres, & que la fécondité des Espèces est toujours proportionelle aux dangers qui menacent les Individus'. For the way Wesley endorsed the views of Bonnet, see Maddox, R.L. 2009. 'John Wesley's Precedent for Theological Engagement with the Natural Sciences' in: *Wesleyan Theological Journal* 44 (1): 23-54. More on this in the main text.

designedly created the Ichneumonidæ with the express intention of their feeding within the living bodies of caterpillars.'[173]

When summarizing Wesley's thoughts as examined thus far, this author appears to argue in line with the majority of contemporary scholars. This is to be expected as in his preface to the first edition of his *Survey*, repeated in the fourth, he paid tribute to natural philosophers from which he borrowed, mentioning Ray, Derham, and Nieuwentijt by name.[174] A properly designed universe requires a balance between death and birth so fine-tuned that no species is lost, but neither expands at the expense of fellow creatures. For this purpose, predation among animals and their deaths are unavoidable. There are no differences between the editions of 1763 and 1784 in the passages selected for quoting, which implies that Wesley expanded his work but did not see any need for revision. Therefore, I conclude that Wesley's views on the subject as summarized above remained the same over this entire period.

In view of this, it is surprising to learn how in Wesley's *sermons*, completely different, even opposite thoughts are expounded, contrary to the content of his *Survey of the Wisdom*. In the sermons, Wesley did not follow the ideas of the Plotinian-inspired scholars he mentioned with esteem in the preface of his *Survey* but endorses the thoughts of Hildrop.[175]

Two sermons that are widely known and often quoted even today deserve attention; both were published in the final decade of Wesley's life. The first to be addressed is a sermon on Genesis 1:31.[176] Herein, Wesley's position is clear. 'The world, at the beginning, was in a totally different state from that wherein we find it now.' There was no predation as 'none of these [the animals] then attempted to devour, or in anyway hurt, one another'. But 'such is the miserably disordered state of the world at present, that innumerable creatures can no otherwise preserve their own lives than by destroying others. But in the beginning it was not so.' On the contrary,

---

173 Darwin to Gray. 22 May 1860. *Darwin Correspondence Project*, "Letter no. 2814," accessed on 14 December 2021, https://www.darwinproject.ac.uk/letter/?docId=letters/DCP-LETT-2814.xml.

174 Wesley, 1763. *Survey of the Wisdom* I: iv; 1784. I: iv.

175 Wesley published an extended extract of Hildrop's *Free Thoughts on the Brute Creation* in twelve successive issues of *The Arminian Magazine for the Year 1783... Volume VI*: 33-36, 90-92, 142-144, 202-204, 259-261, 315-317, 370-371, 424-427, 487-489, 538-539, 596-598, 654-657.

176 Wesley, J. 'Sermon LXI. God's Approbation of His Works' in: Wesley, J. 1853. *The Works of the Rev. John Wesley. Third American Complete and Standard Edition, from the Latest London Edition, with the Last Corrections of the Author... Volume II*. Carlton & Phillips, New York: 25-31. 'And God saw every thing that he had made, and, behold, it was very good.'(KJV)

> [t]he paradisiacal earth afforded a sufficiency of food for all its inhabitants; so that none of them had any need or temptation to prey upon the other. The spider was then as harmless as the fly, and did not then lie in wait for blood. (...) the reptiles of every kind were equally harmless (...) there were no birds or beasts of prey; none that destroyed or molested another (...) He made not death in the animal creation; neither its harbingers, sin and pain.[177]

Opposite to the views he expounded before, Wesley here rejected the view that animal death and predation belong to a well-designed universe. In this approach, he specifically attacks one specific person:

> "Nay," (says a bold man [Mr. S— J—s.], who has since personated a Christian, and so well that many think him one!) "God is not to blame for either the natural or moral evils that are in the world; (for he made it as well as he could;) seeing evil must exist in the very nature of things." It must *in the present nature* of things, supposing man to have rebelled against God: but evil did not exist at all in the original nature of things. It was no more the necessary result of matter, than it was the necessary result of spirit. All things then, without exception, were very good. And how should they be otherwise? There was no defect at all in the power of God, any more than in his goodness or wisdom. His goodness inclined him to make all things good; and this was executed by his power and wisdom. Let every sensible infidel, then, be ashamed of making such miserable *excuses* for his Creator. He needs none of us to make *apologies*, either for him, or for his creation.[178]

In this sermon, Wesley appears to withdraw anything written in his *Survey of the Wisdom*. Things in themselves are not evil, but humans have turned against God. The Creator does not need our defense.

He also seems to have abandoned his agnosticism about the afterlife for animals. This theme was addressed in the other sermon that deserves attention, a sermon on Romans 8:19–22.[179] Here, Wesley first wrote that,

---

177 Wesley, 'God's Approbation': 29-30.
178 Wesley, 'God's Approbation': 30. The initials refer to Soame Jenyns. Wesley's disdain of Jenyns was mutual, Jenyns speaking about Methodists as people 'determined to listen to no reasoning at all, having with all reason and common-sense declared eternal warfare'. In: [Jenyns], *Free Inquiry*: xvii.
179 Wesley, J. 'Sermon LXV. The General Deliverance' in: Wesley, J. 1853. *The Works of the Rev. John Wesley. Third American Complete and Standard Edition, from the Latest London Edition, with the Last Corrections of the Author...Volume II.* Carlton & Phillips, New York: 49-57. 'The earnest expectation of the creature waiteth for the manifestation of the sons of God. For the creature was made subject to vanity, not

in the beginning animals 'were all surrounded (...) with every thing that could give them pleasure, pleasure unmixed with pain; for pain was not yet; it had not entered into paradise. And they too were immortal: For "God made not death; neither hath he pleasure in the death of any living."' The conviction uttered in the previous sermon is repeated. Animal death and predation do not belong to the prelapsarian state. But things have become totally different from what they were in the past:

> [W]hat savage fierceness, what unrelenting cruelty, are invariably observed in thousands of creatures; yea, is inseparable from their natures! Is it only the lion, the tiger, the wolf, among the inhabitants of the forest and plains,—the shark, and a few more voracious monsters, among the inhabitants of the waters,— or the eagle, among birds,— that tears the flesh, sucks the blood, and crushes the bones of their helpless fellow creatures? Nay; the harmless fly, the laborious ant, the painted butterfly, are treated in the same merciless manner, even by the innocent songsters of the grove! The innumerable tribes of poor insects are continually devoured by them.[180]

Next, Wesley wondered whether the animals will always remain in this sad condition. His answer was unambiguous. 'God forbid that we should affirm this; yea, or even entertain such a thought! While "the whole creation groaneth together," (...) their groans are not dispersed in idle air, but enter into the ears of Him that made them'. Indeed, a blissful future awaits the animals:

> The whole brute creation will then [Wesley refers to Revelation 21], undoubtedly, be restored, not only to the vigour, strength, and swiftness which they had at their creation, but to a far higher degree of each than they ever enjoyed. They will be restored, not only to that measure of understanding which they had in paradise, but to a degree of it as much higher than that, as the understanding of an elephant is beyond that of a worm. And whatever affections they had in the garden of God, will be restored with vast increase; being exalted and refined in a manner which we ourselves are not now able to comprehend. The liberty they then had will be completely restored, and they will be free in all their motions.

---

willingly, but by reason of him that subjected it: Yet in hope that the creature itself also shall be delivered from the bondage of corruption, into the glorious liberty of the sons of God. For we know that the whole creation groaneth, and travaileth in pain together until now.' This passage as quoted by Wesley in his sermon slightly differs from the KJV 1611 text.
180 Wesley, 'The General Deliverance': 52-53.

> They will be delivered from all irregular appetites, from all unruly passions, from every disposition that is either evil in itself, or has any tendency to evil. No rage will be found in any creature, no fierceness, no cruelty, or thirst for blood. So far from it that "The wolf shall dwell with the lamb, the leopard shall lie down with the kid; the calf, and the young lion, together; and a little child shall lead them. The cow and the bear shall feed together; and the lion shall eat straw like the ox. They shall not hurt nor destroy in all my holy mountain," Isa. Xi, 6, &c.[181]

This blessed afterlife not only is certain because promised in Scripture, it also serves a particular purpose. 'As a recompence for what they [the whole brute creation] once suffered, while under the "bondage of corruption," when God has "renewed the face of the earth," and their corruptible body has put on incorruption, they shall enjoy happiness suited to their state, without alloy, without interruption, and without end.' Furthermore, the certainty of a blessed afterlife suits another purpose as well.

> [To] furnish us with a full answer to a plausible objection against the justice of God, in suffering numberless creatures, that never had sinned, to be so severely punished? They could not sin, for they were not moral agents. Yet how severely do they suffer!— yea, many of them, beasts of burden in particular, almost the whole time of their abode on earth; so that they can have no retribution here below. But the objection vanishes away, if we consider that something better remains after death for these poor creatures also; that these, likewise, shall one day be delivered from this bondage of corruption, and shall then receive an ample amends for all their present sufferings.[182]

When analyzing Wesley's writings, it is difficult to compile a coherent summary in view of these conflicting and mutually exclusive thoughts. Whereas in his *Survey of the Wisdom of God in the Creation*, Wesley implicitly endorsed the Plotinian view, the notes in his *Sermons* speak differently. It is unlikely that they are due to an intensified spiritual life as an effect of the Aldersgate experience Wesley had in 1738 since the *Wisdom* (that pays less honor to Scripture in comparison with the *Sermons*) was published in 1763, long after that pivotal event.[183]

---

181 Wesley, 'The General Deliverance': 54-55.
182 Wesley, 'The General Deliverance': 56.
183 See Britannica, The Editors of Encyclopaedia. "John Wesley". *Encyclopedia Britannica*, 14 July 2021, https://www.britannica.com/biography/John-Wesley. Accessed on 14 December 2021.

An increased attention for animals' suffering and their recompense by redemption in a blessed afterlife that Wesley developed in the final decade of his life has been addressed by several authors. It is explained by some to be due to Wesley's increased awareness of humanity's place as a link in the *Chain of Being* that Wesley drew from the writings of Charles Bonnet in which the interconnectedness of mankind with the non-human animal world was emphasized.[184] Wesley so highly appreciated Bonnet that he included his thoughts in the third and subsequent editions of his *Survey* as already noted above. In view of the influence of Bonnet on Wesley's thoughts, it may be worthwhile to elaborate at this place on the thoughts of this author as far as relevant for understanding Wesley.

Charles Bonnet (1720-1793) was a Swiss naturalist and philosopher with Huguenot roots.[185] In his view, the earth we now inhabit, is just the latest in an order of successive stages, each new one separated from the preceding by catastrophic events which of course questions the literacy of Scripture, but for Bonnet, 'Moses may have described in the book of the six days only phenomena or appearances, as they would have been offered to the eyes of a spectator then placed on earth'.[186] Each stage has its own specific population of living beings which do not arise from new creations but from surviving indestructible germs created in the beginning of time and in each of the successive epochs assuming an embodiment adapted to the physical conditions of that specific period.[187] So it was in the past, and it will be in the future also. And divine wisdom guarantees that each new stage will surpass the foregoing.

---

184 Maddox, R.L. 2007. 'Anticipating the New Creation: Wesleyan Foundations for Holistic Mission in: *The Ashbury Journal* 62 (1): 49-66; Maddox, 'John Wesley's Precedent'; Pedlar, J.E. 2013. "His Mercy Is over All His Works": John Wesley's Mature Vision of New Creation' in: *Canadian Theological Review* 2 (2): 45-56.
185 For biographical details, see Britannica, The Editors of Encyclopaedia. "Charles Bonnet". *Encyclopedia Britannica*, 16 May 2021, https://www.britannica.com/biography/Charles-Bonnet. Accessed on 14 December 2021.
186 Bonnet, C. 1769. *La Palingénésie Philosophique ou Idées sur l'Etat Passé et sur l'*État *Futur des* Êtres *Vivans. Tome Premier*. Claude Philibert et Barthelemi Chirol, Genève: 174. 'Moyse a pu ne décrire dans l'Ouvrage des six jours, que les Phénomènes ou les Apparences, telles qu'elles se seroient offertes aux yeux d'un Spectateur placé alors sur la Terre.'
187 Lovejoy, *Chain of Being*: 283-286; Glass, B. 'Heredity and Variation in the Eighteenth Century Concept of the Species' in: Glass, B., Temkin, O., Straus Jr, W.L. (eds). 1968. *Forerunners of Darwin: 1745-1859*. The Johns Hopkins Press, Baltimore: 164-170; Bowler, P.J. 1973. 'Bonnet and Buffon: Theories of Generation and the Problem of Species' in: *Journal of the History of Biology* 6 (2): 259-281; Anderson, L. 1976. 'Charles Bonnet's Taxonomy and Chain of Being' in: *Journal of the History of Ideas* 37 (1): 45-58; Gould, S.J. 1977. *Ontogeny and Phylogeny*. The Belknap Press of Harvard University Press, Cambridge (MA): 17-28.

> The same progression that we discover today between the different organized orders of beings will undoubtedly be observed in the future state of our globe: but it will follow other proportions, which will be determined by the degree of perfectibility of each species. Man, then transported to another stay, more suited to the eminence of his faculties, will leave to the monkey or the elephant that first place which he occupied among the animals of our planet. In this universal restitution of animals, there can therefore be found among the monkeys or elephants Newtons and Leibnizs; among the beavers, Perraults & Vaubans, &c.[188]

Wesley probably appreciated the thoughts of Bonnet because of this eschatological perspective that he could accommodate in his thoughts about a blessed afterlife for humanity and the non-human animal kingdom as well. For him, the new creation cannot suffer from less plenitude than the current corrupted one and Bonnet's concept of indestructible germs progressing to higher stages of life with each renewal of the earth suits this conviction very well. A moving upwards in the chain that connects all living beings ensures that the animals' participation in that new world will cure evils that now harm them, thus justifying God in his behavior towards innocent living beings, innocent because they lack a free will.

It, however, remains difficult to understand how Wesley, close to the end of his life, at one side clung to a cosmic fall and redemption and on the other hand in his *Survey* could eulogize the dissolution of animal bodies as source for new life:

> By a law (…) all organized bodies become uncompounded and insensibly change in the earth. Whilst they suffer this kind of dissolution, their volatile parts pass into the air, which transports them every where. So that animals are buried in the atmosphere as well as in the earth and water; we may even doubt whether that portion which the air receives be not the most considerable in bulk. All these particles dispersed here and there, soon enter into new organical wholes, destined to the same

---

[188] Bonnet, *Palingénésie*: 203-204. 'La même Progression que nous découvrons aujourd'hui entre les différens Ordres d'Etres organisés, s'observera, sans doute, dans l'Etat Futur de notre Globe: mais, elle suivra d'autres Proportions, qui seront déterminées par le degré de *Perfectibilité* de chaque Espèce. L'*Homme* , transporté alors dans un autre séjour plus assorti à l'éminence de ses Facultés, laissera au *Singe* ou à *l'Eléphant* cette première Place qu'il occupoit parmi les Animaux de notre Planète. Dans cette Restitution universelle des Animaux, il pourra donc se trouver chés les *Singes* ou les *Eléphants* des Newtons & des Leibnitz; chés les *Castors*, des Perraults & des Vaubans, &c.' Perrault and Vauban were famous French architects.

revolutions as the former. And this circulation, which has subsisted from the beginning of the world, will continue as long as it endures.[189]

The discrepancy between the *Sermons* that speak about a creation without death, also for the non-human animals, and the passage from the *Survey* in which Wesley described a beneficial cycle of life and death 'from the beginning of the world' is evident. Thus far, an explanation for this has not been given by any Wesleyan scholar, at least to the best of my knowledge. The image of Wesley as staunch defender of an idyllic creation now corrupted prevails, and his other thoughts are ignored, especially in literature from young-earth creationist circles.[190]

However this may be, neither in the views expounded in the *Survey*, nor in the thoughts Wesley conveys in the *Sermons*, divine attributes were questioned, natural evils that afflict animals are either unavoidable as connected with an ubiquitous and everlasting circle of life and death or due to Adam's sin. And in the latter case, divine justice was vindicated as they will 'receive an ample amends for all their present sufferings'.

4.6.12. *Thomas Amory (1691?-1788)*

For the dissenting divine *Thomas Amory*,[191] there was no doubt about divine goodness, as can be inferred from the contents of his sermons in which he conformed to thoughts expounded before by others. The miseries of the individuals contribute to the well-being of the whole. Furthermore, each individual serves the role allotted to it as a link in the chain of living beings, serving as food for those placed above and feeding on those below. Furthermore, limited mental capacities of the animals save them from fearing the future and thus enable them an unspoiled joy of the present.[192] That some animals are food for other is no reason for concern, certainly not if we consider that it is better to have enjoyed life—even for a limited time—than not to have lived at all. And furthermore, because the animal souls transmigrate to animate another animal body

---

189 Wesley, 1784, *Survey of the Wisdom* IV: 131.
190 Ury, T.H. 2001. *The Evolving Face of God as Creator: Early Nineteenth-Century Traditionalist and Accommodationist Theological Responses in British Religious Thought to Paleonatural Evil in the Fossil Record.* Dissertations. 158: 86-96. Ury, T.H. 'Luther, Calvin, and Wesley on the Genesis of Natural Evil' in: Mortenson, T., Ury, T.H. 2008. *Coming to Grips with Genesis. Biblical Authority and the Age of the Earth.* Master Books, Green Forest: 408-411.
191 For biographical data, see Stephen, L. 'Amory, Thomas (1691?-1788)' in: *Dictionary of National Biography, 1885-1900, Volume 01.*
192 Amory, T. 1766. *Twenty-two Sermons on the Following Subjects: the Explication and Proof of the Divine Goodness...*T. Becket and P.A. De Hondt, London: 12-13.

upon death, they are continually receiving new and happy lives.[193] For Amory, the death of an animal only meant changing one role for another, an idea that can already be found in Plotinus.

> What does it matter when they are devoured only to return in some new form? It comes to no more than the murder of one of the personages in a play; the actor alters his make-up and enters in a new role. The actor, of course, was not really killed; but if dying is but changing a body as the actor changes a costume, or even an exit from the body like the exit of the actor from the boards when he has no more to say or do, what is there so very dreadful in this transformation of living beings one into another? Surely it is much better so than if they had never existed.[194]

Whereas Bougeant, Ramsay, and Jenyns invoked the transmigration of souls to explain animal suffering as punishment either for fallen angels or for wicked humans, Amory creatively employed this doctrine as an opportunity to increase the amount of joyful events and to offer compensation for suffering in one life with a surplus of happiness in another. Adam and his transgression are out of sight here, as is a prelapsarian creation without predation. Therefore, there are neither any threats to divine attributes. This is understandable since in Amory's views there are no challenges to the divine attributes: creation *as it is* speaks of God's goodness, wisdom, and bounty.

4.6.13. Capel Berrow (1716–1782)

For the Anglican divine *Capel Berrow*,[195] it was a matter of fact that 'brutes are endowed with some degree of reason and reflection, and a sensibility of pain, as well as pleasure'. This worried him. 'Wherefore all these agonizing pains and miseries heaped on an helpless offspring of divine providence ? Are they not flesh and blood ? Do *they* not, as well as *we*, know what sorrow means?'[196] To solve this problem, Berrow supposed that 'every organized body, as well in the brute creation, as in the rational, [is] (…) an allotted *temporary* prison for a *predelinquent* soul'.[197] Both human and animal miseries are to be explained as punishment for

---

193 Amory, *Sermons*: 81-82.
194 Plotinus, *Enneads*: 173.
195 For biographical details, see Grosart, A.B. 'Berrow, Capel' in: *Dictionary of National Biography, 1885-1900, Volume 04.*
196 Berrow, C. 1766. *A Pre-existent Lapse of Human Souls in a State of Pre-existence, the Only Original Sin, and the Ground Work of the Gospel Dispensation.* J. Dodsley et al., London: 109n.
197 Berrow, *A Pre-existent Lapse*: 110n.

indwelling rational souls that, in their pre-existent states (i.e., the state between their creation and the moment the soul 'drops into the womb'), were 'complicated and involved in the guilt of the fallen angels, by an association with those apostate powers'.[198] The animal body is a temporary shelter in which the 'predelinquent' soul is subjected to punishments. And as these punishments are well-deserved, God is not to blame for any suffering.

Berrow was well aware of the objections that can be raised against his hypothesis. 'It may be urged, if the soul did actually exist in a prior state, it is very extraordinary, that that pre-existence should not have been intimated to us in the *mosaic history* of the creation, whereas that evidently supposes the *soul* of man, as well as his *body*, to have been then first formed by the Creator.'[199] To this objection, Berrow answered that 'the silence of Moses, with respect to the pre-existence of souls, [is not] at all to be wondered at, when we consider how many truths of the utmost importance are left totally unnoticed by him'.[200]

Others may ask how it is possible 'that we should have existed in a prior state without being able now to form any idea of that State?'[201] This is no problem because even in our current life there are many things that we have forgotten or that never have entered our consciousness. So, absence of memories of a previous state does not exclude the possibility that such a state existed.[202]

For further substantiation of his argument, Berrow referred to Ramsay[203]—the author already discussed above—and in particular to Origen (cf. § 2.3.1.3), who also ascribed evil as punishment for transgressions a soul had committed between its creation and its descending into a physical body.[204] But in doing so, he apparently overlooked that the Church Father's thoughts were not entirely consistent with his own. 'We think that those views are by no means to be admitted, which some are wont unnecessarily to advance and maintain, *viz.*, that souls descend to such a pitch of abasement that they forget their rational nature and dignity, and sink into the condition of irrational animals, either large or

---

198 Berrow, *A Pre-existent Lapse*: 88n, 78.
199 Berrow, *A Pre-existent Lapse*: 116-117.
200 Berrow, *A Pre-existent Lapse*: 118.
201 Berrow, *A Pre-existent Lapse*: 85.
202 Berrow, *A Pre-existent Lapse*: 95-97.
203 Berrow, *A Pre-existent Lapse*: 23.
204 Berrow, *A Pre-existent Lapse*: 165-189. See for details Origen's doctrine of pre-existence of souls Scott, M.S.M. 2012. *Journey Back to God. Origen on the Problem of Evil.* Oxford University Press, Oxford: in particular pp. 49-73.

small.'[205] That an animal's body would serve as a temporary shelter for the soul on its way back to divine perfection was not an option for Origen. 'For we do not hold the doctrine of the transmigration of the soul and its fall even to irrational animals.'[206]

4.6.14. Richard Dean (fl. 1768)

For *Richard Dean*, no other personal details are available than those mentioned in the title page of the work that justifies his inclusion in the present study, Curate of Middleton.[207] Dean subscribed to the idea that animals have only limited mental capacities so that they can neither remember past sufferings nor fear future ones, but this does not get the divine attributes entirely off the hook. Animal sufferings may 'impeach the divine Goodness; for it appears as if the Principle of Sensibility, in a World where Evils predominate, was a huge Misfortune, and an ungracious Gift, provided that the Creatures endued with it, have no Interest in the Benefits of a better [world]'.[208] This latter point—animals may expect a blessed afterlife as well as humans—was worked out in detail. To refute those who find such a thought far-fetched, Dean referred to other authors who also advocated an afterlife for the animals such as Hildrop and Ramsay, thus showing his acquaintance with the contemporary literature on the subject.[209]

Dean started with questioning the relationship between suffering and sin. It is evident that there is a problem here as one cannot assume that for animals, pain, and disease are consequences of sin. After all, 'Brutes are incapable of committing Sin, and if natural Misery derives only from this Source, how comes it to pass then, that they are so universally subject to it!'[210] But is there perhaps reason to believe that the animals are not as innocent as they seem at first glance, 'in some Respect or other, be

---

205 Origen. 'De Principiis, Chapter VIII. On the Angels' in: Schaff, Ph. (ed.). 1885. *Ante-Nicene Fathers. Volume 4. Fathers of the Third Century: Tertullian, Part Fourth; Minucius Felix; Commodian; Origen, Parts First and Seconds*. Republished by the Christian Classics Ethereal Library, Grand Rapids: 610-613 (I.viii.4). Quote on p. 613.
206 Origen. 1965. *Contra Celsum. Translated with an Introduction & Notes by Henry Chadwick*. Cambridge University Press, Cambridge: 473-474 (VIII.30).
207 Dean, R. 1768. *An Essay on the Future Life of Brutes, Introduced with Observations upon Evil, Its Nature, and Origin. In Two Volumes*. G. Kearsly, London. Dean is also addressed in Morillo, *Rise of Animals and Descent of Man* but without including any biographical details other than Dean being Curate of Middleton and sometimes schoolmaster in the Manchester area (86).
208 Dean, *Essay* I: 21-22.
209 Dean, *Essay* II: ii.
210 Dean, *Essay* I: 106.

supposed to be faulty?'²¹¹ That would make their suffering a consequence of sin as well, but Dean concluded that because of our ignorance, we have to 'leave this Matter to rest here'.²¹² With Dean, we encounter—for the first time since Theophilus made some vague allusions (cf. § 2.3.1.2)—the thought that animals may have sinned because 'God cannot punish his Creatures without a Cause'.²¹³ It makes Dean unique among his contemporaries and it would last till our own days before the idea that animals might sin would be raised again, an issue to which I will return in Chapter 7.

But whereas Dean confessed to be ignorant about the possibility that animals might sin, he is convinced that they will participate with mankind in a blessed afterlife. Assuming that this is not possible because animals would not have an immortal soul does not make sense. 'The Notion that God annihilates the Souls of Brute Animals, is founded on weak Principles, and opposes Arguments much clearer, and stronger for the Continuation of them.'²¹⁴ Denying animals a blessed afterlife offends divine goodness, wisdom, love, and justice, a conviction Dean illustrated by pointing out the inconsistencies arising from such a denial in details that deserve a full quote.

> It reflects upon his Goodness, to suppose that he Subjects to Pains, and Sorrows, such a Number of Beings, whom he never designs to beatify; upon his Wisdom, that he forms them for the miserable Duration of a Moment, without leaving himself a Power to extend their Duration, and better their Condition; upon his Love, that he exposes them to the horrible Evils of Nature, and the cruel Treatment of superior Beings, which a tender Disposition would be concerned to remedy or prevent. And lastly, it reflects upon his Justice, to suppose that he destroys without a Recompense Creatures that he has brought into such a State of Infelicity, and in some Measure capacitated for everlasting Happiness.²¹⁵

Moreover, it could never have been God's intention to create animals for the sole purpose of being each other's food, as if the fly 'was only meant to gratify the Appetite of a Spider, or a Swallow'.²¹⁶ It is therefore likely that the current situation is only provisional, to be replaced by something better. Furthermore, Dean could not imagine that the plenitude of such a

---

211 Dean, *Essay* I: 108.
212 Dean, *Essay* I: 109.
213 Dean, *Essay* I: 109.
214 Dean, *Essay* II: 69.
215 Dean, *Essay* II: 74-76.
216 Dean, *Essay* II: 115.

splendid future creation should be less than nowadays, which would be the case if the animals did not take part in it. God's attributes require 'a Continuation of that mighty Chain of living Beings, which is the Astonishment of all contemplative Minds'.[217]

The properties of God thus vindicated by assuming a future compensation for current miseries, Dean also tried to make the current suffering less by pointing to mankind's cruel behavior towards the animals. Apparently, the mental properties of animals are not only relevant *vis-à-vis* the divine attributes but also for our plights towards our non-human fellow creatures. Abusing them will not go unpunished. Evildoers 'will no doubt be called upon to Account for every Act of Barbarity committed upon Brutes, in the Day when God shall Judge the World by Jesus Christ'.[218]

Reverberations of Dean's views on animal well-being can be found in several contemporary authors as well. The Anglican vicar *James Granger* (1723–1776)[219] advocated for a gentle treatment of animals in a similar way. In his *Sermon on Proverbs xii.* 10—'A righteous man regardeth the life of his beast'—Granger prompted his congregation to 'imitate the extensive care and benevolence of the Divine Providence, that Providence without which not a sparrow falleth to the ground; by shewing our kindness to every living creature under our eye'.[220]

Dean's conviction that animals would get remunerations for current sufferings in a blessed afterlife was shared by *Samuel Jackson Pratt* (1749–1814), who was ordained in the Church of England but later left the Holy Orders because of a scandalous love affair.[221] Pratt intended 'to examine several facts relating to men—animals—and things, in a new manner,— with this ultimate view—to vindicate the ways of God not only to *man*, but to every *other* living creature!'[222] After extensive digressions about the

---

217 Dean, *Essay* II: 116.
218 Dean, *Essay* II: 111.
219 For biographical details, see https://en.wikipedia.org/wiki/James_Granger. Accessed on 14 December 2021.
220 Granger, J. 1774. *An Apology for the Brute Creation, or Abuse of Animals Censured; in a Sermon on Proverbs xii. 10…The Third Edition*. T. Davies, London: 24. In his sermon, Granger referred to the engravings of Hogarth, warning children that 'what is begun in wantonness, may end in murder' (22, cf. § 4.2). He did not refer to the text of Dean. For a discussion of the disastrous reception of this sermon by an audience not amused, see Morillo, *Rise of Animals and Descent of Man*: 80-86.
221 For biographical details, see https://en.wikipedia.org/wiki/Samuel_Jackson_Pratt. Accessed on 14 December 2021. Pratt also wrote to teach children a proper attitude towards animals. For this, see Morillo, *Rise of Animals and Descent of Man*: 55-61.
222 Pratt, S.J. 1783. *Liberal Opinions, or, the History of Benignus, a New Edition, Corrected. Volume II*. G. Robinson and J. Bew, London: 70.

miseries of humans and animals alike, Pratt concluded that nothing else than a future life 'can make the present life supportable, or the present system equitable'.²²³ Thus, just like Dean, Pratt considered the concept of immortal animal souls to be indispensable in vindicating the divine attributes. This view, however, was not universally accepted by contemporary authors, as we will see with the following one.

4.6.15. James Rothwell (fl. 1769)

Only shortly after Dean had published his thoughts about the immortality of the souls of animals, *James Rothwell*, master of the Free Grammar School of Blackrod, Lancashire, replied with a strong rebuttal, probably funded by himself and supported by subscribers as listed in the book pages, since neither publisher nor place of publication are indicated.²²⁴ Rothwell unambiguously rejected the possibility of a future life for animals as well.

> [S]ooner would I believe that a Prometheus could animate a lump of clay, and confer upon it the faculties of reason and speech, than any one shall ever persuade me, that all the brute creation, from the largest elephant to the most diminutive mite; that all the beasts, birds, reptiles, insects, animalcules and those infinite shoals of living creatures that lie hid in the bosom of the deep, must be reanimated and enjoy a state of endless duration and felicity.²²⁵

Invoking support from Scripture as done by Dean does not make sense. 'Is it any where said in scripture, that brutes were in a better or happier condition before, than after the fall of man? Is it any where said, or can it be inferred, that the fall brought any damage to them?'²²⁶ As the state of animals did not change when Adam fell, there is no need for a future restoration.

Not only Dean was under attack but also others as well. On Bougeant's ideas about indwelling evil spirits, Rothwell commented: 'An hypothesis so absurd, so inconsistent with sense and reason, as this is, could only have entered into the fertile brain of a flighty, fantastical Frenchman.'²²⁷ And to Hildrop who wrote that nothing 'should hinder their [the animals]

---

223 Pratt, *Liberal Opinions* II: 75.
224 Rothwell, J. 1769. *A Letter to the Rev. Mr. Dean, of Middleton; Occasioned by Reading His Essay on the Future Life of Brute Creatures.* n.p., n.p. For a discussion of the Dean versus Rothwell controversy, see Morillo, *Rise of Animals and Descent of Man*: 86-90.
225 Rothwell, *A Letter*: 11.
226 Rothwell, *A Letter*: 71n.
227 Rothwell, *A Letter*: 87n.

Continuation in being after the Dissolution of their Bodies'[228], Rothwell answered simply that he on the contrary is 'sure no just reason can be assigned, why they should exist in a future state'.[229]

Furthermore, imagine the problems connected with a universal resurrection of everything that has lived on this earth since the time of creation. The new findings made with the microscope alone make such an idea preposterous. 'The surface of animals is also covered with other animals, which are in the same manners the basis of other animals, that live upon it. (…) And must all these live again to eternity? (…) Is it likely that all the flies and frogs, locusts and lice, which once infested the land of *Egypt*, will be reanimated, and have an endless existence in another state?'[230]

Rothwell was aware of the danger that animal suffering might pose for the divine attributes but objected that we have no judgment on that. 'Hath not the potter power over the clay.'[231] Furthermore, it is likely that the animals' enjoyments prevail over the sufferings. This conviction he supported with the usual arguments: Animals have no fear of the future, are not haunted by the past, and when the time comes, they die a quick and painless death.[232] Rothwell admitted '[t]hat brutes have souls' as can be deduced from the fact that they are 'endued with sensation, passion and a principle of self-motion. But does it therefore follow, that (…) they must live in a future state?'[233]

The Stoic assumption that animals only live in the present is—as for so many other authors—the panacea that served Rothwell very well to save divine benevolence. But their limited mental capacities do not offer a license to treat them inhumanely. 'As they have the same feelings with us, the bruises and wounds they receive, must be painful and afflictive to them. Whoever tortures a beast wantonly and without occasion, is a scandal to his species, and ought to be banished out of human society.'[234]

In his compassion for the animals, Rothwell joined Dean. But not in allowing them access to a blessed afterlife. Animals are only there for our benefit. Therefore, '(…) at the final consummation of all things, as they will then have fully accomplished the end for which they were created, we

---

228 Hildrop, *Free Thoughts* Letter II: 53.
229 Rothwell, *A Letter*: 91.
230 Rothwell, *A Letter*: 94-95.
231 Rothwell, *A Letter*: 103. Rothwell here quoted Romans 9:21. 'Hath not the potter power over the clay, of the same lump to make one vessel unto honour, and another unto dishonour?'(KJV)
232 Rothwell, *A Letter*: 106.
233 Rothwell, *A Letter*: 84.
234 Rothwell, *A Letter*: 113.

may reasonably and safely conclude they will be reduced to a state of annihilation and non-existence'.²³⁵ Here, Rothwell unambiguously harked back to the opinion prevalent in earlier ages that anything was created only for our use. And if we don't need it anymore, it can be thrown away.

4.6.16. John Bruckner (1726–1804)

John Bruckner, born in the Netherlands but spending his life in England was a Lutheran minister.²³⁶ The work relevant for our study was originally written in French but already shortly thereafter translated into English and German.²³⁷ It may be considered as the prime example of the Plotinian conviction already encountered before among the eighteenth-century authors; nowhere is the principle that the common good puts limits on the happiness of the individual worked out in such great detail.

Bruckner started with defining the problem and referred to some approaches employed for solving the apparent conflict between animal suffering and divine benevolence. There are people who blame the first human pair as they see it as 'a necessary consequence' of 'the fall of Adam' while others believe they can save divine goodness by imagining 'a future state, a paradise provided for the wretched martyrs amongst the brutal race'.²³⁸ Both were rejected as inadequate. As things stand, so they should be. 'It is very evident that Providence not only permits, but has designed that animals should devour each other.'²³⁹ Bruckner grew eloquent in propagating this belief.

> See how some animals thirst after the blood of others, how nature has armed them with claws and teeth to put their bloody purpose in execution (…) It is evident (…) that animals are in a state of perpetual war, and that it is the will of their Creator that one should live upon another.--- And what is the consequence? That the works of the Omnipotent are defective, Or that the world, which was created perfect, has since fallen into general depravity? These by no means follow. (…) [T]he law which enjoins the destruction of one animal for the advantage of another, contributes to the increase and happiness of life.²⁴⁰

---

235 Rothwell, *A Letter*: 116-117.
236 For biographical details, see https://en.wikipedia.org/wiki/John_Bruckner. Accessed on 14 December 2021.
237 Bruckner, J.A. 1770. *A Philosophical Survey of the Animal Creation…Translated from the French.* J. Potts, Dublin.
238 Bruckner, *Survey*: 42.
239 Bruckner, *Survey*: 43.
240 Bruckner, *Survey*: 45-46.

Sufferings of one animal increase the happinesses of others. 'Such is the wonderful œconomy of nature.'[241] Nature intends to keep a balance—not allowing one species to overrule others—and has done so since the beginning of time. 'The effects of the carnivorous race, with respect to the other species, are exactly the same as that of the pruning-hook with respect to shrubs which are too luxuriant in their growth, or of the hoe to plants that grow too close together. By the diminution of their numbers, the others arrive at greater perfection.'[242]

It is evident that the Mosaic account of the creation does not contain a trustworthy description of real events: no Edenic past with lions eating grass and toying with lambs. Nature aims to protect every species from extinction and therefore puts restrictions on numbers. Flocks of insects are kept in check by an army of birds, and the animals that reproduce quickly, such as hares, rabbits, rats, and mice, are also confronted with opponents who prevent their unlimited expansion.[243] To persuade those who are not yet convinced that nature works the way it should, Bruckner included a story that illustrated the disastrous outcome of interfering with this balanced system. Farmers, who fought a certain species of birds because of the damage it inflicted on their crops, had to find that they had to face nasty insects which in one day caused more devastation than the birds would have done in twelve months.[244]

Coming at the end of his treatise, Bruckner turned—as befits a good minister—to the application. We have to accept that animal death and predation are needed to maintain the order of the universe. When only looking at the details, the religious man is inclined to doubt the goodness of the Creator whereas the infidel or atheist finds a reason to deny the existence of a Deity at all.[245] But things may not be as miserable as they look at first sight. To reassure those who object that 'to expose one animal to the fury of another is cruel', Bruckner condoned the suffering of the animals by stating that 'they are neither endowed with our penetration nor sensibility'.[246] Again, we are warned against falling into the trap of the pathetic fallacy. Bruckner followed the approach generally employed in this period. Animals are not merely machines, but they lack the mental abilities that are required to make their sufferings comparable with ours.

---

241 Bruckner, *Survey*: 68.
242 Bruckner, *Survey*: 106-107.
243 Bruckner, *Survey*: 108-109.
244 Bruckner, *Survey*: 138.
245 Bruckner, *Survey*: 143-144. The similarity of these considerations to those employed in the current creation-versus-evolution debate is evident.
246 Bruckner, *Survey*: 152-153.

Misconceptions about the relationship between animal life and divine attributes were for Bruckner due to a limited perspective on nature as well as on God. When we stop calling events evil that are not evil at all, all problems vanish. We should study the book of nature alone. This book tells us that everything is designed to preserve animal species from extinction.[247] In this emphasis on the survival of the species at the expense of the individual—no species going extinct—Bruckner apparently ignored, or was unaware, of the fossils and the danger they pose for his defense of divine goodness. Herein, he differed from Ray who had noted this threat already decades ago.

4.6.17. Humphry Primatt (1735-1776/7)
Humphry Primatt was a Church of England clergyman and writer on animal welfare. The latter activity earned him the honor of being acclaimed as a pioneer in the development of an awareness of animal rights and legislation aimed at animal protection.[248] The treatise that gained him this fame was published in 1776, close to the end of his life.[249]

Whereas for most other authors, animals and their lives served as just as many witnesses for the divine wisdom and benevolence, Primatt went one step further. For him, the goodness of the Creator over all his creatures was not merely something to admire and adore, but also an example to follow. This conviction inspired Primatt to warn against cruelty towards animals. To strengthen his point, Primatt emphasized that the 'Creation is a transcript of the divine Goodness; and every leaf in the Book of Nature reads us a lecture on the wisdom and benevolence of its great Author'.[250]

> Every creature is to be considered as a wheel in the great machinery of Nature; and if the whole machine is curious and beautiful, no wheel in it, however small, can be contemptible or useless. In some animals, their usefulness (…) is subservient and owing to their *defects*. Consequently, to despise or abuse them for being defective, is to despise or abuse them for being useful. The most ugly animals, though we knew no other use of them, may be considered as a foil, like the shades in a good picture, to set off the beauties of the more perfect. (…) An Animal, whatever it be, or

---

247 Bruckner, *Survey*: 169-176.
248 Morillo, *Rise of Animals and Descent of Man*: 97-105.
249 Primatt, H. 1834 [1776]. *The Duty of Mercy, and the Sin of Cruelty to Brute Animals*. T. Constable, Edinburgh.
250 Primatt, *Duty of Mercy*: 9.

wherever it is placed in the great Scale of Being, is such, and is so placed by the great Creator and Father of the Universe.[251]

Primatt subscribed to the view that anything in the universe occupies the place needed for the best of the whole, 'a wheel in the great Machinery of Nature'. Nature resembles a well-organized society wherein the subordination of some to others preserves order and notes from previous centuries that sameness would distract from beauty and that shades accentuate the bright colors appear anew. But the fact that mankind and animals occupy different positions of the 'great scale of Being' does not alter that they both 'are all susceptible and sensible of the misery of *Pain*'. Therefore, 'the difference of shape between a man and a brute, cannot give to a man any right to abuse and torment a brute'.[252]

Humankind is obliged to be humane to its fellow creatures because as long as the animal 'lives, he has a right to happiness'.[253] For humans, the fulfillment of that right to happiness can be realized in a blessed afterlife, but Primatt doubted whether this applies to animals as well. Therefore, we should handle them gently as it is likely that their current existence is all they have. '[I]f he is unhappy here, his lot is truly pitiable; and the more pitiable his lot, the more base, barbarous, and unjust in man, must be every instance of cruelty towards him.'[254]

Primatt acknowledged the less bright tones in nature when admitting 'that *there are some Brutes of prey* which wholly subsist on the flesh of other brutes, and whose lives are one continued course of rapine and bloodshed'.[255] But this is not our concern. 'Our principal Duty and Business is to consider the Creatures of the *tame* and domestic kind'; only they 'are assigned over to our care, management, and protection'.[256] With wild animals, things are different.

> The Duty of Men concerning Animals that are *wild* by nature, lies in a very narrow compass—*Let them alone*. Being GOD's property, and in his sight, GOD will provide for them. And it is enough for us, that we invade not their province, - but leave them unmolested and at liberty to perform the tasks, and answer the ends, for which GOD was pleased to create them.[257]

---

251 Primatt, *Duty of Mercy*: 12-13.
252 Primatt, *Duty of Mercy*: 14, 21.
253 Primatt, *Duty of Mercy*: 54.
254 Primatt, *Duty of Mercy*: 46.
255 Primatt, *Duty of Mercy*: 62.
256 Primatt, *Duty of Mercy*: 125.
257 Primatt, *Duty of Mercy*: 124.

The way of life of wild animals is not under our judgment; neither should we interfere. The ends for which God 'was pleased to create them' are obvious, even with those that feed on the flesh of their fellow creatures as they adjust the happiness-versus-misery balance by reducing the amount of the latter. 'God, the Father of Mercies, hath ordained beasts and birds of prey to do that distressed creature the kindness to relieve him from his misery, by putting him to death', thus performing the same act of 'mercy as it is to shoot thy horse or thy dog, when all his teeth are gone, and the happiness of his life is at an end'.[258]

Despite these condoning remarks, Primatt seems also to consider that things could have been otherwise as he feels himself 'emboldened to say, on the principles of divine revelation, that Nature would never have groaned, if Man had not sinned'.[259] This however, does not make God injust because 'in the punishment of a criminal, the effect of his crime may extend to his innocent family'.[260] Animals suffer as guiltless bystanders. 'To suffer pain as Punishment he [the animal] *cannot*: for punishment is due only to Demerit; and demerit being of a moral nature, can be attributed only to *rational* beings.'[261]

There is no reason to blemish God because 'I [Primatt] firmly believe, that no evil which the innocent Brutes suffer from the hand of God (…) is in any respect equal to the pains and miseries they endure from the cruelties of Men. For GOD is merciful even when provoked to judgment, but MAN is cruel without any provocation at all.'[262] It is mankind who is to blame.

When summarizing Primatt's thoughts on the subject, one can say that, on one side, he accepted the common opinion that the goodness of the whole requires that animals prey upon each other. On the other side, he employed human sin as an explanation as well. His main purpose however was to convince his fellow people to 'See that no BRUTE of any kind, whether intrusted to thy care, or coming in thy way, suffer through thy neglect or abuse'.[263] In view of this, his status as pioneer in promoting animal welfare is well-deserved.

4.6.18. *Joseph Priestly (1733–1804)*

The theologian and chemist *Joseph Priestly* belonged to a tribe of Dissenters that advocated that a proper understanding of the natural

---

258 Primatt, *Duty of Mercy*: 64-66.
259 Primatt, *Duty of Mercy*: 272-273.
260 Primatt, *Duty of Mercy*: 274.
261 Primatt, *Duty of Mercy*: 46-47.
262 Primatt, *Duty of Mercy*: 274-275.
263 Primatt, *Duty of Mercy*: 291.

world would eventually bring about the Christian millennium, a conviction that might have been decisive for pursuing a career in science. He paid for his convictions by being forced to flee to the United States after a mob burned down his Birmingham home and church.[264] Today, he is mainly known for the discovery of oxygen and not so much for his thoughts about animal life and death. During his lifetime, this was different, as can be inferred by the attention that contemporary writers paid to his ideas on these issues.[265]

For Priestly, it was evident 'that the author of all things intended the animal creation to be happy, (…) health and enjoyment having a natural and necessary connection through the whole system of nature'.[266] Priestly admitted that people may think otherwise when looking how animals prey upon each other, but we should realize that nature requires death of animals to maintain a healthy balance. Without predation, animal happiness would be less than it is now because when their happiness decreases through physical decay, their demise is quick and painless, and this demise serves the happiness of others.[267] That there might have been a past without corruption and animal death does not play a role. Scriptural data are deemed to be allegorical. 'As to the history of the *fall of man*, and other particulars preceding the time of Moses, and the memory of his immediate ancestors, it may be allowed that there is a mixture of fable, or allegory in it.'[268]

In another text, Priestly addressed questions on state, source, and destination of animal souls.[269] He found it difficult to accept that there should be major differences between humanity and the non-human animal creation.

> [Animals] have the same external senses that we have, [and therefore] they have, of course, all the same *inlets to ideas* that we have; and though, on account of their wanting a sufficient *quantity of brain perhaps*, chiefly, the combination and association of their ideas cannot be so complex as

---

264 Biographical details taken and adapted from McEvoy, J.G. 'Joseph Priestley. English Clergyman and Scientist' in: McEvoy, John G. "Joseph Priestley". *Encyclopedia Britannica*, 10 March 2021, https://www.britannica.com/biography/Joseph-Priestley. Accessed on 14 December 2021.
265 See in Primatt, *Duty of Mercy*: 66.
266 Priestly, J. 1794 [1782]. *Institutes of Natural and Revealed Religion. In Two Volumes… The Third Edition. Volume I.* n.p., London: 15.
267 Priestly, *Institutes*: 18-19.
268 Priestly, *Institutes*: 267.
269 Priestly, J. 1777. *Disquisitions Relating to Matter and Spirit…Especially with Respect to the Doctrine of the Pre-existence of Christ*. J. Johnson, London: 42.

ours (...) they must necessarily have, *in kind* every faculty that we are possessed of. Also since they evidently have *memory, passions, will,* and *judgment* too, as their actions demonstrate, they must, of course, have the faculty that we call *abstraction* as well as the rest.[270]

In writing these lines, Priestly was the first author who explicitly rejected the assumption that animals only live in the present, having no memories from the past and neither expectations of the future as taught by the Stoics and solidified into a doctrine since antiquity. Similarities in anatomy—an observation in which Priestly pays tribute to progress made in biological sciences—implies similarity in function as well.

However, the fact that Priestly assigned mental qualities to animals that differ little from those available to mankind does not mean that he also granted them the prospect of a blessed afterlife. We remain ignorant of this but we can trust that 'the Maker and Judge of all will do what is right'.[271] Passages like Romans 8:18–21 about the liberation of the creation from its bondage to decay or Isaiah 11:6–8 or Isaiah 65:25 about the lion eating straw like the ox—passages by other authors referred to as scriptural support for the assumption of a blessed future for animals—are not considered. It was beyond dispute for Priestly that an excess of happiness in the present justifies divine benevolence, regardless of whether or not the animals share in a blissful afterlife.

4.6.19. *Thomas Balguy (1716–1785)*

Pleasures for the animal in the here and now were also central to the Anglican clergyman *Thomas Balguy*.[272] At first sight, Balguy calculates like a cool mathematician. There is as much divine goodness in assigning happiness to a series of animals in succession as in limiting that same amount of happiness to one and the same animal. 'What one loses, another gains.'[273] Therefore, the fact that animals have 'to make way for others'[274] does not affect God's benevolence.

However, it is not only theoretical calculations that prove that God is benevolent; his goodness is also evident in looking at the pleasures animals enjoy during their lives. The keen observer will see how God has arranged that what is necessary for the maintenance of life is accompanied

---

270 Priestly, *Disquisitions*: 238.
271 Priestly, *Disquisitions*: 240.
272 For biographical details, see Stephen, L. 'Balguy, Thomas' in: *Dictionary of National Biography, 1885-1900, Volume 03*.
273 Balguy, T. 1781. *Divine Benevolence Asserted; and Vindicated from the Objections of Ancient and Modern Sceptics*. Lockyer Davis, London: 17.
274 Balguy, *Divine Benevolence*: 8.

by enjoyments—not necessary in itself if the intended purpose does not go beyond keeping the animal alive. That God added joy to necessity testifies to his goodness.[275] In the next century, William Paley would pay tribute to Balguy in his elaborations about the idea of superadded pleasures as proof of divine benevolence (cf. § 5.4.2).[276]

4.6.20. William Smellie (1740–1795)

The Scotchman *William Smellie* is mainly known as editor of the first edition of the *Encyclopedia Britannica* but he also gained fame for his achievements in natural history.[277] At just twenty-two years old, he already joined the discussion on the theme of good and evil in creation, disputing the view that anything has been created for the benefit of mankind.[278] The seventeen pages of his small *Essay* are full of examples that belie this idea.

First, many animals live in remote and barren areas and shun any contact with humans.[279] Second, quite a lot of animals are noxious, and they, 'instead of being useful, are, to the inhabitants of many places of the world, the very bane of society and mutual intercourse'.[280] And third, the usefulness to humans of many recently discovered animals is unknown, not to mention the existence of many species unknown to date, hidden even from the most diligent naturalists.[281]

Smellie did not lack arguments to demonstrate the folly of anthropocentrism. What about snakes and spiders of whom a single sting or bite is already fatal? Who can believe that such animals were created for our benefit is like a man who thinks 'that whoever drubs him heartily, or beats the eyes out of his head, is upon the whole his real friend, and that it would have been a disadvantage to him if such a man never had existed.'[282] And what benefit do we have from rats and mice that spoil our food and moles that mess up our gardens. They may be created to be food for the cat, but if they had not existed, the cat would not have been needed either.

---

275 Balguy, *Divine Benevolence*: 31.
276 See Paley, W. 1802. *Natural Theology or, Evidences of the Existence and Attributes of the Deity, Collected from the Appearances of Nature*. John Morgan, Philadelphia: 353.
277 Hatch, R.B. 1975. 'William Smellie: Philosopher of Natural History' in: *Studies in Scottish Literature* 12 (3): 159-180; Wolloch, *The Enlightenment's Animals*: 71-87.
278 Smellie, W. 1762. 'Essay I. Whether all Animate and Inanimate Bodies Made for the Immediate Use and Conveniency of Mankind; or, Is that only a Secondary End of Their Existence?' Read before the Newtonian Society of Edinburgh. Republished in: Smellie, A. (ed.). 1800. *Literary and Characteristical Lives...To Which Are Added... Three Essays by the Late William Smellie*. Alex. Smellie et al., Edinburgh: 413-429.
279 Smellie, 'Essay': 415-416.
280 Smellie, 'Essay': 416.
281 Smellie, 'Essay': 417-418.
282 Smellie, 'Essay': 419-421 (421).

Of course, people may accuse him 'to have no idea of that vast chain of nature' in which every organism contributes to the well-being of the whole', the 'chain of utility' that 'advances by low degrees till it arrives at that noble creature Man, whose good is the ultimate end of every created existence'.[283] That may be so, but such criticism can't make him to 'admit that beings are thus linked together for the sole benefit of their chief, without any regard to their own welfare and happiness'. And the idea that the usefulness for the human race would increase the closer the animal is to mankind makes no sense. 'Were this the case, the Ourang Outang, and all the Monkey kind, as approaching nearest to the human species in wisdom and sagacity, should be more serviceable to mankind than horse, sheep, cows, &c. which I am persuaded none will ever take it into their heads so much as to suppose.'[284]

The fact that God has entrusted mankind with dominion over animals cannot mean that our fellow creatures are called in life solely for our benefit. That would be the same as assuming that the 'people would be created for the sake of the King, and the whole world, for the sake of a few ambitious individuals; than which nothing can be more ridiculously absurd'. We have to 'observe here the difference between having the superiority or dominion over any Creature, and the chief end of that Creature's being'.[285] The evil that animals inflict on humanity cannot be explained away by assuming that it ultimately serves mankind's welfare but must be sought elsewhere.

> It is a maxim in Nature, That no blank should be left in the vast scale of being. A strict adherence, I imagine, to this catholic maxim, is the reason why such prodigious troops of animals, not only useless, but even noxious to mankind, are called into life. Accordingly we see, that, lest any void should be left, mankind are suffered to be infested, and, in many instances, actually injured, by creatures which all his ingenuity is unable to turn to any advantage. This, again, throws light upon another maxim, That all partial evil is universal good; for even man, the chief of animals, must submit to many evils and inconveniencies, rather than that the blessings of life should be denied to insects and wild beasts.[286]

---

283 Smellie, 'Essay': 422.
284 Smellie, 'Essay': 423. Augustine, too, had his reservations about a relationship between the place of an animal in the *Great Chain of Being* and its usefulness to man. Cf. Huff, P. 1992. 'From Dragons to Worms: Animals and the Subversion of Hierarchy in Augustine's Theology' in: *Melita Theologica* 43 (2): 27-43.
285 Smellie, 'Essay': 424.
286 Smellie, 'Essay': 428.

To explain why animals may hurt mankind, Smellie harked back to the belief that the creation's perfection requires that there are no open spaces left—the concept of plenitude that we encountered before as one of the three aspects of the great chain of life. All components of this chain have their own interests, and it is impossible that these interests would not occasionally clash. The greater good that is pursued is not the well-being of mankind but the realization of a chain of life in which no link is missing. When some of these links threat others, let it be so. 'Were this doctrine properly pursued, it would, I apprehend, reconcile us to many of the mysteries of Providence, "and justify the ways of God to man",'[287] Smellie thus quoting famous lines from Milton's *Paradise Lost*.[288] Quoting Milton doesn't mean, however, that Smellie agreed with him. Milton, after all is known as the poet whose work epitomized the belief that animals became harmful through humanity's transgression, while Smellie accepted their existence as an inescapable side effect of the fact that the chain of life tolerates no gaps.

At a more advanced age, Smellie returned to the theme of animal behavior, not now with regard to the possible benefit to humanity, but focused on the way they interact with each other. In *The Philosophy of Natural History*, published almost thirty years after his *Essay*, he confessed to worry about the role of animals that are called '*carnivorous* or *rapacious*, because they live chiefly, or entirely, on animal food'.[289] When we realize that 'all herbivorous animals, though not from choice, and even without consciousness, daily devour thousands of insects', the problem takes on awesome proportions. It is painful to face that 'no good can be eat, and no fluid can be drunk, in which animal substances, either in a living or dead state, are not to be found'.[290] This is a troubling subject and 'the reader must not expect to have every difficulty removed, and every question solved'.[291] Nevertheless, Smellie was 'not entirely without hopes of showing several important utilities which result from this almost universal scene of animal devastation'.[292] It is true that we cannot solve the problem, but looking at the benefits predation offers can nevertheless provide some clues.

---

287 Smellie, 'Essay': 429.
288 Milton, J. 1667. *Paradise Lost. A Poem Written in Ten Books*. Peter Parker, London. Book I, lines 25 and 26: 'I may assert th' Eternal Providence, / And justifie the wayes of God to men.'
289 Smellie, W. 1808 [1790-1799]. *The Philosophy of Natural History*. Thomas et al., Dover: 378.
290 Smellie, *Philosophy*: 394.
291 Smellie, *Philosophy*: 379.
292 Smellie, *Philosophy*: 379.

If all animals were to live upon vegetables alone, many species, and millions of individuals, which now enjoy life and happiness, could have no existence; for the productions of the earth would not be sufficient to support them. But, by making animals feed upon each other, the system of animation and of happiness is extended to the greatest possible degree. In this view, Nature, instead of being cruel and oppressive, is highly generous and beneficent. (…) The carnivorous tribes may be compared to the hoe and the pruning hook, which, by diminishing the number of plants when too close, or lopping off their luxuriancies, make the others grow to greater perfection. (…) No species, however, is ever exhausted. The balance between gain and loss is perpetually preserved.[293]

In his youth, Smellie justified animal suffering by seeing it as an inevitable collision of individual interests entailed by the plenitude of creation. The arguments put forward by him in this later work are not much different. Predation not only serves to preserve any species of animals and to maximize the amount of happiness but even makes animals growing 'to greater perfection'. That such a growth into 'greater perfection' could imply development of new species, evolution in a Darwinian sense, lies however beyond Smellie's scope; after all, no species 'is ever exhausted', which refutes any thought that a species could be lost through transformation into another.[294]

At the end of his discourse, Smellie concluded that a 'circle of animation and of destruction goes perpetually round. This is the oeconomy of Nature. Different species of animals live by the mutual destruction of each other.'[295] Even the apparently cruel fate of the caterpillar that serves for the propagation of the ichneumon fly—so vividly described by Hill (cf. § 4.6.9)—fits within this scheme. The 'hairy species [of caterpillars] (…) are the food of the worms which are transformed into those smaller flies that afford nourishment to the birds which reject the hairy caterpillars'.[296] In this way both the numbers of caterpillars and the numbers of ichneumon wasps remain limited.

Events that at first glance raise doubts play a role in maintaining a greater good: a balance between birth and death in which nothing is lost and a maximum amount of happiness is warranted. The Reverend *John*

---

293 Smellie, *Philosophy*: 396-398.
294 Smellie was determined to avoid evolutionary concepts that would upset the Mosaic chronology. Cf. Hatch, 'William Smellie: Philosopher of Natural History'.
295 Smellie, *Philosophy*: 402.
296 Smellie, *Philosophy*: 400.

Toogood (1742/43–1824)²⁹⁷ was of the same conviction. 'The wise and good Creator hath appointed the corruption of all things to effect this great work.(…) In this manner does our gracious Creator produce, from the most disgusting things, inestimable blessings, and draw from the bosom of putrefaction the finest flowres, and the most delicious fruits.'²⁹⁸ Insects are 'furnished with means to seize their prey, or activity to escape their enemy.'²⁹⁹ That there would ever have been a creation in which the animals did not eat each other is far out of sight, let alone that the responsibility for predation would lie with humans.

4.7. Discussion

The above gives an overview of the thoughts about animal death and suffering as put forward by theologians, philosophers, and others throughout the major part of the eighteenth century with the exception of the first decade which was already covered in the previous chapter. This period was, as indicated above (cf. § 4.3 and § 4.4), characterized by scientific developments that made it difficult to hold on to the conviction that the Bible contains a reliable description of events that actually took place. The question now is whether and to what extent this diminished authority of Scripture—at least for the cosmogony as recorded in Genesis—and developments in science had any influence on the contemporary thoughts about the subject of my study: how to reconcile animal suffering and predation with divine goodness and benevolence.

At first glance, it already appears that this period differs from the previous one in two respects. First, it is striking that whereas in the seventeenth century the issue of animal suffering was rarely noticed, in the eighteenth century, almost no author ignored this point. The Cartesian *beast-machine* doctrine had never really been popular, but now did not play a role at all.³⁰⁰ To the contrary, animals were granted mental properties that enabled them to be conscious of happiness as well as misery. So, Jeremy Bentham's often quoted note, 'The question is not *Can they reason?*

---

297 For background of this author, see Morillo, *Rise of Animals and Descent of Man*: 105-107.
298 Toogood, J. [1798?]. *The Book of Nature: a Discourse on Some of those Instances of the Power, Wisdom, and Goodness of God…The Third Edition, Corrected and Enlarged.* Goadby et al., Sherborne: 5.
299 Toogood, *Book of Nature*: 31.
300 Shugg, W. 1968. 'The Cartesian Beast-Machine in English Literature (1663–1750)' in: *Journal of the History of Ideas* 29 (2): 279-292; Strickland, L. 2013. 'God's Creatures? Divine Nature and the Status of Animals in the Early Modern Beast-Machine Controversy' in: *International Journal of Philosophy and Theology* 74 (4): 291-309; Wolloch, *The Enlightenment's Animals*: 49-61.

or *Can they talk?* but *Can they suffer?*,³⁰¹ that was made at the end of the eighteenth century, in fact, was already answered at the beginning of this period.³⁰²

Second, the conviction that animals were created only for humanity's use had lost its strength; nature now was interpreted as consisting of interrelated elements that all had their own value, metaphorically summarized as the chain of life. This loss of anthropocentricity implied that any pain versus pleasure balance had to be sought without invoking advantages or benefits for humans. Evidently, the relationship between humans and animals had changed compared to the past. Their mental properties were not separated from ours by an unbridgeable gap anymore, nor was the animal there solely for humanity's benefit. Below I will go into more detail on how the authors chose to address the issue of animal suffering and divine attributes. For the sake of convenience, opinions of authors discussed are listed in Table 4.1.

4.7.1. Animals Suffer Because Adam Sinned

When comparing Table 4.1 with Table 3.1 (see previous chapter), it is clear that the belief that animals suffer as a consequence of human transgression had lost persuasiveness with the passage of time. Apparently, the changed attitude towards the animals that characterized this century had made the view that 'in the punishment of a criminal, the effect of his crime may extend to his innocent family'³⁰³ less acceptable. The belief that the value of the animal lies in its importance for humans had lost credibility and this change could not but strengthen the belief that God's justice does not allow punishing innocent living beings for the transgressions of mankind.

---

301 Bentham, *An Introduction to the Principles and Morals*: 309n.
302 It should be noted that Bentham's comment is not very relevant to our subject. What matters to him is the justification of our actions towards the animals, rather than the behavior of the animals towards each other. See Steiner, *Anthropocentrism and Its Discontents*: 162-166; Rowlands, M. 'Philosophy and Animals in the Age of Empire' in: Kete, K. (ed.). 2007. *A Cultural History of Animals in the Age of Empire*. Berg, Oxford: 135-152; Wolloch, *The Enlightenment's Animals*: 60-61. That Bentham should not be seen as someone who was concerned with the fate of animals themselves but rather with proper human behavior is also posited by Rob Boddice. Cf. Boddice, *A History of Attitudes and Behaviours toward Animals*: 121-140; Boddice, R. 2010. 'The Moral Status of Animals and the Historical Human Cachet' in: *JAC* 30 (3/4): 457-489.
303 Primatt, *Duty of Mercy*: 274.

| Table 4.1. Animal Sufferings Acknowledged and Divine Justice Vindicated ||||||||
| Year | Author | | Surplus of Happiness Justifies Miseries |||||
		Adam guilty	Punishment of imprisoned wicked souls	Compensation in a blessed afterlife	Compensation for miseries in consecutive lives	Compensation for miseries within one single life	Required for the goodness of the whole
1713	Derham						Yes
1719	Nieuwentijt						Yes
1729	Mandeville	No					Ambiguous
1731	King	No				Yes	Yes
1737	Bougeant		Yes				
1740	Watts	No				Yes	Yes
1742	Hildrop	Yes	No	Yes			
1745	Parker	Yes		Yes			
1748	Ramsay		Yes				
1749	Hartley	Ambiguous		Ambiguous		Yes	No
1752	Hill					Yes	Yes
1753	Jenyns	No	Yes		Yes		Yes
1763	Wesley*	Yes		Yes	Yes		Yes
1766	Amory				Yes		Yes
1766	Berrow	No	Yes				
1768	Dean	No		Yes			
1769	Rothwell	No	No	No		Yes	
1770	Bruckner	No		No		Ambiguous	Yes
1775	Pratt			Yes			
1776	Primatt	Yes		Ambiguous		Yes	Yes
1777	Priestly	No		Ambiguous		Yes	Yes
1781	Balguy					Yes	Yes
1790	Smellie	No				Yes	Yes
1798	Toogood						Yes

* Wesley shows mutually exclusive views on this in his writings. See explanation in text.

4.7.2. Animals Will Be Compensated in a Blessed Afterlife

The idea that animals will enjoy a blissed hereafter had already been propagated in the seventeenth century as I have discussed in the previous chapter. But I have also shown that, at that time, the aim of their presence in the renewed world was not so much a compensation for undeserved miseries but to contribute to the bliss of the redeemed sinners. The increasing awareness that animals have their own independent meaning—irrespective of their importance to humans—made this view untenable. The animals' access to a blessed afterlife was no longer seen to increase the eternal bliss of saved sinners. To the contrary, their access to the blessed hereafter rests on their right to be compensated for current—undeserved—misery. On this, all who propagated that animals will inhabit the renewed earth agreed. They only differed in some details. Hildrop and Wesley explained the fact that the animals have to be compensated by referring to the sin of man; his transgression subjected the animals to suffering. Dean agreed that current suffering will be settled in a blissful afterlife, but without linking animal miseries to human sin. The distinction may not have made much difference to the animals themselves, but it does matter to our appreciation of the divine attributes. For if we believe that animals suffer because of our sins, the knowledge that they receive satisfaction in a blessed hereafter will be a reason to be even more amazed at God's grace. He blots out not only our sins, but also the consequences they brought for our innocent fellow creatures. But if we don't have to feel guilty about the suffering of the animals, then a blessed afterlife for the animals is only the compensation to which they are entitled—the way in which God solves a problem that he first created himself, obliged to do so by his righteousness and not moved by tender mercy.

4.7.3. Animals Suffer as Punishment

God is entitled to punish when his commandments are not respected. This explains adequately why humankind suffers; it is because of Adam's transgression and because of our own sins. It may also explain why animals suffer if one assumes that they have sinned as well. At first sight, this may sound implausible, but it is getting less incredible if we assume that it is not the animals themselves that suffer but some ethereal entities that ensoul them. Descartes's mind-body dualism had found an application that its creator had not foreseen and which he probably would have disagreed with.

Some authors, however, found Descartes sharp distinction between mind and body very useful to reconcile the miseries of animal life with the divine attributes. Animals are just machines that are animated by evil spirits; the senses and perception that are natural properties of the animal body are instruments through which God punishes the imprisoned spirit. 'They [the imprisoned spirits] have no ideas, nor perceptions, but what are relative to the conservation of that parcel of matter, to which they are confined.'[304] The ability to feel pain, which is mandatory to preserve life, is one of the properties that are required to safeguard the integrity of the body which in itself is only soulless matter.

About the nature of these incarcerated evildoers, authors varied; they could be either fallen angels or sinful human souls. These ideas did not gain wide acceptance; they were, on the other hand, vehemently contested by contemporary authors. In spite of this, however, the concept served divine justice very well, both explaining animal suffering as well as (in case of human souls) warranting the appropriate punishment of cruel people that apparently lived long and happy lives.

Justice should be done, if not here and now, then hereafter. In this sense, the mind-body dualism on which this theory was based, worked both ways. Migration of souls enabled both a punishment of evil committed as well as a compensation for miseries unmerited. The latter possibility was, however, less often put forward which is understandable because for compensation, another option was available—the blissful afterlife.

4.7.4. Animals Suffer for the Goodness of the Whole

Some authors justified the suffering of the animals by assuming that the miseries experienced during life are outweighed by a surplus of positive experiences. Most others shared this view, but also legitimated animal suffering by stating that it is needed for the goodness of the whole of creation. As noted by *Gottfried Wilhelm Leibniz* (1646–1716), '(...) one must think of the creation of the best of all possible universes, all the more since God not only decrees to create a universe, but decrees also to create the best of all.'[305] Leibniz's agreeing comment on the text of William King (cf. § 4.6.4) can be considered as exemplary for the line of reasoning that ran throughout this whole period; it reflected the generally shared conviction that improvement of things that we experience as harmful would probably be at the expense of greater disadvantages.[306]

---

304 Ramsay, *Philosophical Principles...Part Second*: 322.
305 Leibniz, *Theodicy*: 249 (196).
306 Leibniz, 'Appendix' in *Theodicy*: 411 (6). Cf. Lovejoy, *Chain of Being*: 144-182, 255-262; Vergata, A. 1988. 'Theodicy and Nature's Economy' in: *Nuncius / Istituto e Museo di Storia della Scienza* 3(1):139-152; Wiertel, 'Theism and Animal Suffering': 682-688.

To accept this explanation, it may be helpful to realize that for animals, pain and pleasure signify something different than for humanity. 'One cannot reasonably doubt the existence of pain among animals; but it seems as if their pleasures and their pains are not so keen as they are in man: for animals, since they do not reflect, are susceptible neither to grief that accompanies pain, nor to the joy that accompanies pleasure.'[307] The Stoic assumption that animals are without memories about the past and worries about the future still prevailed.

Animal suffering was also justified because of its importance in the conservation of any created species. In the balance of life and death that characterizes the well-designed creation, each species has its own particular place. Keeping things in order requires reduction of some to create room for others. Nature aims to preserve the species but not the individual. This was already noted early in the period of the Reformations by the French poet *Guillaume de Saluste*, who wrote:

> Thus dost thou print, O Parent of this all,
> In every breast of brutest animal
> A kind instinct which makes them dread no less
> Their children's danger than their own decease;
> That so each kind may last immortally,
> Though th'individuals pass successively.[308]

The demise of the individual warrants the preservation of the species. This belief had already been propagated in the times of the Early Church by Basil and Ambrose (cf. § 2.3) and came to life again in the early Modern Period as evidenced by the writings of Wilkins, Ray, Hill, Bruckner, and Smellie. As noted above (cf. § 4.4), the fossils could be a reason to abandon this belief but this did not appear to be the case. Ray countered the danger fossils posed to the belief that no animal species has

---

307 Leibniz, *Theodicy*: 281 (250).
308 Sylvester, J. 1908 [1608–1641]. *The Divine Weeks of Josuah Sylvester*...H.M. Youmans, Waukesha: 107-108. Guillaume de Salluste, Sieur Du Bartas (1544-1590) was a French Huguenot and connected with the court of Henry de Navarre, who would become Henry IV of France. His hexameral poem La Sepmaine earned him much fame and was translated into English by Josuah Sylvester. For biographical details of Bartas and discussion of his poem, see Randall, *The Wisdom of the Animals*: 39-59. George Hakewill (cf. § 3.8.7) was among the English authors who quoted from Du Bartas's text and and John Milton was also familiar with it. Cf. Auger. P. 2011. 'The Semaines' Dissemination in England and Scotland until 1641' in: *Renaissance Studies* 26 (5): 625-640. John Swan (cf. § 3.8.5) called him the 'Nightingale of France', see Swan, J. 1643. *Specvlvm Mundi. Or a Glasse Representing the Face of the World...The Second Edition Enlarged*. Roger Daniel, Cambridge: 43.

become extinct since creation by assuming that species apparently extinct species still had living representatives in inaccessible or unexplored parts of the earth. The others even completely ignored or overlooked that the petrified remains of animals not seen anymore could endanger the conviction that God has ordained animal death as the means to save any animal species from extinction. This neglect would soon come to an end, but that is a subject for the next chapter.

4.7.5. Preliminary Summary

At the turn of the eighteenth century, the divine attributes seem to be as resistant to any claims of injustice or malevolence as in earlier periods. A minority still thought that animals suffer because Adam sinned but took refuge in assuming a compensation afterwards to save God from the charge of injustice. Some others believed that it was not the animals themselves that were subject to suffering, but that the animal body served as an instrument to punish an evil spirit trapped within. The majority, however, was convinced that the happiness the animal experiences during life outweighs any troubles—adding that we cannot compare the suffering of animals to what humans experience—and that suffering as such is necessary for the maintenance of a well-ordered universe. Nature bears testimony to the glory of its Creator. However, some dissenting voices could be heard as well.

4.7.6. Dissenting Voices

A few authors disagreed with the prevailing assumption that nature bears testimony of the glory of its Creator. I already noted how Bernard Mandeville concluded that 'all the Calamities we can suffer from Man or Beast, as well as Plagues and all other Diseases, are under a wise Direction that is unfathomable'.[309] Nature displays divine power but no goodness or benevolence. The next step was taken by the anonymous author who asked whether there is 'such a prepollency of good as seems suitable to infinite wisdom, goodness, and power?' and thereafter sighs that 'Nature is inveloped in obscurity. Clouds and darkness surround the throne of God'.[310] The argument from design fails.

Similar notes were written by others in the latter decades of the eighteenth century. The famous Scottish philosopher *David Hume* (1711–1776) refuted the possibility to prove divine attributes from the book of nature in his posthumously published *Dialogues on Natural Theology*. In contrast: 'The whole presents nothing but the idea of a blind Nature, (…)

---

309 Mandeville, *Fable of the Bees* 2: 262.
310 Anonymous, 'A View of the Distresses of Mankind': 231-232.

pouring forth from her lap, without discernment or parental care, her maimed and abortive children!' and therefore, one has to conclude that 'the original source of all things is entirely indifferent to all these principles, and has no more regard to good above ill than to heat above cold, or to drought above moisture, or to light above heavy'.[311]

Charles Darwin's grandfather *Erasmus Darwin* (1731-1802), physician, natural philosopher, and poet,[312] had similar second thoughts. '[T]he stronger locomotive animals devour the weaker ones without mercy. Such is the condition of organic nature! whose first law might be expressed in the words, "Eat or be eaten!" and which would seem to be one great slaughter-house, one universal scene of rapacity and injustice! (…) Where shall we find a benevolent idea to console us amid so much apparent misery?'[313] Such an idea is not available. It is all the 'silent mandates of the Almighty Will; / Whose hand unseen the works of nature dooms / By laws unknown – WHO GIVES, AND WHO RESUMES'.[314]

Mandeville, Hume, and Erasmus Darwin did not deny the existence of God, but they rejected the conviction that any evidence for this might be obtained from the book of nature. The further step, however, that nature being a 'slaughterhouse' could lead to a doubt about the existence of God was not taken.

4.8. Conclusion

Throughout the eighteenth century, animal sufferings did not in general pose any threat to divine goodness, wisdom, and benevolence. That animals could suffer was widely accepted, in contrast with the previous period in which it was largely ignored. A dwindling minority still believed it was the sin of Adam but saved God's benevolence by claiming that the animals would be rewarded for undeserved miseries in a blessed hereafter. Another few propagated that suffering did not afflict the animals themselves but

---

311 Hume, D., 1907 [1779]. *Dialogues Concerning Natural Religion. Reprinted with an Introduction by Bruce M'Ewen*. William Blackwood and Sons, Edinburgh: 159-160. Text quoted is from the imaginary speaker *Philo* who propounds Hume's own thoughts. For identification of Philo as Hume, see Hurlbutt III, R.J. 1956. 'David Hume and Scientific Theism' in: *Journal of the History of Ideas* 17 (4): 486-497. Cf. Thomson, *Before Darwin*: 47-51.
312 Porter, *Flesh in the Age of Reason*: 374-389; Thomson, *Before Darwin*: 210-213; Morillo, *Rise of Animals and Descent of Man*: 155-191. I will return to Erasmus Darwin more extensively in Chapter 5, § 5.3.1.
313 Darwin, E. 1800. *Phytologia; or, the Philosophy of Agriculture and Gardening. With the Theory of Draining Morasses, and with an Improved Construction of the Drill Plough*. J. Johnson, London: 556.
314 Darwin, E. 1803. *The Temple of Nature; or, the Origin of Society: a Poem, with Philosophical Notes*. J. Johnson, London: 156 (Canto IV: 344-346).

wicked souls that animated animal bodies. The majority, however, condoned animal suffering by assuming that, in animal life, happiness predominated above their miseries, which went hand in hand with allotting them limited mental abilities, or that animals suffered for the good of the whole, especially in preserving any species from going extinct.

Although the validity of these considerations as evidence for divine benevolence and other attributes was doubted by a few, none of these dissenters invoked animal suffering as a refutation of God's existence. They just disagreed with the view that nature would reflect a divine design. Whether these latter considerations would gain significance over time will be explored in the next chapter.

Chapter 5: A Tale of Two Darwins

Concerns with Animals in the First Half of the Nineteenth Century (1800–1859)

Abstract
In this chapter, it is shown that in the decades prior to the time that Charles Darwin published his famous book, animal suffering still was not seen as a serious threat to the divine attributes. The discussion at the time might have been complicated by the facts provided by geology—aggravating the problem of death in the non-human animal kingdom—but these new findings did not yield opinions significantly different from those of the past. A few authors still associated animal death and predation with humanity's sin in a remote past, but most saw these events as necessary for the benefit of the whole. Others, deeming these arguments to be inadequate, preferred to leave the problem of how to reconcile divine goodness and benevolence with animal suffering unresolved. Only a few outcasts operating on the fringes of society utilized the events they saw in nature as a convenient ground to deny the existence of God, thoughts that were not much appreciated by their contemporaries. On the eve of the Darwinian era, God's attributes or his existence were not in danger. The loners who questioned God's benevolence were neglected or muzzled by the ruling classes as rebels and threats to a well-ordered society.

5.1. Introduction

The eighteenth century had been characterized by an increased awareness that animals suffer and that it is humankind's duty to prevent such suffering as much as possible. In the first decades of the nineteenth century, this awareness was reflected in developments in society indicating that the concern with animal well-being was no longer restricted to only a few fanatics. In contrast, legislation against cruelty towards animals, bull-baiting being forbidden in 1835 and cock-fighting in 1849, showed that the interests of non-human animals had gained so much support that it could be translated into concrete laws, both to improve the life conditions of the animals as well as to raise the moral level of the lower socio-economic layers of society. It was feared that the spectacle of animals tearing each other to pieces could wake up a tendency to violence dormant in the underclass with all its unpleasant consequences for those who cherished the established order.¹ 'The state must curb animal cruelty in the course of exercising its general responsibility for promoting the citizen's moral growth.'² While in the past (cf. Chapter 3, § 3.8.8) the Puritans had opposed animal sports because they saw these as sin, the contemporary ruling class now outlawed them to keep the mob quiet. This clarifies why legislation focused only on the animal sports that entertained the lower classes, while the amusements of the upper classes—'stag hunting and grouse shooting'—were not a topic of discussion.³

The foundation of the Society for the Prevention of Cruelty to Animals (1824)—elevated to the status of *Royal* in 1840—is another example of the increased social influence of anticruelty sentiments.⁴ The activities of

---

1 Turner, J. 1980. *Reckoning with the Beast. Animals, Pain, and Humanity in the Victorian Mind*. The Johns Hopkins University Press, Baltimore: 15-28, 39-40, 52-59; Thomas, K. 1983. *Man and the Natural World. Changing Attitudes in England 1500-1800*. Penguin Books, Harmondsworth: 150-165; Preece, R. 2002. *Awe for the Tiger, Love for the Lamb: a Chronicle of Sensibility to Animals*. Routledge, London: 406-480; Rowlands, M. 'Philosophy and Animals in the Age of Empire' in: Kete, K. (ed.). 2007. *A Cultural History of Animals in the Age of the Empire*. Berg, Oxford: 135-152; Bates, A.W.H. 2017. *Anti-Vivisection and the Profession of Medicine in Britain. A Social History*. Palgrave MacMillan, London: 15-17. For a contemporary's criticism of the different kinds of animal sports, see Drummond, W.H. 1838. *The Rights of Animals, and Man's Obligation to Treat Them with Humanity*. John Mardon, London: 104-114. Cf. Boddice, R. 2008. *A History of Attitudes and Behaviours toward Animals in Eigtheen- and Nineteenth-Century Britain. Anthropocentrism and the Emergence of Animals*. Edwin Mellen Press, Lewiston: 203-258.

2 Harrison, B. 1973. 'Animals and the State in Nineteenth-Century England' in: *The English Historical Review* 88 (349): 786-820 (815).

3 Desmond, A. 1989. *The Politics of Evolution. Morphology, Medicine, and Reform in Radical London*. The University of Chicago Press, Chicago: 183-192 (187). Not everyone, even among the clergy, however, believed that animal sports should be frowned upon as evidenced by the contents of a letter published in 1801 in the *Sporting Magazine* for August of that year. '[I]f you think it worth your While to come over with a Couple of *Bears*, I can only say that you shall be welcome (…). If you come You must bring a Dog or two with You to run at the Bears—and bring also that Pointer Dog with you that I saw in the Yard when I was at your house. I am, yours, &c. Thomas Newton. Direct, "Revd. Thomas Newton, Parwich, near Ashborne."' Reverend Newton clearly saw no objection to entertaining his parishioners in this way. The *Sporting Magazine* was mandatory reading for any animal sports enthusiast. The journal announced scheduled events, published their outcomes, and provided a platform for discussion about the pros and cons of using animals for public entertainment. Cf. Boddice, *A History of Attitudes and Behaviours toward Animals*: 174, *passim*.

4 Turner, *Reckoning with the Beast*: 39-45, 52-59; Thomas, *Man and the Natural World*: 186; Ritvo, H. 1987. *The Animal Estate. The English and Other Creatures in the Victorian Age*. Harvard University Press, Cambridge (MA): 125-166; Boddice, *A History of*

this organization included not only overseeing that the laws against animal sports were actually observed in practice—for which they even hired employees—but also fostering opposition to experiments with animals, a feeling that was found not only among people who refused to acknowledge the benefits these could bring to science but also within the circles of the scientists themselves. The latter is not as strange as it appears at first sight. If experiments on animals had to offer outcomes useful for humankind, one had to assume a close kinship between both, which raises the question whether it is lawful to let one creature suffer for the benefit of the other. But when the distance between humans and animals is so great that these ethical considerations do not play a role, the question arises whether the results obtained through vivisection still have any scientific use.[5] 'If authorised by analogy, it is both criminal and ferocious; and if justified by a difference of nature, it remains objectless and unworthy of confidence.'[6] Other authors did not even grant this benefit of the doubt. 'In performing experiments which involve the fatal mutilation of animals, we are studying death, not life; we are learning the influence which the removal of an organ has in *killing* an animal, not the influence which its presence has in *keeping* it *alive*.'[7]

The fray between supporters and opponents of vivisection was not simply a conflict between progressives and conservatives or scientists and

---

Attitudes and Behaviours toward Animals: 155-201. Both the legislation and the foundation of societies for the protection of animals did not go unnoticed elsewhere in Europe. The German philosopher Arthur Schopenhauer praised the English for this but on the other hand regretted that 'Christian morality takes no thought for beasts' which made it necessary 'to fill up by legislation the *lacuna* that their religion leaves in morality'. Cf. Schopenhauer, A. 2007 [1840]. Über die Grundlagen der Moral. Mit einer Einleitung, Anmerkungen und einem Register herausgegeben von Peter Welsen. Felix Meiner Verlag, Hamburg: 142-144. The quotes are from Schopenhauer, A. 1903. *The Basis of Morality. Translated with Introduction and Notes by Arthur Brodrick Bullock.* Swan Sonnenschein & Co., London: 222, 224.

5 Franco, N.H. 2013. 'Animal Experiments in Biomedical Research: a Historical Perspective' in: *Animals* 3: 238-273, in particular pp. 246-255.
6 Lordat, M. 1854. 'Mental Dynamics in Relation to the Science of Medicine...Lecture V.' in: *The Journal of Psychological Medicine and Mental Pathology* 7: 252-263 (259).
7 Ryan, M. 1836. 'Importance of Comparative Anatomy' in: *The London Medical and Surgical Journal: Exhibiting a View of the Improvements and Discoveries in the Various Branches of Medical Science* 8: 184-185 (184). For a detailed description of what vivisection encompassed back then, see Drummond, *The Rights of Animals, and Man's Obligation to Treat Them with Humanity*: 145-169. It makes the author sigh that 'myriads of enormous cruelties are perpetrated, as disgraceful to the name of science, as they must be criminal in the sight of that great Being, whose "tender mercies are over all his works"' (154).

lay people.⁸ Other issues also were at stake, and one of them was the general opinion that a decent person should not be concerned with this activity, irrespective of any usefulness that might be obtained. Therefore, the practitioners of the profession believed to benefit most from animal experiments also kept their distance. Doctors wanted to be seen as professionals with compassion for their patients, not as callous torturers of animals. In this way, there is an interesting parallel with dissecting human corpses, then as now considered an activity that may be useful, but which people would rather not talk about.⁹ And finally, the horror stories of the way in which the vivisectionists in France—a country treated with suspicion because of its revolutionary and materialistic character—indulged in the most gruesome experiments were not suited to promote a positive attitude towards acquiring knowledge by cutting up animals alive either.¹⁰

Clearly, it wasn't just compassion for the animals that directed people to reject vivisection. There were also political and social pressures. And it is telling that an uncertainty about the morality of eating meat, which arose around the same time, was largely ignored by the general public.¹¹ This difference in appreciation of experimenting with animals and eating them might be considered a sign that the sensibility for animal suffering as shown by the anti-vivisectionists served also other purposes than only improving the living conditions of the animals themselves. That does, however, not alter the fact that the interests of the animals as such had now gained enough societal and political weight to make them useful as arguments in the public debate, if only to further other interests.

Supporters of natural theology who wished to defend the doctrine that nature offers evidence for divine goodness and benevolence had to cope with this changed attitude towards the animals and one may expect

---

8   Turner, *Reckoning with the Beast*: 83-84, 96-121; Desmond, *Politics of Evolution*: 183-192; Guerrini, A. 2003. *Experimenting with Humans and Animals. From Galen to Animal Rights*. The Johns Hopkins University Press, Baltimore: 74-78.
9   Bates, *Anti-Vivisection and the Profession of Medicine in Britain*: 18-21. Bates points at the parallelism in the ambiguous feelings towards vivisection and anatomizing human cadavers (23). For information on the attitude towards the latter for this period, see Richardson, R. 1988. *Death, Dissection and the Destitute*. Penguin Books, London. It was the time of the so-called resurrectionists, people who made a living from exhuming and selling freshly interred bodies and occasionally even went as far as to murder poor and lonely people to increase their income by selling the corpses thus obtained to anatomists.
10 Recarte, C.A. 2014. 'Anti-French Discourse in the Nineteenth-century. British Antivivisection Movement' in: *Atlantis, Journal of the Spanish Association of Anglo-American Studies* 36 (1): 31-49.
11 Thomas, *Man and the Natural World*: 287-300.

that the higher status now attributed to humankind's fellow creatures would have an impact on the credibility of this conviction. Furthermore, the fossils, an issue largely ignored thus far by those who had concerns about the relationship between the book of nature and the book of Scripture, entered the scene. In this chapter, I will examine whether and to what extent the thoughts about animal suffering and divine attributes were influenced by these developments in society and science.

In § 5.2, I will sketch an outline of the changing role of natural theology and address the significance of the data provided by the fledgling sciences of geology and paleontology. In § 5.3, I will account for the methodology followed in retrieving the sources relevant for obtaining the aim outlined above. The content of these sources is the subject of § 5.4. Data thus collected will be discussed in § 5.5, and the chapter ends with § 5.6 in which some concluding remarks are made.

5.2. Natural Theology and Geology
5.2.1. The Waning Tide of Natural Theology
Several authors have noted that during the first half of the nineteenth century, natural theology had to face a declining persuasiveness.[12] The conviction commonly held before—that natural events perceived as evil were needed for the benefit of the 'Whole' and thus, in reality, are not evil but beneficial—was increasingly being questioned. That was not to be expected. In the previous chapter, I noted that at the end of the eighteenth century, scholars were rather unanimous in their conviction that nature reflects divine wisdom as well as goodness and that anything thought to be evil would turn out not to be evil at all when more closely examined. For example, seemingly evil events were required for preventing famine, species extinction, and other disasters in the non-human animal kingdom. A design with this purpose was obvious for anybody; the study of animals didn't fail to show how precisely the Creator had contrived them for their

---

12 Gascoigne, J. 1988. 'From Bentley to the Victorians: the Rise and Fall of British Newtonian Natural Theology' in: *Science in Context* 2 (2): 219-256; Gillespie, N.C. 1990. 'Divine Design and the Industrial Revolution: William Paley's Abortive Reform of Natural Theology' in: *Isis* 81 (2): 214-229; Topham, J.R. 'Science, Natural Theology and Evangelicalism in Early Nineteenth-Century Scotland' in: Livingstone, D.N., Hart, D.G., Noll, M.A. (eds). 1999. *Evangelicals and Science in Historical Perspective.* Oxford University Press, New York: 142-174; Topham, J.R. 'Biology in the Service of Natural Theology: Paley, Darwin, and the Bridgewater Treatises' in: Alexander, D.R., Numbers, R.L. (eds). 2010. *Biology and Ideology. From Descartes to Dawkins.* The University of Chicago Press, Chicago: 88-113; McGrath, A.E. 2011. *Darwinism and the Divine. Evolutionary Thought and Natural Theology. The 2009 Hulsean Lectures.* University of Cambridge. Wiley-Blackwell, Chichester: 108-142.

specific way of life, all this in spite of Mandeville's (cf. § 4.6.3) and Hume's (cf. § 4.7.6) skeptical notes.

In the first decade of this century, other arguments were added to the time-honored conviction that the complexity of living organisms and their adaptation to their environment mirror divine wisdom. Harmony was found not only within one individual animal but also in the order of the animal kingdom. Taxonomy and classification were not merely arbitrary but disclosed the laws God had devised to create order in his creation. That different animals shared body features that made it possible to divide them in phyla, classes, orders, families, genera, and species was not fortuitous but referred to an underlying divine blueprint; an idealist perspective was added to the teleological, purpose-oriented framework. The unity and the harmony of the whole of nature, not the contrivance of the individual parts were emphasized.[13]

Thus, at the turn of the nineteenth century, natural theology was buttressed in two ways: adaptation of the animal to its specific way of life and an overall order that revealed the Creator's wisdom. In this climate, William Paley, an author to whom I will return shortly, published his almost canonical defense of the doctrine of divine design.[14] Only five decades later, Charles Darwin replaced divine design with natural selection and explained order and harmony in the animal kingdom by common descent.[15] A mere fifty years separated natural theology's zenith from its nadir—a decline to which various developments may have contributed.

First, natural theology lost significance throughout this period because of a concern in some clerical circles that knowledge of God provided by nature was prioritized over the Bible as main source for knowing God and his attributes.[16] It is the book of Scripture and not the book of nature

---

13 Bowler, P.J. 1977. 'Darwinism and the Argument from Design: Suggestions for a Reevaluation' in: *Journal of the History of Biology* 10 (1): 29-43; Livingstone, D.N. 1984. *Darwin's Forgotten Defenders. The Encounter between Evangelical Theology and Evolutionary Thought*. Regent College Publishing, Vancouver: 3-7; Yeo, R.R. 1986. 'The Principle of Plenitude and Natural Theology in Nineteenth-Century Britain' in: *The British Journal for the History of Science* 19 (3): 263-282; Topham, 'Biology in the Service of Natural Theology' in: Alexander & Numbers, *Biology and Ideology*: 88-113; McGrath, *Darwinism and the Divine*: 109.

14 Paley, W. 1802. *Natural Theology: or, Evidences of the Existence and Attributes of the Deity, Collected from the Appearances of Nature*. John Morgan, Philadelphia.

15 Ayala, F.J. 2007. 'Darwin's Greatest Discovery: Design without Designer' in: *Proceedings of the National Academy of Sciences* 104 (Suppl. 1): 8567-8573; Ayala, F.J. 2010. 'Darwin's Explanation of Design: From Natural Theology to Natural Selection' in: *Infection, Genetics and Evolution* 10 (6): 839-842.

16 Bebbington, D.W. 'Science and Evangelical Theology in Britain from Wesley to Orr'

that conveys the message of sin and salvation.[17] '[T]he natural Theologian wholly refuses to read the indelible characters in which the punishment inflicted for disobedience against God is written on this mundane globe',[18] thus wrote *Francis Palgrave* (1788–1861), a Jew converted to Anglican Christianity. The theologian and poet *Samuel Taylor Coleridge* (1772–1834) had a similar opinion: 'I more than fear the prevailing taste for books of natural theology, physico-theology, demonstrations of God from nature, evidences of Christianity, and the like. Evidences of Christianity! I am weary of the word.'[19] These considerations weakened the alliance between science and religion that had characterized British intellectual life thus far. The clergy became less inclined to support faith with arguments derived from the study of the book of nature, and scientists felt less urgency to integrate the results of their activities with their own religious convictions but in contrast became more eager to strengthen their position as people not restricted in their professional activities by the shackles of the book of Scripture.[20] They sought to determine the future of science at the expense of the role of the ecclesiastical authorities.[21]

Second, the persuasiveness of the argument from design had lost a lot of its appeal.[22] Already in 1822, *Jeremy Bentham*, writing under the pseudonym Philip Beauchamp, went thus far that he left no room for the entire concept; in his view, picturing the idea of a well-designed universe

---

in: Livingstone, Hart, Noll, *Evangelicals and Science in Historical Perspective*: 120-141; McGrath, *Darwinism and the Divine*: 109-110, 127-130, 133-134.
17 Topham, 'Biology in the Service of Natural Theology' in: Alexander & Numbers, *Biology and Ideology*: 88-113.
18 Palgrave, F. 1844. *Truths and Fictions of the Middle Ages. The Merchant and the Friar. Second Edition, Revised and Corrected*. John W. Parker, London: 230. Biography of Palgrave in: Bowler, P.J. 1974. 'Sir Francis Palgrave on Natural Theology' in: *Journal of the History of Ideas* 35: 144-147.
19 Coleridge, S.T. 1840. *Aids to Reflection, with a Preliminary Essay, by James Marsh. From the Fourth London Edition, with the Author's Last Corrections*. Edited by Henry Nelson Coleridge. Chauncey Goodrich, Burlington: 348.
20 Moore, J.R. 'Geologists and Interpreters of Genesis in the Nineteenth Century' in: Lindberg, D.C., Numbers, R.L. (eds). 1986. *God & Nature. Historical Essays on the Encounter between Christianity and Science*. University of California Press, Berkeley: 322-350; Stanley, M. 2015. *Huxley's Church & Maxwell's Demon. From Theistic Science to Naturalistic Science*. The University of Chicago Press, Chicago.
21 Turner, F.M. 1978. 'The Victorian Conflict between Science and Religion: a Professional Dimension' in: *Isis* 69 (3): 356-376.
22 Gillespie, 'Divine Design and the Industrial Revolution: William Paley's Abortive Reform of Natural Theology'; Bowler, P.J. 2007. *Monkey Trials and Gorilla Sermons. Evolution and Christianity from Darwin to Intelligent Design*. Harvard University Press, Cambridge (MA): 51-55.

was fiction that only served to promote the interests of the ruling classes, both secular as well as clerical.[23] More moderate contemporary critics limited themselves to pointing out flaws, noting how 'writers are enraptured with the provident arrangement which enables the gazelle, antelope, deer, &c, by their swiftness and watchfulness to escape their natural enemies, and then they express equal admiration that these natural enemies have their feet covered with hair to deaden the sound of their approaching feet'. It is an odd design when the aimed purposes 'counteract each other, one set of animals are qualified by nature to eat the other, and these [the prey] are aided by nature not to be eaten by them'.[24]

And third, different opinions about the way in which the design in nature took shape, turned natural theology into a 'house divided against itself'.[25] Disagreement about the influence of God on animal behavior illustrates this very well: Are animals driven by instinct or could it be that they respond appropriately to external stimuli? In the first case, design becomes apparent by purpose-oriented, innate behavioral patterns, whereas in the second case, design implied that God had equipped the animals with the mental qualities required for adequately responding to the contingent demands made by the environment.[26] The expanding scientific knowledge made it increasingly difficult to achieve a uniform interpretation of nature in terms of design.

But not only the credibility of the book of nature suffered throughout this period; the book of Scripture became a target as well. Its authority was challenged by historians and theologians alike, initially mainly from Germany but eagerly taken over by the British. There appeared to be many inconsistencies and anomalies when one examined the biblical text in the same way as was done with any other historical document; not only the Genesis text was unreliable, but also even the Gospels could not be taken as true in every detail.[27]

---

23 Beauchamp, P. [Jeremy Bentham]. 1822. *Analysis of the Influence of Natural Religion on the Temporal Happiness of Mankind*. R. Carlile, London: 137-140.
24 Ensor, G. 1836. *Natural Theology: the Arguments of Paley, Brougham, and the Bridgewater Treatises on this Subject Examined*...Richard Taylor, London: 10-11.
25 Brooke, J.H. 1977. 'Natural Theology and the Plurality of Worlds: Observations on the Brewster-Whewell Debate' in: *Annals of Science* 34 (3): 221-286 (222). Cf. Brooke, J., Cantor, G. 1998. *Reconstructing Nature. The Engagement of Science and Religion. Glasgow Gifford Lectures*. Oxford University Press, New York: 160-161.
26 Morganti, F. 2015. 'Natural Theology and the Origin of Instincts. Debating the Divine Government of Animals in Early Nineteenth Century Britain' in: *Lo Sguardo - Rivista di Filosofia* 18 (II): 167-187.
27 Moore, 'Geologists and Interpreters of Genesis in the Nineteenth Century' in: Lindberg & Numbers, *God & Nature*: 322-350; Brooke, J.H. 1991. *Science and Religion. Some Historical Perspectives*. Cambridge University Press, Cambridge: 263-274; Jones,

This coincidence of scientific and historical criticism of the Bible on the one hand and the loss of persuasiveness of natural theology on the other may explain why the bond between religion and science began to weaken precisely during this period. This however does not imply that religion itself had lost its impact on society. In Britain, the first half of the nineteenth century witnessed a spiritual revival both within as well as outside the circle of the Church of England but this did not halt the fading of the inclination to buttress religion with observations from nature.[28]

5.2.2. Geology Enters the Scene

As mentioned in the previous chapter, the presence of fossils had raised concern already throughout the eighteenth century. At the turn of the nineteenth century, geology and paleontology had collected so much data about the crust of the earth with its petrified remains of animals not seen anymore that the conclusion that animal species could die out became inescapable.[29] These developments have been amply documented, and reiterating them here lies beyond the scope of this study, especially because the authors that are the subject of our study didn't play any role herein.[30] Till the end of the eighteenth century, British authors had

---

R.H. 2012. *For the Glory of God. The Role of Christianity in the Rise and Development of Modern Science. Volume II: The History of Christian Ideas and Control Beliefs in Science.* University Press of America, Lanham: 240-241.

28 Turner, F.M. 'The Victorian Crisis of Faith and the Faith that Was Lost' in: Helmstadter, R.J., Lightman, B. (eds). 1990. *Victorian Faith in Crisis. Essays on Continuity and Change in Nineteenth-Century Religious Belief.* Stanford University Press, Stanford: 9-38.

29 Black, J. 'The Hermeneutics of Extinction: Denial and Discovery in Scientific Literature' in: Shaffer, E.S. (ed.). 1991. *Comparative Criticism. An Annual Journal. Literature and Science* 13: 147-170; Rudwick, M.J.S. 2008. *Worlds before Adam. The Reconstruction of Geohistory in the Age of Reform.* The University of Chicago Press, Chicago: 237-250; Jones, *For the Glory of God*: 105-115.

30 Lovejoy, A.O. 1904. 'Some Eighteenth Century Evolutionists' in: *Popular Science Monthly* 65: 238-251, 323-340; Lovejoy, A.O. 1909. 'The Argument for Organic Evolution before 'The Origin of Species' in: *Popular Science Monthly* 75: 499-514, 537-549; Lovejoy, A.O. 1936. *The Great Chain of Being. A Study of the History of an Idea. The William James Lectures Delivered at Harvard University 1933.* Harvard University Press, Cambridge: 242-287; Hofsten, N. von. 1936. 'Ideas of Creation and Spontaneous Generation Prior to Darwin' in: *Isis* 25 (1): 80-94; Gillispie, C.C. 1959. *Genesis and Geology. The Impact of Scientific Discoveries upon Religious Beliefs in the Decades before Darwin.* Harper and Row, New York; Greene, J.C. 1961. *The Death of Adam. Evolution and Its Impact on Western Thought.* The New American Library, New York; Haber, F.C. 'Fossils and the Idea of a Process of Time in Natural History' in: Glass, B., Temkin, O., Straus Jr, W.L. (eds). 1968. *Forerunners of Darwin: 1745-1859.* The Johns Hopkins Press, Baltimore: 222-261; Lovejoy, A.O., 'The Argument for Organic Evolution before the Origin of Species 1830-1858' in: Glass, Temkin, Straus, *Forerunners of Darwin*: 356-414; Bowler, P.J. 1974. 'Evolutionism in the Enlightenment' in: *History of Science*

appeared to be rather immune to any thoughts from abroad about the age of the earth and the relationship of the extinct animal species with those species still living. '[T]he country of Darwin had made far less progress in this part of biology than had France and Germany.'[31] Probably, this was because the English people were in general reluctant to accept thoughts from the revolutionary French. This British repugnance towards thoughts from abroad, at least as far as they concerned development and change in the natural world, would only decrease in the first decades of the nineteenth century.

In 1820, James Parkinson—an author I introduced in the previous chapter—deplored the lagging behind of British science in comparison with other European countries: 'In France and Italy, and more particular in Germany, the most ardent and scientific inquiries have indeed been instituted; in consequence of which, discoveries of the most curious and interesting nature have been made. These, however, having been published either in French, German, or Latin; and not having yet appeared in an English dress, it is not to be wondered at that the astonishing information which they impart, is so little known in this country.'[32] Other authors to be discussed below would join Parkinson in his wishes to improve on this.

Most British scholars began to realize that the age of the earth had to be vastly extended, surprisingly, however, not urged to do this by the Scottish geologist *James Hutton* (1726–1797)—their fellow countryman who already had raised the possibility of an old age of the earth at the end of the eighteenth century in his *Theory of the Earth*.[33] Instead, they took

---

12 (2): 159-183; Brooke, *Science and Religion*: 226-231, 243-254; Thomson, K. 2005. *Before Darwin. Reconciling God and Nature*. Yale University Press, New Haven.

31 Gillispie, *Genesis and Geology*: 273nn78, 79. Quote from Lovejoy, 'Some Eighteenth Century Evolutionists' in: *Popular Science Monthly* 65: 340. Cf. Rudwick, *Bursting the Limits of Time. The Reconstruction of Geohistory in the Age of Revolution*. The University of Chicago Press, Chicago: 431-434.

32 Parkinson, J. 1820. *Organic Remains of a Former World…In Three Volumes*. Sherwood et al., London: I: 7.

33 Hutton, J. 1959 [1795]. *Theory of the Earth. With Proofs and Illustrations*. Hafner Publishing Co., New York. Reprinted, originally published by Cadell, Junior et al., London. For reasons why Hutton failed to have impact on his successors in the science of geology, see Porter, R. 1977. *The Making of Geology. Earth Science in Britain 1660-1815*. Cambridge University Press, Cambridge: 184-202. Contemporaries judged his theory to be more based on philosophy and speculations than on Baconian empirics and 'raising spectres which threatened the good name of Earth science in a period of counter-revolutionary intellectual illiberalism' (186). Nor did his statement that he could find 'no vestige of a beginning,—no prospect of an end' (*Theory of the Earth*: 200) met much appreciation as this ignored the evidence for a history deducible from the variation in fossil remains that geology had already revealed. Cf. Gould, S.J. 1991.

their arguments from the work of the French zoologist *Georges Cuvier* (1769-1832)[34] who was introduced to the British public by the Scottish professor of natural history Robert Jameson.[35]

In the previous centuries, the literal interpretation of the story of Eden and the fall had been questioned, as discussed in Chapters 3 and 4, but without abandoning the scriptural chronology. Now, geological data forced scholars to question Scripture on this subject as well[36]—rejected by some[37] but hailed by others. 'In this dark age of geology [now left behind] her science rested on the two assumptions that the world was made in six days, and was afterwards overwhelmed in the waters of an universal deluge', but now, 'our geologists' are liberated from the 'chains forged by a presumptuous theology'.[38] The first verses of Genesis had to be reconsidered. 'In the beginning' could mean an antecedent long period of

---

Time's Arrow, Time's Cycle. Myth and Metaphor in the Discovery of Geological Time. Penguin Books, London: 61-97; Rudwick, *Bursting the Limits of Time*: 158-172.

34 Rudwick, *Bursting the Limits of Time*: 353-388, 510-512; Rudwick, *Worlds before Adam*: 11-23.

35 Jameson, R. 'Preface' in: Cuvier, G. 1813. *Essay on the Theory of the Earth…Translated from the French. By Robert Kerr*. William Blackwood, Edinburgh: iii-ix. For biographical details on Jameson, see Gillispie, *Genesis and Geology*: 66-68. For a description of how Jameson distorted Cuvier's work for his own purposes, see Rudwick, *Bursting the Limits of Time*: 596-598.

36 Gillispie, *Genesis and Geology*: 71-97; Rudwick, M.J.S. 'The Shape and Meaning of Earth History' in: Lindberg, D.C., Numbers, R.L. (eds). 1986. *God and Nature: Historical Essays on the Encounter between Christianity and Science*. University of California Press, Berkeley: 296-321. Reproduced in: Rudwick, M.J.S. 2004. *The New Science of Geology. Studies in the Earth Sciences in the Age of Revolution*. Ashgate, Aldershot; Rudwick, M.J.S. 'Geologist's Time: a Brief History' in: Lippincott, K. (ed.). 1999. *The Story of Time*. Merrell Holberton, London: 1-7. Republished in: Rudwick, *The New Science of Geology*. Cf. Rudwick, *Bursting the Limits of Time*: 115-118.

37 Millhauser, M. 1954. 'The Scriptural Geologists: an Episode in the History of Opinion' in: *Osiris* 11: 65-86; Stiling, R.L. 'Scriptural Geology in America' in: Livingstone, Hart, Noll, *Evangelicals and Science in Historical Perspective*: 177-192; Ury, T.H. 2001. *The Evolving Face of God as Creator: Early Nineteenth-Century Traditionalist and Accommodationist Theological Responses in British Religious Thought to Paleonatural Evil in the Fossil Record*. Dissertations. 158. Andrews University, Berriens Springs; O'Connor, R. 2007. 'Young-Earth Creationists in Early Nineteenth-Century Britain? Towards a Reassessment of 'Scriptural Geology'' in: *History of Science* 45: 357-403.

38 Anonymous. 1837. 'Art. I.—Geology and Mineralogy Considered with Reference to Natural Theology. By the Rev. William Buckland' in: *The Edinburgh Review or Critical Journal for April,…..July 1837* 65: 1-39 (3, 12). *The Edinburgh Review, or The Critical Journal* was published from 1802 to 1929 and was widely esteemed for its political and literary criticism. Cf. Britannica, The Editors of Encyclopaedia. "The Edinburgh Review, or The Critical Journal". *Encyclopedia Britannica*, 7 August 2019, https://www.britannica.com/topic/The-Edinburgh-Review-or-The-Critical-Journal. Accessed on 14 December 2021.

time about which Scripture does not provide details, or, alternatively, the six days of creation had not to be taken for real days but successive epochs of an undefined length.[39] Moreover, it had to be recognized that the human race was a relative latecomer, a long history of an earth teeming with animal life predating its appearance.[40]

Some tried to save the trustworthiness of the Genesis text—to be understood as a reliable record including the specific time indications—by advocating that the geological data referred to an *apparent* age, in the same way as a tree created in a full-grown stage suggests a past that never was[41] or by holding that fossils had not necessarily been 'animated structures' and thus lacked convincing evidence for 'the existence of this earth many ages before man was created.'[42] Most people, however, accepted the fossils as the remains of living beings now extinct; they were explained as the remnants of separate consecutive acts of the Creator who

---

39 Bebbington, 'Science and Evangelical Theology in Britain from Wesley to Orr' in: Livingstone, Hart, Noll, *Evangelicals and Science in Historical Perspective*: 120-141.
40 Rudwick, *Bursting the Limits of Time*: 275-287; Rudwick, *Worlds before Adam*: 407-422.
41 Gosse, P.H. 1857. *Omphalos: an Attempt to Untie the Geological Knot*. John van Voorst, London. Philip Gosse is the most widely known advocate for this conviction, the title of his book—*Omphalos*—even becoming proverbial for the conviction named *omphalism,* which holds that God created a world with an apparent age. His thoughts were widely shared at the time and were also advanced elsewhere in Europe. In his sermons on the *Catechism of Heidelberg*, the Dutch divine D. Molenaar came up with this idea even earlier than Gosse—already in 1852 rejecting the idea of an old earth. '[W]aarom zouden wij dan geloof geven aan menschelijke vindingen van lateren tijd, die ons wijs willen maken, dat er, omdat men hier en daar natuurverschijnselen vindt, welke aan eenen hoogeren ouderdom doen denken (lavabeddingen en beenderen van diersoorten, welke er niet meer zijn) eene vroegere schepping heeft plaats gehad, en het verhaal Gen. 1, slechts van eene herschepping moet worden opgevat? Immers vergeet men bij zulk eene opvatting, dat vele dingen, gelijk de mensch, in eenen volwassenen staat zijn voorgebragt [sic]' in: Molenaar, D. 1852. *De Heidelbergsche Catechismus in Leerredenen*. J.W. Swaan, Arnhem: 172. In translation [mine]: 'Why, then, should we give credence to human inventions of later times, which would make us believe that, because one finds here and there natural phenomena, which are reminiscent of a higher age (lava beds and bones of animal species that no longer exist) an earlier creation has taken place, and the story of Gen. 1, must be understood only of a re-creation? For one forgets with such an opinion that many things, like man, are brought forth in an adult state.' By courtesy of Dr. John van Eck who brought this source to my attention. Cf. McIver, T.A. 1989. *Creationism. Intellectual Origins, Cultural Context, and Theoretical Diversity*. PhD Thesis, University of California, Los Angeles.
42 Anonymous. 1853. *A Brief and Complete Refutation of the Anti-Scriptural Theory of Geologists. By a Clergyman of the Church of England*. Wertheim and Macintosh, London: 7, 6.

destroyed and created, thus subscribing to Cuvier's doctrine of catastrophism.[43]

The objections against catastrophism that were raised from 1830 onwards by *Charles Lyell* (1797-1875),[44] who advocated uniformitarianism—the earth surface in the past was shaped by processes similar to those active nowadays, obeying natural laws that do not change throughout time, either in rate or in intensity[45]—above the sudden changes of catastrophism are less important for the purpose of my study. Both catastrophism as well as uniformitarianism had to understand themselves with countless years of death in the animal kingdom.[46]

These developments implied that scholars in the first decades of the nineteenth century had to cope with a new problem: how to justify the benevolence of a Creator who time and again wiped out living beings to make room for others, thus personally annihilating multitudes of animals without any apparent benefit for the greater good of a smoothly running universe. This consequence did not go unnoticed. Already in 1817, Cuvier's ideas and Jameson's introduction to them raised objections. After having pointed out that these thoughts imply that multitudes of animals perished before humans were created, a certain H.S. Boyd concluded:

---

43 Gillispie, *Genesis and Geology*: 98-120; Greene, *Death of Adam*: 130. The extent to which the adoption of a divine intervention did justice to Cuvier's own views is a topic of discussion. Possibly, his disciples went further than the master in this. See von Hofsten, 'Ideas of Creation and Spontaneous Generation Prior to Darwin': 87; Hooykaas, R. 1959. *Natural Law and Divine Miracle. A Historical-Critical Study of the Principle of Uniformity in Geology, Biology and Theology.* E.J. Brill, Leiden: 197-198; Palmer, T. 1999. *Controversy. Catastrophism and Evolution. The Ongoing Debate.* Springer, New York: 45-47; Rudwick, *Bursting the Limits of Time*: 596-598; Rudwick, *Worlds before Adam*: 356-361. The results of French science were more often adapted to the British mindset, see Bowler, P.J. 1976. *Fossils and Progress. Paleontology and the Idea of Progressive Evolution in the Nineteenth Century.* Science History Publications, New York: 15-44; Brooke, J.H. 1989. 'Scientific Thought and Its Meaning for Religion: the Impact of French Science on British Natural Theology, 1827-1859' in: *Revue de Synthèse* 110 (1): 33-59.
44 Rudwick, *Worlds before Adam*: 201-207.
45 Gould, *Time's Arrow, Time's Cycle*: 117-126.
46 Cf. Hooykaas, *Natural Law*: 225. 'From the religious point of view, it makes no difference whether geological changes be paroxysmal or uniform, whether scientific theories bear a more catastrophic or a more uniformitarian character.' For an in-depth study on Lyell's defense of uniformitarianism against catastrophism and his ultimate submission to Darwin's theory of species evolving and not static, see Bartholomew, M. 1973. 'Lyell and Evolution: an Account of Lyell's Response to the Prospect of an Evolutionary Ancestry for Man' in: *The British Journal for the History of Science* 6 (23): 261-303; Gould, *Time's Arrow, Time's Cycle*: 99-179; Rudwick, *Worlds before Adam*: 310-312, 347-361, 467-481.

> That if there had been no sin, there would have been no suffering; that suffering of every kind is the effect of sin; that Adam was constituted the head and representative of the whole creation; and consequently that all the animals participated in the consequences of his disobedience. But in this [Cuvier's] respect, the Christian doctrine is overturned, and, I may say, annihilated, by the system of geologists. According to them, whole races of carnivorous animals inhabited both the sea and the dry land before the creation of man; consequently the brute creation must have been in a state of pain and suffering before Adam fell.[47]

Nevertheless, the idea that fossils were the remains of previous divine acts remained alive, in spite of the consequences as played in poetry by *Alfred Tennyson* (1809-1892) in words that have been quoted many times and appear here again:

> Are God and Nature then at strife,
> That Nature lends such evil dreams ?
> So careful of the type she seems,
> So careless of the single life,
> (…)
> So careful of the type?' but no.
> From scarped cliff and quarried stone
> She cries, 'A thousand types are gone:
> I care for nothing, all shall go.
> (…)
> Who trusted God was love indeed
> And love Creation's final law—
> Tho' Nature, red in tooth and claw
> With ravin, shriek'd against his creed—[48]

'Scarped cliff and quarried stone' are the cemeteries of countless beings once alive; geology did not allow any other conclusion. Apparently, it had pleased the Creator to replace the inhabitants of the earth with new creatures from time to time, each new generation surpassing the previous

---

47 Boyd, H.S. 1817. 'LXII. On Cosmogony' in: *The Philosophical Magazine and Journal…*50: 375-378 (377).
48 Tennyson, A. 1895 [1850]. *In Memoriam. Edited with Notes by William J. Rolfe*. Houghton Mifflin Company, Boston: 61-62. For details about the background of Tennyson's poem, see Shepherd, H.E. 1893. 'Tennyson's "In Memoriam"' in: *The Sewanee Review* 1 (4): 402-409; Hough, G. 1947. 'The Natural Theology of In Memoriam' in: *The Review of English Studies* 23 (91): 244-256; Weiss, K.M. 2010. '"Nature, Red in Tooth and Claw", So What?' in: *Evolutionary Anthropology* 19: 41-45.

one. Such a surpassing should, however, not being understood as an improved adaptation to their surroundings that would cast doubt on God's skills as a Creator as if he couldn't make a perfect fit all at once. That he didn't have to try was obvious because the fossils showed that in each period each animal was 'provided by its Author with such powers and habits, with such organs and constitutions as adapted it precisely to the condition of things in which it was to live'.[49] It was increased diversity and presence of 'higher' forms of life that counted as progression, not improved adaptation.[50]

The alternative explanation, known as transmutation or transformation, was heavily rejected. This view holds that the fossils are the antecessors of organisms now populating the earth, arisen by gradual change in morphology throughout time; it was extensively addressed in a work published anonymously in 1844.[51] Many critics unanimously believed that transmutation lacked any empirical support because there existed no forms intermediate between fossils and contemporary living organisms.[52]

---

49 Whewell, W. 1832. 'Art. IV.—Principles of Geology...By Charles Lyell... Vol. II. London. 1832' in: *The Quarterly Review, Volume XLVII*, Published in March & July, 1832. John Murray, London: 103-132 (117).
50 Rudwick, *Worlds before Adam*: 430-449. What is exactly meant by 'higher' apparently was clear without further explanation. Possibly, the adjective refers to a higher or lower position in the *Great Chain of Being*. This traditionally static concept had meanwhile acquired a more dynamic character. See Lovejoy, *The Great Chain of Being*: 242-287. Incidentally, the problem of how to classify organisms in terms of higher and lower remains problematic even now, see Shanahan, T. 2000. 'Evolutionary Progress?' in: *Bioscience* 50 (5): 451-459; Bailey, C. 2011. 'Kinds of Life: on the Phenomenological Basis of the Distinction between "Higher" and "Lower" Animals' in: *Environmental Philosophy* 8 (2): 47-68; Clough, D.L. 2012. *On Animals. Volume 1. Systematic Theology*. T&T Clark International, London: 51-64. For more details on the contemporary thoughts about the relationship between the successive faunas as revealed by paleontology, see Bowler, *Fossils and Progress*; Ospovat, D. 1978. 'Perfect Adaptation and Teleological Explanation: Approaches to the Problem of the History of Life in the Mid-nineteenth Century' in: *Studies in the History of Biology* (2): 33-56.
51 [Chambers, R.] 1844. *Vestiges of the Natural History of Creation*, John Churchill, London. Robert Chambers, a Scottish publisher and author wanted to remain anonymous for the controversial content of his book. Only in 1884, thirteen years after his death, was his identity as author revealed. See Secord, J.A. 2003. *Victorian Sensation. The Extraordinary Publication, Reception, and Secret Authorship of Vestiges of the Natural History of Creation*. The University of Chicago Press, Chicago: 525.
52 Lyell, C. 1832. *Principles of Geology, Being an Attempt to Explain the Former Changes of the Earth's Surface, by Reference to Causes Now in Operation. Volume the Second*. John Murray, London: 18-35; Lyons, S.L. 1993. 'Thomas Huxley: Fossils, Persistence, and the Argument from Design' in: *Journal of the History of Biology* 26 (3): 545-569; Rudwick, *Bursting the Limits of Time*: 589-591.

Still worse, it might imply that 'the human family may be (...) of many species, and all sprung from apes'.[53]

But whereas the doctrine of transmutation threatened God's attributes because it ignored the responsibility of the 'creative power which envelopes the Supreme Being'[54] for the emergence of new species, neither was the idea of successive creations without potential harm. As already mentioned above, this theory not only implied animal death on an unimaginable scale but also raised concerns about the Creator's skills. Why did he create only to destroy? Was he unsatisfied with the outcome of his work and was each new creation an attempt to ameliorate perceived defects in the antecedent one? These arguments prompted the author of the *Vestiges of the Natural History of the Creation* to prefer transmutation above catastrophism; the aforementioned argument that in each separate period the animals are perfectly adapted to their contemporary living environment apparently did not convince him.

In Chambers's view, the facts provided by geology and contemporary comparative anatomy provided evidence for transmutation. The idea of successive creations is unlikely given the presence of 'abortive or rudimentary organs'. They serve no purpose whatsoever and 'could be regarded in no other light than as blemishes or blunders'—an idea that is 'irreconcilable with that idea of Almighty Perfection which a general view of nature so irresistibly conveys'. But if, on the other hand, we assume that the different life forms evolve from each other, then, '(...) we see nothing in these abortive parts but harmless peculiarities of development, and interesting evidences of the manner in which the Divine Author has been pleased to work'.[55] Rudimentary organs—animal parts without any obvious function are incompatible with divine design, but become understandable when interpreted as remnants inherited from antecessors now extinct. A wise Creator cannot be supposed to saddle animals with useless parts.

The *Vestiges* evoked much consternation.[56] Now, not only divine providence manifesting itself in successive creative acts was questioned but also the ability of God as a wise designer was in danger. *Adam Sedgwick* (1785-1873)—Anglican clergyman and professor of geology at

---

53 Sedgwick, A. 1845. 'Vestiges of the Natural History of Creation ' in: *The Edinburgh Review or Critical Journal for July, 1845...October, 1845* 82: 1-85 (11).
54 Whewell, 'Art. IV.—Principles of Geology': 126.
55 Chambers, *Vestiges*: 198.
56 Gillispie, *Genesis and Geology*: 149-183; Secord, *Victorian Sensation*; Bowler, *Monkey Trials and Gorilla Sermons*: 55-78; Rudwick, *Worlds before Adam*: 546-548.

Cambridge[57]—took the lead in refuting these blasphemous thoughts.[58] 'Who is it that dares to tax the God of nature with blemishes and blunders?'[59] Mankind should know its place. 'We know little of what creation is: and by the light of Nature we know nothing of those inner movements of Almighty Will from which creation sprang. How little do we know of the great scheme of Nature!'[60] This thundering of Sedgwick did, however, not imply that the high age of the earth and the succession of animal species were contested issues. The stumbling block was the proposed continuity between the animal species presently alive and those extinct. Looking back to the period of the great reptiles, man could possibly count even a '*Patriarchosauros*' among his ancestors, so quipped William Whewell.[61]

Up to the end of the eighteenth century, animal suffering and death had been justified as a means to keep each species of animals within its allotted boundaries, thus ensuring the preservation of the kind. Obviously, data provided by geology in these first decades of the nineteenth century had deprived this argument of any persuasion. Now, one had to face a Creator who apparently did not care about the species, creating and destroying as it pleased him—intentionally wiping out animal species to replace them by others.[62] Furthermore, God's skills in creating—or an apparent lack of them—had become a matter of concern. All of this must have come as a shock to the pious mind! The question now is to what extent these developments influenced theorizing about the relationship between divine benevolence and animal suffering.

5.3. Method

In the following parts of this chapter I will investigate how authors approached the vicissitudes of animal life in relation to God's attributes for a period ranging from grandfather Erasmus Darwin to grandson Charles Darwin. Eighteen authors or groups of authors who addressed *animal death and predation as related to the attributes of God* could be

---

57 Brooke & Cantor, *Reconstructing Nature*: 268-274; Roberts, M.B. 2009. 'Adam Sedgwick (1785–1873): Geologist and Evangelical' in: *Geological Society, London, Special Publications* 310: 155-170.
58 Gillispie, *Genesis and Geology*: 147-183; Secord, *Victorian Sensation*: 231-247.
59 Sedgwick, 'Vestiges of the Natural History of Creation': 63.
60 Sedgwick, A. 1850. *A Discourse on the Studies of the University of Cambridge. The Fifth Edition, with Additions, and a Preliminary Dissertation.* John W. Parker, London: ccxli. Cf. Roberts, 'Adam Sedgwick': 158-161.
61 Whewell, 'Art. IV.—Principles of Geology': 117.
62 Black, 'The Hermeneutics of Extinction' in: Shaffer, *Comparative Criticism*: 147-170.

found for this period, either in secondary sources[63] or through references in texts by contemporary authors. During this period North American authors also entered the debate; hence a description of their thoughts is included. After examination of the sources, data thus collected will be discussed, and the chapter ends with a conclusion.

5.4. The Literary Sources
5.4.1. *Erasmus Darwin (1731-1802)*
Erasmus Darwin, the grandfather of Charles, was mentioned in passing in the previous chapter as the author who, at the end of the eighteenth century, introduced the 'slaughterhouse' metaphor when speaking about animal life. As most of his writings were published after the turn of the nineteenth century, including this member of the Darwin family among the authors examined in this chapter is justified, all the more because his groundbreaking and unorthodox views had their influence in this period.

Erasmus Darwin gained fame as scientist and inventor, a combination that earned him the qualification of 'a sort of British Da Vinci'.[64] His activities and professions encompassed, among others, medicine, botany, and zoology. Furthermore, he fathered nineteen children with three different women. Regarding Darwin's orthodoxy, scholars disagree, some calling him 'a theist who (…) fully accepted God as the creator of the universe', whereas others believe him to be a radical deist.[65]

Darwin unfolded his thoughts in three books. The first is his *Zoonomia*, followed by *Phytologia*, and by his posthumously published *Temple of Nature*.[66] Whether the 'mosaic history of Paradise and of Adam and Eve'

---

63 Greene, *Death of Adam*; Gillispie, *Genesis and Geology*; Glass, Temkin, Straus, *Forerunners of Darwin*; Livingstone, *Darwin's Forgotten Defenders*; Livingstone, Hart, Noll, *Evangelicals and Science in Historical Perspective*; Ury, *The Evolving Face of God as Creator*; Secor, *Victorian Sensation*; Thomson, *Before Darwin*; Rudwick, *Bursting the Limits of Time*; Rudwick, *Worlds before Adam*; Alexander & Numbers, *Biology and Ideology*.

64 Morillo, J. 2018. *The Rise of Animals and Descent of Man, 1660-1800. Toward Posthumanism in British Literature between Descartes and Darwin*. University of Delaware Press, Lanham: 155-203 (155). Cf. Porter, R. 2003. *Flesh in the Age of Reason. How the Enlightenment Transformed the Way We See Our Bodies and Souls*. Penguin Books, London: 374-388.

65 Quoted from Gillispie, *Genesis and Geology*: 33. Cf. Primer, I. 1964. 'Erasmus Darwin's Temple of Nature: Progress, Evolution, and the Eleusinian Mysteries' in: *Journal of the History of Ideas* 25 (1): 58-76; Fara, P. 2012. *Erasmus Darwin. Sex, Science, & Serendipity*. Oxford University Press, Oxford: 16-29, 60-61; Morillo, *Rise of Animals and Descent of Man*: 180, 188n15.

66 Darwin, E. 1794. *Zoonomia; or, the Laws of Organic Life. Volume I*. J. Johnson, London; Darwin, E. 1800. *Phytologia; or, the Philosophy of Agriculture and Gardening…* J. Johnson, London; Darwin, E. 1803. *The Temple of Nature or the Origin of Society…*J.

played a significant role in Darwin's thinking is doubtful; this may after all only be 'a sacred allegory, designed to teach obedience to divine commands, and to account for the origin of evil'.[67] It is uncertain to what extent these considerations were Darwin's own but the fact that he wrote these lines without any comment makes this at least likely, all the more when we look at his other writings on nature and creation.

In his *Phytologia*, we encounter a statement of the problem that is relevant for my study: 'Such is the condition of organic nature! whose first law might be expressed in the words, "Eat or be eaten!" and which would seem to be one great slaughter-house, one universal scene of rapacity and injustice!'[68] This problem cries out for a solution: 'Where shall we find a benevolent idea to console us amid so much apparent misery?' Such consolation is, however, available; we just have to face that nature strives to maximize happiness and to minimize miseries. Because old and feeble living beings are less capable to experience happiness, termination of their existence makes their 'organized matter' available for new and more vigorous organisms who do not yet have to contend with such a diminished capacity to enjoy their lives. The replacement of the old for the young and the weak for the strong ensures a reduction of suffering and an increase in pleasure. Furthermore, '(…) the aged and infirm, from their present state of inirratibility and insensibility, lose their lives with less pain, and which ceases instantly with the stroke of death'.[69]

This justification was extended to its limits (or maybe beyond) when we read how Darwin—pretending that this text was not his own but was added to his manuscript by an anonymous author—wrote that it consoled him to contemplate how the corpses of fallen soldiers could contribute to the lives of 'millions of microscopic animals, vegetables, and insects, and afterwards of quadrupeds and men; the sum of whose happiness is perhaps much greater than that of the harassed soldiers, by whose destruction they have gained their existence!'[70] The happiness of millions of microscopic animals far outweighs the misery of a few thousand fallen soldiers. In his *Temple of Nature*, Darwin expressed similar thoughts in poetry:

Johnson, London.
67 Darwin, 'Additional Notes. X. Eve from Adam's Rib' in: *Temple of Nature*: 42.
68 Darwin, *Phytologia*: 556.
69 Darwin, *Phytologia*: 557.
70 Darwin, *Phytologia*: 558. See comment on authorship in Morillo, *Rise of Animals and Descent of Man*: 163 and notes.

> Organic forms with chemic changes strive,
> Live but to die, and die but to revive!
> Immortal matter braves the transient storm,
> Mounts from the wreck, unchanging but in form.—[71]

Death is merely a metamorphosis, a notion we came across already in Chapter 4 with Charles Wesley (cf. § 4.6.11) and Thomas Amory (cf. § 4.6.12). Old and disabled living matter returns in blossoming youth.

> While Nature sinks in Time's destructive storms,
> The wrecks of Death are but a change of forms;
> Emerging matter from the grave returns,
> Feels new desires, with new sensations burns;
> With youth's first bloom a finer sense acquires,
> And Loves and Pleasures fan the rising fires.—
> Thus sainted Paul, 'O Death!' exulting cries,
> 'Where is thy sting? O Grave! thy victories?'[72]

Even the crust of the earth bears testimony to past happiness. '[A]ll the calcareous mountains [i.e., fossilized organic beings] (…) are MONUMENTS OF THE PAST FELICITY OF ORGANIZED NATURE!—AND CONSEQUENTLY OF THE BENEVOLENCE OF THE DEITY.'[73]

Darwin's ideas evoked outcries of horror and disgust. Humans only being a link in a chain of blinking and sinking—a temporary clustering of living matter destined to be raw material for new organisms in due time—was an indigestible idea. In the conservative political periodical *Anti-Jacobin Review and Magazine*,[74] a reviewer qualified the *Temple of Nature* as a work that denies 'any interference of a Deity in the Creation and preservation of every thing that exists, and an obstinate adherence to a system of materialism'. Its content is the more detestable because it 'degrade[s] the pretension of the patriot or the hero to a lasting fame in the memory of posterity, to the hope of breeding maggots like a dead

---

71 Darwin, *Temple of Nature*: 46 (Canto II: 41-44).
72 Darwin, *Temple of Nature*: 161 (Canto IV: 397-404). The quote in the final lines is from 1 Corinthians 15:55.
73 Darwin, *Phytologia*: 560. Similar thoughts are brought up in *Temple of Nature*: 165 (Canto IV: 447-450) and in *Zoonomia*: 509.
74 The *Anti-Jacobin Review and Magazine* was published from 1798-1821 and can be seen as a reaction to the ideals of the French Revolution. https://en.wikipedia.org/wiki/Anti-Jacobin_Review. Accessed on 14 December 2021.

dog'.⁷⁵ Darwin's ideas about universal happiness outweighing universal miseries could not find grace in the eyes of others either; in another contemporary journal, the reviewer told his readers to be 'full of horror'.⁷⁶ Others scoffed at Darwin's way of condoning animal suffering, poetically paraphrasing his note about soldiers killed in action. 'That when the Russians logger-headed, / Were kill'd by Frenchmen, ever dreaded, / Darwin rejoic'd the filthy creatures / Would serve for stock to make musquitoes.'⁷⁷ There is nothing to worry about when realizing that 'death is but a trivial thing, / Because a toadstool, or a king / Will, after death, be sure to rise / In bats and bed-bugs, fleas and flies'.⁷⁸

Until now, the metaphor of the balance between pain and pleasure had only been used to justify animal suffering; that the happiness of animals could compensate for human suffering was unheard of. By itself, the way Darwin explained animal suffering was not different from the thoughts prevalent in the previous century—animals' ailments served a greater good—but expanding this conviction to include humanity as well was a bridge too far for many. Justifying God's goodness is fine but not at any cost. The thoughts of the author to be discussed next received a much more favorable welcome.

5.4.2. William Paley (1743–1805)

After being educated in Cambridge, *William Paley* pursued a clerical career that took him ultimately to the position of archdeacon. In terms of authorship, he mainly published works devoted to apologetics. Among those, it was his book on natural theology that would make his name famous till the present day.⁷⁹ His 'watch analogy' became proverbial as evidence for divine design within nature.⁸⁰ 'It is only by the display of

---

75 Anonymous. 1803 'The Temple of Nature…By Erasmus Darwin…' in: *The Anti-Jacobin Review and Magazin*…16: 170-173 (172).
76 Anonymous. 1804. 'Art. X. The Temple of Nature…By Erasmus Darwin…' in: *British Critic* 23: 169-174 (174).
77 Caustic, C. 1803. *Terrible Tractoration!! A Poetical Petition against Galvanising Trumpery, and the Perkinistic Institution…Second Edition, with Great Additions*. T. Hurst and J. Ginger, London: 113-121 (114-115).
78 Caustic, *Terrible Tractoration*: 120.
79 Paley, W. 1802. *Natural Theology*. For Paley's impact, see Thomson, *Before Darwin*: 14-18; Topham, 'Biology in the Service of Natural Theology' in: Alexander & Numbers, *Biology and Ideology*: 88-113; McGrath, *Darwinism and the Divine*: 85-107.
80 Actually, Paley did not invent the 'watch analogy'. This metaphor was already used before by the Dutch philosopher Bernard Nieuwentijt, an author discussed in Chapter 4. Hence, contemporary authors accused Paley of plagiarism. McGrath acquits Paley from this charge, see McGrath, *Darwinism and the Divine*: 88-91.

contrivance, that the existence, the agency, the wisdom of the Deity, could be testified to his rational creatures.'[81]

For the purpose of our study, the chapter on 'the Goodness of the Deity' is the most important. Already in the first sentences, Paley made his point clear: '(…) in a vast plurality of instances in which contrivance is perceived, the design of the contrivance is *beneficial*.'[82] This view did not blind Paley to less agreeable aspects. He admitted that 'two cases which appear to me to have the most of difficulty in them, as forming the most of the appearance of exception to the representation here given, are those of *venomous* animals, and of animals *preying* upon one another.'[83] Nevertheless, Paley held to his conviction. Venomous bites and stings of animals were explained as beneficial, either for defense of the animal itself or as an act of mercy preventing prey animals to be swallowed alive.[84]

In clarifying why some animals devour others, Paley harked back to the explanations given in the previous century. 'Without [animal] death there could be no generation, no sexes, no parental relation, i. e. as things are constituted, no animal happiness.' Furthermore, without predation, the world would be filled 'with drooping, superannuated, half starved, helpless and unhelped animals.' Beasts of prey save the less fit animals such a miserable fate. Next, '(…) we have no reason to suppose, that their [the animals'] happiness is much molested by their fears. Their danger exists continually (…) but it is only when the attack is actually made upon them, that they appear to suffer from it.' As so often, attributing animals limited mental abilities offers a solution. 'To contemplate the insecurity of their condition with anxiety and dread, requires a degree of reflection, which (happily for themselves) they do not possess.'[85] Finally, one has to realize that 'there is no species of terrestrial animals whatever, which would not overrun the earth, if it were permitted to multiply in perfect safety (…). It is necessary, therefore, that the effects of such prolific faculties be curtailed.'[86] Predation is needed to maintain a harmonious creation in which no species of animals is allowed to push another into extinction.

Paley's thoughts thus summarized did not contain any consideration not yet already brought up by authors in previous centuries. Animal death from predation contributes to the benefit of the creation as this

---

81 Paley, *Natural Theology*: 29.
82 Paley, *Natural Theology*: 339.
83 Paley, *Natural Theology*: 348.
84 Paley, *Natural Theology*: 349.
85 Paley, *Natural Theology*: 351-352.
86 Paley, *Natural Theology*: 355.

prevents animals from prolonged suffering when they enter a stage of sickness or debility, it keeps each species within its allotted space, and limited mental capacities ensure that the enjoyments outweigh the mishaps. Plotinian and Stoic philosophy serve as they did before. But Paley had more in store.

After addressing the benefits of a design that includes predation, Paley introduced a second line of thoughts in which he attempts to demonstrate not only divine power and wisdom but goodness as well. A feeling of hunger would be enough to induce an animal to eat. 'Why add pleasure to the act of eating; sweetness and relish to food? Why a new and appropriate sense for the perception of the pleasure? Why should the juice of a peach applied to the palate, affect the part so differently from what it does when rubbed upon the palm of the hand?'[87] Not only divine power and wisdom but also divine benevolence are vindicated. '[T]he Deity has added pleasure to animal sensations beyond what was necessary for any other purpose; or when the purpose, so far as it was necessary, might have been effected by the operation of pain.' Therefore, 'we are authorized to ascribe to the Deity the character of benevolence.'[88]

Pain and death bear also witness to divine wisdom and power. 'Of *bodily* pain the principal observation, (…) is, that the annexing of pain to the means of destruction is a salutary provision: inasmuch as it teaches vigilance and caution; both gives notice of danger, and excites those endeavours which may be necessary to preservation.' And death, '(…) as a mode of removal and of succession, is so connected with the whole order of our animal world, that almost every thing in that world must be changed, to be able to do without it'. Animal death is not an issue to be concerned about. 'Brutes are in a great measure delivered from all anxiety on this account by the inferiority of their faculties; or rather they seem to be armed with the apprehension of death just sufficiently to put them upon the means of preservation, and no further.'[89] The animals have received sufficient mental abilities to strive to stay alive, but no more than that. A century earlier, William King (cf. § 4.6.4) wrote already something similar: 'An Animal in the present State of things, must therefore either, be obnoxious to these [pain] or quickly perish.'[90]

---

87 Paley, *Natural Theology*: 358. In this emphasis on superadded pleasure, Paley pays tribute to Thomas Balguy, an author addressed in Chapter 4, § 4.6.19, see Balguy, T. 1781. *Divine Benevolence Asserted, and Vindicated from the Objections of Ancient and Modern Sceptics*. Lockyer Davis, London: 30-31, 78.
88 Paley, *Natural Theology*: 363-364.
89 Paley, *Natural Theology*: 366-370.
90 King, W. 1731. *An Essay on the Origin of Evil. Translated from the Latin…With Some Account of the Origin of the Passions and Affections*. W. Thurlbourn, Cambridge: 115.

Paley's work was in general greatly applauded, but there were critical notes as well.[91] An anonymous reviewer wrote in the *Edinburgh Review or Critical Journal*[92] that 'found[ing] his [Paley's] reasoning for the *absolute* goodness of the Deity, upon the marks of beneficent contrivance, *in a great plurality of instances*' fell short 'since the infinite *malevolence* of the Deity might be inferred, in the same manner from the incalculably great number of beings who are occasionally subjected to suffering'.[93]

Other reviewers were more concerned about Paley's failure to observe Scripture. In the *Christian Observer*, a journal that served the evangelical branch within the Church of England,[94] the anonymous reviewer complained about neglecting the fact that 'the world is not now in the state in which it originally proceeded from the hand of the Creator, but that it is evidently in a state of degradation and ruin'.[95] In the same vein, another reviewer wrote in the *Evangelical Magazine*[96] to be 'not without fear, that some readers will sit down satisfied with natural theology, and dangerously conclude, that no other religion is necessary to their eternal salvation'.[97] The objections of these latter two reviewers related not so much to Paley's way of condoning animal suffering but rather to his lack of attention for Scripture. Natural theology in Paley's style with an emphasis on God's benevolence while at the same time neglecting the fact that we live in a corrupted world could obfuscate the message of sin and mercy.

This criticism did not inhibit Paley's thoughts from finding many followers, both among his contemporaries as well as long afterwards as history has shown. They prompted a less well-known author to write that '[t]he circumstance of animals preying upon each other (…) is, perhaps,

---

91 Fyfe, A. 1997. 'The Reception of William Paley's Natural Theology in the University of Cambridge' in: *The British Journal for the History of Science* 30: 321-335.
92 The *Edinburgh Review or Critical Journal* was published from 1802 to 1829, and was intended as an outlet for liberal views. Cf. Britannica, The Editors of Encyclopaedia. "The Edinburgh Review, or The Critical Journal". *Encyclopedia Britannica*, 7 August 2019, https://www.britannica.com/topic/The-Edinburgh-Review-or-The-Critical-Journal. Accessed on 14 December 2021.
93 Anonymous. 1806. 'Art. III. Natural Theology…By William Paley…' in: *The Edinburgh Review or Critical Journal for Oct. 1802…Jan. 1803, Fifth Edition*: I: 287-305 (304).
94 See https://en.wikipedia.org/wiki/Christian_Observer. Accessed on 14 December 2021.
95 Anonymous. 1803. 'XCVIII. Paley's Natural Theology' in: *The Christian Observer… Volume II. From First of January, to Thirty-First of December, 1803*: 369-374 (373).
96 A monthly journal for Christians committed to Calvinism, both inside and outside the Church of England, published from 1793 to 1904. https://en.wikipedia.org/wiki/Evangelical_Magazine. Accessed on 14 December 2021.
97 Anonymous. 1803. 'Natural Theology…By William Paley, D.D.' in: *The Evangelical Magazine for the Year 1803* XI: 494-495 (495).

one of the most striking instances of the divine *goodness*. For, by these means, certain sensitive beings are furnished with temporary enjoyments which could not have existed without this economy', adding that '[t]hose who wish to see the proofs of the *divine goodness*, from the view of nature, exhibited in greater detail, may consult Payley [sic], and other writers, on Natural Religion.'[98] However, dissidents also remained. Thomas Gisborne, the author to be discussed next, was one of them.

5.4.3. *Thomas Gisborne (1758-1846)*

Thomas Gisborne, Anglican priest and poet, graduated from St. John's College in Cambridge. Within the Church of England, he belonged to the Clapham Sect, whose members aimed at social reform including the abolition of slavery.[99] Thoughts that are relevant to my study are found in his *Testimony of Natural Theology to Christianity*.[100]

Gisborne criticized Paley for ignoring that the earth 'cannot be supposed to have originally proceeded thus from the forming hand of its Creator'.[101] Because of humanity's sin, the book of nature contains pages with dark colors as well. This also concerns the suffering of the animals. 'It was not until the nature of animals and the state of the earth on which they were to dwell, were altered in consequence of human transgression, that life was taken away, or that blood was shed, by any living existence for food.'[102]

Gisborne was aware of the fact that not everybody will share this view. After all, why should guiltless animals also suffer from evil. He recognizes the problem. '[A]nimals are incapable of moral agency; and consequently, are not placed under moral responsibility', but, so continues Gisborne, 'They suffered as under human governments individuals are frequently involved in the participation of national calamity, to the introduction of which they had not knowingly contributed'.[103] Furthermore, 'God can in any case give compensation, superabundant compensation, antecedently to the suffering which it is to counterbalance. (...) To vindicate the justice and the benignity of God towards any one of His creatures, this fact alone

---

98 Brown, W.L. 1816. *An Essay on the Existence of a Supreme Creator...and Deducing from the Whole Subject, the Most Important Practical Inferences. Vol. I.* T. Hamilton et al., London: 235, 237.
99 For biographical details, see https://en.wikipedia.org/wiki/Thomas_Gisborne. Accessed on 14 December 2021.
100 Gisborne, T. 1818. *The Testimony of Natural Theology to Christianity*. M. Thomas, Philadelphia.
101 Gisborne, *Testimony*: 7.
102 Gisborne, *Testimony*: 142.
103 Gisborne, *Testimony*: 122.

can be requisite; that the being of that creature, whenever or in whatever manner terminated, shall have been to it on the whole a blessing.'[104]

Gisborne employed the happiness-versus-misery balance to reconcile the vicissitudes of animal life with divine justice. God's justice warrants that the outcome of this balance will be positive, thus compensating animals during their life for the adverse effects of the fall. There is no prospect for a remuneration in a blessed afterlife; that is not necessary because the compensation is given 'antecedently to the suffering which it is to counterbalance'.

At a first glance, Gisborne's thoughts are similar to those of Hartley and Bruckner, authors addressed in the previous chapter. There is however one major difference; Hartley and Bruckner considered the positive outcome of a happiness-versus-misery balance necessary for compensating any animal suffering that is required for the greater good. For Gisborne, on the contrary, this positive outcome is necessary to remunerate innocent bystanders for the miseries they suffer because of Adam's transgression. For Hartley and Bruckner, divine power and wisdom were at stake; for Gisborne, divine justice had to be vindicated.

Gisborne's orthodoxy also determined how data provided by contemporary science should be interpreted. 'On the authority of certain writers on geology it may be alleged, that the present earth was constructed from the materials of a former globe; and that the shells and other organic remains imbedded in our existing strata belonged to animals inhabiting that globe.' Gisborne considered this hypothesis 'gratuitous and unnecessary'.[105] The presence of fossils may well be a consequence of the deluge, and, moreover, it cannot be excluded that animals that we now think are extinct still exist in remote areas of the earth[106]—a view that was more widely held at that time, as I discussed in the previous chapter.

5.4.4. Alexander Crombie (1760-1842)
Whereas Gisborne criticized Paley for ignoring Scripture, *Alexander Crombie* disagreed for other reasons. This Scottish Presbyterian minister who would leave his clerical office to become a schoolmaster later in his life wrote a two volumes *Natural Theology*[107]—a book recommended as a

---

104 Gisborne, *Testimony*: 123-124.
105 Gisborne, *Testimony*: 28.
106 Gisborne, *Testimony*: 28-33.
107 Crombie, A. 1829. *Natural Theology; or Essays on the Existence of Deity and of Providence, on the Immateriality of the Soul, and a Future State. In Two Volumes*. R. Hunter and T. Hookham, London.

'clear and judicious one'[108] by the North American philosopher James McCosh to whom I will return in the next chapter. Crombie's aim was to 'contribute towards the prevention or correction of an evil which would extirpate religion, virtue, and human happiness' and to 'confirm those, who acknowledge no other guide, than the light of nature, in their Belief of Deity, Providence, and a Future state'.[109]

Crombie acknowledged that there is a paradox. 'Is the evil, which man, and the inferior creation are doomed to bear, reconcileable with the hypothesis of the infinite power, the infinite wisdom, and the infinite goodness of their Maker?'[110] The problem thus defined, Crombie continued by surveying the arguments to vindicate the divine attributes hitherto, but only to find them inconclusive. Could evils that are considered incidental—teeth formed to masticate, and not to ache—not have been foreseen and prevented? And why should a minor evil be needed for the production of a greater good? Could the intended aim not have been attained anyhow? And those who maintain that suffering from disasters and griefs 'furnish exercise for the most exalted virtues' should realize that this does not apply to 'the numerous evils, which the inferior creation suffer'. Others refer to universal laws that may have unpleasant consequences. But could he who makes those laws not have been 'capable of ordaining laws, which shall be universally productive of good'?[111] All the arguments put forward do not do justice to the divine omnipotence. Hence, Paley's explanation of evil as the result of 'defects in contrivance'—not intended but inseparable from the main purpose[112]—fails. 'A defect in contrivance, as imputed to unlimited intelligence' is an absurdity. Crombie did not lack words for his disapproval: 'How monstrous the notion, that there can be a defect of wisdom in a Being, the fountain of all knowledge, and whose all-seeing eye no cause, no effect, can possibly escape, and whose power nothing created can control!'[113] For a solution, we have to look elsewhere, to the philosophical system of the *Great Chain of Being*.

According to Crombie, a universe in which each being has been allotted the highest possible happiness would be no universe at all because such a world would only comprise beings like God himself, which obviously is absurd. There is gradation, and that implies that there should

---

108 McCosh, J. 1875. *The Scottish Philosophy. Biographical, Expository, Critical from Hutcheson to Hamilton*. MacMillan and Co., London: 266. For biographical details of Crombie, see pp. 265-266.
109 Crombie, *Natural Theology* I: vii.
110 Crombie, *Natural Theology* II: 199.
111 Crombie, *Natural Theology* II: 201-202.
112 Paley, *Natural Theology*: 347.
113 Crombie, *Natural Theology* II: 210-211.

be different levels of enjoyment as well. If there were no different levels of enjoyment, God could not augment those enjoyments which would put limits on his omnipotence. Furthermore, '(...) if we had no conception of greater or less happiness, no experience of evil, we should have no feeling, no notion of benevolence'.[114] It appears that for Crombie, the mixture of good and evil serves humanity's moral improvement. And when asked why that purpose could not be reached otherwise, the Presbyterian minister answered that we should submit, '(...) with due humility, our weak reason to the counsels of Eternal and Unerring wisdom'. The faithful will 'regard every evil as an ordination for good, and ultimately to issue in higher enjoyment'.[115] A similar attitude towards God's way of acting with his creation can be found with another Scottish Presbyterian, Thomas Chalmers.

5.4.5. Thomas Chalmers (1780–1847)

The Scottish theologian and Presbyterian minister *Thomas Chalmers* played a major role in church politics. He was one of the founders of the Free Church of Scotland, a denomination born out of a schism within the Church of Scotland.[116] Its members were—at least by some contemporaries—dismissed as an 'obstructing group of ignorant zealots'.[117] Next to church politics, natural theology was also one of his subjects of interest.[118]

Several of his works are relevant for my study. The first of these, *Remarks on Cuvier's Theory of the Earth*[119]—written in 1814 and reprinted in 1848—addressed the implications of geology for Scripture. In this booklet, Chalmers promoted the so-called *gap theory*. The first part of

---

114 Crombie, *Natural Theology* II: 220.
115 Crombie, *Natural Theology* II: 248-249.
116 The conflict that is known as 'The Great Disruption' concerned among others the right of a congregation to choose its own minister without interference by the local nobility. See for more details https://www.scotland.org.uk/history/disruption. Accessed on 14 December 2021.
117 For biographical details, see Britannica, The Editors of Encyclopaedia. "Thomas Chalmers". *Encyclopedia Britannica*, 26 May 2021, https://www.britannica.com/biography/Thomas-Chalmers. Accessed on 14 December 2021. Disqualifying note is quoted from Secord, *Victorian Sensation*: 85.
118 Livingstone, *Darwin's Forgotten Defenders*: 7-9; Topham, 'Science, Natural Theology and Evangelicalism in Early Nineteenth-Century Scotland' in: Livingstone, Hart, Noll, *Evangelicals and Science in Historical Perspective*: 142-174.
119 Chalmers, T. [1814]. 'Remarks on Cuvier's Theory of the Earth; in Extracts from a Review of that Theory Which Was Contributed to "the Christian Instructor" in 1814.' in: Chalmers, T. 1848. *Tracts and Essays Religious and Economical*. Thomas Constable, Edinburgh: 347-372.

Genesis 1:1 refers to ages of unknown length that allow the periods of time suggested by the geological data; Scripture summarizes these past ages and almost immediately proceeds with describing how God resumed to create when the final of those 'geological revolutions' had changed the earth into a formless void covered with darkness.[120]

Similar notes were made in a book published a few years later. '[D]oes he [Moses] ever say, that there was not an interval of many ages betwixt the first act of creation, described in the first verse of the book of Genesis, and said to have been performed at the *beginning*; and those more detailed operations, the account of which commences at the second verse (...)?'[121] Chalmers concentrated on the problem of time when reconciling data from geology and Scripture.[122] Questions that may arise when finding fossilized animals long before the appearance of humanity in the geological strata are answered by assuming successive acts of creation to replace extinct genera by new ones.[123] Apparently, Chalmers took animal death for granted and not in any way associated with the sins of the first pair of humans.

> When we look to the animal creation, we behold an endless diversity there between the various species, in respect both of their capacities for enjoyment, and of the disabilities, nay the pains and sufferings to which they are subjected by the very nature which God hath bestowed on them. It is not for men to complain that they are not angels, any more than it is for reptiles to complain that they are not creatures of a better and nobler existence than themselves. We can give no absolute vindication of these things, any more than we can of men being formed in the likeness of their fallen parent, instead of being formed in his likeness when unfallen.[124]

Just as it is a mystery why Adam's fall is imputed to us, so is the way God deals with the animals; both elude all vindication. Some—including Paley, whom Chalmers mentioned by name—may 'attempt to strike a sort of arithmetical balance between the good and ill of our world' and assume that a surplus of happiness would justify suffering. Chalmers did

---

120 Chalmers, 'Remarks': 370.
121 Chalmers, T. 1817. *The Evidence and Authority of the Christian Revelation.* Anthony Finley, Philadelphia: 174.
122 The *gap theory* may reconcile geology and Scripture regarding the chronology but does not solve the problem why God allows that animals die and species go extinct—both in the presumed previous creations now destroyed as well as in the current one.
123 Chalmers, T. *Posthumous Works of the Rev. Thomas Chalmers. Volume VII.* Edited by the Rev. William Hanna. 1849. Harper & Brothers, New York: 102-106.
124 Chalmers, *Posthumous Works*: 487.

not agree with this. 'We should imagine it exceedingly difficult, nay impracticable, to form aught like a precise estimate, first of the felicities, and then of the distresses of life; and then to take the summation of each so as to come at the difference betwixt them.'[125]

In his contribution to the *Bridgewater Treatises,* a book series 'on the Power, Wisdom, and Goodness of God, as Manifested in the Creation',[126] Chalmers addressed the divine attributes by pointing to the efficiency of design—craftsmanship, as it were—and not so much with the aim to vindicate divine benevolence. It seems that for Chalmers, divine design is morally neutral. Teeth may serve to inflict damage as well as to process food and a dentition fitted for its purpose is a proof of divine power and wisdom anyhow, regardless of its use and the serpent's properties and behavior are proof of divine design, not the outcome of a disastrous event in a remote past.[127] Seen in this way, an old earth with mortality in the non-human animal kingdom long before the human race appeared on the scene will not be a problem either.

A later document, however, showed that Chalmers was not entirely satisfied with his solution thus provided. In his *On Natural Theology*, he held that 'the mental phenomena speak more distinctly and decisively for the character of God than do the material phenomena of creation'.[128] God's attributes are not so much reflected in the events in the natural world as by the processes these events elicit in the human mind. The fact that exposure to another's sufferings drives us to compassion is clear evidence of God's benevolence; it could also have left us unconcerned. It appears that Chalmers goes back—probably without being aware of this—to the thoughts of Aquinas who also saw a benefit in animal suffering as a learning tool to develop our ability to pity (cf. § 2.3.2.2). His contemporary and fellow Presbyterian Alexander Crombie had uttered similar thoughts as I have shown above.

---

125 Chalmers, *Posthumous Works*: 126.
126 The *Bridgewater Treatises* were funded from a generous legacy left by the eighth Earl of Bridgewater, Francis Henry Egerton (1756-1829). Their contents played a major role in the position of natural theology throughout the thirties and subsequent decades of the nineteenth century. See Robson, J.M. 'The Fiat and Finger of God: the Bridgewater Treatises' in: Helmstadter & Lightman, *Victorian Faith in Crisis*: 71-125; Topham, J. 1992. 'Science and Popular Education in the 1830s: the Role of the "Bridgewater Treatises"' in: *The British Journal for the History of Science* 25 (4): 397-430; McGrath, *Darwinism and the Divine*: 119-126.
127 Chalmers, T. 1835. *The Bridgewater Treatises …Treatise I. On the Adaptation of External Nature, to the Moral and Intellectual Constitution of Man.* Carey et al., Philadelphia: 31.
128 Chalmers, T. 1840. *The Works of Thomas Chalmers. Volume First. On Natural Theology.* Robert Carter, New York: 289-292 (291).

5.4.6. William Buckland (1784–1856)

William Buckland was Oxford University's first reader in geology.[129] He is considered the main British proponent of catastrophism, the theory that explains the geological data by assuming that the earth's crust and surface have been shaped by successive catastrophic events over a long period of time. In this sense, he was a faithful follower of the ideas of Cuvier (cf. § 5.2.2).[130]

The first text to be examined is Buckland's inaugural lecture (1820), delivered with the aim to 'shew that the study of geology has a tendency to confirm the evidences of natural religion and that the facts developed by it are consistent with the accounts of the creation and deluge recorded in the Mosaic writings'.[131] Buckland referred to the treasures to be mined from the earth. These are 'the wreck and ruins of disturbances that affected our planet long before the existence of the human race', from which we can 'trace the finger of an Omnipotent Architect providing for the daily wants of its rational inhabitants [humans], not only at the moment in which he laid the first foundations of the earth, but also through the long series of shocks and destructive convulsions which he has caused subsequently to pass over it'.[132] Long before people roamed the globe, God began to provide for their needs. At first glance, this may collide with the Mosaic record, but that is only an appearance when we realize that 'though Moses confines the detail of his history to the preparation of this globe for the reception of the human race, he does not deny the prior existence of another system of things'.[133]

In this inaugural lecture, Buckland discussed the discrepancies between the Genesis text and the geological data with only brief remarks on the existence of successive animal kingdoms, conceiving these as admirable proofs of divine 'design and intelligence'.[134] This subject was more extensively addressed in his contribution to the *Bridgewater Treatises*

---

129 Greene, M.T. 'Genesis and Geology Revisited: the Order of Nature and the Nature of Order in Nineteenth-Century Britain' in: Lindberg, D.C., Numbers, R.L. (eds). 2003. *When Science & Christianity Meet*. The University of Chicago Press, Chicago: 139-159; Rudwick, *Bursting the Limits of Time*: 600-602.
130 Gillispie, *Genesis and Geology*: 98-120; McGrath, *Darwinism and the Divine*: 110-111; Thomson, *Before Darwin*: 191-193; Topham, 'Biology in the Service of Natural Theology' in: Alexander & Numbers, *Biology and Ideology*: 88-113.
131 Buckland, W. 1820. *Vindiciae Geologicae; or the Connexion of Geology with Religion*... Oxford University Press, Oxford: letter of dedication, page not numbered.
132 Buckland, *Vindiciae*: 12.
133 Buckland, *Vindiciae*: 24. From the context, it may be inferred that in speaking of 'things', Buckland includes anything created, both alive and lifeless.
134 Buckland, *Vindiciae*: 18.

(1836).¹³⁵ 'The myriads of petrified Remains which are disclosed by the researches of Geology all tend to prove, that our Planet has been occupied in times preceding the Creation of the Human Race, by extinct species of Animals and Vegetables, made up, like living Organic Bodies, of "Clusters of Contrivances," which demonstrate the exercise of stupendous Intelligence and Power.'¹³⁶ The physico-theological argument of design not only serves to demonstrate God and his attributes as exemplified in the present but in the past as well. Paleontological data that could be explained by assuming repeated acts of creation provided effective arguments to refute the deist conception of a clockwork universe governed by natural laws, the legislator remaining idle after having finished his initial activities.

In explaining animal death, Buckland employed the same arguments as forwarded in the previous century. 'Thus the great drama of universal life is perpetually sustained; and though the individual actors undergo continual change, the same parts are ever filled by another and another generation; renewing the face of the earth, and the bosom of the deep, with endless successions of life and happiness.'¹³⁷ But how about pre-Adamite death and suffering? This issue was left unmentioned thus far, but it was discussed in Buckland's last text to be addressed, a sermon delivered for an academic audience, possibly in reply to the objections of a group of authors to whose thoughts I will return shortly.¹³⁸ His aim is clear: '(…) the hope of shewing the unfounded nature of an opinion entertained by many persons, that death was inflicted on the entire animal creation, as a penal dispensation consequent upon the sin of the parents of the human race'. Clarifying notes on this topic are urgently needed. 'It has not unfrequently been proposed to me, as a theological objection to the credibility of the great amount of death, which Geology shows to have prevailed among extinct races that formerly inhabited our earth, that such phenomena are irreconcileable with the idea, *supposed* to be derived from Scripture, that no animals would ever have died, had it not been for the Fall of Man.'¹³⁹

In this sermon, Buckland expounded his view that death, '(…) though most clearly inflicted as a punishment *on man*, it is by no inspired writer

---

135 Buckland, W. 1836. *The Bridgewater Treatises…Treatise VI. Geology and Mineralogy …In Two Volumes*. William Pickering, London.
136 Buckland, *Geology and Mineralogy* I: viii.
137 Buckland, *Geology and Mineralogy* I: 134.
138 Buckland, W. 1839. *An Inquiry whether the Sentence of Death Pronounced at the Fall of Man Included the Whole Animal Creation or Was Restricted to the Human Race…* John Murray, London.
139 Buckland, *Inquiry*: v.

spoken of as a penal dispensation to any other living creature excepting Adam and his posterity'. Therefore, '(…) the brute creation death is in no way connected with the moral misconduct of the human race, and that whether Adam had, or had not, ever transgressed, a termination by death is, and always has been, the condition on which life was given to every individual'.[140]

After this introduction, Buckland continued by addressing the scriptural passages that seem to indicate otherwise. Referring to Romans 5 and 1 Corinthians 15, Buckland emphasized that these biblical verses speak about the death of humans as opposed to the life that comes from the sacrifice of Christ. In the same way, the words written by Paul in Romans 8 about the groaning of creation only relate to the fate and prospect of humanity and are not to be applied to the non-human animal kingdom.[141] 'It is', so continued Buckland, 'apparent from this brief review, that (…) we are free to adopt (…) the dispensation of death throughout all the inferior races of God's creatures, as a matter which Scripture does not teach us to associate in any way with the consequences of the fall of our first parents from Paradise.'[142] Neither do some passages from the prophet Isaiah as these apply 'only *prospectively* to things that should arrive at a *future* period, under a future dispensation; and is affirmative of nothing respecting *past* events'.[143]

Geology not only provided signs of God's power, wisdom, and goodness in eras now bygone but also served more elevated purposes; the same author who had welcomed the liberation of geology from its theological chains (cf. § 5.2.2) advocated that geology even might offer spiritual lessons as 'among the prostrate relics of a once breathing world, he [humanity] reads the lesson of his own mortality; and in the new forms of being which have marked the commencement of every succeeding cycle, he recognises the life-giving hand by which the elements of his own mouldered frame are to be purified and recombined'.[144] In this panegyric to the cycle of life and death, this anonymous reviewer joined— probably unconsciously—Charles Wesley and Erasmus Darwin, who had propagated a similar view (cf. § 4.6.11 and § 5.4.1). Decomposing bodies are a precious raw material for creating new life. In Buckland's view, death

---

140 Buckland, *Inquiry*: 12.
141 Buckland, *Inquiry*: 16-17. Buckland referred to Romans 5:12 and 17–18, 1 Corinthians 15:21, and Romans 8:22.
142 Buckland, *Inquiry*: 17.
143 Buckland, *Inquiry*: 27. Buckland referred to Isaiah 11:6–8 and 65:25.
144 Anonymous. 1837. 'Art. I.—Geology and Mineralogy Considered with Reference to Natural Theology. By the Rev. William Buckland' in: *The Edinburgh Review or Critical Journal for April,…July, 1837* 65: 1-39 (39).

and predation were no instruments for punishment but required for the benefit of the universe, both now and in past times. Creation glorifies its Creator. The author to be discussed next agreed.

5.4.7. Charles Bell (1774–1842)

Charles Bell, born the son of a clergyman of the Episcopal Church of Scotland, was a famous anatomist who spent his life in the academy, teaching and practicing medicine. In medical circles, his name has survived for his description of the affliction of the facial nerve[145] that bears his name as eponym: Bell's palsy. His commitment to the Christian faith is shown from letters he wrote in which he confessed a reverence for both the Creator and his creation.[146] His contribution to the *Bridgewater Treatises* breathes the same tenor as Buckland's.

Bell accepted the data provided by geology without any comment. 'The most obvious appearances and the labours of the geologist give us reason to believe that the earth has not always been in the state in which it is now presented to us.'[147] But this does not mean that the way in which animals interacted in past ages is also different from the present as we may suppose that, just as in the present time, every creature faced natural enemies, suffered from lack of food and from disease, and that the equilibrium as it exists today also existed in the past.[148] Predation is required for a healthy balance, as are animal pain and death. After all, 'Pain, whilst it is a necessary contrast to its opposite pleasure, is the great safeguard of the frame.'[149] I assume that his medical work had convinced Bell of the grave consequences of insensitivity to pain.

Bell agreed in his considerations with thoughts that are well-known from the majority of philosophers from the previous centuries (cf. Chapters 3 and 4), but he also honored the new data provided by geology. The Plotinian notion that individual mishaps may serve the good of the whole, justifies animal miseries both now and in eras past.

After this conclusion, Bell could have stopped, but this is not what he did. He is also confronting the other—new—threat that geology poses to divine attributes that I spoke about in the introduction. Why did God choose to create successive worlds instead of finishing the complete work at once? Was he learning by so doing? Bell rejected this idea emphatically.

---

145 The facial nerve is the nerve that innervates the muscles of the face.
146 Spector, B. 1942. 'Sir Charles Bell and the Bridgewater Treatises' in: *Bulletin of the History of Medicine* 12: 314-322.
147 Bell, C. 1836. *The Bridgewater Treatises…Treatise IV. The Hand, Its Mechanism and Vital Endowment as Evincing Design.* Carey et al., Philadelphia: 111.
148 Bell, *The Hand*: 27.
149 Bell, *The Hand*: 2.

When we acknowledge that animals have been created in succession and with an increasing complexity of parts, we are not to be understood as admitting that there is here proof of a growing maturity of power, or an increasing effort in the Creator; (…) It is not (…) a greater power that we see in operation, but a power manifesting itself in the perfect and successive adaptation of one thing to another—or vitality and organization to inorganic matter. (…) There is extreme grandeur in the thought of an anticipating or prospective intelligence: in reflecting that what was finally accomplished in man, was begun in times incalculably remote, and antecedent to the great revolutions which the earth's surface has undergone.[150]

Successive creations are not due to an increase of the Creator's intelligence or power but the revelation of an intended design in which there is *grandeur*. Could it be that Bell's lines inspired Charles Darwin when he wrote the concluding sentences of his *Origin*: 'There is *grandeur* in this view of life'?[151]

5.4.8. Peter Mark Roget (1779-1869)

Peter Mark Roget, the son of a Swiss clergyman, practiced both medicine and philology. As a medical professional, he was involved in founding the medical school at Manchester. His *Thesaurus of English Words and Phrases*, still popular in modern editions, is the lasting fruit of his second occupation.[152] His scientific track record, which included the office of the Royal Society's Secretary, brought him the honor to be invited as one of the *Bridgewater Treatise* authors.[153] Similar to the other contributors, animal life was one of the subjects he addressed, which justifies his inclusion in the present study.

When considering animal predation, Roget started with remarking that '[o]n first contemplating this extensive destruction of animal life, by modes the most cruel and revolting to all our feelings, we naturally recoil with horror from the sanguinary scene; and cannot refrain from asking how all this is consistent with the wisdom and benevolence so conspicuously manifested in all other parts of the creation'. Many have

---

150 Bell, *The Hand*: 111-112.
151 Darwin, C. 2009 [1859]. *On the Origin of Species by Means of Natural Selection, or the Preservation of Favoured Races in the Struggle for Life*. Reprint of the first edition, edited with an Introduction by William Bynum. Penguin Books, London: 427 [italics mine].
152 For biographical details see Desmond, *Politics of Evolution*: 222-235, 427.
153 Brock, W.H. 1966. 'The Selection of the Authors of the Bridgewater Treatises' in: *Notes and Records of the Royal Society of London* 21 (2): 162-179.

already puzzled over this. 'The best theologians have been obliged to confess that a difficulty does here exist, and that the only plausible solution which it admits of, is to consider the pain and suffering thus created, as one of the necessary consequences of those general laws which secure, on the whole, the greatest and most permanent good.'[154]

For Roget, this line of reasoning was acceptable. After all, a design that makes one animal to serve for the sustenance of another warrants animal activity and the pleasure connected.[155] Without the activities connected with preying or escaping predation, animals' enjoyments would have been less. In the same way, pain is a precious gift and not to be despised 'for, had this property been omitted, the animal system would have been but of short duration, exposed, as it must necessarily be, to perpetual casualties of every kind'.[156] Furthermore, without the capacity to feel pain, there is no capacity to have pleasure either. Predation as well as pain both are proofs of design and divine benevolence as they serve to increase the enjoyments the animals experience. Nowhere, any threat or blemish for God is perceived in the way he creates and sustains. The enjoyments outweigh the miseries.

5.4.9. William Prout (1785-1850)

William Prout, son of a farmer, devoted his professional career to medicine. Furthermore, he earned laurels from his investigations on the chemistry of body fluids,[157] and therefore, the choice for Prout to deal with chemistry in the *Bridgewater Treatise* volumes was obvious.[158]

Prout, however, not only wrote about chemistry but also about meteorology, and this may explain the specific color of his contribution to the discussion about the relationship between the fate of animals and divine benevolence and other attributes. Without predation, the balance between the animal species would be lost, but God has ordained the means to prevent this, thereby taking everything into account. 'While in temperate climates we have cats and spiders, designed as checks on over productiveness (…) [in] the Tropics, the same wise purpose is executed

---

154 Roget, P.M. 1836. *The Bridgewater Treatises…Treatise V. Animal and Vegetable Physiology…In Two Volumes. Volume II*. Carey et al., Philadelphia: 53-54.
155 Roget, *Animal and Vegetable Physiology* II: 54.
156 Roget, *Animal and Vegetable Physiology* II: 262.
157 For biographical details, see Britannica, The Editors of Encyclopaedia. "William Prout". *Encyclopedia Britannica*, 5 April 2021, https://www.britannica.com/biography/William-Prout. Accessed on 14 December 2021. Prout also stood at the cradle of the periodic table of elements, see Brink, G. van den. 2004. *Een Publieke Zaak. Theologie tussen Geloof en Wetenschap*. Boekencentrum, Zoetermeer: 85-86.
158 Brock, 'The Selection of the Authors of the Bridgewater Treatises': 168-169.

by the Tiger and by the Rattlesnake.'[159] Design is apparent, not only from predation itself but also in the accommodation of the size and fierceness of the predators to the different climates on the globe. Requirements to keep a balance between birth and decay in areas where life is exuberant differ from those in which life is less intense.

After this description of the bare facts and their interpretation as evidence of design by a wise and powerful Deity, Prout nevertheless was still left with the question why the world is as it is. 'Such questions, the Great Author of the universe alone can answer.' But this did not alter the fact that Prout was convinced that 'within those narrow limits by which our observations are bounded, wherever we can trace His designs, we see that His works are never without an object'. From this, it follows that 'we cannot doubt that in determining their [the earth's inhabitants'] perpetual change, there is no less an object; though it be above our comprehension'. This is where Prout halted. '[T]o speculate further on points so utterly beyond our capacity, would be presumptuous: for who can "know the mind of God, or who hath been His counsellor?"'[160] We have to trust that God knows what he does and that none of his deeds are without purpose. Sometimes, we can guess what he intends but more often not.

For Prout, death and predation among animals were no threat to God's attributes. 'Animals have not only been destined to prey on each other; but all created beings are the food of those progressively higher than themselves.'[161] The possibility that animals suffer was completely ignored, let alone the need for any compensation for this. And in agreement with the other authors of the *Bridgewater Treatises* discussed thus far, there are no references to Adam and his fall as an explanation for predation. Neither did Prout contest the contemporary findings of geology. 'The world itself (…) appears to have been, at intervals, subjected to changes involving even the fundamental laws by which it is governed.'[162] The author to be discussed next, however, thought otherwise, both about Scripture and science.

5.4.10. William Kirby (1759-1850)
As with many contemporaries, *William Kirby* combined the duties of an Anglican clergyman with studying nature. The latter activity brought him

---

159 Prout, W. 1834. *The Bridgewater Treatises…Treatise VIII. Chemistry Meteorology and the Function of Digestion…*William Pickering, London: 392.
160 Prout, *Chemistry*: 542-543. Probably, Prout cited Romans 11:34.
161 Prout, *Chemistry*: 538.
162 Prout, *Chemistry*: 541.

wide recognition as a pioneer in the study of insects,[163] but this fame did not protect him from being accused of 'quaint fundamentalism' as well.[164] Possibly, the reason for this contemptuous characterization was Kirby's conviction that Scripture should be taken literally; in this, he differed from the more commonly held belief that the biblical text should be interpreted in view of the data provided by contemporary science.

Kirby disagreed. For him, the ideas of the geologists that 'the Saurians were the mighty masters, as well as monsters, of the primeval animal kingdom, and the lords of the creation before the existence of the human race (…) cannot be reconciled with the account of the creation of animals as given in the first chapter of Genesis'.[165] Neither can the hypothesis that there were carnivorous animals before humanity had transgressed. 'Had Adam not fallen, this sad change [i.e., the emergence of carnivores] would, probably, never have taken place.'[166]

Because of humanity's violation of the divine command, 'Divine Providence (…) did not leave all things to the action of the original laws which had received his awful sanction before the fall, but altered those by which this system, especially our own globe, was guided and governed before that fatal event, to suit them to what had taken place, and to the altered and deteriorated moral state of man'.[167]

In his mercy, God took the measures that, given the new situation, were necessary for general well-being. Predation became needed 'to balance the respective numbers of the different kinds of animals, from the invisible monad to the gigantic whale, that a certain proportion may be preserved, with regard to their numbers, between them, so that each may be in sufficient force to accomplish the end for which it was created'.[168] But even in this corrupted stage, creation glorifies its Creator, '(…) combining into harmony almost universal discord, and out of seeming death and destruction bringing forth life and health and universal joy!'[169]

From this point of view, the reproduction method of the Ichneumon wasp that would become proverbial for cruelty in nature after Darwin was no problem for Kirby either. 'The active Ichneumon braves every

---

163 For biographical details, see Bettany, G.T. 'Kirby, William' in: *Dictionary of National Biography, 1885-1900, Volume 31.*
164 Brock, 'The Selection of the Authors of the Bridgewater Treatises': 174.
165 Kirby, W. 1835. *The Bridgewater Treatises…Treatise VII. On the History Habits and Instincts of Animals. In Two Volumes. Vol. I [Second Edition].* William Pickering, London: 36.
166 Kirby, *History* I: 10.
167 Kirby, *History* I: 41.
168 Kirby, *History* I: 200.
169 Kirby, *History* I: 137.

danger, and does not desist until her courage and address have ensured subsistence for one of her future progeny.'[170] When examining the book of nature, we note 'that the doctrine of the sufferings of one creature, by the will of God, being necessary to promote the welfare of another, is irrefragably established by every thing we see in nature; and further, that there is an unseen hand directing all to accomplish this great object, and taking care that the destruction shall in no case exceed the necessity'.[171]

Suffering promotes the greater benefit and is no reason for blemishing the Lord. On the contrary, 'this (…) war of one part of the creation upon another' illustrates 'that the sacrifice of a part maintains the health and life of the whole'. So we see that 'the great doctrine of *vicarious suffering* forms an article of physical science; and we discover (…) that the sufferings and death of one being may be, in the Divine counsels, and consistently with what we know of the general operations of Providence, the cause and instrument of the spiritual life and final salvation of infinite hosts of others'. Thus reasoning, Kirby came to the conclusion that 'the animal kingdom, in some sort, PREACH THE GOSPEL OF CHRIST'.[172] Nature reflects not only the attributes of God the Father but also the sacrificing love of God the Son.

Among the contributors to the *Bridgewater Treatises*, Kirby occupies a special position in his conviction that Scripture has to be taken literally. The consequences of this conviction are twofold. First, nature as seen nowadays is not the same as initially intended; animals were not created to feed on their fellow creatures. After humanity's fall, God in his mercy took the measures needed to maintain a creation fitted to accommodate human and animal life; the current situation in fact has to be characterized

---

170 Kirby, W., Spence, W. 1818. *An Introduction to Entomology: or Elements of the Natural History of Insects: with Plates. Third Edition. Vol. I.* Longman et al., London: 343-345 (344). For more details on the way Darwin's contemporaries dealt with the Ichneumon wasp see Gould, S.J. 1982. 'Nonmoral Nature' in: *Natural History* 91 (2): 19-26. Republished in Gould, S. J. 1994. *Hen's Teeth and Horse's Toes. Further Reflections in Natural History.* W.W. Norton & Company, New York: 32-45.

171 Kirby, W. 1835. *The Bridgewater Treatises…Treatise VII. On the History Habits and Instincts of Animals. In Two Volumes. Vol. II.* William Pickering, London: 526. In his remark on the 'unseen hand', Kirby probably referred here to the metaphor coined by the economist Adam Smith (1723–1790) that, although intended for the support of a *laissez faire* economy, found its application in natural science as well. See Paley, *Natural Theology*: 255; Gould, S.J. 1993. 'Darwin and Paley Meet the Invisible Hand' in: *Eight Little Piggies. Reflections in Natural History.* W.W. Norton & Company, New York: 138-152; Rothschild, E. 1994. 'Adam Smith and the Invisible Hand' in: *The American Economic Review* 84 (2). *Papers and Proceedings of the Hundred and Sixth Annual Meeting of the American Economic Association*: 319-322.

172 Kirby, *History* II: 62.

as 'next-best'. Kirby agreed with the others in interpreting predation and animal suffering as needed for the good of the whole and therefore he found no reason for any critical notes about the attributes of the Creator; on the other side, however, he acknowledged that things could have been better. But Kirby saw benefit from loss as well: in spite of being corrupted, creation nevertheless reveals divine grace. One suffers for the salvation of 'infinite hosts of others'.

Fig. 5.01. Frontispiece of Gideon Mantell's *Wonders of Geology* entitled 'The Country of the Iguanodon, restored from the Geological Discoveries of the Author. By John Martin.' The central part of the picture shows an iguanodon attacked by a megalosaurus and a crocodile. Mantell adds an extensive description, emphasizing that the 'vigour and beauty of this successful conception of the distinguished artist are equalled by the fidelity of its details'.[173]

Second, according to Kirby, the Genesis text offers no room for a long pre-Adamite period. The divine attributes at stake because 'who can think that a Being of unbounded power, wisdom, and goodness should create a world merely for the habitation of a race of monsters, without a single

---

173 Mantell, G.A. 1839. *The Wonders of Geology...Vol. I. First American, from the Third London Edition.* A.H. Maltby, Newhaven: after p. 428.

rational being in it to glorify and serve him?'[174] To whom are the heavens telling the glory of God and for whom does the firmament proclaim his handiwork if there are no people to take this message?[175]

Kirby's thoughts evoked a firm rebuttal from the Methodist-born obstetrician and geologist *Gideon Mantell* (1790-1852),[176] who could not accept the idea that a literal interpretation of Scripture should prevail above obvious scientific facts. Mentioning Kirby in particular, Mantell criticized those who hold to the view 'that the supposition of the earth

---

174 Kirby, *History* I: 39.
175 Kirby's idea that a creation without humans does not fulfill the purpose of God was not new. Similar considerations had already prompted the seventeenth-century theologian Isaac la Peyrère to propagate that countless other humans had been created prior to and together with Adam. 'Want God zou schijnen wat te vergeefs gedaen te hebben/ en wat onschiklijks: zoo hij op dien eygen dagh/ op welken hij had bestemt/ dat die geschapen dingen den mensch zouden dienen/ de menschen op dien eygen tijd niet geschapen had gehadt/ die haar zouden gebruyken/ 't zij in wat deel des werelts de zelve voortgebracht waren geweest. Maer zoo wij Adam voor den eersten en eenigen mensch stellen willen/ van welk daer nae alle menschen door de heele werelt voortgekomen zijn: waer toe dan soo veel tijds genomen/ dewijl de geheele wereld door deze eenige en alleene wijsheyt hare heeren en verzameling van menschen kond hebben: waer toe/ zeg ik/ zouden de landen van Mesopotamien/ d'Antipodes/ kruijden en moes voortgebraght hebben? Voor wien zouden de boomen in die landen vrucht voortgebragt hebben? tot wiens dienst zouden die beesten geweest hebben?' In: [Peyrère, I. la]. 1661. *Praeadamieten of Oefening Over het 12, 13, en 14. Vers des Vijfden Capittels van den Brief des Apostels Pauli tot den Romeynen, Waer Door Geleert Wort: Datter Menschen voor Adam Geweest Zijn*. [Johannes Janssonius, Amsterdam]: 250-256 (253). In translation [mine]: 'For God would seem to have acted in vain and unsuitable if he had on that own day to whom he had intended that those created things should serve man at that time had not created the people who would use them, be it in what part of the world they had been produced. But if we want to present Adam as the first and only human being, from which all people throughout the whole world have come forth, what time had it taken, until the whole world through this one and only wisdom has its lords and collection of people? For what purpose, I say would the countries of Mesopotamia, the Antipodes, herbs and vegetables have grown? For whom would the trees in those lands bear fruit? to whose service would those beasts have been?' For more details on this author, see Popkin, R.H. 1987. *Isaac la Peyrère (1595-1676). His Life, Work and Influence*. Brill, Leiden; Asselt, W. van. 'Adam en Eva als Laatkomers. De Pre-Adamitische Speculaties van Isaac La Peyrère' in: Goris, H., Hennecke, S. (eds). 2005. *Adam en Eva in het Paradijs. Actuele Visies op Man en Vrouw uit 2000 Jaar Christelijke Theologie* [Utrechtse Studies, 7]. Meinema, Zoetermeer: 99-115. The idea that creation only acquires its value through man's knowledge of it was contested by the *Bridgewater Treatise* author *William Whewell* who pointed out that large parts of this globe were inaccessible to humans, not to mention the extent of the universe. See [Whewell, W.] 1853. *Of the Plurality of Worlds. An Essay*. John W. Parker and Son, London: in particular pp. 103-108.
176 Gillispie, *Genesis and Geology*: 138-139; Rudwick, *Worlds before Adam*: 61-69.

having been peopled by other creatures before the existence of man, is incompatible with the evident design of the Creator'. These ideas are untenable. '[S]urely, the discoveries of geology ought not to be rejected because they instruct us that ere man was called into existence, this planet was the object of the Almighty's care, and teeming with life and happiness.' After all, it 'is the sublime truth revealed to us by geology—*that for countless ages our globe was the abode of myriads of living forms of happiness, enjoying all the blessings of existence*'.[177]

Geological data allow indeed a reliable reconstruction of this past, but I doubt that the past presented in this way deserves the positive words of Mantell (Fig. 5.1). Others would join the discussion as will be seen next; for some of them, supposing a prehistoric world full of death and destruction meant a blow in the face of the Creator. In the decades preceding the publication of Charles Darwin's *Origin,* this point became more and more a bone of contention.

5.4.11. *The 'Scriptural Geologists'*

As already mentioned above (cf. § 5.2.2), not everybody endorsed the idea that geological data could be reconciled with the Genesis text. The main stumbling block appeared to be the idea that death had been an essential part of creation from the very beginning and did not appear on the scene with the fall of Adam. For these dissenters, animal death had to be due to human sin; thinking otherwise was blasphemous.[178] Later authors identified those who took this position as 'Scriptural Geologists'[179]—a name probably derived from the title of a two-volume work named *Scriptural Geology* that was published in 1826 and 1827 by the Anglican clergyman *George Bugg* (1769–1851).[180] His views will be further investigated, along with those of others also considered to be representative.[181]

---

177 Mantell, G. 1838. *The Wonders of Geology. Vol. II.* Relfe and Fletcher, London: 443-447 (445, 447).
178 Bebbington, 'Science and Evangelical Theology in Britain from Wesley to Orr' in: Livingstone, Hart, Noll, *Evangelicals and Science in Historical Perspective*: 120-141.
179 Millhauser, 'The Scriptural Geologists'; Brooke & Cantor, *Reconstructing Nature*: 57-62; Stiling, 'Scriptural Geology in America' in: Livingstone, Hart, Noll, *Evangelicals and Science in Historical Perspective*: 177-192; Ury, *The Evolving Face of God as Creator*. O'Connor, 'Young-Earth Creationists in Early Nineteenth-Century Britain?'
180 Bugg, G. 1826, 1827. *Scriptural Geology; or, Geological Phenomena Consistent only with the Literal Interpretation of the Sacred Scriptures...*Hatchard and Son, London. For biographical details, see https://en.wikipedia.org/wiki/George_Bugg. Accessed on 14 December 2021. Bugg does not seem to have been a very compliant person; during his career, he was discharged from three church positions due to complaints from some members.
181 Ury, *The Evolving Face of God as Creator*: 161-170.

Starting with Bugg, it is noted that he derived from the Scriptures that 'animals were *not created carnivorous*'. To the contrary, '(...) they actually lived for twelve months in the Ark, on *vegetable* food only. Carnivorous animals have, therefore, degenerated into their present habit; but, it is more than probable they could, even now, be brought gradually to live on vegetable food again.'[182] Assuming that it had been otherwise creates insurmountable difficulties, for two reasons. The first is a practical one. 'If animals were created carnivorous they would instantly have fed upon their fellow creatures. Then unless *many* of one kind had been created at first the animals upon which the others fed would have immediately become extinct.' The other objection is theological. 'If animals were *created carnivorous*, "death," even violent death must have been common in the creation from the very beginning.' But that goes against Scripture. After all, we are taught that death entered the world by sin. After putting forward this theological argument, Bugg returned to the practical problems that arise when we assume that the animals were created carnivorous: 'Had lions and tigers, &c. been as voracious from the first as they are now the earth must have been in danger of being depopulated; And Adam himself would not have been safe from destruction by voracious animals.'[183]

After emphasizing that death, also animal death, entered into the world after—and due to—humanity's violation of the divine law, Bugg also addressed the consequences for the divine attributes arising from the doctrine of multiple creations for thousands or maybe even millions of years. '[T]o attribute such procedure to the "*only wise God*," is little better than *charging "God foolishly*".'[184] The ridiculousness of this view is clear to everyone:

> will any Christian Divine who regards his Bible, or will any Philosopher who believes that the Almighty works no "superfluous miracles", and does nothing in vain, advocate the absurdity that a wise, just, and benevolent Deity has, "numerous" times, wrought miracles, and gone out of his usual way for the sole purpose of destroying whole generations of animals, that he might *create others* very like them (...)!![185]

Thus, modern geology threatens divine attributes in two ways. It makes God not only responsible for animal suffering but also degrades him to a careless tinkerer.

---

182 Bugg, *Scriptural Geology* I: 221-222.
183 Bugg, *Scriptural Geology* I: 145-146.
184 Bugg, *Scriptural Geology* I: 109.
185 Bugg, *Scriptural Geology* I: 319.

The next scriptural geologist to be addressed, the Scottish clergyman *George Young* (1777–1848), who served one of the many seceded Presbyterian denominations,[186] wrote similar notes. '[I]n the sacred volume, the misery and destruction of the creatures are represented as the bitter fruits of man's transgression; and how then can we admit, that the catastrophes belonging to the formation system, were antecedent to the introduction of sin, and even to the creation of man?'[187] And like Bugg, Young thought that the idea that the earth has existed for a long time and was the scene of successive creations is nonsense. 'Some have alleged, in proof of the pre-adamite theory, that in tracing the beds upwards, we discern among the inclosed bodies, a gradual progress from the more rude and simple creatures, to the more perfect and completely organized; as if the Creator's skill had improved by practice.'[188]

To suppose that many centuries preceded the creation of Adam is folly. First, '(...) it seems scarcely consistent with the wisdom of the Divine Being, any more than with the declarations of his word, that a succession of creations, all beautiful and interesting, should occupy our globe throughout long ages, without any intelligent creatures, to enjoy the scene, and praise the Creator'. And second, 'it was man's disobedience that brought death into the world', which obviously excludes that 'death had reigned and triumphed on the globe, in the destruction of numerous races of creatures, thousands of years before man existed'.[189]

Contemporary geology not only made God responsible for the animal death associated with predation but also detracted from his glory by supposing that he created without ensuring the presence of creatures who could rationally praise him for this. With the latter point, the unthinkable fact of a creation without rational admirers, Young joined Kirby who wrote similar notes. The notion of rational man as the pinnacle of creation is palpable here.

Furthermore, those who think 'that the carnivorous creatures lived on animal food before the fall of man' should consider that for Adam and Eve, '(...) the sight of a cruel tiger destroying a lamb, and the cries of the innocent victim piercing their ears, might be quite compatible with their

---

186 For biographical details, see Cooper, T. 'Young, George (1777-1848)' in: *Dictionary of National Biography, 1885-1900, Volume 63.*
187 Young, G., Bird, J. 1828. *A Geological Survey of the Yorkshire Coast...Second Edition...*R. Kirby, Whitby: 342.
188 Young, G. 1840. *Scriptural Geology; or an Essay on the High Antiquity Ascribed to the Organic Remains Imbedded in Stratified Rocks...Second Edition: with an Appendix...* Simpkin, Marshall, and Co., London: 9.
189 Young, *Scriptural Geology*: 41-42.

state of perfect bliss!'[190] Bugg noted that carnivorousness in Paradise brought the first human couple the risk of becoming victims of predation. Young apparently supposed that God would protect them against such an unhappy fate, but not against witnessing unpleasant spectacles.

The last author from this group, *William Honyman Gillespie* (1808–1875)—designated by his biographer as one whose 'writings denote him as a man of faith, of prayer, of mediation, and of evangelical convictions'[191]— painted this spectacle in even shriller colors. Imagine 'innocent happy Adam eyeing contemplatively the carnivora tearing their victims limb from limb! And soft-hearted blessed Eve, too, looking on at all that shedding of blood, without the least diminution of her happiness!'[192] Gillespie did not lack words to reject the maleficent views of the contemporary geologists. They conflicted not only with the story of the creation as told in Genesis, but also with what the apostle Paul tells us in Romans 8:20-22. There we read that the creation groans and expects to be delivered from the bondage of corruption.[193]

Gillespie was convinced that this passage from Romans not only explains why mankind is subjected to death but also offer adequate support for the doctrine that animals suffer because of humanity's transgression which apparently excludes pre-Adamite animal death. To suppose the latter contradicts not only Scripture but also the image with which God reveals himself. Could it be that 'the God of the Old Testament, so full of love, and mercy, and tender pity, even to the lowest creatures, is on the same level with that Creator discovered by the geologists, who sent, directly from His hands, fishes, reptiles, mammals, to tear each other to pieces, till death closed the scene with race after race in those successions of murderers?'[194]

The ideas of contemporary geologists are not only refuted by Scripture but also collide with natural theology. 'One of those truths of Natural Theology is this, That the First Cause of all is necessarily free from that imperfectness which is, at bottom, the only supposable cause of malignant feelings. Therefore, the Great First Cause could not create monstrous animal natures, delighting in the infliction of tortures on their fellows.'[195]

---

190 Young, *Scriptural Geology*: 103-104.
191 Urquhart, J. 1920. *William Honyman Gillespie of Torbanehill. Scottish Metaphysical Theist. Prepared on Behalf of the Trustees of Mrs. Honyman Gillespie of Torbanehill.* T&T Clark, Edinburgh: 384.
192 Gillespie, W. 1859. *The Theology of Geologists as Exemplified in the Cases of the Late Hugh Miller, and Others.* Adam and Charles Black, Edinburgh: 58.
193 Gillespie, *Theology of Geologists*: 14.
194 Gillespie, *Theology of Geologists*: 20.
195 Gillespie, *Theology of Geologists*: 37.

This is against Christian as well as natural theology. Mankind is the evildoer.

The fact, however, that humans are to blame for the death of the animals does not solve all problems because humanity's responsibility for animal suffering and predation does not include the power to transform animals that once were herbivorous into beasts and birds of prey. Therefore, the question who them made so, pops up. 'By what medium did the races of those animals come to be what the palaeontologists find them to have actually been?'[196] In broaching this problem—ignored by Bugg and Young—Gillespie harked back to ideas brought up in the previous century and that offered an opportunity to accept the geologist's concept of deep time and pre-Adamite death. Could it be that 'those horrible lizards, and other still more horrible monsters, were the outer shells of devilish souls'? We cannot be sure that 'the fossil remains of the monsters, so familiar to our geologists, decide that these creatures came, in that condition of monstrosity, from the hands of the Creator'.[197]

Their phenotype as inferred from their petrified remains may be the result of corruption from indwelling evil spirits. Support from this idea is provided by Scripture in the narration of the demons and the herd of swine. When we read that demons were allowed 'to lodge for a while, however brief, in the bodies of swine', then we may also assume that something similar 'occurred again and again, during the long geological periods'.[198] With this line of reasoning, Gillespie killed two birds with one stone: God is acquitted from introducing death among the animals before humanity entered the scene and had sinned, as well as from creating those horrible prehistoric beasts. Both were attributed to the devil and his household, but how the evil spirits managed to transform animals into these hideous creatures remains hidden from us.[199]

Authors mentioned in the previous chapter invoked the concept of indwelling evil spirits as punishment for those spirits, the animals themselves being nothing other than a physical shell. In Gillespie's thoughts, on the other hand, the animals' appearance and behavior reflect the effect of evil powers, not divine punishment. Gillespie did not make

---

196 Gillespie, *Theology of Geologists*: 78.
197 Gillespie, *Theology of Geologists*: 81, 82.
198 Gillespie, *Theology of Geologists*: 83.
199 Gillespie, *Theology of Geologists*: 80. Cf. Ter. Tisanthrope [Gillespie, W.H.] 1873. *The Origin of Evil; a Celestial Drama*. n.p., n.p. In this latter text Gillespie depicted, herein following the style of John Milton's *Paradise Lost*, how the devil and his henchmen deliberated on how best to confuse God's intentions with his creation. 'We, therefore,—glory evermore, that we / Shall make all ravenous and noisome monsters, / To tear each other, limb from limb, to pieces.—' (109).

clear whether these considerations made deep time with all its consequences for him more acceptable; neither did he address the question of why God allowed the evil spirits to spoil his creation. Furthermore, this author appears somewhat ambivalent in his considerations. On the one hand, the suffering of the animals is explicitly attributed to Adam's sin, but on the other hand, it is assumed to be caused by the fallen angels before mankind appeared on the scene.

A review of the thoughts of these authors as described so far makes me suspect that they were especially anxious to defend the literal reading of the creation story as expressed in Genesis. This—rather than a desire to reconcile animal suffering with divine benevolence—may have led them to dismiss that there would have been life and death on this globe long before Adam had transgressed the divine command. Referring to animal suffering as incompatible with the goodness of the Creator was in that case not really an end in itself, but primarily intended to reinforce the belief that Scripture should be taken literally in all its details.

Support for my presumption is provided by the writings of Darwin's contemporary *Robert Dabney*. This North American Presbyterian divine took efforts to prioritize Scripture above science by questioning the chronology of the geologists. In the past, God may have seen 'fit to construct these *strata*, and to sow them with vegetable and animal life with a prodigal profusion now unknown; and to hurry the maturing of *strata*, and the early death and entombment of these thronging creatures, with a speed very different from the speculations of geology'. In this way, this author endeavors to maintain the scriptural authority—realistically-historically understood—against the data provided by science. That this aim goes before the interests of the animals becomes evident from what Dabney wrote next when speaking about the apparent waste of life that follows from squeezing the entire life history of the earth in only a few thousand years. 'Why this seeming, prodigal waste? It is no duty of mine to account for it. But God acts so!'[200] Scripture must be defended, not the way God deals with the animals. That is up to him.

The thoughts of Bugg and his kinsmen did not remain undisputed; Sedgwick called them people suffering from 'a shameful want of knowledge

---

200 Dabney, R.L. 1873. 'The Caution against Anti-Christian Science Criticised by Dr. Woodrow' in: *Southern Presbyterian Review* 24: 539-586 (585). Reprinted in Vaughan, C.R. (ed.). 1892. *Discussions by Robert L. Dabney. Vol III. Philosophical.* Presbyterian Committee of Publication, Richmond: 137-180 (179-180). For more details on Dabney and the context in which he unfolded his thoughts, see Livingstone, D.N. 2014. *Dealing with Darwin. Place, Politics, and Rhetoric in Religious Engagements with Evolution. The Gifford Lectures, 2014.* Johns Hopkins University Press, Baltimore: 117-156.

of the fundamental facts they presume to write about'.[201] Thomas Chalmers expressed himself in a similar negative sense. 'We regret that (…) our Scriptural geologists, should have entered upon this controversy without a sufficient preparation of natural science (…) and so landing themselves at times in a situation of most humiliating exposure to the argument or ridicule of their adversaries.'[202] After the 1850s, the scriptural geologists fell silent; their ideas slumbered until they were awakened to new life at the turn of the century to come as I will show in the next chapter.

5.4.12. John Pye Smith (1774–1851)

None of the authors in these pre-Darwinian decades took so much efforts in justifying God for having created predatory animals (now as well as in the past) as the Congregationalist Church leader *John Pye Smith*. His aim was 'to show that the prejudices against the new science, which extensively obtained among the orthodox, were utterly groundless'.[203] First, the role of death and decay were addressed. The data provided by nature should guide our interpretation of Scripture, and the former demonstrate beyond doubt that there has never been a time when animals did not die.[204] Without death, life would be impossible.

Pye Smith realized that some scriptural data seem to suggest otherwise. He referred to texts like Romans 5:12 and 1 Corinthians 15:21 that tell us that 'by one man, sin entered into the world, and death by sin' and that 'by man came death'. This is not about the death of the animals. To the contrary, these passages should be considered as only 'declaring that in this manner death acquired dominion over the first man and his posterity'.[205] Therefore, '(…) those predictions of the peace and happiness of the Messiah's reign, which picture the ferocious and venomous animals as becoming herbivorous and harmless, must be understood, as they are by Christian expositors generally, as beautiful poetry, expressing the moral influence of the gospel'.[206]

---

201 Sedgwick, *A Discourse on the Studies of the University of Cambridge*: 111-114 (112). For a detailed description of Sedgwick's ideas about the 'follies' of the scriptural geologists, see Roberts, 'Adam Sedgwick (1785–1873): Geologist and Evangelical': 161-165.
202 Chalmers, *On Natural Theology*: 254.
203 Davies, J.H. 1854. 'A Short Sketch of the Literary Life of the Author' in: Pye Smith, J. *The Relation between the Holy Scriptures and Some Parts of Geological Science. Fifth Edition*…Henry G. Bohn, London: ix-lxiii (liii).
204 Pye Smith, *Relation*: 86-89.
205 Pye Smith, *Relation*: 263.
206 Pye Smith, *Relation*: 264.

After explaining Scripture in this way, Pye Smith returned to emphasizing that a system of nature without death is unimaginable. Without death in general, all animal life would run out of supply, and death by predation is even beneficial as this saves old and diseased animals from a miserable withering away by offering them a quick demise—arguments often heard before.[207] Pye Smith ended with a kind of summary of his thoughts on this topic that deserves to be quoted full length.

> Some have proposed the hypothesis that the carnivorous tribes were not created till after the fall, or even after the deluge. This hypothesis (...) overlooks the fact that the grasses, leaves, seeds, and fruits, which are the food of the herbivorous races, swarm with insect life. The supposition that the carnivorous animals could at any time have fed upon vegetables, cannot be entertained for a moment, except it were by a person quite ignorant of the anatomical structure of those animals. (...) What, then, is the meaning of Rom. viii. 20 (...)? I reply, that here the word (...) denotes the part of the created universe which is immediately related to man, or comes under his influence; and that "vanity" denotes the frustration of high and holy purposes to which that part of the universe is subjected by the wickedness of mankind, ungratefully towards God and cruelly towards sentient animals, abusing the gifts of Providence.[208]

Absence of death before Adam fell is biologically impossible and not supported by Scripture. When asked by a member of the Congregationalist's community about this issue,[209] Pye Smith answered in terms similar to those quoted above.[210] The positive acceptance in Congregationalist circles of the facts provided by geology was also shown by the favorable review of Buckland's contribution to the *Bridgewater Treatises* (cf. § 5.4.6), the anonymous author being convinced 'that opposition between science and revelation is absolutely impossible, when the facts in nature are correctly observed, and divine truth is correctly interpreted'.[211]

A similar consenting response from the Congregationalist denomination towards science is displayed elsewhere; successive creations do

---

207 Pye Smith, *Relation*: 320--322.
208 Pye Smith, *Relation*: 322.
209 [T.K.] 1837. 'A Question in Geology' in: *The Congregational Magazine for the Year 1837*: 710.
210 Pye Smith, J., 1837. 'Suggestions on the Science of Geology, in Answer to the Question of T.K.' in: *The Congregational Magazine for the Year 1837*: 765-766.
211 Anonymous. 1837. 'Geology and Mineralogy Considered with Reference to Natural Theology, by the Rev. Dr. Buckland. 2 Vols...' in: *The Congregational Magazine for the Year 1837*: 42-47 (43).

not, as brought up by some aforementioned authors (cf. § 5.4.11), blemish the Creator for want of craftsmanship. In contrast, from viewing a gradually unfolding creation we may suppose 'that in this way the Almighty would impress his finite intelligent creatures [humanity] with renewed and perpetually increasing evidences of his wisdom, power, and skill'.[212] Neither should we care so much about the fact that Adam saw how animals devoured each other. Whereas authors discussed in the previous paragraph considered such a spectacle to be incompatible with a state of happiness, Pye Smith took it as it is. It made the first couple understand the concept of death: '(...) the denunciation in Gen, ii. 17 would seem to imply that they understood *what* the penalty was, in consequence of their having witnessed the pangs of death in the inferior animals.'[213]

The Presbyterian divine *David King* (1806-1883)—minister of Glasgow's United Secession Church[214]—agreed that the death Paul refers to in his letters only concerns humanity and that the 'death of animals is a fact in the course of nature, the truth of which all parties must admit'.[215] The life and death of animals have been inextricably linked from the beginning of creation.

5.4.13. Hugh Miller (1802-1856)

After a youth spent in poverty, *Hugh Miller* became an influential writer in Scottish intellectual circles; similar to the aforementioned Thomas Chalmers, he played a major role in the Disruption that led to the establishment of the Free Church as a Presbyterian denomination independent from the Church of Scotland.[216] His untimely death at the age of fifty-four years by committing suicide urged a contemporary to write how Miller's 'very intellect, his reason,—God's most precious gift,—a gift dearer than life,—perished in the great endeavor to harmonize the works and word of the Eternal'.[217]

---

212 Anonymous. 1837. 'The Scripture Cosmogony, Illustrated and Confirmed by the Discoveries and Conclusions of Geology' in: *The Congregational Magazine for the Year 1837*: 706-710 (708).
213 Pye Smith, *Relation*: 322.
214 Secord, *Victorian Sensation*: 286, 288.
215 King, D. 1850. *The Principles of Geology Explained, and Viewed in Their Relations to Revealed and Natural Religion...*Johnstone and Hunter, London: 50-53 (53).
216 For biographical details, see Gillispie, *Genesis and Geology*: 170-181; Livingstone, *Darwin's Forgotten Defenders*: 9-16; Brooke, J.H. 'The History of Science and Religion. Some Evangelical Dimensions in: Livingstone, Hart, Noll, *Evangelicals and Science in Historical Perspective*: 17-40.
217 Hanna, W. 'Memorials of the Death and Character of Hugh Miller, with an Account of His Funeral Obsequies' in: Miller, H. 1867 [1857]. *The Testimony of the Rocks; or,*

From the books that he wrote on the subject of geology, his posthumously published *Testimony of the Rocks*[218] is the most relevant, for in this text, the topic of pre-Adamite animal life and suffering was addressed in great detail. Miller made his point clear: 'Ever since animal life began upon our planet, there existed in all the departments of being, carnivorous classes, who could not live but by the death of their neighbours.'[219] And that has nothing to do with the sin of man. To the contrary, 'untold ages ere man had sinned or suffered, the animal creation exhibited exactly its present state of war.'[220] Miller was aware that this situation might blemish God, but he had other thoughts about that, as can be inferred from the text below, fully quoted to preserve both style and content.

> It has been weakly and impiously urged (…) that such an economy of warfare and suffering,—of warring and of being warred upon,—would be(…) unworthy of an all-powerful and all-benevolent Providence, and in effect a libel on his government and character. But that grave charge we leave the objectors to settle with the great Creator himself. (…) Be it enough for the geologist rightly to interpret the record of creation,—to declare the truth as he finds it,—to demonstrate, from evidence no clear intellect ever yet resisted, that he, the Creator, from whom even the young lions seek their food, and who giveth to all the beasts, great and small, their meat in due season, ever wrought as he now works in his animal kingdom,—that he gave to the primeval fishes their spines and their stings,—to the primeval reptiles their trenchant teeth and their strong armor of bone,—to the primeval mammals their great tusks and their sharp claws,—that he of old divided all his creatures, as now, into animals of prey and the animals preyed upon,—that from the beginning of things he inseparably established among his non-responsible existences the twin laws of generation and of death,—nay, further, passing from the established truths of *Geologic* to one of the best established truths of *Theologic* science,—God's eternal justice and truth,—let us assert, that in the Divine government the matter of fact always determines the question of right, and that whatever has been done by him who rendereth no

---

Geology in Its Bearings on the Two Theologies, Natural and Revealed... With Memorials of the Death and Character of the Author. Gould and Lincoln, Boston: 16. Cf. Hooykaas, *Natural Law*: 202-203, 218-222.
218 Miller, H. 1867 [1857]. *The Testimony of the Rocks*. Gould and Lincoln, Boston.
219 Miller, *Testimony*: 99.
220 Miller, *Testimony*: 103.

account to man of his matters, he had in all ages, and in all places, an unchallengeable right to do.[221]

Miller rejected any attempt to save divine benevolence. God is God, and he does not have to justify himself to us. Miller's image of God is evidently that of voluntarist. God doesn't do things because they are good, but things are good because he does them. Natural facts, also those provided by geology, morally vindicate God's actions. In such an approach, animal suffering can be something regrettable, but not an issue threatening the attributes of God. Elsewhere in the same work, Miller uttered similar thoughts, telling that, by the data provided by geology, '(…) we are the better enabled to appreciate the impressive directness of the sublime message to Job, when the "Lord answered him out of the whirlwind, and said, Where wast thou when I laid the foundations of the earth?"'[222]

Humanity is not in the position to pose questions about divine acts; similar to Job, we should know our place. It is the Lord who puts us to the test and not the other way around. And whereas others exhaust themselves in their attempts to save God's attributes, not so with Hugh Miller. Nowhere in his writings, neither in the *Testimony*, nor in any of his other books[223] do we encounter the words 'benevolence' or 'goodness' when it comes to the fate of the animals past and present.

In defending his views, Miller did not shy away from sarcasm when speaking about 'a most Protestant lecturer who addressed (…) that, though God created all the wild animals, it was the devil who made the flesh-eaters among them fierce and carnivorous; and, of course, shortened their bowels, lengthened their teeth, and stuck formidable claws into the points of their digits'.[224] Apparently, the negligence of the zoological problems posed by a change in diet annoyed Miller. What also annoyed him was that this speaker did not only 'exert himself in demolishing the geologists as infidel', but that 'he denounced also as unsound the theology of good old Isaac Watts' by claiming that the 'lines taught us in our infancy,—"Let dogs delight to bark and bite / For God hath made them

---

221 Miller, *Testimony*: 103-104.
222 Miller, *Testimony*: 262. Millers refers to Job 38:1-4.
223 Miller, H. 1851. *The Old Red Sandstone...From the Fourth London Edition*. Gould and Lincoln, Boston; Miller, H. 1854. *The Two Records: the Mosaic and the Geological. A Lecture Delivered before the Young Mens' Christian Association, in Exeter Hall*. Gould and Lincoln, Boston; Miller, H. 1858. *The Foot-Prints of the Creator: or, the Asterolepis of Stromness. From the Third London Edition. With a Memoir of the Author by Louis Agassiz*. Gould and Lincoln, Boston.
224 Miller, *Testimony*: 394-395.

so," were (…) decidedly heterodox. They ought to have run instead,— "Let dogs delight to bark and bite / *Satan* hath made them so"!!!'[225]

Hugh Miller differs from all other authors addressed so far that he does not make the slightest effort to justify animal death and predation by taking recourse to the Plotinian view so often used, in which any suffering is explained away as needed for the greater good or to maximize the amount of happiness. Instead, the Calvinistic Scotchman joined the naming Reformer who wrote that 'if we find it strange that He punishes the animals, which are not guilty in our way of thinking, let us realize that it is not our role to oversee His judgments, which surpass all human understanding'.[226] For Miller, this humble attitude was more appropriate than saving the divine attributes by questioning the geological data as done by the scriptural geologists (cf. § 5.4.11). By referring to the battle between Galileo and the ecclesiastical authorities, Miller warned against falling into the same trap. '[I]t is the class who term themselves the "Mosaic geologists" (…) who essay to "find natural philosophy in the first chapter of Genesis," and that too a demonstrably false natural philosophy'[227]—thus agreeing with Sedgwick and Chalmers, who had made similar negative judgments.

5.4.14. *John Anderson (1796–1864)*

Whereas people like Buckland, Pye Smith, and Miller saw no problems in reconciling Scripture with the data provided by geology, *John Anderson*, clergyman in the Church of Scotland[228]—someone qualified by Hugh Miller as a 'dabbler in geology who found a [fossil] fish in the Old Red

---

225 Miller, *Testimony*: 395n. The quoted verse lines are from Isaac Watts's *Poems of Home: II. For Children*. The next two lines are also relevant: 'Let bears and lions growl and fight / For 't is their nature too.' http://www.theotherpages.org/poems/watts01.html. Accessed on 14 December 2021.
226 Calvin, J. 2000. *Sermons sur la Genèse Chapitres 1,1–20,7*, Supplementa Calviniana 11/1-2, ed. M. Engammare, Neukirchen-Vluyn, Vol. 11/1, 479, ll. 21-23: 'Et si nous trouvons estrange qu'il punisse les bestes, qui ne sont point coulpables comme nostre opinion le porte, cognoissons que ce n'est point à nous de controller ses jugemens qui surmontent tous sens humain.' English translation from Calvin, J. 2009. 'Sermon 43' in: *Sermons on Genesis. Chapters 1:1-11:4. Forty-Nine Sermons Delivered in Geneva between 4 September 1559 and 23 January 1560. Translated into English by Rob Roy McGregor*. The Banner of Truth Trust, Edinburgh: 736.
227 Miller, *Testimony*: 386.
228 For biographical details, see https://www.nationalgalleries.org/art-and-artists/9272/rev-dr-john-anderson-1796-1864-newburgh-church-scotland-minister-archaeologist-and-geologist. Accessed on 14 December 2021.

Sandstone, and described it as a beetle'[229]—had a different opinion. According to this author, geology could provide information about successive layers in the crust of the earth, but 'in estimating *the time* that elapsed during the formation of the various sedimentary strata, are geologists warranted in assuming such principles of calculation as have been adopted?'[230] Anderson had his doubts; he wanted to stick to the scriptural chronology of six days of creation, although he reluctantly admitted that these six days each might have been longer periods.[231] But the fossil records themselves do not offer proof for deep time, as 'betwixt *great* periods of time, and the *gradual* increase of animal life, there is no necessary connection'.[232] And in his problems with a late arrival of humans, he agreed with Kirby and Young. '[W]ithout a fitting audience, the brilliancy of the representation loses half its attractions.'[233]

Despite those reservations, Anderson had no troubles with animal death and predation as part of God's initial creation. On the contrary, it has 'been the course of creation in all the present, and in every past epoch, that races [i.e., species], like individuals, have their terms of existence,— that all die out or are violently exterminated,—and that new families are created, adapted to the changes which have taken place, and organically distinct from all that preceded them'. We don't have to worry about that because this 'view of things is in every stage of it visibly dependent upon His will, as it emanates directly from His appointment'.[234]

The death of animals and even the extinction of entire species are included in God's divine plan, both in creating as well as in his providential care. 'Animals preyed likewise upon each other and by this means kept up then, as now, the general average and balance of life.'[235] Nowhere did Anderson refer to Adam's fall as an explanation for animal death. 'The various tribes and orders had their own limits of organization, their own sphere within which the functions of each were to be performed, and adapted to the condition in which they were placed, each reaped the full enjoyment that divine benevolence had appointed.'[236]

---

229 Miller, H. 1843. 'The Disruption' in: *Witness,* 20 May 1843. Republished in Miller, H. 1865. *The Headship of Christ*...Gould and Lincoln, Boston: 475-482 (479). Quoted from the latter source.
230 Anderson, J. 1851. *The Course of Creation*. Wm. H. Moore & Co., Cincinnati: 330.
231 Anderson, *Course of Creation*: 363.
232 Anderson, *Course of Creation*: 341.
233 Anderson, *Course of Creation*: 291.
234 Anderson, *Course of Creation*: 310.
235 Anderson, *Course of Creation*: 320.
236 Anderson, *Course of Creation*: 308. Adaptation should not be interpreted here as a result of natural selection as Darwin did, but as the result of a careful act of creation, so proof of design.

Whereas Miller was convinced of the earth's old age, Anderson in contrast took efforts to save the literal interpretation of Scripture concerning the chronology of creation. Furthermore, Anderson was not entirely blind to the interests of the animals; at their assigned place, they have their own enjoyments and serve the interests of the greater whole as well. Miller did not have any such considerations.

5.4.15. Paton James Gloag (1823-1906)

Unlike Anderson, *Paton James Gloag*, a pastor also serving the Church of Scotland,[237] accepted the results of geological enquiries. 'If the heavens declare the glory of God, the rocks do not less strikingly proclaim His wisdom and benevolence. If astronomy unfolds to us the wonders of creation in the immensity of space, geology displays these wonders in the immensity of time.'[238] The significance of data provided by science should not be neglected. Ignoring them bears grave consequences 'for nothing is more calculated to undermine a man's belief than the discovery that the demonstrated facts of science are in manifest and irreconcilable opposition to what he has been accustomed to regard as the revelation of Scripture.'[239]

Whereas Scripture, properly explained, does not offer arguments against an earth of old age, neither does it offer a reason to question pre-Adamite animal death. 'The tree of life was expressly planted and provided for Adam; but we read of no tree of life to which the lower animals might repair, and eat, and live for ever.' Therefore, we may be sure 'that even before the fall, beasts tore and devoured each other as now,—that then as now the lower creation was divided into animals of prey and animals preyed upon,—and that then as now there existed the ravenous lion, the ferocious tiger, and the venomous serpent,—and that then as now there was, as regards the lower animals, a constant circle of life and death'.[240]

The idea that animal death entered the world with the sin of humanity lacks any proof from the Genesis text; the often quoted passages from Paul's epistles or Isaiah's prophecies which seem to teach the same fall short as well. Wherever the apostle speaks of death in his letters, this death 'is limited to the human race', and as to his notes on the bondage of the creation, Gloag remarked that 'even although it should be so extended as to embrace all creatures, yet it does not assert that the death of the

---

237 For biographical details, see Bayne, T.W. 'Gloag, Paton James' in: *Dictionary of National Biography, 1912 Supplement, Volume 2.*
238 Gloag, P.J. 1859. *The Primeval World: a Treatise on the Relations of Geology to Theology.* T&T Clark, Edinburgh: 11.
239 Gloag, *Primeval World*: 51.
240 Gloag, *Primeval World*: 123.

inferior creatures was caused by sin; the utmost that it asserts is that they suffer, as in many ways they do by cruelties and oppressions, from the sins of men.' And as for the passages from the prophet that speak about the wolf dwelling with the lamb, '(…) it is evident that these are expressions, conceived in the happiest spirit of poetry, denoting the great moral changes which shall be effected by the prevalence of the Gospel'.[241]

But if animal death is no punishment, why then should animals die? A benevolent Creator could have saved them from that fate. Gloag had no worries about this. For 'the lower animals, death is merely the law of their nature. They die, because they were so constituted; their existence necessarily and inevitably leads to death. With regard to them, there is no connexion between sin and death; they are not morally accountable creatures, they are incapable of moral obedience or disobedience toward God.'[242] Their death is no punishment but, in contrast, 'a benevolent disposition'.[243]

In the same way as many other authors did before, Gloag justified animal death and predation by pointing (1) to the limited resources that would put limits on the number of animals and, as a result, limits on the amount of happiness as well, (2) to the grace of a quick, although violent, death when old age arrives with all its infirmities, and (3) to the need to prevent an excessive increase of any particular species. Furthermore, 'beasts are not troubled with fears and anxieties about the future; they enjoy the present hour, and know not what awaits them the next'.[244] The new problems that arise from geology are solved with old remedies: the Plotinian philosophy in which suffering of the individual is justified by the benefit of the whole, and the Stoic thoughts that put limits on animals' mental abilities. And that was no different in the past than in the present.

> The same kindness and care, which God now exercises toward the inferior animals, were exercised during the past geological ages. In the fossil organic remains we find as numerous instances of benevolent design and contrivance as in living animals. Each animal then, as now, was provided for by the care of our heavenly Father; each then, as now, had its appropriate food, was endowed with its peculiar instincts, and was adapted to the climate in which it lived; and therefore, we conclude that each then, as now, was an object of the Divine benevolence. It is this

---

241 Gloag, *Primeval World*: 126-127. Here Gloag apparently refers to Romans 5:12, Romans 8:19-22, 1 Corinthians 5:21, and Isaiah 11:6.
242 Gloag, *Primeval World*: 127-128.
243 Gloag, *Primeval World*: 128.
244 Gloag, *Primeval World*: 128-132 (131).

extension of the same benevolence, which is now exercised toward the inferior animals, to the immeasurable ages of the past, that constitutes the disclosure of geology. The goodness of God is thus seen in a far vaster number and greater variety of living creatures, and the manifestations of it are thus multiplied and increased indefinitely.[245]

Gloag's considerations prompted the aforementioned author William Gillespie to a vehement rebuttal, accusing him of the 'most false and dangerous assertions'.[246] Others like the Cambridge graduate and Anglican clergyman *John Henry Pratt* (1809–1871)[247] came to Gloag's help. This author shared Gloag's belief 'that the discoveries of Science are opposed to the declarations of Holy Scripture, is as mischievous as it is false, because it tends both to call in question the Inspiration of the Sacred Volume and to throw discredit upon scientific pursuits'.[248] He also agreed with Gloag that 'the lesson we learn from the Apostle [Paul] is, not that Death had never appeared even in the irrational world before the Fall of Man, but that (…) [d]eath received its horrors when its sentence fell upon man'.[249] Pratt did not address the question whether animal death had any consequences for the way in which we perceive God's goodness and justice, but his opinion, however, that it had nothing to do with human sin is crystal clear.

5.4.16. New Ideas from the New World
The writings of the geologists found their way into the former British colonies in North America as well. In 1854, the Congregationalist minister and geologist *Edward Hitchcock* (1793–1864)[250] entered the debate. In his compilation of lectures on the subject, he included praise for the work of British geologists like Pye Smith and others and expressed his

---

245 Gloag, *Primeval World*: 173-175 (175).
246 Gillespie, *Theology of Geologists*: 42.
247 For biographical details, see "Pratt, John Henry ." Complete Dictionary of Scientific Biography. Retrieved November 25, 2021 from Encyclopedia.com: https://www.encyclopedia.com/science/dictionaries-thesauruses-pictures-and-press-releases/pratt-john-henry-0. Accessed on 14 December 2021.
248 Pratt, J.H. 1859. *Scripture and Science not at Variance; with Remarks on the Historical Character, Plenary Inspiration, and Surpassing Importance of the Earlier Chapters of Genesis*. Thomas Hatchard, London: 1.
249 Pratt, *Scripture and Science not at Variance*: 43.
250 Wright, C. 1941. 'The Religion of Geology' in: *The New England Quarterly* 14 (2): 335-358; Guralnick, S.M. 1972. 'Geology and Religion before Darwin: the Case of Edward Hitchcock, Theologian and Geologist (1793–1864)' in: *Isis* 63 (4): 529-543; Livingstone, *Darwin's Forgotten Defenders*: 16-20.

dissatisfaction with those who tried to discredit their work as incompatible with Scripture.[251]

Pre- as well as post-Adamite animal suffering and death were explained and justified in the usual way: no pleasure without pain, carnivorous animals are needed to prevent the herbivorous ones from exhausting the earth's resources, and one can be sure that the amount of happiness exceeds the amount of miseries. Observation of nature teaches that there must have been death, long before mankind's transgression. And in the often quoted passages from the letters to the Romans and the Corinthians,[252] Paul speaks of death due to sin for mankind only.[253] Probably, the fabrications of Milton in his *Paradise Lost* (cf. § 3.2) have had more impact on the mind of the theologians than the biblical text itself.[254] People who question the data provided by geology are like those who dare to criticize Greek authors without mastering the Greek alphabet.[255]

Thus far, Hitchcock did not leave the well-trodden path in his attempts to reconcile present and past animal suffering with divine benevolence but he added another element that deserves to be considered in more detail. '[T]he certainty of man's [future] apostasy might have been the grand reason in the divine mind for giving to the world its present constitution, and subjecting animals to death.'[256] Hitchcock assumed that God foresaw that Adam would sin and thereby incur death. As co-existence of mortal and immortal creatures in the same natural environment is unthinkable, the animals—anticipating Adam's transgression—had to be created as mortal, because the alternative—immortal animals that became subject to death and decay after the fall—is unthinkable as well.[257]

One might object that it is 'inconsistent with divine benevolence, to place the inferior, irrational animals in a condition of suffering because man would transgress, and thus punish creatures incapable of sinning for his transgression.'[258] Hitchcock refuted this objection by again referring to the arguments with which he—along with many others—has shown that animal suffering is not so bad because enjoyments outweighing sufferings.

---

251 Hitchcock, E. 1854. *The Religion of Geology and Its Connected Sciences. Ninth Thousand.* Phillips, Sampson, and Company, Boston: 1-32.
252 Romans 5:12; 1 Corinthians 15:21.
253 Hitchcock, *Religion*: 72-73.
254 Hitchcock, *Religion*: 80-81.
255 Hitchcock, *Religion*: vii.
256 Hitchcock, *Religion*: 104-111 (105).
257 Hitchcock, *Religion*: 104-111, 247-248.
258 Hitchcock, *Religion*: 247.

We should acknowledge that for humanity, death is necessary as a deliverance from the corrupt flesh and as an entry into eternal life. And because—as mentioned above—the combination of a mortal humanity with an immortal animal world is not possible, the animals must die too, although for them not as punishment but as a logical consequence of the interdependence of everything that lives.

The assumption that God anticipated Adam's fall when creating was not entirely new. In the seventeenth century, it had been brought up by Willet and Gott. For them, it circumvented the problem of animals suddenly changing from herbivores to carnivores (cf. § 3.8), thus reconciling Scripture with zoology. Now, a similar approach served to unite Scripture with geology.

That animal suffering and divine benevolence could be reconciled by assuming a retroactive influence of a foreseen human transgression was endorsed by *J.Jay Dana*, a minister who also served the Congregationalist denomination.[259] This author joined Hitchcock in stating that '[w]e are not to regard sin as an accident which came unexpectedly upon the world, but as a thing which was foreseen. The whole constitution of things was formed in view of the fact that sin would enter the world. Humans were created with bodies fitted to a world of probation, and inferior animals were also adapted to a world where they should meet with death.'[260]

Anyone who objects to this by maintaining that the death of animals is a consequence of Adam's sin, must realize that this thought has no basis in Scripture. On the contrary, '(…) by coupling the death of animals with the sin of our first parents, we thereby teach that animals which knew not good or evil, and of course have done neither, were visited with evil for a sin in which they had no agency or participation; and that this view is more prejudicial to the Divine benevolence than the other'.[261] Furthermore, 'we find nothing in the Bible which intimates that his [Adam's] sin was the cause of the death of the inferior races'. That humans die is because they have sinned, but 'the Bible does not recognize the capability of

---

259 Biographical details for this author are limited. His name is mentioned several times in the *Minutes of the General Association of Massachusetts, 1848*. Crocker and Brewster, Boston. These minutes concern a Congregationalist conference, and hence, it can be concluded that Dana served this denomination as minister. J. Jay Dana should not be confused with his namesake James Dwight Dana who also wrote on geology and religion and also belonged to the Congregationalists, see Wright, 'The Religion of Geology'.
260 Dana, J.J. 1853. 'The Religion of Geology' in: *Bibliotheca Sacra* 10: 505-522 (521).
261 Dana, J.J. 1846. 'Article IV. On the Relations between Geology and Religion' in: Bidwell, W.H. (ed.). *Biblical Repository and Classical Review. Third Series*. Published by the Proprietor, New York: 297-320 (308-309).

sinning, in a being without reason or conscience. And hence the death of such beings can have no connexion with sin'. And for those who point to the words of Paul about the groaning of creation as written in Romans 8:19–22, Dana had his answer ready as well. 'That this passage refers to the brute creation remains to be established.'[262]

To whoever objected to a fall that works retroactively, Dana pointed out that such a person must also object to an atonement effective retroactively. Long before Christ suffered on Calvary, the faithful from the Old Testament received forgiveness for their sins.[263] This idea of these two North-American Congregationalist theologians offered an entirely new and original view on the issue of animal death, human responsibility, and divine benevolence. It would be revived one century and a half later by the present-day mathematician and philosopher William Dembski, who reintroduced the idea of a fall retroactively responsible for animal suffering from the beginning of time.[264]

Furthermore, Dana deserves to be included in the discussion because he explicitly rejected the idea that it would be below the dignity of the Creator to have been active for so many epochs without intelligent beings around that could praise him for his works as forwarded by authors like Bugg, Kirby, and Young. That is not the case. On the contrary, the data provided by geology only add to the glory of the Creator because they give mankind an impression of God's work over a period of time that far exceeds the time that mankind lived on the earth. 'Nature has provided for us in her grand Herbarium, specimens of ancient plants, and has made the earth's strata a vast anatomical museum.'[265] God is not ashamed of his works, neither for what he is doing now nor for what he has done in the past. 'The fact that He has thus displayed them, manifest in Him a consciousness that they will bear the strictest scrutiny of men of every grade of mind, without thereby causing the infinity of his Goodness to be called in question.'[266]

Not only the 'heavens are telling the glory of God'.[267] The fossils found in the crust of the earth and revealed by geology convey an identical message. The fact that the different animal species follow each other in a sequence of emerging, flowering, and perishing is no reason to doubt

---

262 Dana, 'On the Relations Between Geology and Religion': 319-320.
263 Dana, 'The Religion of Geology': 521.
264 Dembski, W. 2009. *The End of Christianity. Finding a Good God in an Evil World.* B&H Publishing Group, Nashville: 124-126, 142-155.
265 Dana, 'On the Relations Between Geology and Religion': 299.
266 Dana, 'On the Relations Between Geology and Religion': 307.
267 Psalm 19:1. (NRSV)

God's benevolence—even if this implies death and destruction. Not everyone, however, shared this rosy view as I will show next.

5.4.17. Flies in the Ointment

That animal suffering could be an argument to doubt God's goodness and benevolence had not been a major issue in the British Isles as shown thus far. On the other side of the Strait of Dover, things were different. Here, the French materialist *Paul-Henri Thiry,* Baron *d'Holbach* (1723–1789),[268] wrote at the end of the eighteenth century that '[o]ne animal, or mite, that suffers, furnishes invincible arguments against divine providence and its infinite goodness',[269] adding that 'if he [God] allow [sic] machines, whom he has created sensible, to experience sorrow, he is destitute of bounty'.[270]

His ideas were adopted by the atheistic and anarchistic philosopher *William Godwin* (1756–1836),[271] who agreed that the suffering of even a single living being was an adequate argument against divine benevolence: 'Let us not amuse ourselves with a pompous and delusive survey of the whole, but let us examine parts severally and individually.' After expounding on the miseries for animals such a survey reveals, Godwin concluded that 'the creed of optimism, or an opinion bearing some relation to that creed, has done much harm in the world'.[272]

These thoughts however failed to impress the British public that remained immune to ideas that came over from the fiercely anticlerical French atheists[273] as well as from their fellow countryman Godwin. The aforementioned Scottish divine Thomas Chalmers was one of the first to take up the cudgels. In his contribution to the *Bridgewater Treatises,* he

---

268 Cushing, M.P. 1920. 'A Forgotten Philosopher' in: *The Monist* 30: 311-316. Cf. Roe, S.A. 'Biology, Atheism, and Politics in Eighteenth-century France' in: Alexander & Numbers, *Biology and Ideology*: 36-60.

269 d'Holbach, P.H. 1795. *Common Sense: or, Natural Ideas Opposed to Supernatural. Translated from the French.* n.p., New York: 47.

270 d'Holbach, P.H. 1889 [1770]. *The System of Nature: or, Laws of the Moral and Physical World...Two Volumes in One.* J.P. Mendum, Boston: 354.

271 For biographical details, see Britannica, The Editors of Encyclopaedia. "William Godwin". *Encyclopedia Britannica,* 3 April 2021, https://www.britannica.com/biography/William-Godwin. Accessed on 14 December 2021. His daughter Mary Shelley was the author of the gothic novel *Frankenstein.* Cf. Shelley, M. 2016 [1818]. *Frankenstein, or the Modern Prometheus. Edited, Annotated, and Illustrated by M. Grant Kellermeyer. The Third Edition.* Oldstyle Tales Press, Fort Wayne.

272 Godwin, W. 1798. *Enquiry Concerning Political Justice, and Its Influence on Morals and Happiness. The Third Edition Corrected. In Two Volumes. Vol. I.* G.G. and J. Robinson, London: 458.

273 Buckley, M.J. 1987. *At the Origins of Modern Atheism.* Yale University Press, New Haven and London: 255-256.

contested d'Holbach's atheism by maintaining that nature bears 'the most impressive signatures of a Deity'.[274] A few years later, even stronger notes were employed when he qualified d'Holbach as an author whose work is 'characterized more by its magniloquence than its magnificence, its plausibility than its power' and it is to be deplored that '[i]ts circulation has been much extended of late by the infidel press of our own country—where it is (…) working mischief among the half-enlightened classes of British society'.[275] The politician *Henry Brougham* (1778–1868)[276] had the same opinion, considering d'Holbach's attempts to persuade people to atheism to be convincing only for those who 'take for granted the thing to be proved'.[277]

The reluctance to question divine providence, let alone God's existence, also had a political background. Just as nature mirrors benevolent divine design—everything is in the place required for serving the benefit of the whole—in the same way reflects society a divinely imposed and sustained order.[278] William Kirby, whom we met before as one of the contributors to the *Bridgewater Treatises,* had no doubts on this. '[T]hose powers that rule under God (…) in his physical universe [also] have power in his church, or over his people.' Scripture is clear on this:

> St. Paul, describing the creation of all things by the Son of God, whether *visible* or *invisible*, mentions particularly *four* ruling powers in nature and grace—*Thrones, dominions, principalities, and powers*. This may be *interpreted* of all rule and government both in heaven and upon earth;

---

274 Chalmers, *On the Adaptation of External Nature*: 21-22 (22). The *System of Nature* was originally published under the pen name J.B. Mirabaud. Hence, Chalmers used this name in his criticism. See https://www.britannica.com/topic/System-of-Nature. Accessed on 14 December 2021.
275 Chalmers, *On Natural Theology*: 163.
276 For biographical details, see Britannica, The Editors of Encyclopaedia. "Henry Peter Brougham, 1st Baron Brougham and Vaux". *Encyclopedia Britannica*, 15 September 2021, https://www.britannica.com/biography/Henry-Peter-Brougham-1st-Baron-Brougham-and-Vaux. Accessed on 14 December 2021.
277 Brougham, H. 1856. *Works of Henry, Lord Brougham. Volume VI. Natural Theology...* Richard Griffin and Company, London: 144-151 (145). Cf. Brooke & Cantor, *Reconstructing Nature*: 195-200.
278 Brooke & Cantor, *Reconstructing Nature*: 157-158. For details about how science education should serve public interests, see Topham, 'Science and Popular Education in the 1830s'. For discussion how the validity of divine design was invoked in pursuit of political goals, see Jacyna, L.S. 1983. 'Immanence or Transcendence: Theories of Life and Organization in Britain, 1790–1835' in: *Isis* 74 (3): 310-329, in particular pp. 321-328; Brooke, J.H. 1992. 'Natural Law in the Natural Sciences: the Origins of Modern Atheism?' in: *Science & Christian Belief* 4 (2): 83-103, in particular pp. 98-101.

which is all derived from Christ, as King of Kings and Lord of Lords, to whom *All power is given in heaven and earth*: who is (…) acting by all the powers that he hath created, whether physical or metaphysical, whether civil, ecclesiastical, or spiritual; for *He upholdeth all things by the word of his power.*[279]

Questioning divine design in nature thus threatened the prevailing social order. Hence, it is not surprising that atheism was at the time mainly found in those circles that wanted to overthrow that order.[280] For a short period (1841–1843) they had the *Oracle of Reason* as their mouthpiece— 'the only exclusively ATHEISTICAL print that has appeared in any age or country.'[281]

Church and society were not the only targets. The Creator also received his share, pointing to animal suffering served those who already disputed the existence of God. 'To the Atheist, a moth in the candle's flame, or a poor fly in the fangs of a spider, is a *proof* that the world could not have been designed by one being, infinitely wise, infinitely good, and infinitely powerful. Infinite goodness would not desire evil, infinite power would not have created it, nor could an artist infinitely wise fashion an imperfect universe.'[282]

Attempts to justify God for any evil were dismissed. Declaring that 'they [evils] are necessary, to enable us to appreciate the good which exists, or, that god, in his inscrutable wisdom, has undoubtedly a reason, good and sufficient, for creating such circumstances' does not make sense. 'This worse than ridiculous—this vilely pernicious teaching, the atheist rejects with contempt and disgust—contempt for those who would enforce such principles, and disgust for principles thus sought to be enforced.'[283] Not only does the book of nature counter the attributes traditionally assigned to God but the book of Scripture does not support

---

279 Kirby, *History* I: xcix-c. Kirby quotes from respectively Colossians 1:16: 'For by him were all things created, that are in heaven, and that are in earth, visible and invisible, whether they be thrones, or dominions, or principalities, or powers: all things were created by him, and for him.'; Matthew 28:18: 'And Jesus came and spake unto them, saying, All power is given unto me in heaven and in earth.'; Hebrews 1:3: 'Who being the brightness of his glory, and the express image of his person, and upholding all things by the word of his power' (KJV). Cf. Desmond, *Politics of Evolution*: 114-116.
280 Desmond, A. 1987. 'Artisan Resistance and Evolution in Britain, 1819-1848' in: *Osiris* 3: 77-110; Desmond, *Politics of Evolution*: 185, 408.
281 Anonymous. 1842. 'Preface' in: *The Oracle of Reason, or, Philosophy Vindicated* 1: ii.
282 Southwell, C. 1842. 'Is there a God? VIII' in: *The Oracle of Reason, or, Philosophy Vindicated* 1: 109-111 (111).
283 Chilton, W. 1843. 'Theory of Regular Gradation XLVIII' in: *The Oracle of Reason, or, Philosophy Vindicated* 2: 378-380 (379).

them either as can be seen from the commentary that one of them made on the scriptural record of the deluge—reflecting elaborately on the text which reads that 'it repented the Lord that he had made man on the earth'.[284] Any paraphrasing or summarizing would detract from the vitriolic sarcasm shown by this contribution that is therefore quoted full-length.

> The Being of whom it is said in another portion of the Bible, that he is not a man that he should repent, is here represented like some bungling workman lamenting over a bad job—vexed with himself that he should have been so incompetent to the undertaking. How an omniscient and omnipotent Being should have thus been foiled by a serpent, and be made to confess not only his incapacity, but his weakness, is a riddle much beyond our comprehension. If the attributes assigned by theologians to God have any existence at all, the representation of the Lord given in the previous quotations must be a caricature. For an omniscient being would have constructed all things for the best, to meet all present and future contingencies—an omnipotent being would have been powerful enough to prevent any departure from the intention of omniscience, and an unchangeable being, consequently, would never, in the language of erring and short-sighted man, have repented of anything he had done; for repentance is characteristic of weakness and error, and can never be predicated of omniscience and omnipotence. Noah's God is only a localized changeable personage, and a proof of the very gross and foolish notions entertained by the Jews on the subject of Deity. As the earth was so "corrupt" and " full of violence," and as all beasts, and creeping things, and fowls, whether mice or elephants, fleas or scorpions, cock-robins or eagles, had gone astray, and become great sinners, one would have thought the easiest way of setting all right, would have been either to change their natures to that state of innocence and simplicity, we are led to suppose, they presented before the fall, or else to have annihilated the whole, and made an entirely new race. Neither plans, however, were adopted; for instead of vigorously going to work, to put things into proper order, the Lord having decided upon drowning the world, resolves to preserve a male and female of every species, to perpetuate the breed. This does not appear to us a very satisfactory mode of removing the "corruptions of all flesh," thus merely to drown the earth in freak of vengeance, and at the same time, to perpetuate the tainted species, which had been at the bottom of all mischief.[285]

---

284 Genesis 6:6. (KJV)
285 Chilton, W. 1842. 'Mosaic Account of the Deluge' in: *The Free-Thinker's Information for the People* 2: 9-16 (9-10). This text could have been written nowadays by authors like Richard Dawkins or his likes.

The author hit several targets with one shot. First, God's attributes were put in a bad light. Omnipotence and omniscience are incompatible with repentance. Second, God was depicted as only a Jewish fancy, and third, the solution offered for correcting the animals' wickedness is illogical. And in passing, sin was mocked by ridiculing that animals could also be intentional perpetrators.[286]

The ideas of these authors were not much appreciated; some of them were even sent to jail on accusation of blasphemy. The ruling classes preferred the protection of a society that derived its justification from the doctrine that its present order was designed by God above providing room for the revolutionary thoughts of what they saw as an unruly underclass. Young children learned this order when they were taught to sing: 'The rich man in his castle / The poor man at his gate / God made them high and lowly / And ordered their estate.'[287] Those who contested the fairness of this order were muzzled.

5.4.18. *Charles Darwin (1809-1882)*
Authors discussed thus far saw in the suffering and death of animals as no reason to doubt God's attributes, let alone his existence. Animal pleasures were considered to outweigh animal sufferings and sufferings were justified because they served a greater good. With Charles Darwin, that would change.[288] As early as 1837—twenty-two years before he published his *Origin*—Darwin already wrote about the animals as being 'our fellow brethren in pain, disease, death, suffering and famine.'[289] Nature is not as pleasant as it seems at first sight; we have to envisage 'that the birds which

---

286 At this place I am ignoring the possibility that animals may indeed sin as some present-day theologians assume. This point is dealt with in Chapter 7.
287 From 'Maker of Heaven and Earth', an Anglican hymn written by Cecil Frances Alexander and published in the bundle *Hymns for Little Children*, see: Alexander, C.F. 1852 [1848]. *Hymns for Little Children. Fifth Edition*. Joseph Masters, London: 27.
288 Literature on Darwin is voluminous. For concise overviews for the way Darwin developed his theory, see Moore, J.R. 1979. *The Post-Darwinian Controversies. A Study of the Protestant Struggle to Come to Terms with Darwin in Great Britain and America 1870-1900*. Cambridge University Press, Cambridge: 314-326; Livingstone, *Darwin's Forgotten Defenders*: 28-40; Bowler, *Monkey Trials and Gorilla Sermons*: 79-102; Darwin, *Origin*: xv-lx; Berry, R.J. 'Biology since Darwin' in: Robinson, A. (ed.). 2012. *Darwinism and Natural Theology. Evolving Perspectives*. Cambridge Scholars Publishing, Newcastle upon Tyne: 12-38; Jones, *For the Glory of God*: 115-121.
289 Darwin, C. 1887. *The Life and Letters of Charles Darwin, Including an Autobiographical Chapter. Edited by His Son, Francis Darwin. In Three Volumes:—Vol. II*. John Murray, London: 6.

are idly singing round us mostly live on insects or seeds, and are thus constantly destroying life' and 'we forget how largely these songsters, or their eggs, or their nestlings, are destroyed by birds and beasts of prey'.[290] Similar notes on the miseries of animals can be found in Darwin's letters. His writings about the propagation of the Ichneumon wasp[291] and other 'horridly cruel works of nature'[292]—more extensively quoted in Chapter 1—are widely known.

These gloomy thoughts did not imply that Darwin ignored any attempts to justify or mitigate animal miseries. Admittedly, there is a 'struggle for life', but '[w]hen we reflect on this struggle, we may console ourselves with the full belief, that the war of nature is not incessant, that no fear is felt, that death is generally prompt, and that the vigorous, the healthy, and the happy survive and multiply'.[293] The pain of death is not made worse by prior awe and the total amount of pleasure increases when the weak perish and those better equipped for joyful experiences take their place—thoughts in which Darwin harkens back (unconsciously?) to his grandfather Erasmus Darwin who wrote similar themes about animal death as a tool to minimize pain and to maximize happiness. Actually, it is surprising to read Darwin's conviction that 'happiness decidedly prevails' although he admitted in the same sentence that 'this would be very difficult to prove'.[294]

But whereas in the past, emphasis on animal pleasures as prevailing above miseries served as proof for beneficial divine design, not so for Darwin. There are too many imperfections. 'We need not marvel at the sting of the bee causing the bee's own death; at drones being produced in such vast numbers for one single act, and being then slaughtered by their sterile sisters; at the astonishing waste of pollen by our fir-trees; at the instinctive hatred of the queen bee for her own fertile daughters; at ichneumonidæ feeding within the live bodies of caterpillars; and at other such cases.'[295] Such examples illustrate that '[t]he old argument of design

---

290 Darwin, *Origin*: 65.
291 Darwin to Gray. 22 May 1860. *Darwin Correspondence Project*, "Letter no. 2814," accessed on 14 December 2021, https://www.darwinproject.ac.uk/letter/?docId=letters/DCP-LETT-2814.xml
292 Darwin to Hooker. 13 July 1856. *Darwin Correspondence Project*, "Letter no. 1924," accessed on 14 December 2021, https://www.darwinproject.ac.uk/letter/?docId=letters/DCP-LETT-1924.xml
293 Darwin, *Origin*: 79.
294 Darwin, C. 1958 [1887]. *The Autobiography of Charles Darwin 1809–1882. With the Original Omissions Restored. Edited and with Appendix and Notes by His Granddaughter Nora Barlow*. Collins, London: 88.
295 Darwin, *Origin*: 412.

in nature, as given by Paley (…) fails'.[296] Animals are not designed for the environment they inhabit by a divine creative act, but they adapt to their environment throughout successive generations, natural selection weeding out those that fail to adapt.

Darwin replaced design and purpose by selection and randomness, thus loosening the connection between God and his creation.[297] Whether this indicates that Darwin questioned any involvement of God with nature entirely, let alone God's existence, is less clear. On one hand, he ponders that 'the sufferings of millions of the lower animals throughout almost endless time' is a very strong argument 'against the existence of an intelligent first cause'.[298] But on the other hand, he feels 'compelled to look to a First Cause having an intelligent mind' when considering 'the extreme difficulty or rather impossibility of conceiving this immense and wonderful universe (…) as the result of blind chance or necessity'.[299]

Darwin's wavering on this theme is also shown in his correspondence with the Dutchman *Nicolaas Dirk Doedes*.[300] Doedes—who had left the study of theology because he could 'believe no more in the existence of God'—had asked Darwin for his opinion on this subject.[301] Thus challenged, Darwin replied that 'the impossibility of conceiving that this grand and wondrous universe, with our conscious selves, arose through chance, seems to me the chief argument for the existence of God', but added that he, on the other side, could not 'overlook the difficulty from the immense amount of suffering through the world. (…) The safest conclusion seems to be that the whole subject is beyond the scope of man's intellect.'[302] Our mental capacities fall short. We come across similar thoughts elsewhere. 'A dog might as well speculate on the mind of

---

296 Darwin, *Autobiography*: 87.
297 Brooke, *Science and Religion*: 255-263; Ayala, 'Darwin's Greatest Discovery'; Ayala, 'Darwin's Explanation of Design'; McGrath, *Darwinism and the Divine*: 143-182.
298 Darwin, *Autobiography*: 90.
299 Darwin, *Autobiography*: 92.
300 For biographical details, see https://www.dbnl.org/tekst/_jaa003190701_01/_jaa003190701_01_0013.php. Accessed on 14 December 2021.
301 Doedes to Darwin. 27 March 1873. *Darwin Correspondence Project*, "Letter no. 8828," accessed on 14 December 2021, https://www.darwinproject.ac.uk/letter/?docId=letters/DCP-LETT-8828.xml. For a detailed record of the contact between Darwin and Doedes and Darwin's reluctance to speak out about the existence of God as Creator, see Heide, J. van der. 2006. 'Darwin's Young Admirers' in: *Endeavour* 30 (3): 103-107.
302 Darwin to Doedes. 2 April 1873. *Darwin Correspondence Project*, "Letter no. 8837," accessed on 14 December 2021, https://www.darwinproject.ac.uk/letter/?docId=letters/DCP-LETT-8837.xml

Newton.'³⁰³ Attempts to find proofs for God from reading the book of nature put us 'in much the same frame of mind as an old Gorilla would be in if set to learn the first book of Euclid'.³⁰⁴

A similar cloud of ambivalence surrounds Darwin concerning to what extent he saw the 'struggle for life' as serving a higher purpose. Some phrases from his *Origin* could indicate this when he speaks of a 'general law, leading to the advancement of all organic beings',³⁰⁵ or—in the concluding paragraph of the *Origin*—how he wrote that:

> from the war of nature, from famine and death, the most exalted object which we are capable of conceiving, namely, the production of the higher animals, directly follows. There is grandeur in this view of life, with its several powers, having been originally breathed into a few forms or into one; and that, whilst this planet has gone cycling on according to the fixed law of gravity, from so simple a beginning endless forms most beautiful and most wonderful have been, and are being, evolved.³⁰⁶

It is difficult to read anything else in these phrases than that animal suffering serves a greater good. But whether this implies divine contrivance or only the unintended outcome of properties inherent in nature still remains a subject of debate among scholars today.³⁰⁷

---

303 Darwin to Gray. 22 May 1860. *Darwin Correspondence Project*, "Letter no. 2814," accessed on 14 December 2021, https://www.darwinproject.ac.uk/letter/?docId=letters/DCP-LETT-2814.xml

304 Darwin to Gray. 11 December 1861. *Darwin Correspondence Project*, "Letter no. 3342," accessed on 14 December 2021, https://www.darwinproject.ac.uk/letter/?docId=letters/DCP-LETT-3342.xml

305 Darwin, *Origin*: 220.

306 Darwin, *Origin*: 427.

307 Bowler, *Fossils and Progression*: 117-147; Ospovat, D. 1980. 'God and Natural Selection: the Darwinian Idea of Design' in: *Journal of the History of Biology* 13 (2): 169-194; Cornell, J.F. 1987. 'God's Magnificent Law: the Bad Influence of Theistic Metaphysics on Darwin's Estimation of Natural Selection' in: *Journal of the History of Biology*, 20 (3): 381-412; Kohn, D. 1989. 'Darwin's Ambiguity: the Secularization of Biological Meaning' in: *The British Journal for the History of Science* 22 (2): 215-239; England, R. 2001. 'Natural Selection, Teleology, and the Logos: from Darwin to the Oxford Neo-Darwinists, 1859-1909' in: *Osiris* 16: 270-287; Richards, R.J. 2009. 'Darwin's Place in the History of Thought: a Reevaluation' in: *Proceedings of the National Academy of Sciences* 106 (Suppl. 1): 10056-10060; Lightman, B. 2010. 'Darwin and the Popularization of Evolution' in: *Notes & Records of the Royal Society* 64: 5-24; Brink, G. van den, Cook, H. 2020. '"I Am Inclined to Look at Everything as Resulting from Designed Laws": Charles Darwin's Origin of Species as a Specimen of Natural Theology' in: *Christian Scholar's Review* 50 (1): 25-37.

Darwin himself rejected any blame for promoting disbelief in spite of his ambiguities about design and purpose: '(…) I have never been an atheist in the sense of denying the existence of a God'.[308] But it cannot be denied—in spite of these reassuring words—that Darwin had opened a door that had remained closed hitherto. Now, the possibility that animal suffering could threaten the attributes of God or challenge his existence was suggested by a respectable upper class author and not only propagated by a few rebellious misfits.

Darwin's thoughts did not come out of the blue entirely. I have shown above how elements like an old age of the earth and a succession of animal species that emerged, flourished, and perished had already become commonplace in the nineteenth century decades prior to the publication of the *Origin*. But now—with Darwin—the issue at stake was about the relationship between animal species now alive and those inhabiting the earth in the past; did the former have the latter as precursors or had they emerged as a new creation? One may assume that this does not make so much difference to the problem of animal suffering because in both cases animals die but for Darwin the crucial thing was that in the former case the animals had to die as a result of natural laws while in the latter God is directly responsible. In reply, one could argue that this also makes no difference as God is the one who designed the laws of nature—and hence remains accountable. This is also true, but creating a distance between God and his creation by inserting laws of nature as an intermediary agency is but one step away from removing him from the stage entirely. For that you only have to consider the laws of nature as a property of organized matter and not as laws given to us from heaven.[309] Darwin's

---

308 Darwin to Fordyce. 7 May 1879. *Darwin Correspondence Project*, "Letter no. 12041," accessed on 14 December 2021, https://www.darwinproject.ac.uk/letter/?docId= letters/DCP-LETT-12041.xml. See for Darwin's opinion about religion also Brown, B.F. 1986. 'The Evolution of Darwin's Theism' in: *Journal of the History of Biology* 19 (1): 1-45; Livingstone, D.N. 'Re-placing Darwinism and Christianity' in: Lindberg & Numbers, *When Science & Christianity Meet*: 183-202; Brooke, J.H. 'Darwin and Victorian Christianity' in: Hodge, J., Radick, G. (eds) 2009. *The Cambridge Companion to Darwin. Second Edition.* Cambridge University Press, Cambridge: 197-218, in particular pp: 204-207; Brooke, J.H. 2010. 'Darwin and Religion: Correcting the Caricatures' in: *Science and Education* 19 (4-5): 391-405; White, P. 2010. 'Darwin's Church' in: *Studies in Church History* 46: 333-352; Brooke, J.H. 2018. 'Myth, Mutual Interaction, and Poetry. Darwin and Christianity: Truth and Myth' in; Zygon (3): 836-849.

309 That the laws of nature neither confirm nor refute the presence and activity of God in his creation is aptly summed up by Brooke in his discussion of Newton's law of gravitation: 'There is nothing (…) which settles the question whether the power of attraction is an inherent and defining property of matter, a contingent property

theory could make such a step imaginable and therefore welcome to any atheist as grist to her or his mill.

Table 5.1. Opinions on animal suffering and death

Author	Adam is to blame	Required for the greater good	Reasons beyond our understanding
Darwin sr.		X	
Paley		X	
Gisborne	X		
Crombie			X
Chalmers			X
Buckland		X	
Bell		X	
Roget		X	
Prout		X	X
Kirby	X		
Scriptural Geologists	X		
Pye Smith		X	
Miller			X
Anderson		X	
Gloag		X	
Hitchcock		X*	
Dana		X*	
Darwin Jr		X#	

* For the benefit of a fallen humanity
# Occasionally, Darwin referred to progression as outcome of natural selection. See § 5.4.18 for this issue.

---

freely added by a deity, a divine emanation or a direct and immediate expression of the divine will.' In: Brooke, 'Natural Law in the Natural Sciences: the Origins of Modern Atheism?': 94-95. Such reasoning applies equally to other laws of nature. Cf. Jaeger, L. 'The Twin Truths of Divine Immanence and Transcendence: Creation, Laws of Nature and Human Freedom' in: Fuller, M., Evers, D. et al. (eds). 2020. *Issues in Science and Theology: Nature—and Beyond. Transcendence and Immanence in Science and Theology.* Springer, Cham: 41-56; Southgate, C. 'Beyond the Disguised Friend: Immanence, Transcendence and Glory in a Darwinian World' in: Fuller, Evers et al., *Issues in Science and Theology*: 57-68.

5.5. Discussion

The above survey summarizes the ideas and thoughts about animal death and suffering as expressed by theologians, philosophers and others during the first six decades of the nineteenth century. As noted in the introduction of this chapter, natural theology began to lose persuasiveness in this time, while for the fledgling science of geology, the opposite was the case. The question is whether and to what extent these developments influenced the contemporary thoughts about the relationship between animal death and predation on one side and divine goodness and benevolence on the other. And what are the consequences of the doctrine of deep time with animal populations replacing each other successively? In the previous periods, God's justice, goodness, and benevolence were at stake, but now, even God's skills in creation could be questioned. Opinions had changed since 1710 when Wilkins wrote that the creation was perfect from the beginning, not in need of any 'mending' afterwards.[310]

For the purpose of clarity, opinions of the authors examined in this chapter are listed in Table 5.1. When comparing this table with Table 4.1 in the previous chapter, it will be seen that in this period, the thoughts about the reasons why animals suffer are much less varied whereas the idea that animal death serves a greater good is still the most prevalent one. In this sense, there is some continuity. On the other hand, there is also loss of continuity as we no longer come across the idea—so popular in the eighteenth century—that animals would be compensated for their suffering in a blessed afterlife.

This does not mean that the idea of an afterlife for the animals was completely off the table—in his Bible Commentary on Paul's letter to the Romans, the Methodist theologian and biblical scholar *Adam Clarke* wrote that 'as they [the animals] have not lost their happiness through their own fault, both the beneficence and justice of God are bound to make them a reparation'. To realize this, 'it is reasonable to conclude, thatas from the present constitution of things, they cannot have the happiness designed for them in *this state*, they must have it in *another*'.[311] The idea that animals will be rewarded for their current misery in a blessed afterlife still lived, but the need to use this as an argument to justify God's attributes in the discussion in general was apparently no longer felt as none of the aforementioned authors—Clarke of course

---

310 Wilkins, J. 1710. *Of the Principles and Duties of Natural Religion: Two Books. The Sixth Edition*. R. Chiswell et al., London: 78.
311 Clarke, A. 1833. *The New Testament of Our Lord and Saviour Jesus Christ. ...Designed as a Help to a Better Understanding of the Sacred Writings. Volume II*. B. Waugh and T. Mason, New York: 101.

excepted—made any allusion to this. In the following paragraphs, I will discuss the options listed in the table in more detail. Those who solved the problem by denying the existence of God are not dealt with here. For them, the suffering of the animals supported their atheistic point of view since vindicating the attributes of someone who does not exist anyhow makes no sense.

5.5.1. Adam Is to Blame

Only a few authors attributed animal death to Adam's transgression: the Anglican scholars Gisborne, Kirby, and Bugg; the Presbyterian minister Young, and the theologian-philosopher Gillespie, the latter however assuming a causal role for fallen angels as well. They all agreed that animals were not created to prey upon each other, but it was only Gisborne who recognized that punishing animals for humanity's faults poses a problem for divine justice; to solve this problem, he supposed that God will compensate them for these undeserved miseries but only in the here and now, satisfaction being given 'antecedently to the sufferings' and not in a blessed afterlife as suggested in the previous century. The others were silent on this point; they overlooked or ignored that it may stand against God's justice to punish innocent animals.

5.5.2. For the Goodness of the Whole

The majority of authors in the period addressed in this chapter considered predation and the death of animals to be signs of divine wisdom and benevolence. In general, their arguments were the same as those brought up by the eighteenth-century authors. Death is required to save the animals from a miserable death when getting old and destitute and serves to keep animal species within their allotted space. Moreover, the animals' limited mental capacities ensure that enjoyments prevail over miseries.

In this way, a maximum of happiness and a minimum of pain is obtained, either for each individual in particular, or, as advocated by Erasmus Darwin, applicable to a larger circle of living beings; this circle may even include humanity—the miseries of a few fallen soldiers being compensated by the joys of countless maggots feeding on their bodies. For North American geologists Hitchcock and Dana, the greater good to which the death of the animals contributed even crosses the boundaries of time. Mankind's death puts an end to a sinful earthly existence and gives access to eternal life, but this implies—because of the intertwining of everything that lives—that the animals also have to die. The minor evil of animal death and suffering is justified by the greater good of a blessed afterlife for humanity.

The concept of successive creations with their own populations of animals did not threaten divine wisdom and benevolence although one would expect that the observation that there had been several massive extinctions of animals in the past should make the argument that predation is needed to preserve each species less plausible. Why, after all, would the Creator take efforts to keep a healthy balance between the various kinds of animals when he himself wiped them out at his pleasure? And why did he create only to destroy?

This was indeed a stumbling block for the scriptural geologists as I have mentioned above, but not for the 'suffering serves a greater good' advocates like Buckland, Bell, Pye Smith, Dana, and Gloag, to mention only some of them: the higher the number of successive creations, the greater the wisdom and goodness of him who made them and the greater the number of living beings to enjoy life. Later generations would make harsher judgments about this, asking why God 'behaved after the manner of a lazy and incompetent architect', apparently not being able to create other than by trial and error:

> [T]he thing that now impresses us in the theory is its extraordinarily irreligious, not to say blasphemous, character. (...) [I]t is hard to see how any one could suppose it in any degree advantageous to religion. (...) For no man out of a madhouse ever behaved in such a manner as that in which, by this hypothesis, the Creator of the universe was supposed to have behaved. Ascribing to him both the ability and the disposition to intervene with absolute freedom in natural (...) phenomena, the theory also represented him as incapable of intervening intelligently or effectually.[312]

Could it be that such thoughts, written at the turn of the twentieth century, already played a role in Darwin's thinking? Considerations like

---

312 Lovejoy, 'The Argument for Evolution before "The Origin of Species"': 548-549. Cf. Lovejoy, "The Argument for Organic Evolution 1830–1858' in: Glass, Temkin, Straus, *Forerunners of Darwin*: 411-414. On this point, it is interesting to note that the question of why God did not create everything at once, but extended the work over a longer period of time, has been raised before. According to the seventeenth-century theologian John Swann (cf. § 3.8.5) it 'was, not because he [God] was unable to make all the world perfect in an instance; but because he would not,' adding that working in this way 'is so farre from eclipsing his power, that it rather doth demonstrate both his power and wisdom to be infite'. We can learn from this that God took his time in making the world fit for mankind and that we should not rush either when we take on an important work. In: Swan, J. 1643. *Specvlvm Mundi. Or a Glasse Representing the Face of the World...The Second Edition Enlarged*. Roger Daniel, Cambridge: 45-46 (45).

these may have contributed to his ambivalence about the existence of design and purpose in nature to which his letters and books testify. But for now, the belief that animal suffering is justifiable because of the higher purpose it serves seems almost unassailable.

5.5.3. Beyond Our Understanding

Thus far, presumed causes for the way in which God deals with his creation have been addressed, God being justified for allowing predation and animal death by referring to the fall or by pointing out the inescapable demands that are connected with a lawful behavior of nature. In both lines of reasoning, attempts were made to understand why God acts as he does. God has to be just, good, benevolent, and powerful and so on, and cases where the contrary is suggested require a conclusive explanation. Some authors, however, abstained from such statements. The Scottish Presbyterians Crombie, Chalmers, Miller, and Anderson fall in this category. Crombie pleaded for humble submission to the 'counsels of Eternal and Unerring wisdom' and Chalmers wrote that 'we can give no vindication of these things'. Miller even went so far that he expressed the conviction that 'in the Divine government the matter of fact always determines the question of right' and Anderson is on the same line when noting that everything is 'visibly dependent upon His will'.

It is obvious that any attempt to reconcile animal suffering and death with divine justice and benevolence was considered idle by these authors who rejected the assumption that God acts in accordance with human considerations; probably, the Calvinistic roots of the Scottish Presbyterians lie at the root of this conviction. At first sight, noting that similar thoughts can be found with the Englishman Prout who wrote that nobody can 'know the mind of God' might refute this idea, but since this latter author obtained his academic education at the University of Edinburgh, he might have imbibed Scottish Presbyterianism as well. Whatever the case, the notion that God's actions cannot be fathomed was not found outside the Scottish region. Elsewhere on the British Isles, most authors took efforts to rescue the divine attributes by supposing a positive outcome of a happiness-versus-misery balance either applicable to each individual living being or calculated for a larger whole or they stuck to the traditional fall-explanation. In this intellectual climate, Darwin published his *Origin*, the influence of which will be discussed in the next chapter.

5.5.4. Just a Stick to Beat the Dog?

Reviewing everything I have found so far for this period has raised some doubts with me whether the suffering of the animals indeed weighed so heavily. It seems that concerns about animal suffering were not always as real as is pretended but rather something that only plays a role in supporting a position already taken or useful to refute an opponent's arguments.

For the *Bridgewater Treatises* authors and those who wrote similar notes, it was beyond dispute that nature and society both testify to a divine benevolent design, which for them implied that doubting the former threatened the credibility of the latter. Therefore, the apparent miseries of animal life had to be accepted as necessary for the greater good of a much valued established order designed by God himself. If that greater good requires animal suffering, so be it. This attitude may also explain why hardly any author of that time condoned animal suffering— as opposed to a century earlier, as I showed in the previous chapter—by assuming a lower sensitivity to pain.[313] It was only the zoologist *Richard Owen* (1804-1892)[314] who reverted to this approach by assigning animals—at least the lower ranks—the privilege of an existence guided by reflexes without conscious sensations. There is no other way to reconcile an apparent scene of suffering 'with the dispensations of a Creation founded on Benevolence.'[315]

The reference to a higher purpose makes it understandable how Charles Bell, one of the *Bridgewater Treatises* authors, could subject animals to painful experiments without any qualms.[316] And Thomas Chalmers—also from this group of authors—argued for careful handling of the animals, but did not reject vivisection either. '[W]e do not foresee, but with the perfecting of the two sciences of anatomy and physiology, the abolition of animal experiments; but we do foresee a gradual, and, at length, a complete abandonment of the experiments of illustration, which

---

313 This is not to say that the belief that animals would feel less pain than humans had fallen into oblivion. It had not but it had found a new application, justifying vivisection rather than defending God's goodness. Cf. Boddice, *A History of Attitudes and Behaviours toward Animals*: 304-317.
314 For biographical details, see Desmond, *Politics of Evolution*: 426.
315 From Richard Owen's unpublished 1842 Hunterian Lectures at the Royal College of Surgeons. The manuscript of this is housed at the Natural History Museum in London: *Manuscripts, Notes, and Synopses. Owen. 1842–48, Owen Collection 38*. The quote is from his 'Hunterian Lectures on the Nervous System 1842: Lecture 1,' 5 April 1842: 33.
316 Berkowitz, C. 2014. 'Defining a Discovery: Priority and Methodological Controversy in Early Nineteenth-Century Anatomy' in: *Notes & Records of the Royal Society Journal of the History of Science* 68 (4): 357-372. Bell's claim that he was the first to clarify the function of the nerves that originate from the spinal cord was disputed by the notorious French vivisectionist François Magendie.

are at present a thousand-fold more numerous than the experiments of humane discovery.'[317] Animal experiments that are only done to illustrate something that has been known since long are objectionable, but that does not apply to the greater good of cutting-edge research because this contributes to the well-being of humans. This lukewarmness towards vivisection supports my assumption that upholding a divinely designed social order took precedence over protecting the interests of the animals.

The scriptural geologists cared less about the suffering of the animals than about defending their view on how the Bible should be interpreted; the latter was their motivation to reject a pre-Adamite death of the animals; not because a long period of animal suffering and death would contend with God's benevolence and justice. And those who aimed to overthrow the social order invoked the animal miseries to proclaim that any belief in a designer who wants the best for his creatures is ridiculous.

In previous centuries, it was thought that the animals were created only for our convenience, at that time in a physical sense—for food and power. Now, they even appeared to be of use in buttressing entrenched positions about society and Scripture. As in the past, animals are 'only for our use', albeit now not so much physically but rather ideologically. Seen in this way, the increased attention to animal suffering that arose during this period indeed has some social impact. But the animal itself had little benefit from that; neither did it steer the debate about the divine attributes in a certain direction.

5.6. Conclusion

In the decades prior to the time when Charles Darwin published his famous book, there were, as in the prior periods, hardly any negative comments on the relationship between divine attributes and animal suffering. The discussion had been complicated by the facts provided by geology that aggravated the amount of death in the non-human animal kingdom, but these new findings did not yield significantly different viewpoints. Neither did a diminishing persuasiveness of natural theology and an increase in awareness of the interests of animals pose a threat. Some authors still explained animal death and predation as the outcome of humanity's sin in a remote past, but most considered these events to be required for the benefit of the whole. Only a few deemed such arguments to be inadequate and preferred to leave the problem of how to reconcile divine goodness and benevolence with animal suffering unresolved. For even less, operating at society's fringe, animal suffering had become an

---

[317] Chalmers, T. 1826. *On Cruelty to Animals: a Sermon, Preached in Edinburgh, on the 5th of March, 1826. Second Edition.* Chalmers & Collins, Glasgow: 28.

argument to propagate atheism. At the eve of the Darwinian era, however, God's attributes or his existence were not widely questioned in spite of these lone opposing voices. To what extent Darwin's troubles with divine benevolence would change this common feeling will be discussed in the next chapter.

Chapter 6: After Darwin

The Divine Attributes at Stake (1860–1961)

Abstract

Before Darwin published his theory of evolution by natural selection, the belief that animal life in all its aspects reflected divine providential care was only rarely doubted. This chapter examines the extent to which this belief persisted after Darwin's theory came to prominence. Examination of the texts written by Darwin's contemporaries and the following generations up to the 1960s shows that the first half century after Darwin did not bring many changes. The majority of the authors who addressed the theme of animal suffering and death in relation to divine wisdom and benevolence saw, despite Darwin's gloomy thoughts on the subject, no reason to adjust their own more optimistic view. As it is, it is good. Others resorted to a strict separation between faith and science; the existence of God is not contested, but it is disputed that nature would reflect his goodness and wisdom. A veil hides him from our eyes. Only a few would break the tacit consensus between science and religion, emphasizing that a nature 'red in tooth and claw' is difficult to reconcile with a benevolent God. For them, God and nature are at strife. In doing so, they adopted the conviction of anti-evolutionist Christian writers that a benevolent God would never create by means of death and destruction—but they drew an opposite conclusion: apparently, there is no God. Darwin appears to be only indirectly involved in the shifts that have occurred in conceptions of the relationship between God and animals. The anti-evolutionists gave birth to the 'incompatibility view', which was then eagerly adopted and nurtured by their atheistic opponents.

6.1. Introduction

As has been amply outlined in Chapter 1, nowadays, nature is often considered to be 'red in tooth and claw', a spectacle of gruesome animal suffering, whereas in the past it was experienced as offering testimony to God's glory. In the seventeenth century, an author could write without any worries about *The Creatures Praying God*,[1] whereas nowadays we are

---

1 Goodman, G. 1622. *The Creatvres Praysing God: or, the Religion of Dumbe Creatures. An Example and Argument for the Stirring vp of Our Deuotion and for the Confusion of Atheisme*...Felik Kingston, London.

told that '[t]he total amount of suffering per year in the natural world is beyond all decent contemplation. During the minute it takes me [Richard Dawkins] to compose this sentence, thousands of animals are being eaten alive; others are running for their lives, whimpering with fear; others are being slowly devoured from within by rasping parasites; thousands of all kinds are dying of starvation, thirst and disease.'[2]

In order to trace the historical roots of this shift in opinion, I have investigated views regarding the relationship between animal suffering and divine attributes—in particular, God's benevolence—for a period extending from late antiquity up to the year in which Darwin published his *Origin of Species*.[3] This preliminary endpoint was chosen to prevent a confounding effect on the findings by any discussion on creation by divine fiat versus evolution by natural selection.

Having arrived at the final stage of this historical overview, it appears that until the end of the fifties of the nineteenth century, God's attributes had remained largely unquestioned. This does not imply that the reality of animal suffering was overlooked or denied. On the contrary, as we have seen, various attempts were made over time to reconcile divine goodness with animal suffering; but such attempts left divine attributes like goodness, power, and wisdom themselves beyond doubt. The vicissitudes of animal behavior and suffering could not endanger belief in them. Rather, this belief determined the interpretation of observations that at first sight suggested otherwise, and various approaches were employed to solve the conflict—if a conflict was perceived. For example, some sought mitigating circumstances, whereas others accepted that 'God moves in a mysterious way'.[4] Thus far, animal suffering had not raised serious questions about God's goodness, let alone had it caused doubts about his existence. It appears that before Darwin published his *Origin*, progress in science and an increased appreciation of the interests of animals had not yet ended up in a denial of God's goodness and benevolence towards his creation; this denial—so widespread nowadays—thus seems to have emerged (in Britain) only after 1859. The question is whether this is coincidental or whether Darwin played a decisive role in this changed view on the relationship between the Creator and his creation.

---

2 Dawkins, R. 1995. *River out of Eden. A Darwinian View of Life*. Weidenfeld & Nicholson, London: 131-132.
3 Darwin, C. 2009 [1859]. *On the Origin of Species by Means of Natural Selection, or the Preservation of Favoured Races in the Struggle for Life*. Reprint of the first edition, edited with an Introduction by William Bynum. Penguin Books, London.
4 First line of a hymn written by William Cowper (1731–1800). 'Judge not the Lord by feeble sense / But trust Him for His grace / Behind a frowning providence / He hides a smiling face.'

To address this topic, I will examine developments from the year that Darwin published his *Origin* until 1961. This end point is chosen because in that year John Whitcomb and Henry Morris published their (in)famous *Genesis Flood*,[5] which represented the outburst of a conflict that had been smouldering for decades between Christians who clung to a young earth while ignoring conflicting scientific data and Christians who wished to harmonize Genesis and geology.[6] For the first group, an old age that included pre-Adamite animal suffering was in blatant contradiction not only with Scripture but also with God's wisdom and benevolence; the latter group, by contrast, denied that there was a conflict here.[7]

I realize that throughout this long period, the thoughts about the validity of Darwin's theory did not remain the same.[8] Darwinism was even considered to be moribund in the early twentieth century, and only from the 1920s onwards neo-Darwinism emerged as a synthesis of Darwin's theory of natural selection with genetics based on Mendel's discoveries.[9] But shifts in ideas about Darwin's theory and the mechanisms of evolution do not necessarily affect the problem at hand. For the question is: how did authors view the position of God in relation to animal suffering in an age when the conviction that nature reflects divine design had to compete with the belief that nature is governed by

---

5   Whitcomb, J.C., Morris, H.M. 1961. *The Genesis Flood. The Biblical Record and Its Scientific Implications*. Presbyterian and Reformed Publishing Co., Phillipsburg.
6   Bowler, P.J. 2007. *Monkey Trials and Gorilla Sermons. Evolution and Christianity from Darwin to Intelligent Design*. Harvard University Press, Cambridge (MA): 189-228; Gayon, J. 'From Darwin to Today in Evolutionary Biology' in: Hodge, J., Radick, G. (eds). 2009. *The Cambridge Companion to Darwin. Second Edition.* Cambridge University Press, Cambridge: 277-301; Matzke, N.J. 2010. 'The Evolution of Creationist Movements' in: *Evolution: Education and Outreach* 3: 145-162.
7   McIver, T.A. 1989. *Creationism. Intellectual Origins, Cultural Context, and Theoretical Diversity*. PhD Thesis, University of California, Los Angeles, Chapter 2; Numbers, R.L. 2006. *The Creationists. From Scientific Creationism to Intelligent Design. Expanded Edition*, Harvard University Press, Cambridge (MA): 206-238; Rios, C.M. 2014. *After the Monkey Trial. Evangelical Scientists and a New Creationism*. Fordham University Press, New York: 54-72.
8   Moore, J. 1991. 'Deconstructing Darwinism: The Politics of Evolution in the 1860s' in: *Journal of the History of Biology* 24 (3): 353-408; Richards, R.J. 2009. 'Darwin's Place in the History of Thought: a Reevaluation' in: *Proceedings of the National Academy of Sciences* 106 (Suppl. 1): 10056-10060; Lightman, B. 2010. 'Darwin and the Popularization of Evolution' in: *Notes & Records of the Royal Society* 64: 5-24.
9   Bowler, P.J. 2005. 'Revisiting the Eclipse of Darwinism. The "Darwinian Revolution": Whether, What and Whose?' in: *Journal of the History of Biology* 38 (1): 19-32; Largent, M.A. 2009. 'The So-Called Eclipse of Darwinism' in: *Transactions of the American Philosophical Society, New Series* 99 (1): 3-21.

'unintelligent forces'?[10] So it is not in Darwin per se that we are interested, but in the possible influence of upcoming evolutionary theories on the awareness of animal suffering as a serious issue.

For the purpose thus outlined, secondary sources devoted to the interaction of science and theology were screened to map out the variety of opinions about animal suffering and divine benevolence circulating from 1859 till 1961 and to identify authors who can be considered representative of the different views on this theme.[11] Next, the number of authors found in this way could be increased by using these authors' references and other bibliographic data as an additional source. The ideas of the authors identified in this two-step approach are discussed in the next sections. I start with a brief survey of the contemporary intellectual climate (§ 6.2). Thereafter, in § 6.3, I discuss the views of those who—either rejecting Darwinian evolution (§ 6.3.1) or accepting it (§ 6.3.2)—continued the natural theology tradition. It is shown how they, one way or another, managed to combine animal suffering with divine benevolence. Next, I turn to authors who broke with the natural theology tradition. Among them the general conviction is that the fate of animals cannot be reconciled with a design that proclaims divine wisdom and benevolence, and in order to save God, they dispute that he reveals himself in nature. (§ 6.4). Finally, I examine those who refrained from any compromise. According to them—given Darwinian evolution—animal suffering is incompatible with God's perfections. It is either Darwinian evolution or the traditional conception of God as the one who even clothes the grass of the field that should therefore be rejected (§ 6.5). For the three categories,

---

10 Ellegård, A. 1990. *Darwin and the General Reader. The Reception of Darwin's Theory of Evolution in the British Periodical Press, 1859–1872.* The University of Chicago Press, Chicago: 114-140 (129).

11 Moore, J.R. 1975. 'Evolutionary Theory and Christian Faith: a Bibliographic Guide to the Post-Darwinism Controversies' in: *Christian Scholar's Review* 4 (3): 211-230; Moore, J.R. 1979. *The Post-Darwinian Controversies. A Study of the Protestant Struggle to Come to Terms with Darwin in Great Britain and America 1870–1900.* Cambridge University Press, Cambridge; Livingstone, D.N. 1984. *Darwin's Forgotten Defenders. The Encounter Between Evangelical Theology and Evolutionary Thought.* Regent College Publishing, Vancouver; Ellegård, *Darwin and the General Reader*; Brooke, J.H. 1991. *Science and Religion. Some Historical Perspectives.* Cambridge University Press, Cambridge: 275-320; Livingstone, D.N., Hart, D.G., Noll, M.A. (eds). 1999. *Evangelicals and Science in Historical Perspective.* Oxford University Press, New York; Bowler, P.J. 2001. *Reconciling Science and Religion. The Debate in Early-Twentieth-Century Britain.* The University of Chicago Press, Chicago; McGrath, A.E. 2011. *Darwinism and the Divine. Evolutionary Thought and Natural Theology. The 2009 Hulsean Lectures.* University of Cambridge. Wiley-Blackwell, Chichester; Livingstone, D.N. 2014. *Dealing with Darwin, Place, Politics, and Rhetoric in Religious Engagements with Evolution. The Gifford Lectures, 2014.* Johns Hopkins University Press, Baltimore.

I will present the various authors in chronological order, so that it is possible to trace certain developments. In § 6.6, I discuss the results of my explorations in view of the core question—the emergence of doubts about the possibility to square animal suffering with divine benevolence and Darwin's role in this—and in § 6.7, a conclusion is formulated.

6.2. Background

As discussed in Chapter 5, in the decades that predate the publication of Darwin's *Origin*, the idea that the earth was of old age and had been populated by a multitude of life forms during large periods of time had become widely accepted. The difference between the chronologies of Genesis and geology was explained by assuming either that the creation days represented periods of an undetermined length or that there had been earlier worlds antedating the events described in Genesis. In both scenarios, now extinct animal species had been replaced by others, and in this way, the glory of the Creator came out even better. Also, many of those who did not subscribe to either a 'day-age view' or a 'gap theory' held that God's creative acts had not been limited to only one week, but formed an ongoing process that covered countless years. Both theologians and scientists agreed with this view in peaceful co-existence.

The importance attached to such a peaceful relationship between religion and science in the British Isles at that time becomes apparent in a note of the anthropologist *James Hunt*. In 1864, Hunt published an English translation of a treatise about humanity's place in nature written by the German scholar *Carl Vogt* (1817–1895).[12] In his preface, he apologized for some passages that could be envisaged as offensive. 'If M. Vogt had been an Englishman I should certainly have highly censured a man of such profound and extensive views for wasting his energies in attacking the opinions of theologians. (...) Sometimes the author conveys the impression that he writes merely with a view of destroying belief in generally received theological dogmas.'[13] In this climate of mutual respect, Darwin's theory of evolution by natural selection proved to be easily adaptable to the contemporary theological views by assuming that God could guide the development of animals and species just as well by overseeing selection and variation as by consecutive creative acts.[14]

---

12 Carl Vogt was a notorious materialist, who advocated a polygenist evolution of the human race; in his view, black people were closely related to the apes. See Wolpoff, M., Caspari, R. 1997. *Race and Human Evolution*. Simon & Schuster, New York: 128-131.

13 Hunt, J. 1864. 'Editor's Preface' in: Vogt, C. *Lectures on Man: His Place in Creation, and in the History of the Earth*. Longman et al., London: xiii-xiv.

14 Moore, *Post-Darwinian Controversies*: 193-345; Phipps, W.E. 1983. 'Darwin and Cambridge Natural Theology' in: *Bios* 54 (4): 218-227; Brooke, *Science and Religion*:

The acceptance or rejection of evolution by natural selection appeared to depend more on local circumstances than on scientific or theological considerations. Presbyterians in Edinburgh had less troubles with evolution but were more occupied with fighting the attacks on the authority of the Bible. Their brethren in Belfast on the other hand loathed evolutionary theory from the bottom of their hearts. They had been shocked by the hostility of science towards religion shown by some representatives of the British Association for the Advancement of Science—a hostility that, however, was not so much directed against religion as such (as was the case with the aforementioned German scholar Carl Vogt)—but against the clergy's claim that science should be subordinate to religion.[15] It was generally recognized that Darwin's theory implied an increased role of chance at the expense of providential control, an intensification of the problem of evil, and a challenge to humanity's presumed superiority to the animals.[16] In actual practice, however, it was mainly the latter point that was experienced as a potential threat to traditional belief.[17]

Already earlier in the nineteenth century, Robert Chambers's *Vestiges of the Natural History of Creation*[18] had evoked much consternation on

---

275-320; Livingstone, *Darwin's Forgotten Defenders*: 57-145; Ellegård, *Darwin and the General Reader*: 114-140; England, R. 2001. 'Natural Selection, Teleology, and the Logos: From Darwin to the Oxford Neo-Darwinists, 1859-1909' in: *Osiris* 16: 270-87; Roberts, J.H. 'That Darwin Destroyed Natural Theology' in: Numbers, R.L. (ed.). 2009. *Galileo Goes to Jail and Other Myths about Science and Religion*. Harvard University Press, Cambridge (MA): 161-169; Sollereder, B. 2010. 'The Darwin–Gray Exchange' in: *Theology and Science* 8 (4): 417-432; Berry, R.J. 'Biology since Darwin' in: Robinson, A. (ed.). 2012. *Darwinism and Natural Theology. Evolving Perspectives*. Cambridge Scholars Publishing, Newcastle upon Tyne: 12-38; Brooke, J.H. 'Christian Darwinians' in: Robinson, *Darwinism and Natural Theology*: 47-67.

15 Barton, R. 1987. 'John Tyndall, Pantheist: a Rereading of the Belfast Address' in: *Osiris* 3: 111-134; Livingstone, D.N. 'Situating Evangelical Responses to Evolution' in: Livingstone, Hart, Noll, *Evangelicals and Science in Historical Perspective*: 193-219; Livingstone, *Dealing with Darwin*: 27-88, 197-207. For additional description of the way in which questions about the authority of Scripture and ecclesiastical controversies within the Church of England interfered with the acceptance or rejection of Darwinism, see Gregory, F. 'The Impact of Darwinian Evolution on Protestant Theology in the Nineteenth Century' in: Lindberg D.C., Numbers, R.L. (eds). 1986. *God & Nature. Historical Essays on the Encounter between Christianity and Science*. University of California Press, Berkeley: 369-390, in particular pp. 372-374.

16 Jones, R.H. 2012. *For the Glory of God. The Role of Christianity in the Rise and Development of Modern Science. Volume II: The History of Christian Ideas and Control Beliefs in Science*. University Press of America, Lanham: 121-125; Fergusson, D. 'Natural Theology after Darwin' in: Robinson, *Darwinism and Natural Theology*: 78-95, in particular pp. 83-92.

17 Ellegård, *Darwin and the General Reader*: 293-331, 332-337.

18 [Chambers, R.] 1844. *Vestiges of the Natural History of Creation*. John Churchill, London.

specifically this issue, as we saw in the previous chapter. Darwin may have postponed the treatment of this tricky subject until later in his life,[19] but the consequences of his ideas for the descent of humanity could not be ignored. Referring to Darwin, the famous Baptist preacher *Charles Haddon Spurgeon* (1834–1892) told his audience that '[a]ny bearded gentleman here who chooses, may claim relationship with the oyster; and others may imagine that they themselves are only developed gorillas, but I, on my own part, believe there is a great gulf fixed between us, so that they who would pass from us to you [addressing a stuffed gorilla on display] cannot; neither can they come to us who would pass from thence'.[20] Not only Spurgeon thought so, but with him and after him many others. The bones studied by the paleoanthropologists would remain bones of contention for the time to come.[21] Moreover, the theme of human descent became an inexhaustible source of entertainment (Fig. 6.1).[22]

---

19 Darwin, C. 1871. *The Descent of Man, and Selection in Relation to Sex. In Two Volumes.* John Murray, London.

20 Spurgeon, C.H. 1861. *The Gorilla and the Land He Inhabits. A Lecture Delivered by the Rev. C.H. Spurgeon in the Metropolitan Tabernacle, Newington on Tuesday, October 1st 1861.* n.p., n.p.: 9. Note the allusion to the parable of the rich man and Lazarus in Luke 16:26: 'And beside all this, between us and you there is a great gulf fixed: so that they which would pass from hence to you cannot; neither can they pass to us, that would come from thence.' (KJV). The debate on human descent was heavily influenced by the contemporary discovery of the gorilla, see Reel, M. 2013. *Between Man and Beast. An Unlikely Explorer, the Evolution Debates, and the African Adventure that Took the Victorian World by Storm.* Doubleday, New York. Spurgeon's reluctance to accept an ape as ancestor of humankind did, however, not prevent him from accepting a high age of the earth. 'We know not how remote the period of the creation of this globe may be—certainly many millions of years before the time of Adam. Our planet has passed through various stages of existence, and different kinds of creatures have lived on its surface, all of which have been fashioned by God.' Quoted from Spurgeon, C.H. 'Sermon VI. The Power of the Holy Ghost' in: Spurgeon, C.H. 1856. *"The Modern Whitfield." Sermons of the Rev. C.H. Spurgeon, of London; with an Introduction and Sketch of his Life by E.L. Magoon.* Sheldon, Blakeman and Company, New York: 112-133 (115).
   Cf. VanDoodewaard, W. 2015. *The Quest for the Historical Adam. Genesis, Hermeneutics, and Human Origins.* Reformation Heritage Books, Grand Rapids: 148n52.

21 Bowler, *Reconciling Science and Religion*: 287-328; VanDoodewaard, *The Quest for the Historical Adam*; Mortenson, T. (ed.). 2016. *Searching for Adam. Genesis & the Truth about Man's Origin.* Master Books, Green Forest; Brink, G. van den. 2020. *Reformed Theology and Evolutionary Theory.* Wm. B. Eerdmans, Grand Rapids: 136-159; Craig, W.L. 2021. *In Quest of the Historical Adam. A Biblical and Scientific Exploration.* Wm. B. Eerdmans, Grand Rapids.

22 Clark, C.A. 2009. '"You Are Here": Missing Links, Chains of Being, and the Language of Cartoons' in: *Isis* 100 (3): 571-589.

Fig. 6.1. Spurgeon's lecture on the gorilla evoked much upheaval, not only in print but also in picture. At the backside of this photograph, one reads the following text. 'We are now to be entertained by Mr. Spurgeon on the "Gorilla" (laughter). But in after ages -- according to the development theory -- we shall doubtless have a Gorilla lecturing on Mr. Spurgeon" (Roars of Laughter). (Extract from the speech of the Rt. Honorable AH Layard MP at Mr Spurgeon's Lecture.)" https://www.worthpoint.com/worthopedia/cdv-charles-spurgeon-cartoon-carte-de-visite. Accessed on 15 February 2022.

The speaker referred to was Austen Layard, the Parliament member representing the South London district where Spurgeon's lecture hall was located. He took the opportunity to deliver an introductory talk to Spurgeon's lecture as a God-given opportunity to address so many potential voters at one time. And with his sneering remark that with the passage of time gorillas with the ability to lecture on Spurgeon would likely emerge, he struck the right chord for an audience that was already skeptical of the idea that mankind and ape share a common ancestor. For the complete story of Spurgeon's foray into a field fraught with sensitivities and the subsequent uproar that struck him so that for some weeks, he was unable to deliver his Sunday sermons, see Reel, M. 2013. *Between Man and Beast. An Unlikely Explorer, the Evolution Debates, and the African Adventure that Took the Victorian World by Storm*. Doubleday, New York: 138-141, 161-167.

Compared to the focus on human descent, the fact that Darwin's theory could also have implications for the problem of the unpleasant aspects of the lives of animals in relation to God's goodness and wisdom, evoked less upheaval.[23] People had already known for a long time that nature deals roughly with her subjects; in that sense, Darwin's theory of the *survival of the fittest* did not pose a problem not already encountered before. What was new, however, was that Darwin rejected the arguments put forward thus far to alleviate this problem. Hitherto—before Darwin—

---

23 Ellegård, *Darwin and the General Reader*: 114-140.

people had tried to save divine attributes by assuming that animal sufferings served an intended higher purpose, but for Darwin—as addressed in Chapter 5 (cf. § 5.4.18)—these arguments fell short. '[W]hat advantage can there be in the sufferings of millions of the lower animals throughout almost endless time?'[24]

The question waiting for an answer is whether and to what extent Darwin's refusal to associate animal suffering with divine design had any influence on a wider circle in the decades that would follow. The next three sections are devoted to this issue. I will start with discussing those for whom animal suffering posed no serious problem for the divine attributes. Thereafter, I pay attention to those that found the case of reconciling divine benevolence with animal suffering less straightforward and I will end with those who were convinced that animal suffering and divine benevolence are irreconcilable and therefore came to deny God's existence.

6.3. Whatever Is Is Right
As discussed in Chapter 5, animal suffering had not been a major issue in the decades predating the publication of Darwin's *Origin*. Death and predation in the non-human animal kingdom could be explained as necessary to maintain the harmonious balance between the different animal species and to provide a quick delivery from bodily decay in case of disease, accidental injuries, and from the decrepitude that comes with advanced age. Hence, death and predation were not without purpose. Darwin, however, now had deprived nature of its purposefulness by replacing divine design with the law of natural selection upon random variations. That raised the question of whether animal suffering still could be justified by referring to such a purpose, or whether it was entirely meaningless. Thus, a new reflection on the problem of animal suffering became necessary. In this challenge put forward by Darwin, two options were available to those who did not want to drop the concept of a benevolent divine design. Some rejected Darwin's thoughts entirely, considering them either unscientific or a dethronement of God as Creator, or both. Others were less irreconcilable and interpreted Darwin's theory as a mechanism that God could employ to reach his intended purpose. For the sake of clarity, I discuss the considerations about animal suffering as put forward by the authors from these two groups separately, starting with the first one—the hardcore anti-Darwinians. Was their rejection of Darwin's theory of evolution based on the belief that the emerging of new animal species by natural selection robs animal suffering of its purpose and thereby

---

24 Darwin, C. 1887. *The Autobiography of Charles Darwin 1809–1882. With the Original Omissions Restored. Edited and with Appendix and Notes by His Grand-daughter Nora Barlow*. Collins, London: 90.

a threat to God's goodness, or was it based on other reasons such as (alleged) insufficient scientific evidence?

6.3.1. Christian Anti-Darwinians About Animal Suffering and Divine Benevolence

The Presbyterian *John William Dawson* (1820–1899), a Nova Scotia–born geologist and graduate of the University of Edinburgh who had returned to Canada,[25] was one of the first to enter the fray against Darwin. Already in April 1860, less than six months after the publication of the *Origin*, he wrote a strongly negative review of the book—stating that 'the struggle for existence is a myth, and its employment as a means of improvement still more mythical'.[26] Nature offers no evidence of this idea, as among the fossils no transitional forms between species are present.

In rejecting the concept of one species developing into another by an accumulation of minute changes, Dawson joined the ranks of the pre-Darwinian geologists (including Lyell) discussed in the previous chapter, who had unanimously rejected this idea as well. New species only arose by direct divine creation.[27] This conviction stamped the first book Dawson wrote about the relationship between nature and Scripture. Interestingly, however, Dawson did accept an old earth with countless species predating the advent of humans for long periods of time. Therefore, the question how the massive suffering and dying of so many animals could be reconciled with God's wisdom and goodness could have bothered him. But it did not. In his view, death had ruled the world since the introduction of animals. Thinking otherwise 'would be the extremest folly, and would involve at once a misinterpretation of the geologic record, and a denial of the agency of an intelligent Designer as revealed in scripture, and indicated by the succession of beings'.[28] Similar notes can be found in one of Dawson's later publications. 'For countless ages the earth had been inhabited by creatures wonderful in their structures and instincts, and mutely testifying, as their buried remains still do, to the Creator's glory.'[29]

---

25 Cornell, J.F. 1983. 'From Creation to Evolution: Sir William Dawson and the Idea of Design in the Nineteenth Century' in: *Journal of the History of Biology* 16 (1): 137-170; Livingstone, *Dealing with Darwin*: 91-99.
26 Dawson, J.W. 1860. 'Review of "Darwin on the Origin of Species by Means of Natural Selection"' in: *Canadian Naturalist and Geologist* 5 (2): 100-120 (113).
27 Cornell, 'From Creation to Evolution.'
28 Dawson, J.W. 1860. *Archaia or Studies of the Cosmogony and Natural History of the Hebrew Scriptures*. B. Dawson & Son, Montreal: 353-354 (354).
29 Dawson, J.W. 1877. *The Origin of the World, According to Revelation and Science*. Harper & Brothers, New York: 235-236 (235).

Being aware that many animals are carnivorous by nature, Dawson even approvingly quoted from Tennyson's *In Memoriam*. 'Nature red in tooth and claw' represents the way in which God carries out his 'progressive' plan—ancient forms of life being replaced by newly created ones.[30] When the writer of Genesis informs us that the animals were only given green herbs for food, he probably has in mind the group of animals that humans had to deal with in the Garden of Eden or—in case all animals are meant—that ultimately the total animal kingdom will depend on plants for its food.[31] What it means for the animals themselves to be part of a cycle of life and death was left unaddressed. There is no reason to believe that for Dawson animal suffering formed a threat to divine benevolence as he was silent on this issue, in contrast with earlier authors from the realm of Scottish Presbyterianism like Thomas Chalmers (cf. § 5.4.5) and Hugh Miller (cf. § 5.4.13). Possibly, he considered this problem already sufficiently covered by them, being aware of at least the work of Miller from which he quoted repeatedly.[32]

Such neglect of animal suffering was not an option for the dedicated warrior against vivisection, *Francis Orpen Morris* (1810–1893).[33] This Anglican cleric and ornithologist gained fame—or notoriety—by his relentless crusade against Darwinism, which he felt was not supported by the facts of nature. There are no gradual transitions between different animal species, and, still more importantly, Scripture tells us that each animal species emerged through divine intervention.[34] To come to terms with animal suffering, Morris took his refuge to the time-honored concept of a future compensation in a blessed afterlife, an idea already cherished for several centuries as shown in the Chapters 3–5. There is no other way to compensate the animals for their sufferings that are, 'the necessary consequence of the fall of man, and too frequently aggravated unnecessarily by him.'[35] It is all our fault and 'we increase our debt every day'.[36]

---

30 Dawson, *The Origin*: 222. The relevant lines of Tennyson's poem are quoted on pp. 222-223.
31 Dawson, *The Origin*: 240-241.
32 Dawson, *The Origin*: 123, 135, 140. He does not quote Miller on the topic of animal suffering, though.
33 Morris, M.C.F. 1897. *Francis Orpen Morris. A Memoir*...John C. Nimmo, London: 213-231; Kofoid, C.A. 1938. 'Francis Orpen Morris: Ornithologist and Anti-Darwinist' in: *The Auk* 55 (3): 496-500; Moore, *Post-Darwinian Controversies*: 196-197.
34 Morris, F.O. 1869. *Difficulties of Darwinism*...Longmans et al., London; Morris, F.O. 1882. *All the Articles of the Darwin Faith. Re-redoubled Edition*. William Poole, London.
35 Morris, F.O. 1861. *Records of Animal Sagacity and Character. With a Preface on the Future Existence of the Animal Creation*. Longman et al., London: xx. Cf. Hamilton, J. 1877. *Animal Futurity: a Plea for the Immortality of the Brutes*. C. Aitchison, Belfast.
36 Catechism of Heidelberg, Q & A 13.

It may be that it was not so much scientific objections or reverence for Scripture but rather his sympathy for the animals that led this author to condemn Darwinism. Morris may have felt that a sense of guilt toward the animals evoked by the awareness that they suffer because of our sins would keep us from treating them cruelly or negligently. With Darwinism, which separates animal suffering from human sin, such a humbling sense of culpability is lost. And the fact that Darwin himself recommended vivisection as a tool for progression in science will not have contributed to the good relations either.[37]

Other contemporary authors who disagreed with Darwin did not share Morris's concerns about the animals' fate, let alone worry about who might be responsible for it. They disputed—as Dawson did—that new species could arise by modification through natural selection but saw no trouble in accepting that animal death predated Adam's sin. One of the most prolific of them was the Methodist minister *Luther T. Townsend* (1838–1922).[38] Townsend did not see a problem in the thought that there had already been catastrophic events on the earth before humanity entered the scene.[39] Therefore, 'the world is not improperly represented as being at that time a vast and silent burial-ground'.[40] In the earth's crust we see indications of large periods in which the fish, amphibians, saurians, giant birds, and pre-glacial mammals successively held sway, periods that were sometimes accompanied by unimaginable violence.[41] Obviously, it was not the idea of an old earth with death and destruction before Adam that urged Townsend to dismiss evolution as 'a theory that tends to dethrone God'.[42] Neither did this author show much

---

37 Darwin, C. 1881. 'Mr. Darwin on Vivisection' in: *The British Medical Journal* 1 (23 April): 660. Vivisection was a hotly debated topic in these decades, so much so that a government-appointeded committee considered whether legislation in this area was desirable. Darwin's positive attitude toward vivisection is also evident in the minutes of this committee. 'I am fully convinced that physiology can progress only by the aid of experiments on living animals. I cannot think of any one step which has been made in physiology without that aid.' In: *Report of the Royal Commission on the Practice of Subjecting Live Animals to Experiments for Scientific Purposes; with Minutes of Evidence and Appendix. Presented to Both Houses of Parliament by Command of Her Majesty.* 1876. George Edward Eyre and William Spottiswoode, London: 233-234 (234). I will return to this subject in Chapter 7, § 7.2.7.
38 Numbers, *The Creationists*: 28-29.
39 Townsend, L.T. 1881. *The Mosaic Record and Modern Science*. Howard Gannett, Boston: 24.
40 Townsend, L.T. 1896. *Evolution or Creation. A Critical Review of the Scientific and Scriptural Theories of Creation and Certain Related Subjects*. Fleming H. Revell Company, New York: 168.
41 Townsend, L.T. 1904. *Adam and Eve. History or Myth?* The Chapple Publishing Co., Boston: 78-80.
42 Townsend, L.T. 1905. *Collapse of Evolution...* National Magazine Company, Boston: 56.

concern with the vicissitudes of the animals; birth, growth, decay and death are the fate of every living being and nothing to be worried about.[43] Rather, it was the elevation of some animals at the expense of humanity—the fact that evolution tends to 'elevate monkeys and degrade men', as he put it—that sparked his resistance.[44]

Neither the Presbyterian Dawson nor the Anglican Morris or the Methodist Townsend saw the suffering of the animals as caused by the influence of evil forces that had corrupted God's creation, as had been the view of William Honyman Gillespie in the decades before Darwin (cf. § 5.4.11). They could have done that; Dawson at least was aware of this idea. He refers in passing to the possibility of an earth predating humanity and governed by fallen angels at the time, but he did not elaborate on that, neither in the affirmative nor in the negative.[45] It was a theologian belonging to the Plymouth Brethren, *George Pember* (1837–1910),[46] who—several years after the appearance of the *Origin*—revived the idea of a catastrophe antedating the appearance of humanity. According to Pember, in our era animal death and predation are due to Adam's fall, but animal death predating humanity took place in a world that was subjected to the rule of fallen angels. This view arose not so much out of compassion for the animals as from the fact that for Pember, death was inseparable from sin.[47]

It is obvious by now that rejecting Darwin's theory did not imply that one should also reject an old earth with all that it encompasses. On the other side of the Atlantic Ocean, an anonymous author wrote in *The Fundamentals* of 1912, that 'the evolutionary theory was conceived in agnosticism, and born and nurtured in infidelity', but also wrote a statement of adhesion to Townsend. This latter author had—as we have seen above—no problems with an old age of the earth, and apparently,

---

43 Townsend, *Collapse of Evolution*: 16.
44 Townsend, *Collapse of Evolution*: 56.
45 Dawson, *Archaia*: 365.
46 For biographical details, see https://peoplepill.com/people/g-h-pember/. Accessed on 14 December 2021.
47 Pember took his starting point in the gap theory. Prior to the present world, there had been an earlier one that ended in the chaos described in Genesis 1:2. This first world fell prey to decay and destruction because Satan, created as Lucifer and appointed steward over this first world, withdrew from God's rule. In this way, the geologically irrefutable fact of death in the animal kingdom long before Adam came on the scene is explained. Death is due to sin, both in the first creation that ended in chaos and in the present one that will be renewed by fire. In both, the animals suffer as innocent bystanders. See Pember, G.H. 1889. *Earth's Earliest Ages; and Their Connection with Modern Spiritualism and Theosophy. Fifth Edition.* Hodder and Stoughton, London: 33-77. Pember's book went through numerous reprints, the last one in 1975.

this anonymous author did not either.[48] Evolution—in a Darwinian sense or otherwise—puts God offside *and* degrades man, and that is the problem Christians have to tackle, not the vicissitudes of animal life. An old age of the earth—including pre-human animal life and death—was not a predominant point of contestation by then. This is nicely illustrated by the famous 'monkey trial', in which the issue of teaching evolution at public schools was at stake: the defender of the anti-evolutionists' case, *William Jennings Bryan*, confessed to believing that the Genesis days of creation represented large periods of time.[49]

The authors mentioned so far—the outsider Morris excepted—adhered to the views of the pre-Darwinian geologists like Sedgwick, Buckland, and Pye Smith, to name but a few (cf. § 5.4). Given this continuity, I conclude that for this group of authors, Darwin's theory was only an incentive to clarify their own point of view and not an impulse to change their ideas about nature or the suffering of animals, ideas already held before Darwin entered the scene. One of their most prominent reasons to reject Darwinian evolution even was that it seemed to elevate the status of animals at the expense of humans; thus, it was not that they pitied the fate of animals under Darwinian conditions, but the fate and status of humanity! That their rejection of Darwinian evolution was not inspired by their concern for animals is clear from the fact that they did accept an old age of the earth, on which processes of death and dying in the animal kingdom had been going on for millions of years. The only difference was that in their view new species came into existence by divine special creation, not by evolution. The authors to be discussed next had more flexibility of mind *vis-à-vis* Darwinian evolution.

6.3.2. Christian Darwinists About Animal Suffering and Divine Benevolence
The authors addressed thus far rejected Darwin's theory that new animal species arose by natural selection and not by divine intervention, but

---

48 Anonymous. 1912. 'Evolutionism in the Pulpit' in: *The Fundamentals. A Testimony to the Truth Volume VIII*. Testimony Publishing Company, Chicago: 27-35 (31, 30).

49 Larson, E.J. 'The Scopes Trial in History and Legend' in: Lindberg, D.C., Numbers, R.L. (eds). 2003. *When Science & Christianity Meet*. The University of Chicago Press, Chicago: 245-264. Cf. Numbers, *The Creationists*: 51-87, 120-207; Rios, *After the Monkey Trial*: 14-40. That later authors as well did not always make a sound distinction between rejecting evolution and rejecting the old age of the earth can be deduced from the text of Alfred Rehwinkel (1951). Rehwinkel referred to geologists like Hugh Miller, John Pye Smith, and William Dawson as 'eminent scientists' who nevertheless remained 'faithful believers and defenders of the Bible' while Rehwinkel himself rejected an old earth for biblical reasons. See Rehwinkel, A.M. 1951. *The Flood in the Light of the Bible, Geology, and Archaeology*. Concordia Publishing House, St. Louis: xviii.

there were other voices heard as well. This is illustrated in one of the first recorded responses to Darwin's book, which came from the Anglican cleric and university professor *Charles Kingsley* (1819–1875). Having seen a preprint of the *Origin*, he wrote in a letter to Darwin, dated on 18 November 1859—six days before the book became available to the public on 24 November—that 'it is just as noble a conception of Deity, to believe that he created primal forms capable of self development into all forms needful pro tempore & pro loco, as to believe that He required a fresh act of intervention to supply the lacunas which he himself had made'.[50] Twelve years later, Kingsley expressed the same opinion in words that are more often quoted: 'We knew of old that God was so wise that He could make all things; but behold, He is so much wiser than even that, that He can make all things make themselves.' That this God-designed capacity for self-development implied a struggle for existence, should not be seen as a threat for his attributes. After all, Scripture 'reveals a God not merely of love, but of sternness – a God in whose eyes physical pain is not the worst of evils, nor animal life (…) the most precious of objects'.[51]

Kingsley did not stand alone in this view. In 1868, the influential Anglican cleric *John Henry Newman* (1801–1890), who converted to Roman Catholicism in 1845,[52] had no troubles in accepting evolution either. In his letter to another cleric, he wrote that he did not see why one has to deny evolution:

> As to the Divine *Design*, is it not an instance of incomprehensibly and infinitely marvellous Wisdom and Design to have given certain laws to matter millions of ages ago, which have surely and precisely worked out, in the long course of those ages, those effects which He from the first proposed. Mr Darwin's theory *need* not then be atheistical, be it true or

---

50 Kingsley to Darwin. 18 November 1859. *Darwin Correspondence Project*, "Letter no. 2534," accessed on 14 December 2021, https://www.darwinproject.ac.uk/letter/?docId=letters/DCP-LETT-2534.xml. These lines were quoted almost *verbatim* by Darwin in the second edition of the *Origin* at p. 481. 'A celebrated author and divine has written to me that "he has gradually learnt to see that it is just as noble a conception of the Deity to believe that He created a few original forms capable of self-development into other and needful forms, as to believe that He required a fresh act of creation to supply the voids caused by the action of His laws."' Darwin, C. 1860. *On the Origin of Species by Means of Natural Selection…Fifth Thousand*. John Murray, London: 481.
51 Kingsley, C. 1871. 'The Natural Theology of the Future' in: *MacMillan's Magazine* 23: 370-378 (377).
52 For biographical details, see Aquino, F.D., King, B.J. (eds). 2018. *The Oxford Handbook of John Henry Newman*. Oxford University Press, Oxford.

not; it may simply be suggesting a larger idea of Divine Prescience and Skill.⁵³

It is obvious that for Newman, Darwinism does not threaten the Christian faith; it is only a theory that describes how God has worked out his plan for creation throughout the ages. Worries about the amount of animal suffering that comes with it—a source of concern for Darwin himself— were lost on Newman. In his view, animal suffering is no matter of concern anyhow. 'Brutes feel far less than man, because they cannot think of what they feel.'⁵⁴ To this neo-Cartesian interpretation of animals' feelings, Newman even gave a remarkable theological twist when saying that in the same way as 'men are superior to brute animals and are affected by pain more than they, (...) so in like manner our Lord [referring to Christ's passion] felt pain of the body with an advertence and a consciousness (...) which none of us can possibly fathom or compass.'⁵⁵ For this Roman-Catholic author, creation and evolution were compatible and animal suffering an issue of minor significance. His fellow Roman Catholic, the biologist *St. George Mivart* (1827–1900),⁵⁶ had the same opinion: the level of pain highly depends on the mental abilities of the sufferer.⁵⁷ Authors belonging to other Christian denominations would soon follow the same track.

In 1872, the Quaker politician *Edward Fry* (1827–1918)⁵⁸ acknowledged that Darwin's theory could be shocking because of the violence associated

---

53 Newman, J.H. 1868. 'To J. Walker of Scarborough' in: *The Letters and Diaries of John Henry Newman. Electronic Edition. Volume XXIV: A Grammar of Assent (January 1868 to December 1869)*: 77-78. For more details on the attitude of the Roman Catholic Church to evolution, see Hess, P.M.J. 'Evolution, Suffering, and the God of Hope in Roman Catholic Thought after Darwin' in: Bennett, G. et al. (eds). 2008. *The Evolution of Evil*. Vandenhoeck & Ruprecht, Göttingen: 234-254.
54 Newman, J.H. 1862 [1849]. *Discourses Addressed to Mixed Congregations. Third Edition*. James Duffy, Dublin: 379-380.
55 Newman, *Discourses*: 383. On the continent, upcoming materialism had led to a renewed attention for Descartes as a way to save the distinction between the material and the mental realm, but whether this had influenced Newman's ideas is unclear. See Zijlstra, C. P. 2005. *The Rebirth of Descartes: the Nineteenth-Century Reinstatement of Cartesian Metaphysics in France and Germany*. PhD Thesis, University of Groningen, Groningen.
56 St. George Jackson Mivart tried to reconcile Darwinism with the Catholic faith but ended his life rejected by both. See Richards, R.J. 1987. *Darwin and the Emergence of Evolutionary Theories of Mind and Behavior*. The University of Chicago Press, Chicago: 353-363.
57 Mivart, St. G. 1871. *On the Genesis of Species*. MacMillan and Co., London: 260.
58 Anonymous. 1918. 'The Right Hon. Sir Edward Fry, G.C.B., F.R.S.' in: *Nature* 102: 169-170.

with the struggle for life. However, when we realize that in this way nature strives for life forms better adapted to their environment, we should admit that 'no more remarkable instance of design in a law or of an abiding tendency towards perfection can possibly be conceived.'[59] This point is important for our purposes, since according to Fry this 'tendency towards perfection' justifies appalling events like—quoting Darwin's example—'the larvae of ichneumonidae, which feed on the live bodies of caterpillars'.[60] Darwin had refused to connect animal suffering with purposeful design, but for Fry, the end—a better adaptation of the animals to their habitat—justified such miseries. The same applies to the author who now demands our attention.

In 1884, *Frederick Temple* (1821–1902),[61] the Anglican bishop who was to become archbishop of Canterbury in 1896, delivered his lectures entitled *The Relations between Religion and Science*,[62] two of which were devoted to the subject of evolution. Already before, the Anglican cleric had uttered a positive response to Darwin's theory[63] and the thoughts expounded in these lectures breathe the same spirit. 'What is touched by this doctrine [evolution] is not the evidence of design but the mode in which the design was executed. (…) In the one case the execution follows the design by the effect of a direct act of creation; in the other case the design is worked out by a slow process.'[64] This slow process may encompass a lot of pain and waste, but this is justified by a perpetual progress.

> The very phrase which we commonly use to sum up Darwin's teaching, the survival of the fittest, implies a perpetual diminution of pain and increase of enjoyment for all creatures that can feel. If they are fitter for their surroundings, most certainly they will find life easier to live. And, as if to mark still more plainly the beneficence of the whole work, the less developed creatures, as we have every reason to believe, are less sensible of pain and pleasure; so that enjoyment appears to grow with the capacity

---

59 Fry, E. 1872. *Darwinism and Theology. Reprinted with Slight Alterations from the 'Spectator' of the 7th, 14th, and 21st September, 1872.* Henry Sotheran and Co., London: 19.
60 Fry, *Darwinism and Theology*: 20.
61 For biographical details, see Britannica, The Editors of Encyclopaedia. "Frederick Temple". *Encyclopedia Britannica*, 26 November 2021, https://www.britannica.com/biography/Frederick-Temple. Accessed on 14 December 2021.
62 Temple, F. 1885. *The Relations between Religion and Science. Eight Lectures Preached before the University of Oxford in the Year 1884. On the Foundation of the Late Rev. John Bampton, M.A. Canon of Salisbury.* Macmillan and Co., London.
63 Frederick Temple had preached a sermon at the 1860 meeting of the British Association for the Advancement of Science that witnessed the famous Huxley-Wilberforce encounter. See Brooke, *Science and Religion*: 274.
64 Temple, *The Relations between Religion and Science*: 114.

for enjoyment, and suffering diminishes as sensitivity to suffering increases.[65]

In these notes, Temple connected, possibly unconsciously, Darwinian evolution with the thoughts that Darwin's grandfather Erasmus Darwin already had advocated. When estimating the outcome of the pleasure-pain balance, we should not look at the individual organism but at the entire universe (cf. § 5.4.1). But whereas Darwin senior could only reckon with a redistribution of a fixed amount of pleasure, his grandson had, at least according to Temple, opened a way by which the total amount of happiness could even increase; for if evolution leads to an increase in mental faculties, the ability to experience happiness and the acumen to avoid suffering increases as well. Thus, far from testifying against divine beneficence, evolution 'leaves the argument for an intelligent Creator and Governor of the world stronger than it was before'.[66] The vicissitudes of the animals (even if they suffer and die) are part of a well-considered design directed at their perfection. Yet this doesn't remove the boundary between humans and animals. There remains an unbridgeable gap between us and them. The increase in mental facilities over time within the non-human animal kingdom does not end in humankind, since that would mean that humans were hardly more than big-brained apes. Rather, already very early in evolution a separate branch was formed that would lead to humankind.[67] A consequence of this conviction was that animal suffering could not be justified as necessary for the emergence of humanity as the intended pinnacle of a divinely guided evolution. It was this argument, though, that became propagated by the authors to be discussed next.

Across the ocean, the Harvard professor of botany *Asa Gray* (1810–1888), Presbyterian in his youth but joining the Congregational denomination later in life,[68] also subscribed to the view that God attains his purposes through evolution.[69] Darwin's theory even explains the less agreeable aspects of animal life. As this touches the core of my study, a full-length quote to illustrate this point is needed:

> Finally, Darwinian teleology has the special advantage of accounting for the imperfections and failures as well as for successes. It not only accounts

---

65 Temple, *The Relations between Religion and Science*: 117-118.
66 Temple, *The Relations between Religion and Science*: 122.
67 Temple, *The Relations between Religion and Science*: 174-176.
68 For biographical details, see Moore, *Post-Darwinian Controversies*: 269-280; Livingstone, *Darwin's Forgotten Defenders*: 60-64.
69 Gray, A. 1888 [1876]. 'Evolutionary Teleology' in: *Darwiniana: Essays and Reviews Pertaining to Darwinism*. D. Appleton and Company, New York: 354-390.

for them, but turns them to practical account. It explains the seeming waste as being part and parcel of a great economical process. Without the competing multitude, no struggle for life; and without this, no natural selection and survival of the fittest, no continuous adaptation to changing surroundings, no diversification and improvement, leading from lower up to higher and nobler forms. So the most puzzling things of all to the old-school teleologists are the *principia* of the Darwinian. In this system the forms and species, in all their variety, are not mere ends in themselves, but the whole a series of means and ends, in the contemplation of which we may obtain higher and more comprehensive, and perhaps worthier, as well as more consistent, views of design in Nature than heretofore. At least, it would appear that in Darwinian evolution we may have a theory that accords with if it does not explain the principal facts, and a teleology that is free from the common objections.[70]

Note that concepts like 'waste' and 'struggle for life' almost necessarily include animal suffering, starvation, and death. Whereas Darwin himself considered such phenomena as evidence against divine design, Gray was of the opposite opinion.[71] In his view, instead of questioning God's attributes, Darwin's theory actually supported them. Yet, there is not much concern with the animals themselves in this note; they are just means to reach a preconceived higher purpose. Gray accepted that achieving this purpose may be accompanied by much animal suffering. Apparently, the outcome—the emergence of 'higher and nobler forms' (obviously culminating in humanity)—justifies the costs.[72]

That mankind could indeed be considered the intended outcome of the evolutionary process had not been self-evident for Gray immediately. Initially, he had expressed his doubts about an apish ancestry for humanity in his review of Darwin's *Origin*, emphasizing the lack of 'a common progenitor'.[73] Until more evidence is produced, 'we must needs believe in the separate and special creation of man'.[74] But after having read the *Descent of Man*, he wrote to Darwin: 'Almost thou persuadest me to have been "a hairy quadruped, of arboreal habits, furnished with a tail and

---

70 Gray, 'Evolutionary Teleology' in: *Darwiniana*: 378.
71 About the compatibility of design with evolution, there is an extensive exchange of letters between Darwin and Gray, see by example Sollereder, 'The Darwin-Gray Exchange'.
72 England, 'Natural Selection, Teleology, and the Logos': 277.
73 Gray, A. 1860. 'The Origin of Species by Means of Natural Selection' in: *American Journal of Science and Arts, March 1860*. Republished in *Darwiniana*: 9-61 (50).
74 Gray, A. 1860. 'Natural Selection not Inconsistent with Natural Theology' in: *Atlantic Monthly for July, August, and October, 1860*. Republished in *Darwiniana*: 83-128 (92).

pointed ears" &c.'⁷⁵ The 'almost' subsequently turned into a 'certainly'. In his *Natural Science and Religion*, Gray wrote that he could not believe that any special position of mankind should depend on the manner of its creation.⁷⁶ Even the intellectual gap he had emphasized before had lost significance, Gray now writing how difficult it is to draw 'a line between the simpler judgments and affections of man and those of the highest-endowed brutes'.⁷⁷

His fellow countryman *Joseph LeConte* (1823–1901)⁷⁸ fully agreed with this. LeConte was a pupil of *Louis Agassiz* (1807–1873)—the Swiss-born American geologist who became famous for his work on the glacial periods but notorious because over against Darwin he subscribed to progressive creation as the origin of species.⁷⁹ Yet he did not follow in the footsteps of his teacher. In his very popular *Evolution and its Relation to Religious Thought*,⁸⁰ he acknowledged that a struggle for life is the necessary condition of evolution, but that this is no reason for concern:

> Shall we call that evil which was the necessary condition of the progressive elevation which culminated so gloriously? Evil doubtless it seemed to the individual, struggling animal, but is this worthy to be weighed in comparison with the evolution of the whole organic kingdom until it culminated in man? Is it not rather a *good* in disguise?⁸¹

To ask the question is to answer it. LeConte's book was very well received in clerical as well as in scientific circles,⁸² and leading authors like *Aubrey*

---

75 Gray to Darwin, 14 April 1871, *Darwin Correspondence Project*, "Letter no. 7683," accessed on 14 December 2021, https://www.darwinproject.ac.uk/letter/?docId=letters/DCP-LETT-7683.xml. In this letter Gray almost *verbatim* quoted Darwin, who had written in the *Descent of Man* that '[w]e thus learn that man is descended from a hairy quadruped, furnished with a tail and pointed ears, probably arboreal in its habits (…).' See Darwin, *Descent of Man* II: 389.
76 Gray, A. 1880. *Natural Science and Religion. Two Lectures Delivered to the Theological School of Yale College*. Charles Scribner's Sons, New York: 100.
77 Gray, 'Evolutionary Teleology' in: *Darwiniana*: 360. Cf. Moore, *Post-Darwinian Controversies*: 279-280 for a description of how Gray over the years changed his mind on the topic of human evolution.
78 Martin, J.M. 1964. 'Joseph LeConte and the Reconciliation of Science and Religion' in: *The Georgia Review* 18 (1): 78-91.
79 For biographical details, see Jordan, D.S. "Louis Agassiz". *Encyclopedia Britannica*, 10 December 2021, https://www.britannica.com/biography/Louis-Agassiz. Accessed on 14 December 2021.
80 LeConte, J. 1888. *Evolution and Its Relation to Religious Thought*. D. Appleton and Company, New York.
81 LeConte, *Evolution and Its Relation to Religious Thought*: 329.
82 Martin, 'Joseph LeConte and the Reconciliation of Science and Religion': 88.

Moore and *George Romanes*—both to be discussed below—held LeConte in high regard.[83] Apparently, viewing mankind's development as progression from an apish ancestry had become less controversial in these circles. As a result, animal suffering now could even be justified as an instrument for attaining humanity's elevated status, at least by those theologians who had—albeit after some hesitation as seen with Gray— started to accept this ultimate outcome of a divinely guided evolution.

Efforts to connect the fate of animals in the evolutionary process with the virtues of the Creator are found with other authors as well. 'The birth and death of plants, animals, and men (…) may be the ever-evolving, ever-dissolving creation of an immanent yet independent Creator,'[84] wrote the Princeton professor *Charles Woodruff Shields* (1825–1904) one year after LeConte.[85] But it requires a prepared mind to recognize this. Viewed superficially, there is in nature only survival at the expense of the other. But when looking with an eye of faith, we see how '[o]rder, plan and purpose will be found pervading the universe through all its gradations and cycles, with the ever-growing virtue and happiness of creatures, for the glory of the Creator', each animal 'fulfilling its own end, while contributing to the general good of nature'.[86] Shields justified—in the same way as Temple did—animals' miseries because in his view all in all they lead to an increase in happiness. Interestingly, however, he added that this interpretation requires faith—a *caveat* also found with the author to be addressed next.

Aubrey Moore (1848–1890) was an Anglican clergyman belonging to the ranks of the liberal Anglo-Catholic theologians.[87] In his *Science and the Faith*, Moore urged—while quoting from the Bible that 'God's mercy is over all His works' and that 'not a sparrow falls to the ground without His knowledge'—that we must believe there to be purpose and design in every place. But this does not imply that the intended purpose and signs of divine benevolence are always clear. The wisdom and goodness of God

---

83 Moore, A.L. 1905 [1889]. *Science and the Faith. Essays on Apologetic Subjects. With an Introduction…Sixth Edition*. Kegan Paul et al., London: 211; Romanes, G.J. 1896. *The Life and Letters of George John Romanes. Written and Edited by His Wife. New Edition*. Longmans et al., London: 237-243. Cf. Pleins, J.D. 2014. *In Praise of Darwin. George Romanes and the Evolution of a Darwinian Believer*. Bloomsbury, New York: 281-282, 287-288.
84 Shields, C.W. 1889. *Philosophia Ultima or Science of the Sciences. Volume II. The History of the Sciences and the Logic of the Sciences*. Sampson Low et al., London: 350.
85 Livingstone, *Darwin's Forgotten Defenders*: 111-112.
86 Shields, *Philosophia Ultima*: 351.
87 For biographical details, see Blakiston, H.E.D. 'Moore, Aubrey Lackington' in: *Dictionary of National Biography, 1885-1900, Volume 38*.

are postulates of faith. We are convinced 'that God is good, and cannot be the cause of meaningless and unnecessary pain. And our faith is not staggered by much which seems, as yet, like useless suffering.'[88] For Moore, as for Shields, one needs the eye of faith to endorse design and to trust that suffering has a higher goal. Apparently, it was no longer, as in the natural theology tradition up to Temple and Gray, nature that speaks for itself, since we now need the light of faith to interpret nature correctly. Is this a sign that the suffering of so many animals is gradually becoming a real issue?

Moore's eye of faith not only may have played a role in clinging to divine design as a fact beyond doubt, but also in refuting the idea that Darwin's theory must inevitably lead to atheism. Moore even became famous for arguing that, whereas '[s]cience had pushed the deist's God farther and farther away, (…) at the moment when it seemed as if He would be thrust out altogether, Darwinism appeared, and, under the disguise of a foe, did the work of a friend'.[89] He thought so since in his view Darwin's theory—which presupposes a continuously effective natural selection—assumed the omnipresence of God's creative power, interpreting natural law as a manifestation of direct divine action and thus refuting Deism with its absent Deity. God's ongoing activities are actually visible in the working of the natural laws. Those who wrote Scripture knew very well the details of human procreation, but this did not withhold them from writing that God 'fashions the child in the womb'.[90] What unfolds as a result of natural laws is the outcome of unceasing divine intervention.

Moore's colleague *John Richardson Illingworth* (1848–1915),[91] who belonged to the same branch within the Church of England, also took efforts to reconcile divine goodness with animal suffering. The problem touched him more deeply than we have seen thus far, as can be inferred from his note that the 'universality of pain throughout the range of the

---

88 Moore, *Science and the Faith*: 199.
89 Moore, A. 'The Christian Doctrine of God' in: Gore, C. (ed.). 1890. *Lux Mundi. A Series of Studies in the Religion of the Incarnation. Tenth Edition.* John Murray, London: 57-109 (99). Cf. Southgate, C. 'Beyond the Disguised Friend: Immanence, Transcendence and Glory in a Darwinian World' in: Fuller, M., Evers, D. et al. (eds). 2020. *Issues in Science and Theology: Nature—and Beyond. Transcendence and Immanence in Science and Theology.* Springer, Cham: 57-68, in particular pp. 57-58.
90 Moore, 'The Christian Doctrine of God': 94-95. Cf. England, 'Natural Selection, Teleology, and the Logos': 278-281.
91 Patrick, J. 2009. 'John Richardson Illingworth and Reason's Romance: the Idealist Apology in Late-Victorian England' in: *Anglican and Episcopal History* 78 (3): 249-278.

animal world, reaching back into the distant ages of geology, (...) is without doubt among the most serious problems which the Theist has to face'.[92] He removed the sting out of this problem, however, by emphasizing that it is not the number of suffering animals that counts but the suffering of the individual. 'No one animal suffers more because a million suffer likewise. And what we have to consider is the amount which an individual animal suffers.'[93] As to the problem that animals had to suffer before Adam's fall, we don't have to 'commit ourselves to the statement that suffering was introduced into the world by sin, which is not a Christian dogma, though it is often thought to be so'.[94] In rejecting that it is humanity's fault that animals have to suffer, Illingworth did not deviate from opinions uttered since the time of the Early Church, as has been demonstrated in the previous chapters. New was his emphasis on the suffering of the individual as a means to mitigate the seriousness of the problem. As we have seen (§ 5.4.3), for Baron d'Holbach it was, by contrast, a means to highlight the problem: the suffering of only one innocent insect would damage the divine attributes beyond repair.[95]

The unanimous view among the authors discussed thus far that divine benevolence and animal suffering did not conflict with each other did not imply, however, that they were blind to the vulnerability of this belief or that they ignored the need to defend it against attacks of outsiders. One of those who entered the fray was the Reverend *Theodore Wood (1863–1923)*.[96] Wood delivered a lecture on this subject at the Victoria Institute, in which he aimed to refute the arguments against divine wisdom and benevolence brought forward by 'a certain class of infidels'. He admitted that 'a wise Creator could have avoided [animal death and destruction] and a merciful Creator would have prevented it'.[97] But in view of the

---

92 Illingworth, R.J. 'The Problem of Pain: Its Bearing on Faith in God' in: Gore, *Lux Mundi*: 111-126 (113).
93 Illingworth, 'The Problem of Pain': 114.
94 Illingworth, 'The Problem of Pain': 117.
95 d'Holbach, P.H. 1795. *Common Sense: or, Natural Ideas Opposed to Supernatural. Translated from the French*. n.p., New York: 47.
96 Theodore Wood was trained to become Church of England cleric but gained more fame with his books about natural history. https://www.pipspatch.com/2020/04/07/memories-of-a-beetle-collector/. Acessed on 14 December 2021.
97 Wood, T. 1892. 'The Apparent Cruelty of Nature' in: *Journal of the Transaction of the Victoria Institute or Philosophical Society of Great Britain* 25: 253-278 (253, 254). The Victoria Institute (which still exists) was founded in 1865 with the purpose to defend 'the great truths revealed in Holy Scripture (...) against the oppositions of science, falsely so-called'. Fellows of the Royal Society were among its members. See Moore, *Post-Darwinian Controversies*: 85; Numbers, *The Creationists*: 162-166, 175-179; Rios, *After the Monkey Trial*: 23-25.

limited mental abilities of animals, 'the so-called cruelty of Nature is cruelty only in appearance; in reality, it is a blessing and a boon'.[98] Wood's opinion was shared by the audience, as can be inferred from the minutes attached to the text of his speech. 'God being beneficent, there can be no cruelty in Nature,' concluded the chairman when closing the meeting.[99] The Scottish Free Church professor *James Iverach* (1839–1922)[100] didn't have much trouble either. In his view, complaints about the struggle for life are 'exaggerated', and he wondered 'whether it is not a kind of anthropomorphism, whether it is not a reading of man's practices into the cosmos'. The struggle in the animal kingdom is nothing compared to the ferocity with which people attack each other literally and figuratively. The desires of an animal are limited; when it has had its meal, no one has any danger to fear. Mankind, on the other hand, is insatiable.[101]

It seems that things had not changed much since the archdeacon of Carlisle had written his canonical treatise on natural theology. 'We might accept all that Mr. Darwin (...) has so learnedly and so acutely written on physical science, and yet preserve our natural theology on exactly the same basis as that on which (...) Paley left it,' thus told Kingsley his audience in the same lecture in which he praised God for being able to 'make all things make themselves'.[102] Frederick Temple had the same opinion, also stating that evolution does not affect the power of Paley's arguments at all. There is still design, only the way this design is implemented differs because it is not so much aimed at maintaining a harmonic *status quo* as at a development from lower to higher forms of life.[103] In the same way as in the previous century the Lisbon earthquake had shocked the earth but not the trust in divine providence[104] did

---

98 Wood, 'The Apparent Cruelty of Nature': 270.
990 Wood, 'The Apparent Cruelty of Nature': 278.
100 For biographical details of Iverach, see Moore, *Post-Darwinian Controversies*: 253-259. The Free Church of Scotland had separated from the established Church of Scotland in 1843, an event known as the Disruption. Thomas Chalmers and Hugh Miller, both discussed in Chapter 5, were among its founding members.
101 Iverach, J. 1894. *Christianity and Evolution*. Thomas Whittaker, New York: 179-184 (181). In this critical note, Iverach specifically aimed at Thomas Huxley as an example of those who suffer from the ailment of anthropomorphism. Huxley's contribution to the debate on animal suffering and divine design will be addressed in § 6.4.
102 Kingsley, 'The Natural Theology of the Future ': 376.
103 Temple, *The Relations between Religion and Science*: 99-123.
104 This analogy may be instructive indeed. It is generally believed that the Lisbon earthquake (1755) had caused serious damage to human trust in divine providence as intending the well-being of humankind, but the prevailing view was that earthquakes belong to the normal course of events and that God cannot be considered to suspend the laws imposed by himself for the sake of humanity. Alternatively, the

Darwin's theory not cause insurmountable problems for those who continued to be convinced that the Creator seeks the best for all his creatures. Among those examined so far, only Shields and Moore hesitated, pointing out that it takes faith to see a benevolent design.

The transition to higher life forms could justify animal suffering.[105] Writing in 1890, the Presbyterian Princeton professor *James McCosh* (1811-1894)[106] had expressed this general feeling concisely. 'There is nothing atheistic in the creed that God proceeds by instruments, which we may find to be for the good of his creatures. (…) In the geological development I am privileged as it were to enter God's workshop and see his modes of operation.'[107] McCosh acknowledged animal suffering but accepted it as something necessary. '[Nature] is groaning, but it is to be delivered from a load. It is travailing, but it is for a birth. It is not perfect, but it is going on toward perfection.'[108]

McCosh's younger contemporary and countryman, the Congregational clergyman and amateur geologist *George Frederick Wright* (1838-1921)[109] had neither troubles to square divine attributes with past and present animal life. 'The truth is, that the rose-colored views (…) of the pietistic interpreters of natural theology, are built upon a very narrow basis of

---

earthquake might represent a divine punishment, rightly applied to Lisbon—a city in which the Inquisition had shed the blood of so many pious. Marques, J.O.A. 2005. 'The Paths of Providence: Voltaire and Rousseau on the Lisbon Earthquake' in: *Cadernos de História e Filosofia da Ciência*. Campinas: CLE_Unicamp, Série 3, v. 15 (1): 33-57. J.J. Dana, the North American Congregationalist theologian discussed in Chapter 5 (cf. § 5.4.16), wrote that the 'earthquake and the volcano often destroy multitudes of the human family, yet Geology shows these to be necessary for the safety of the whole system, and hence are evils small in comparison with what would take their place, were they removed' in: Dana, J.J. 'On the Relations between Geology and Religion' in: Bidwell, W.H. (ed.), 1846. *Biblical Repository and Classical Review*. Wiley & Putnam, London: 297-320 (308).

105 See for the wide spread of this conviction Moore, *Post-Darwinian Controversies*: 221-241; Ellegård, *Darwin and the General Reader*: 114-140, 267-279; Jones, *For the Glory of God*: 126-135.
106 McCosh had emigrated from Northern Ireland to the US in 1863. Cf. on him Moore, *Post-Darwinian Controversies*: 245-251; Livingstone, *Darwin's Forgotten Defenders*: 106-111; Livingstone, *Dealing with Darwin*: 157-196.
107 McCosh, J. 1890. *The Religious Aspect of Evolution. Enlarged and Improved Edition*. Charles Scribner's Sons, New York: 5-8 (8).
108 McCosh, *The Religious Aspect of Evolution*: 110.
109 Numbers, *The Creationists*: 33-50. It should be noted that, later in life, Wright abandoned his position of a Christian Darwinist, assigning a more important role for active divine intervention, see Wright, G.F. [1910]. 'The Passing of Evolution' in: *The Fundamentals. A Testimony to the Truth Volume VII*. Testimony Publishing Company, Chicago. Cf. Numbers, R.L. 1988. 'George Frederick Wright: from Christian Darwinist to Fundamentalist' in: *Isis* 79 (4): 624-645.

facts.'[110] Obviously, the 'sensational happiness of all organic creatures, from the lowest animalcule to that of the most highly organized animal form, is an element to be considered in that general good of being', but the 'pleasurable sensations of the intellect, investigating and interpreting the ways of God as displayed in the creation, are likewise a part of that good included in the end for which all things were made.'[111] Hence, '(…) it is of more account to God's creatures as a whole that the universe be capable of interpretation, and that the method of God in his works be manifested, than that any amount of temporary good should occur during the earlier stages of the process of development'.[112]

This unbroken view on the compatibility between animal suffering and divine attributes persisted till the first decades of the twentieth century. Authors who wrote on the subject repeated the warning of James Iverach that we should not read our own feelings into the mind of the animals and agreed with LeConte and Gray that the aim—the emergence of humanity—justified the means. This approach, condoning animal suffering and justifying it by the outcome, would become the leading one for the next two decades.

In 1912, the Scottish Presbyterian *James Y. Simpson* (1873–1934), who taught biology at the Free Church's New College and the University of Edinburgh—and served the British Empire as a diplomat[113]—wrote that it is misplaced anthropomorphic reasoning to assume that animals live in a constant fear of suffering and death.[114] Hence, a description of nature as 'the more or less enduring suffering which is the meed of both vanquished and victor' was dismissed by Simpson as wrongly assuming that 'many wild animals lead lives on planes of intelligence and happiness scarcely attained by humanity'.[115] And if we wonder whether the troubles of the animals are justified by their intended purpose, the answer can be nothing but affirmative. '[I]n the creation of human personality we can not unreasonably discern the temporary goal of the world's development.'[116]

---

110 Wright, G.F. 1882. *Studies in Science and Religion*. Warren F. Draper, Andover: 185.
111 Wright, *Studies in Science and Religion*: 194.
112 Wright, *Studies in Science and Religion*: 195.
113 For biographical details, see Bowler, *Reconciling Science and Religion*: 236-240.
114 Simpson, J.Y. 1912. *The Spiritual Interpretation of Nature. Second Edition*. Hodder and Stoughton, London: 158.
115 Simpson, *The Spiritual Interpretation of Nature*: 154. In this text, Simpson quotes from Huxley, T.H. 1895. *Collected Essays. Volume IX. Evolution & Ethics and Other Essays*. MacMillan and Co., London: 200. 'But he must shut his eyes if he would not see that more or less enduring suffering is the meed of both vanquished and victor.' The contribution of Huxley to the debate on divine attributes and animal suffering is addressed in more detail in § 6.4.
116 Simpson, *The Spiritual Interpretation of Nature*: 272.

If there were any animal suffering at all, it had to be accepted as the birth pangs for humanity. We should not lose sight of that higher purpose. If interpreted allegorically, the meaning of animal suffering extended even beyond time, into eternity.

> Suffering itself is service, and vicarious suffering is its highest expression. The principle of vicarious self-sacrifice pervades creation, and is most marvellously provocative of service in others. At Calvary the Creator draws men to Him by His own submission to this one great law of sacrifice. Viewed in this light the misery and seeming waste associated with the struggle for existence are seen to be not wholly unconnected with the profoundest fact in history.'[117]

In this interpretation of animal suffering as referring to a spiritual good, Simpson joined the *Bridgewater Treatise* author Kirby (cf. § 5.4.10).[118] And in his opinion that we should not put too much weight on animal suffering, Simpson agreed with his fellow Free Church member James Iverach, who as we saw had forwarded similar thoughts just before the turn of the twentieth century.

The low views on animal suffering held by Iverach and Simpson were to survive the Great War unmodified, as they were repeated in the early 1920s by the Congregationalist minister *Ebenezer Griffith-Jones* (1860–1942).[119] According to Griffith-Jones, the fact that people had started to sympathize with animals was only a recent phenomenon.[120] In the past, animals had never been a matter of concern. 'The fact that the lower creatures in a state of nature were liable to causes which, at least in the case of human beings, would produce acute pain and suffering did not seem to raise any difficulty, or suggest a lack of benevolent regard on the part of the Creator.'[121] Observations reported by zoologists also confirm that the extent and intensity of animal suffering is greatly overdramatised.[122]

---

117 Simpson, *The Spiritual Interpretation of Nature*: 167.
118 Simpson did not refer to Kirby, however.
119 For biographical details of Griffith-Jones, see Bowler, *Reconciling Science and Religion*: 219-222, 233-235.
120 Griffith-Jones, E. 1925. *Providence—Divine and Human. A Study of the World-Order in the Light of Modern Thought. Volume I. Some Problems of Divine Providence.* Hodder and Stoughton, London: 225-235. With this view, this author apparently ignored all previous attempts to come on terms with animal suffering.
121 Griffith-Jones, *Providence—Divine and Human*: 226.
122 Griffith-Jones, *Providence—Divine and Human*: 233-240 (233). Griffith Jones referred to contemporary zoologists who emphasized that in animal life, the enjoyments far surpass the miseries.

So, there is no reason to suppose that God falls short in wisdom or goodness.[123] Concerns with animal sufferings rather are the products of the fantasies of 'arm-chair naturalists who grow pale over the supposed agonies resulting from the fierce struggle for existence among animals'.[124]

Griffith-Jones agreed with his older contemporaries about the relative innocence of animal suffering as well as its intended purpose—the emergence of humanity—and praised God for having designed such an admirable way to achieve this result'.[125] And Griffith-Jones also propagated the opinion, just as Simpson had done, that suffering points to a spiritual reality. The care that parents show for their young and the risks they take to protect them testify to the presence of sacrificial love, 'a principle that finds its highest expression in the Cross of Christ'.[126]

Finally, Griffith-Jones paid attention to the role of personified evil. He did so in response to an anonymous author who had attributed all evil in nature to Satan's disruption of God's plan from the beginning of time[127]—a concept also raised several years earlier by the Oxford don *Clement Charles Julian Webb*.[128] Webb had explained animal suffering in the same way by the 'activity of an evil will or wills antecedent to the appearance of man.[129] Several years later, the Oxford professor of divinity *Norman Powell Williams* (1883–1943)[130] made the same claim and added that such evil 'would necessarily manifest itself in a development of organic life permeated through and through with the spirit of selfishness, manifested in ferocious competition and in a bloodthirsty struggle for existence'.[131]

---

123 Griffith-Jones, *Providence—Divine and Human*: 141. In this rebuttal, Griffith-Jones aimed at John Stuart Mill who had written that the 'notion of a providential government by an omnipotent Being for the good of his creatures must be entirely dismissed', see Mill, J.S. 1874. *Nature, the Utility of Religion and Theism. Second Edition.* Longmans et al., London: 243. For discussion of Mill, see § 6.5.
124 Griffith-Jones, *Providence—Divine and Human*: 236.
125 Griffith-Jones, *Providence—Divine and Human*: 190.
126 Griffith-Jones, *Providence—Divine and Human*: 245.
127 Anonymous. 1899. *Evil & Evolution. An Attempt to Turn the Light of Modern Science on to the Ancient Mystery of Evil. By the Author of 'the Social Horizon'. Fourth Impression.* MacMillan and Co., London. Other sources mention George Francis Millin as author; for biographical details, see https://www.myheritage.nl/names/george_millin. Accessed on 14 December 2021.
128 For biographical details, see Britannica, The Editors of Encyclopaedia. "Clement Charles Julian Webb". *Encyclopedia Britannica*, 1 October 2021, https://www.britannica.com/biography/Clement-Charles-Julian-Webb. Accessed on 14 December 2021.
129 Webb, C.C.J. 1911. *Problems in the Relations of God and Man.* James Nisbet & Co., London: 268-272 (269).
130 For biographical details, see https://peoplepill.com/people/norman-powell-williams. Accessed on 14 December 2021.
131 Williams, N.P. 1927. *The Ideas of the Fall and of Original Sin. A Historical and Critical*

In Griffith-Jones's view, it makes, however, no sense to take refuge in the hypothesis of an interfering 'Evil Spirit' of whatsoever kind as this 'only postpones the problem, and either enthrones a permanent dualism at the heart of things, or makes God still ultimately responsible for the mystery of suffering'.[132] His contemporary *Ernest William Barnes* (1874–1953),[133] the Anglican bishop of Birmingham, had the same opinion. He called the idea of a pre-mundane fall something that 'shows how amazingly unscientific in temper some of our theologians continue to be'.[134] For Barnes, evil and suffering in the natural world are justified by the outcome. 'The fittest have survived in a process of struggle wherein, to our thinking, profuse waste and continuous carnage abound', but '[o]ut of the witches' cauldron man has emerged'.[135] What it means to the animals to be only ingredients for the witch concoction from which the human race was born, this author did not add. Another contemporary, the theologian *Charles Raven* (1885-1964)[136] condoned the harsh fate of animals throughout time in a similar way: "That, in spite of a myriad delays and a myriad failures, through bloodshed and horror, organisms have achieved the ascent of man, is proof perhaps that the agony of the ages has not been in vain.'[137] As it took blood to redeem humans, so it

---

Study. Being Eight Lectures Delivered before the University of Oxford, in the Year 1924, on the Foundation of the Rev. John Bampton, Canon of Salisbury. Longmans et al., London: xxxi-xxxv, 522-537 (527). This author did not associate evil with the devil but conceived it as a vitiated expression of God's creative power. That power is said to have detached itself from God and, as an independent entity, to have set its own will against God's will. It should be something akin to Plato's World Soul or Henri Bergson's élan vital, but in a perverted form. Cf. Lloyd, M. 'The Fallenness of Nature. Three Nonhuman Suspects' in: Rosenberg, S.P. (ed.). 2018. *Finding Ourselves After Darwin. Conversations on the Image of God, Original Sin, and the Problem of Evil*. Baker Academic, Grand Rapids: 262-279, in particular pp. 263-266.

132 Griffith-Jones, *Providence—Divine and Human*: 232-233.
133 For biographical details of Barnes, see Bowler, *Reconciling Science and Religion*: 260-270.
134 Barnes, E.W. 'Religion and Science. The Present Phase. A Sermon Preached in Westminster Abbey on Sunday, September 25th, 1927' in: Barnes, E.W. 1927. *Should Such a Faith Offend? Sermons and Addresses*. Hodder and Stoughton, London: 309-317 (312).
135 Barnes, E.W. 'God. A Sermon Preached before the University of Cambridge on Sunday, May 16th, 1926' in: Barnes, *Should Such a Faith Offend*: 289-299 (290).
136 For more details about this author, see Bowler, *Reconciling Science and Religion*: 277-286.
137 Raven, C.E. 1928. *The Creator Spirit. A Survey of Christian Doctrine in the Light of Biology, Psychology and Mysticism. The Hulsean Lectures, Cambridge, 1926-7. The Noble Lectures Harvard, 1926. With an Appendix on Biochemistry and Mental Phenomena*. Harvard University Press, Cambridge (MA): 122.

took blood to create them. '[W]oven into the very woof and warp of this universe is the pattern of the Cross'.[138]

In endorsing this anthropocentric view on the matter, Barnes and Raven both epitomized the general trend seen since the turn of the twentieth century. By connecting animal suffering with progress towards humanity, any threat for divine benevolence was effectively defused. The fact that Barnes did not even mention it illustrates this development as does Raven's comment that it is doubtful whether the animals can feel pain 'without a frontal cortex, a fore-plan in mind, and a love which can put itself in the place of another'. To assume that the suffering of animals resembles our own 'is to set up the bogey of a nightmare as truth'.[139] Between the 1920s and the 1950s, it was only the apologist and philosopher C.S. Lewis (1998–1963)[140] who felt compelled to 'defend' God for the suffering of the animals. Lewis resorted to a moderate neo-Cartesianism combined with the assumption of an influence of demonic counterforces corrupting animal life from long before the advent of mankind.[141]

For the authors discussed in this section, the acceptance of Darwin's theory was no reason to adjust or change their conviction that animal life reflects benevolent divine design, any more than those who rejected Darwin's theory saw reason to do so. However, not everyone adopted such a reconciliatory position, as the next section will show.

6.4. Behind the Veil

While providential care was predominantly seen as being focused on the creature's physical well-being and thus as cause for praise, its less pleasant aspects did not go unnoticed entirely. For this topic, we have to go back to the time Darwin published his *Origin*. One of the authors who questioned a rosy view of nature was the Congregational minister *Horace Bushnell* (1802–1876).[142] He could not agree with a natural theology in Paley's line that in his view dealt with the suffering in the world too superficially. Animal suffering testified against a benevolent design; for Bushnell, the concept of design took on a different content. Design is often ambiguous; predation may serve to keep animals and species within their allotted spaces but 'how easy was it for the Creator to keep down the over-population of the animal races, by making them less fruitful, or

---

138 Raven, *The Creator Spirit*: 124.
139 Raven, *The Creator Spirit*: 120-121.
140 McGrath, A. 2013. *C.S. Lewis – A Life: Eccentric Genius, Reluctant Prophet*. Thomas Nelson, Nashville.
141 Lewis, C.S. 1986 [1940]. *The Problem of Pain*. Collins, Glasgow: 103-114.
142 Cf. Lane, B.C. 2011. *Ravished by Beauty. The Surprising Legacy of Reformed Spirituality*. Oxford University Press, New York: 228-233.

shortening the time of their life!'¹⁴³ We must not dismiss the reality of animal suffering with sought-after explanations. To the contrary, we should face it as a consequence of our sin—not in the sense that it followed sin in time, for the world has known pain from its first beginnings—but because God foresaw future events. This is why 'the whole creation was groaning, in all orders and degrees, from the rocks upward, before the arrival of the occupant and his sin, prefiguring and symbolizing the great, sad history to come, and preparing fit environment for it.'¹⁴⁴

Bushnell's ideas about the divine attributes are, to say the least, not the same as those of Paley and the *Bridgewater* authors. Divine goodness and wisdom were not denied but Bushnell gave these a different meaning than intended by them.

> The really existent God, as we can see with our eyes, is such a being as can use contrivance in adjusting the due apparatus, both of prey and of poison. And we need not scruple to confess a degree of satisfaction in this kind of discovery, showing that goodness is no such innocent, mawkishly insipid character, no such mollusc softness swimming in God's bosom as many affect to suppose; that it has resolve, purpose, thunder in it, able to contrive hard things, when hard are wanted. (…) Elemental forces, grinding hard about us and upon us, are necessary to the due unfolding of our moral and religious ideas, and it is in just these severities of discipline that we afterward discover the deepest counsels of beneficence, and the highest culminations of eternal goodness itself.¹⁴⁵

God aims at our moral improvement and does not shy away from a harsh approach to reach this goal. The vicissitudes of animal life have to be considered from this point of view. They are part of a purposeful design indeed, but it is not a design that is focused on humankind's earthly comfort; it is for our moral benefit.¹⁴⁶

Bushnell's thoughts were not new. The North American geologists Hitchcock and Dana, both addressed in Chapter 5, had also forwarded that God had anticipated future events and that natural evil, including 'prey and poison', should serve the moral improvement of a fallen

---

143 Bushnell, H. 1869. *Moral Uses of Dark Things*. Strahan and Company, London: 321.
144 Bushnell, *Moral Uses*: 110-111.
145 Bushnell, *Moral Uses*: 328-329.
146 Bushnell, *Moral Uses*: 343-344.

humanity (cf. § 5.4.16).[147] For them, animal suffering was not contrary to the divine design; design simply had to be interpreted differently.

But whereas the aforementioned authors either continued in the style of Paley or adopted a more sophisticated notion of design like Bushnell, there were others who had more difficulties in reconciling animal suffering with divine attributes. A 'nature red in tooth and claw' could never have been the intention of a benevolent Creator. This conviction permeates the writings of *George John Romanes* (1848–1894), Cambridge graduate and friend of Darwin. His mother was Presbyterian whereas his father held holy orders in the Anglican Church. Contacts with Darwin's theory and—perhaps even more influential—personal contacts with Darwin himself are thought to be the cause of his slide in to disbelief as a young scientist, but just before his premature death at the age of just forty-six, he returned to the bosom of the Anglican Church.[148]

In his *A Candid Examination of Theism*,[149] Romanes refuted, just as Bushnell had done, sweet-toothed thoughts about natural theology. He felt particularly challenged here by the thoughts of *Robert Flint* (1838–1910)[150]—a Scottish theologian and professor of Divinity at the University of Edinburgh who followed the well-trodden pathways. Referring to the aforementioned author LeConte, Flint summarized the benefits of the ability to feel pain, concluding that we are entitled 'to hold that pain is an evidence of the benevolence of God'.[151]

Romanes was of a different opinion. He attributed Flint's ideas to the fact that those who believe in God will be reluctant to make conclusions that detract from his goodness; such people ignore, possibly unconsciously,

---

147 It is uncertain whether Bushnell borrowed from Hitchcock and Dana; he did not mention their names in his *Moral Uses*. It is however likely he did, as all belonged to the same ecclesiastical denomination.

148 Anonymous. 1948. 'George John Romanes (1848-94)' in: *Nature* 161: 757; Moore, *Post-Darwinian Controversies*: 107-109; Brooke, *Science and Religion*: 316; Schwartz, J.S. 1995. 'George John Romanes's Defense of Darwinism: the Correspondence of Charles Darwin and His Chief Disciple' in: *Journal of the History of Biology* 28 (2): 281-316. For his biography in terms of religious convictions and the way they influenced his thoughts about Darwin's theory, see Richards, *Darwin and the Emergence of Evolutionary Theories of Mind and Behavior*: 334-374; Pleins, *In Praise of Darwin*: 1-14, 265-294.

149 Physicus [Romanes, G.J.] 1878. *A Candid Examination of Theism*. Trübner & Co., London.

150 O'Sullivan, L. 2009. 'Robert Flint: Theologian, Philosopher of History and Historian of Philosophy' in: *Intellectual History Review* 19 (1): 45-63.

151 Flint, R. 1877. *Theism Being the Baird Lecture for 1876*. William Blackwood and Sons, Edinburgh: 247-249 (249).

the evidence that the world shows little evidence of divine benevolence.[152] For Romanes, nature is full of miseries and has been so for years untold. Everywhere, '(...) we find we find teeth and talons whetted for slaughter, hooks and suckers moulded for torment—everywhere a reign of terror, hunger, and sickness, with oozing blood and quivering limbs, with gasping breath and eyes of innocence that dimly close in deaths of brutal torture!'[153]

To be sure, this dim situation does not argue against design itself, but the question is whether this design points to a benevolent designer. Romanes doubted it. A spring-trap to catch a rabbit can show a lot of ingenuity, but 'if I could believe that there is a being who, with yet higher faculties of thought and knowledge, and with an unlimited choice of means to secure his ends, has contrived untold thousands of mechanisms no less diabolical than a spring-trap; I should call that being a fiend, were all the world besides to call him God.'[154]

The refutation that we would not be able to judge the purposes of God is not sufficient. For Romanes, any attempt to reconcile divine benevolence with the miseries of animal life is idle and speculations about a balance between pain and pleasure or a greater good either here and now or later are useless. Those who still hold on to the idea of a benevolent God, consciously close themselves to reality. According to Romanes, we have to conclude that, assuming that God exists, he is either limited in the means available to him or not benevolent in his design. Let us imagine what a benevolent design that was not characterized by competition but by collaboration could have looked like! 'Organic species might then have been likened to a countless multitude of voices, all singing to their Creator in one harmonious psalm of praise.'[155]

In his posthumously published *Thoughts on Religion*, Romanes struck similar chords. 'Most of the instances of special design which are relied upon by the natural theologian to prove the intelligent nature of the First Cause, have as their end or object the infliction of painful death or the escape from remorseless enemies.'[156] If we assume that a higher power is involved, then we must conclude that it is not guided by any moral consideration in view of 'the total disregard of animal suffering.'[157]

---

152 [Romanes], *A Candid Examination*: 170-171.
153 [Romanes], *A Candid Examination*: 171.
154 [Romanes], *A Candid Examination*: 171-172.
155 [Romanes], *A Candid Examination*: 177.
156 Romanes, G.J. 1895. *Thoughts on Religion. Edited by Charles Gore*. The Open Court Publishing Company, Chicago: 76-85 (76).
157 Romanes, *Thoughts on Religion*: 85.

Unlike the authors discussed in the previous section, Romanes saw no possibility to explain the events in nature—so often appalling—from an underlying divine design. Neither could natural selection be taken as a synonym for divine action.[158] Romanes joined Pascal, who, along with many others, had already pointed out that no evidence for the existence of God could be inferred from nature.[159] It is better to abandon this concept altogether. 'I do not perceive any evidences of Design in Nature the value or cogency of which I am in any degree able to estimate.'[160] God reveals himself in a different way; he is only 'knowable (if knowable at all) by intuition and not by reason'.[161] Romanes's return to the faith of his youth at the end of his life was not due to any proofs from nature but because '[t]he heart has its reasons, which reason knows not'.[162] It was a move not appreciated by some of his contemporaries: 'As Abraham went out to sacrifice his only son Isaac, so Romanes seriously tried to slaughter his reason on the altar of faith.'[163]

The lines written at the end of Romanes's *Darwin, and after Darwin* that are quoted *verbatim* in his *Life and Letters* let themselves be read as the confession of faith of a seeker who has discovered that the ground for that faith cannot be found in nature. Events in the external world may shock the religious mind, but 'when this cry of Reason pierces the heart of Faith, it remains for Faith to answer now, as she has always answered

---

158 This opinion evoked an exchange of thoughts with the North American theologian and botanist Asa Gray, who thought otherwise. Further exploration of this topic lies beyond the scope of my study. See Moore, *Post-Darwinian Controversies*: 276-278; Richards, *Darwin and the Emergence of Evolutionary Theories of Mind and Behavior*: 342-346; Pleins, *In Praise of Darwin*: 266-272.
159 Romanes, *Thoughts on Religion*: 178. When mentioning Pascal, a specific reference is missing. Romanes probably referred to: 'It is a remarkable fact that no canonical writer has ever employed nature to prove God. All tend to make him be believed. David, Solomon and others have never said: "There is no vacuum, therefore there is a God." They must have been cleverer than the cleverest in after days who have all used this argument. This is well worth considering.' Pascal, B. 1901. *The Thoughts of Blaise Pascal. Translated from the Text of M. Auguste Molinier by C. Kegan Paul.* George Bell and Sons, London: 204. Obviously, Romanes considered the contributions of the majority of theologians that saw no problem in invoking teleology as proof for divine truths to be unconvincing.
160 Gildea, W.L., Alexander, S., Romanes, G.J. 1889-1890. 'Symposium: Is there Evidence of Design in Nature?' in: *Proceedings of the Aristotelian Society* 1 (3): 49-76 (76).
161 Romanes, *Thoughts on Religion*: 146. Cf. Richards, *Darwin and the Emergence of Evolutionary Theories of Mind and Behavior*: 370-374; Pleins, *In Praise of Darwin*: 265-294.
162 Pascal, *The Thoughts of Pascal*: 306.
163 Carus, P. 1894. 'The Late Professor Romanes's Thoughts on Religion' in: *The Monist* 5: 385-400 (398).

before—and answered with that trust which is at once her beauty and her life—Verily thou art a God that hidest thyself."[164]

Others shared Romanes's belief that the problems of reconciling animal suffering with divine design did not necessarily constitute evidence against the existence of God himself.[165] *S. Alexander*, the vice president of the Aristotelean Society, admitted that the facts from nature may suggest a designer who is 'at once the most exquisite of craftsmen, and the most blundering of bunglers, at once the object of worship and the object of execration, at once a merciful and long-suffering ruler, and the most bloodthirsty and reckless of tyrants', but added that this, however, did 'not imply the untruth of Theism, but only of one kind of Theism'.[166] Even Darwin's bulldog *Thomas Huxley* (1825–1895),[167] who wrote that the idea that 'the sentient world is, on the whole, regulated by principles of benevolence, does but ill stand the test of impartial confrontation with the facts of the case'[168]—words that earned him firm rebuttals from Iverach and Simpson as addressed above—did not exploit these notes as an argument against God's existence. 'That there is no evidence of the existence of such a being as the God of the theologians is true enough; but strictly scientific reasoning can take us no further.'[169]

In the first decade of the twentieth century, it was the influential Cambridge philosopher *Frederick Robert Tennant* (1866–1957)[170] who

---

164 Romanes, G.J. 1892. *Darwin, and after Darwin. An Exposition of the Darwinian Theory and a Discussion of Post-Darwinian Questions. I. The Darwinian Theory.* Longmans et al, London: 418; Romanes, *Life and Letters*: 299.
165 Bowler, *Reconciling Science and Religion*: 16.
166 Gildea, Alexander, Romanes, 'Symposium': 64, 63.
167 For biographical details, see Desmond, A.J. "Thomas Henry Huxley". *Encyclopedia Britannica*, 25 June 2021, https://www.britannica.com/biography/Thomas-Henry-Huxley. Accessed on 14 December 2021.
168 Huxley, 'The Struggle for Existence in Human Society' in: *Collected Essays. Volume IX. Evolution & Ethics and Other Essays*: 195-236 (196).
169 Thomas Henry Huxley to M. Henri Gadeau de Kerville, February 1, 1887. Quoted in Huxley, L. 1901. *Life and Letters of Thomas Henry Huxley. By His Son Leonard Huxley. In Two Volumes. Vol II.* D. Appleton and Company, New York: 172. For a discussion of Huxley's view on the relationship between science and religion, see Ellegård, *Darwin and the General Reader*: 140; Bowler, *Reconciling Science and Religion*: 16-17; Lightman, B. 2002. 'Huxley and Scientific Agnosticism: the Strange History of a Failed Rhetorical Strategy' in: *The British Journal for the History of Science* 35 (3): 271-289; Stanley, M. 2015. *Huxley's Church & Maxwell's Demon. From Theistic Science to Naturalistic Science.* The University of Chicago Press, Chicago: 81-85.
170 For biographical details, see Britannica, The Editors of Encyclopaedia. "Frederick Robert Tennant". *Encyclopedia Britannica*, 5 September 2021, https://www.britannica.com/biography/Frederick-Robert-Tennant. Accessed on 14 December 2021. Cf. Hick, J. 1968 [1966]. *Evil and the God of Love.* Collins, London: 250-255. Hick

also had trouble connecting divine design with animal suffering. With Romanes, Tennant acknowledged that evolution in a Darwinian sense involves a lot of animal suffering.[171] In its interpretation, they, however, parted company. Tennant attempted—unlike Romanes who refrained from any attempt to discern divine design in nature—to understand why animals suffer. This led him to conclude that 'in the interests of Christian theodicy, it is necessary [to postulate] (…) that much which belongs to the divine world-plan belongs to it only incidentally, as a necessary accompaniment or by-product, without being in itself a divine end at all'.[172] The need to uphold God's benevolence forced Tennant to assume that animal sufferings are an inescapable side effect which God has to face on the road to his intended goal.

It is obvious that none of the authors addressed in this section subscribed to the idea that nature offers us signs of God's benevolence toward his creation; the statements made by others to justify the animal suffering are inadequate. In this, they agreed, but the alternatives they proposed are different. Bushnell saved the concept of design by expanding its content; nature does not aim to obtain a positive outcome of a pain-versus-pleasure balance but to improve the moral quality of humanity. Romanes, in contrast, abandoned the concept of design as a mirror of God's benevolence entirely, and Tennant saved divine design by considering animal suffering to be unavoidable as nobody, not even God, can make—metaphorically spoken—an omelette without breaking eggs.

The authors addressed in the previous section managed to uphold a belief in perceiving benevolent design in the life of animals after Darwin. The authors examined in this section disagreed. They had their worries about the suffering of animals, but their concerns had not led them to reject the existence of God as incompatible with the results of science or, conversely, to doubt the results of science because they would cast doubt on the existence of God. The authors who did not shy away from making a choice either for God or for science are discussed in the next section.

---

characterizes Tennant as the last natural theologian defending theism as an explanatory principle to understand the world as a whole, and at the same time an exponent of the Irenaean theodicy in which suffering is justified as a means of moral and spiritual improvement of humanity (cf. § 2.4.2.2).

171 Tennant, F.R. 1909. 'The Influence of Darwinism upon Theology' in: *Quarterly Review* 211: 418-440.
172 Tennant, F.R. 1908. *The Origin and Propagation of Sin Being the Hulsean Lectures Delivered before the University of Cambridge in 1901–2.* University Press, Cambridge: 126.

6.5. God and Nature at Strife

The first texts in which God as Creator was put under discussion were—as discussed in Chapter 5—from the Frenchman Baron d'Holbach[173] and the Englishman William Godwin,[174] both living several decades before Darwin. At that time, these considerations failed to meet acceptance among the British public for reasons already mentioned (cf. § 5.4.17). In Darwin's time, it was the utilitarian philosopher *John Stuart Mill* (1806–1873)[175] who revived the thoughts of d'Holbach and Godwin when writing that '[t]he notion of a providential government by an omnipotent Being for the good of his creatures must be entirely dismissed'.[176] His contemporaries rejected Mill's thoughts as a 'monstruous assertion'[177] or criticized them in less intense terms.[178] The same fate befell the traveler and journalist *William Winwood Reade* (1838–1875).[179]

Confessed to be influenced by Darwin's *Origin*,[180] this author, who made no secret of his wish to destroy Christianity,[181] wrote about the book of nature as a book 'inscribed in blood and tears' that illustrates 'how illusive is this theory that God is Love'.[182] Reade grew eloquent in expounding the absurdities of those who take refuge to mitigating comments:

> It is useless to say that pain has its benevolence, that massacre has its mercy. Why is it so ordained that bad should be the raw material of good? Pain is not less pain because it is useful; murder is not less murder because

---

173 d'Holbach, *Common Sense*.
174 Godwin, W. 1798. *Enquiry Concerning Political Justice, and Its Influence on Morals and Happiness. The Third Edition Corrected. In Two Volumes. Vol. I.* G.G. and J. Robinson, London.
175 For biographical details, see Anschutz, R.P. "John Stuart Mill". *Encyclopedia Britannica*, 16 May 2021, https://www.britannica.com/biography/John-Stuart-Mill. Accessed on 14 December 2021.
176 Mill, *Nature the Utility of Religion and Theism*: 243.
177 James, W.P. 1885. 'On Pessimism, and Its Modern Champions' in: *Journal of the Transactions of the Victoria Institute or Philosophical Society of Great Britain* 18: 228-252 (235).
178 Over 50 references to Mill in Romanes's *A Candid Examination* and 25 references in his *Thoughts on Religion* show the efforts taken by him to address, and sometimes refute, Mill's atheistic thoughts.
179 For biographical details, see https://www.darwinproject.ac.uk/william-winwood-reade. Accessed on 14 December 2021.
180 Reade to Darwin. 31 January 1871. *Darwin Correspondence Project*, "Letter no. 7468," accessed on 14 December 2021, https://www.darwinproject.ac.uk/letter/?docId=letters/DCP-LETT-7468.xml
181 Reade, W. 1872. *The Martyrdom of Man*. Trübner & Co., London: 525.
182 Reade, *The Martyrdom of Man*: 520.

it is conducive to development. *Here is blood upon the hand still, and all the perfumes of Arabia will not sweeten it.* To this then we are brought with the much-belauded theory of a semi-human Providence, an anthropoid Deity, a Constructive Mind, a Deus Paleyensis, a God created in the image of a watchmaker.[183]

Nature clearly teaches that 'Christianity is false' and that 'God-worship is idolatry'.[184] But neither as with Mill was Reade's criticism well received. *Alfred Russel Wallace* (1823-1913)—Darwin's co-discoverer of the theory of species emerging by natural selection[185]—dismissed the writings of Reade simply as 'greatly exaggerated', the 'supposed "torments" and "miseries" of animals' being but 'the reflection of the imagined sensations of cultivated men and women'.[186] Thoughts like Reade's were not appreciated in North America either. The lawyer and politician *Robert G. Ingersoll* (1833-1899) could then ask himself if there was anyone who 'can appreciate the mercy of so making the world that all animals devour animals; so that every mouth is a slaughterhouse, and every stomach a tomb?'[187] but thereby deprived himself of a successful political career.[188]

Voices that propagated that cruelties in nature argue against the existence of God remained scarce, at least till the turn of the twentieth century. Thereafter, the discussion would become more widespread, albeit not initiated by those who disputed God's existence. At the beginning of the twentieth century, the Seventh-Day Adventist *George McCready Price* (1870-1963)[189] actively propagated the conviction that it is impossible to reconcile God as he reveals himself in Scripture with animal suffering, having the same opinion as Mill and Reade but with the opposite aim. In his *Outlines of Modern Christianity and Modern*

---

183 Reade, *The Martyrdom of Man*: 520-521.
184 Reade, *The Martyrdom of Man*: 523.
185 For biographical details, see Camerini, J.R. 'Alfred Russel Wallace. British Naturalist' in: Camerini, J.R. "Alfred Russel Wallace". *Encyclopedia Britannica*, 3 November 2021, https://www.britannica.com/biography/Alfred-Russel-Wallace. Accessed on 14 December 2021.
186 Wallace, A.R. 1889. *Darwinism. An Exposition of the Theory of Natural Selection with Some of Its Applications…Second Edition*. MacMillan and Co., London: 37.
187 Ingersoll, R.G. 1878. *The Gods and Other Lectures*. C.P. Farrell, Washington, D.C.: 71.
188 For biographical details, see Britannica, The Editors of Encyclopaedia. "Robert G. Ingersoll". *Encyclopedia Britannica*, 7 August 2021, https://www.britannica.com/biography/Robert-G-Ingersoll. Accessed on 14 December 2021.
189 Numbers, *The Creationists*: 88-119; Vulikovsky, A. 2007. 'Creation and Genesis: a Historical Survey' in: *Creation Research Society Quarterly* 43: 206-219; Weinberg, C. 2014. '"Ye Shall Know Them by Their Fruits": Evolution, Eschatology, and the Anticommunist Politics of George McCready Price' in: *Church History* 83 (3): 684-722.

Science,¹⁹⁰ this author is quite clear on the issue. The Bible teaches that death, even animal death, is the result sin but 'with evolution we have countless millions of years of creature suffering, cruelty, and death before man appeared at all, cruelty and death that (…) have no moral meaning at all, save as the work of a fiend creator, or a bungling and incompetent one'.¹⁹¹ The idea of evolution with its pre-Adamite death 'makes the whole Scripture a jargon of unmeaning folly'.¹⁹²

Clearly, Price harked back on the views of the 'Scriptural Geologists' (cf. § 5.4.11). These authors had also recognized that God's skills as Creator could come in danger if the thoughts of an old earth with successive creations were to be accepted, making him a tinkerer who needed several attempts to achieve the required result. And they also had exploited this supposed blemish on God's blazon as a means to sustain the only correct reading—in their opinion—of the biblical story of creation which cannot be anything else than encompassing six days of twenty-four hours each. In view of the latter purpose, Price and his predecessors seem to be concerned not so much with the suffering of the animals as with the inerrancy of Scripture.

Ten years later, in the well-known volume of *The Fundamentals* that marked—as noted by the historian David Livingstone—the shift from a scholarly discussion about cosmogenesis towards an aggressive anti-evolutionism,¹⁹³ the Reverend *Henry Beach* wrote that because Darwinism is founded on 'the destruction of the weak and defenseless', it metamorphoses God into 'an Ivan the terrible'.¹⁹⁴ Evolution cannot be true because it presupposes a cruelty in God that refutes everything that the Bible reveals about him. Others endorsed this incompatibility between God and evolution, not, however to contest evolution but for the opposite purpose.

One of the first to exploit this controversy to promote atheism was the philosopher *Bertrand Russell* (1872–1970).¹⁹⁵ 'Do you think that, if you were granted omnipotence and omniscience and millions of years in which to perfect your world, you could produce nothing better than the

---

190 Price, G.E. McCready. 1902. *Outlines of Modern Christianity and Modern Science*. Pacific Press Publishing Company, Oakland.
191 Price, *Outlines of Modern Christianity*: 116.
192 Price, *Outlines of Modern Christianity*: 248.
193 Livingstone, *Darwin's Forgotten Defenders*: 146-168 (152). Cf. Numbers, *The Creationists*: 51-119.
194 Beach, H.H. 1912. 'Decadence of Darwinism' in: *The Fundamentals. A Testimony to the Truth Volume VIII*: 36-48 (44). Testimony Publishing Company, Chicago.
195 Bowler, *Reconciling Science and Religion*: 341-343.

Ku Klux Klan or the Fascists?'[196] This same author also expressed his astonishment that religion had 'accommodated itself to the doctrine of evolution' but did not explain why the Creator did not go straight to his goal but via a detour of animals that 'were torturing each other with ferocious horns and agonizing strings'.[197] Nature reflecting divine design is nonsense. '[S]ince the time of Darwin we understand much better why living creatures are adapted to their environment. It is not that their environment was made to be suitable to them but that they grew to be suitable to it, and that is the basis of adaptation. There is no evidence of design about it.'[198] Those who consider evolution and God incompatible are right; they only draw the wrong conclusion.[199]

Almost at the same time, it was *Chapman Cohen* (1868–1954),[200] chairman of the Secular Society,[201] who emphasized that God and evolution cannot co-exist. He grasped the 'monkey trial' (see above) as an excellent opportunity to ridicule any attempt to harmonize evolution with Christianity. Those who try to do so should explain why we find in nature a process so full of obvious errors, so full of fumbles.[202] Arguments to vindicate God by assuming a higher purpose don't convince. 'A tiger may well glorify the cosmic order every times it dines off a sheep, but there surely remains the sheep's point of view.'[203] And a justification by pointing to a progression towards higher forms of life neither does for '[w]hat profit is it to the myriads of animals that have been crushed out in the struggle for existence that some hundreds of thousands of year later a

---

196 Russell, B. 1957. *Why I Am Not a Christian: And Other Essays on Religion and Related Subjects.* Simon & Schuster, New York: 10.
197 Russell, B. 1935. *Religion and Science. [The Home University Library of Modern Knowledge].* Thornton Butterworth, London: 79-80.
198 Russell, *Why I Am Not a Christian*: 10.
199 Cf. Munday, J.C. 'Animal Pain: Beyond the Threshold?' in: Miller, K.B. (ed.). 2003. *Perspectives on an Evolving Creation.* Wm. B. Eerdmans, Grand Rapids: 435-468. 'Non-Christians, perhaps taking their cue from young-Earth creationists, use the arguments about evolution's wastage but in converse fashion; they claim that young-Earth creationists are wrong both about evolution and about God' (451).
200 For biographical details, see https://www.secularism.org.uk/chapman-cohen.html. Accessed on 14 December 2021.
201 Bowler, *Reconciling Science and Religion*: 351-352. The Secular Society was formed in 1898. One of its objects was 'to promote the principle that human conduct should be based upon natural knowledge, and not upon supernatural belief'. See Cohen, C. [1925]. *God and Evolution.* The Pioneer Press, London: postscript, page not numbered. Other writings published by this organization carry titles such as *The Faults and Failings of Jesus Christ* or *The Bible: What Is It Worth*.
202 Cohen, *God and Evolution*: 32.
203 Cohen, *God and Evolution*: 33.

perfect form of life may exist?'[204] Any attempt to harmonize the existence of the world with the essence of a God as Scripture reveals is doomed to fail.[205]

With Russell and Cohen, we see—now more than half a century after Mill and Reade—that the cruelties connected with animal death and predation were revived as evidence against God. But whereas Mill and Reade had met severe criticism at the time, Russell and Cohen did not come across similar refutations. Times had apparently changed since Darwin. People had lost interest in defending divine design, either because they had given up on faith altogether, or because they had concluded that design as vehicle of divine revelation had failed; God reveals himself in Scripture and not in nature.[206] This did not imply that there was no discussion about the relationship between faith and science anymore, but the problem of animal suffering and divine benevolence was no longer part of this debate.[207]

This silence on the subject of animal suffering and divine attributes has also been noted by others,[208] and usually, the profound influence of the Swiss theologian *Karl Barth* (1886–1968), fierce critic of any form of natural theology, is held responsible for this situation.[209] Barth's lack of interest in science did not do much to encourage attempts to make science relevant for theology or *vice versa*. His influence on the Anglican theologians as well on their colleagues in the other British denominations was profound as has been amply documented.[210] Speaking of natural theology in this period has been described as 'to tread on confessional

---

204 Cohen, *God and Evolution*: 35.
205 Cohen, *God and Evolution*: 37.
206 Bowler, *Reconciling Science and Religion*: 193-214.
207 Bowler, *Reconciling Science and Religion*: 122-159, 376-405; Numbers, *the Creationists*: 88-207; Bowler, *Monkey Trials and Gorilla Sermons*: 134-228; Rios, *After the Monkey Trial*: 41-72.
208 Murray, M.J. 2008. *Nature Red in Tooth and Claw: Theism and the Problem of Animal Suffering.* Oxford University Press, Oxford: 1-5; Southgate, C. 2008. *The Groaning of Creation. God, Evolution, and the Problem of Evil.* Westminster John Knox Press, Louisville: 10-12; Sollereder, B.N. 2019. *God, Evolution, and Animal Suffering. Theodicy without a Fall.* Routledge, London: 44.
209 Roberts, 'That Darwin Destroyed Natural Theology' in: Numbers, *Galileo Goes to Jail*: 161-169; Clapman, P. 'Barth and Darwin: Can They Talk' in: Robinson, *Darwinism and Natural Theology*: 154-159; Clough, D.L., 2012. *On Animals. Volume 1. Systematic Theology.* T&T Clark, London: 16-19; McGrath, A.E. 2017. *Re-Imagining Nature. The Promise of a Christian Natural Theology.* Wiley Blackwell, Chichester: 130-132, 144-149.
210 Bowler, *Reconciling Science and Religion*: 277-286, 288-289, 318-321; Bowler, *Monkey Trials and Gorilla Sermons*: 187-188.

eggshells'.[211] Furthermore, the atrocities of the Great War had prompted both theologians as well as the common public to find their solace in meditations on divine grace and mercy and not in contemplating nature as a mirror of divine love anymore.[212] And finally, the social and economic iniquities of twentieth-century society had killed every thought that the social order would reflect divine design which of course also affected the conviction that nature reflected a divine design.[213]

It would—aside from a lonely voice like Lewis's as addressed above—last till the 1950s before there were again authors who would pay attention to the ambiguous relationship between a good Creator and the suffering in creation. One of the first to reopen the discussion was the Baptist theologian *Bernard Ramm* (1916–1992).[214] In 1954, he published *The Christian View of Science and Scripture* in which he emphasized that the presence of death in the animal kingdom is inseparable from creation. Those who have difficulty in calling such a creation good must revise their definition of the term *good*. 'The cycle of Nature is an amazing thing, and the relationship of life to life sets up a magnificent *balance* of *Nature*.'[215]

The publication of this book, marked as 'a pivotal event for evangelicals concerned with the relation between science and Christian faith',[216] did not go unnoticed. It prompted the young-earth creationists *John Whitcomb* and *Henry Morris* to publish their well-known *Genesis Flood*,[217] a firm rebuttal against Ramm as evidenced by the forty references to this latter author the book contains.[218] 'Does the Book of Genesis, honestly

---

211 McGrath, *Darwinism and the Divine*: 18.
212 Hick, *Evil and the God of Love*: 243-250.
213 Moore, *Post-Darwinian Controversies*: 350.
214 Anonymous. 1979. 'Bernard Ramm' in: *Journal of the American Scientific Affiliation* 31 (4): 178.
215 Ramm, B. 1954. *The Christian View of Science and Scripture*. Wm. B. Eerdmans, Grand Rapids: 331-335 (335). Acceptance of old age and pre-Adamite death did not imply that Ramm subscribed to Darwinism as well. He clung to the idea of special creation, all animal species both extinct or still around having emerged through special divine creative acts. In this way, he continued the tradition of the pre-Darwinian geologists and the authors discussed in § 6.3.1.
216 Haas, J.W. 1979. 'The Christian View of Science and Scripture' in: *Journal of the American Scientific Affiliation* 31 (4): 177.
217 Whitcomb, J.V., Morris, H.M. 1961. *The Genesis Flood: the Biblical Record and Its Scientific Implications*. Presbyterian and Reformed Publishing Co., Phillipsburg. For details on the role of this book in shaping the creationist movement, see Matzke, 'The Evolution of Creationist Movements': 153.
218 For more details on the background of the Ramm versus Whitcomb & Morris encounter, see McIver, *Creationism*: Chapter 2; Numbers, *The Creationists*: 206-238; Rios, *After the Monkey Trial*: 54-72; Defoe, T. 2019. *An Analysis of Bernard Ramm's Influence on Young Earth Creationism*. www.academia.edu/39527102/an_analysis_of_

studied in the light of the New Testament, allow for a reign of tooth and claw and death and destruction before the Fall of Adam?'[219] The fortress raised half a century ago by George McCready Price and Henry Beach was manned again.

While Whitcomb and Morris were preparing for a renewed battle against a science considered by them to be unscriptural, others convened for handling this issue more peacefully. The 1956 annual conference of the Research Scientists' Christian Fellowship (RCSF)[220] was devoted to the 'Problem of Pain, Suffering and Evil'.[221] In the proceedings of this conference, the classical exegesis of Genesis 3 as source of all and any evil—both moral and natural—was addressed first by the Reverend M.R.W. Farrar.[222] He spoke about nature as touched by sin, not, however, because of Adam but by an angelic rebellion antedating humankind.[223] This concept, nature corrupted through sin, was challenged by the authors of the second paper who referred to the 'evidence geology can give about conditions on the earth before the fall, that is, before the appearance of *homo sapiens*'. Already before humanity entered the scene 'carnivores existed, having big canine teeth'.[224] The authors admitted that the earth is subjected to frustration, thereby referring to Romans 8:20,[225] but '[t]his frustration in nature is a challenge to man and forms a world suitable for his development.' And this frustration 'did not prevent God from seeing it as very good, because it had been imposed for a good purpose'.[226] Again it is, as with so many authors before, the end that justifies the means.

It is clear that around the middle of the twentieth century, the theme of suffering in creation as a threat for the attributes of God was in the

---

  Bernard_Ramms_influence_on_young_earth_creationism. Accessed on 14 December 2021.
219 Whitcomb & Morris, *The Genesis Flood*: 455.
220 Research Scientists' Christian Fellowship was a British association founded in 1944 with the aim to develop a Christian view on problems of science and faith. See Rios, *After the Monkey Trial*: 75-104. In 1988 it changed its name into *Christians in Science*. See https://en.wikipedia.org/wiki/Christians_in_Science. Accessed on 14 December 2021.
221 Rios, *After the Monkey Trial*: 93-94.
222 No further details on this author could be retrieved.
223 Farrar, M.R.W. 1958. 'The Problem of Pain and Suffering. Part I: A Traditional View' in: *The Christian Graduate* 11: 51-54.
224 [A Cambridge R.S.C.F. Group]. 1958. 'The Problem of Pain and Suffering, Part 2: A Scientific Interpretation' in: *The Christian Graduate* 11: 55-59 (56). It should be noticed that, in their rebuttal, these authors apparently missed the point that carnivorousness may be due to an angelic rebellion in a remote past, long before there were humans around as forwarded by the first contributor.
225 'For the creature was made subject to vanity,' (KJV)
226 [A Cambridge R.S.C.F. Group], 'The Problem of Pain and Suffering, Part 2': 55, 56.

spotlights again—either as a problem asking for a solution or as a 'Shibboleth'[227] that separates the true Christians from those who falsely call themselves that.

6.6. Discussion

Both the authors who rejected Darwin's theory of animal species originating by natural selection, as well as those who accepted Darwin's thoughts—either unmodified or adulterating natural selection with some form of divine involvement—acknowledged that animal suffering somehow may conflict with the belief in a wise and benevolent Creator. However, as with pre-Darwinian authors, animal suffering was minimized by taking recourse to a neo-Cartesian approach whereas predation was seen as beneficial because it served the greater good of maintaining a harmonious balance between competing animal species and it minimized suffering by ensuring a quick demise in case of failing health.

For some authors, Darwin's theory even made the problem of the animal miseries connected with the struggle for survival less acute because this struggle had contributed to the emergence of the human species as the pinnacle of creation. Darwin himself might have written in the sixth edition of his *Origin* that 'natural selection or the survival of the fittest, does not necessarily include progressive development'[228] but for his contemporaries, Darwin's theory—albeit modified to accommodate the concept of progression—offered additional arguments to justify the Creator in his acts.[229] And to the problem that animal death and suffering

---

227 'Whenever one of the fugitives of Ephraim said, "Let me go over," the men of Gilead would say to him, "Are you an Ephraimite?" When he said, "No," they said to him, "Then say Shibboleth," and he said, "Sibboleth," for he could not pronounce it right. Then they seized him and killed him at the fords of the Jordan.' Judges 12:5–6. (NRSV)

228 Darwin, C. 1872. *The Origin of Species by Means of Natural Selection, or the Preservation of Favoured Races in the Struggle for Life. Sixth Edition, with Additions and Corrections (Eleventh Thousand.).* John Murray, London: 98. Cf. the letter of Charles Darwin to Alpheus Hyatt. 4 December 1872: 'After long reflection I cannot avoid the conviction that no innate tendency to progressive development exists, as is now held by so many able naturalists, & perhaps by yourself. It is curious how seldom writers define what they mean by progressive development; but this is a point which I have briefly discussed in the Origin.' *Darwin Correspondence Project*, "Letter no. 8658," accessed on 14 December 2021, https://www.darwinproject.ac.uk/letter/?docId=letters/DCP-LETT-8658.xml

229 It cannot be denied that Darwin himself provided clues for this progressionists's interpretation of his theory as in the second edition of the *Descent of Man* he wrote about 'natural selection [to] have sufficed to raise man to his present high position in the organic scale' and about 'Man, the wonder and glory of the Universe'. See Darwin, C. 2004 [1879]. *The Descent of Man, and Selection in Relation to Sex. With Illustrations.* John Murray, London. Reprint of the second edition with an introduction by James

reigning throughout long ages could jeopardize God's skills as Creator, Darwin's theory did not pose problems not encountered before. This issue was already raised before Darwin as addressed in Chapter 5. Darwin's theory of species originating through natural selection did not aggravate this problem. Apparently, Darwinism was not the death blow for natural theology.[230]

Some, however, found all these arguments wanting and chose to forgo any effort to reconcile animal suffering with divine benevolence. Instead, they rejected the concept of design altogether or changed its meaning. In the latter case, animal suffering was justified as a reference to God's awesomeness or understood as an unintended but unavoidable side effect of God's plan for this world. But their denial that nature points to a benevolent God did not cause them to question the existence of God himself.

The preliminary conclusion is that Darwin's worries about the tension between the goodness of the Creator and the observed miseries of his creatures found little resonance with his contemporaries and the generation thereafter.[231] The same arguments that were considered persuasive before Darwin turned out to be useful after him, at least for those who wanted to hold fast to the belief that nature reflects God's benevolence.

Those who in the decades after Darwin opposed that nature would reflect divine design did so for other reasons than worrying about the fate of the animals; they were more concerned with liberating the common public from anything that smelled of superstition and determined to loosen the grip of the clergy on matters scientific and social.[232] It was not about finding arguments against the existence of God, but about delivering

---

Moore and Adrian Desmond. Penguin Books, London: 85, 193. For Darwinism and progression, see also Bowler, P.J. 1976. *Fossils and Progress. Paleontology and the Idea of Progressive Evolution in the Nineteenth Century.* Science History Publications, New York: 117-147.

230 Greene, J.C. 1959. 'Darwin and Religion' in: *Proceedings of the American Philosophical Society* 103 (5): 716-725; Brooke, J.H. 'Darwin and Victorian Christianity' in: Hodge & Radick, *The Cambridge Companion to Darwin*: 197-218.

231 Bowler, *Reconciling Science and Religion*: 19-24; 27-58, 122-159.

232 Turner, F.M. 1978. 'The Victorian Conflict between Science and Religion: a Professional Dimension' in: *Isis* 69 (3): 356-376; Barton, R. 1990. 'An Influential Set of Chaps': the X-Club and Royal Society Politics 1864–85' in: *The British Journal for the History of Science* 23 (1): 53-81; Bowler, *Reconciling Science and Religion*: 59-86; Livingstone, D.N. 'Re-placing Darwinism and Christianity' in: Lindberg & Numbers, *When Science & Christianity Meet*: 183-202.

science from restrictions imposed by church or society as has recently convincingly been documented by the historian Matthew Stanley.[233]

My own research supports the view that rejecting the traditional conception of design mirroring divine benevolence did not imply that God himself was also referred to the realm of fiction. Attempts to exploit events in nature as arguments against the existence of God were few in the nineteenth century and would only become more influential with the 1920s, at that time the outcome of a fateful marriage between anti-evolutionists and atheists. The former had given birth to the thought that God and evolution cannot co-exist to support their biblical literalism and to reject evolution in any case. The other party also subscribed to the view that Scripture teaches a special creation of six days but held that science makes this claim untenable and hence Scripture cannot be considered to be reliable.[234] For them, it was not science but the Bible that was in doubt.

These early twentieth-century skirmishes between evolutionists and anti-evolutionists deserve attention not only because they are the roots of the debate as it continues to this day, but also because they support the belief that in the British Isles, the post-Darwinian battle between science and religion was not about the existence of God, but about the free conduction of science. It was the monkey trial in Dayton, USA—an outright attack on the freedom to teach science without religious restrictions—that incensed the wrath of the British atheist Cohen and inspired him to exploit the cruelty in nature to deny the existence of God.[235] The idea that God and evolution are mutually exclusive did not emerge within the British scientific community, but was conceived and brought up in the former colonies, several decades after Darwin's death.[236]

Why precisely around the 1960s theologians and others resumed the discussion about the relationship between God's goodness and animal

---

233 Stanley, M. 2015. *Huxley's Church & Maxwell's Demon. From Theistic Science to Naturalistic Science.* The University of Chicago Press, Chicago.
234 Fraser, L.J. 2015. 'The Secret Sympathy: New Atheism, Protestant Fundamentalism, and Evolution' in: *Open Theology* 1: 445-454.
235 Cohen, *God and Evolution.* See § 6.5.
236 For further explanation of the observation that the notion that God and evolution are mutually exclusive originated in North America and not in England, see Stanley, *Huxley's Church & Maxwell's Demon*: 267. First, it would be related to a different educational system which would make the American public less knowledgeable in the principles of science than the English. Second, the lack of a single dominant church meant that the attacks that scholars in Britain launched on the Anglican clergy by the Americans were interpreted as being directed against Christianity in a more general sense. That a lack of understanding of science and the misconception that criticism of the church includes criticism of God, are the ideal conditions for a conflict between faith and science needs no further explanation.

suffering is not entirely clear, natural theology itself becoming fashionable again only several decades later.[237] Possibly, it may be due to an increased awareness of the intrinsic value of the non-human creation evoked by man-made ecological problems,[238] but may be also elicited by an atheistic scientism initially propagated by Bertrand Russell and Chapman Cohen (see above), and more recently rekindled by *Jacques Monod*, the latter pretending to be 'surprised that a Christian would defend the idea that this [the cruel process of elimination and destruction] is the process which God more or less set up in order to have evolution'.[239] Others would follow suit.[240]

Since the end of the time period discussed in this chapter, the discussion of the relationship between God's involvement with his creation and the suffering that afflicts animals has continued unabated. In the next and final chapter, I will investigate to what extent the arguments from the past are considered still valid by present-day authors who address the subject and to what extent they are influenced by Darwin's theory.

6.7. Conclusion

Before Darwin published his theory of evolution by natural selection, the idea that nature was under God's providential care was only rarely doubted. The life of the animals as we see it today did not cause problems for divine benevolence and wisdom and neither did a past as revealed by the geologists. In the first half century after Darwin, this did not change much. Most authors saw opportunities to reconcile Darwinism with traditional views and if that was a step too far, abandoning the belief that God reveals himself in nature became an option, without, however, disputing his existence as such. Only from the 1920s, vociferous atheists would advocate that the cruelties they observed in nature could not coexist with the belief in a benevolent God—in this way exploiting arguments put forward by anti-evolutionists to support the reliability of

---

237 Holder, R.D. 'Natural Theology in the Twentieth Century' in: Manning, R.R. (ed.). 2013. *The Oxford Handbook of Natural Theology*. Oxford University Press, Oxford: 118-134; McGrath, *Re-Imagining Nature*: 168-173.

238 Carson, R. 1962. *Silent Spring*. Houghton Mifflin, Boston; White Jr, L. 1967. 'The Historical Roots of Our Ecologic Crisis' in: *Science* 155: 1203-1207. Cf. Southgate, *Groaning of Creation*: 11.

239 On 10 June 1976, the Australian Broadcasting Commission Science Unit broadcasted a tribute to Jacques Monod (1910-1976) which was entitled 'The Secret of Life.' https://creation.com/jacques-monod-and-theistic-evolution. Accessed on 14 December 2021.

240 *The Four Horseman - Hitchens, Dawkins, Dennet, Harris*. 2007. https://www.youtube.com/watch?v=n7IHU28aR2E. Accessed on 14 December 2021. For a rebuttal, see Plantinga, A. 2011. *Where the Conflict Really Lies. Science, Religion, and Naturalism*. Oxford University Press, New York: 55-63.

Scripture as evidence for the opposite. So Darwin is not to blame for turning nature from a theatre of God's glory into a bloody horror spectacle but hard-nosed scripturalists who provided the ammunition thereafter so eagerly exploited by atheistic scientists to fight their own battle.

Chapter 7: Epilogue

A Comparison of Past and Present Arguments

Abstract
Building on the analysis in the previous chapters, in which it was shown that the introduction of Darwin's evolution theory did not radically change the debate on animal suffering in relation to the divine benevolence, in this chapter a systematic comparison is given of contemporary and past arguments regarding this issue. It is shown that almost all present-day arguments have been defended in the past, also by pre-Darwinian thinkers: animals do not suffer at all; that animals suffer does not matter; pleasure outweighs their pain; animal suffering serves a positive purpose; it is the fault of Adam or the devil; animals will be rewarded in a blissful eschatological existence. Ignoring this continuity in opinions is regrettable because it gives birth to the erroneous thought that concerns about animal suffering emerged only with (and because of) Darwin's theory of evolution. In fact, these concerns had been there before, which means that the tension between a good Creator and suffering beings is neither solved by merely denying evolutionary history, nor increased by accepting it.

7.1. Introduction

In the previous chapter, I have shown that Darwin's theory of evolution did not much change the prevailing thoughts about the relationship between animal suffering and divine benevolence. Arguments to reconcile the doctrine of a good and benevolent Creator with the obvious suffering of his creatures that had been forwarded before Darwin did not lose persuasion after him. In any case, they remained valid for those who adhered to the belief that God sustains all creatures through his providential care, although, of course, it cannot be ruled out that the number of those who had this conviction may have diminished over time.

Apparently, Darwin's evolution theory was not a watershed in this regard, at least not until the 1960s, the period so far investigated. This is surprising since nowadays Darwin is commonly seen as the visionary or—alternatively—the bugbear who has given birth to the belief that nature refutes rather than confirms the existence of a benevolent creator. This view of Darwin as being responsible for this belief is evident in the following quotation, to which many others could be added:

> What kind of God can one infer from the sort of phenomena epitomized by the species on Darwin's Galápagos Islands? The evolutionary process is rife with happenstance, contingency, incredible waste, death, pain and horror. (...) To quote Darwin, "I cannot persuade myself that a beneficent and omnipotent God would have designedly created the *Ichneumonidae* with the express intention of their feeding within the living bodies of caterpillars." Whatever the God implied by evolutionary theory and the data of natural history may be like, He is not the Protestant God of waste not, want not. He is also not a loving God who cares about His productions. He is not even the awful God portrayed in the book of Job. The God of the Galapágos is careless, wasteful, indifferent, almost diabolical. He is certainly not the sort of God to whom anyone would be inclined to pray.[1]

Thus, through Darwin we now know that the Christian God of love and care for his creatures does not exist. Christian anti-evolutionists agree that Darwin's theory of evolution is indeed incompatible with the concept of a God who cares about the weak, but their appreciation of this outcome of Darwin's gloomy view on nature is quite different.

> If this is God's "method of creation", it is strange that He would use such cruel, haphazard, inefficient, wasteful processes. Furthermore, the idea of the "survival of the fittest", whereby the stronger animals eliminate the weaker in the "struggle for existence" is the essence of Darwin's theory of evolution by natural selection, and this whole scheme is flatly contradicted by the Biblical doctrine of love, of unselfish sacrifice, and of Christian charity. The God of the Bible is a God of order and of grace, not a God of confusion and cruelty.[2]

God can't be someone who allows that the strong flourish at the expense of the weak, and therefore, 'We (...) deny that the millions of years of

---

1 Hull, D.L. 1991. 'The God of the Galápagos, Review of *Darwin on Trial* by Philip E. Johnson' in: *Nature* 352: 485-486 (486). The author made these critical remarks when reviewing a book combating evolution. It is interesting to note that it is anti-evolutionist sentiments that provoked such harsh statements about God and nature. In the 1920s, the anti-evolutionary monkey trial prompted Chapman Cohen to a similar atheistic outburst, as I described in Chapter 6. For a critical analysis of Hull's considerations, see Southgate, C. 2002. 'God and Evolutionary Evil: Theodicy in the Light of Darwinism' in: *Zygon* 37 (4): 803-824, in particular pp. 803-806; Southgate, C. 2008. *The Groaning of Creation. God, Evolution, and the Problem of Evil*. Westminster John Knox Press, Louisville: 7-10.
2 Morris, H.M. *Evolution and the Bible*. https://www.icr.org/article/53/. Accessed on 14 December 2021. Initially published as Morris, H.M. June 1973. *Evolution and the Bible*. ICR Impact Series No. 5.

death, disease, violence, and extinction occurred in the animal world before the Fall and thereby deny that those millions of years claimed by the evolutionary scientific establishment ever happened'.[3] Letting go of God as someone who cares about the weak had already caused much misery and much more harm was to be expected.

> Dangerous ideas have always had negative consequences, as is tragically seen in the 20th century, which reaped so much bitter fruit in the wake of philosophies which implemented Darwin's ideas. Few more chilling examples of the fallout of Darwinism can be found than Nazism and communism, which consciously applied Darwinian principles, and radically affected millions of lives. Our Western world, once so firmly grounded on Judeo-Christian principles, is now deeply into its post-Christian phase illustrated by partial-birth abortions, marriage radically redefined, euthanasia, etc. This decline shows no sign of abating.[4]

I suppose that these quotes are convincing enough to show that nowadays both friend and foe hold Darwin responsible for the fact that the belief that there is a God who cares about everything is less plausible than it was in the past. The question addressed in this chapter is to what extent he is indeed responsible for this shift in opinion.

As in the past, Christian authors nowadays are struggling to square the suffering of animals with the Creator's supposed goodness, and they are deeply divided on the issue. It seems that the problem has not become easier since Darwin.[5] But did it indeed become more difficult? In view of my findings to date, that remains to be seen. In any case, it was not experienced as having become more difficult by Darwin's contemporaries and those after him, at least up to the 1920s. For them, Darwin's theory presented no problems with regard to animal suffering that had not been encountered and discussed before. Thus, the influence of Darwin's theory of natural selection on the problem of animal suffering *vis-à-vis* divine benevolence was only marginal at that time, and it may be that this—contrary to popular belief that holds Darwin accountable—also applies to the current debate.

In order to test this hypothesis, I will compare the thoughts on this theme as published since 1962 with the findings brought to light in the

---

3 Mortenson, T., Ury, T.H. (eds). 2008. *Coming to Grips with Genesis. Biblical Authority and the Age of the Earth.* Master Books, Green Forest: 456.
4 Mortenson & Ury, *Coming to Grips with Genesis*: 425.
5 Schneider, J.R. 2020. *Animal Suffering and the Darwinian Problem of Evil.* Cambridge University Press, Cambridge: 1-47.

previous chapters, limiting myself to the writings of those authors whom I could identify—through research of the literature in this field—as contributing to the contemporary discussion on the tension between animal suffering and divine benevolence. Unlike before, the voices of female theologians are now also joining the discussion, a finding that reflects the generally increased contribution of women to science.[6]

Whether, and if so to what extent, there are differences between opinions forwarded since the 1960s, and those in the time before Darwin, I will analyze in §7.2, concluding the discussion of each option with a brief note on its weaknesses, if any. In § 7.3, I will reflect upon the outcome of my search, and in § 7.4, I will offer some personal reflections on animal suffering and its bearing on the creation-versus-evolution debate. I will end with a final conclusion in § 7.5. One cautionary note has to be added here. I am aware that present-day theology has far more to tell about (animal) theodicy than discussed in this chapter. Given the scope of this study, however, I restrict myself to examining those proposals that stick to classical notions of divine goodness and omnipotence. Therefore, I will ignore contemporary concepts in which a solution for the problem of animal suffering is sought in a redefinition of the divine attributes—in particular omnipotence—as, for example, proposed in process theology.[7] Excellent surveys that offer a more complete theological perspective can be found elsewhere.[8]

7.2. Past and Present Views Compared
7.2.1. *Animals Do Not Suffer at All*
The option that animals do not suffer at all is especially associated with the Cartesian 'beast-machine doctrine' that was developed in the seventeenth century by its name-giver René Descartes. For those who subscribed to the view that animal suffering implies divine punishment, the theological advantages of this option are obvious. After all, God has the right to punish a sinful humanity but no reason to let animals suffer since animals are guiltless of sin and thus do not deserve any reprobation. When their suffering is only apparent and not real, God is absolved from being unjust. But in spite of the theological advantages, almost none of

---

6 *Women in Science*. 2020. Unesco Fact Sheet No. 60. fs60-women-in-science-2020-en.pdf (unesco.org). Accessed on 14 December 2021.

7 Haught, J.F. 2005. 'The Boyle Lecture 2003: Darwin, Design and the Promise of Nature' in: *Science & Christian Belief* 17 (1): 5-20. For criticism on this approach, see Berry, R.J. 2005. 'The Lions Seek Their Prey from God: a Commentary on the Boyle Lecture' in: *Science & Christian Belief* 17 (1): 41-56.

8 E.g. in Sollereder, B.N. 2019. *God, Evolution, and Animal Suffering. Theodicy without a Fall*. Routledge, London: 44-91.

the British authors addressed in this study endorsed this view; for most of them, denying animals any sensibility ran counter to common sense, as has been amply demonstrated. Only in the seventeenth century and the first decade of the eighteenth, a few authors supported this view, as has been addressed in Chapter 3. The overwhelming majority of the relevant authors found the idea that animals were senseless brutes preposterous and not worthy of much serious attention. This has remained the case ever since, as appeared from my survey throughout the centuries till Darwin entered the scene.

Before Darwin, people had acknowledged that 'the lower animals, like man, manifestly feel pleasure and pain, happiness and misery',[9] and in this sense, Darwin's theory did not offer a perspective that was entirely new. It is not surprising, therefore, that Darwin's contemporaries and successors also accepted that animals can suffer and continued to minimize the scope of that suffering in the same ways as their pre-Darwinian predecessors had done. In this connection, the conviction that animals (1) have a lower level of consciousness than humanity, (2) do not have memories to pain experienced in the past, and (3) do not fear pains that will come in the future, served pre- and post-Darwinian authors alike. '[W]e have good grounds for believing that, although the lower animals are sensitive to pain, they are far less sensitive than man, and that the lower we descend in the scale of animal life, the less sensitive it becomes', a belief that 'should strengthen our belief in the mercy and benevolence of the Creator.'[10]

A similar downplaying of animals' suffering can still be encountered nowadays. In the early nineties of the previous century, the historian Peter Harrison claimed that '[n]o strict argument can be mounted for or against the existence of animal pain'.[11] A more recent example of someone being agnostic on the issue of animal suffering is the medical doctor *Jon Garvey*, who holds that 'when asking if, and how, animals feel pain, we should also fully understand our lack of any real knowledge on anything

---

9   Darwin, C. 1879. *The Descent of Man, and Selection in Relation to Sex. With Illustrations*. John Murray, London. Reprinted with an Introduction by James Moore and Adrian Desmond. 2004. Penguin Books, London: 89.

10 Collier, W. 1889. 'The Comparative Insensibility of Animals to Pain' in: *The Nineteenth Century: a Monthly Review*: 26 (152): 622-627 (627). Cf. Raven, C.E. 1928. *The Creator Spirit. A Survey of Christian Doctrine in the Light of Biology, Psychology and Mysticism. The Hulsean Lectures, Cambridge, 1926-7. The Noble Lectures Harvard, 1926. With an Appendix on Biochemistry and Mental Phenomena*. Harvard University Press, Cambridge (MA): 120-121.

11 Harrison, P. 1989. 'Theodicy and Animal Pain' in: *Philosophy* 64 (247): 79-92 (81). Cf. Harrison, P. 1991. 'Do Animals Feel Pain?' in: *Philosophy* 66 (255): 25-40.

that could even make sense of the question', and adds that 'our profound ignorance of what it is like to be an animal makes it supremely arrogant to accuse God of creating a world of extreme cruelty'.¹² The neuroscientist *Joseph LeDoux* approaches the problem from a different angle and emphasizes the importance of the distinction between conscious and nonconscious behavior: '[W]e should not assume that the observation of one of the nonconscious behavioral consequences means that a conscious feeling of pain or pleasure has occurred.'¹³

Other contemporary authors, however, show more concern about the problem of animal pain and refrain from making mitigating notes. Admittedly, there is, in the words of *Michael Murray*,¹⁴ no convincing proof for the assumption that animals have experiences similar to us, but absence of evidence does not imply evidence of absence. We have to envisage the possibility that, to quote *Trent Dougherty*, 'morally significant pain is widespread through the non-human population of the animal kingdom'.¹⁵ After all, a similarity in neurobiological sense should be acknowledged. 'In fact, because many non-human species have all the neural substrates that are likely to be essential for the emergence of feeling, and exhibit behavioral manifestations that are consistent with feelings and emotion, the parsimonious assumption should be that feelings are present in these species.'¹⁶

---

12 Garvey, J. 2019. *God's Good Earth. The Case for an Unfallen Creation.* Cascade Books, Eugene: 147-167 (166-167).

13 LeDoux, J. 2019. *The Deep History of Ourselves. The Four-Billion-Year Story of how We Got Conscious Brains.* Viking, New York: 218-219, 335-371 (218). Cf. Lewis, C.S. 1986 [1940]. *The Problem of Pain.* Collins, Glasgow: 103-106; Hick, J. 1968 [1966]. *Evil and the God of Love.* Collins, London: 345-350; Carruthers, P. 1989. 'Brute Experience' in: *The Journal of Philosophy* 86 (5): 258-269; Harrison, P. 1989. 'Theodicy and Animal Pain'; Swinburne, R. 1998. *Providence and the Problem of Evil.* Oxford University Press, Oxford: 173-175; Harrison, P. 1991. 'Do Animals Feel Pain?'; Corey, M.A. 2000. *Evolution and the Problem of Natural Evil.* University Press of America, Lanham: 154-157.

14 Murray, M.J. 2008. *Nature Red in Tooth and Claw: Theism and the Problem of Animal Suffering.* Oxford University Press, Oxford: 41-72 (57).

15 Dougherty T. 2014. *The Problem of Animal Pain. A Theodicy for All Creatures Great and Small.* Palgrave MacMillan, Basingstoke: 56-95 (95). Cf. Dawkins, M.S. 2006. 'Through Animal Eyes: What Behaviour Tells Us' in: *Applied Animal Behaviour Science* 100: 4-10; Mashour, G.A., Alkire M.T. 2013. 'Evolution of Consciousness: Phylogeny, Ontogeny, and Emergence from General Anesthesia' in: *Proceedings of the National Academy of Sciences* 110 (Suppl. 2): 10357-10364; Srokosz, M, Kolstoe, S. 2016. 'Animal Suffering, the Hard Problem of Consciousness, and a Reflection on why We Should Treat Animals Well' in: *Science & Christian Belief* 28 (1):3-19.

16 Damasio, A., Carvalho, G.B. 2013. 'The Nature of Feelings: Evolutionary and Neurobiological Origins' in: *Nature Reviews Neuroscience* 14 (2): 143-152 (148).

Determining whether animals can suffer and, if so, to what extent, remains, however, a challenge. We have no access to the mental life of animals,[17] and therefore we have to infer their emotions and feelings from their behavior as the only available source of information on this subject.[18] Occasionally, this behavior seems to be so appropriate and adapted to the situation that accepting that animals have mental lives is more obvious than denying it. It might be worthwhile to recall here that one of the objections against the Cartesian beast-machine doctrine was that it made God a deceiver: Creating animals that seem to be guided by sensation and intelligence in their behavior would be misleading if in fact they lacked these qualities; that would turn nature into a puppeteer theatre (cf. Chapter 3, § 3.9.2.2, Box 3.1). Similarly, denying animals the capability to suffer may save God's goodness, but at the expense of his trustworthiness. On the other hand, however, our intuition may deceive us and ascribing experiences of suffering to animals may be a case of anthropomorphism, defined as 'the tendency to imbue the real or imagined behavior of nonhuman agents with humanlike characteristics, motivations, intentions, or emotions'.[19] Plain observation suggests that the sun circles around the earth whereas science tells us the opposite. In the same way, our intuition may entice us to attribute abilities to other organisms that they may not possess and lead us to believe that their behavior is associated with mental states similar to ours.[20] This can even go so far that we assign mental properties to man-made devices like robots.[21]

---

17 Cf. the famous paper of Nagel, T. 1974. 'What Is It Like to Be a Bat?' in: *The Philosophical Review* 83 (4): 435-450.
18 Waal, F.B.M. de. 2011. 'What Is an Animal Emotion?' in: *Annals of the New York Academy of Sciences* 1224: 191-206.
19 Epley, N., Waytz, A., Cacioppo, J.T. 2007. 'On Seeing Human: a Three-Factor Theory of Anthropomorphism' in: *Psychological Review* 114: 864-886. Anthropomorphism as a scientifically valid method for interpreting animal behavior and thus for ascribing real suffering to animals, is defended in: Gregory, N.G. 2004. *Physiology and Behaviour of Animal Suffering.* Blackwell, Oxford: 7-8, 183; Bailey, C. 2011. 'Kinds of Life: on the Phenomenological Basis of the Distinction between "Higher" and "Lower" Animals' in: *Environmental Philosophy* 8 (2): 47-68; Proctor, H. 2012. 'Animal Sentience: Where Are We and Where Are We Heading?' in: *Animals* 2: 628-639.
20 Povinelli, D.J., Vonk, J. 2003. 'Chimpanzee Minds: Suspiciously Human?' in: *Trends in Cognitive Sciences* 7 (4): 157-160; Tallis, R. 2011. *Aping Mankind. Neuromania, Darwinitis and the Misrepresentation of Humanity.* Acumen, Durham: 157-161, 238-242; LeDoux, *The Deep History of Ourselves*: 16.
21 Epley, Waytz, Cacioppo, 'On Seeing Human: a Three-Factor Theory of Anthropomorphism'; Waytz, A., Cacioppo, J., Epley, N. 2010. 'Who Sees Human? The Stability and Importance of Individual Differences in Anthropomorphism' in: *Perspectives on Psychological Sciences* (3): 219-232; Broadbent, E. 2017. 'Interactions with Robots: the Truths We Reveal about Ourselves' in: *Annual Review of Psychology* 68: 627-652.

In any case, it is clear that unadulterated Cartesianism, which states that animals cannot suffer, is not endorsed by any of the contemporary authors. Some restrict themselves to saying that we cannot rule out the possibility of animal suffering; others move beyond this and consider the capacity for suffering an indisputable fact. Similar views were already commonplace before Darwin as I have shown in Chapter 3, and this did not change after him. The issue of whether animals could suffer had already been debated in the opening decades of the eighteenth century.

7.2.2. Animal Suffering Does Not Count as Evil
If there is uncertainty about the extent to which animals can suffer, accepting such suffering but denying that it is morally significant is a second strategy that can help to save the divine attributes. In discussing the relationship between the mishaps of animal life and these attributes, it is usually taken for granted that God is subject to the same standards of good and evil as we humans are. If it is morally reprehensible for us to let animals suffer, then also for God. But if we drop this point of view, we can assume that neither for God nor for us humans should the suffering of animals be seen as *evil*. This approach was followed by most authors from the Early Church till the Period of the Reformers, as addressed in Chapter 2. Animals were created for the benefit of humanity and what this meant to themselves was not a theme for moral reflection. And when any moral reflections on the relationship between God and the non-human animal kingdom emerged with the advent of the Early Modern Period, moral indifference to animal suffering could easily be turned into accepting it as something about which we should have no judgment. In this section, we will briefly retrieve from earlier chapters how this view was expounded in the past and then examine some contemporary authors uttering a similar (or even the same) opinion.

As we have seen, an author following this latter approach was John Calvin. In discussing this Reformer (cf. § 2.3.3.2), I reported that he warned against criticizing God's actions. We see a similar reticence in the first decades of the nineteenth century. The *Bridgewater Treatise* authors Thomas Chalmers (cf. § 5.3.4) and William Prout (cf. § 5.3.8) both accepted that we do not have the right to condemn God's acts because we do not understand them. The Scottish geologist Hugh Miller, who passed away three years before the publication of the *Origin* (cf. § 5.3.12), went a step further when he wrote that 'in the Divine government the matter of fact always determines the question of right, and (…) whatever has been done by him who rendereth no account to man of his matters, he had in all ages, and in all places, an unchallengeable right to do'.[22]

The assumption that the Scottish Presbyterian showed his Calvinistic roots here will not be too far-fetched. More in general, it is remarkable—as argued by historian James Moore—that those who embraced Protestant orthodoxy had less problems with the 'bloody' aspects of Darwin's theory than more liberal believers, who were inclined to propose modifications that made Darwin's thoughts more palatable and more befitting their belief in progress. The former had since long accepted that God's acts and aims are beyond our understanding, whereas the latter could not resist the view that God's purposes are within our comprehension. Conceiving natural selection as a form of God's purposeful action fitted seamlessly into their frame of thought.[23]

Moore's hypothesis definitely contains some truth. Yet, not every Presbyterian went so far as to declare animal suffering morally irrelevant. For example, as we saw in the previous chapter, James McCosh (cf. § 6.3.2) argued 'that God proceeds by instruments, which we may find to be for the good of his creatures'.[24] This seems to imply that we humans must be able (and actually are able) to demonstrate that, from the divine perspective, animal suffering is justified since it serves a higher goal that could not be reached otherwise. Therefore, a relationship between Presbyterianism and justifying animal suffering by referring to God's inscrutability is not as straightforward as Moore assumed.

Moving to the present, the scarcity of authors appealing to divine sovereignty as a justification for animal suffering in the past is reflected in a similar paucity of contemporary authors holding this conviction. One of the few who does, is the Presbyterian natural scientist *David Snoke*, who holds that '[t]he Bible (…) is full of statements which give God the credit for creating all things, including all kinds of cruel things'.[25] Another author, the French Evangelical theologian *Henri Blocher*, points to our inveterate anthropomorphism that the Bible corrects. 'There is no trace

---

22 Miller, H. 1867 [1856]. *The Testimony of the Rocks; or, Geology in Its Bearings on the Two Theologies, Natural and Revealed…With Memorials of the Death and Character of the Author*. Gould and Lincoln, Boston: 104.
23 Moore, J.R. 1979. *The Post-Darwinian Controversies. A Study of the Protestant Struggle to Come to Terms with Darwin in Great Britain and America 1870–1900*. Cambridge University Press, Cambridge: 299-345.
24 McCosh, J. 1890. *The Religious Aspect of Evolution. Enlarged and Improved Edition*. Charles Scribner's Sons, New York: 8. Cf. § 6.3.2.
25 Snoke, D. 2004. 'Why Were Dangerous Animals Created?' in: *Perspectives on Science and Christian Faith* 56 (2): 117-125 (119).

in Scripture about this aspect [pain and suffering] of animal life.'[26] Westminster Theological Seminary professor *William Edgar* also believes that the Bible gives little cause for concern about animal suffering, pointing out that Scripture often uses predator behavior to illustrate how 'creation reflects the power of God'.[27] And finally, the philosophical theologian *Wesley Wildman*—serving at Boston University School of Theology[28]—takes a stand against what he sees as an overly anthropomorphic representation of God's goodness and benevolence, God not being 'good in a humanly recognizable way'.[29]

Whereas authors like Snoke and others invoke God's sovereignty or inscrutability to save the divine attributes, Roman Catholic philosopher *Peter Geach*[30] opts for an even more radical approach. In his view, the divine mind is totally different from the human and the animal, which implies that 'God cannot share with his creatures (…) the virtue of sympathy with physical suffering'.[31] Just as it is folly to attribute to God the human virtues of chastity, courage, or gratitude, so it is to ascribe to God sympathy with the pains of animals. 'God is not an animal as men are, and if he does not change his designs to avoid pain and suffering to animals he is not violating any natural sympathies (…). Only anthropomorphic imagination allows us to accuse God of cruelty in this regard.'[32] And any 'protest that we ought not so to love and admire him

---

26 Blocher, H. 'The Theology of the Fall and the Origins of Evil' in: Berry, R.J., Noble, T.A. (eds). 2009. *Darwin, Creation and the Fall. Theological Challenges*. Apollos, Nottingham: 149-172 (168). In this connection, Blocher refers to 1 Corinthians 9:9. 'Is it for oxen that God is concerned?' (NRSV)

27 Edgar, W. 'Adam, History, and Theodicy' in: Madueme, H., Reeves, M. (eds). 2014. *Adam, the Fall and Original Sin. Theological, Biblical, and Scientific Perspectives*. Baker Academic, Grand Rapids: 307-321 (316).

28 The Boston University School of Theology belongs to the Methodist denomination. https://en.wikipedia.org/wiki/Boston_University_School_of_Theology. Accessed on 14 December 2021.

29 Wildman, W.J. 'Incongruous Goodness, Perilous Beauty, Disconcerting Truth: Ultimate Reality and Suffering in Nature' in: Murphy, N., Russell, R.J., Stoeger, W.R. (eds). 2007. *Physics and Cosmology: Scientific Perspectives on the Problem of Natural Evil*. Vatican Observatory and Center for Theology and the Natural Sciences, Vatican City and Berkeley: 267-294 (293).

30 Kenny, A. 2015. 'Peter Thomas Geach, 1916–2013' in: *Biographical Memoirs of Fellows of the British Academy* 14: 185-203.

31 Geach, P. 1977. *Providence and Evil. The Stanton Lectures 1971–2*. Cambridge University Press, Cambridge: 77-80 (79).

32 Geach, *Providence and Evil*: 80. For a critical analysis of this view, see Wennberg, R. 1991. 'Animal Suffering and the Problem of Evil' in: *Christian Scholar's Review* 21: 120-140. 'To conclude that there are evils that we, but not God, recognize and abhor is to attribute to God an unacceptable moral ignorance' (125).

[God] if he does not share the moral perfections proper to his creatures is a mere impertinence'.[33] Furthermore, animal pains 'belong to the order of nature that is woven in warp and woof on the loom of predation and parasitism'.[34] Nor should we attach more meaning to the words of Christ about the fall of the sparrow than intended. On the contrary, 'it is false sentiment to picture God as concerned and pitiful for the sparrow when it falls'. The text only communicates that nothing happens outside of God's providence. '[N]o detail of the universe is too petty for the Divine knowledge and will.'[35]

A similar, but somewhat less provocatively phrased opinion was uttered by the former Calvin College professor *John Schneider*. Schneider argues that 'God has "rightfully," or "justly," and not immorally or amorally, decided to make and to shape the world (…) in this unexpected, undeserved, and painful way, including inexplicably great violence, disorder, suffering, and injustice'.[36] God has the right to do so because he 'is not constrained by all the ethical conditions that we rightly impose on ordinary (non-divine) persons'.[37] *Quod licet Iovi, non licet bovi.*

The arguments of the authors discussed in this section all have the same vulnerability. The idea that animal suffering does not count as evil seems to sacrifice God's love at the altar of God's power—an intolerable thought for the majority of the authors that we previously examined, and probably not an option for most contemporary Christians either. If we want to 'save' the divine attributes, pain must have either a justification or a purpose. In the next sections, I will examine how each of these two alternatives fares today.

7.2.3 *Animals Have Deserved Their Sufferings*
Something that could pass for a justification is the assumption that animals are not innocent after all. In view of the supposed evolutionary—and hence possibly also moral—continuity between humanity and the non-human animal kingdom, it has been suggested that, just like humans,

---

33 Geach, *Providence and Evil*: 79. Geach's emphasis on divine sovereignty does not imply sympathies for Calvinism. On the contrary: 'the predestinarian doctors have divinized cruelty, wrath, fury, vengeance and all the blackest vices'.
34 Geach, *Providence and Evil*: 104.
35 Geach, *Providence and Evil*: 116. Geach refers to Matthew 10:29. 'Are not two sparrows sold for a penny? Yet not one of them will fall to the ground apart from your Father.' (NRSV)
36 Schneider, J.R. 2010. 'Recent Genetic Science and Christian Theology on Human Origins: an "Aesthetic Supralapsarianism"' in: *Perspectives on Science and Christian Faith* 6 (3): 196-213 (207).
37 Schneider, *Animal Suffering and the Darwinian Problem of Evil*: 71.

animals may *sin*, and thus could rightfully be punished for their faults. In the time of the Fathers of the Church, some allusions in this direction were already made by Theophilus (cf. § 2.3.1.2), and in the eighteenth century, such an explanation for animal suffering was tentatively suggested by Richard Dean (cf. § 4.6.15)—in both cases totally detached from any evolutionary context.

Furthermore, the records of legal or ecclesiastical proceedings conducted against animals over the centuries could be considered a sign that the ability to sin was indeed occasionally attributed to animals. These procedures, however, may also be seen as a means to restore a disturbed social order or to rob an animal's indwelling evil spirit from its hiding place.[38] These alternative interpretations call into question whether people at that time really thought that animals could sin.

Nowadays, the concept that animals may deliberately violate divine rules has been revived.[39] *Christopher Southgate* may well say that he 'remain[s] to be convinced how meaningful it is to extend the concept of sin, understood as the freely chosen rejection of God and God's ways, beyond *Homo sapiens*',[40] other voices are also heard. Methodist theologian *David Clough* derives support for the view that animals can sin from their actual behavior. Clough suggests that the habit of infanticide that is widespread among the entire non-human animal kingdom—stretching from invertebrates on one side to the great apes on the other—should be considered as deliberate murder and hence sinful. In his view, internecine animal behavior shown throughout the ages is a matter of moral concern. For support, he refers to texts from the Old Testament where God prescribes how to handle animals that behave inappropriately and to the aforementioned legal and ecclesiastic procedures in the Middle Ages and the Early Modern Period.[41]

---

38 Evans, E.P. 1906. *The Criminal Prosecution and Capital Punishment of Animals*. William Heinemann, London; Cohen, E. 'Animals in Medieval Perceptions. The Image of the Ubiquitous Other' in: Manning, A., Serpell, J. (eds). 1994. *Animals and Human Society: Changing Perspectives*. Routledge, London: 59-80, in particular pp: 71-75.

39 Clough, D.L. 2012. *On Animals. Volume 1. Systematic Theology*. T&T Clark International, London, in particular Chapter 5 *Atonement*: 104-130; Moritz, J.M. 2014. 'Animal Suffering, Evolution, and the Origins of Evil: towards a "Free Creatures" Defense' in: *Zygon* 49 (2): 348-380.

40 Southgate, C. 2018. 'Response with a Select Bibliography' in: *Zygon* 53 (3): 909-930 (923-924).

41 Clough, *On Animals*: 108-119. For criticism of Clough's ideas, see Southgate, C. 2015. 'God's Creation Wild and Violent, and Our Care for Other Animals' in: *Perspectives on Science and Christian Faith* 67 (4): 245-253. In general, it is assumed that the ability to suppress impulses distinguishes humans from animals and that this ability also draws the boundary line between *Homo sapiens* and its more primitive predecessors. Not

Another theologian who propagates that animals may behave sinfully—*Joshua Moritz*—substantiates this view along different lines. The evolutionary continuity between humankind and its predecessors brings him to the conclusion 'that there is in reality no absolute or sharp dividing line between human morality and the morality of nonhuman primates'. Therefore, 'moral culpability can likewise be envisioned as existing in a variety of gradations'.[42] He finds support for this idea in the serpent speaking in the garden of Eden; for Moritz, this presupposes that there has been a fall within the animal world, predating that of Adam and hence making the animals culpable of their own transgressions.[43]

A moral continuity between humans and animals is also presupposed by the New Zealand scientist and theologian *Nicola Hoggard Creegan*.[44] 'Animals (…) are corrupted in part in the same way that humans are, with tendencies toward aggression and rivalry and certainly selfishness. The sharp theological exclusive boundary between humanity and animals has been broken.'[45] Whether in her view this makes the animals guilty—and thus can explain animal suffering as punishment—is not entirely clear. On the one hand, we are told 'that humans have crossed a threshold that takes us into the realm of bearing responsibility for our actions', but on the other hand she wonders why, unlike animals, humans 'who often have very little awareness of what they are doing and the consequences of their actions' are held morally culpable.[46] Possibly the solution to this

---

using this ability is sin. See Tennant, F.R. 1909. 'The Influence of Darwinism upon Theology' in: *Quarterly Review* 211: 418-440; Brink, G. van den. 2020. *Reformed Theology and Evolutionary Theory*. Wm. B. Eerdmans, Grand Rapids: 164-165, 193-195, 236-241. Other examples of animal behavior that we would despise as immoral when seen in humans are mentioned in Domning D.P., Hellwig, M.K. 2016 [2006]. *Original Selfishness. Original Sin and Evil in the Light of Evolution*. Routledge, Abingdon: e-book without page numbering, Section 8.1: 'The Selfish Behavior of Primates and Other Animals'; Hoggard Creegan, N. 2013. *Animal Suffering and the Problem of Evil*. Oxford University Press: 27-43, 138-142.

42 Moritz, 'Animal Suffering': 367, 374.
43 Moritz, J.M. 2011. 'The Search for Adam Revisited: Evolution, Biblical Literalism, and the Question of Human Uniqueness' in: *Theology and Science* 9 (4): 367-377; Moritz, 'Animal Suffering': 360-361.
44 Hoggard Creegan, *Animal Suffering and the Problem of Evil*, in particular pp. 27-43 and pp. 138-153. Hoggard Creegan draws on North American theologian André LaCocque, who finds evidence of a more general fall in the animal kingdom (predating the transgression of the first human couple) in the presence of the serpent in the Eden story: '[T]he rebellious snake is symbolically the head of a universal conspiracy'. See LaCocque, A. 2006. *The Trial of Innocence. Adam, Eve, and the Yahwist*. Cascade Books, Eugene: 141-189 (188).
45 Hoggard Creegan, *Animal Suffering and the Problem of Evil*: 26.
46 Hoggard Creegan, *Animal Suffering and the Problem of Evil*: 74-75.

ambivalence lies in the fact that Hoggard Creegan is more concerned with people who are unable to keep their inherited impulses under control than with blaming the animals:

> Recognition of this shared propensity to sinfulness and the deep roots into our animal past could make us more compassionate of others and more focused on redemption and renewal rather than punishment. After all, only humans have access to the story that makes redemption possible, which might lift us out of this quagmire of inevitability and into the possibility of forgiveness. If there is human uniqueness, it is in the sharing of the possibility of forgiveness and not in violence, sin, or death.[47]

Here, the similarity between humans and animals in showing reprehensible behavior is not used to hold the animals guilty for failing to meet moral standards but to foster understanding of our own failures.

Lastly, next to Clough, Moritz and perhaps Hoggard Creegan German theologian *Gregor Etzelmüller* should be mentioned in this connection. Etzelmüller also interprets animal behavior that we consider cruel as sinful. 'While the fact that life lives at the expense of life must be attributed to the shadow side of creation, the cruelty that may result from this can be understood as an expression of sin, which continually distorts God's good intentions with creation.'[48]

If we compare such views with those of authors writing around the time of Charles Darwin, we see a clear difference: Darwin's contemporaries would certainly have rejected these ideas. In 1849, ten years before Darwin published his *Origin*,[49] John Henry Newman wrote that 'the wild emotions of wrath, hatred, desire, greediness, cruelty are no sin in the brute creation, which has neither the means nor the command to repress them',[50] adding that animals, because of their '[r]age, wanton cruelty, hatred, sullenness, jealousy, revenge, cunning, malice, envy, lust, vainglory, gluttony (...) look like sinners, though they be not'.[51] In other words, animals cannot sin because they lack the necessary mental equipment.

---

47 Hoggard Creegan, *Animal Suffering and the Problem of Evil*: 42.
48 Etzelmüller, G. 2014. 'The Evolution of Sin' in: *Religion & Theology* 21 (1): 107-124 (111).
49 Darwin, C. 2009 [1859]. *On the Origin of Species by Means of Natural Selection, or the Preservation of Favoured Races in the Struggle for Life*. Reprint of the first edition, edited with an Introduction by William Bynum. Penguin Books, London.
50 Newman, J.H. 1862 [1849]. *Discourses Addressed to Mixed Congregations. Third Edition*. James Duffy, Dublin: 173.
51 Newman, *Discourses*: 317-318.

This view remained dominant in the next decades. To St. George Mivart it was beyond doubt 'that there is no trace in brutes of any actions simulating morality which are not explicable by the fear of punishment, by the hope of pleasure, or by personal affection'.[52] Similar objections were raised by Frederick Temple:

> Evolution may lead the creature to say what is hateful and what is loveable, what is painful and what is delightful, what is to be feared and what is to be sought; it may develop the sentiment which comes nearest of all to the sentiment of reverence, namely, the sentiment of shame; but it cannot reveal the eternal character of the distinction between right and wrong.[53]

In their behavior, animals are guided by the principles of pleasure and pain and not by a transcendent moral law. This line of thought is traceable till the first decades of the following century. In 1908, the aforementioned theologian Frederick Robert Tennant (cf. § 6.4) wrote that it may be 'overwhelmingly probable that there is continuity between the physical constitution of man and that of the lower animals,' but added that the '[c]ontinuity of mental development is an infinitely more difficult question to dogmatize upon in the present state of our knowledge of animal psychology'.[54] This uncertainty, however, did not withhold him from the firm statement that '[h]ad evolution stopped short at the stage of lower animal life and not proceeded until human experience appeared, there would have been, indeed, no sin'.[55] Similar thoughts were expressed by the aforementioned authors Simpson, Griffith-Jones, and Williams (cf. § 6.3.2) who also defined sin as a willful transgression of an externally imposed rule, a capacity that in their view the animals lack. 'Sin emerges only with the will, and consciousness of alternative action.'[56] For acquiring the ability to sin, mere consciousness has to evolve into self-consciousness. Only '[a]t this stage sin becomes possible'.[57] It is not even certain that our

---

52 Mivart, St. G. 1871. *On the Genesis of Species.* MacMillan and Co., London: 196.
53 Temple, F. 1885. *The Relations between Religion and Science. Eight Lectures Preached before the University of Oxford in the Year 1884. On the Foundation of the Late Rev. John Bampton...*Macmillan and Co., London: 179.
54 Tennant, F.R. 1908. *The Origin and Propagation of Sin. Being the Hulsean Lectures Delivered before the University of Cambridge in 1901–2.* University Press, Cambridge: 86.
55 Tennant, *The Origin and Propagation of Sin*: 139.
56 Simpson, J.Y. 1912. *The Spiritual Interpretation of Nature. Second Edition.* Hodder and Stoughton, London: 342.
57 Griffith-Jones, E. 1925. *Providence—Divine and Human. A Study of the World-Order in the Light of Modern Thought. Volume I. Some Problems of Divine Providence.* Hodder and Stoughton, London: 284.

distant ancestors who looked like us had the capacity to sin. On the contrary: '[T]he birth of a moral law, consciously recognized as such, must have taken place many thousands of years after the emergence of man as a distinct zoological species.'[58] Identical skulls do not necessarily house identical minds.[59]

It is evident that none of these theologians, working and living contemporaneously with Darwin or in the decades after him, would have endorsed the view that animals could sin; all restricted the ability to sin exclusively to humans, because only they possess the mental capabilities necessary to consciously turn their backs on God. This view is joined by present-day theologians *Celia Deane-Drummond, Christopher Southgate* and *Daryl Domning*. All three emphasize that it is the possibility to transgress a transcendently imposed rule that qualifies behavior as sinful.

Sin implies 'a deliberate turning way from God',[60] Deane-Drummond wrote in 2008, and she repeated this view in 2017 when stating that she 'prefer[s] not to use the term "sin" for other animals [other than humans], as this speaks of a more deliberative characteristic in relation to the divine'.[61] Crucial are mental abilities because 'sin, properly so called, amounts to a self-conscious turning away from God'.[62] Southgate concurs: 'There seems to me no demonstrable parallel to the human sense of knowing the right and yet doing the wrong, or yet of knowing (from

---

58 Williams, N.P. 1927. *The Ideas of the Fall and of Original Sin. A Historical and Critical Study. Being Eight Lectures Delivered before the University of Oxford, in the Year 1924, on the Foundation of the Rev. John Bampton, Canon of Salisbury*. Longmans et al., London: 516.

59 It is interesting to connect these notes made one hundred years ago with the current debate about what makes *Homo sapiens* human. Cf. Bergström, A. et al. 2021. 'Origins of Modern Human Ancestry' in: *Nature* 590: 229-237.

60 Deane-Drummond, C. 2008. 'Shadow Sophia in Christological Perspective: the Evolution of Sin and the Redemption of Nature' in: *Theology and Science* 6 (1): 13-32 (15).

61 Deane-Drummond, C. 'In Adam All Die? Questions at the Boundary of Niche Construction, Community Evolution, and Original Sin' in: Cavanaugh, W.T., Smith J.K.A. (eds). 2017. *Evolution and the Fall*. Wm. B. Eerdmans, Grand Rapids: 23-47 (44n67).

62 Deane-Drummond, C. 2018. 'Perceiving Natural Evil Through the Lens of Divine Glory? A Conversation with Christopher Southgate' in: *Zygon* 53 (3): 792-807 (799). The author leaves open to what extent animals have these properties. 'Of course, this raises the difficult question of how far and to what extent we can really think of animals as self-conscious beings (persons) able to make decisions, a characteristic more usually associated with *imago Dei*'. In: Deane-Drummond, 'Shadow Sophia in Christological Perspective': 15. Cf. Deane-Drummond, C. 'Are Animals Moral? Taking Soundings through Vice, Virtue, Conscience and *Imago Dei*' in: Deane-Drummond, C., Clough, D. (eds). 2009. *Creaturely Theology: on God, Humans and Other Animals*. SCM Press, London: 190-210.

revelation) what God might desire and turning along the opposite path, and these, to my mind, constitute the essence of human sin.'[63] A more extensive quote from Domning and his co-author *Monika Hellwig* summarizes the issue at stake.

> The appearance in history of creatures capable of self-conscious reflection (...) gave a moral dimension to acts that previously had lacked such a dimension. The acts themselves did not change; what was new was the actors' consciousness that they were free to choose among alternatives that would differ in their harmful or beneficial effects on others, and were even free to make their own self-interest the measure of morality – to claim for themselves, in the biblical allegory, the godlike Knowledge of (that is, sovereignty over) Good and Evil.[64]

Darwin himself would also have disagreed with the idea that animals can sin. It is true that he recognized the existence of moral behavior in some animal species, but for him, such behavior is driven by instincts that have been refined in the course of evolution. It is focused on the interests of the group over those of the individual and not a consequence of voluntary obedience to a rule imposed by God.[65] Consequently, Darwin would not label animal behavior that we disapprove as sinful. After all, evolution has made the female hive bees to kill their brothers and the mothers to kill their fertile daughters, a behavior that could not have evolved if it had not served the well-being of the beehive in the long term.[66] From Darwin's point of view, it is far-fetched to consider the infanticide among chimpanzees that so disturbs some contemporary authors (like David Clough) as sinful, since it is a means to improve the reproductive fitness of the group.[67] Mandeville's comment—made a century and a half ago—that private vices serve public benefits apparently got a new application with Darwin.[68]

---

63 Southgate, 'God's Creation Wild and Violent, and Our Care for Other Animals': 248.
64 Domning & Hellwig, 'The Moral Divide' in: *Original Selfishness*, Section 9.1. e-book, pages not numbered.
65 Darwin, *The Descent of Man*: 119-152. Cf. Richards, R.J. 'Darwin on Mind, Morals and Emotions' in: Hodge, J., Radick, G. (eds). 2009. *The Cambridge Companion to Darwin. Second Edition.* Cambridge University Press, Cambridge: 96-119.
66 Darwin, *The Descent*: 129.
67 See for this view Rohr, C.R. von, Burkart, J.M., Schaik, C.P. van. 2011. 'Evolutionary Precursors of Social Norms in Chimpanzees: a New Approach' in: *Biology and Philosophy* 26 (1): 1-30.
68 Cf. Chapter 4, § 4.6.3.

Not only these theologians have their doubts about animals obeying moral rules; present-day *scientists* like *Thomas Suddendorf* and the aforementioned Joseph LeDoux are not convinced either. They deny that animals have moral senses with the qualities needed to play a role in guiding their behaviors.[69] *Raymond Tallis* even rejects outright the idea that morality could apply to animals. We should not assume that the feelings that determine our behavior are the same in animals.[70] 'Morality is a human construct and is therefore not amenable to explanation in biological terms.'[71] Animal behavior may be interpreted in terms of virtuous or vicious when we set standards as they pertain to people, but it does not follow that such conduct is the outcome of an informed decision based on considering and rejecting alternatives.[72] And since arguably deliberate decisions are a *conditio sine qua non* for moral culpability, it is not only early twenty-first-century theologians but also modern secular ethologists who deny animals the capacity to sin– the latter concept understood as the violation of abstract moral rules. Even the famous primatologist *Frans de Waal*—well-known for his books in which he consistently humanizes the great apes[73]—states that apes 'may not, like humans, feel any obligation to be good, or experience guilt and shame whenever they fail'[74] and confines the capacity of 'careful weighing of

---

69   Suddendorf, T. 2013. *The Gap. The Science of What Separates Us from Other Animals.* Basic Books, New York, in particular pp. 185-213; LeDoux, *The Deep History of Ourselves*: 313-334, 372-379.
70   Tallis, R. 'Biological Reasons for Being Cheerful?' in: Tallis, R. 2014. *In Defence of Wonder and Other Philosophical Reflections.* Routledge, London: 95-100.
71   Tallis, *Aping Mankind*: 317-320 (320).
72   Flack, J.C., Waal, F.B.M. de. 2000. ''Any Animal Whatever'. Darwinian Building Blocks of Morality in Monkeys and Apes' in: *Journal of Consciousness Studies* 7 (1-2): 1-29; Ayala, F.J. 2010. 'The Difference of Being Human: Morality' in: *Proceedings of the National Academy of Sciences* 107 (Suppl. 2): 9015-9022; Clement, G. 2013. 'Animals and Moral Agency: the Recent Debate and Its Implications' in: *Journal of Animal Ethics* 3 (1): 1-14; Joyce, R. 2014. 'The Origins of Moral Judgment' in: *Behaviour* 151 (2-3): 261-278; Musschenga, A.W. 2015. 'Moral Animals and Moral Responsibility' in: *Les Ateliers de l'Éthique / The Ethics Forum* 10 (2): 38-59; Fitzpatrick, S. 2017. 'Animal Morality: What Is the Debate About?' in: *Philosophy and Biology* 32 (6): 1151-1183; Tomasello, M. 2018. 'How We Learned to Put Our Fate in one Another's Hand. The Origins of Morality' in: *Scientific American* September: 70-75.
73   Waal, F.B.M. de. 2013. *The Bonobo and the Atheist. In Search of Humanism among the Primates*. W.W. Norton & Company, New York; Waal, F.B.M. de. 2019. *Mama's Last Hug. Animal Emotions and What They Tell Us about Ourselves*. W.W. Norton & Company, New York.
74   Waal, F.B.M. de. 2014. 'Natural Normativity: the 'Is' and 'Ought' of Animal Behavior' in: *Behaviour* 151 (2-3): 185-204 (200).

what one did against what one could or should have done' to humans.[75] The community strengthening benefits that result from obeying the commandments of a 'transcendent policeman' are only available to beings that have sufficient mental capacities to invent and obey such an 'unobserved observer'. Animals, Philip Kitcher adds, typically don't display such capacities.[76] And even if we accept that animals could sin, they anyhow lack the ability to shed tears of repentance for their wickedness.[77]

It seems that theologians go beyond the boundaries set by science when they extend the capacity to sin so as to include animals, as this presupposes a continuity in mental properties between humans and animals that is not supported by animal psychology. 'An animal cannot be judged or held responsible for following its strongest impulses.'[78] And even if some animals were to possess the mental apparatus necessary to consciously choose between good and evil—and thus could be justly punished for committing sins—the assumption that animals can sin falls short as an explanation for animal suffering in general because it leaves unexplained the suffering of those animals that lack this ability.

7.2.4. Adam Is to Blame

An explanation for animal death and predation that is especially prevalent in Evangelical and orthodox Protestant circles is the thought that these phenomena are due to Adam's fall into sin, which allegedly caused a cosmic catastrophe: the so-called Cosmic Fall. The divine curse evoked by this sin turned a kingdom of peace into a hell of violence and terror. So

---

75 Waal, F. de. 'The Tower of Morality' in: Macedo, S., Ober, J. (eds). 2006. *Primates and Philosophers. How Morality Evolved.* Princeton University Press, Princeton: 161-181 (175).
76 Kitcher, P. 2014. 'Is a Naturalized Ethics Possible?' in: *Behaviour* 151 (2-3): 245-260 (249-250). The idea that somewhere in its evolution humanity developed a sense for a transcendent authority is known as the 'Supernatural Punishment Theory'. See Bering, J.M., Johnson, D.P. 2005. '"O Lord…You Perceive My Thoughts from Afar": Recursiveness and the Evolution of Supernatural Agency' in: *Journal of Cognition and Culture* 5 (1-2): 118-142; Johnson, D.P., Bering, J.M. 2006. 'Hand of God, Mind of Man: Punishment and Cognition in the Evolution of Cooperation' in: *Evolutionary Psychology* (4): 219-233; Johnson, D. 2015. *God Is Watching You. How the Fear of God Makes Us Human.* Oxford University Press, New York.
77 Gračanin, A., Bylsma, L.M., Vingerhoets, A.J.J.M. 2018. 'Why only Humans Shed Emotional Tears. Evolutionary and Cultural Perspectives' in: *Human Nature* 29: 104-133. Cf. Southgate, C. 2011. 'Re-Reading Genesis, John, and Job: a Christian Response to Darwinism' in: *Zygon* 46 (2): 370-396 (373).
78 Korsgaard, C.M. 'Morality and the Distinctiveness of Human Action' in: Macedo & Ober, *Primates and Philosophers*: 98-119 (118).

Adam is to blame for all the sufferings that affect animals. When looking back to the authors addressed in this study, it appears that this interpretation of the Genesis text regarding the fall is of a fairly recent date. In the time of the Fathers of the Church, the way animals lived their lives—predation included—was usually taken for granted and not a subject of discussion or moral consideration anyhow.[79] Consequences of the fall were restricted to a loss of humanity's dominion over the animal kingdom; as a result of this loss, animals, at least some of them, now threatened their former masters. Only at the turn of the Early Modern Period did animal predation become connected with the transgression of the first human couple. This is particularly clear in the writings of Martin Luther and John Calvin and their followers, as I have demonstrated in Chapters 2 and 3 and as was recently confirmed by Jon Garvey.[80] Today, its supporters are mainly found among those who defend a young (and initially peaceful) earth.[81]

As we have seen, from the time of the Church Fathers until now, authors have considered this explanation of animal suffering to be inadequate and to lack support from Scripture.[82] Unless one accepts the idea that animals themselves might sin—a possibility addressed in the previous subsection—it would be against the justice of God to punish animals for the fault of other beings. Furthermore, it became—in view of the increasing knowledge of animal anatomy as related to dietary habits—difficult to understand how animals could have turned from herbivores into carnivores without losing their identity. And more recently, geology offered evidence for widespread animal death predating humanity. This

---

[79] As discussed in Chapter 2, only Irenaeus and Theophilus believed that predation was a consequence of the fall; none of the other Late Antique theologians joined them. For more details on this, see Chapter 2, § 2.3.1.1, § 2.3.1.2, and § 2.3.1.13.

[80] Garvey, *God's Good Earth*: 91-95.

[81] Smith Jr, H.B. 2007. 'Cosmic and Universal Death from Adam's Fall: an Exegesis of Romans 8:19–23a' in: *Journal of Creation* 21 (1): 75-85; Stambaugh, J. 'Whence Cometh Death? A Biblical Theology of Physical Death and Natural Evil' in: Mortenson & Ury, *Coming to Grips with Genesis*: 373-397; Anderson, D. 'Creation, Redemption, and Eschatology' in: Nevin, C.N. (ed.). 2009. *Should Christians Embrace Evolution? Biblical and Scientific Responses*. Inter-Varsity Press, Nottingham: 73-92.

[82] For contemporary discussion, see Hick, *Evil and the God of Love*: 281-287; Bimson, J.J. 2006. 'Reconsidering a 'Cosmic Fall'' in: *Science & Christian Belief* 18 (1): 63-81; Southgate, *Groaning of Creation*: 28-35; Osborn, R.E. 2014. *Death before the Fall. Biblical Literalism and the Problem of Animal Suffering*. InterVarsity Press, Downers Grove: 96-112; Southgate, *Theology in a Suffering World*: 112-114; Garvey, *God's Good Earth*: 22-68, 91-115; Sollereder, *God, Evolution, and Animal Suffering*: 13-43; Van den Brink, *Reformed Theology and Evolutionary Theory*: 110-119. For a contemporary analysis of the story of the fall as written in Genesis 3, see Harris, M. 2013. *The Nature of Creation. Examining the Bible and Science*. Routledge, Abingdon: 131-146.

evidence ruled out any responsibility of Adam for this dark side of nature, unless one accepts a retroactive influence of the fall. As we have seen, this was proposed in the seventeenth century by Andrew Willet (cf. § 3.8.3) and Samuel Gott (cf. § 3.8.15) and in the nineteenth by the pre-Darwinian North American geologists Edward Hitchcock and Jay Dana (cf. § 5.3.16), and Darwin's contemporary Horace Bushnell (cf. § 6.4).[83]

Among present-day authors, it is particularly *William Dembski* who assumes something similar: '(…) an omnipotent God unbound by time can make natural evil predate the Fall and yet make the Fall the reason for natural evil.'[84] In this way, it is possible to maintain the relationship between natural evils like 'death, predation, parasitism, disease, drought, floods, famines, earthquakes, and hurricanes,'[85] and human sin. That connection must not be lost as it is clear to Dembski that 'in the Fall humans rebelled against God and thereby invited evil into the world.'[86] Neglect of this connection leads mankind not to fully realize what it has done with this rebellion, while its recognition makes the redemption brought about by God in Christ all the more precious.[87] Against the obvious objection that it is not just to make animals suffer for the sin of man, Dembski responds by pointing out the special position humanity occupies in creation. 'If God's relation with the covenant head goes awry, so does his relation with all that the covenant head represents.'[88]

Efforts such as the above to maintain the link between human sin and animal suffering do not alter that blaming Adam for animal suffering is not, and never has been, a very common response to the problem of animal suffering, given the theological and scientific problems that beset

---

83 Cf. Van den Brink, *Reformed Theology and Evolutionary Theory*: 118n59 for discussion of continental theologians who endorsed this view. David Clough also addresses trans-temporal effects of events in sacred history, not however pointing to the fall but to Christ's death and resurrection as a source of reconciliation for anything created throughout all times: see Clough, *On Animals*: 125-126.
84 Dembski, W. 2009. *The End of Christianity. Finding a Good God in an Evil World*. B&H Publishing Group, Nashville: 48-54,124-126, 142-155 (50). Dembki's concept is analyzed in Ventureyra, S. 2015. 'Dembski's Theodicy in Dialogue with Domning and Hellwig's Original Selfishness: a Potentially Fruitful Approach to Understanding the Intersection of Evolution, Sin, Evil and the Fall' in: *The American Journal of Biblical Theology* 16 (39): 1-22 and criticized in Lloyd, M. 'Theodicy, Fall, and Adam' in: Rosenberg, S.P. (ed.). 2018. *Finding Ourselves After Darwin. Conversations on the Image of God, Original Sin, and the Problem of Evil*. Baker Academic, Grand Rapids: 244-261.
85 Dembski, *The End of Christianity*: 145.
86 Dembski, *The End of Christianity*: 145.
87 Dembski, *The End of Christianity*: 43-46.
88 Dembski, *The End of Christianity*: 147.

this view. And although the developments in the nineteenth century—fledgling geology pointing to an old earth with prelapsarian animal death—may have contributed to a rejection of the doctrine of the 'cosmic Fall', these events were not the initiators. There had been doubts about its robustness as an explanation for animal suffering ever since it was first considered as a real option during the advent of the Early Modern Period, as I have shown in Chapters 2 and 3.

7.2.5. Evil Spirits Are to Blame

The considerations outlined in the previous subsection do not imply that the idea of *evil spirits* as a cause of animal suffering had to be rejected as well. On the contrary, animal suffering could indeed—without assuming any involvement of Adam as actor or mediator—be linked to evil spirits. As we have seen in Chapter 4, this was especially the case in the eighteenth century. Animal suffering was interpreted as divine punishment for imprisoned evil spirits, either of fallen angels or of deceased sinners; in this view, the animal body was only a physical shell, equipped with just enough abilities as was needed to preserve life and to enable a perception of punishment for the incarcerated evil spirit. In this way, divine justice was vindicated as it was not the animal but the indwelling evil spirit that suffered.

Nineteenth and early-twentieth-century authors turned the tables by changing the evil spirits from victims into actors. They assumed that these spirits—as angels that, led by Lucifer or the devil himself, had become rebellious and had therefore been expelled from heaven—had spoiled God's good creation already before Adam had entered the scene. Thus they solved not only the problem of contemporary animal suffering but also pre-human animal suffering while safeguarding the divine justice, albeit in another way.[89] It was not God who was responsible for animals' suffering as we see around us today or the existence of the pre-Adamite murderous monsters that had been discovered in the fossils but the devil and his henchmen.

---

89 Gillespie, W.H. 1873. *The Origin of Evil. A Celestial Drama.* n.p., n.p: 122; Pember, G.H. 1889. *Earth's Earliest Ages; and Their Connection with Modern Spiritualism and Theosophy. Fifth Edition.* Hodder and Stoughton, London: 33-37, 73-77; Webb, C.C.J. 1911. *Problems in the Relations of God and Man.* James Nisbet & Co., London: 268-272; Williams, N.P. 1927. *The Ideas of the Fall and of Original Sin*: 522-530; Gunning Jr, J.H. 1929. *Blikken in de Openbaring.* J.M. Bredée, Rotterdam. Vol. 1: 323-344; cf. Flipse, A. 2014. *Christelijke Wetenschap. Nederlandse Rooms-Katholieken en Gereformeerden over de Natuurwetenschap, 1880-1940.* PhD Thesis, Vrije Universiteit Amsterdam: 94, 154.

Not everyone embraced the activity of evil spirits as an adequate explanation for pre-Adamite death, since the metaphysical dualism involved was experienced as sub-Christian. When discussing the influence of the theory of evolution on the theologians' thoughts on the origin of evil, the aforementioned Bishop Barnes (cf. § 6.3.2) made a harsh judgment. 'The theory [that some outburst of insurgent evil before the world was made is responsible for natural evil] is only worth mentioning as illustrating the way in which educated men, when in difficulty, will turn anew to myths that seemed long dead. Of course such play of fancy is useless in serious theological reconstruction.'[90]

These scathing notes notwithstanding, there are present-day theologians who still follow the line of thought so despised by Barnes. C.S. Lewis, *Robert Wennberg, Gary Emberger, Michael Lloyd, Stephen H. Webb* and *Nathan O'Holloran* all assume a role of fallen angels in connection with animal suffering.[91] 'As Wennberg (to quote just one of them) says: '(…) the supposition of an angelic rebellion enables us to preserve the principle that God never directly wills or creates evil; he uses evil that others have created, brings good out of evil but does not himself call into existence the evil he employs for his own good ends.'[92]

Other theologians agree that there is an evil counterforce but do not attribute it to the activity of fallen angels. Hoggard Creegan postulates a mysterious adversary who sows tares among the wheat but leaves the nature of that adversary unspecified: 'It [the parable of the wheat and the tares] doesn't tell us who or what is evil; the ontology of evil I believe will always be inscrutable.'[93] This concept of a mysterious adversary is made a

---

90   Barnes, E.W. 1933. *Scientific Theory and Religion. The World Described by Science and Its Spiritual Interpretation. The Gifford Lectures at Aberdeen 1927–1929.* University Press, Cambridge: 521.

91   Lewis, *The Problem of Pain*: 107-108; Wennberg, R. 1991. 'Animal Suffering and the Problem of Evil' in: *Christian Scholar's Review* 21:120-140; Emberger, G. 1994. 'Theological and Scientific Explanations for the Origin and Purpose of Evil' in *Perspectives on Science and Christian Faith* 46: 150-158; Lloyd, M. 'Are Animals Fallen?' in: Linzey, A., Yamamoto, D. (eds). 1998. *Animals on the Agenda. Questions about Animals for Theology and Ethics.* University of Illinois Press, Urbana: 147-160; Webb, S.H. 2010. *The Dome of Eden. A New Solution to the Problem of Creation and Evolution.* Cascade Books, Oregon: 139-180; O'Halloran, N.W. 2015. 'Cosmic Alienation and the Origin of Evil: Rejecting the "Only Way" Option' in *Theology and Science* 13 (1): 43-63; Lloyd, 'The Fallenness of Nature. Three Nonhuman Suspects' in: Rosenberg, *Finding Ourselves After Darwin*: 262-279. For a survey of this position, see Murray, *Nature Red in Tooth and Claw*: 73-106; Sollereder, *God, Evolution, and Animal Suffering*: 67-70.

92   Wennberg, 'Animal Suffering and the Problem of Evil': 134.

93   Hoggard Creegan, *Animal Suffering and the Problem of Evil*: 82-96 (93), 127-137. Cf. Hoggard Creegan, N. 2018. 'Theodicy: a Response to Christopher Southgate' in: *Zygon* 53 (3): 808-820. For the parable of the tares among the wheat, see Matthew 13:24-30.

little more concrete by Celia Deane-Drummond; taking her cue from Eastern Orthodox notions, she assumes the influence of 'shadow Sophia', an evil power that has its origins in God but has separated itself from Him and thus has become perverted.[94] Finally, *Neil Messer* should be mentioned here—also a theologian who postulates the existence of a mysterious counterforce that thwarts God's purpose in creation.[95]

I conclude that throughout history a role has been assigned to evil spirits of various sorts as instrumental to the massive occurrence of animal suffering and predation. In the past these spirits were supposed to suffer, incarcerated as they were in animal bodies, whereas in the present they usually represent a more anonymous and impersonal counterforce. It is tempting to speculate about the cause of this change in opinion. Possibly, the latter fits better in a scriptural framework, the former requiring the transmigration of souls which sits uneasily with the Christian faith.[96] Yet the natural question to be asked in this connection, namely, why God (assuming that God is almighty) would allow an evil counterforce to spoil his creation, remains unanswered. Perhaps as a result of this, this form of animal theodicy never gained much traction.

7.2.6. Biology Is a 'Package Deal'

In general, it is taken for granted that life thrives on death. Maintenance of animal life requires the constant availability of resources that can only be supplied by other living beings. Life as we know it aims at conservation and propagation which by definition implies things like feeding to sustain life, fighting in a competition for food or mates, fleeing to avoid life-threatening danger, and sexual behavior to propagate. These are the basic and most primal drives that all animals, including humans, share and on

---

94 Deane-Drummond, 'Shadow Sophia in Christological Perspective': 20-24; Deane-Drummond, 'Perceiving Natural Evil through the Lens of Divine Glory?': 802-804. I detect an analogy here with Norman Powell Williams's thoughts on a corrupted *World Soul*. Cf. § 6.3.2.

95 Messer, N. 2018. 'Evolution and Theodicy: How (Not) to Do Science and Theology' in: *Zygon* 53 (3): 821-835.

96 The idea that animals could serve as a bodily host for demons has recently been revived by Michael Gilmour with reference to Matthew 8:28-32 and the other synoptic Gospels. This author, however, regards the indwelling of demons in animals as something that actually *benefits* these demons. Living in a body postpones their exile to the abyss and thus implies a delay of punishment and not the punishment itself, as in the traditional interpretation. The pigs sacrifice their lives by throwing themselves into the sea, and so they liberate the world from a legion of demons that now, deprived of their temporary embodiment, perishes. This interpretation is original but obviously cannot serve as a justification for animal suffering. See Gilmour, M.J. 2014. *Eden's Other Residents. The Bible and Animals*. Cascade Books, Eugene: 83-87.

which all life depends.[97] Plain observation of nature makes this clear and the analysis done in this study reveals that this conviction has served from of old to reconcile animal death, and even predation, with a benevolent Creator. The Church Fathers and the medieval scholastics as well as the majority of the theologians of the Modern Period endorsed this view, as has been amply demonstrated above. Throughout the past, it was widely held that God had ordered death to maintain the fertility of the earth and to keep each species of animal within its allotted boundaries.

Nowadays, different words might be used to convey the same message, but the view that there is no life without death has not lost its persuasiveness,[98] nor has the idea that there can be no life without the ability to feel pain.[99] This was already noted by Augustine who wrote that pain is indispensable for maintaining the unity of the organism.[100] The benefit of being alive compensates for the disadvantages that arise from the ability to feel pain. In philosophical terms, one might say that the outcome of the good-harm analysis is at least neutral.[101] There is no reason to blame the Creator for giving the animals the capacity to suffer pain.

Today, this notion of pain as necessary for the maintenance of life has even found wider application. It has become more obvious that obtaining

---

97 Pribram, K.H. 1960. 'A Review of Theory in Physiological Psychology' in: *Annual Review of Psychology* 60 (1): 1-40.
98 Alexander, D.R. 2014. *Creation or Evolution. Do We Have to Choose. Second Edition Revised and Updated.* Monarch Books, Oxford: 369; Garvey, *God's Good Earth*: 147-167; Hick, *Evil and the God of Love*: 333-338, 345-353; Southgate, *Groaning of Creation*: 47-48; Southgate, C. 2018. *Theology in a Suffering World. Glory and Longing.* Cambridge University Press, Cambridge: 138, 146.
99 Domning D.P., Wimmer J.F. 2008. *Evolution and Original Sin. Accounting for Evil in the World.* Washington Theological Consortium, Washington: 12-13 (12); Garvey, *God's Good Earth*: 147-167; Murray, *Nature Red in Tooth and Claw*: 112-121. Another source often referred to to emphasize the impossibility of life without pain is Brand, P., Yancey, P. 1993. *The Gift of Pain. Why We Hurt & What We Can Do about It.* Zondervan, Grand Rapids. However, this is a less good source for two reasons. First, Brand only speaks about pain in humans, 'pain being a privilege of the human species' (13), and second, he describes the possibility that harmful stimuli can lead to protective reactions of the body without penetrating into consciousness (173-176). So Brand could be read as endorsing a neo-Cartesian stance as well.
100 Augustine, 'The Literal Meaning of Genesis' in: Rotelle, J.E. (ed.). 2017. *The Works of Saint Augustine. A Translation for the 21st Century. On Genesis I/13...4th printing.* New City Press, New York: 246-247 (III.16.25).
101 Sollereder, *God, Evolution, and Animal Suffering*: 51-52; Southgate, *Groaning of Creation*: 48; Southgate, C., Robinson, A. 'Varieties of Theodicy: an Exploration of Responses to the Problem of Evil Based on a Typology of Good-Harm Analysis' in: Murphy, Russell, Stoeger, *Physics and Cosmology: Scientific Perspectives on the Problem of Natural Evil*: 67-90.

the sustenance necessary for survival, or finding a mate for procreation, may force an animal to inflict pain to chase away or outlive a competitor. This line of thought is further elaborated by present-day authors Domning and Wimmer. In their view, the 'package deal' encompasses both the ability to feel pain as well as the ability to *inflict* pain. '[P]ain and death (…) play essential, *constructive* roles in the evolution of life.'[102]

In the pre-Darwinian past such arguments appeared sufficient to protect God from blame[103] and even at the turn of the twentieth century Frederick Tennant thought so, as shown in the previous chapter (cf. § 6.4). Nowadays, however, a neutral (or positive) outcome of the good-harm analysis is no longer taken for granted.[104] The package deal approach has no answer to the question whether an almighty Creator could not have achieved his goals without subjecting his creatures to suffering and death or forcing them to inflict this on others. Obviously, the answer could be 'no' since divine omnipotence (on most construals) does not include the possibility to perform what is logically or physically impossible. But the absence of pain could have been a possibility in view of scientific data that indicate that the protection of the body by the activity of nociceptors[105] does not necessarily require conscious awareness of pain.[106] Moreover, supposing that the ability to feel pain provides no other benefit than simply staying alive is no longer seen as convincing when one wants to justify divine wisdom and benevolence—it suggests that God lacked power to do more to compensate animals for their often miserable fate.

The package deal argument is perceived as problematic by many because it seems to imply that in creating God is bound to the constraints

---

102 Domning & Wimmer, *Evolution and Original Sin*: 53. Cf. Ventureyra, 'Dembski's Theodicy in Dialogue with Domning and Hellwig's Original Selfishness.'
103 Rowell, G.A. 1847. 'On the Beneficent Distribution of the Sense of Pain' in: *The Edinburgh New Philosophical Journal, Exhibiting a View of the Progressive Discoveries and Improvements in the Sciences and the Arts* 43: 385-395. '[T]he sense of pain is for the preservation of animals, by compelling them to take due care of themselves' (392).
104 Rowe, W.L. 1979. 'The Problem of Evil and some Varieties of Atheism' in: *American Philosophical Quarterly* 16 (4): 335-341; in this paper, Rowe introduces the famous example of a fawn whose terrible death by burning does not serve any greater good—not even a lesson for humans since the fawn slowly dies unbeknownst to anyone. Smith, Q. 1991. 'An Atheological Argument from Evil Natural Laws' in: *International Journal for Philosophy of Religion* 29 (3): 159-174.
105 Dubin, A.E., Patapoutian, A. 2010. 'Nociceptors: the Sensors of the Pain Pathway' in: *The Journal of Clinical Investigation* 120 (11): 3760-3772.
106 Brand & Yancey, *The Gift of Pain*: 173-176, 201-218.

of matter—an old Gnostic heresy.[107] So it is not surprising that over the centuries there have also been theologians—both before and after Darwin—who were convinced that the suffering of animals should bring them more benefits than merely a 'dodging of death'.[108] I will explore this option in the next section.

7.2.7. Animal Suffering Is a Necessary Condition for Securing Greater Goods

In the package deal theory, animal pain is required to maintain life. But it is also conceivable that it serves the achievement of a greater profit. After all, those who cannot suffer cannot have pleasant experiences either, and the ability to have pleasant feelings is inextricably linked up with the sensitivity to pain. This was already noted by those seventeenth-century authors who rejected the Cartesian beast-machine doctrine, arguing that although this doctrine 'saved' animals from having pain, it also deprived them of any possibility to have pleasure. Nowadays, modern research has even provided a neurobiological foundation for the intertwining of the abilities to experience pain and pleasure, showing that the brain employs the same neuronal pathways and neurotransmitters for both.[109] The ability to feel pain is not only required to sustain life, but also opens the door to positive experiences that would be out of reach without this capacity. This means that life, even if it is accompanied by pain, is better than no life at all—a thought already expressed in the eighteenth century by William King (cf. § 4.6.4) and which finds a contemporary retrieval in the work of Ruth Page.[110] Moreover, it has been argued that pain and pleasure are strong motivators for guiding intentional behavior, since living beings seek pleasure and intend to avoid pain. Without these incentives, the animal would feel no need or reason to do anything and in that way be condemned to a dim existence, being nothing more than a plaything of fate. By contrast, an animal life focused on the realization of ambitions

---

107 This point has been amply discussed by Southgate who, on the one hand, endorses the view that God is bound in creation by what is logically possible but, on the other hand, seeks compensation for the resulting inevitable suffering in the belief that God co-suffers with all his creatures and that a better future awaits them. See Southgate, *Groaning of Creation*: passim; Southgate, 'Re-Reading Genesis, John, and Job'; Southgate, 'God's Creation Wild and Violent, and Our Care for Other Animals': 245-253; Southgate, 'Response with a Select Bibliography': 912-916.
108 Farrer, A. 1962. *Love Almighty and Ills Unlimited*. Wm. Collins Sons & Co., London: 81.
109 Leknes, S., Tracey, I. 2008. 'A Common Neurobiology for Pain and Pleasure' in: *Nature Reviews Neuroscience* 9 (4): 314–320.
110 Page, R. 1996. *God and the Web of Creation*. SCM Press Ltd, London: 91-105. For a critical analysis of this author, see Southgate, C. '"Free-Process" and the "Only Way" Arguments' in: Rosenberg, *Finding Ourselves After Darwin*: 293-305, in particular pp. 297-299.

may be considered as of more value, since it may safely be assumed that whereas an animal life without intentional acts carries less risks, it also provides less satisfaction.[111] This line of reasoning was occasionally followed in the past as I have demonstrated in the previous chapters with authors like Henry More (cf. § 3.8.11) and Mark Roget (cf. § 5.3.7). Pain may indeed be a condition for securing greater goods. It does not only serve to preserve life as discussed in the previous section but, because of its connectedness with pleasure, serves also to encourage the animal to strive for an active life with worthwhile experiences.

The greater good principle could also be applied to a wider circle; the suffering of one animal may serve the well-being of another, or of its group, or its species, or even the entire biosphere—as advocated by Plotinus and a row of successors (cf. the previous chapters, in particular 4 and 5). In the time period studied in this chapter, *Austin Farrer* focuses in this regard on the interests of the individual, emphasizing that '[t]heir [the animals'] bent is towards the fulfilment of the pattern in which each finds its being' and that 'in the pursuit of their own success, they trample their neighbours'.[112] *Holmes Rolston III* applies the greater good principle in an overall way: 'The living materials flow through food chains, destroyed to be recreated', which implies that '[s]omething is always dying, and something is always living on. For all the struggle, violence, and transition, there is [however] abiding, escalating value.'[113] Erasmus Darwin could have written the same.

More particularly, *John Hick*, *Richard Swinburne*, and *Michael Corey* advocate that animal suffering is necessary because (1) the animals have 'to fulfil a role in relation to the continuing divine creation of man',[114] (2) animal suffering serves to 'provide us (…) with much knowledge',[115] and (3) it contributes to humanity's growth to perfection as animals' sufferings provide 'a potent physical referent for those psychospiritual evils that are capable of parasitizing our innermost souls if they are allowed to do so'.[116]

---

111 Swinburne, *Providence and the Problem of Evil*: 171-173; Murray, *Nature Red in Tooth and Claw*: 108-112; Miller, K.B. 2011. ''And God Saw that It Was Good': Death and Pain in the Created Order' in: *Perspectives on Science and Christian Faith* 63 (2): 85-94.
112 Farrer, *Love Almighty and Ills Unlimited*: 77-105 (82).
113 Rolston III, H. 2018. 'Redeeming a Cruciform Nature' in: *Zygon* 53 (3): 739-751 (745).
114 Hick, *Evil and the God of Love*: 345-353 (353).
115 Swinburne, *Providence and the Problem of Evil*: 189-192, 217-219 (190).
116 Corey, *Evolution and the Problem of Natural Evil*: 151-166 (158). Corey says here in a complex way that animal suffering alerts us to the evil that resides within ourselves and, by making us aware of it, encourages us to fight against it. It is fascinating to see how Corey harks back here to the idea—prevailing in the Late Antique Period and

Denis Lamoureux joins this triumvirate by stating that 'pain, suffering, and death are part of the Creator's very good creation and function to test our souls.'[117]

Christopher Southgate contends that not only beauty but also ugliness (as manifest in for example animal suffering) bears witness to God's glory[118] and adds—herein referring to Karl Barth—that 'we need to attend to the silent music of other creatures' praise, and that that praise may be a source of instruction.'[119] The pedagogical significance of animal suffering is clear here. '[T]he creation still manifests (…) glory' but it is 'a glory full of 'groaning'.'[120] From this position, Southgate draws far-reaching consequences.

> The hyena pack that seize a newborn impala calf and tear it apart before extracting with great skill every last bit of nutrition from the bones is not in any conventional sense acting beautifully, but is acting characteristically, praising God in its action, manifesting its creatureliness in a way that is a sign of the work of its Creator. Even a more magnificent creature like an orca acts in a way most would call ugly when two orca toss a sea lion between them, apparently, just for fun, before killing it. But that too is a characteristic action, orca being themselves, and so part of creaturely praise, part of the manifestation of *Gloria mundi*.[121]

Such an interpretation of nature not only allows for an effortless acceptance of Darwin's theory but also may give the 'survival of the fittest' a deeper meaning. The assumption that evolution has humanity as its intended result had already made the animal suffering associated with evolution acceptable as I have shown above (cf. § 6.3.2), but in this way 'nature red in tooth and claw' can even be understood as serving a much loftier goal. The evolutionary process finds its fulfilment not merely in the creation of humanity as an end in itself, but in the emergence of conscious

---

the Middle Ages—that the animal world reflects the human mind and thus functions as a repository of moral lessons.

117 Lamoureux, D.O. 2020. 'Toward an Evangelical Evolutionary Theodicy' in: *Theology and Science* 18 (1): 12-30 (19). 'Our' obviously refers to the human race here.
118 Glory is not conceived here as beauty but as the a awe-inspiring character of any manifestation of divine action or presence. See Southgate, *Theology in a Suffering World*: 17-44; cf. Southgate, C. 2014. 'Divine Glory in a Darwinian World' in: *Zygon* 49 (4): 784-807.
119 Southgate, *Theology in a Suffering World*: 96-148 (133).
120 Southgate, *Theology in a Suffering World*: 107.
121 Southgate, *Theology in a Suffering World*: 132.

beings that can notice and praise God's awesomeness.[122] Whether Darwin would have agreed with this interpretation is, however, debatable to say the least, given his own objection to any teleological interpretation of his theory (cf. § 5.3.18).

The greater good connected to animal suffering can also be situated in other values – values that have to do with personal self-denial and sanctification. This could be found in the past *inter alia* in Aquinas, who wrote that 'if a man practice a pitiful affection for animals, he is all the more disposed to take pity on his fellow-men' (cf. § 2.3.2.2).[123] Since then, the idea that animals have to suffer in order to give us humans opportunities for showing compassion and thereby improving our moral sensitivity has had its adherents until the present day. For Austin Farrer '[o]ne of the functions of pain (…) is to awaken compassion',[124] and Richard Swinburne writes the same: 'all animal pain gives knowledge and opportunity for compassion.'[125] Shortly before Darwin, Thomas Chalmers had made the same comment (cf.§ 5.3.5).[126]

---

122 The idea that God's creation only comes to its destination when there are conscious observers who praise him was also propagated in the first half of the nineteenth century by the *Bridgewater Treatise* author William Kirby and contemporaries (cf. § 5.4.10). For a nuanced discussion of humanity as God's intended goal of creation, see Southgate, *Groaning of Creation*: 37, 43, 92-115. 'I propose, then, that the evolutionary struggle of creation can be read as being the "travail" to which God subjected creation in hope that the values of complex life, and ultimately freely choosing creatures such as ourselves, would emerge' (95). For the most desirable outcome of that free choice, see Southgate, 'Re-Reading Genesis, John, and Job': 373-377 and Southgate, *Theology in a Suffering World*: 227-234: '[T]he perfectly free return of the divine gift of self-giving love (…) can be seen as the most distinctive emergent in the history of humanity, and therefore constituting the ultimate fulfilment of the creative process' (230).
123 Aquinas. 'Question 102. Of the Causes of the Ceremonial Precepts. Article 6. Whether There Was Any Reasonable Cause for the Ceremonial Observances? Reply to Objection 1' in: Aquinas, T. 2020 [1920]. *The Summa Theologiae of St. Thomas Aquinas. Literally Translated by Fathers of the English Dominican Province. First Part of the Second Part*. The Collected Works of St. Thomas Aquinas. Electronic Edition. http://www.newadvent.org/summa/
124 Farrer, *Love Almighty and Ills Unlimited*: 102.
125 Swinburne, *Providence and the Problem of Evil*: 217.
126 Similar notes had been written at the turn of the nineteenth century by the German philosopher Immanuel Kant, who contended that ignoring the suffering of animals 'weakens a natural tendency which is very serviceable to morality in relation to other men'. It led to a heavy reproach from Arthur Schopenhauer: 'So one is only to have compassion on animals for the sake of practice, and they are as it were the pathological phantom on which to train one's sympathy with men!' From: Schopenhauer, A. 1903. *The Basis of Morality. Translated with Introduction and Notes by Arthur Brodrick Bullock*. Swan Sonnenschein & Co., London: 94. For the original text: Kant, I. 1800.

The ideas of the present-day theologians mentioned above indicate that Darwin's contributions did not change the feeling of some that animal suffering should make us more sensitive to suffering in general. This is surprising since one would have expected that the thought that the suffering of animals benefits humanity—physically or spiritually—would have lost persuasiveness because of Darwin's theory. After all, a common descent for humanity and the non-human animal kingdom may downgrade humans and upgrade animals, thus making the view that the suffering of the latter is to the benefit of the former less acceptable. This appears not to be the case, however, not even with Darwin himself. Although Darwin wrote extensively about the similarities between humans and animals in many respects, this did not lead him to question their subservience to the needs of humanity.[127] His thoughts about vivisection bear witness of this conviction: 'I know that physiology cannot possibly progress except by means of experiments on living animals, and I feel the deepest conviction that he who retards the progress of physiology commits a crime against mankind.'[128] Common descent does not automatically imply equal rights or equal moral value. '[T]he much vaunted claim that increased sensibility to animals was stimulated by Charles Darwin's theory of evolution does not stand up to careful scrutiny.'[129] The medieval doctrine that animals are 'only for our use'

Metaphysische Anfangsgründe der Tugendlehre. Zweite Auflage. Ludwig Christian Kehr, Kreuznach: 146 and Schopenhauer, A. 2007 [1840]. Über die Grundlagen der Moral. Mit einer Einleitung, Anmerkungen und einem Register herausgegeben von Peter Welsen. Felix Meiner Verlag, Hamburg: 60. I mention these German philosophers here because Bullock's translation of Kant's notes and Schopenhauer's criticism may have contributed to the formation of opinions on the matter among British authors. That someone took the trouble to translate their work supports this assumption.

127 Steiner, G. 2005. *Anthropocentrism and Its Discontents. The Moral Status of Animals in the History of Western Philosophy*. University of Pittsburgh Press, Pittsburgh: 190-197. This text provides an excellent entry to Darwin's thoughts on this subject by referring to sources across many of Darwin's works.
128 Darwin, C. 1881. 'Mr. Darwin on Vivisection' in: *The British Medical Journal* 1 (23 April): 660.
129 Preece, R. 2005. *Brute Souls, Happy Beasts, and Evolution. The Historical Status of Animals*. UBC Press, Vancouver: 359. That Darwinism changed little or nothing about the moral status accorded to animals at the time is shown in several studies devoted to the relationship between vivisection and Darwinism. Cf. Preece, R. 2003. 'Darwinism, Christianity, and the Great Vivisection Debate' in: *Journal of the History of Ideas* 64 (3): 399-419; Preece, *Brute Souls, Happy Beasts, and Evolution*: 331-358; Boddice, R. 2008. *A History of Attitudes and Behaviours toward Animals in Eighteenth- and Nineteenth-Century Britain. Anthropocentrism and the Emergence of Animals*. Edwin Mellen Press, Lewiston: 317-339; Boddice, R. 2010. "The Moral Status of

might have lost strength in theory since the beginning of the Early Modern Period, but it is still very much alive in practice.[130]

Yet while the aforementioned authors had no problems with an anthropocentric application of the 'greater good approach', other voices can be heard today as well. Among these, it is in particular David Clough who addresses this point *in extenso*. First, he surveys the history of anthropocentrism as related to Christianity,[131] and thereafter, he explains the shortcomings of this doctrine by invoking relevant biblical texts other than Genesis 1:28[132]– texts which emphasize that the animals have their own particular place in the eyes of their Creator.[133] Similar critical notes can be found with Ruth Page, *John Haught*, Michael Murray and *Bethany Sollereder*, all of whom dispute the validity of a theodicy that ignores the sufferings of the individual and places the interests of humanity above those of the animals.[134] This negative attitude towards anthropocentrism may also explain why today we no longer come across the idea—put forward in the past by the pre-Darwinian author Kirby (cf. § 5.4.10) and the post-Darwinian theologians Simpson, Griffith-Jones, and Raven (cf. § 6.3.2)—that animal suffering fosters our spiritual life because it reflects the vicarious suffering of Christ.

The currently low popularity of the idea that the interests of the animals are subordinate to those of humankind may also be a reason why present-day theologians no longer assign a role to animals as God's instruments to show his wrath over an apostate humanity, with the aim to move them to repentance or to destroy stubborn enemies. As shown in Chapters 2 and 3, this view was widely held in the past. The long-standing view that the primordial fall had deprived humans of their authority over the animals also fits into this context. A now hostile non-human animal

---

Animals and the Historical Human Cachet' in: *JAC* 30 (3/4): 457-489; Boddice, R. 2011. 'Vivisecting Major. A Victorian Gentleman Scientist Defends Animal Experimentation, 1876-1885' in: *Isis* 102 (2): 215-237. In fact, Darwinism has strengthened the arguments in favor of vivisection; common descent implies common life processes, and that makes more plausible the belief that findings obtained through vivisection are relevant to understanding human physiology.

130 Rowlands, M. 'Philosophy and Animals in the Age of Empire' in: Kete, K. (ed.). 2007. *A Cultural History of Animals in the Age of the Empire*. Berg, Oxford: 135-152.
131 Clough, *On Animals*: xvi-xx, 6-15,
132 '(...) and have dominion over the fish of the sea and over the birds of the air and over every living thing that moves upon the earth.' (NRSV)
133 Clough, *On Animals*: 26-77, in particular pp. 43-44 and pp. 76-77.
134 Page, *God and the Web of Creation*: 63-80; Haught, 'The Boyle Lecture 2003: Darwin, Design and the Promise of Nature'; Murray, *Nature Red in Tooth and Claw*: 7-8, 149-157, 186-192; Sollereder, *God, Evolution, and Animal Suffering*: 48-62.

world constantly reminded people of their sins and urged them to repentance, not because of compassion with the animals but because of regret over a lost dominion. It is remarkable that of the contemporary Christian writers it is only Dembski who points to this pedagogical aspect of animal suffering. In this sense, the content of the suffering-for-the-greater-good argument has changed, but it does not seem that Darwinian evolution has anything to do with this transition.[135]

7.2.8. Animals Receive After-life Compensation

The main stumbling block with the suffering-for-the-greater-good approach is the idea that animals should suffer for the benefit of humankind (or the biosphere at large), as I have shown in the previous section. Our sense of justice requires that each individual, either animal or human, should be compensated individually for endured miseries—if not in the present, then, perhaps, in the hereafter. This observation leads us to a final option that we come across in the relevant literature, both in the past and in the present.

The idea that animals somehow will receive afterlife compensation for endured sufferings when they join humanity in a new and better world can be found already in the Early Church. For example, Irenaeus wrote that animals will somehow participate in a restored creation (cf. § 2.3.1.1).[136] Since then, this idea has met support from a lot of writers, both in times before Darwin and in Darwin's own lifetime.[137] In the present, it

---

[135] Rather, it might be related to a changed image of God in which paternal care prevails over a punishing hand. Further exploration of this transition is beyond the scope of my research; let it suffice to say that its background seem much more of a cultural than of a scientific nature.

[136] Irenaeus, and many following him, base their view that on the new earth there will also be animals on the prophetic texts that speak of a future where 'the lion shall eat straw like the ox' (Isaiah 11:7; 65:25, NRSV). The same prophet, however, also writes that 'the Lord of hosts will make for all peoples a feast (…) of rich food filled with marrow' (Isaiah 25:6, NRSV), a text that, according to Faro, could imply that on the new earth, people will eat meat. Cf. Faro, I. 2015. 'The Question of Evil and Animal Death before the Fall' in: *Trinity Journal* 36: 1-21 (13n45). Obviously, the interpretation of these prophecies is fraught with difficulties for if we take them literally, we must assume that in the future, the lions have to content themselves with eating straw while humans will still be able to feast on slaughtered animals. We usually imagine the new earth differently.

[137] For concise but nevertheless adequate historical surveys, see Morris, F.O. 1861. *Records of Animal Sagacity and Character: with a Preface on the Future Existence of the Animal Creation*. Longman et al., London: vii-xxvii; Wennberg, R.N. 2003. *God, Humans, and Animals. An Invitation to Enlarge Our Moral Universe*. Wm. B. Eerdmans, Grand Rapids: 318-321; Preece, *Brute Souls, Happy Beasts, and Evolution*: 116-165; Roedell, C.A. 2005. *The Beasts that Perish: the Problem of Evil and the Contemplation of the Animal Kingdom in English Thought, c.1660–1839*. PhD Thesis, Georgetown University, Washington, D.C.: 191-226. Cf. § 3.9.2.6 and § 4.7.2.

is put forward by *Jay McDaniel* and Michael Murray, to mention only two examples among many others (most of whom do not refer to any earlier instantiations of the view).[138] But although the idea itself appears to have a long history, its content has not always been the same, and it is therefore worthwhile to elaborate on this view.

Assigning animals a place in a new, restored creation does not automatically imply that these animals should be the very same beings as those that once inhabited the not yet renewed earth; it has also been considered conceivable that God will create *other* animals, thus replenishing his new creation with a new fauna—a thought broadly adhered to in the Early Modern Period (as addressed in Chapter 3).[139] If that were the case, however, there would be no compensation for endured suffering.

Today, the idea that the new earth will be populated by an animal world specially created for that purpose finds little support.[140] This current unpopularity is understandable, because this solution does not meet the purpose of compensating animals in the future for current sufferings; this purpose requires that each animal is personally raised to new life and also has the memories of its earlier life, for in the absence of such a memory the animal cannot interpret the blessings of the new life as a compensation for past misery.[141] The views expressed in the eighteenth century better

---

138 McDaniel, J.B. 1989. *Of God and Pelicans. A Theology of Reverence for Life*. Westminster/John Knox Press, Louisville: 41-47; Willey, P., Willey, E., 'Will Animals Be Redeemed' in: Linzey & Yamamoto, *Animals on the Agenda*: 190-200; Murray, *Nature Red in Tooth and Claw*: 122-129; Russell, R.J. 'The Groaning of Creation. Does God Suffer with All Life?' in: Bennett, G. et al. (eds). 2008. *The Evolution of Evil*. Vandenhoeck & Ruprecht, Göttingen: 120-140, in particular pp. 138-140; Southgate, *Groaning of Creation*: 78-91; Clough, *On Animals*: 131-172; Dougherty, *The Problem of Animal Pain*: 134-178; Johnson E.A. 2014. *Ask the Beasts. Darwin and the God of Love*. Bloomsbury, London: 211-235; Peters, T. 2018. 'Extinction, Natural Evil, and the Cosmic Cross' in: *Zygon* 53 (3): 691-710; Southgate, 'Response with a Select Bibliography': 912-913; Hausoul, R.R. 2019. *Gods Toekomst voor de Dieren*. KokBoekencentrum Uitgevers, Utrecht: 179-198; Sollereder, *God, Evolution, and Animal Suffering*: 75-78, 156-182. For a critical contemporary note see Badham, P. 'Do Animals Have Immortal Souls?' in: Linzey & Yamamoto, *Animals on the Agenda*: 181-189.
139 Waite, J. 1650. *Of the Creatures Liberation...*Tho. Broad, York. Cf. § 3.9.2.6 and references therein.
140 For a concise but excellent overview of the various contemporary opinions on afterlife compensation for animals, see Sollereder, *God, Evolution, and Animal Suffering*: 161-165.
141 For some authors, either some or all animals do not possess this kind of memory, which for them is a reason to deny these animals an afterlife. See Hick, *Evil and the God of Love*: 352; Lewis, *The Problem of Pain*: 109-114. Both common sense and

met this goal (as we saw in Chapter 4), since at that stage various authors started to assign an immortal soul to animals, thus ensuring their 'transtemporal psychic unity'.[142]

Nowadays, some authors prefer to speak of God 'redeeming' animals rather than 'remunerating' them because they want to emphasize God's love and to avoid the impression that God would owe something to the animals.[143] The basic idea, however, that God has something in store for the animals that would let them understand and even approve of past sufferings is widely accepted.[144] Other authors, on the other hand, are critical of this idea because of practical problems to be expected, which may seem intractable: 'A bull-frog can lay twenty-five thousand eggs in a clutch and lay more than one clutch a season. If all survive, and these descendants continue repeating the cycle, the number of frogs in bullfrog heaven is soon approaching infinity.'[145] Similar notes were already written in the past: 'Is it likely that all the flies and frogs, locusts and lice, which once infested the land of *Egypt*, will be reanimated, and have an endless

---

modern animal psychology, however, do not support this view. See Anderson, D.J., Adolphs, R. 2014. 'A Framework for Studying Emotions Across Species' in: *Cell* 157 (1): 187-200. How memory functions in animals is uncertain, but the fact that a renewed exposure to the environment in which the animal has had an unpleasant experience in the past evokes negative emotions in the present is irrefutable. Re-seeing a stick that has struck him in the past visibly upsets the dog. At the new earth, the stick may change from something associated with pain into an object of pleasure when it has—for example—become part of a game. In that case, the pleasure of fetching the stick compensates for the pain inflicted with this object earlier. The pleasure may even be greater than if the stick had merely been a neutral object in the animal's perception, unburdened by past experience. This type of memory does not, however, invalidate the argument that animals suffer less than humankind because they have no memories of past miseries or fear for the future, as this latter type of memory requires mental representation without an evoking external clue—in this example the stick. Whether animals possess this latter type of memory remains a matter of dispute. See LeDoux, *The Deep History of Ourselves*: 324-328.

142 Term coined by Adams, M. McCord. 1999. *Horrendous Evils and the Goodness of God*. Cornell University Press, Ithaca: 28.
143 Clough, *On Animals*: 144-148. For an overview of what redemption entails, see Edwards, D. 'The Redemption of Animals in an Incarnational Theology' in: Deane-Drummond & Clough, *Creaturely Theology*: 81-99.
144 For a critical analysis of the contemporary views on the subject, see Schneider, *Animal Suffering and the Darwinian Problem of Evil*: 219-269. His claim that the idea that animals also have a place on the new earth is of a recent date is, however, incorrect. As far back as the seventeenth century, there were already theologians who felt that way, as discussed in Chapter 3.
145 Rolston III, 'Redeeming a Cruciform Nature': 747.

existence in another state?'[146] Apparently, it is especially an expected multitude of frogs that questions the possibility of a wonderful future for the animals.

Yet the idea that suffering animals will join humankind on a new earth is rather popular nowadays, despite practical concerns. This may be due to the vagueness of the concept, so that everyone can adapt it to their own preferences, while the problems related to their privately cherished vision of the future often go unmentioned.[147] That was already the case before Darwin and that has not much changed ever since.

7.3. New Wine in Old Wineskins?

When I reflect on the outcome of my search so far, it seems that Darwin's theory of evolution has not led to major changes in the arguments put forward to justify God's dealings with the animals. Though we have definitely seen some changes in popularity of the different approaches to the theodicy problem, none of these were instigated by the work of Darwin. Moreover, almost all considerations deemed to be valid in the past are still being forwarded today (although some are not so widely shared anymore as in the past). It is surprising to see that (with a few exceptions) most contemporary writers on the subject fail to acknowledge this, while they nevertheless reason and argue in the same way.[148] Ignoring this continuity is regrettable, first, because it does not do justice to the work done in the past and, second, because it overlooks the fact that the debate about animal suffering in relation to divine attributes did not

---

146 Rothwell, J. 1769. *A Letter to the Rev. Mr. Dean, of Middleton; Occasioned by Reading His Essay on the Future Life of Brute Creatures*. n.p., n.p.: 94-95. Some nineteenth century authors solved this problem by assuming a transfer of the resurrected animals to other planets or even distant galaxies, see Hamilton, J. 1877. *Animal Futurity: a Plea for the Immortality of the Brutes*. C. Aitchison, Belfast: 98-99. For the history of the debate around the plurality of worlds and their possible inhabitants, see Yeo, R.R. 1986. 'The Principle of Plenitude and Natural Theology in Nineteenth-Century Britain' in: *The British Journal for the History of Science* 19 (3): 263-282; Fara, P. 2004. 'Heavenly Bodies: Newtonianism, Natural Theology and the Plurality of Worlds Debate in the Eighteenth Century' in: *Journal for the History of Astronomy* 35 (2): 143-160.

147 Rolston III, 'Redeeming a Cruciform Nature': 747. 'The claim seems vaguely reasonable so long as it is kept reasonably vague.'

148 References to Irenaeus and Augustine can be found in Hick, *Evil and the God of Love*: 92-93, 271-221, 262-266. Southgate briefly mentions Aquinas in 'God and Evolutionary Evil' (807, 819) and Augustine and Hume in *Groaning of Creation* (3, 10). Clough addresses the thoughts of some eighteenth-century authors about an afterlife for the animals in *On Animals* (133-153) and Garvey discusses the contributions of a wide panel of Church Fathers and also the thoughts of Luther, Calvin, and Wesley in *God's Good Earth* (71-102).

originate with the theory of evolution; in fact, it had already been a live issue for centuries. This continuity also implies that those who reject the theory of evolution today because of its incompatibility with their conception of God as a benevolent Father caring for even the lowliest of his creatures, must realize that animal suffering is a problem anyhow (*i.e.*, irrespective of evolutionary theory).

Long before Darwin, Christians were already struggling with the same question: how to reconcile a good Creator with a creation that suffered so much? Pointing to Adam's sin as an explanation was not sufficient by then either, since it questioned the divine justice—an objection that current defenders of Adam's responsibility for animal suffering usually ignore. And in the same sense, the often heard complaint that Darwin and the nineteenth-century geologists predating him are to be blamed for questioning the credibility of Scripture on this point should be rejected.[149] A *prima facie* interpretation of the first chapters of Genesis was already questioned in the first decades of the seventeenth century, as I have shown in Chapter 3. Darwin may have intensified this debate, but he did not initiate it.[150]

It is true that Darwin himself highlighted that there is a conflict between God's attributes on the one hand and animal suffering on the other; but once again, similar thoughts had been advanced earlier. Already more than a century before Darwin, Mandeville had written that nature, by itself, gave more reason to think of an evil than of a benevolent 'First Cause' (cf. § 4.6.3) and in the nineteenth-century decades predating Darwin, authors had not been reluctant to question the divine attributes for this reason either (cf. § 5.3.17). After Darwin, many years would elapse before authors like Bertrand Russell and Chapman Cohen referred to cruelty in nature as a reason to doubt the existence of God—so there is not even a sign that Darwin in fact *intensified* this debate. Therefore, to consider Darwin's troubles in reconciling animal suffering with divine design as one of the causes of modern atheism is debatable, to say the least. Darwin's gloomy image of God may only have offered a final push towards abandoning the faith to deists who already had exchanged God as depicted in Scripture for a remote cause of a mechanical universe that

---

149 See for this conviction a.o. MacArthur, J. 'Foreword' in: Mortenson & Ury, *Coming to Grips with Genesis*: 9-13; Mortenson, '"Deep Time" and the Church's Compromise: Historical Background' in: Mortenson & Ury, *Coming to Grips with Genesis*: 70-104.
150 Brooke, J.H. 2010. 'Darwin and Religion: Correcting the Caricatures' in: *Science and Education* 19 (4-5): 391-405.

obeys laws once imposed on it and that since then has been left alone.[151] They may have taken advantage of Darwin's bleak view of the image of God, so that their appeal to Darwin was rather a symptom of the emerging modern atheism than its cause.

Neither can the roots of modern *secularization* be situated in Darwin's work. Authors such as Charles Taylor and Callum Brown (and many others) have emphasized that secularization broke through in the period after World War II, when the disappearance of ecclesiastical and social structures that were perceived as oppressive led to major changes in the structure of society.[152] In such a climate, any argument to disparage God is welcome and useful. This would also explain why, as we have seen, books about the incompatibility of a good Creator and a cruel nature did not appear until the 1970s.[153]

But those who did not want to jettison their Christian faith had little trouble in accepting and Christianizing evolutionary theory; on the contrary, assuming that evolution represented a divinely guided progression to higher life forms—culminating in humankind—made it even easier to reconcile the suffering of the animals with divine benevolence, as has been shown in Chapter 6.

Nor should Darwin be seen as the first to render God as Creator superfluous by devising a purely materialistic explanation for the origin of the world that was also intellectually satisfactory. Richard Dawkins may write that 'Darwin made it possible to be an intellectually fulfilled atheist',[154] but he overlooks that such an intellectual satisfaction had already been available before Darwin. As early as in the 1780s, scholars had formulated theories in which divine design was replaced by matter-bound organizing principles.[155] Here, too, Darwin did not bring up

---

151 Cf. Buckley, M.J. 1987. *At the Origins of Modern Atheism*. Yale University Press, New Haven: 37-67, 341-363; Brooke, J.H. 1992. 'Natural Law in the Natural Sciences: the Origins of Modern Atheism?' in: *Science & Christian Belief* 4 (2): 83-103; Brooke, J., Cantor, G. 1998. *Reconstructing Nature. The Engagement of Science and Religion*. Glasgow Gifford Lectures. Oxford University Press, New York: 161-166; Jones, R.H. 2012. *For the Glory of God. The Role of Christianity in the Rise and Development of Modern Science. Volume II: The History of Christian Ideas and Control Beliefs in Science*. University Press of America, Lanham: 237-243; McGrath, A.E. 2017. *Re-Imagining Nature. The Promise of a Christian Natural Theology*. Wiley Blackwell, Chichester: 138-143.
152 Taylor, Ch. 2018 [2007]. *A Secular Age*. Harvard University Press, Cambridge (MA): 471-535; Brown, C.G. 2009. *The Death of Christian Britain. Understanding Secularisation, 1800-2000*. Routledge, London.
153 Cf. Dawkins, R. 1976. *The Selfish Gene*. Oxford University Press, New York.
154 Dawkins, *The Blind Watchmaker*: 6.
155 Gliboff, S. 2000. 'Paley's Design Argument as an Inference to the Best Explanation, or, Dawkins' Dilemma' in: *Studies in History and Philosophy of Biological and*

something that had not been the subject of discussion previously.[156] Dawkins also ignores that many of Darwin's contemporaries thought the empirical basis of his theory was meagre, its two cornerstones—the emergence of one species from another and the random nature of the variations on which natural selection acted—being unproven assumptions.[157] And for quite a lot, combining the theory of evolution with the Christian faith turned out to be at least as successful in providing intellectual satisfaction.[158]

In Chapter 6, I concluded that Darwin's theory added little to contemporary debates about animal suffering and benevolent divine design, a conclusion supported by the observation that it would take until the 1920s for authors to name Darwin's view on animal life to support their atheistic worldview.[159] It will be clear that this applies equally to the

Biomedical Sciences 31 (4): 579-597. German biologists from the university of Göttingen developed the concept of *Bildungstrieb* that became widely known in France and Britain as well. In the same way as Newton's gravitation theory offered the best explanation for the movements of the celestial bodies, the *Bildungstrieb* served to explain a lot of biological phenomena. The predictability of, for example, developmental processes in an embryo suggested an indwelling organizing principle. For more details, see Richards, R.J. 2000. 'Kant and Blumenbach on the Bildungstrieb: a Historical Misunderstanding' in: *Studies in History and Philosophy of Biological and Biomedical Sciences* 31 (1) 11-32.

156 Zirkle, C. 1941. 'Natural Selection before the "Origin of Species"' in: *Proceedings of the American Philosophical Society* 84 (1): 71-123; Lovejoy, A.O. 'The Argument for Organic Evolution before the Origin of Species 1830-1858' in: Glass, B., Temkin, O., Straus Jr, W.L. (eds). 1968. *Forerunners of Darwin: 1745-1859*. The Johns Hopkins Press, Baltimore: 356-414.

157 Ellegård, A. 1957 'The Darwinian Theory and Nineteenth-Century Philosophies of Science' in: *Journal of the History of Ideas* 18 (3): 362-393; Hull, D.L. 'Darwin's Science and Victorian Philosophy of Science' in: Hodge & Radick, *The Cambridge Companion to Darwin*: 173-196.

158 Cf. Ruse, M. 1998. 'Darwinism and Atheism: Different sides of the Same Coin?' in: *Endeavour* 22 (1): 17-20; Ruse, M. 'Belief in God in a Darwinian Age' in: Hodge & Radick, *The Cambridge Companion to Darwin*: 368-389; Lamoureux, D.O. 2012. 'Darwinian Theological Insights: toward an Intellectually Fulfilled Christian Theism – Part I. Divine Creative Action and Intelligent Design in Nature' in: *Perspectives on Science and Christian Faith* 64 (2): 108-119; Lamoureux, D.O. 2012. 'Darwinian Theological Insights: toward an Intellectually Fulfilled Christian Theism – Part II. Evolutionary Theodicy and Evolutionary Psychology' in: *Perspectives on Science and Christian Faith* 64 (3): 166-177; Brink, G. van den, Cook, H. 2020. '"I am Inclined to Look at Everything as Resulting from Designed Laws": Charles Darwin's Origin of Species as a Specimen of Natural Theology' in: *Christian Scholar's Review* 50 (1): 25-37.

159 Cohen, C. [1925]. *God and Evolution*. Pioneer Press, London; Russell, B. 1935. *Religion and Science. [Home University Library]*. Thornton Butterworth, London. Cf. Bowler, P.J. 2001. *Reconciling Science and Religion. The Debate in Early-Twentieth-Century*

exchange of ideas on the issue that takes place today: Darwin should not make much of a difference. Our finding that the range of arguments put forward by present-day theologians to reconcile animal suffering with divine design is not fundamentally different from pre-Darwinian views on the matter, indicates that acclaiming Darwin as the one who has opened humanity's eyes to this problem—as is done so much today—does not do justice to the historical reality. His significance mainly lies in the new perspective on animal suffering he offered, *viz.* as instrumental in the process of evolution.

The purpose for which God allowed animal suffering may have changed. Prior to Darwin, it was the God-ordained means of preserving animal species from extinction; after Darwin that turned into God's means of creating new animal species with humanity as the intended outcome. The debates on whether such purposes might justify the presence of animal suffering, continued unabated.

7.4. Brief Theological Postscript

Obviously, the fact that Darwin had only a minor influence on the debate about the tension between divine design and animal suffering does not imply that such a tension does not exist. Having come at the end of my investigations, I would like to reflect briefly on what my findings could mean for present-day theistic believers in dealing with the tensions that we have discussed throughout this book. After all, for agnostics and atheists, any discussion on the bearing of animal suffering on the divine attributes is at best interesting for theoretical reasons (if not entirely irrelevant); for the theist, however, the friction between the attributes of God as revealed in Scripture and the troubling observations of the fate of animals in nature remains a matter of concern. 'What are we to make of a creation in which the routine activity is for organisms to be tearing others apart with teeth of all types—biting, grinding flesh, plants stalks, bones between molars, pushing the pulp greedily down the gullet with delight, incorporating its essence into one's own organization, and then excreting with foul stench and gasses the residue?'[160]

Especially in the context of the evolution *versus* creation debates, the data provided by the book of nature may be conceived as incompatible with the attributes of the Creator as depicted in the book of Scripture.[161]

Britain. The University of Chicago Press, Chicago: 72-76; Bowler, P.J. 2007. *Monkey Trials and Gorilla Sermons. Evolution and Christianity from Darwin to Intelligent Design*. Harvard University Press, Cambridge (MA): 198-203.

160   Becker, E. 1973. *The Denial of Death*. Simon & Schuster, New York: 282.
161   Haught, 'The Boyle Lecture 2003: Darwin, Design and the Promise of Nature'; Berry, 'The Lions Seek Their Prey from God: a Commentary on the Boyle Lecture';

Nature, after all, testifies of a long history of animal species either becoming extinct or developing into new ones at the expense of countless other animals, 'a nightmare spectacular taking place on a planet that has been soaked for hundreds of millions of years in the blood of all its creatures'.[162]

Thus, how to reconcile God's providential care with the suffering of animals was not only a problem in the past but continues to be so in the present, especially now that generally speaking we have become more sensitive to the similarities between animals and humans. In this regard, it is important to note that animal suffering is a problem both for those who subscribe to the concept of theistic evolution—God created the world in the way that is disclosed by contemporary geology, biology and related sciences—as well as for those who reject evolution and 'deep time' altogether. Animal suffering endangers belief in the divine goodness, power, and wisdom in the present no less than it did in the past.[163] Arguably, the suffering and death of one innocent animal is no less problematic for God's goodness and justice than the death and suffering of countless numbers of them.[164]

The significance of evolution for the debate about animal suffering and divine benevolence is further put into perspective when we realize that it does not matter to the animals themselves whether they are part of an evolutionary process or not. What has happened before that animal was born or what will happen after its death does not add to or detract from its private sufferings or enjoyments. Hence, evolution does not aggravate or ameliorate the amount of suffering at the level of the individual animal and can be considered morally neutral in terms of God's providential care over his creatures.[165] For that reason, the rejection

---

Conradie, E.M., 2018, 'The Christian Faith and Evolution: an Evolving, Unresolved Debate' in: *Verbum et Ecclesia* 39(1): a1843; Van den Brink, *Reformed Theology and Evolutionary Theory*: 99-135.

162   Becker, *The Denial of Death*: 283.
163   Cf. Munday Jr, J.C., 'Animal Pain: Beyond the Threshold?' in: Miller, K.B. (ed.). 2003. *Perspectives on an Evolving Creation*. Wm. B. Eerdmans, Grand Rapids: 435-468. 'All the issues [violent death through predation, sickness and other causes of suffering] must be satisfied by a conception of God's justice, whether or not evolution is true' (447).
164   Middleton, T. 2017. 'Objecting to Theodicy and the Legitimacy of Protesting against Evil' in: *Science & Christian Belief* 29 (1): 3-19. Cf. Lewis, *The Problem of Pain*: 103. '[N]o more pain is felt when a million suffer than when one suffers.'
165   Some will argue against this reasoning that the fact that evolution always eliminates the weak is at odds with God's character as revealed in the Bible, and that evolution therefore makes the question of natural evil more poignant after all, see e.g. Peels, R. 2018. 'Does Evolution Conflict with God's Character?' in: *Modern Theology* 34 (4):

of evolution as cruel and hence incompatible with divine goodness does not make sense and, *vice versa*, also refutes the arguments of those who, because of the suffering caused by evolution, think they must give up their belief in a personal God.[166] Divine goodness, benevolence, etc. are at stake anyhow, regardless of whether or not there is evolution.[167]

More than a century ago, James McCosh (cf. § 6.3.2) noted that '[n]o difficulty arises on the theory of development [= evolution], which does not meet us on the theory of the immediate creation of every new individual and species. The works of nature are equally the works of God on the one supposition as on the other, and the mysteries [evils, disease and death] bear against God in the one case as in the other.'[168] Regarding those mysteries, George Frederick Wright (cf. § 6.3.2) asserted that '[f]or what we know we should be thankful' and '[w]ith respect to what is beyond our comprehension we should be humble inquirers.'[169]

Personally, I think that this is the wisest approach when thinking about the relationship between God's attributes and the miseries afflicting the animals, both in the evolutionary past and in the present. As we have seen, all attempts to save the divine benevolence come with their own problems and are highly dependent on assumptions that cannot be verified in any way.[170] Moreover, attempts to explain away the suffering by attributing 'meaning' to 'the seemingly monstrous randomness of nature's violence' do not do justice to those who are affected by it, as is so impressively brought up by *David Hart* in his 2005 article with the telling

---

544-564. Against this it can be argued that it remains to be seen whether God's special care for the weak includes animals. The (indeed many) biblical texts that speak of God's special care for the weak and vulnerable are mainly about frail and threatened human beings.

166 As done by the minister I quoted in the intro of Chapter 1.

167 It could be objected that the long time frame of evolution involves the suffering of many more animals than the shorter time frame of the young-earth creationists. Against this, it can be argued that during this long period the Earth was predominantly populated by primitive organisms lacking the nervous system necessary to experience suffering, while modern animals with more advanced brains only appear in the penultimate stage.

168 McCosh, *The Religious Aspect of Evolution*: 68.

169 Wright, G.F. 1882. *Studies in Science and Religion*. Warren F. Draper, Andover: 190.

170 For a recent critical and instructive analysis that shows the shortcomings of commonly followed roads to reconcile animal suffering with divine benevolence, see Peels, 'Does Evolution Conflict with God's Character?'. Whether the view of this author 'that a Darwinian evolutionary process makes possible genuine moral choices and allows for human responsibility' (364) offers an acceptable way out is debatable. Referring to the emergence of humans as a justification for evolutionary animal suffering was popular in the early decades after Darwin, yet today is seen as unwarranted anthropocentrism.

title *Tsunami and Theodicy*. For him, such attempts only serve to make 'a fine case for a rejection of God, or of faith in divine goodness.'[171] Therefore, like others in the Reformed theological tradition (as we have seen before), I prefer to leave the issue of animal suffering and divine benevolence unsolved while trusting that it will one day become clear. 'You do not know now what I am doing, but later you will understand.'[172] I consider this attitude—known as skeptical theism—the most appropriate.[173]

7.5. Conclusion

Historically, Charles Darwin's theory of evolution did not form a watershed in the debate about animal suffering. This can be deduced from the observation that the arguments to save God's benevolence that are endorsed by present-day theologians are not much different from those advanced in the period before Darwin. There is only one exception to this rule: the thought that animals suffer because of their own sins. This view, held by only a minority of the authors we examined, can indeed be traced back to Darwin's idea of a moral continuity between humans and animals—with the *caveat* that Darwin himself did not go so far as to see in that continuity a reason to attribute the capacity to sin to the animals.

Ignoring the similarities in the debate as it was conducted before and after Darwin is regrettable, because it gives birth to the erroneous thought that concerns about animal suffering only emerged with, and are bound up with, the Darwinian theory of evolution. As a matter of fact, these concerns had been around long before, which means that the tension between a good Creator and suffering animals cannot be released by rejecting the theory of evolution. Neither is this problem increased by accepting this theory.

---

171 Hart, D.B. 2005. 'Tsunami and Theodicy' in: *First Things*. March. Hart is talking about natural evils that affect people, but his arguments apply equally to the non-human animal world. https://www.firstthings.com/article/2005/03/tsunami-and-theodicy. Accessed on 14 December 2021.
172 John 13:7. (NRSV)
173 Faro, 'The Question of Evil and Animal Death before the Fall'; Van den Brink, *Reformed Theology and Evolutionary Theory*: 122-123, 134.

Summary

Many people today think that nature provides conclusive evidence for the belief that God does not exist. They believe that all the evil and suffering in nature, including the vast amount of suffering and death that occur in the animal world—proverbially summed up as "nature red in tooth and claw"—is incompatible with the belief in a benevolent God who takes care of all living beings. In the past, however, God's hand was noticed everywhere in nature—'the heavens declare the glory of God, and the firmament declares the work of his hands.' But awareness of the suffering that afflicts animals has undermined the credibility of this idea to modern humans ('God cannot be like that'). It is often assumed that Charles Darwin's theory of evolution played a decisive role in this change. Whether this is correct is the question that prompted the present study. There is reason to be skeptical of this hypothesis in advance, because it was clear long before Darwin that there is a constant struggle for survival in the animal world. The novelty Darwin brought in was that new species emerge from this struggle—something that does little to add to or detract from the suffering of each individual animal.

To trace the historical roots of this change in interpretation of nature, I investigated how people in the past were able to reconcile belief in a benevolent Creator and Sustainer on the one hand with seeing the evil that the animals do to each other on the other. The research first focuses on a time frame that begins in late antiquity and initially ends with the year in which Darwin published his theory of evolution. I chose this provisional end point to gain a picture of the discussion in a period in which Darwin and his theory did not yet play a role. I then discuss developments since Darwin with the aim of considering whether it is appropriate to hold the emergence of Darwin's theory of natural selection responsible for the fact that nature, instead of being a mainstay of belief in God appears to have turned into evidence to the contrary.

In **Chapter 1**, I describe the above change in nature interpretation (§1.1) and link to it my research question (§1.2). It reads as follows:

To what extent does the change of feeling about the praiseworthiness of the Creator's work in relation to the animal world go back to developments that already took place before Darwin and are thus not directly linked to the concept of evolution by natural selection?

This question can be answered by examining the extent to which a less favorable view of the Creator's work in relation to the animal world already played a role in the time preceding Darwin and therefore cannot have arisen through his theory of evolution.

After some notes on the relevance of the research for the current creation-versus-evolution debate (if Darwin's theory plays no decisive role in the discussion, the suffering of animals cannot be used as an anti-evolution argument; §1.3) and the method followed (§1.4), I give an overview of the content of the chapters (§1.5). First, I examine the views of authors who lived from the time of the Early Church to the time of the Reformers (Chapter 2). Next, my research focuses specifically on English-language literature between the early seventeenth century and the 1960s (Chapters 3-6). This limitation is necessary to keep the amount of data manageable, and it is justified because it is precisely in the English-speaking areas that the discussion of our research topic was abundant both before and after Darwin. The results thus obtained form the basis for the final phase—an examination of whether current arguments for exempting God from the charge of injustice to animals differ from what was said about them in the past and whether they show any influence from Darwin's theory of evolution (Chapter 7).

In **Chapter 2,** I describe the views on the relationship between God and his creation in the period beginning with the Church Fathers and ending in 1600, the year in which the Reformation more or less took shape. After outlining the intellectual climate of late antiquity as far as relevant to the debate about God and his creation (§ 2.1) and giving a justification for the method I followed (§ 2.2), I discuss the authors relevant to my topic (§ 2.3). Their thoughts are then summarized and analyzed in § 2.4.

It appears that the majority of authors believed that both the fact that animals die and that some serve as food for others is part of creation as it came from God's hand. The only exceptions to this were Irenaeus of Lyons and Theophilus of Antioch; for them, it is certain that the existence of predators is a consequence of the fall, which does not mean, however, that they also attributed the death of animals to this fall. God created the animals as mortal beings; immortality is the privilege of mankind alone.

Other Early Church fathers who are believed to have included the suffering and death of animals among the consequences of the fall—the Cappadocians Basil the Great and Gregory of Nyssa—appear to be at two ends of the spectrum when their texts are carefully examined. On the one hand, they wrote that in the uncorrupted creation, no predators existed and animals did not die; on the other hand, they refuted their own claims by praising God for having, in creating carnivorous animals, provided them with the sharp teeth and claws they needed to obtain the food intended for them. Such ambivalence is lacking among the other theologians of the Early Church. Their thoughts can be summarized with words of Augustine: that the animals eat each other does not matter, and it is normal for the weaker to lose out in the confrontation with the stronger.

In general, one limited the consequences of the fall—as far as animals are concerned—to a disruption of the relationship between mankind and the animals. Man's dominion over animals was diminished by the fall, and as a result, some animals now pose a threat to humans and their livestock. This remained the prevailing view for over thirteen centuries. Adam's sin did not change the nature of the animal, according to Thomas Aquinas. Only with Luther and Calvin did the idea that the existence of predators is a consequence of the fall return, understandably because they—as befits the Reformers—emphasize the importance of the literal interpretation of the Bible. In Genesis we read that God gave the animals of the field the green herb for food. That it is different now cannot but be a result of Adam's transgression. But that does not imply that they then also argued that God would have created the animals immortal and that they only became mortal after, or even through, Adam's fall. Luther explicitly denied this and Calvin is silent on the matter.

That the suffering of animals could raise questions about the existence and role of God remained out of the picture during this period. None of the authors considered the option that the existence of predators and the death of animals could be grounds for doubting God's benevolence. Immortality is limited to mankind and animals are made to meet the needs of humanity. On the doorstep of the early Modern Era, the possibility that animals themselves might suffer was hardly a consideration. And, moreover, it is not for humans to pass judgment on the way God treats animals, at least according to Calvin—who thus apparently sensed that something could be going wrong here.

In **Chapter 3** I focus on the texts of authors from the early modern period (1600–1709). In § 3.1, I discuss how the Reformation changed the way the Bible was interpreted. I illustrate the implications of this with a brief discussion of three poems (§ 3.2) after which I show how through this development the Bible became both a subject of scholarly research (§ 3.3) and a source of inspiration for the study of nature (§ 3.4). Then I outline the political and ecclesiastical situation of this period in § 3.5 and in § 3.6 I discuss the state of science in the broader sense at that time. After explaining the methodology (§ 3.7), I discuss the opinions of the relevant authors in § 3.8 whose texts I then analyze in § 3.9.

The changing view of the Bible yielded new insights, but it also created new problems; this period saw the first skirmishes over the relationship between Scripture and science. That God—according to Genesis 1—created all animals as herbivores is difficult to reconcile with the close relationship between dentition and digestive tract on the one hand and diet on the other, brought to light by the burgeoning study of nature. Some authors saw this as a reason not to take this Bible text literally while others resorted to the assumption that the predators may have already been created as carnivores but had to postpone their first meal until after the fall of Adam. God had foreseen what would happen and made the appropriate arrangements.

The view of nature itself also changed during this period. Whereas in the past it was primarily seen as a mirror of God's glory, there was now a conviction that it also provided insight into the purpose for which God had created it. That purpose could be—given the fact that God is a benevolent God—nothing else than the welfare of all His creatures. It will be clear that such a belief makes it important to find a satisfactory explanation for everything in creation which at first sight seems to contradict this goodness. Hence it was precisely in this period that the fate of the animals also became part of the theodicy problem. Furthermore, the many biological similarities between humans and animals necessitated reflection on what really distinguishes humans from their fellow creatures. Whether these many similarities mean that animals therefore also have a soul—whether immortal or not—became a highly contested issue.

However, the arguments put forward during this period to absolve God of the charge of cruelty to animals reflected little or nothing of these new insights. First of all, it was debatable whether animals could suffer at all, something that supporters of Descartes in particular denied. Descartes's theory that animals are devoid of sense—merely machines driven by reflexes—met with little appreciation from the British public. Most authors were convinced that animals could indeed suffer. They therefore looked for other ways to resolve the tension between the beyond all doubt goodness of God and the visible misery that afflicts the animals. Some of them argued that the suffering of animals is outweighed by the more pleasurable experiences they also have; others assumed that the suffering the animals endure is necessary to ensure the smooth running of creation; the happiness of the individual is secondary to the well-being of the greater whole.

A few wanted to hold on to the belief that the death of animals and the existence of predators is man's fault. We have forsaken our stewardship and brought death into the world through sin; therefore, creation is now subject to futility and unable to fulfill the purpose to which God called it into being. Others, however, explicitly rejected this idea. Punishing innocent animals for something Adam had done wrong, they say, is inconsistent with God's justice. Hence, they limited the consequences of the fall of Adam—as far as animals are concerned—to a disruption of the relationship between humans and animals. That disruption is expressed in a weakening of man's dominion over animals. Through sin, we have not so much plunged the animals into misfortune as harmed our own interests.

That the animals did not matter is also evident from the role assigned to them on the new earth; if there is such a role, it is only as a contribution to the bliss of redeemed sinners and not as compensation for any suffering in the present world. The conviction that the animal is there solely for the benefit of humankind was still undisputed in this period. Yet this does not say everything. There were also glimmers of something new; in a few people the realization dawned that God may have created the animals not only for the benefit of man, but also for themselves.

In **Chapter 4**, I discuss the remaining part of the eighteenth century, from 1709 to 1800. In § 4.1, I give a brief summary of the developments that contribute to the change in the position of animals that occurs in this period. In § 4.2, I elaborate on this by showing that people began to see that animals were not there solely to meet the needs of humans. In stories and poems, animals appear as protagonists, and in sermons and other texts, theologians address the reprehensibility of cruelty to our fellow creatures. Then in § 4.3, I discuss how nature is given a role as an independent revelation of God after which in § 4.4 the advances in the knowledge of nature are addressed. In § 4.5, I discuss the method I followed in surveying the sources and these sources themselves are discussed in § 4.6 and commented on in § 4.7.

As interest in the interests of the animal grew, the significance of the Bible as an interpretive framework for animal life continued to decline. That the presence of predators would be a consequence of the fall had already been questioned in the last century, and new developments made this assumption even more unlikely than it already was. The microscope showed that everything was teeming with life; consequently, every bite of grass or sip of water meant the death of countless small animals. This increased the already existing doubts about the possibility of a creation without carnivorous animals. The changed position of the animal also meant that the idea that animals suffer was no longer disputed. As a result, finding an explanation that absolves God of the accusation of treating animals unjustly or cruelly gained urgency.

Some still assumed that the suffering of the animals is a result of Adam's sin, but added—to absolve God from the charge of punishing innocent animals for the sins of man—that the animals will receive reparation for their undeserved misery in a blissful afterlife. The idea that there will also be animals on the new earth was not new in itself but the purpose to which they are granted this privilege changes. Previously it was seen as a contribution to God's glory and possibly to the eternal well-being of the saved sinner; now, according to the authors concerned, the animals are given this position because they are entitled to it. This too shows the increased attention to the animal as a being with its own rights and interests.

Others believed that the suffering affected not the animals themselves, but fallen angels or sinful human souls. The doctrine of transmigration of souls, which stems from Greek philosophy, comes in handy to shield God from the accusation that he allows animals to suffer for no reason. The fact that animals suffer is only an illusion: in reality, souls imprisoned in animal bodies are being punished for crimes committed in a previous existence.

A third approach assumed that animals experience more moments of happiness than of suffering during their lives; a surplus of positive experiences offsets the negative ones. Moreover, the animal is not tormented by memories of suffering endured or fears of what the future holds, which significantly reduces the severity of suffering. And lastly, it was assumed that animals must die to maintain order and cohesion in creation. God has so ordained to ensure that no one species displaces another and thus would detract from the completeness of creation. That the fossils—mostly of animal species that had gone extinct—disprove this argument did not become an issue until the early nineteenth century.

Not everyone was convinced of the credibility of the arguments put forward to resolve the tension between God's benevolence and justice on the one hand and the fate of the animals on the other, but none of these critics saw in the suffering of the animals a reason to question the goodness of God, let alone his existence. They only rejected that nature could say anything about God's attributes or intentions. For reliable information on this, one had to turn to Scripture.

In **Chapter 5** I deal with the part of the nineteenth century that precedes the year in which Charles Darwin made his theory of evolution public (1800–1859). In § 5.1, I discuss the relationship between animals and society. Then, in § 5.2, I discuss what the unfolding study of nature means for the persuasiveness of nature as an independent revelation of God. In § 5.3, I show how I identified the authors relevant to my research. Their ideas are discussed in § 5.4 and I comment on them in § 5.5.

It was the period in which the increasing attention for the position of the animal also took shape socially; through legislation the government aimed to improve the lives of animals and personal initiative led to the establishment of organizations that pursued the same goal. Moreover, natural theology—the systematic elaboration of the belief that creation reflects God's goodness and wisdom and provides insight into what He intends for the world—was now experiencing its zenith with the book of Anglican clergyman William Paley and the series of books published several decades later known as the *Bridgewater Treatises*. Sometimes there were critical comments about this natural theology, but they did not seriously challenge the belief that everything in the universe is designed to provide as much happiness as possible to as many individuals as possible.

Against this background, it is not surprising that—as in previous periods—there were effectively no moral questions raised about the way God treats animals. Most authors advocated the traditional view that each animal species has its own role in maintaining the order laid down by God in creation; predators are one of the means established by God to maintain this order. After all, they ensure that no species of animal increases in number to the point that another becomes extinct as a result, so that none of the species of animal that God created simply disappears from the scene. And if the fossils show that animal species can indeed become extinct, this did not affect confidence in God's power and wisdom. On the contrary, a past so rich in animal life emphasizes all the more the glory of God as Creator.

There are also authors who referred to God's sovereignty in explaining the suffering of animals. They were found mainly among the Scottish Presbyterians, kindred spirits of John Calvin who had also taught that we must unconditionally submit to God's wise counsel. However, this did not mean that these authors also unconditionally submitted to the literal interpretation of Scripture also prescribed by Calvin. They realized that creation as described in the first chapters of Genesis is difficult to reconcile with the picture that emerges from the findings of geology and therefore they interpreted the six days of creation as equally longer periods or assumed that what is described in Genesis 1 is preceded by a long period of earthly life about which the Bible is otherwise silent. Such a view, of course, rules out the possibility that it is only through the fall of Adam that death enters the world and that man would be responsible for the suffering of animals.

Others recognized that animal suffering cannot be due to Adam's sin given the irrefutable evidence of death and destruction in the animal kingdom long before mankind appeared on the scene, but could not accept that so much suffering would be God's intention. God cannot be like that and therefore an explanation other than an appeal to God's sovereign will must be sought. They found it in the fallen angels spoken of in some texts at the periphery of the canon (2 Peter 2:4, Jude:6). These would have been responsible for the existence of death and violence in God's creation from the very beginning of time. Or could it be that God had already foreseen that Adam would fall and had anticipated this when He created the world? Because of sin, mankind would forfeit the ability to become immortal, and therefore the animals had to be mortal as well. After all, a mortal human surrounded by immortal animals was unthinkable. Thus, God was absolved from responsibility for evil without also denying or ignoring the information provided by geology.

A third group wanted to hold not only to the traditional belief that death and violence in the animal kingdom resulted from the fall of Adam, but also to the literal interpretation of the creation story as recorded in the first chapters of Genesis. This conviction forced them to question the credibility of the geological record that provides evidence of animal death long before mankind arrived on earth. With them arose the conflict between Scripture and science that has continued unabated ever since. All the suffering in the world—including that of animals—came from man's disobedience; by assuming that animals died before Adam's fall, so they said, we turn God into a cruel tyrant who allows animals to suffer for no apparent reason.

What the above approaches have in common, despite all their differences, is that in none of them was the suffering of animals seen as a threat to the attributes of God, let alone his existence. One justified God's dealings with the animals by subordinating their welfare to a higher interest, by blaming Adam or fallen angels (or possibly other evil spirits), or by appealing to God's sovereignty that eludes our judgment. Criticism of God for allowing the animals to suffer was unthinkable for the vast majority of authors. Indeed, that would make God an incompetent architect, which also endangered the legitimacy of the prevailing social order that—just as nature—was seen as designed and willed by God. Condoning animal suffering therefore also served a social purpose. Hence, in this period we also see that a small number of authors did not condone animal suffering but, on the contrary, emphasized it. By referring to the misery of animals, they tried to cast doubt on God's existence and thereby robbed the ruling social order of its legitimacy.

Pretending to care about animals as a cover for pursuing something else did not only occur to those who preached revolution. It also occurred with those who, in the face of the science of the day, wanted to stick to the literal reading of Scripture. By arguing that the death of animals without Adam's guilt would degrade God to a cruel tyrant, they tried to make their view that the Bible must be interpreted literally—even as it relates to the creation story in Genesis—more convincing. And for those who emphasized harmony in the animal kingdom in the face of animal suffering, it was primarily a matter of justifying the prevailing social order. Whether or not the animals suffered had become an argument in discussions that were actually about something else.

In **Chapter 6**, I outline developments as they occurred after Darwin published his theory of the origin of species by natural selection. Before him, as we saw, the idea that animal life in all its aspects reflects God's providential care was only rarely questioned, although animal suffering had gradually received more attention. In this chapter I examine whether the conviction that God is benevolent endured after him. After giving a short introduction and an explanation of my research method in § 6.1, I discuss in § 6.2 how Darwin's theory of evolution was received by the public. Next, the authors relevant to my topic are discussed, divided into three categories according to their position in the debate on the relationship between God's benevolence and animal suffering: no problem (§ 6.3), a solvable problem (§ 6.4), or an unsolvable problem (§ 6.5). The role Darwin's theory of evolution plays in this discussion is the theme of § 6.6.

The texts written by Darwin's contemporaries and subsequent generations show that not much changes in the first decades after Darwin. The majority of them managed to interpret Darwin's thoughts as a description of the way God has shown his benevolence and wisdom over the centuries. In a way, condoning the suffering of animals even became easier, because Darwin's theory gives a positive meaning to death and decay in the animal kingdom. After all, the death of weak organisms led to the emergence of ever new and better adapted species, a process that culminated in the creation of humanity. That lofty goal justified all means.

If Darwinism was rejected, it was not because of Darwin's emphasis on animal suffering or because of the idea of an ancient earth with animals dying long before Adam appeared on the scene. Both those who accepted evolution by natural selection and those who assumed repetitive creation saw in the death of animals or the extinction of animal species no reason to doubt the existence of God or his goodness. On the contrary, both the petrified past and the living present testified to the glory of the Creator.

Some refused to accept that not Adam but God Himself would be responsible for the presence of death and violence in the animal kingdom and still wanted—but without denying the findings of geology—to insist that the suffering that afflicts the animals is Adam's fault. They joined the idea already put forward earlier that God had foreseen that Adam would sin and had taken this into account when he brought the world into being. To bring fallen humanity to penance and repentance, God created an animal world in which death and violence also emphasize his power and majesty.

There were also authors who attribute the existence of the bloodthirsty dinosaurs and similar prehistoric monsters preceding Adam to the influence of the devil and his angels; they have—after having already been driven out of heaven in the dawn of creation—corrupted God's creation. With this assumption, God could also be absolved of responsibility for death and violence in the animal kingdom; after all, these are due to the devil.

It was not until the 1920s that authors broke the tacit consensus between science and religion by emphasizing that a violent nature makes the existence of a benevolent God implausible. In doing so, they responded to contemporary anti-evolution writers who implicitly adopted the cultural upgrading of the animal's moral status, and therefore argued that God would never create through death and destruction in the animal kingdom. God and evolution therefore do not go together. But while the anti-evolution writers saw the incompatibility of the two as grounds for denying the existence of evolution, these authors came to the opposite conclusion: that evolution exists, cannot be denied, and thus God cannot exist. In short, it was not because of Darwin that beliefs about the relationship between God and animals changed. The anti-evolutionists conceived the 'incompatibility view,' and it was then eagerly adopted and nurtured by their atheist opponents.

In **Chapter 7**, I examine the extent to which the arguments put forward in the past to safeguard God from responsibility for the suffering of animals are reflected in the present-day discussion of this topic and to what extent Darwin plays a role in this debate. After giving a short introduction and an account of the method I followed to select the sources for my research (§ 7.1), I discuss in § 7.2 how authors nowadays deal with the above problem. Conclusions about a possible influence of Darwin's theory of evolution are drawn in § 7.3 and the significance of my findings for the discussion about creation and evolution as it is conducted today between young-earth creationists and theistic evolutionists is discussed in § 7.4.

Today, both friend and foe are convinced that Darwin's theory of evolution has profoundly influenced our view of God. Darwin's (atheist) followers tirelessly emphasize that their hero has rendered the existence of a Creator implausible, in part by opening our eyes to the cruelty that characterizes nature. Darwin's (Christian) opponents, on the other hand, regard him as the bogeyman who changed the image of a creation sustained by God's providential care to that of a vale of tears.

My research, however, has shown that neither is right. The assumption that the gradual transition between humans and animals assumed by

Darwin would lead to an increased sensitivity to the suffering that affects the animals is not supported by the historical data; Darwin added no new insights to the debate about the relationship between animal suffering and the divine attributes at odds with it. If Darwin's theory mattered, it was in arousing the fear of bestializing mankind rather than promoting the interests of animals (cf. the famous Wilberforce – Huxley debate). That animals resemble humans in structure and behavior was already clear enough before Darwin and whether that was the result of common design or common ancestor did not matter. And further, I would even dare to say that removing the boundary between mankind and animal as done by Darwin has usually had a negative effect on the interests of the animals. Biological similarities support the belief that animal experiments produce relevant results relevant for promoting human health and nowadays even provide a rationale for breeding pigs as suppliers of organs for xenotransplantation.

Even before Darwin, there were debates about the relationship between God's goodness and the suffering of animals, and it appeared that the arguments made by present-day theologians in this regard are not substantially different from those of the past. Now as in the past, some assume that animals have less refined mental qualities so that their suffering would be less severe than the misery that humans have to endure—a view that was already promoted by the Greek Stoic philosophers. Others adhere to the view first found among seventeenth-century Calvinist theologians that God is not subject to our standards of good and evil so that it is up to him how he deals with animals. Still others emphasize that life and death are simply inseparable because the death of one provides food for the other—a view also already expressed in late antiquity. And finally, there are authors who see suffering as a necessary evil for achieving a greater good, just as in a painting both bright and dark colors have their place, also a view with a long history.

It was not only because of Darwin's theory of evolution that people began to wonder what the suffering of animals meant for the belief in a God who lovingly cares for all living beings; they had been thinking about this since at least the first decades of the seventeenth century. The view that animals suffer because of Adam's sin or because of the evil influence of fallen angels, for example, dates from long before Darwin; the same is true of the conviction that justice will be done to the animals on the renewed earth. Some influence of Darwin is detectable only among the theologians who assume that the animals suffer because of their own sins; a gradual transition from animal to human also means, in their view, a gradual emergence of the possibility of deliberately turning one's back on God.

The assumption that Darwin's theory of evolution represents a turning point in our thinking about the relationship between the Creator and the sea of suffering that sweeps through nature is thus refuted by the historical record. From early modern times onward, people were aware that the suffering of animals was at odds with their belief in a loving God who intended the well-being of all his creatures, and sought ways to come to terms with this tension. Rejecting evolution does not solve this problem, and accepting evolution does not make it worse.

Bibliography

Primary Sources

Addison, J. 1730. *The Evidences of the Christian Religion: by the Right Honorable Joseph Addison, Esq; to Which Are Added, Several Discourses against Atheism and Infidelity, and in Defence of the Christian Revelation, Occasionally Published by Him and Others: and now Collected into One Body, and Digested under Their Proper Heads. With a Preface, Containing the Sentiments of Mr. Boyle, Mr. Lock, and Sir Isaac Newton, Concerning the Gospel-Revelation*. J. Tonson, London.

Alexander, C.F. 1852 [1848]. *Hymns for Little Children. Fifth Edition*. Joseph Masters, London.

Ambrose. 'Saint Ambrose, Hexameron, Paradise, and Cain and Abel. Translated by John J. Savage' in: Deferrari, R.J. et al. (eds). 1961. *The Fathers of the Church. A New Translation. Volume 42*. Fathers of the Church, New York.

Amory, T. 1766. *Twenty-two Sermons on the Following Subjects: the Explication and Proof of the Divine Goodness. The Goodness of God Illustrated in Creation, Particularly in the Frame of Man. In Providence, and in Redemption. The Principal Properties of the Divine Goodness. The Objections Drawn from Moral and Natural Evil, and Future Punishments, Answered. The Evidences of a Future State. The Necessity of Holiness. The Proper Temper for Inquiring after Eternal Life, and Jesus Christ the Best Guide to It*. T. Becket and P.A. de Hondt, London.

Anderson, J. 1851. *The Course of Creation*. Wm. H. Moore & Co., Cincinnati.

Anderson, R. (ed.). 1794. *The Works of the British Poets. With Prefaces, Biographical and Critical. Volume Eight*. John & Arthur Arch, London.

Anonymous. 1760. 'A View of the Distresses of Mankind, and of the Brute Animals' in: *The Universal Magazine of Knowledge and Pleasure* 27: 231-233.

Anonymous. 1803. 'Art. X. The Temple of Nature, or the Origin of Society, a Poem, with Philosophical Notes. By Erasmus Darwin, M.D. F.R.S. Author of the Botanic Garden, of Zoonomia, and of Phytologia. 4to. 298 pp. il. 15s. Johnson. 1803' in: *British Critic* 1804, 23: 169-174.

Anonymous. 1803. 'XCVIII. Paley's Natural Theology' in: *The Christian Observer, Conducted by Members of the Established Church. Volume II. From First of January, to Thirty-First of December, 1803*: 369-374.

Anonymous. 1803. 'Natural Theology; or Evidences of the Existence and Attributes of the Deity, Collected from the Appearances of Nature. By William Paley, D.D.' in: *The Evangelical Magazine for the Year 1803*. Vol. XI: 494-495.

Anonymous. 1803. 'The Temple of Nature, or, the Origin of Society. A Poem with Philosophical Notes. By Erasmus Darwin, M.D. F.R.S. Author of the Botanic Garden, &c. Quarto. Pp. 298. 1l. 5s. Johnson' in: *The Anti-Jacobin Review and Magazine, or, Monthly Political and Literary Censor from September to December (Inclusive)—1803—with an Appendix Containing an Ample Review of Foreign Literature* 16: 170-173.

Anonymous. 1804. 'Art. X. The Temple of Nature, or the Origin of Society, a Poem, with Philosophical Notes. By Erasmus Darwin, M.D. F.R.S. Author of the Botanic Garden, of Zoonomia, and of Phytologia. 4to. 298 pp. il. 15s. Johnson. 1803' in: *British Critic* 23: 169-174.

Anonymous. 1806. 'Art. III. Natural Theology: or, Evidences of the Existence and Attributes of the Deity, Collected from the Appearances of Nature. By William Paley, D.D. Archdeacon of Carlisle. London. 1802, 8vo. pp. 586' in: *The Edinburgh Review or Critical Journal for Oct. 1802…Jan. 1803, Fifth Edition*. Vol. I: 287-305.

Anonymous. 1837. 'Art. I.—Geology and Mineralogy Considered with Reference to Natural Theology. By the Rev. William Buckland' in: *The Edinburgh Review or Critical Journal for April,…July, 1837* 65: 1-39.

Anonymous. 1837. 'Geology and Mineralogy Considered with Reference to Natural Theology, by the Rev. Dr. Buckland. 2 Vols. 8vo. pp. 727. Plates. London: Pickering' in: *The Congregational Magazine for the Year 1837*: 42-47.

Anonymous. 1837. 'The Scripture Cosmogony, Illustrated and Confirmed by the Discoveries and Conclusions of Geology' in: *The Congregational Magazine for the Year 1837*: 706-710.

Anonymous. 1842. 'Preface' in: *The Oracle of Reason, or, Philosophy Vindicated* 1: ii.

Anonymous. 1853. *A Brief and Complete Refutation of the Anti-Scriptural Theory of Geologists. By a Clergyman of the Church of England*. Wertheim and Macintosh, London.

Anonymous. 1899. *Evil & Evolution. An Attempt to Turn the Light of Modern Science on to the Ancient Mystery of Evil. By the Author of 'the Social Horizon'. Fourth Impression*. MacMillan and Co., London.

Anonymous. 1912. 'Evolutionism in the Pulpit' in: *The Fundamentals. A Testimony to the Truth Volume VIII*. Testimony Publishing Company, Chicago: 27-35.

Apostle, H.G. 2021 [1981]. *Aristotle's on the Soul. Translated with Commentaries and Glossary*. Thomas More College Press, Merrimack.

Aquinas, T. 2003. *On Evil. Translated by Richard Regan. Edited with an Introduction and Notes by Brian Davies*. Oxford University Press, Oxford.

Aquinas, T. 2020 [1920]. *The Summa Theologiae of St. Thomas Aquinas. Literally Translated by Fathers of the English Dominican Province*. The Collected Works of St. Thomas Aquinas. Electronic Edition. http://www.newadvent.org/summa/

Arnobius, 'The Seven Books of Arnobius Adversus Gentes, Translated by Archd. Hamilton Bryce and Hugh Campbell' in: Roberts, A., Donaldson, J. (eds). 1871. *Ante-Nicene Christian Library. Translations of the Writings of the Fathers Down to A.D. 325. Volume XIX*. T&T Clark, Edinburgh.

Athanasius. 'On the Incarnation of the Word' in: Schaff, Ph. (ed.). 1891. *Nicene and Post-Nicene Fathers Series II, Volume 4. Athanasius*. T&T Clark, Edinburgh. Republished by Wm. B. Eerdmans, Grand Rapids: 249-333.

Augustine. 'On the Morals of the Manichaeans' in: Schaff, Ph. (ed.). 1887. *A Select Library of the Nicene and Post-Nicene Fathers of the Christian Church. Volume IV. St. Augustin: the Writings against the Manichaeans and against the Donatists*. T&T Clark, Edinburgh. Republished by Wm. B. Eerdmans, Grand Rapids: 112-156.

Augustine. 'The Catholic Faith Concerning Infants' in: Schaff, Ph. (ed.). 1887. *A Select Library of the Nicene and Post-Nicene Fathers of the Christian Church. Volume V. St. Augustin: Anti-Pelagian Writings*. T&T Clark, Edinburgh. Republished by Wm. B. Eerdmans, Grand Rapids: 1093.

Augustine. 'St. Augustine. The Problem of Free Choice. Translated and Annotated by Dom Mark Pontifex' in: Quasten, J., Plumpe, J.C. (eds). 1955. *Ancient Christian Writers. The Works of the Fathers in Translation No. 22*. The Newman Press, Westminster.

Augustine. 'Saint Augustine against Julian, Translated by Matthew A. Schumacher' in: Deferrari, R.J. et al. (eds). 1957. *The Fathers of the Church. A New Translation. Volume 35*. Fathers of the Church, New York.

Augustine. 1960. *The City of God Against the Pagans. Books XVII.36-XX. With an English Translation by William Chase Greene*. Harvard University Press, Cambridge (MA).

Augustine. 1966. *The City of God Against the Pagans. Books XII-XV. With an English Translation by Philip Levine*. Harvard University Press, Cambridge (MA).

Augustine. 1968. *The City of God Against the Pagans. Books VIII-XI. With an English Translation by David S. Wiesen*. Harvard University Press, Cambridge (MA).

Augustine. 2016. *Confessions. Books 9-13.* Edited and Translated by Carolyn J.-B. Hammond. Harvard University Press, Cambridge (MA).

Augustine in: Rotelle, J.E. (ed.). 2017. *The Works of Saint Augustine. A Translation for the 21st Century. On Genesis I/13. On Genesis: A Refutation of the Manichees (De Genesi Adversus Manichaeos), Unfinished Literal Commentary on Genesis (De Genesi ad Litteram Liber Imperfectus), Litteral Meaning of Genesis (De Genesi ad Litteram).* Introductions, Translations and Notes by Edmund Hill. 4th printing. New City Press, New York.

Balguy, T. 1781. *Divine Benevolence Asserted; and Vindicated from the Objections of Ancient and Modern Sceptics.* Lockyer Davis, London.

Barnes E.W. 1927. *Should Such a Faith Offend? Sermons and Addresses.* Hodder and Stoughton, London.

Barnes, E.W. 'Religion and Science. The Present Phase. A Sermon Preached in Westminster Abbey on Sunday, September 25th, 1927' in: Barnes, E.W. 1927. *Should Such a Faith Offend? Sermons and Addresses.* Hodder and Stoughton, London: 309-317.

Barnes, E.W. 'God. A Sermon Preached before the University of Cambridge on Sunday, May 16th, 1926' in: Barnes, E.W. 1927. *Should Such a Faith Offend? Sermons and Addresses.* Hodder and Stoughton, London: 289-299.

Barnes, E.W. 1933. *Scientific Theory and Religion. The World Described by Science and Its Spiritual Interpretation. The Gifford Lectures at Aberdeen 1927–1929.* University Press, Cambridge.

Basil. 1995. *The Syriac Version of the Hexaemeron by Basil of Caesarea.* Translated by Robert W. Thomson. Peeters, Leuven.

Basil. 2005. *St. Basil the Great. On the Human Condition.* Translation and Introduction by Nonna Verna Harrison. St. Vladimir's Seminary Press, New York.

Baxter, R. 1667. *The Reasons of the Christian Religion. The First Part, of Godliness: Proving by Natural Evidence the Being of God, the Necessity of Holiness, and a Future Life of Retribution; the Sinfulness of the World; the Desert of Hell, and what Hope of Recovery Mercies Intimate. The Second Part, of Christianity: Proving by Evidence Supernatural and Natural, the Certain Truth of the Christian Belief: and Answering the Objections of Unbelievers.* Fran. Titon, London.

Bayle, P. 1734 [1697]. *The Dictionary Historical and Critical of Mr Peter Bayle. The Second Edition, Carefully Collated with the Several Editions of the Original; in Which Many Passages Are Restored, and the Whole Greatly Augmented, Particularly with a Translation of the Quotations from Eminent Writers in Various Languages. To Which is Prefixed, the Life of the Author, Revised, Corrected, and Enlarged, by Mr Des*

Maizeaux, Fellow of the Royal Society. Volume The First. A—Bi. J.J. and P. Knapton et al., London.

Bayle, P. 1737 [1697]. *The Dictionary Historical and Critical of Mr Peter Bayle. The Second Edition, Carefully Collated with the Several Editions of the Original; in Which Many Passages Are Restored, and the Whole Greatly Augmented, Particularly with a Translation of the Quotations from Eminent Writers in Various Languages. To Which is Prefixed, the Life of the Author, Revised, Corrected, and Enlarged, by Mr Des Maizeaux, Fellow of the Royal Society. Volume The Fourth. M—R.* D. Midwinter et al., London.

Beach, H.H. 1912. 'Decadence of Darwinism' in: *The Fundamentals. A Testimony to the Truth Volume VIII*: 36-48. Testimony Publishing Company, Chicago.

Beauchamp, P. [Jeremy Bentham]. 1822. *Analysis of the Influence of Natural Religion on the Temporal Happiness of Mankind.* R. Carlile, London.

Bell, C, 1836. *The Bridgewater Treatises on the Power, Wisdom, and Goodness of God, as Manifested in the Creation. Treatise IV. The Hand, Its Mechanism and Vital Endowment as Evincing Design.* Carey et al., Philadelphia.

Bentham, J. 1789. *An Introduction to the Principles of Morals and Legislation. Printed in the Year 1780, and now First Published.* T. Payne, and Son, London.

Bentley, R. 1699 [1692]. *The Folly and Unreasonableness of Atheism Demonstrated from the Advantage and Pleasure of a Religious Life, the Faculties of Humane Souls, the Structure of Animate Bodies, & the Origin and Frame of the World: in Eight Sermons Preached at the Lecture Founded by the Honourable Robert Boyle, Esquire in the First Year, MDCXCII. The Fourth Edition Corrected.* H. Mortlock, London.

Berrow, C. 1766. *A Pre-existent Lapse of Human Souls in a State of Pre-existence, the Only Original Sin, and the Ground Work of the Gospel Dispensation.* J. Dodsley et al., London.

Blount, C. 1695 [1679]. 'Anima Mundi; or an Historical Narration of the Opinions of the Ancients Concerning Man's Soul after this Life: According to Unenlightened Nature' in: *The Miscellaneous Works of Charles Blount...* n.p., n.p.: 11-133.

Bochart, S. 1712 [1663]. *Samuelis Bocharti Opera Omnia. Hoc Est Phaleg, Chanaan, et Hierozoicon. Quibus Accesserunt Dissertationes Variæ ad Illustrationem Sacri Codicis Aliorumque Monumentorum Veterum. Præmittitur Vita Auctoris à Stephano Morino Descripta et Paradisi Terrestris Delineatio ad Mentem Bocharti. Indices Denique Accurati & Mappæ Geographicæ Suis Locis Insertæ Sunt. Editio Quarta.* Cornelius Boutesteyn et al., Leiden.

Bonnet, C. 1764. *Contemplation de la Nature. Tome Premier.* Marc-Michel Rey, Amsterdam

Bonnet, C. 1770. *La Palingénésie Philosophique ou Idées sur l'Etat Passé et sur l'État Futur des Êtres Vivans. Ouvrage Destiné à server de Supplément aux Derniers Écrits de l'Auteur, et Qui Contient Principalement le Précis de Ses Recherches sur le Christiansime. Tome Premier.* Claude Philibert et Barthelemi Chirol, Genève.

Bougeant, G.H. 1740. *A Philosophical Amusement upon the Language of Beasts and Birds, Written Originally in French by Father Bougeant, a Famous Jesuit; now Confined at La Fleche on Account of this Work. The Second Edition Corrected.* T. Cooper, London.

Boyd, H.S. 1817. 'LXII. On Cosmogony' in: *The Philosophical Magazine and Journal Comprehending the Various Branches of Science, the Liberal and Fine Arts, Geology, Agriculture, Manufactures and Commerce* 50: 375-378.

Boyle, R. 1690. *The Christian Virtuoso Shewing, that by Being Addicted to Experimental Philosophy, a Man Is Rather Assisted, than Indisposed, to Be a Good Christian: The First Part.* John Taylor, London.

Boyle, R. 1715. *The Theological Works of the Honourable Robert Boyle, Epitomized by Richard Boulton. Vol. II.* W. Taylor, London.

Bradford, J. [1555]. 'The Restoration of All Things' in: Townsend, A. (ed.). 1848. *The Writings of John Bradford, Containing Sermons, Meditations, Examinations, &c.* Cambridge University Press: 350-364.

Brougham, H. 1856. *Works of Henry, Lord Brougham. Volume VI. Natural Theology, Comprising a Discourse of Natural Theology, Dialogues on Instinct, and Dissertations of the Cells of Bees and on Fossil Osteology.* Richard Griffin and Company, London.

Brown, W.L. 1816. *An Essay on the Existence of a Supreme Creator...and Deducing from the Whole Subject, the Most Important Practical Inferences. Vol. I.* T. Hamilton et al., London.

Browne, T. 1658. *Pseudodoxia Epidemica: or, Enquiries into Very Many Received Tenents and Common'y Presumed Truths. The Fourth Edition. With Marginal Observations, and a Table Alphabetical.* Edward Dod, London.

Browne, T. 1898 [1642]. *Religio Medici.* George Bell and Sons, London.

Bruckner, J.A. 1770. *A Philosophical Survey of the Animal Creation, an Essay. Wherein the General Devastation and Carnage, that Reign among the Different Classes of Animals, Are Considered in a New Point of View; and the Vast Increase of Life and Enjoyment Derived to the Whole from this Institution of Nature is Clearly Demonstrated. Translated from the French.* J. Potts, Dublin.

Buckland, W. 1820. *Vindiciae Geologicae; or the Connexion of Geology with Religion Explained, in an Inaugural Lecture Delivered before the University of Oxford, May 15, 1819, on the Endowment of a Readership in Geology by His Royal Highness the Prince Regent.* Oxford University Press, Oxford.

Buckland, W. 1836. *The Bridgewater Treatises on the Power Wisdom and Goodness of God as Manifested in the Creation. Treatise VI. Geology and Mineralogy Considered with Reference to Natural Theology. In Two Volumes.* William Pickering, London.

Buckland, W. 1839. *An Inquiry whether the Sentence of Death Pronounced at the Fall of Man Included the Whole Animal Creation or Was Restricted to the Human Race. A Sermon Preached in the Cathedral of Christ-Church before the University of Oxford. January 27, 1839.* John Murray, London.

Buckley, M.J. 1987. *At the Origins of Modern Atheism.* Yale University Press, New Haven.

Bugg, G. 1826, 1827. *Scriptural Geology; or, Geological Phenomena Consistent only with the Literal Interpretation of the Sacred Scriptures, upon the Subjects of the Creation and Deluge; in Answer to an "Essay on the Theory of the Earth," by M. Cuvier, Perpetual Secretary of the French Institute, &c. &c. and to Professor Buckland's Theory of the Caves.* Hatchard and Son, London.

[Burnet, T.] 1692. *Archaeologiae Philosophicae: Sive Doctrina Antiqua de Rerum Originibus. Libri Duo.* Gualterus Kettilby, London.

Burnet, T. 1729. *Archaeologiae Philosophicae: or the Ancient Doctrine Concerning the Originals of Things. Written in Latin by Thomas Burnet, Faithfully Translated into English, with Remarks thereon by Mr. Foxton. Part I. Being a Critique on the Mosaic Creation.* E. Curll, London.

Bushnell, H. 1869. *Moral Uses of Dark Things.* Strahan and Company, London.

Calvin, J. n.d. *Commentaries on the First Book of Moses Called Genesis by John Calvin. Translated from the Original Latin, and Compared with the French Edition by John King. Volume First.* Christian Classics Ethereal Library. Grand Rapids.

Calvin, J. n.d. *Commentary on the Book of the Prophet Isaiah by John Calvin. Translated from the Original Latin by William Pringle. Volume First.* Christian Classics Ethereal Library. Grand Rapids.

Calvin, J. n.d. *Commentary on the Book of the Prophet Isaiah by John Calvin. Translated from the Original Latin by William Pringle. Volume Fourth.* Christian Classics Ethereal Library. Grand Rapids.

Calvin, J. n.d. *Commentaries on the Twelve Minor Prophets by John Calvin. Now First Translated from the Original Latin by John Owen. Volume First. Hosea.* Christian Classics Ethereal Library. Grand Rapids.

Calvin, J. n.d. *Commentaries on the Epistle of Paul the Apostle to the Romans by John Calvin. Translated and Edited by John Owen*. Christian Classics Ethereal Library. Grand Rapids.

Calvin, J. 1559. *Institvtio Christianæ Religionis, in Libros Quator nunc Primùm Digesta, Certísque Distincta Capitibus, ad Aptissimam Methodum: Aucta etiam tam Magna Accessione vt Propemodum Opus Nouum Haberi Possit*. Oliua Roberti Stephani, Geneva.

Calvin, J. 1574. *Sermons of Master Iohn Caluin, vpon the Booke of IOB. Translated out of French by Arthur Golding*. Lucas Harison and George Bishop, London.

Calvin, J. 1960 [1559]. *Calvin: Institutes of the Christian Religion. In Two Volumes. Edited by John T. McNeill. Translated and Indexed by Ford Lewis Battles*. The Westminster Press, Philadelphia.

Calvin, J. 2000. *Sermons sur la Genèse Chapitres 1,1–20,7*, Supplementa Calviniana 11/1–2, ed. M. Engammare, Neukirchen-Vluyn.

Calvin, J. 2009. *Sermons on Genesis. Chapters 1:1-11:4. Forty-Nine Sermons Delivered in Geneva between 4 September 1559 and 23 January 1560. Translated into English by Rob Roy McGregor*. The Banner of Truth Trust, Edinburgh.

[A Cambridge R.S.C.F. Group]. 1958. 'The Problem of Pain and Suffering, Part 2: A Scientific Interpretation' in: *The Christian Graduate* 11: 55-59.

Caustic, C. 1803. *Terrible Tractoration!! A Poetical Petition against Galvanising Trumpery, and the Perkinistic Institution. In Four Cantos. Most Respectfully Addressed to the Royal College of Physicians. Second Edition, with Great Additions*. T. Hurst and J. Ginger, London.

Chalmers, T. [1814]. 'Remarks on Cuvier's Theory of the Earth; in Extracts from a Review of that Theory Which Was Contributed to "the Christian Instructor" in 1814.' in: Chalmers, T. 1848. *Tracts and Essays Religious and Economical*. Thomas Constable, Edinburgh: 347-372.

Chalmers, T. 1817. *The Evidence and Authority of the Christian Revelation*. Anthony Finley, Philadelphia.

Chalmers, T. 1826. *On Cruelty to Animals: a Sermon, Preached in Edinburgh, on the 5th of March, 1826. Second Edition*. Chalmers & Collins, Glasgow.

Chalmers, T. 1835. *The Bridgewater Treatises on the Power, Wisdom, and Goodness of God, as Manifested in the Creation. Treatise I. On the Adaptation of External Nature, to the Moral and Intellectual Constitution of Man*. Carey et al., Philadelphia.

Chalmers, T. 1840. *The Works of Thomas Chalmers. Volume First. On Natural Theology*. Robert Carter, New York.

Chalmers, T. 1848. *Tracts and Essays Religious and Economical*. Thomas Constable, Edinburgh.

Chalmers, T. 1849. *Posthumous Works of the Rev. Thomas Chalmers. Volume VII. Edited by the Rev. William Hanna*. Harper & Brothers, New York.

[Chambers, R.] 1844. *Vestiges of the Natural History of Creation*. John Churchill, London.

Charles, R.H. (ed.). 1913. *The Apocrypha and Pseudepigrapha of the Old Testament in English with Introductions and Critical and Explanatory Notes to the Several Books. Volume II. Pseudepigrapha*. Clarendon Press, Oxford.

Charnock, S. 1815 [1682]. *The Works of the Late Rev. Stephen Charnock, B.D. In Nine Volumes. With a Prefatory Dedication and Memoir by Edward Parsons*. Baynes et al., London.

Charnock, S. 1853 [1682]. *Discourses upon the Existence and Attributes of God. With His Life and Character, by William Symington. In Two Volumes*. Robert Carter & Brothers, New York.

Charron, P. 1707 [1601]. *Of Wisdom. Three Books. Written Originally in French by the Sieur de Charron. With an Account of the Author. Made English by George Stanhope. The Second Edition, Corrected*. R. Bonwick et al., London.

Chilton, W. 1842. 'Mosaic Account of the Deluge' in: *The Free-Thinker's Information for the People* 2: 9-16.

Chilton, W. 1843. 'Theory of Regular Gradation XLVIII' in: *The Oracle of Reason, or, Philosophy Vindicated* 2: 378-380.

Chrysostom. 'Homily XIV' in: Schaff, Ph. (ed.). 1889. *A Select Library of the Nicene and Post-Nicene Fathers of the Christian Church. Series I, Volume 11. Saint Chrysostom: Homilies on the Acts of the Apostles and the Epistle to the Romans*. T&T Clark, Edinburgh. Republished by Wm. B. Eerdmans, Grand Rapids: 784-804.

Chrysostom. 1986. *Saint John Chrysostom. Homilies on Genesis 1–17. Translated by Robert C. Hill*. The Catholic University of America Press. Washington D.C.

Clarke, A. 1833. *The New Testament of Our Lord and Saviour Jesus Christ. The Text Carefully Printed from the Most Correct Copies of the Present Authorised Version Including the Marginal Readings and Parallel Texts. With a Commentary and Critical Notes. Designed as a Help to a Better Understanding of the Sacred Writings. Volume II*. B. Waugh and T. Mason, New York.

Cohen, C. [1925]. *God and Evolution*. The Pioneer Press, London.

Cole, C.N. (ed.). 1791. *The Works of Soame Jenyns, Esq. In Two Volumes. Including Several Pieces never before Published. To Which Are Prefixed, Short Sketches of the History of the Author's Family and also of His Life. Vol. I*. P. Wogan et al., Dublin.

Coleridge, S.T. 1840. *Aids to Reflection, with a Preliminary Essay, by James Marsh. From the Fourth London Edition, with the Author's Last Corrections. Edited by Henry Nelson Coleridge*. Chauncey Goodrich, Burlington.

Collier, W. 1889. 'The Comparative Insensibility of Animals to Pain' in: *The Nineteenth Century: a Monthly Review*: 26 (152): 622-627.

Coolman, B.T., Coulter, D.M. (eds). 2013. *Trinity and Creation. A Selection of Works of Hugh, Richard, and Adam of St Victor*. New City Press, New York.

Crombie, A. 1829. *Natural Theology; or Essays on the Existence of Deity and of Providence, on the Immateriality of the Soul, and a Future State. In Two Volumes*. R. Hunter and T. Hookham, London.

Cudworth, R.C. 1845 [1678]. *The True Intellectual System of the Universe: wherein All the Reason and Philosophy of Atheism Is Confuted, and Its Impossibility Demonstrated. With a Treatise Concerning Eternal and Immutable Morality. To Which Are Added the Notes and Dissertations of Dr. J.L. Mosheim, Translated by John Harrison. In Three Volumes*. Thomas Tegg, London.

Cuvier, G. 1813. *Essay on the Theory of the Earth. Translated from the French of M. Cuvier, Perpetual Secretary of the French Institute, Professor and Administrator of the Museum of Natural History, &c. &c. By Robert Kerr. With Mineralogical Notes, and an Account of Cuvier's Geological Discoveries, by Professor Jameson*. William Blackwood, Edinburgh.

Cyril, 1839. 'The Catechetical Lectures of S. Cyril, Archbishop of Jerusalem, Translated, with Notes and Indices' in: *A Library of Fathers of the Holy Catholic Church, Anterior to the Division of the East and West. Translated by Members of the English Church, Volume II*. John Henry Parker, Oxford.

Dabney, R.L. 1873. 'The Caution against Anti-Christian Science Criticised by Dr. Woodrow' in: *Southern Presbyterian Review* 24: 539-586.

Dana, J.J., 1846. 'Article IV. On the Relations between Geology and Religion' in: Bidwell, W.H. (ed.). *Biblical Repository and Classical Review. Third Series*. Published by the Proprietor, New York: 297-320.

Dana, J.J. 1853. 'The Religion of Geology' in: *Bibliotheca Sacra* 10: 505-522.

Daniel, G. 1694. *A Voyage to the World of Cartesius. Written Originally in French. Translated into English by T. Taylor. The Second Edition*. Thomas Bennet, London.

Darwin to Hooker. 13 July 1856. *Darwin Correspondence Project*, "Letter no. 1924," accessed on 14 December 2021, https://www.darwinproject.ac.uk/letter/?docId=letters/DCP-LETT-1924.xml

Darwin, C. 2009 [1859]. *On the Origin of Species by Means of Natural Selection, or the Preservation of Favoured Races in the Struggle for Life.* Reprint of the first edition, edited with an Introduction by William Bynum. Penguin Books, London.

Darwin, C. 1860. *On the Origin of Species by Means of Natural Selection, or the Preservation of Favoured Races in the Struggle for Life. Fifth Thousand.* John Murray, London.

Darwin to Gray. 22 May 1860. *Darwin Correspondence Project,* "Letter no. 2814," accessed on 14 December 2021, https://www.darwinproject.ac.uk/letter/?docId=letters/DCP-LETT-2814.xml

Darwin to Gray. 11 December 1861. *Darwin Correspondence Project,* "Letter no. 3342," accessed on 14 December 2021, https://www.darwinproject.ac.uk/letter/?docId=letters/DCP-LETT-3342.xml

Darwin, C. 1871. *The Descent of Man, and Selection in Relation to Sex. In Two Volumes.* John Murray, London.

Darwin to Hyatt. 4 December 1872. *Darwin Correspondence Project,* "Letter no. 8658," accessed on 14 December 2021, https://www.darwinproject.ac.uk/letter/?docId=letters/DCP-LETT-8658.xml

Darwin, C. 1872. *The Origin of Species by Means of Natural Selection, or the Preservation of Favoured Races in the Struggle for Life. Sixth Edition, with Additions and Corrections (Eleventh Thousand.).* John Murray, London.

Darwin to Doedes. 2 April 1873. *Darwin Correspondence Project,* "Letter no. 8837," accessed on 14 December 2021, https://www.darwinproject.ac.uk/letter/?docId=letters/DCP-LETT-8837.xml

Darwin to Fordyce. 7 May 1879. *Darwin Correspondence Project,* "Letter no. 12041," accessed on 14 December 2021, https://www.darwinproject.ac.uk/letter/?docId=letters/DCP-LETT-12041.xml

Darwin, C. 2004 [1879]. *The Descent of Man, and Selection in Relation to Sex. With Illustrations.* John Murray, London. Reprint of the second edition with an introduction by James Moore and Adrian Desmond. Penguin Books, London.

Darwin, C. 1881. 'Mr. Darwin on Vivisection' in: *The British Medical Journal* 1 (23 April): 660.

Darwin, C. 1887. *The Life and Letters of Charles Darwin, Including an Autobiographical Chapter. Edited by His Son Francis Darwin. In Three Volumes:—Volume II.* John Murray, London.

Darwin, C. 1958 [1887]. *The Autobiography of Charles Darwin 1809–1882. With the Original Omissions Restored. Edited and with Appendix and Notes by His Grand-daughter Nora Barlow.* Collins, London.

Darwin, E. 1794. *Zoonomia; or, the Laws of Organic Life. Volume I.* J. Johnson, London.

Darwin, E. 1800. *Phytologia; or, the Philosophy of Agriculture and Gardening. With the Theory of Draining Morasses, and with an Improved Construction of the Drill Plough.* J. Johnson, London.

Darwin, E. 1803. *The Temple of Nature; or, the Origin of Society: a Poem, with Philosophical Notes.* J. Johnson, London.

Davies, J.H. 1854. 'A Short Sketch of the Literary Life of the Author' in: Pye Smith, J. 1854. *The Relation between the Holy Scriptures and Some Parts of Geological Science. Fifth Edition. With a Short Sketch of the Literary Life of the Author, by John Hamilton Davies.* Henry G. Bohn, London: ix-lxiii.

Dawson, J.W. 1860. *Archaia; or, Studies of the Cosmogony and Natural History of the Hebrew Scriptures.* B. Dawson & Son, Montreal.

Dawson, J.W. 1860. 'Review of "Darwin on the Origin of Species by Means of Natural Selection"' in: *Canadian Naturalist and Geologist* 5 (2): 100-120.

Dawson, J.W. 1877. *The Origin of the World, According to Revelation and Science.* Harper & Brothers, New York.

Dean, R. 1768. *An Essay on the Future Life of Brutes, Introduced with Observations upon Evil, Its Nature, and Origin. In Two Volumes.* G. Kearsly, London.

Deferrari, R.J. et al. (eds). 1957. *The Fathers of the Church. A New Translation, Volume 35.* Fathers of the Church, New York.

Deferrari, R.J. et al. (eds). 1961. *The Fathers of the Church. A New Translation, Volume 42.* Fathers of the Church, New York.

Derham, W. 1754 [1713]. *Demonstration of the Being and Attributes of God from His Works of Creation. Being the Substance of Sixteen Sermons Preached in St. Mary-le-Bow Church, London. At the Honourable Mr. Boyle's Lectures, in the Years 1711, and 1712. With Large Notes, and Many Curious Observations. The Twelfth Edition.* W. Innys and J. Richardson, London.

Descartes, R. 2008. *A Discourse on the Method. A New Translation by Ian Maclean.* Oxford University Press, Oxford.

Digby, K. 'Observations upon Religio Medici Occasionally Written by Sir Kenelm Digby' in: Browne, T. 1898 [1642]. *Religio Medici.* George Bell and Sons, London: 143-187.

Digby, K. 1645. *Two Treatises: In the One of Which, the Nature of Bodies; in the Other, the Nature of Mans Soule, Is Looked into: In Way of Discovery, of the Immortality of Reasonable Soules.* Iohn Williams, London.

Doedes to Darwin. 27 March 1873. *Darwin Correspondence Project*, "Letter no. 8828," accessed on 14 December 2021, https://www.darwinproject.ac.uk/letter/?docId=letters/DCP-LETT-8828.xml

Donne, J. 1639 [1610]. 'To Sr. Edward Herbert, Now Lord Herbert of Cherbury, Being at the Siege of Iulyers' in: *Poems, by J.D. With Elegies on the Authors Death*. John Marriot, London.

Draxe, T. 1613. *The Earnest of Our Inheritance: together with a Description of the New Heaven and the New Earth, and a Demonstration of the Glorious Resurrection of the Bodie in the Same Substance. Preached at Pauls Crosse the Second Day of August. 1612*. George Norton, London.

Drummond, W.H. 1838. *The Rights of Animals, and Man's Obligation to Treat Them with Humanity*. John Mardon, London.

Edwards, J. 1693. *A Discourse Concerning the Authority, Stile, and Perfection of the Books of the Old and New Testament. With a Continued Illustration of Several Difficult Texts of Scripture throughout the Whole Work*. Richard Wilkin, London.

Edwards, J. 1694. *A Discourse Concerning the Authority, Stile, and Perfection of the Books of the Old and New Testament. Vol. II. Wherein the Author's Former Undertaking Is further Prosecuted, viz. an Enquiry into Several Remarkable Texts Which Contain Some Difficulty in Them, with a Probable Resolution of Them*. Jonathan Robinson and John Wyat, London.

Edwards, J. 1695. *A Discourse Concerning the Authority, Stile, and Perfection of the Books of the Old and New Testament. Vol. III. Treating of the Excellency and Perfection of the Holy Scriptures. Wherein Are also Several Remarkable Texts Interpreted According to the Author's Particular Judgment*. Jonathan Robinson et al., London.

Edwards, J. 1696. *A Demonstration of the Existence and Providence of God, from the Contemplation of the Visible Structure of the Greater and the Lesser World. In Two Parts. The First, Shewing the Excellent Contrivance of the Heavens, Earth, Sea, &c. The Second, the Wonderful Formation of the Body of Man*. Jonathan Robinson and John Wyat, London.

Edwards, T. 1646. *The First and Second Part of Gangræna: or a Catalogue and Discovery of Many of the Errors, Heresies, Blasphemies and Pernicious Practices of the Sectaries of this Time, Vented and Acted in England in these Four Last Yeers*. Ralph Smit, London.

Elton, E. 1653 [1618]. *Three Excellent and Pious Treatises, viz. 1. The Complaint of a Sanctified Sinner. 2. The Triumph of a True Christian. 3. The Great Mystery of Godliness Opened. In Sundry Sermons upon the Whole Seventh, Eight, and Ninth Chapters of the Epistle to the Romans*. Christopher Meredith, London.

Emes, T. 1702. *Vindiciae Mentis. An Essay of the Being and Nature of Mind: wherein the Distinction of Mind and Body, the Substantiality, Personality, and Perfection of Mind Is Asserted; and the Original of Our*

Minds, Their Present, Separate, and Future State, Is Freely Enquir'd into, in Order to a More Certain Foundation for the Knowledge of God, and Our Selves, and the Clearing All Doubts and Objections that Have Been, or May Be Made Concerning the Life and Immortality of Our Souls. In a New Method, by a Gentleman. H. Walwyn, London.

Ensor, G. 1836. *Natural Theology: the Arguments of Paley, Brougham, and the Bridgewater Treatises on this Subject Examined and also the Doctrines of Brougham and the Immaterialists Respecting the Soul.* Richard Taylor, London.

Farrar, M.R.W. 1958. 'The Problem of Pain and Suffering. Part I: A Traditional View' in: *The Christian Graduate* 11: 51-54.

Fisher, A. (ed.). 1807. *The Pleasing Instructor; or, Entertaining Moralist: Consisting of Select Essays, Relations, Visions, and Allegories, Collected from the Most Eminent English Authors, to Which Are Prefixed New Thoughts on Education.* J. Brambles et al., London.

Flavel, J. 1824 [1674]. *Husbandry Spiritualized; or the Heavenly Use of Earthly Things, in Which Hushbandmen Are Directed to an Excellent Improvement of Their Common Employments. Whereunto Are Added, Occasional Meditations upon Birds, Beasts, Trees, Flowers &c. Also, the Touchstone of Sincerity. And Extracts from a Token for Mourners.* J.A. Boswell, Middletown.

Flint, R. 1877. *Theism Being the Baird Lecture for 1876.* William Blackwood and Sons, Edinburgh.

Franck, R. 1687. *A Philosophical Treatise of the Original and Production of Things. Writ in America in a Time of Solitudes.* John Gain, London.

Fry, E. 1872. *Darwinism and Theology. Reprinted with Slight Alterations from the 'Spectator' of the 7th, 14th, and 21st September, 1872.* Henry Sotheran and Co., London.

Gibbons, N. 1601. *Questions and Disputations Concerning the Holy Scripture wherein Are Contained, Briefe, Faithfull and Sound Expositions of the Most Difficult and Hardest Places: Approued by the Testimony of the Scriptures Themselues: Fully Correspondent to the Analogie of Faith, and the Consent of the Church of God; Conferred with the Iudgment of the Fathers of the Church, and Interpreters of the Scripture, Nevv and Old. Wherein also the Euerlasting Truth of the Word of God Is Freed from the Errors and Slaunders of Atheists, Papists, Philosophers, and All Heretikes. The First Part of the First Tome.* Felix Kyngston, London.

Gildea, W.L., Alexander, S., Romanes, G.J. 1889–1890. 'Symposium: Is there Evidence of Design in Nature?' in: *Proceedings of the Aristotelian Society* 1 (3): 49-76.

Gillespie, W.H. 1859. *The Theology of Geologists as Exemplified in the Cases of the Late Hugh Miller, and Others.* Adam and Charles Black, Edinburgh.

Gillett, E.H. 1874. *God in Human Thought; or, Natural Theology Traced in Literature, Ancient and Modern, to the Time of Bishop Butler. With a Closing Chapter on the Moral System, and an English Bibliography, from Spenser to Butler. In Two Volumes.* Scribner, Armstrong & Co., New York.

Gisborne, T. 1818. *The Testimony of Natural Theology to Christianity.* M. Thomas, Philadelphia.

Glanvill, J. 1676. *Essays on Several Important Subjects in Philosophy and Religion.* John Baker, London.

Gloag, P.J. 1859. *The Primeval World: a Treatise on the Relations of Geology to Theology.* T&T Clark, Edinburgh.

Godwin, W. 1798. *Enquiry Concerning Political Justice, and Its Influence on Morals and Happiness. The Third Edition Corrected. In Two Volumes. Vol. I.* G.G. and J. Robinson, London.

Goodman, G. 1616. *The Fall of Man, or the Corrvption of Natvre, Proved by the Light of our Naturall Reason. Which Being the First Grovnd and Occasion of Ovr Christian Faith and Religion, May Likewise Serve for the First Step and Degree of the Naturall Mans Conuersion. First Preached in a Sermon, since Enlarged, Reduced to the Forme of a Treatise, and Dedicated to the Queenes Most Excellent Maiestie.* Felix Kyngston, London.

Goodman, G. 1622. *The Creatvres Praysing God: or, the Religion of Dumbe Creatures. An Example and Argument, for the Stirring vp of Our Deuotion, and for the Confusion of Atheisme. Benedicite Omnia Opera Domini Domino; Laudate & Superexaltate Eum in Secula.* Felik Kingston, London.

Gore, C. (ed.). 1890. *Lux Mundi. A Series of Studies in the Religion of the Incarnation. Tenth Edition.* John Murray, London.

Gosse, P.H. 1857. *Omphalos: an Attempt to Untie the Geological Knot.* John van Voorst, London.

Gott, S. 1670. *The Divine History of the Genesis of the World Explicated & Illustrated.* Henry Eversden, London.

Granger, J. 1774. *An Apology for the Brute Creation, or Abuse of Animals Censured; in a Sermon on Proverbs xii. 10. Preached in the Parish Church of Shiplake, in Oxfordshire, October 18, 1772. The Third Edition.* T. Davies, London.

Gray, A. 1860. 'The Origin of Species by Means of Natural Selection' in: *American Journal of Science and Arts, March 1860.* Republished in Gray, A. 1888. *Darwiniana: Essays and Reviews Pertaining to Darwinism.* D. Appleton and Company, New York: 9-61.

Gray, A. 1860. 'Natural Selection not Inconsistent with Natural Theology' in: *Atlantic Monthly for July, August, and October, 1860.* Republished in Gray, A. 1888. *Darwiniana: Essays and Reviews Pertaining to Darwinism.* D. Appleton and Company, New York: 83-128.

Gray to Darwin. 14 April 1871, *Darwin Correspondence Project,* "Letter no. 7683," accessed on 14 December 2021, https://www.darwinproject.ac.uk/letter/?docId=letters/DCP-LETT-7683.xml

Gray, A. 1880. *Natural Science and Religion. Two Lectures Delivered to the Theological School of Yale College.* Charles Scribner's Sons, New York.

Gray, A. 1888 [1876]. 'Evolutionary Teleology' in: *Darwiniana: Essays and Reviews Pertaining to Darwinism.* D. Appleton and Company, New York: 354-390.

Gray, A. 1888. *Darwiniana: Essays and Reviews Pertaining to Darwinism.* D. Appleton and Company, New York.

Gregory of Nyssa. 'On the Making of Man.' in: Schaff, Ph. (ed.). 1892. *Nicene and Post-Nicene Fathers Series II, Volume 5. Gregory of Nyssa.* T&T Clark, Edinburgh. Republished by Wm. B. Eerdmans, Grand Rapids: 714-795.

Gregory of Nyssa. 'On the Soul and the Resurrection' in: Schaff, Ph. (ed.). 1892. *Nicene and Post-Nicene Fathers Series II, Volume 5. Gregory of Nyssa.* T&T Clark, Edinburgh. Republished by Wm. B. Eerdmans, Grand Rapids: 799-870.

Griffith-Jones, E. 1925. *Providence—Divine and Human. A Study of the World-Order in the Light of Modern Thought. Volume I. Some Problems of Divine Providence.* Hodder and Stoughton, London.

Gunning Jr, J.H. 1929. *Blikken in de Openbaring. Tweede Onveranderde Druk.* J.M. Bredée, Rotterdam.

Hakewill, G. 1627. *An Apologie of the Povver and Prouidence of God in the Gouerment of the World. Or An Examination and Censvre of the Common Errour Tovching Natvres Perpetvall and Vniuersall Decay Diuided into Fovre Books.* Iohn Lichfield and William Turner, Oxford.

Hakewill, G. 1635. *An Apologie or Declaration of the Povver and Providence of God in the Government of the World. Consisting in an Examination and Censure of the Common Errovr Tovching Natvres Perpetuall and Universall Decay, Divided into Six Bookes. The Third Edition Revised, and in Sundry Passages and Whole Sections Augmented by the Authour; Besides the Addition of Two Entire Bookes not Formerly Published.* William Turner, Oxford.

Hale, M. 1677. *The Primitive Origination of Mankind, Considered and Examined According to the Light of Nature.* William Shrowsbery, London.

Hamilton, J. 1877. *Animal Futurity: a Plea for the Immortality of the Brutes.* C. Aitchison, Belfast.

Hanna, W. 'Memorials of the Death and Character of Hugh Miller, with an Account of His Funeral Obsequies' in: Miller, H. 1867 [1857]. *The Testimony of the Rocks; or, Geology in Its Bearings on the Two Theologies, Natural and Revealed...With Memorials of the Death and Character of the Author.* Gould and Lincoln, Boston.

Hartley, D. 1749. *Observations on Man, His Frame, His Duty, And His Expectations. In Two Parts.* James Leake and Wm. Frederick, London. Republished in 1966 with an Introduction by Theodore L. Huguelet. Scholars' Facsimiles & Reprints, Gainesville.

Hildrop, J. 1742. *Free Thoughts upon the Brute-Creation: or, an Examination of Father Bougeant's Philosophical Amusement, &c. In Two Letters to a Lady.* R. Minors, London.

Hill, J. 1752. *Essays in Natural History and Philosophy Containing a Series of Discoveries, by the Assistance of Microscopes.* J. Whiston et al., London.

Hitchcock, E. 1854. *The Religion of Geology and Its Connected Sciences. Ninth Thousand.* Phillips, Sampson, and Company, Boston.

Hobbes, T. 1651. *Leviathan or the Matter, Forme, & Power of a Commonwealth Ecclesiasticall and Civill.* Andrew Crooke, London.

Hodges, T. 1675. *The Creatures Goodness, as They Came out of God's Hands, and the Good Mans Mercy to the Brute Creatures, Which God Hath Put under His Feet. In Two Sermons, the First Preached before the University of Oxford, the Second at the Lecture at Brackley.* Tho. Parkhurst, London.

D'Holbach, P.H. 1795. *Common Sense: or, Natural Ideas Opposed to Supernatural. Translated from the French.* n.p., New York.

D'Holbach, P.H. 1889 [1770]. *The System of Nature: or, Laws of the Moral and Physical World. A New and Improved Edition, with Notes by Diderot. Translated, for the First Time, by H.D. Robinson. Two Volumes in One.* J.P. Mendum, Boston.

Hooke, R. 1705. *The Posthumous Works of Robert Hooke Containing His Cutlerian Lectures and Other Discourses, Read at the Meetings of the Illustrious Royal Society...Illustrated with Sculptures. To these Discourses Is Prefixt the Author's Life, Giving an Account of His Studies and Employments, with an Enumeration of the Many Experiments, Instruments, Contrivances and Inventions, by Him Made and Produc'd as Curator of Experiments to the Royal Society.* Richard Waller, London.

Hume, D., 1907 [1779]. *Dialogues Concerning Natural Religion. Reprinted with an Introduction by Bruce M'Ewen.* William Blackwood and Sons, Edinburgh.

Hutton, J. 1959 [1795]. *Theory of the Earth. With Proofs and Illustrations.* Hafner Publishing Co., New York. Reprinted, originally published by Cadell Junior et al., London.

Huxley, T.H. 1895. *Collected Essays. Volume IX. Evolution & Ethics and Other Essays.* MacMillan and Co., London

Huxley, T.H. 'The Struggle for Existence in Human Society' in: Huxley, T.H. 1895. *Collected Essays. Volume IX. Evolution & Ethics and Other Essays.* MacMillan and Co., London: 195-236.

Huxley, L. 1901. *Life and Letters of Thomas Henry Huxley. By His Son Leonard Huxley. In Two Volumes. Vol II.* D. Appleton and Company, New York.

Illingworth, R.J. 'The Problem of Pain: Its Bearing on Faith in God' in: Gore, C. (ed.). 1890. *Lux Mundi. A Series of Studies in the Religion of the Incarnation. Tenth Edition.* John Murray, London: 111-126.

Ingersoll, R.G. 1878. *The Gods and Other Lectures.* C.P. Farrell, Washington, D.C.

Irenaeus. 'Against Heresies' in: Schaff, Ph. (ed.). 1885. *Ante-Nicene Fathers. Volume 1. The Apostolic Fathers, Justin Martyr, Irenaeus.* Christian Classics Ethereal Library, Grand Rapids: 833-1391.

Irenaeus. 'Proof of the Apostolic Preaching, Translated and Annotated by Joseph P. Smith' in: Quasten, J., Plumpe, J.C. (eds). 1952. *Ancient Christian Writers. The Works of the Fathers in Translation, No. 16.* The Newman Press, Westminster.

Iverach, J. 1894. *Christianity and Evolution.* Thomas Whittaker, New York.

Jago, R. 'An Elegy on a Blackbird' in: Fisher, A. (ed.). 1807. *The Pleasing Instructor; or, Entertaining Moralist: Consisting of Select Essays, Relations, Visions, and Allegories, Collected from the Most Eminent English Authors, to Which Are Prefixed New Thoughts on Education.* J. Brambles et al., London: 321-323.

Jameson, R. 'Preface' in: Cuvier, G. 1813. *Essay on the Theory of the Earth. Translated from the French of M. Cuvier, Perpetual Secretary of the French Institute, Professor and Administrator of the Museum of Natural History &c. &c. by Robert Kerr. With Mineralogical Notes, and an Account of Cuvier's Geological Discoveries by Professor Jameson.* William Blackwood, Edinburgh: v-ix.

[Jenyns, S.] 1756. Untitled Letter in: *The Gentleman's Magazine, and Historical Chronicle. Volume XXVI. For the Year M.DCC.LVI*: 65-67.

[Jenyns, S.] 1761. *A Free Inquiry into the Nature and Origin of Evil. In Six Letters to—. The Fourth Edition. With an Additional Preface, and Some Explanatory Notes.* R. and J. Dodsley, London.

Jenyns, S. 1782. *Disquisitions on Several Subjects.* J. Dodsley, London.

Johnston, J. 1657. *An History of the Wonderful Things of Nature: Set Forth in Ten Severall Classes. Wherein Are Contained I. The Wonders of the Heavens. II. Of the Elements. III. Of Meteors. IV. Of Minerals. V. Of Plants. VI. Of Birds. VII. Of Four-footed Beasts. VIII. Of Insects, and Things Wanting Blood. IX. Of Fishes. X. Of Man. Written by Johannes Jonstonus, and now Rendred into English by a Person of Quality.* John Streater, London.

Kant, I. 1800. *Metaphysische Anfangsgründe der Tugendlehre. Zweite Auflage.* Ludwig Christian Kehr, Kreuznach.

King, D. 1850. *The Principles of Geology Explained, and Viewed in Their Relations to Revealed and Natural Religion. With Notes and an Appendix by John Scouler.* Johnstone and Hunter, London.

King, W. 1731. *An Essay on the Origin of Evil. Translated from the Latin, with Large Notes; Tending to Explain and Vindicate Some of the Author's Principles against the Objections of Bayle, Leibnitz, the Author of a Philosophical Enquiry Concerning Human Liberty; and Others. To Which Is Prefix'd a Dissertation Concerning the Fundamental Principle and Immediate Criterion of Virtue as also, the Obligation to, and Approbation of It. With Some Account of the Origin of the Passions and Affections.* Law, E. (ed.). W. Thurlbourn, Cambridge.

Kingsley to Darwin. 18 November 1859. *Darwin Correspondence Project*, "Letter no. 2534," accessed on 14 December 2021, https://www.darwinproject.ac.uk/letter/?docId=letters/DCP-LETT-2534.xml

Kingsley, C. 1871. 'The Natural Theology of the Future' in: *MacMillan's Magazine* 23: 370-378.

Kirby, W. 1835. *The Bridgewater Treatises on the Power Wisdom and Goodness of God as Manifested in the Creation. Treatise VII. On the History Habits and Instincts of Animals. In Two Volumes.* William Pickering, London.

Kirby, W., Spence, W. 1818. *An Introduction to Entomology: or Elements of the Natural History of Insects: with Plates. Third Edition. Volume I.* Longman et al., London.

Lactantius. 'The Divine Institutes. Books I-VII. Translated by Mary Francis McDonald' in: Dressler, H. et al. (eds). 1964. *The Fathers of the Church. A New Translation Volume 49.* The Catholic University of America Press, Washington, D.C.

LeConte, J. 1888. *Evolution and Its Relation to Religious Thought.* D. Appleton and Company, New York.

Leibniz, G.W. 1951 [1710]. *Theodicy: Essays on the Goodness of God, the Freedom of Man, and the Origin of Evil. Edited with an Introduction by Austin Farrer. Translated by E.M. Huggard from C.J. Gerhardt's Edition of the Collected Philosophical Works, 1875-90*. Routledge & Kegan Paul, London.

Lewis, C.S. 1986 [1940]. *The Problem of Pain*. Collins, Glasgow.

Locke J. 1836 [1689]. *An Essay Concerning Human Understanding. Twenty-Seventh Edition, with the Author's Last Additions and Corrections. Complete in One Volume, with Notes and Illustrations, and an Analysis of Mr. Locke's Doctrine of Ideas*. T. Tegg and Son, London.

Lordat, M. 1854. 'Mental Dynamics in Relation to the Science of Medicine. A Course of Lectures Delivered by M. Lordat, Professor of Physiology in the University of Montpellier. Arranged and Translated by S. Templeman Speer. Lecture V.' in: *The Journal of Psychological Medicine and Mental Pathology* 7: 252-263.

Luther, M. 1535. *Ein Christlicher Schöner Trost inn Allerley Leiden und Trübsal / Aus dem Achten Cap. Zun Römern / Sampt der Auslegung des Euangelion Auff den Vierden Sontag nach Trinitatis / Gepredigt durch D. Mart. Luth*. Georg Rhau, Wittemberg.

Luther, M. in: Pelikan, J. (ed.). 1958. *Luther's Works. Volume 1. Lectures on Genesis. Chapters 1-5*. Concordia Publishing House, St. Louis.

Luther, M. in: Pelikan, J., Oswald, H.C. (eds). 1969. *Luther's Works. Volume 16. Lectures on Isaiah. Chapters 1-39*. Concordia Publishing House, St. Louis.

Luther, M. in: Oswald, H.C. (ed.). 1969. *Luther's Works. Volume 17. Lectures on Isaiah. Chapters 40-66*. Concordia Publishing House, St. Louis.

Luther, M. in: Oswald, H.C. (ed.). 1972. *Luther's Works. Volume 25. Lectures on Romans. Glosses and Scholia*. Concordia Publishing House, St. Louis.

Luther, M. in: Oswald, H.C. (ed.). 1976. *Luther's Works. Volume 11. First Lectures on the Psalms II. Psalms 76-126*. Concordia Publishing House, St. Louis.

Lyell, C. 1832. *Principles of Geology, Being an Attempt to Explain the Former Changes of the Earth's Surface, by Reference to Causes now in Operation. Volume the Second*. John Murray, London.

Macaulay, T.B. 1849. *The History of England from the Accession of James the Second. Vol. I*. Bernhard Tauchnitz, Leipzig.

Maerlant, J. van. 1952. *Het Boek der Natuur. Samenstelling en Vertaling door P. Burger*. Querido, Amsterdam.

Malebranche, N. de. 1700. *Father Malebranche His Treatise Concerning the Search after Truth. The Whole Work Complete. To Which Is Added* the Author's Treatise of Nature and Grace Being a Consequence of the Principles Contained in the Search. Together with His Answer to the Animadversions upon the First Volume: His Defence against the Accusations of Monsieur de la Ville, &c. Relating to the Same Subject. All Translated by T. Taylor. The Second Edition, Corrected with Great Exactness. With the Addition, of a Short Discourse upon Light and Colours, by the Same Author. Communicated in Manuscript to a Person of Quality in England: and never before Printed in Any Language. Thomas Bennet et al., London.

Mandeville, B. 1732. *An Enquiry into the Origin of Honour, and the Usefulness of Christianity in War*. John Brotherton, London.

Mandeville, B. 1924 [1729, 1732]. *The Fable of the Bees: or, Private Vices, Publick Benefits. With a Commentary Critical, Historical, and Explanatory by F.B. Kaye. Two Volumes*. Clarendon Press, Oxford.

Mandeville, B. 1962 [1795] *The Fable of the Bees or Private Vices, Publick Benefits. Newly Edited, with an Introduction by Irwin Primer*. Capricorn Books, New York.

Mantell, G. 1838. *The Wonders of Geology. Vol. II*. Relfe and Fletcher, London.

Mantell, G.A. 1839. *The Wonders of Geology; Edited by Professor Silliman, with an Introduction. In Two Volumes. Vol. I. First American, from the Third London Edition*. A.H. Maltby, Newhaven.

McCosh, J. 1875. *The Scottish Philosophy. Biographical, Expository, Critical from Hutcheson to Hamilton*. MacMillan and Co., London.

McCosh, J. 1890. *The Religious Aspect of Evolution. Enlarged and Improved Edition*. Charles Scribner's Sons, New York.

Mill, J.S. 1874. *Nature, the Utility of Religion and Theism. Second Edition*. Longmans et al., London.

Miller, H. 1851. *The Old Red Sandstone; or, New Walks in an Old Field. Illustrated with Numerous Engravings. From the Fourth London Edition*. Gould and Lincoln, Boston.

Miller, H. 1854. *The Two Records: the Mosaic and the Geological. A Lecture Delivered before the Young Mens' Christian Association, in Exeter Hall*. Gould and Lincoln, Boston.

Miller, H. 1858. *The Foot-Prints of the Creator: or, the Asterolepis of Stromness. From the Third London Edition. With a Memoir of the Author by Louis Agassiz*. Gould and Lincoln, Boston.

Miller, H. 1865. *The Witness Papers. The Headship of Christ, and the Rights of the Christian People, a Collection of Essays, Historical and Descriptive Sketches, and Personal Portraitures. With the Author's Celebrated Letter to Lord Brougham. Edited, with a Preface by Peter Bayne*. Gould and Lincoln, Boston.

Miller, H. 1867 [1856]. *The Testimony of the Rocks; or, Geology in Its Bearings on the Two Theologies, Natural and Revealed... With Memorials of the Death and Character of the Author.* Gould and Lincoln, Boston.

Milton, J. 1667. *Paradise Lost. A Poem Written in Ten Books.* Peter Parker, London.

Mivart, St.G. 1871. *On the Genesis of Species.* MacMillan and Co., London.

Molenaar, D. 1852. *De Heidelbergsche Catechismus in Leerredenen.* J.W. Swaan, Arnhem.

Montaigne, M. 1885 [1580, 1603]. *The Essayes of Michael Lord of Montaigne Translated by John Florio. Edited with an Introduction and a Glossary by Henry Morley.* George Routledge and Sons, London.

Moore, A. 'The Christian Doctrine of God' in: Gore, C. (ed.). 1890. *Lux Mundi. A Series of Studies in the Religion of the Incarnation. Tenth Edition.* John Murray, London: 57-109.

Moore, A.L. 1905 [1889]. *Science and the Faith. Essays on Apologetic Subjects. With an Introduction...Sixth Edition.* Kegan Paul et al., London.

More, H. 1653. *Conjectura Cabbalistica or, a Conjectural Essay of Interpreting the Minde of Moses, According to a Threefold Cabbala: viz. Literal, Philosophical, Mystical, or, Divinely Moral.* William Morden, Cambridge.

More, H. 1655. *An Antidote against Atheism or, an Appeal to the Naturall Faculties of the Minde of Man, whether there Be Not a God... The Second Edition Corrected and Enlarged: with an Appendix thereunto Annexed.* William Morden, Cambridge.

More, H. 1743 [1668]. *Divine Dialogues, Containing Disquisitions Concerning the Attributes and Providence of God. In Three Volumes.* Robert Foulis, Glasgow.

Morris, F.O. 1861. *Records of Animal Sagacity and Character. With a Preface on the Future Existence of the Animal Creation.* Longman et al., London.

Morris, F.O. 1869. *Difficulties of Darwinism. Read before the British Association at Norwich and Exeter in 1868 and 1869. With a Preface and a Correspondence with Professor Huxley.* Longmans et al., London.

Morris, F.O. 1882. *All the Articles of the Darwin Faith. Re-redoubled Edition.* William Poole, London.

Morris, M.C.F. 1897. *Francis Orpen Morris. A Memoir by His Son the Rev. M.C.F. Morris, B.C.L., M.A. Rector of Nunburnholme, Yorkshire. With Portrait and Illustrations.* John C. Nimmo, London.

Newman, J.H. 1862 [1849]. *Discourses Addressed to Mixed Congregations. Third Edition.* James Duffy, Dublin.

Newman, J.H. 1868. 'To J. Walker of Scarborough' in: *The Letters and Diaries of John Henry Newman. Electronic Edition. Volume XXIV: A Grammar of Assent (January 1868 to December 1869)*: 77-78.

Nieuwentijt, B. 1715. *Het Regt Gebruik der Wereltbeschouwingen ter Overtuiginge van Ongodisten en Ongelovigen Aangetoont...Met Kopere Platen*. Weduwe J. Wolters en J. Pauli, Amsterdam.

Nieuwentyt. B. 1719. *The Religious Philosopher: or, the Right Use of Contemplating the Works of the Creator. I. In the Wonderful Structure of Animal Bodies, and in Particular Man. II. In the no Less Wonderful and Wise Formation of the Elements. and Their Various Effects upon Animal and Vegetable Bodies. And, III. In the Most Amazing Structure of the Heavens, with All Its Furnitures. Design'd for the Conviction of Atheists and Infidels. Vol. II. Throughout Which, All the Late Discoveries in Anatomy, Philosophy and Astronomy, together with the Various Experiments Made Use of to Illustrate the Same, are most Copiously Handled by that Learned Mathematician, Dr. Nieuwentyt. Translated from the Original, by John Chamberlayne*. J. Senex and W. Taylor, London.

Norris, J. 1704. *An Essay towards the Theory of the Ideal or Intelligible World. Being the Relative Part of It. Wherein the Intelligible World is Consider'd with Relation to Humane Understanding. Whereof some Account Is here Attempted and Proposed. Part II*. S. Manship, London.

Origen. 'De Principiis, Chapter VIII. On the Angels' in: Schaff, Ph. (ed.). 1885. *Ante-Nicene Fathers. Volume 4. Fathers of the Third Century: Tertullian, Part Fourth; Minucius Felix; Commodian; Origen, Parts First and Seconds*. Republished by the Christian Classics Ethereal Library, Grand Rapids: 610-613 (I.viii.4).

Origen. 1965. *Contra Celsum. Translated with an Introduction & Notes by Henry Chadwick*. Cambridge University Press, Cambridge.

Oswald, H.C. (ed.). 1969. *Luther's Works. Volume 17. Lectures on Isaiah 40-66*. Concordia Publishing House, St. Louis.

Oswald, H.C. (ed.). 1972 [1540]. *Luther's Works. Volume 25. Lectures on Romans. Glosses and Scholia*. Concordia Publishing House, St. Louis.

Oswald, H.C. (ed.). 1976. *Luther's Works. Volume 11. First Lectures on the Psalms II. Psalms 76-126*. Concordia Publishing House, St. Louis.

Overton, R. 1655. *Man Wholly Mortal; or, a Treatise wherein 'T is Proved, both Theologically and Philosophically, that as Whole Man Sinned, so Whole Man Died; contrary to that Common Distinction of Soul and Body: and that the Present Going of the Soul into Heaven or Hell Is a Meer Fiction: and that at the Resurrection Is the Beginning of Our Immortality; and then Actual Condemnation and Salvation, and not before. With Doubts and Objections Answered and Resolved, both by*

Scripture and Reason, Discovering the Multitude of Blasphemies and Absurdities that Arise from the Fancie of the Soul. Also, Divers Other Mysteries; as, of Heaven, Hell, the Extent of the Resurrection, the New Creation, &c. Opened, and Presented to the Tryal of Better Judgments. The Second Edition, by the Author Corrected and Enlarged. n.p., London.

Paley, W. 1802. *Natural Theology: or, Evidences of the Existence and Attributes of the Deity, Collected from the Appearances of Nature.* John Morgan, Philadelphia.

Palgrave, F. 1844. *Truths and Fictions of the Middle Ages. The Merchant and the Friar. Second Edition, Revised and Corrected.* John W. Parker, London.

Parker, B. 1734. *Philosophical Meditations with Divine Inferences.* Printed for the Author, London.

P[arker], B. [1745?]. *An Essay Proving the Immateriality and Immortality of the Spirits of the Whole Animal Creation; both from Scripture and Reason: wherein the Objections Generally Made to this Doctrine Are Distinctly Answer'd. The State of Spirits between Death and the Resurrection Consider'd: and, the Nature of Spiritual Bodies after the Resurrection, Inquired into. The Second Edition.* Printed for the Author, London.

Parker, B. 1745. *A Survey of the Six Days Works of the Creation: Philosophically Proving the Truth of the Account Thereof, as Deliver'd by Moses in the First Chapter of Genesis.* Printed for the Author, London.

Parkinson, J. 1820. *Organic Remains of a Former World. An Examination of the Mineralized Remains of the Vegetables and Animals of the Antediluvian World; Generally Termed Extraneous Fossils. In Three Volumes.* Sherwood et al., London.

Pascal, B. 1901. *The Thoughts of Blaise Pascal. Translated from the Text of M. Auguste Molinier by C. Kegan Paul.* George Bell and Sons, London.

Pelikan, J. (ed.). 1958. *Luther's Works Volume 1. Lectures on Genesis. Chapters 1-5.* Concordia Publishing House, St. Louis.

Pelikan, J. 1961. 'Cosmos and Creation: Science and Theology in Reformation Thought' in: *Proceedings of the American Philosophical Society* 105: 464-469.

Pelikan, J., Oswald, H.C. (eds). 1969. *Luther's Works. Volume 16. Lectures on Isaiah. Chapters 1-39.* Concordia Publishing House, St. Louis.

Pember, G.H. 1889. *Earth's Earliest Ages; and Their Connection with Modern Spiritualism and Theosophy. Fifth Edition.* Hodder and Stoughton, London.

Perkins, W. 1606. *The Whole Treatise of the Cases of Conscience Distinguished into Three Bookes: the First whereof Is Revised and*

Corrected in Sundrie Places, and the Other Two Annexed. Taught and Deliuered by M. W. Perkins in His Holy-day Lectures, Carefully Examined by His Owne Briefes, and now Published together for the Common Good, by T. Pickering Bachelour of Diuinity. Whereunto Is Adioyned a Twofold Table: One of the Heads and Number of the Questions Propounded and Resolued; Another of the Principall Texts of Scripture vvhich Are either Explaned, or Vindicated from Corrupt Interpretation. Printed by Iohn Legat, Printer to the University of Cambridge, [Cambridge].

[Peyrère, I. la]. 1661. *Praeadamieten of Oefening over het 12, 13, en 14. Vers des Vijfden Capittels van den Brief des Apostels Pauli tot den Romeynen, waer door Geleert Wort: Datter Menschen voor Adam Geweest Zijn.* [Johannes Janssonius, Amsterdam].

Physicus [Romanes, G.J.] 1878. *A Candid Examination of Theism.* Trübner & Co., London.

Plotinus. 1956. *The Enneads. Translated by Stephen MacKenna, Second Edition Revised by B.S. Page. With a Foreword by Professor E.R. Dodds and an Introduction by Professor Paul Henry.* Faber and Faber, London.

Pope, A. 1713. 'On Cruelty to the Brute Creation' in: *The Guardian,* Tuesday May 21: 90.

Pope, A. 1881 [1734]. *Essay on Man. Edited by Mark Pattison. Sixth Edition.* Clarendon Press, Oxford.

Porphyry. 1655. *Porphyrii Philosophi Pythagorici. De Abstinentia ab Animalibus Necandis. Libri Quatuor.* Lucas Holstenius, Hamburg.

Pratt, J.H. 1859. *Scripture and Science not at Variance: with Remarks on the Historical Character, Plenary Inspiration, and Surpassing Importance of the Earlier Chapters of Genesis.* Thomas Hatchard, London.

Pratt, S.J. 1783. *Liberal Opinions, or, the History of Benignus, a New Edition, Corrected. Volume II.* G. Robinson and J. Bew, London.

Price, G.E. McCready. 1902. *Outlines of Modern Christianity and Modern Science.* Pacific Press Publishing Company, Oakland.

Priestly, J. 1777. *Disquisitions Relating to Matter and Spirit. To Which is Added, the History of the Philosophical Doctrine Concerning the Origin of the Soul, and the Nature of Matter; with Its Influence on Christianity, Especially with Respect to the Doctrine of the Pre-existence of Christ.* J. Johnson, London.

Priestly, J. 1794 [1782]. *Institutes of Natural and Revealed Religion. In Two Volumes. To Which Is Prefixed, an Essay on the Best Method of Communicating Religious Knowledge to the Members of Christian Societies. The Third Edition. Volume I.* n.p., London.

Primatt, H. 1834 [1776]. *The Duty of Mercy, and the Sin of Cruelty to Brute Animals.* T. Constable, Edinburgh.

Proba. '*Cento Vergilianus de Laudibus Christi.* Quoted in Latin and Translated in English' in: Evans, J.M. 1968. *Paradise Lost and the Genesis Tradition.* Clarendon Press, Oxford: 116-118.

Prout, W. 1834. *The Bridgewater Treatises on the Power Wisdom and Goodness of God as Manifested in the Creation. Treatise VIII. Chemistry Meteorology and the Function of Digestion Considered with Reference to Natural Theology.* William Pickering, London.

Pye Smith, J., 1837. 'Suggestions on the Science of Geology, in Answer to the Question of T.K.' in: *The Congregational Magazine for the Year 1837*: 765-766.

Pye Smith, J. 1854. *The Relation between the Holy Scriptures and Some Parts of Geological Science. Fifth Edition. With a Short Sketch of the Literary Life of the Author, by John Hamilton Davies.* Henry G. Bohn, London.

Quasten, J., Plumpe, J.C. (eds). 1952. *Ancient Christian Writers. The Works of the Fathers in Translation No. 16.* The Newman Press, Westminster.

Quasten, J., Plumpe, J.C. (eds). 1955. *Ancient Christian Writers. The Works of the Fathers in Translation No. 22.* The Newman Press, Westminster.

Ramm, B. 1954. *The Christian View of Science and Scripture.* Wm. B. Eerdmans, Grand Rapids.

Ramsay, Chevalier, A.M. 1748. *The Philosophical Principles of Natural and Revealed Religion. Unfolded in a Geometrical Order.* Robert Foulis, Glasgow; *Idem, Part Second.* Robert and Andrew Foulis, Glasgow.

Ray, J. 1722 [1691]. *The Wisdom of God Manifested in the Works of the Creation. In Two Parts. Viz. The Heavenly Bodies, Elements, Meteors, Fossils, Vegetables, Animals, (Beasts, Birds, Fishes, and Insects); more particularly in the Body of the Earth, It's Figure, Motion, and Consistency; and in the Admirable Structure of the Bodies of Man, and Other Animals ; as also in Their Generation, &c. With Answers to Some Objections. The Eighth Edition, Corrected.* William and John Innys, London.

Ray, J. 1713. *Three Physico-Theological Discourses, Concerning I. the Primitive Chaos, and Creation of the World. II. the General Deluge, Its Causes and Effects. III. The Dissolution of the World and Future Conflagration…The Third Edition, Illustrated with Copper–Plates, and Much More Enlarged than the Former Editions, from the Author's own MSS.* William Innys, London.

Reade to Darwin. 31 January 1871. *Darwin Correspondence Project*, "Letter no. 7468," accessed on 14 December 2021, https://www.darwinproject.ac.uk/letter/?docId=letters/DCP-LETT-7468.xml

Reade, W. 1872. *The Martyrdom of Man*. Trübner & Co., London.

Rehwinkel, A.M. 1951. *The Flood in the Light of the Bible, Geology, and Archaeology*. Concordia Publishing House, St. Louis.

Report of the Royal Commission on the Practice of Subjecting Live Animals to Experiments for Scientific Purposes; with Minutes of Evidence and Appendix. Presented to Both Houses of Parliament by Command of Her Majesty. 1876. George Edward Eyre and William Spottiswoode, London.

Roberts, A., Donaldson, J. (eds). 1871. *Ante-Nicene Christian Library. Translations of the Writings of the Fathers Down to A.D. 325. Volume XIX*. T&T Clark, Edinburgh.

Robinson, T. 1709. *An Essay towards a Natural History of Westmorland and Cumberland. Wherein an Account Is Given of Their Several Mineral and Surface Productions, with Some Directions how to Discover Minerals by the External and Adjacent Strata and Upper Covers, &c. To Which Is Annexed, a Vindication of the Philosophical and Theological Paraphrase of the Mosaick System of the Creation, &c*. W. Freeman, London.

Roget, P.M. 1836. *The Bridgewater Treatises on the Power, Wisdom, and Goodness of God, as Manifested in the Creation. Treatise V. Animal and Vegetable Physiology, Considered with Reference to Natural Theology. In Two Volumes. Volume II*. Carey et al., Philadelphia.

Romanes, G.J. 1892. *Darwin, and after Darwin. An Exposition of the Darwinian Theory and a Discussion of Post-Darwinian Questions. I. The Darwinian Theory*. Longmans et al., London.

Romanes, G.J. 1895. *Thoughts on Religion. Edited by Charles Gore*. The Open Court Publishing Company, Chicago.

Romanes, G.J. 1896. *The Life and Letters of George John Romanes. Written and Edited by His Wife. New Edition*. Longmans et al, London.

Rotelle, J.E. (ed.). 2017. *The Works of Saint Augustine. A Translation for the 21st Century. On Genesis I/13. On Genesis: A Refutation of the Manichees (De Genesi Adversus Manichaeos), Unfinished Literal Commentary on Genesis (De Genesi ad Litteram Liber Imperfectus), Litteral Meaning of Genesis (De Genesi ad Litteram). Introductions, Translations and Notes by Edmund Hill. 4th printing*. New City Press, New York.

Rothwell, J. 1769. *A Letter to the Rev. Mr. Dean, of Middleton; Occasioned by Reading His Essay on the Future Life of Brute Creatures*. n.p., n.p.

Rowell, G.A. 1847. 'On the Beneficent Distribution of the Sense of Pain' in: *The Edinburgh New Philosophical Journal, Exhibiting a View of the Progressive Discoveries and Improvements in the Sciences and the Arts* 43: 385-395.

Russell, B. 1935. *Religion and Science. [The Home University Library of Modern Knowledge].* Thornton Butterworth, London.

Russell, B. 1957. *Why I Am Not a Christian: And Other Essays on Religion and Related Subjects.* Simon & Schuster, New York.

Ryan, M. 1836. 'Importance of Comparative Anatomy' in: *The London Medical and Surgical Journal: Exhibiting a View of the Improvements and Discoveries in the Various Branches of Medical Science* 8: 184-185.

Schaff, Ph. (ed.). 1885. *Ante-Nicene Fathers. Volume 1. The Apostolic Fathers, Justin Martyr, Irenaeus.* Christian Classics Ethereal Library, Grand Rapids.

Schaff, Ph. (ed.). 1885. *Ante-Nicene Fathers. Volume 4. Fathers of the Third Century: Tertullian, Part Fourth; Minucius Felix; Commodian; Origen, Parts First and Seconds.* Republished by the Christian Classics Ethereal Library, Grand Rapids.

Schaff, Ph. (ed.). 1887. *A Select Library of the Nicene and Post-Nicene Fathers of the Christian Church. Volume IV. St. Augustin: the Writings against the Manichaeans and against the Donatists.* T&T Clark, Edinburgh. Republished by Wm. B. Eerdmans, Grand Rapids.

Schaff, Ph. (ed.). 1887. *A Select Library of the Nicene and Post-Nicene Fathers of the Christian Church. Volume V. St. Augustin: Anti-Pelagian Writings.* T&T Clark, Edinburgh. Republished by Wm. B. Eerdmans, Grand Rapids.

Schaff, Ph. (ed.). 1889. *A Select Library of the Nicene and Post-Nicene Fathers of the Christian Church. Series I, Volume 11. Saint Chrysostom: Homilies on the Acts of the Apostles and the Epistle to the Romans.* T&T Clark, Edinburgh. Republished by Wm. B. Eerdmans, Grand Rapids.

Schaff, Ph. (ed.). 1891. *Nicene and Post-Nicene Fathers Series II, Volume 4. Athanasius.* T&T Clark, Edinburgh. Republished by Wm. B. Eerdmans, Grand Rapids.

Schaff, Ph. (ed.). 1892. *Nicene and Post-Nicene Fathers Series II, Volume 5. Gregory of Nyssa.* T&T Clark, Edinburgh. Republished by Wm. B. Eerdmans, Grand Rapids.

Schedel, H. 1493. *Schedelsche Weltchronik.* Anton Koberger, Nürnberg.

Schopenhauer, A. 1903. *The Basis of Morality. Translated with Introduction and Notes by Arthur Brodrick Bullock.* Swan Sonnenschein & Co., London.

Schopenhauer, A. 2007 [1840]. *Über die Grundlagen der Moral. Mit einer Einleitung, Anmerkungen und einem Register herausgegeben von Peter Welsen.* Felix Meiner Verlag, Hamburg.

Sedgwick, A. 1845. 'Vestiges of the Natural History of Creation' in: *The Edinburgh Review or Critical Journal for July, 1845…October* 82: 1-85.

Sedgwick, A. 1850. *A Discourse on the Studies of the University of Cambridge. The Fifth Edition, with Additions, and a Preliminary Dissertation.* John W. Parker, London.

Shields, C.W. 1889. *Philosophia Ultima or Science of the Sciences. Volume II. The History of the Sciences and the Logic of the Sciences.* Sampson Low et al., London.

Simpson, J.Y. 1912. *The Spiritual Interpretation of Nature. Second Edition.* Hodder and Stoughton, London.

Smets, A, Esbroeck, M. van. 1970. *Basile de Césarée. Sur l'Origine de l'Homme. (Hom. X et XI de l'Hexaéméron).* Introduction, Texte Critique, Traduction et Notes (Sources Chrétiennes 160). Les Éditions du Cerf, Paris.

Smellie, A. (ed.). 1800. *Literary and Characteristical Lives of John Gregory, M.D., Henry Home, Lord Kames. David Hume, Esq. and Adam Smith, L.L.D. To Which Are Added a Dissertation on Public Spirit; and Three Essays by the Late William Smellie.* Alex. Smellie et al., Edinburgh.

Smellie, W. 1762. 'Essay I. Whether all Animate and Inanimate Bodies Made for the Immediate Use and Conveniency of Mankind; or, Is that only a Secondary End of Their Existence?' Read before the Newtonian Society of Edinburgh. Republished in: Smellie, A. (ed.). 1800. *Literary and Characteristical Lives of John Gregory, M.D., Henry Home, Lord Kames. David Hume, Esq. and Adam Smith, L.L.D. To Which Are Added a Dissertation on Public Spirit; and Three Essays by the Late William Smellie.* Alex. Smellie et al., Edinburgh: 413-429.

Smellie, W. 1808 [1790–1799]. *The Philosophy of Natural History.* Thomas et al., Dover.

Sommerville, W. 'The Officious Messenger' in: Anderson, R. (ed.). 1794. *The Works of the British Poets. With Prefaces, Biographical and Critical. Volume Eight.* John & Arthur Arch, London: 529-531.

Southwell, C. *1842.* 'Is there a God? VIII' in: *The Oracle of Reason, or, Philosophy Vindicated* 1: 109-111.

Spurgeon, C.H. 'Sermon VI. The Power of the Holy Ghost' in: Spurgeon, C.H. 1856. *"The Modern Whitfield." Sermons of the Rev. C.H. Spurgeon, of London; with an Introduction and Sketch of his Life by E.L. Magoon.* Sheldon, Blakeman and Company, New York: 112-133.

Spurgeon, C.H. 1856. *"The Modern Whitfield." Sermons of the Rev. C.H. Spurgeon, of London; with an Introduction and Sketch of his Life by E.L. Magoon.* Sheldon, Blakeman and Company, New York.

Spurgeon, C.H. 1861. *The Gorilla and the Land He Inhabits. A Lecture Delivered by the Rev. C.H. Spurgeon in the Metropolitan Tabernacle, Newington, on Tuesday, October 1st, 1861.* n.p., n.p.

St. Victor, H. 1991. *The Didascalicon of Hugh of Saint Victor. A Medieval Guide to the Arts. Translated from the Latin with an Introduction and Notes by J. Taylor.* Columbia University Press, New York.

St. Victor, H. 'On the Three Days'. Introduction and Translation by H. Feiss in: Coolman, B.T., Coulter, D.M. (eds). 2013. *Trinity and Creation. A Selection of Works of Hugh, Richard, and Adam of St Victor.* New City Press, New York: 49-102.

Swan, J. 1643. *Specvlvm Mundi. Or a Glasse Representing the Face of the World Shevving both that It Did Begin, and Must also End: the Manner hovv, and Time when, Being Largely Examined. Whereunto Is Joyned an Hexameron, or a Serious Discourse of the Causes, Continuance, and Qualities of Things in Nature; Occasioned as Matter Pertinent to the VVork Done in the Six Dayes of the Worlds Creation. The Second Edition Enlarged.* Roger Daniel, Cambridge.

Sylvester, J. 1908 [1608-1641]. *The Divine Weeks of Josuah Sylvester. Mainly Translated from the French of William de Saluste, Lord of the Bartas. Edited, with Introduction, Notes, Emendations and Excisions, by Theron Wilber Haight. Collated with the Quarto Editions of 1608, 1611 and 1613, and the Folios of 1621, 1633 and 1641.* H.M. Youmans, Waukesha.

[T.B., R.S.] 1728 [1693]. 'That Brutes Have No Souls but Are Pure Machines, or a Sort of Clockwork, Devoid of Any Sense of Pain, Pleasure, Desire, Hope, Fear, &c.' in: *Athenian Oracle.* 1728. *The Athenian Oracle. Being an Entire Collection of All the Valuable Questions and Answers in the Old Athenian Mercuries Intermix'd with Many Cases in Divinity, History, Philosophy, Mathematics, Love, Poetry; never before Publish'd. To Which Is Added, an Alphabetical Table for the Speedy Finding of Any Questions. By a Member of the Athenian Society. The Third Edition. Vol. I.* J. and J. Knapton et al., London: 504-512.

Temple, F. 1885. *The Relations between Religion and Science. Eight Lectures Preached before the University of Oxford in the Year 1884. On the Foundation of the Late Rev. John Bampton, M.A. Canon of Salisbury.* Macmillan and Co., London.

Tennant, F.R. 1908. *The Origin and Propagation of Sin Being the Hulsean Lectures Delivered before the University of Cambridge in 1901–2.* University Press, Cambridge.

Tennant, F.R. 1909. 'The Influence of Darwinism upon Theology' in: *Quarterly Review* 211: 418-440.

Tennyson, A. 1895 [1850]. *In Memoriam. Edited with Notes by William J. Rolfe.* Houghton Mifflin Company, Boston.

Ter, Tisanthrope [Gillespie, W.H.] 1873. *The Origin of Evil: a Celestial Drama.* n.p., n.p.

Theophilus. 1970. *Theophilus of Antioch ad Autolycum. Text and Translation by Robert M. Grant.* Clarendon Press, Oxford.

Toogood, J. 1798 [?] *The Book of Nature: a Discourse on Some of those Instances of the Power, Wisdom, and Goodness of God, Which Are within the Reach of Common Observation. The Third Edition, Corrected and Enlarged.* Goadby et al., Sherborne.

Topsell, E. 1599. *Times Lamentation: or, an Exposition on the Prophet Ioel, in Sundry Sermons or Meditations.* George Potter, London.

Topsell, E. 1658 [1607]. *The History of Four-footed Beasts and Serpents Describing at Large Their True and Lively Figure, Their Several Names, Conditions, Kinds, Virtues (Both Natural and Medicinal) Countries of Their Breed, Their Love and Hatred to Mankind, and the Wonderful Work of God in Their Creation, Preservation, and Destruction. Interwoven with Curious Variety of Historical Narrations out of Scriptures, Fathers, Philosophers, Physicians, and Poets: Illustrated with Divers Hieroglyphicks and Emblems, &c. both Pleasant and Profitable for Students in All Faculties and Professions. Collected out of the Writings of Conradus Gesner and Other Authors, by Edward Topsel. Whereunto Is now Added, the Theater of Insects; or, Lesser Living Creatures: as Bees, Flies, Caterpillars, Spiders, Worms, &c. A Most Elaborate Work: by T. Muffet, Dr. of Physick. The Whole Revised, Corrected, and Inlarged with the Addition of Two Useful Physical Tables, by J.R.M.D.* G. Sawbridge et al., London.

Townsend, A. (ed.). 1848. *The Writings of John Bradford, Containing Sermons, Meditations, Examinations, &c.* Cambridge University Press.

Townsend, L.T. 1881. *The Mosaic Record and Modern Science.* Howard Gannett, Boston.

Townsend, L.T. 1896. *Evolution or Creation. A Critical Review of the Scientific and Scriptural Theories of Creation and Certain Related Subjects.* Fleming H. Revell Company, New York.

Townsend, L.T. 1904. *Adam and Eve. History or Myth?* The Chapple Publishing Co., Boston.

Townsend, L.T. 1905. *Collapse of Evolution [Bible League, Credo Series, No.2].* National Magazine Company, Boston.

Ursinus, Z. 1598. *Explicationvm Catecheticarvm D. Zachariae Vrsini Silesii Absolvtvm Opvs: Totivsqve Theologiae Purioris Quasi Nouum Corpus. Davidis Parei D. Operâ Extremâ Recognitum. Causas Recognitionis, & Quid in Ea Sit Praestitum, Praefatio Docebit. Cum Gemino Indice: Altero Capitum: Altero Rerum & Verborum. Nec Non Miscellaneis Catecheticis Seorsvm Excusis: Quibus Oratio de Vita & Obitu D. Vrsini est Addita.* Widow of Matthäus Harnisch, Neustadt.

Ursinus, Z. 1888. *The Commentary of Dr. Zacharias Ursinus, on the Heidelberg Catechism. Translated from the Original Latin, by the Rev. G.W. Williard. Fourth American Edition.* Elm Street Printing Company, Cincinnati.

Vogt, C. 1864. *Lectures on Man: His Place in Creation, and in the History of the Earth, Edited by James Hunt.* Longman et al., London.

Waite, J. 1650. *Of the Creatures Liberation from the Bondage of Corruption. Wherein Is Discussed I. What Is Most Probably Meant by (the Creature) II. The Vanitie or Corruption from Which It Shall Be Delivered, and Its Unwillingnesse to that Vanitie. III. The Manner or Way of Its Deliverance. IV. What Creatures Are Conceived as Most Capable of This, and of Their Use after Restauration. V. And Lastly Is Discussed that Glorious Libertie of the Sonnes of God, into Which the Creature Is to Be Reduced.* Tho. Broad, York.

Walker, G. 1641. *The History of the Creation, as It Is Written by Moses in the First and Second Chapters of Genesis, Plainly Opened and Expounded in Severall Sermons Preached in London. Whereunto Is Added a Short Treatise of Gods Actuall Providence, in Ruling, Ordering, and Governing the World and All Things therein.* John Bartlet, London.

Walker, G. 1641. *God Made Visible in His Workes, or, a Treatise of the Externall Workes of God: First, in Generall, out of the Words of the Psalmist, Psal. 135.6. Secondly, in Particular of the Creation, out of the Words of Moses, Genesis, Chap. 1. and 2.; Thirdly, of Gods Actuall Providence.* John Bartlet, London.

Wallace, A.R. 1889. *Darwinism. An Exposition of the Theory of Natural Selection with Some of Its Applications. With a Portrait of the Author, Map and Illustrations. Second Edition.* MacMillan and Co., London.

Watts, I. 1740. *The Ruin and Recovery of Mankind: or, an Attempt to Vindicate the Scriptural Account of these Great Events upon the Plain Principles of Reason. With an Answer to Various Difficulties...Whereto Are Subjoin'd Three Short Essays...* R. Hett and J. Brackstone, London.

Webb, C.C.J. 1911. *Problems in the Relations of God and Man.* James Nisbet & Co., London.

Wells, L.S.A. 'The Books of Adam and Eve' in: Charles, R.H. (ed.). 1913. *The Apocrypha and Pseudepigrapha of the Old Testament in English with Introductions and Critical and Explanatory Notes to the Several Books. Volume II. Pseudepigrapha.* Clarendon Press, Oxford: 123-154.

Wesley, J. 1763. *A Survey of the Wisdom of God in the Creation: Or a Compendium of Natural Philosophy. In Two Volumes.* William Pine, Bristol.

Wesley, J. 1783. 'An Extract from a Book Entitled Free Thoughts on the Brute Creation [by John Hilldrop, [sic] D.D.]' in: *The Arminian*

Magazine for the Year 1783. Consisting of Extracts and Original Treatises on Universal Redemption. Volume VI: 33-36, 90-92, 142-144, 202-204, 259-261, 315-317, 370-371, 424-427, 487-489, 538-539, 596-598, 654-657.

Wesley, J. 1784. *A Survey of the Wisdom of God in the Creation. Or, a Compendium of Natural Philosophy. In Five Volumes. The Fourth Edition.* J. Paramore, London.

Wesley, J. 'Sermon LXI. God's Approbation of His Works' in: Wesley, J. 1853. *The Works of the Rev. John Wesley. Third American Complete and Standard Edition, from the Latest London Edition, with the Last Corrections of the Author. Comprehending also Numerous Translations, Notes, and an Original Preface, etc., by John Emory. In Seven Volumes, Volume II.* Carlton & Phillips, New York: 25-31.

Wesley, J. 'Sermon LXV. The General Deliverance' in: Wesley, J. 1853. *The Works of the Rev. John Wesley. Third American Complete and Standard Edition, from the Latest London Edition, with the Last Corrections of the Author. Comprehending also Numerous Translations, Notes, and an Original Preface, etc., by John Emory. In Seven Volumes, Volume II.* Carlton & Phillips, New York: 49-57.

Wesley, J. 1853. *The Works of the Rev. John Wesley. Third American Complete and Standard Edition, from the Latest London Edition, with the Last Corrections of the Author. Comprehending also Numerous Translations, Notes, and an Original Preface, etc., by John Emory. In Seven Volumes, Volume II.* Carlton & Phillips, New York.

Whewell, W. 1832. 'Art. IV.—Principles of Geology, Being an Attempt to Explain the Former Changes of the Earth's Surface, by Reference to Causes now in Operation. By Charles Lyell, Esq., F.R.S., Professor of Geology in King's College, London. Volume II. London. 1832' in: *The Quarterly Review, Volume XLVII, Published in March & July, 1832.* John Murray, London.

[Whewell, W.] 1853. *Of the Plurality of Worlds. An Essay.* John W. Parker and Son, London.

Whitcomb, J.C., Morris, H.M. 1961. *The Genesis Flood. The Biblical Record and Its Scientific Implications.* Presbyterian and Reformed Publishing Co., Phillipsburg.

Wilkins, J. 1668. *An Essay towards a Real Character, and a Philosophical Language.* Sa. Gellibrand and John Martyn, London.

Wilkins, J. 1710. *Of the Principles and Duties of Natural Religion: Two Books. The Sixth Edition.* R. Chiswell et al., London.

Willet, A. 1620 [1611]. *Hexapla: That Is, a Six-fold Commentarie vpon the Most Diuine Epistle of the Holy Apostle S. Paul to the Romanes: Wherein According to the Authors Former Method Six Things Are Obserued in*

Euery Chapter. 1. the Text with the Diuers Readings. 2. Argument and Method. 3. the Questions Discussed. 4. Doctrines Noted. 5. Controuersies Handled. 6. Morall Uses Obserued. VVherein Are Handled the Greatest Points of Christian Religion: Concerning Iustification by Faith, c.3,4. the Fall of Man, c.5. the Combat betweene the Flesh and the Spirit, c.7. Election, c.9. the Vocation of the Iewes, c.11. With Many Other Questions and Controuersies Summed in the End of the Table. Diuided into Two Bookes. The First vnto the 12. Chapter, Containing Matter of Doctrine: the Second Belonging to Exhoration, in the Fiue last Chapters. The First Booke. Cantrell Legge, Cambridge.

Willet, A. 1633 [1605]. *Hexapla in Genesin & Exodum: that Is, a Sixfold Commentary upon the Tvvo First Bookes of Moses, Being Genesis and Exodus. VVherein these Translations Are Compared together: 1. The Chalde. 2. The Septuagint. 3. The Vulgar Latine. 4. Pagnine. 5. Montanus. 6. Iunius. 7. Vatablus. 8. The Great English Bible. 9. The Geneva Edition. And 10. The Hebrew Originall. Together with a Sixfold Use of Every Chapter, Shewing 1. The Method or Argument: 2. The Divers Readings: 3. The Explanation of Difficult Questions and Doubtfull Places: 4. The Places of Doctrine: 5. Places of Confutation: 6. Morall Observations. In Which Worke, about Three Thousand Theologicall Questions Are Discussed: above Forty Authors Old and New Abridged: and together Comprised whatsoever Worthy of Note, either Mercerus out of the Rabbines, Pererius out of the Fathers, or Marlorat out of the New Writers, Have in Their Learned Commentaries Collected. Now the Fourth Time Imprinted, with the Authors Corrections before His Death.* Iohn Grismond, London.

Williams, N.P. 1927. *The Ideas of the Fall and of Original Sin. A Historical and Critical Study. Being Eight Lectures Delivered before the University of Oxford, in the Year 1924, on the Foundation of the Rev. John Bampton, Canon of Salisbury.* Longmans et al., London.

Witty, J. 1705. *An Essay towards a Vindication of the Vulgar Exposition of the Mosaic History of the Creation of the World, and of the Fall of Adam. In Two Parts.* John Wyat, London.

Wood, T. 1891-1892. 'The Apparent Cruelty of Nature' in: *Journal of the Transactions of the Victoria Institute or Philosophical Society of Great Britain* 25: 253-278.

Wright, G.F. 1882. *Studies in Science and Religion.* Warren F. Draper, Andover.

Wright, G.F. [1910]. 'The Passing of Evolution' in: *The Fundamentals. A Testimony to the Truth Volume VII.* Testimony Publishing Company, Chicago.

Young, G. 1840. *Scriptural Geology, or an Essay on the High Antiquity Ascribed to the Organic Remains Imbedded in Stratified Rocks; Communicated, in Abstract, to the Geological Section of the British Association, at the Annual Meeting Held in Newcastle: in Two Parts. Part I.—Proving that the Strata, Instead of Requiring Myriads of Ages for Their Formation, May Have Been Deposited nearly about One Period. Part II.—Shewing that the Deluge Was the Period, when All the Secondary and Tertiary Rocks Were Formed. Second Edition: with an Appendix, Containing Strictures on Some Passages in the Rev. Dr. J. Pye Smith's Lectures, Entitled Scripture and Geology; Particularly His Theory of a Local Creation, and Local Deluge.* Simpkin, Marshall, and Co., London.

Young, G., Bird, J. 1828. *A Geological Survey of the Yorkshire Coast: Describing the Strata and Fossils Occurring between the Humber and the Tees, from the German Ocean to the Plain of York: Illustrated with Numerous Engravings. Second Edition, Much Improved and Enlarged, Embellished with More than One Hundred New Figures.* R. Kirby, Whitby.

Secondary Sources

Adams, M. McCord. 1999. *Horrendous Evils and the Goodness of God*. Cornell University Press, Ithaca.

Alexander, D.R. 2014. *Creation or Evolution. Do We Have to Choose? Second Edition Revised and Updated.* Monarch Books, Oxford.

Alexander, D.R., Numbers, R.L. (eds). 2010. *Biology and Ideology. From Descartes to Dawkins.* The University of Chicago Press, Chicago.

Almond, P.C. 1999. *Adam and Eve in Seventeenth-Century Thought.* Cambridge University Press, Cambridge.

Amand, D. 1971. 'Alexis Smets, S.J. et Michel van Esbroeck, S.J., *Basile de Césarée. Sur l'Origine de l'Homme.* (Homélies X et XI de l'Hexaéméron). Introduction, Texte Critique, Traduction et Notes [compte-rendu]' in: *L'Antiquité Classique* 40 (1): 295-297.

Anderson, D. 'Creation, Redemption, and Eschatology' in: Nevin, C.N. (ed.). 2009. *Should Christians Embrace Evolution? Biblical and Scientific Responses.* Inter-Varsity Press, Nottingham: 73-92.

Anderson, D.J., Adolphs, R. 2014. 'A Framework for Studying Emotions Across Species' in: *Cell* 157 (1): 187-200.

Anderson, L. 1976. 'Charles Bonnet's Taxonomy and Chain of Being' in: *Journal of the History of Ideas* 37 (1): 45-58.

Andrews, J. et al. 1997. *The History of Bethlem.* Routledge, London.

Anonymous. 1918. 'The Right Hon. Sir Edward Fry, G.C.B., F.R.S.' in: *Nature* 102: 169-170.

Anonymous. 1948. 'George John Romanes (1848-94)' in: *Nature* 161: 757.
Anonymous. 1979. 'Bernard Ramm' in: *Journal of the American Scientific Affiliation* 31 (4): 178.
Anschutz, R.P. „John Stuart Mill". *Encyclopedia Britannica*, 16 May 2021, https://www.britannica.com/biography/John-Stuart-Mill. Accessed 14 December 2021.
Aquino, F.D., King, B.J. (eds). 2018. *The Oxford Handbook of John Henry Newman*. Oxford University Press, Oxford.
Ashworth Jr, W.B. 'Christianity and the Mechanistic Universe' in: Lindberg, D.C., Numbers, R.L. (eds). 2003. *When Science & Christianity Meet*. The University of Chicago Press, Chicago: 61-84.
Asselt, W.J. van. 'De Neus van de Bruid. De 'Profetische' en Zinnebeeldige' Godgeleerdheid van Henricus Groenewegen en Johannes d'Outrein' in: Broeyer. F.G.M., Honée, E.M.V.M. (eds). 1997. *Profetie en Godsspraak in de Geschiedenis van het Christendom. Studies over de Historische Ontwikkeling van een Opvallend Verschijnsel*. Boekencentrum, Zoetermeer.
Asselt, W. van. 'Adam en Eva als Laatkomers. De Pre-Adamitische Speculaties van Isaac La Peyrère' in: Goris, H., Hennecke, S. (eds). 2005. *Adam en Eva in het Paradijs. Actuele Visies op Man en Vrouw uit 2000 Jaar Christelijke Theologie* [Utrechtse Studies, 7]. Meinema, Zoetermeer: 99-115.
Attfield, R. 1983. 'Christian Attitudes to Nature' in: *Journal of the History of Ideas* 44 (3): 369-386.
Auger, P. 2011. 'The Semaines' Dissemination in England and Scotland until 1641' in: *Renaissance Studies* 26 (5): 625-640.
Ayala, F.J. 2007. 'Darwin's Greatest Discovery: Design without Designer' in: *Proceedings of the National Academy of Sciences* 104 (Suppl. 1): 8567-8573.
Ayala, F.J. 2010. 'Darwin's Explanation of Design: From Natural Theology to Natural Selection' in: *Infection, Genetics and Evolution* 10 (6): 839-842.
Ayala, F.J. 2010. 'The Difference of Being Human: Morality' in: *Proceedings of the National Academy of Sciences* 107 (Suppl. 2): 9015-9022.
Badham, P. 'Do Animals Have Immortal Souls?' in: Linzey, A., Yamamoto, D. (eds). 1998. *Animals on the Agenda. Questions about Animals for Theology and Ethics*. University of Illinois Press, Urbana: 181-189.
Bailey, C. 2011. 'Kinds of Life: on the Phenomenological Basis of the Distinction between "Higher" and "Lower" Animals' in: *Environmental Philosophy* 8 (2): 47-68.
Barber, R. 1992. *Bestiary Being an English Version of the Bodleian Library*. The Boydell Press, Woodbridge.

Bartelink, G.J.M. 'Die Beeinflussung Augustins durch die Griechischen Patres' in: Boeft, J. den, Oort, J. van. 1987. *Augustiniana Traiectina. Communications Présentées au Colloque International d'Utrecht, 13-14 Novembre 1986. Études* Augustiniennes, Paris: 9-24.

Bartholomew, M. 1973. 'Lyell and Evolution: an Account of Lyell's Response to the Prospect of an Evolutionary Ancestry for Man' in: *The British Journal for the History of Science* 6 (23): 261-303.

Barton, R. 1987. 'John Tyndall, Pantheist: a Rereading of the Belfast Address' in: *Osiris* 3: 111-134.

Barton, R. 1990. 'An Influential Set of Chaps': the X-Club and Royal Society Politics 1864–85' in: *The British Journal for the History of Science* 23 (1): 53-81.

Bates, A.W.H. 2017. *Anti-Vivisection and the Profession of Medicine in Britain. A Social History*. Palgrave MacMillan, London.

Bayne, R. 'Gibbon, Nicholas (fl. 1600)' in: *Dictionary of National Biography, 1885-1900, Volume 21*

Bayne, T.W. 'Gloag, Paton James' in: *Dictionary of National Biography, 1912 Supplement, Volume 2*.

Bebbington, D.W. 'Science and Evangelical Theology in Britain from Wesley to Orr' in: Livingstone, D.N., Hart, D.G., Noll, M.A. (eds). 1999. *Evangelicals and Science in Historical Perspective*. Oxford University Press, New York: 120-141.

Becker, E. 1973. *The Denial of Death*. Simon & Schuster, New York.

Beeke, J., Pederson, R.J. 2006. *Meet the Puritans. With a Guide to Modern Reprints*. Reformation Heritage Books, Grand Rapids.

Beirne, P. 2013. 'Hogarth's Animals' in: *Journal of Animal Ethics* 3 (2): 133-162.

Benjamins, R. 'The Analogy between Creation and the Biblical Text in Origen of Alexandria' in: Vanderjagt, A., Berkel, K. van. (eds). 2005. *The Book of Nature in Antiquity and the Middle Ages*. Peeters, Leuven: 13-20.

Bennett, G., Hewlett, M.J., Peters T., Russell, R.J. (eds). 2008. *The Evolution of Evil*. Vandenhoeck & Ruprecht, Göttingen.

Bergström, A., Stringer, C., Hajdinjak, M., Scerri, E.M.L., Skoglund, P. 2021. 'Origins of Modern Human Ancestry' in: *Nature* 590: 229-237.

Bering, J.M., Johnson, D.P. 2005. '"O Lord…You Perceive My Thoughts from Afar": Recursiveness and the Evolution of Supernatural Agency' in: *Journal of Cognition and Culture* 5 (1-2): 118-142.

Berkel, K. van, Vanderjagt, A. (eds). 2006. *The Book of Nature in Early Modern and Modern History*. Peeters, Leuven.

Berkman, J.R. 'Towards a Thomistic Theology of Animality' in: Deane-Drummond, C., Clough, D. (eds). 2009. *Creaturely Theology: on God, Humans and Other Animals*. SCM Press, London: 21-40.

Berkowitz, C. 2014. 'Defining a Discovery: Priority and Methodological Controversy in Early Nineteenth-Century Anatomy' in: *Notes & Records of the Royal Society Journal of the History of Science* 68 (4): 357-372.

Berry, R.J. 2005. 'The Lions Seek Their Prey from God: a Commentary on the Boyle Lecture' in: *Science & Christian Belief* 17 (1): 41-56.

Berry, R.J. 'Biology since Darwin' in: Robinson, A. (ed.). 2012. *Darwinism and Natural Theology. Evolving Perspectives.* Cambridge Scholars Publishing, Newcastle upon Tyne: 12-38.

Berry, R.J., Noble, T.A. (eds) 2009. *Darwin, Creation and the Fall. Theological Challenges.* Apollos, Nottingham.Bettany, G.T. 'Kirby, William' in: *Dictionary of National Biography, 1885-1900, Volume 31.*

Bidwell, W.H. (ed.). 1846. *Biblical Repository and Classical Review Third Series,* Wiley & Putnam, London.

Bimson, J.J. 2006. 'Reconsidering a 'Cosmic Fall"' in: *Science & Christian Belief* 18 (1): 63-81.

Black, J. 1991. 'The Hermeneutics of Extinction: Denial and Discovery in Scientific Literature' in: Shaffer, E.S. (ed.). *Comparative Criticism. An Annual Journal. Literature and Science* 13: 147-170.

Blakiston, H.E.D. 'Moore, Aubrey Lackington' in: *Dictionary of National Biography, 1885-1900, Volume 38.*

Blancke, S. 'Lord Monboddo's *Ourang-Outang* and the Origin and Progress of Language' in: Pina, M., Gontier, N. (eds). 2014. *The Evolution of Social Communication in Primates.* Springer International Publishing, Switzerland.

Blocher, H. 'The Theology of the Fall and the Origins of Evil' in: Berry, R.J., Noble, T.A. (eds). 2009. *Darwin, Creation and the Fall. Theological Challenges.* Apollos, Nottingham: 149-172.

Boddice, R. 2008. *A History of Attitudes and Behaviours toward Animals in Eighteenth- and Nineteenth-Century Britain. Anthropocentrism and the Emergence of Animals.* Edwin Mellen Press, Lewiston.

Boddice, R. 2010. 'The Moral Status of Animals and the Historical Human Cachet' in: *JAC* 30 (3/4): 457-489.

Boddice, R. 2011. 'Vivisecting Major. A Victorian Gentleman Scientist Defends Animal Experimentation, 1876-1885' in: *Isis* 102 (2): 215-237.

Boeft, J. den, Oort, J. van. 1987. *Augustiniana Traiectina. Communications Présentées au Colloque International d'Utrecht, 13-14 Novembre 1986. Études* Augustiniennes, Paris.

Boehrer, B. (ed.). 2007. *A Cultural History of Animals in the Renaissance.* Berg, Oxford.

Boehrer, B. 'The Animal Renaissance, Introduction' in: Boehrer, B. (ed.). 2007. *A Cultural History of Animals in the Renaissance.* Berg, Oxford: 1-26.

Bouteneff, P.C. 2008. *Beginnings. Ancient Christian Readings of the Biblical Creation Narratives.* Baker Academic, Grand Rapids.

Bowden, M. 1982. *The Rise of the Evolutionary Fraud.* Sovereign Publications, Bromley.

Bowler, P.J. 1973. 'Bonnet and Buffon: Theories of Generation and the Problem of Species' in: *Journal of the History of Biology* 6 (2): 259-281.

Bowler, P.J. 1974. 'Evolutionism in the Enlightenment' in: *History of Science* 12 (2): 159-183.

Bowler, P.J. 1974. 'Sir Francis Palgrave on Natural Theology' in: *Journal of the History of Ideas* 35: 144-147.

Bowler, P.J. 1976. *Fossils and Progress. Paleontology and the Idea of Progressive Evolution in the Nineteenth Century.* Science History Publications, New York.

Bowler, P.J. 1977. 'Darwinism and the Argument from Design: Suggestions for a Reevaluation' in: *Journal of the History of Biology* 10 (1): 29-43.

Bowler, P.J. 2001. *Reconciling Science and Religion. The Debate in Early-Twentieth-Century Britain.* The University of Chicago Press, Chicago.

Bowler, P.J. 2005. 'Revisiting the Eclipse of Darwinism. The "Darwinian Revolution": Whether, What and Whose?' in: *Journal of the History of Biology* 38 (1): 19-32.

Bowler, P.J. 2007. *Monkey Trials and Gorilla Sermons. Evolution and Christianity from Darwin to Intelligent Design.* Harvard University Press, Cambridge (MA).

Brand, P., Yancey, P. 1993. *The Gift of Pain. Why We Hurt & What We Can Do about It.* Zondervan, Grand Rapids.

Breathnach, C.S. 2005. 'Sir Thomas Browne' in: *Journal of the Royal Society of Medicine* 98: 33-36.

Brink, G. van den. 2004. *Een Publieke Zaak. Theologie tussen Geloof en Wetenschap.* Boekencentrum, Zoetermeer.

Brink, G. van den. 2020. *Reformed Theology and Evolutionary Theory.* Wm. B. Eerdmans, Grand Rapids.

Brink, G. van den, Cook, H. 2020. '"I Am Inclined to Look at Everything as Resulting from Designed Laws": Charles Darwin's Origin of Species as a Specimen of Natural Theology' in: *Christian Scholar's Review* 50 (1): 25-37.

Broadbent, E. 2017. 'Interactions with Robots: the Truths We Reveal about Ourselves' in: *Annual Review of Psychology* 68: 627-652.

Brock, W.H. 1966. 'The Selection of the Authors of the Bridgewater Treatises' in: *Notes and Records of the Royal Society of London* 21 (2): 162-179.

Broeyer, F.G.M., Honée, E.M.V.M. (eds). 1997. *Profetie en Godsspraak in de Geschiedenis van het Christendom. Studies over de Historische*

Ontwikkeling van een Opvallend Verschijnsel. Boekencentrum, Zoetermeer.

Brooke, J.H. 1977. 'Natural Theology and the Plurality of Worlds: Observations on the Brewster-Whewell Debate' in: *Annals of Science* 34 (3): 221-286.

Brooke, J.H. 1989. 'Scientific Thought and Its Meaning for Religion: the Impact of French Science on British Natural Theology, 1827–1859' in: *Revue de Synthèse* 110 (1): 33-59.

Brooke, J.H. 1991. *Science and Religion. Some Historical Perspectives.* Cambridge University Press, Cambridge.

Brooke, J.H. 1992. 'Natural Law in the Natural Sciences: the Origins of Modern Atheism?' in: *Science & Christian Belief* 4 (2): 83-103.

Brooke, J.H. 'The History of Science and Religion. Some Evangelical Dimensions in: Livingstone, D.N., Hart, D.G., Noll, M.A. (eds). 1999. *Evangelicals and Science in Historical Perspective.* Oxford University Press, New York: 17-40.

Brooke, J.H. 2000. "Wise Men nowadays Think Otherwise': John Ray, Natural Theology and the Meanings of Anthropocentrism' in: *Notes and Records of the Royal Society of London* 54 (2): 199-213.

Brooke, J.H. 'Darwin and Victorian Christianity' in: Hodge, J., Radick, G. (eds). 2009. *The Cambridge Companion to Darwin. Second Edition.* Cambridge University Press, Cambridge: 197-218.

Brooke, J.H. 2010. 'Darwin and Religion: Correcting the Caricatures' in: *Science and Education* 19 (4-5): 391-405.

Brooke, J.H. 'Christian Darwinians' in: Robinson, A. (ed.). 2012. *Darwinism and Natural Theology. Evolving Perspectives.* Cambridge Scholars Publishing, Newcastle upon Tyne: 47-67.

Brooke, J.H. 2018. 'Myth, Mutual Interaction, and Poetry. Darwin and Christianity: Truth and Myth' in; Zygon (3): 836-849.

Brooke, J., Cantor, G. 1998. *Reconstructing Nature. The Engagement of Science and Religion. Glasgow Gifford Lectures.* Oxford University Press, New York.

Brown, B.F. 1986. 'The Evolution of Darwin's Theism' in: *Journal of the History of Biology* 19 (1): 1-45.

Brown, C.G. 2009. *The Death of Christian Britain. Understanding Secularisation, 1800-2000.* Routledge, London.

Brown, P.R.L. "St. Ambrose". *Encyclopedia Britannica*, 1 Jan. 2021, https://www.britannica.com/biography/Saint-Ambrose. Accessed 14 December 2021.

Brown, R.F. 1975. 'On the Necessary Imperfection of Creation: Irenaeus' *Adversus Haereses IV, 38*' in: *Scottish Journal of Theology* 28 (1): 17-25.

Byers, S. 'Augustine and the Philosophers' in: Vessey, M. (ed.). 2012. *A Companion to Augustine*. Blackwell, Chichester: 175-187.

Bynum, W.F. 1973. 'The Anatomical Method, Natural Theology, and the Functions of the Brain' in: *Isis* 64 (4): 444-468.

Calloway, K. 2010. *God's Scientists: the Renovation of Natural Theology in England, 1653-1692*. PhD Thesis, University of British Columbia, Vancouver.

Camerini, J.R. "Alfred Russel Wallace". *Encyclopedia Britannica*, 3 Nov. 2021, https://www.britannica.com/biography/Alfred-Russel-Wallace. Accessed 14 December 2021.

Carruthers, P. 1989. 'Brute Experience' in: *The Journal of Philosophy* 86 (5): 258-269.

Carson, R. 1962. *Silent Spring*. Houghton Mifflin, Boston.

Carus, P. 1894. 'The Late Professor Romanes's Thoughts on Religion' in: *The Monist* 5: 385-400.

Cavanaugh, W.T., Smith J.K.A. (eds). 2017. *Evolution and the Fall*. Wm. B. Eerdmans, Grand Rapids.

Cizewski, W. 1987. 'Reading the World as Scripture: Hugh of St. Victor's De Tribus Diebus' in: *Florilegium* 9 (1): 65–88.

Clapman, P. 'Barth and Darwin: Can They Talk' in: Robinson, A. (ed.). 2012. *Darwinism and Natural Theology. Evolving Perspectives*. Cambridge Scholars Publishing, Newcastle upon Tyne: 154-159.

Clark, C.A. 2009. '"You Are Here": Missing Links, Chains of Being, and the Language of Cartoons' in: *Isis* 100 (3): 571-589.

Clark, G. 'The Fathers and the Animals: The Rule of Reason?' in: Linzey, A., Yamamoto, D. (eds). 1988. *Animals on the Agenda. Questions about Animals for Theology and Ethics*. University of Illinois Press, Urbana: 67-79.

Clarke, T.E. 1958. 'St. Augustine and Cosmic Redemption' in: *Theological Studies* 19 (2): 133-164.

Clement, G. 2013. 'Animals and Moral Agency: the Recent Debate and Its Implications' in: *Journal of Animal Ethics* 3 (1): 1-14.

Clough, D. 'The Anxiety of the Human Animal: Martin Luther on Non-human Animals and Human Animality' in: Deane-Drummond, C., Clough, D. (eds). 2009. *Creaturely Theology: on God, Humans and Other Animals*. SCM Press, London: 41-60.

Clough, D.L. 2012. *On Animals. Volume 1. Systematic Theology*. T&T Clark International, London.

Cogswell, T., Cust, R., Lake, P. (eds). 2002. *Politics, Religion and Popularity in Early Stuart Britain. Essays in Honour of Conrad Russell*. Cambridge University Press, Cambridge.

Cohen, E. 'Animals in Medieval Perceptions. The Image of the Ubiquitous Other' in: Manning, A., Serpell, J. (eds). 1994. *Animals and Human Society: Changing Perspectives.* Routledge, London: 59-80.

Cohen, L.D.M.A. 1936. 'Descartes and Henry More on the Beast-Machine—A Translation of Their Correspondence Pertaining to Animal Automatism' in: *Annals of Science* 1 (1) 48-61.

Colas, G., Colas-Chauhan U. 2017. 'An 18th Century Jesuit "Refutation of Metempsychosis" in Sanskrit' in: *Religions* 8: 192, subsequent pages not numbered.

Collins, C.J. 2006. *Genesis 1-4. A Linguistic, Literary, and Theological Commentary.* P&R Publishing Company, Phillipsburg.

Conradie, E.M., 2018, 'The Christian Faith and Evolution: an Evolving, Unresolved Debate' in: *Verbum et Ecclesia* 39 (1): a1843.

Cooper, T. 'Young, George (1777-1848)' in: *Dictionary of National Biography, 1885-1900, Volume 63.*

Corey, M.A. 2000. *Evolution and the Problem of Natural Evil.* University Press of America, Lanham.

Cornell, J.F. 1983. 'From Creation to Evolution: Sir William Dawson and the Idea of Design in the Nineteenth Century' in: *Journal of the History of Biology* 16 (1): 137-170.

Cornell, J.F. 1987. 'God's Magnificent Law: the Bad Influence of Theistic Metaphysics on Darwin's Estimation of Natural Selection' in: *Journal of the History of Biology*, 20 (3): 381-412.

Cottingham, J. 1978. "'A Brute to the Brutes?': Descartes' Treatment of Animals' in: *Philosophy* 53 (206): 551-559.

Craig, W.L. 2021. *In Quest of the Historical Adam. A Biblical and Scientific Exploration.* Wm. B. Eerdmans, Grand Rapids.

Crane, R.S. 1934. 'Suggestions toward a Genealogy of the "Man of Feeling"' in: *Journal of English Literary History* 1 (3): 205-230.

Cunningham, A. 1988. 'Getting the Game Right: Some Plain Words on the Identity and Invention of Science' in: *Studies in History and Philosophy of Science Part A* (3): 365-389.

Cunningham, A. 1991. 'How the *Principia* Got Its Name' in: *History of Science* (4): 377-392.

Cunningham, A. 2000. 'The Identity of Natural Philosophy. A Response to Edward Grant' in: *Early Science and Medicine* 5 (3): 259-278.

Cunningham, A., Williams, P. 1993. 'De-Centring the "Big Picture": "The Origins of Modern Science" and the Modern Origins of Science' in: *The British Journal for the History of Science* 26 (4): 407-432.

Curley, M.J. 2009. *Physiologus. A Medieval Book of Nature Lore.* The University of Chicago Press, Chicago.

Cushing, M.P. 1920. 'A Forgotten Philosopher' in: *The Monist* 30: 311-316.
Damasio, A. 2018. 'Why Your Biology Runs on Feelings' in: Biology – Neuroscience. http://nautil.us/issue/56/perspective/why-your-biology-runs-on-feelings. Accessed on 14 December 2021.
Damasio, A., Carvalho, G.B. 2013. 'The Nature of Feelings: Evolutionary and Neurobiological Origins' in: *Nature Reviews Neuroscience* 14 (2):143-152.
Dawkins, M.S. 2006. 'Through Animal Eyes: What Behaviour Tells Us' in: *Applied Animal Behaviour Science* 100: 4-10.
Dawkins, R. 1976. *The Selfish Gene.* Oxford University Press, New York.
Dawkins, R. 1995. *River out of Eden. A Darwinian View of Life.* Weidenfeld & Nicholson, London.
Dawkins, R. 1996. *The Blind Watchmaker. Why the Evidence of Evolution Reveals a Universe without Design. With a New Introduction.* W.W. Norton & Company, New York.
Dawkins, R. 2006. *The God Delusion.* Bantam Press, London.
Deane-Drummond, C. 2008. 'Shadow Sophia in Christological Perspective: the Evolution of Sin and the Redemption of Nature' in: *Theology and Science* 6 (1): 13-32.
Deane-Drummond, C. 'Are Animals Moral? Taking Soundings through Vice, Virtue, Conscience and *Imago Dei*' in: Deane-Drummond, C., Clough, D. (eds). 2009. *Creaturely Theology: on God, Humans and Other Animals.* SCM Press, London: 190-210.
Deane-Drummond, C. 'In Adam All Die? Questions at the Boundary of Niche Construction, Community Evolution, and Original Sin' in: Cavanaugh, W.T., Smith, J.K.A. (eds). 2017. *Evolution and the Fall.* Wm. B. Eerdmans, Grand Rapids: 23-47.
Deane-Drummond, C. 2018. 'Perceiving Natural Evil through the Lens of Divine Glory? A Conversation with Christopher Southgate' in: *Zygon* 53 (3): 792-807.
Deane-Drummond, C., Clough, D. (eds). 2009. *Creaturely Theology: on God, Humans and Other Animals.* SCM Press, London.
Deason, G.B. 'Reformation Theology and the Mechanistic Conception of Nature' in: Lindberg, D.C., Numbers, R.L. (eds). 1986. *God & Nature. Historical Essays on the Encounter between Christianity and Science.* University of California Press, Berkeley: 167-191.
Defoe, T. 2019. *An Analysis of Bernard Ramm's Influence on Young Earth Creationism.* www.academia.edu/39527102/an_analysis_of_Bernard_Ramms_influence_on_young_earth_creationism. Accessed on 14 December 2021.
Dembski, W. 2009. *The End of Christianity. Finding a Good God in an Evil World.* B&H Publishing Group, Nashville.

Desmond, A.J. "Thomas Henry Huxley". *Encyclopedia Britannica*, 25 June 2021, https://www.britannica.com/biography/Thomas-Henry-Huxley. Accessed 14 December 2021.

Desmond, A. 1987. 'Artisan Resistance and Evolution in Britain, 1819-1848' in: *Osiris* 3: 77-110.

Desmond, A. 1989. *The Politics of Evolution. Morphology, Medicine, and Reform in Radical London*. The University of Chicago Press, Chicago.

Domning, D.P., Hellwig, M.K. 2016 [2006]. *Original Selfishness. Original Sin and Evil in the Light of Evolution*. Routledge, Abingdon.

Domning, D.P., Wimmer, J.F. 2008. *Evolution and Original Sin. Accounting for Evil in the World*. Washington Theological Consortium. https://washtheocon.org/wp-content/uploads/2012/10/EvolutionOriginalSin1-corrected.pdf. Accessed on 14 December 2021.

Dougherty, T. 2014. *The Problem of Animal Pain. A Theodicy for All Creatures Great and Small*. Palgrave MacMillan, Basingstoke.

Dubin, A.E., Patapoutian, A. 2010. 'Nociceptors: the Sensors of the Pain Pathway' in: *The Journal of Clinical Investigation* 120 (11): 3760-3772.

Duncan, I.J.H. 2006. 'The Changing Concept of Animal Sentience' in: *Applied Animal Behaviour Science* 100: 11-19.

Ebbersmeyer, S. (ed.). 2012. *Emotional Minds*. De Gruyter, Berlin.

Edgar, W. 'Adam, History, and Theodicy' in: Madueme, H., Reeves, M. (eds). 2014. *Adam, the Fall and Original Sin. Theological, Biblical, and Scientific Perspectives*. Baker Academic, Grand Rapids: 307-321.

Edwards, D. 'The Redemption of Animals in an Incarnational Theology' in: Deane-Drummond, C., Clough, D. (eds). 2009. *Creaturely Theology: on God, Humans and Other Animals*. SCM Press, London: 81-99.

Ellegård, A. 1957. 'The Darwinian Theory and Nineteenth-Century Philosophies of Science' in: *Journal of the History of Ideas* 18 (3): 362-393.

Ellegård, A. 1990. *Darwin and the General Reader. The Reception of Darwin's Theory of Evolution in the British Periodical Press, 1859–1872*. The University of Chicago Press, Chicago.

Emberger, G. 1994. 'Theological and Scientific Explanations for the Origin and Purpose of Evil' in: *Perspectives on Science and Christian Faith* 46: 150-158.

England, R. 2001. 'Natural Selection, Teleology, and the Logos: from Darwin to the Oxford Neo-Darwinists, 1859–1909' in: *Osiris* 16: 270-287.

Epley, N., Waytz, A., Cacioppo, J.T. 2007.' On Seeing Human: a Three-Factor Theory of Anthropomorphism' in: *Psychological Review* 114: 864-886.

Etzelmüller, G. 2014. 'The Evolution of Sin' in: *Religion & Theology* 21 (1): 107-124.

Evans, E.P. 1906. *The Criminal Prosecution and Capital Punishment of Animals*. William Heinemann, London.

Evans, J.M. 1968. *Paradise Lost and the Genesis Tradition*. Clarendon Press, Oxford.

Fara, P. 2004. 'Heavenly Bodies: Newtonianism, Natural Theology and the Plurality of Worlds Debate in the Eighteenth Century' in: *Journal for the History of Astronomy* 35 (2): 143-160.

Fara, P. 2012. *Erasmus Darwin. Sex, Science, & Serendipity*. Oxford University Press, Oxford.

Faro, I. 2015. 'The Question of Evil and Animal Death before the Fall' in: *Trinity Journal* 36: 1-21.

Farrer, A. 1962. *Love Almighty and Ills Unlimited*. Wm. Collins Sons & Co, London.

Felleman, L.B. 2006. 'John Wesley's Survey of the Wisdom of God in Creation: A Methodological Inquiry' in: *Perspectives on Science and Christian Faith* 58 (1): 68-73.

Fergusson, D. 'Natural Theology after Darwin' in: Robinson, A. (ed.). 2012. *Darwinism and Natural Theology. Evolving Perspectives*. Cambridge Scholar Publishing, Newcastle upon Tyne: 78-95.

Fergusson, D. 2014. *Creation*. Wm. B. Eerdmans, Grand Rapids.

Fergusson, D. 2018. *The Providence of God. A Polyphonic Approach*. Cambridge University Press, Cambridge.

Fincham, K., Taylor, S. 'Episcopalian Identity, 1640–1662' in: Milton, A. (ed.). 2019. *The Oxford History of Anglicanism. Volume 1. Reformation and Identity*. Oxford University Press, Oxford: 455-482.

Fitzpatrick, S. 2017. 'Animal Morality: What Is the Debate about?' in: *Philosophy and Biology* 32 (6): 1151-1183.

Flack, J.C., Waal, F.B.M. de. 2000. ''Any Animal Whatever'. Darwinian Building Blocks of Morality in Monkeys and Apes' in: *Journal of Consciousness Studies* 7 (1-2): 1-29.

Flasch, K. 2004. *Eva und Adam. Wandlungen eines Mythos*. Verlag C.H. Beck, München.

Flipse, A. 2014. *Christelijke Wetenschap. Nederlandse Rooms-Katholieken en Gereformeerden over de Natuurwetenschap, 1880–1940*. PhD Thesis, Vrije Universiteit, Amsterdam.

Force, J.E., Popkin, R.H. (eds). 1994. *The Books of Nature and Scripture: Recent Essays on Natural Philosophy, Theology, and Biblical Criticism in the Netherlands of Spinoza's Time and the British Isles of Newton's Time*. Kluwer Academic Publishers, Dordrecht.

Franco, N.H. 2013. 'Animal Experiments in Biomedical Research: a Historical Perspective' in: *Animals* 3: 238-273.

Fraser, K.J. 1994. 'John Hill and the Royal Society in the Eighteenth Century' in: *Notes and Records of the Royal Society of London* 48 (1): 43-67.

Fraser, L.J. 2015. 'The Secret Sympathy: New Atheism, Protestant Fundamentalism, and Evolution' in: *Open Theology* 1: 445-454.

Fuller, M., Evers, D. et al. (eds). 2020. *Issues in Science and Theology: Nature— and Beyond. Transcendence and Immanence in Science and Theology.* Springer, Cham.

Fyfe, A. 1997. 'The Reception of William Paley's Natural Theology in the University of Cambridge' in: *The British Journal for the History of Science* 30: 321-335.

Garvey, J. 2019. *God's Good Earth. The Case for an Unfallen Creation.* Cascade Books, Eugene.

Gascoigne, J. 1988. 'From Bentley to the Victorians: the Rise and Fall of British Newtonian Natural Theology' in: *Science in Context* 2 (2): 219-256.

Gayon, J. 'From Darwin to Today in Evolutionary Biology' in: Hodge, J., Radick, G. (eds). 2009. *The Cambridge Companion to Darwin. Second Edition.* Cambridge University Press, Cambridge: 277-301.

Geach, P. 1977. *Providence and Evil. The Stanton Lectures 1971–2.* Cambridge University Press, Cambridge.

Gillespie, N.C. 1987. 'Natural History, Natural Theology, and Social Order: John Ray and the "Newtonian Ideology"' in: *Journal of the History of Biology* 20 (1): 1-49.

Gillespie, N.C. 1990. 'Divine Design and the Industrial Revolution: William Paley's Abortive Reform of Natural Theology' in: *Isis* 81 (2): 214-229.

Gillispie, C.C. 1959. *Genesis and Geology. A Study in the Relations of Scientific Thought, Natural Theology, and Social Opinion in Great Britain, 1790–1850.* Harper & Row, New York.

Gilmour, M.J. 2014. *Eden's Other Residents. The Bible and Animals.* Cascade Books, Eugene.

Glass, B. 'Heredity and Variation in the Eighteenth Century Concept of the Species' in: Glass, B., Temkin, O., Straus Jr, W.L. (eds). 1968. *Forerunners of Darwin: 1745–1859.* The Johns Hopkins Press, Baltimore: 164-170.

Glass, B., Temkin, O., Straus Jr, W.L. (eds). 1968. *Forerunners of Darwin: 1745–1859.* The Johns Hopkins Press, Baltimore.

Gliboff, S. 2000. 'Paley's Design Argument as an Inference to the Best Explanation, or, Dawkins' Dilemma' in: *Studies in History and Philosophy of Biological and Biomedical Sciences* 31 (4): 579–597.

Goodwin, G. 2011. 'Emes, Thomas' in: *Dictionary of National Biography, 1885-1900. Volume 17.*

Goris, H., Hennecke, S. (eds). 2005. *Adam en Eva in het Paradijs. Actuele Visies op Man en Vrouw uit 2000 Jaar Christelijke Theologie* [Utrechtse Studies, 7]. Meinema, Zoetermeer.

Gould, S.J. 1977. *Ontogeny and Phylogeny*. The Belknap Press of Harvard University Press, Cambridge (MA).

Gould, S.J. 1982. 'Nonmoral Nature' in: *Natural History* 91 (2): 19-26. Republished in Gould, S. J. 1983. *Hen's Teeth and Horse's Toes. Further Reflections in Natural History*. W.W. Norton & Company, New York: 32-45.

Gould, S.J. 1983. *Hen's Teeth and Horse's Toes. Further Reflections in Natural History*. W.W. Norton & Company, New York.

Gould, S.J. 1991. *Time's Arrow, Time's Cycle. Myth and Metaphor in the Discovery of Geological Time*. Penguin Books, London.

Gould, S.J. 'Darwin and Paley Meet the Invisible Hand' in: Gould, S.J. 1993. *Eight Little Piggies. Reflections in Natural History*. W.W. Norton & Company, New York: 138-152.

Gould, S.J. 1993. *Eight Little Piggies. Reflections in Natural History*. W.W. Norton & Company, New York.

Gračanin, A., Bylsma, L.M., Vingerhoets, A.J.J.M. 2018. 'Why only Humans Shed Emotional Tears. Evolutionary and Cultural Perspectives' in: *Human Nature* 29: 104-133.

Grant, E. 2000. 'God and Natural Philosophy: the Late Middle Ages and Sir Isaac Newton' in: *Early Science and Medicine* 5 (3): 279-298.

Grant, R.M. 1947. 'Theophilus of Antioch to Autolycus' in: *The Harvard Theological Review* 40 (4): 227- 256.

Grant, R.M. 1999. *Early Christians & Animals*. Routledge, London.

Greenblatt, S. 2017. *The Rise and Fall of Adam and Eve*. W.W. Norton & Company, New York.

Greene, J.C. 1959. 'Darwin and Religion' in: *Proceedings of the American Philosophical Society* 103 (5): 716-725.

Greene, J.C. 1961. *The Death of Adam. Evolution and Its Impact on Western Thought*. The New American Library, New York.

Greene, M.T. 'Genesis and Geology Revisited: the Order of Nature and the Nature of Order in Nineteenth-Century Britain' in: Lindberg, D.C., Numbers, R.L. (eds). 2003. *When Science & Christianity Meet*. The University of Chicago Press, Chicago: 139-159.

Gregory, F. 'The Impact of Darwinian Evolution on Protestant Theology in the Nineteenth Century' in: Lindberg, D.C., Numbers, R.L. (eds). 1986. *God & Nature. Historical Essays on the Encounter between Christianity and Science*. University of California Press, Berkeley: 369-390.

Gregory, N.G. 2004. *Physiology and Behaviour of Animal Suffering*. Blackwell, Oxford.

Groh, D. 'The Emergence of Creation Theology. The Doctrine of the Book of Nature in the Early Church Fathers in the East and the West up to Augustine' in: Vanderjagt, A., Berkel, K. van. (eds). 2005. *The Book of Nature in Antiquity and the Middle Ages*. Peeters, Leuven: 21-34.

Grosart, A.B. 'Berrow, Capel' in: *Dictionary of National Biography, 1885-1900, Volume 04*.

Guerrini, A. 1989. 'The Ethics of Animal Experimentation in Seventeenth-Century England' in: *Journal of the History of Ideas* 50 (3): 391-407.

Guerrini, A. 2003. *Experimenting with Humans and Animals. From Galen to Animal Rights*. The Johns Hopkins University Press, Baltimore.

Guerrini, A. 'Natural History, Natural Philosophy, and Animals, 1600–1800' in: Senior, M. (ed.). 2007. *A Cultural History of Animals in the Age of Enlightenment*. Berg, Oxford: 121-144.

Guralnick, S.M. 1972. 'Geology and Religion before Darwin: the Case of Edward Hitchcock, Theologian and Geologist (1793–1864)' in: *Isis* 63 (4): 529-543.

Haas, J.W. 1979. 'The Christian View of Science and Scripture' in: *Journal of the American Scientific Affiliation* 31 (4): 177.

Haber, F.C. 'Fossils and the Idea of a Process of Time in Natural History' in: Glass, B., Temkin, O., Straus Jr, W.L. (eds). 1968. *Forerunners of Darwin: 1745-1859*. The Johns Hopkins Press, Baltimore: 222-261.

Harris, M. 2013. *The Nature of Creation. Examining the Bible and Science*. Routledge, Abingdon.

Harrison, B. 1973. 'Animals and the State in Nineteenth-Century England' in: *The English Historical Review* 88 (349): 786-820.

Harrison, P. 1989. 'Theodicy and Animal Pain' in: *Philosophy* 64 (247): 79-92.

Harrison, P. 1991. 'Do Animals Feel Pain?' in: *Philosophy* 66 (255): 25-40.

Harrison, P. 1992. 'Descartes on Animals' in: *The Philosophical Quarterly* 42 (167): 219-227.

Harrison, P. 1993. 'Animal Souls, Metempsychosis, and Theodicy in Seventeenth-Century English Thought' in: *Journal of the History of Philosophy* 31: 519-544.

Harrison, P. 1998. *The Bible, Protestantism, and the Rise of Natural Science*. Cambridge University Press, Cambridge.

Harrison, P. 1998. 'The Virtues of Animals in Seventeenth-Century Thought' in: *Journal of the History of Ideas* 59 (3): 463-484.

Harrison, P. 1999. 'Subduing the Earth: Genesis 1, Early Modern Science, and the Exploitation of Nature' in: *The Journal of Religion* 79: 86-109.

Harrison, P. '"The Book of Nature" and Early Modern Science' in: Berkel, K. van, Vanderjagt, A., (eds). 2006. *The Book of Nature in Early Modern and Modern History*. Peeters, Leuven: 1-26.

Harrison, P. 2007. *The Fall of Man and the Foundations of Science.* Cambridge University Press, Cambridge.
Harrison, P. 'The Cultural Authority of Natural History in Early Modern Europe' in: Alexander, D.R., Numbers, R.L. (eds). 2010. *Biology and Ideology. From Descartes to Dawkins.* The University of Chicago Press, Chicago: 11-35.
Harrison, P. 2015. *The Territories of Science and Religion.* The University of Chicago Press, Chicago.
Hart, D.B. 2005. 'Tsunami and Theodicy' in: *First Things.* https://www.firstthings.com/article/2005/03/tsunami-and-theodicy. Accessed on 14 December 2021.
Harth, P. 1969. 'The Satiric Purpose of The Fable of the Bees' in: *Eighteenth-Century Studies* 2 (4): 321-340.
Hatch, R.B. 1975. 'William Smellie: Philosopher of Natural History' in: *Studies in Scottish Literature* 12 (3): 159-180.
Haught, J.F. 2005. 'The Boyle Lecture 2003: Darwin, Design and the Promise of Nature' in: *Science & Christian Belief* 17 (1): 5-20.
Hausoul, R.R. 2019. *Gods Toekomst voor de Dieren.* KokBoekencentrum Uitgevers, Utrecht.
Heide, J. van der. 2006. 'Darwin's Young Admirers' in: *Endeavour* 30 (3): 103-107.
Helmstadter, R.J., Lightman, B. (eds). 1990. *Victorian Faith in Crisis. Essays on Continuity and Change in Nineteenth-Century Religious Belief.* Stanford University Press, Stanford.
Henning, B.D. (ed.). 1983. 'Gott, Samuel (1614-71)' in: *The History of Parliament: the House of Commons.* Boydell and Brewer, Martlesham.
Hepburn, R.W. 1955. 'George Hakewill: the Virility of Nature' in: *Journal of the History of Ideas* 16 (2): 135-150.
Hess, P.M.J. 'Evolution, Suffering, and the God of Hope in Roman Catholic Thought after Darwin' in: Bennett, G, Hewlett, M.J., Peters, T., Russell, R.J. (eds). 2008. *The Evolution of Evil.* Vandenhoeck & Ruprecht, Göttingen: 234-254.
Hick, J. 1968 [1966]. *Evil and the God of Love.* Collins, London.
Hiestand, G. 2018. 'A More Modest Adam: an Exploration of Irenaeus' Anthropology in Light of the Darwinian Account of Pre-Fall Death' in: *Bulletin of Ecclesial Theology* 5 (1): 55-72.
Hiestand, G. 2019. '"And Behold It Was Very Good": St. Irenaeus' Doctrine of Creation' in: *Bulletin of Ecclesial Theology* 6 (1): 1-27.
Hodge, J., Radick, G. (eds). 2009. *The Cambridge Companion to Darwin.* Second Edition. Cambridge University Press, Cambridge.
Hofsten, N. von. 1936. 'Ideas of Creation and Spontaneous Generation Prior to Darwin' in: *Isis* 25 (1): 80-94.

Hoggard Creegan, N. 2013. *Animal Suffering & the Problem of Evil.* Oxford University Press, Oxford.
Hoggard Creegan, N. 2018. 'Theodicy: a Response to Christopher Southgate' in: *Zygon* 53 (3): 808-820.
Holder, R.D. 'Natural Theology in the Twentieth Century' in: Manning, R.R. (ed.). 2013. *The Oxford Handbook of Natural Theology.* Oxford University Press, Oxford: 118-134.
Holder, R.D. 2016. *Natural Theology. Faraday Paper 19.* The Faraday Institute for Science and Religion, Cambridge.
Hooykaas, R. 1959. *Natural Law and Divine Miracle. A Historical-Critical Study of the Principle of Uniformity in Geology, Biology and Theology.* E.J. Brill, Leiden.
Hough, G. 1947. 'The Natural Theology of In Memoriam' in: *The Review of English Studies* 23 (91): 244-256.
Huff, P. 1992. 'From Dragons to Worms: Animals and the Subversion of Hierarchy in Augustine's Theology' in: *Melita Theologica* 43 (2): 27-43.
Huff, P.A. 1999. 'Calvin and the Beasts: Animals in John Calvin's Theological Discourse' in: *Journal of the Evangelical Theological Society* 42 (1): 67-75.
Hull, D.L. 1991. 'The God of the Galápagos, Review of *Darwin on Trial* by Philip E. Johnson' in: *Nature* 352: 485-486.
Hull, D.L. 'Darwin's Science and Victorian Philosophy of Science' in: Hodge, J., Radick, G. (eds). 2009. *The Cambridge Companion to Darwin. Second Edition.* Cambridge University Press, Cambridge: 173-196.
Hunter, C.G. 2001. *Darwin's God: Evolution and the Problem of Evil.* Brazos Press, Grand Rapids.
Hurlbutt III, R.J. 1956. 'David Hume and Scientific Theism' in: *Journal of the History of Ideas* 17 (4): 486-497.
Hutton, S. 'More, Newton, and the Language of Biblical Prophecy' in: Force, J.E., Popkin, R.H. (eds). 1994. *The Books of Nature and Scripture: Recent Essays on Natural Philosophy, Theology, and Biblical Criticism in the Netherlands of Spinoza's Time and the British Isles of Newton's Time.* Kluwer Academic Publishers, Dordrecht: 39-53.
Ickert, S. 'Luther and Animals: Subject to Adam's Fall?' in: Linzey, A., Yamamoto, D. (eds). 1998. *Animals on the Agenda. Questions about Animals for Theology and Ethics.* University of Illinois Press, Urbana: 90-99, 269n5.
Iliffe, R. '"Making a Shew": Apocalyptic Hermeneutics and the Sociology of Christian Idolatry in the Work of Isaac Newton and Henry More' in: Force, J.E., Popkin, R.H. (eds). 1994. *The Books of Nature and Scripture: Recent Essays on Natural Philosophy, Theology and Biblical*

Criticism in the Netherlands of Spinoza's Time and the British Isles of Newton's Time. Kluwer Academic Publishers, Dordrecht: 55-88.

Israel, J.I. 2001. *Radical Enlightenment. Philosophy and the Making of Modernity 1650–1750*. Oxford University Press, Oxford.

Jacyna, L.S. 1983. 'Immanence or Transcendence: Theories of Life and Organization in Britain, 1790–1835' in: *Isis* 74 (3): 310-329.

Jaeger, L. 'The Twin Truths of Divine Immanence and Transcendence: Creation, Laws of Nature and Human Freedom' in: Fuller, M., Evers, D. et al. (eds). 2020. *Issues in Science and Theology: Nature—and Beyond. Transcendence and Immanence in Science and Theology*. Springer, Cham: 41-56.

James, W.P. 1885. 'On Pessimism, and Its Modern Champions' in: *Journal of the Transactions of the Victoria Institute or Philosophical Society of Great Britain* 18: 228-252.

Johnson, D. 2015. *God Is Watching You. How the Fear of God Makes Us Human*. Oxford University Press, New York.

Johnson, D., Behring, J.M. 2006. 'Hand of God, Mind of Man: Punishment and Cognition in the Evolution of Cooperation' in: *Evolutionary Psychology* (4): 219-233.

Johnson, E.A. 2014. *Ask the Beasts. Darwin and the God of Love*. Bloomsbury, London.

Jones, R.F. 1961. *Ancients and Moderns. A Study of the Rise of the Scientific Movement in Seventeenth-Century England. Second Edition with an Index, New Preface, and Minor Revisions*. Washington University Studies, St. Louis.

Jones, R.H. 2012. *For the Glory of God. The Role of Christianity in the Rise and Development of Modern Science. Volume II: The History of Christian Ideas and Control Beliefs in Science*. University Press of America, Lanham.

Jordan, D.S. "Louis Agassiz". *Encyclopedia Britannica*, 10 Dec. 2021, https://www.britannica.com/biography/Louis-Agassiz. Accessed 14 December 2021.

Jorink, E. 2010. *Reading the Book of Nature in the Dutch Golden Age, 1575–1715*. Brill, Leiden.

Joyce, R. 2014. 'The Origins of Moral Judgment' in: *Behaviour* 151 (2-3): 261-278.

Kaldas, S. 2015. 'Descartes versus Cudworth on the Moral Worth of Animals' in: *Philosophy Now. A Magazine of Ideas* 108: 28-31.

Kalof, L. 2007. *Looking at Animals in Human History*. Reaktion Books, London.

Kalof, L. (ed.). 2007. *A Cultural History of Animals in Antiquity*. Berg, Oxford.

Kenny, A. 2015. 'Peter Thomas Geach, 1916–2013' in: *Biographical Memoirs of Fellows of the British Academy* 14: 185–203.

Kete, K. (ed.). 2007. *A Cultural History of Animals in the Age of Empire*. Berg, Oxford.

Kishlansky, M. 1997. *A Monarchy Transformed. Britain 1603–1714*. Penguin Books, London.

Kitcher, P. 2007. *Living with Darwin. Evolution, Design, and the Future of Faith*. Oxford University Press, New York.

Kitcher, P. 2014. 'Is a Naturalized Ethics Possible?' in: *Behaviour* 151 (2-3): 245-260.

Kofoid, C.A. 1938. 'Francis Orpen Morris: Ornithologist and Anti-Darwinist' in: *The Auk* 55 (3): 496-500.

Kohn, D. 1989. 'Darwin's Ambiguity: the Secularization of Biological Meaning' in: *The British Journal for the History of Science* 22 (2): 215-239.

Korsgaard, C.M. 'Morality and the Distinctiveness of Human Action' in: Macedo, S., Ober, J. (eds). 2006. *Primates and Philosophers. How Morality Evolved*. Princeton University Press, Princeton: 98-119.

LaCocque, A. 2006. *The Trial of Innocence. Adam, Eve, and the Yahwist*. Cascade Books, Eugene.

Ladner, G.B. 1958. 'The Philosophical Anthropology of Saint Gregory of Nyssa' in: *Dumbarton Oaks Papers* 12: 59-94.

Ladouceur, P. 2013. 'Evolution and Genesis 2–3: the Decline and Fall of Adam and Eve' in: *St. Vladimir's Theological Quarterly* 57 (1): 135-176.

Lake, P. '"Puritans" and "Anglicans" in the History of the Post-Reformation English Church' in: Milton, A. (ed.). 2019. *The Oxford History of Anglicanism. Volume 1. Reformation and Identity*. Oxford University Press, Oxford: 352-379.

Lamoureux, D.O. 2012. 'Darwinian Theological Insights: toward an Intellectually Fulfilled Christian Theism – Part I. Divine Creative Action and Intelligent Design in Nature' in: *Perspectives on Science and Christian Faith* 64 (2): 108-119.

Lamoureux, D.O. 2012. 'Darwinian Theological Insights: toward an Intellectually Fulfilled Christian Theism – Part II. Evolutionary Theodicy and Evolutionary Psychology' in: *Perspectives on Science and Christian Faith* 64 (3): 166-177.

Lamoureux, D.O. 2020. 'Toward an Evangelical Evolutionary Theodicy' in: *Theology and Science* 18 (1): 12-30.

Lamprecht, S.P. 1926. 'Innate Ideas in the Cambridge Platonists' in: *The Philosophical Review* 35 (6): 553-573.

Lane, A.N.S. 'Irenaeus on the Fall and Original Sin' in: Berry, R.J., Noble, T.A. (eds). 2009. *Darwin, Creation and the Fall. Theological Challenges*. Apollos, Nottingham: 130-148.

Lane, B.C. 2011. *Ravished by Beauty. The Surprising Legacy of Reformed Spirituality.* Oxford University Press, New York.

Lane Fox, R. 1986. *Pagans and Christians.* Viking, Harmondsworth.

Langdon-Brown, W. 1941. 'David Hartley: Physician and Philosopher (1705-1757)' in: *Proceedings of the Royal Society of Medicine* 34 (5): 233-239.

Largent, M.A. 2009. 'The So-Called Eclipse of Darwinism' in: *Transactions of the American Philosophical Society, New Series* 99 (1): 3-21.

Larson, E.J. 'The Scopes Trial in History and Legend' in: Lindberg, D.C., Numbers, R.L. (eds). 2003. *When Science & Christianity Meet.* The University of Chicago Press, Chicago: 245-264.

LeDoux, J. 2019. *The Deep History of Ourselves. The Four-Billion-Year Story of how We Got Conscious Brains.* Viking, New York.

Lee, S. 'Goodman, Godfrey' in: *Dictionary of National Biography, 1885-1900, Volume 22.*

Leknes, S., Tracey, I. 2008. 'A Common Neurobiology for Pain and Pleasure' in: *Nature Reviews Neuroscience* 9 (4): 314–320.

Lightman, B. 2002. 'Huxley and Scientific Agnosticism: the Strange History of a Failed Rhetorical Strategy' in: *The British Journal for the History of Science* 35 (3): 271-289.

Lightman, B. 2010. 'Darwin and the Popularization of Evolution' in: *Notes & Records of the Royal Society* 64: 5-24.

Lindberg, D.C. 1983. 'Science and the Early Christian Church' in: *Isis* 74 (4): 509-530.

Lindberg, D.C., Numbers, R.L. (eds). 1986. *God & Nature. Historical Essays on the Encounter between Christianity and Science.* University of California Press, Berkeley.

Lindberg, D.C., Numbers, R.L. (eds). 2003. *When Science & Christianity Meet.* The University of Chicago Press, Chicago.

Linden, C. ter. 2013. *Wat Doe Ik hier in GODSNAAM? Een Zoektocht.* Uitgeverij De Arbeiderspers, Utrecht.

Linzey, A., Yamamoto, D. (eds). 1998. *Animals on the Agenda. Questions about Animals for Theology and Ethics.* University of Illinois Press, Urbana.

Linzey, A. 'Is Christianity Irredeemably Speciesist?' in: Linzey, A., Yamamoto, D. (eds). 1998. *Animals on the Agenda. Questions about Animals for Theology and Ethics.* University of Illinois Press, Urbana: xi-xx.

Lippincott, K. (ed.). 1999. *The Story of Time.* Merrell Holberton, London.

Livingstone, D.N. 1984. *Darwin's Forgotten Defenders. The Encounter between Evangelical Theology and Evolutionary Thought.* Regent College Publishing, Vancouver.

Livingstone, D.N. 'Situating Evangelical Responses to Evolution' in: Livingstone, D.N., Hart, D.G., Noll, M.A. (eds). 1999. *Evangelicals and Science in Historical Perspective.* Oxford University Press, New York: 193-219.

Livingstone, D.N. 'Re-placing Darwinism and Christianity' in: Lindberg, D.C., Numbers, R.L. (eds). 2003. *When Science & Christianity Meet.* The University of Chicago Press, Chicago: 183-202.

Livingstone, D.N. 2014. *Dealing with Darwin, Place, Politics, and Rhetoric in Religious Engagements with Evolution. The Gifford Lectures, 2014.* Johns Hopkins University Press, Baltimore.

Livingstone, D.N., Hart, D.G., Noll, M.A. (eds). 1999. *Evangelicals and Science in Historical Perspective.* Oxford University Press, New York.

Lloyd, M. 'Are Animals Fallen?' in: Linzey, A., Yamamoto, D. (eds). 1998. *Animals on the Agenda. Questions about Animals for Theology and Ethics.* University of Illinois Press, Urbana: 147-160.

Lloyd, M. 'Theodicy, Fall, and Adam' in: Rosenberg, S.P. (ed.). 2018. *Finding Ourselves After Darwin. Conversations on the Image of God, Original Sin, and the Problem of Evil.* Baker Academic, Grand Rapids: 244-261.

Long, H.S. 1948. 'Plato's Doctrine of Metempsychosis and Its Source' in: *The Classical Weekly* 41 (10): 149-155.

Louth, A. (ed.). 2001. *Ancient Christian Commentary on Scripture. Old Testament I. Genesis 1-11.* InterVarsity Press, Downers Grove.

Lovejoy, A.O. 1904. 'Some Eighteenth Century Evolutionists' in: *Popular Science Monthly* 65: 238-251, 323-340.

Lovejoy, A.O. 1909. 'The Argument for Evolution before 'The Origin of Species" in: *Popular Science Monthly* 75: 499-514, 537-549.

Lovejoy, A.O. 1936. *The Great Chain of Being. A Study of the History of an Idea. The William James Lectures Delivered at Harvard University, 1933.* Harvard University Press, Cambridge (MA).

Lovejoy, A.O., 'The Argument for Organic Evolution before the Origin of Species 1830-1858' in: Glass, B., Temkin, O., Straus Jr, W.L. (eds). 1968. *Forerunners of Darwin: 1745-1859.* The Johns Hopkins Press, Baltimore: 356-414.

Lyons, S.L. 1993. 'Thomas Huxley: Fossils, Persistence, and the Argument from Design' in: *Journal of the History of Biology* 26 (3): 545-569.

MacArthur, J. 'Foreword' in: Mortenson, T., Ury, T.H. (eds). 2008. *Coming to Grips with Genesis. Biblical Authority and the Age of the Earth.* Master Books, Green Forest: 9-13.

Macedo, S., Ober, J. (eds). 2006. *Primates and Philosophers. How Morality Evolved.* Princeton University Press, Princeton.

MacIntosh, J.J. 1996. 'Animals, Morality and Robert Boyle' in: *Dialogue* 35 (3): 435-472.

MacKenzie, I.M. 2002. *God's Order and Natural Law. The Works of the Laudian Divines.* Ashgate, Aldershot.

Maddox, R.L. 2007. 'Anticipating the New Creation: Wesleyan Foundations for Holistic Mission in: *The Ashbury Journal* 62 (1): 49-66.

Maddox, R.L. 2009. 'John Wesley's Precedent for Theological Engagement with the Natural Sciences' in: *Wesleyan Theological Journal* 44 (1) 23-54.

Madueme, H., Reeves, M. (eds). 2014. *Adam, the Fall, and Original Sin. Theological, Biblical, and Scientific Perspectives.* Baker Academic, Grand Rapids.

Maehle, A.H. 'Cruelty and Kindness to the 'Brute Creation'. Stability and Change in the Ethics of the Man-Animal Relationship, 1600–1850' in: Manning, A., Serpell, J. (eds). 1994. *Animals and Human Society: Changing Perspectives.* Routledge, London: 86-87.

Mahoney, E.P. 1987. 'Lovejoy and the Hierarchy of Being' in: *Journal of the History of Ideas* 48 (2): 211-230.

Mandelbrote, S. 'Isaac Newton and Thomas Burnet: Biblical Criticism and the Crisis of late Seventeenth-Century England' in: Force J.E., Popkin R.H. (eds). 1994. *The Books of Nature and Scripture. Recent Essays on Natural Philosophy, Theology, and Biblical Criticism in the Netherlands of Spinoza's Time and the British Isles of Newton's Time.* Kluwer Academic Publishers, Dordrecht: 149-178.

Mandelbrote, S. 2007. 'The Uses of Natural Theology in Seventeenth-Century England' in: *Science in Context* 20 (3): 451-480.

Mandelbrote, S. 'Early Modern Natural Theologies' in: Manning, R.R. (ed.). 2013. *The Oxford Handbook of Natural Theology.* Oxford University Press, Oxford: 75-99.

Manning, A., Serpell, J. (eds). 1994. *Animals and Human Society: Changing Perspectives.* Routledge, London.

Manning, R.R. (ed.). 2013. *The Oxford Handbook of Natural Theology.* Oxford University Press, Oxford.

Marques, J.O.A. 2005. 'The Paths of Providence: Voltaire and Rousseau on the Lisbon Earthquake' in: *Cadernos de História e Filosofia da Ciência.* Campinas: CLE_Unicamp, Série 3, v. 15 (1): 33-57.

Marshall, W.W. 2016. *Puritanism and Natural Theology.* Pickwick Publications, Oregon.

Martin, J.M. 1964. 'Joseph LeConte and the Reconciliation of Science and Religion' in: *The Georgia Review* 18 (1): 78-91.

Mashour, G.A., Alkire, M.T. 2013. 'Evolution of Consciousness: Phylogeny, Ontogeny, and Emergence from General Anesthesia' in: *Proceedings of the National Academy of Sciences* 110 (Suppl. 2): 10357-10364.

Matzke, N.J. 2010. 'The Evolution of Creationist Movements' in: *Evolution: Education and Outreach* 3: 145-162.

McClure, M.T. 1934. 'The Greek Conception of Nature' in: *The Philosophical Review* 43 (2): 109-124.

McColley, G. 1938. 'The Ross-Wilkins Controversy' in: *Annals of Science* 3 (2): 153-189.

McDaniel, J.B. 1989. *Of God and Pelicans. A Theology of Reverence for Life*. Westminster/John Knox Press, Louisville.

McDowell, N. 2005. 'Ideas of Creation in the Writings of Richard Overton the Leveller and "Paradise Lost"' in: *Journal of the History of Ideas* 66 (1): 59-78.

McEvoy, J.G. "Joseph Priestley". *Encyclopedia Britannica*, 10 Mar. 2021, https://www.britannica.com/biography/Joseph-Priestley. Accessed 14 December 2021.

McGrath, A.E. 2011. *Darwinism and the Divine. Evolutionary Thought and Natural Theology. The 2009 Hulsean Lectures. University of Cambridge*. Wiley-Blackwell, Chichester.

McGrath, A. 2013. *C.S. Lewis – A Life: Eccentric Genius, Reluctant Prophet*. Thomas Nelson, Nashville.

McGrath, A.E. 2017. *Re-Imagining Nature. The Promise of a Christian Natural Theology*. Wiley Blackwell, Chichester.

McIver, T.A. 1989. *Creationism. Intellectual Origins, Cultural Context, and Theoretical Diversity*. PhD Thesis, University of California, Los Angeles.

McMahon, S. 2000. 'John Ray (1627–1705) and the Act of Uniformity 1662' in: *Notes and Records of the Royal Society of London* 54 (2): 153-178.

Meijering, E. P. 1974. 'God Cosmos History. Christian and Neo-Platonic Views on Divine Revelation' in: *Vigiliae Christianae* 28: 248-276.

Messer, N. 2018. 'Evolution and Theodicy: How (Not) to Do Science and Theology' in: *Zygon* 53 (3): 821-835.

Middleton, T. 2017. 'Objecting to Theodicy and the Legitimacy of Protesting against Evil' in: *Science & Christian Belief* 29 (1): 3-19.

Miles, W. 1949. 'Sir Kenelm Digby, Alchemist, Scholar, Courtier, and Man of Adventure' in: *Chymia* 2: 119-128.

Miller, I. 'Cosmos and Exegesis in Late Antiquity' in: Vanderjagt, A., Berkel, K. van. (eds). 2005. *The Book of Nature in Antiquity and the Middle Ages*. Peeters, Leuven: 57-69.

Miller, K.B. (ed.). 2003. *Perspectives on an Evolving Creation*. Wm. B. Eerdmans, Grand Rapids.

Miller, K.B. 2011. '"And God Saw that It Was Good": Death and Pain in the Created Order' in: *Perspectives on Science and Christian Faith* 63 (2): 85-94.

Millhauser, M. 1954. 'The Scriptural Geologists: an Episode in the History of Opinion' in: *Osiris* 11: 65-86.

Milton, A. (ed.). 2017. *The Oxford History of Anglicanism. Volume I. Reformation and Identity. c.1520-1662.* Oxford University Press, Oxford.

Milton, A. 'Reformation, Identity, and "Anglicanism"' in: Milton, A. (ed.). 2017. *The Oxford History of Anglicanism. Volume I. Reformation and Identity. c.1520-1662.* Oxford University Press, Oxford: 1-25.

Milton, A. 'Unsettled Reformations, 1603-1662' in: Milton, A. (ed.). 2017. *The Oxford History of Anglicanism. Volume I. Reformation and Identity. c.1520-1662.* Oxford University Press, Oxford: 63-83.

Moore, J.R. 1975. 'Evolutionary Theory and Christian Faith: a Bibliographic Guide to the Post-Darwinism Controversies' in: *Christian Scholar's Review* 4 (3): 211-230.

Moore, J.R. 1979. *The Post-Darwinian Controversies. A Study of the Protestant Struggle to Come to Terms with Darwin in Great Britain and America 1870-1900.* Cambridge University Press, Cambridge.

Moore, J.R. 'Geologists and Interpreters of Genesis in the Nineteenth Century' in: Lindberg, D.C., Numbers, R.L. (eds). 1986. *God & Nature. Historical Essays on the Encounter between Christianity and Science.* University of California Press, Berkeley: 322-350.

Moore, J. 1991. 'Deconstructing Darwinism: the Politics of Evolution in the 1860s' in: *Journal of the History of Biology* 24 (3): 353-408.

Morgan, J. 1979. 'Puritanism and Science: a Reinterpretation' in: *The Historical Journal* 22 (3): 535-560.

Morgan, J. 'The Puritan Thesis Revisited' in: Livingstone, D.N., Hart, D.G., Noll, M.A. (eds). 1999. *Evangelicals and Science in Historical Perspective.* Oxford University Press, New York: 43-74.

Morganti, F. 2015. 'Natural Theology and the Origin of Instincts. Debating the Divine Government of Animals in Early Nineteenth Century Britain' in: *Lo Sguardo - Rivista di Filosofia* 18 (II): 167-187.

Morillo, J. 2018. *The Rise of Animals and Descent of Man, 1660-1800. Toward Posthumanism in British Literature between Descartes and Darwin.* University of Delaware Press, Lanham.

Moritz, J.M. 2011. 'The Search for Adam Revisited: Evolution, Biblical Literalism, and the Question of Human Uniqueness' in: *Theology and Science* 9 (4): 367-377.

Moritz, J.M. 2014. 'Animal Suffering, Evolution, and the Origins of Evil: towards a "Free Creatures" Defense' in: *Zygon* 49 (2): 348-380.

Morris, A.D. 1959. '"Sir" John Hill, M.A., M.D. (1706-1775). Apothecary, Botanist, Playwright, Actor, Novelist, Journalist' in: *Proceedings of the Royal Society of Medicine* 53: 55-60.

Morris, H.M. *Evolution and the Bible*. https://www.icr.org/article/53/. Accessed on 14 December 2021.Initially published as Morris, H.M. June 1973. *Evolution and the Bible*. ICR Impact Series No. 5.

Mortenson, T., Ury, T.H. (eds). 2008. *Coming to Grips with Genesis. Biblical Authority and the Age of the Earth*. Master Books, Green Forest.

Mortenson, T. '"Deep Time" and the Church's Compromise: Historical Background' in: Mortenson, T., Ury, T.H. (eds). 2008. *Coming to Grips with Genesis. Biblical Authority and the Age of the Earth*. Master Books, Green Forest: 70-104.

Mortenson, T. (ed.). 2016. *Searching for Adam. Genesis & the Truth about Man's Origin*. Master Books, Green Forest.

Munday Jr, J.C. 1992. 'Creature Mortality: from Creation of the Fall?' in: *Journal of the Evangelical Theological Society* 35 (1): 51-68.

Munday Jr, J.C., 'Animal Pain: Beyond the Threshold?' in: Miller, K.B. (ed.). 2003. *Perspectives on an Evolving Creation*. Wm. B. Eerdmans, Grand Rapids: 435-468.

Muratori, C. 2012. 'Henry More on Human Passions and Animal Souls' in: Ebbersmeyer, S. (ed.). 2012. *Emotional Minds*. De Gruyter, Berlin: 207-224.

Muratori, C. 2017. '"In Human Shape to Become the Very Beast!" – Henry More on Animals' in: *British Journal for the History of Philosophy* 25 (5): 897-915.

Murphy, N., Russell, R.J., Stoeger, W.R. (eds). 2007. *Physics and Cosmology: Scientific Perspectives on the Problem of Natural Evil*. Vatican Observatory and Center for Theology and the Natural Sciences, Vatican City and Berkeley.

Murray, M.J. 2008. *Nature Red in Tooth & Claw: Theism and the Problem of Animal Suffering*. Oxford University Press, Oxford.

Musschenga, A.W. 2015. 'Moral Animals and Moral Responsibility' in: *Les Ateliers de l'Éthique / The Ethics Forum* 10 (2): 38-59.

Nagel, T. 1974. 'What Is It Like to Be a Bat?' in: *The Philosophical Review* 83 (4): 435-450.

Nevin, N.C. (ed.). 2009. *Should Christians Embrace Evolution? Biblical and Scientific Responses*. Inter-Varsity Press, Nottingham.

Newmyer, S.T. 1999. 'Speaking of Beasts: the Stoics and Plutarch on Animal Reason and the Modern Case against Animals' in: *Quaderni Urbinati di Cultura Classica, New Series* 63 (3): 99-110.

Newmyer, S.T. 'Animals in Ancient Philosophy. Conceptions and Misconceptions' in: Kalof, L. (ed.). 2007. *A Cultural History of Animals in Antiquity*. Berg, Oxford: 151-174.

Nicholson, A. 'Robinson, Thomas' in: *Dictionary of National Biography, 1885-1900, Volume 49.*

Niekerk, C.H. 2004. 'Man and Orangutan in Eighteenth-Century Thinking: Retracing the Early History of Dutch and German Anthropology' in: *Monatshefte* 96 (4): 477-502.

Numbers, R.L. 1988. 'George Frederick Wright: from Christian Darwinist to Fundamentalist' in: *Isis* 79 (4): 624-645.

Numbers, R.L. 2006. *The Creationists. From Scientific Creationism to Intelligent Design. Expanded Edition.* Harvard University Press, Cambridge (MA).

Numbers, R.L. (ed.). 2009. *Galileo Goes to Jail and Other Myths about Science and Religion.* Harvard University Press, Cambridge (MA).

O'Connor, R. 2007. 'Young-Earth Creationists in Early Nineteenth-Century Britain? Towards a Reassessment of "Scriptural Geology"' in: *History of Science* 45: 357-403.

O'Halloran, N.W. 2015. 'Cosmic Alienation and the Origin of Evil: Rejecting the "Only Way" Option' in: *Theology and Science* 13 (1): 43-63.

Ophuijsen, J.M. van, 'The Two-Fold Action of Mind in Aristotle's Proto-Book of Nature' in: Vanderjagt, A., Berkel, K. van (eds). 2005. *The Book of Nature in Antiquity and the Middle Ages.* Peeters, Leuven: 1-11.

Osborn, R.E. 2014. *Death before the Fall. Biblical Literalism and the Problem of Animal Suffering.* InterVarsity Press, Downers Grove.

Osborne, C. 2007. 'On the Transmigration of Souls: Reincarnation into Animal Bodies in Pythagoras, Empedocles, and Plato' in: *Dumb Beasts and Dead Philosophers: Humanity and the Humane in Ancient Philosophy and Literature.* Chapter 3. Published to Oxford Scholarship Online: May 2008.

Ospovat, D. 1978. 'Perfect Adaptation and Teleological Explanation: Approaches to the Problem of the History of Life in the Mid-nineteenth Century' in: *Studies in the History of Biology* (2): 33-56.

Ospovat, D. 1980. 'God and Natural Selection: the Darwinian Idea of Design' in: *Journal of the History of Biology* 13 (2): 169-194.

Oster, M.R. 1989. 'The 'Beame of Diuinity': Animal Suffering in the Early Thought of Robert Boyle' in: *The British Journal for the History of Science* 22 (73): 151-179.

O'Sullivan, L. 2009. 'Robert Flint: Theologian, Philosopher of History and Historian of Philosophy' in: *Intellectual History Review* 19 (1): 45-63.

Page, R. 1996. *God and the Web of Creation.* SCM Press Ltd, London.

Palmén, R. 2016. 'The Experience of Beauty: Hugh and Richard of St. Victor on Natural Theology' in: *Journal of Analytic Theology* 4: 234-253.

Palmer, T. 1999. *Controversy. Catastrophism and Evolution. The Ongoing Debate.* Springer, New York.

Palmeri, F. (ed.). 2006. *Humans and Other Animals in Eighteenth-Century British Culture. Representation, Hybridity, Ethics.* Ashgate, Aldershot.

Papazian, M.A. (ed.). 2003. *John Donne and the Protestant Reformation, New Perspectives.* Wayne State University Press, Detroit.

Patrick, J. 2009. 'John Richardson Illingworth and Reason's Romance: the Idealist Apology in Late-Victorian England' in: *Anglican and Episcopal History* 78 (3): 249-278.

Pedlar, J.E. 2013. '"His Mercy Is over All His Works": John Wesley's Mature Vision of New Creation' in: *Canadian Theological Review* 2 (2): 45-56.

Peels, R. 2018. 'Does Evolution Conflict with God's Character?' in: *Modern Theology* 34 (4): 544-564.

Peters, T. 2018. 'Extinction, Natural Evil, and the Cosmic Cross' in: *Zygon* 53 (3): 691-710.

Petto A.J., Godfrey, L.R. (eds). 2007. *Scientists Confront Creationism. Intelligent Design and Beyond.* W.W. Norton & Company, New York.

Phipps, W.E. 1983. 'Darwin and Cambridge Natural Theology' in: *Bios* 54 (4): 218-227.

Pina, M., Gontier, N. (eds). 2014. *The Evolution of Social Communication in Primates. A Multidisciplinary Approach.* Springer International Publishing, Switzerland.

Plantinga, A. 2011. *Where the Conflict Really Lies. Science, Religion, & Naturalism.* Oxford University Press, New York.

Pleins, J.D. 2014. *In Praise of Darwin. George Romanes and the Evolution of a Darwinian Believer.* Bloomsbury, New York.

Poole, W. 2010. 'The Evolution of George Hakewill's Apologie or Declaration of the Power and Providence of God, 1627–1637: Academic Contexts, and Some New Angles from Manuscripts' in: *Electronic British Library Journal* 7:1-32.

Popkin, R.H. 1987. *Isaac la Peyrère (1596–1676). His Life, Work and Influence.* E.J. Brill, Leiden.

Popkin, R.H. 'Spinoza and Bible Scholarship' in: Force, J.E., Popkin R.H. (eds). 1994. *The Books of Nature and Scripture. Recent Essays on Natural Philosophy, Theology, and Biblical Criticism in the Netherlands of Spinoza's Time and the British Isles of Newton's Time.* Kluwer Academic Publishers, Dordrecht: 1-20.

Porter, R. 1977. *The Making of Geology. Earth Science in Britain 1660–1815.* Cambridge University Press, Cambridge.

Porter, R. 2003. *Flesh in the Age of Reason. How the Enlightenment Transformed the Way We See Our Bodies and Souls.* Penguin Books, London.

Povinelli, D.J., Vonk, J. 2003. 'Chimpanzee Minds: Suspiciously Human?' in: *Trends in Cognitive Sciences* 7 (4): 157-160.

Preece, R., Fraser, D. 2000. 'The Status of Animals in Biblical and Christian Thought: a Study in Colliding Values' in: *Society & Animals* 8 (3): 245-263.

Preece, R. 2002. *Awe for the Tiger, Love for the Lamb: a Chronicle of Sensibility to Animals.* Routledge, London.

Preece, R. 2003. 'Darwinism, Christianity, and the Great Vivisection Debate' in: *Journal of the History of Ideas* 64 (3): 399-419.

Preece, R. 2005. *Brute Souls, Happy Beasts, and Evolution. The Historical Status of Animals.* UBC Press, Vancouver.

Pribram, K.H. 1960. 'A Review of Theory in Physiological Psychology' in: *Annual Review of Psychology* 60 (1): 1-40.

Primer, I. 'Introduction' in: Mandeville, B. 1962 [1795] *The Fable of the Bees or Private Vices, Publick Benefits. Newly Edited, with an Introduction by Irwin Primer.* Capricorn Books, New York: 1-17.

Primer, I. 1964. 'Erasmus Darwin's Temple of Nature: Progress, Evolution, and the Eleusinian Mysteries' in: *Journal of the History of Ideas* 25 (1): 58-76.

Proctor, H. 2012. 'Animal Sentience: Where Are We and Where Are We Heading?' in: *Animals* 2: 628-639.

Raber, K. 'From Sheep to Meat, from Pets to People. Animal Domestication 1600-1800' in: Senior, M. (ed.). 2007. *A Cultural History of Animals in the Age of Enlightenment.* Berg, Oxford: 73-99.

Raggio, O. 1958. 'The Myth of Prometheus: Its Survival and Metamorphoses up to the Eighteenth Century' in: *Journal of the Warburg and Courtauld Institutes* 21 (1/2): 44-62.

Randall, C. 2014. *The Wisdom of the Animals: Creatureliness in Early Modern French Spirituality.* University of Notre Dame Press, Notre Dame.

Recarte, C.A. 2014. 'Anti-French Discourse in the Nineteenth-century. British Antivivisection Movement' in: *Atlantis, Journal of the Spanish Association of Anglo-American Studies* 36 (1): 31-49.

Redwood, J.A. 1974. 'Charles Blount (1654–93), Deism, and English Free Thought' in: *Journal of the History of Ideas* 35 (3): 490-498.

Reel, M. 2013. *Between Man and Beast. An Unlikely Explorer, the Evolution Debates, and the African Adventure that Took the Victorian World by Storm.* Doubleday, New York.

Reeves, M., Madueme, H. 'Threads in a Seamless Garment. Original Sin in Systematic Theology' in: Madueme, H., Reeves, M. (eds). 2014. *Adam, the Fall and Original Sin. Theological, Biblical, and Scientific Perspectives*. Baker Academic, Grand Rapids: 209-224.

Richards, R.J. 1987. *Darwin and the Emergence of Evolutionary Theories of Mind and Behavior*. The University of Chicago Press, Chicago.

Richards, R.J. 2000. 'Kant and Blumenbach on the Bildungstrieb: a Historical Misunderstanding' in: *Studies in History and Philosophy of Biological & Biomedical Sciences* 31 (1) 11-32.

Richards, R.J. 2009. 'Darwin's Place in the History of Thought: a Reevaluation' in: *Proceedings National Academy of Sciences* 106 (Suppl. 1): 10056-10060.

Richards, R.J. 'Darwin on Mind, Morals and Emotions' in: Hodge, J., Radick, G. (eds). 2009. *The Cambridge Companion to Darwin. Second Edition*. Cambridge University Press, Cambridge: 96-119.

Richardson, R. 1988. *Death, Dissection and the Destitute*. Penguin Books, London.

Rios, C.M. 2014. *After the Monkey Trial. Evangelical Scientists and a New Creationism*. Fordham University Press, New York.

Ritvo, H. 1987. *The Animal Estate. The English and Other Creatures in the Victorian Age*. Harvard University Press, Cambridge (MA).

Roberts, J.H. 'That Darwin Destroyed Natural Theology' in: Numbers, R.L. (ed.). 2009. *Galileo Goes to Jail and Other Myths about Science and Religion*. Harvard University Press, Cambridge (MA): 161-169.

Roberts, M.B. 2009. 'Adam Sedgwick (1785-1873): Geologist and Evangelical' in: *Geological Society, London, Special Publications* 310: 155-170.

Robinson, A. (ed.). 2012. *Darwinism and Natural Theology. Evolving Perspectives*. Cambridge Scholar Publishing, Newcastle upon Tyne.

Robinson, C.J. 'Edwards, John (1637-1716)' in: *Dictionary of National Biography, 1885-1900, Volume 17*.

Robson, J.M. 'The Fiat and Finger of God: the Bridgewater Treatises' in: Helmstadter, R.J., Lightman, B. (eds). 1990. *Victorian Faith in Crisis. Essays on Continuity and Change in Nineteenth-Century Religious Belief*. Stanford University Press, Stanford: 71-125.

Roe, S.A. 'Biology, Atheism, and Politics in Eighteenth-century France' in: Alexander, D.R., Numbers, R.L. (eds). 2010. *Biology and Ideology. From Descartes to Dawkins*. The University of Chicago Press, Chicago: 36-60.

Roedell, C.A. 2005. *The Beasts that Perish: the Problem of Evil and the Contemplation of the Animal Kingdom in English Thought, c.1660-1839*. PhD Thesis. Georgetown University, Washington, D.C.

Rohr, C.R. von, Burkart, J.M., Schaik, C.P. van. 2011. 'Evolutionary Precursors of Social Norms in Chimpanzees: a New Approach' in: *Biology and Philosophy* 26 (1): 1-30.

Rolston III, H. 2018. 'Redeeming a Cruciform Nature' in: *Zygon* 53 (3): 739-751.

Rose, S. 2011. *Genesis, Creation, and Early Man. The Orthodox Christian Vision.* St. Herman of Alaska Brotherhood, Platina.

Rosenberg, S.P. (ed.). 2018. *Finding Ourselves After Darwin. Conversations on the Image of God, Original Sin, and the Problem of Evil.* Baker Academic, Grand Rapids.

Rosenberg, S.P. 'Can Nature Be "Red in Tooth and Claw" in the Thought of Augustine' in: Rosenberg, S.P. (ed.). 2018. *Finding Ourselves After Darwin. Conversations on the Image of God, Original Sin, and the Problem of Evil.* Baker Academic, Grand Rapids: 226-243.

Rothschild, E. 1994. 'Adam Smith and the Invisible Hand' in: *The American Economic Review* 84 (2). *Papers and Proceedings of the Hundred and Sixth Annual Meeting of the American Economic Association*: 319-322.

Rowe, W.L. 1979. 'The Problem of Evil and Some Varieties of Atheism' in: *American Philosophical Quarterly* 16 (4): 335-341.

Rowlands, M. 'Philosophy and Animals in the Age of Empire' in: Kete, K. (ed.). 2007. *A Cultural History of Animals in the Age of Empire.* Berg, Oxford: 135-152.

Rudrum, A. 1989. 'Henry Vaughan, the Liberation of the Creatures, and Seventeenth-Century English Calvinism' in: *The Seventeenth Century* 4: 33-54.

Rudwick, M.J.S. 'The Shape and Meaning of Earth History' in: Lindberg, D.C., Numbers, R.L. (eds). 1986. *God and Nature: Historical Essays on the Encounter between Christianity and Science.* University of California Press, Berkeley: 296-321.

Rudwick, M.J.S. 'Geologist's Time: a Brief History' in: Lippincott, K. (ed.). 1999. *The Story of Time.* Merrel Holberton, London: 1-7.

Rudwick, M.J.S. 2004. *The New Science of Geology. Studies in the Earth Sciences in the Age of Revolution.* Ashgate, Aldershot.

Rudwick, M.J.S. 2005. *Bursting the Limits of Time. The Reconstruction of Geohistory in the Age of Revolution.* The University of Chicago Press, Chicago.

Rudwick, M.J.S. 2008. *Worlds before Adam. The Reconstruction of Geohistory in the Age of Reform.* The University of Chicago Press, Chicago.

Ruse, M. 1998. 'Darwinism and Atheism: Different Sides of the Same Coin?' in: *Endeavour* 22 (1): 17-20.

Ruse, M. 'Belief in God in a Darwinian Age' in: Hodge, J., Radick, G. (eds). 2009. *The Cambridge Companion to Darwin. Second Edition.* Cambridge University Press, Cambridge: 368-389.

Ruse, M. 'Natural Theology: the Biological Sciences' in: Manning, R.R. (ed.). 2013. *The Oxford Handbook of Natural Theology.* Oxford University Press, Oxford: 397-417.

Russel, R.J. 'The Groaning of Creation. Does God Suffer with All Life?' in: Bennett, G., Hewlett, M.J., Peters T., Russell, R.J. (eds). 2008. *The Evolution of Evil.* Vandenhoeck & Ruprecht, Göttingen: 120-140.

Sailor, D.B. 1962. 'Cudworth and Descartes' in: *Journal of the History of Ideas* 23 (1): 133-140.

Schneider, J.R. 2010. 'Recent Genetic Science and Christian Theology on Human Origins: an "Aesthetic Supralapsarianism"' in: *Perspectives on Science and Christian Faith* 6 (3): 196-213.

Schneider, J.R. 2020. *Animal Suffering and the Darwinian Problem of Evil.* Cambridge University Press, Cambridge.

Schwartz, J.S. 1995. 'George John Romanes's Defense of Darwinism: the Correspondence of Charles Darwin and His Chief Disciple' in: *Journal of the History of Biology* 28 (2): 281-316.

Scott, M.S.M. 2012. *Journey Back to God. Origen on the Problem of Evil.* Oxford University Press, Oxford.

Sebastiani, S. 2019. 'A 'Monster with Human Visage': the Orangutan, Savagery, and the Borders of Humanity in the Global Enlightenment' in: *History of the Human Sciences* 32 (4): 80-99.

Secord, J.A. 2003. *Victorian Sensation. The Extraordinary Publication, Reception, and Secret Authorship of Vestiges of the Natural History of Creation.* The University of Chicago Press, Chicago.

Sellin, P.R. '"Souldiers of One Army". John Donne and the Army of the States General as an International Protestant Crossroads, 1595–1625' in: Papazian, M.A. (ed.). 2003. *John Donne and the Protestant Reformation, New Perspectives.* Wayne State University Press, Detroit: 143-192.

Senior, M. (ed.). 2007. *A Cultural History of Animals in the Age of Enlightenment.* Berg, Oxford.

Senior, M. 'The Souls of Men and Beasts, 1630-1764' in: Senior, M. (ed.). 2007. *A Cultural History of Animals in the Age of Enlightenment.* Berg, Oxford: 23-45.

Shagan, E.H. 2018. *The Birth of Modern Belief. Faith and Judgment from the Middle Ages to the Enlightenment.* Princeton University Press, Princeton.

Shanahan, T. 2000. 'Evolutionary Progress?' in: *Bioscience* 50 (5): 451-459.

Shelley, M. 2016 [1818]. *Frankenstein, or the Modern Prometheus. Edited, Annotated, and Illustrated by M. Grant Kellermeyer. The Third Edition.* Oldstyle Tales Press, Fort Wayne.

Shelton, J.A. 'Beastly Spectacles in the Ancient Mediterranean World' in: Kalof, L. (ed.). 2007. *A Cultural History of Animals in Antiquity.* Berg, Oxford: 97-126.

Shepherd, H.E. 1893. 'Tennyson's "In Memoriam"' in: *The Sewanee Review* 1 (4): 402-409.

Shugg, W. 1968. 'The Cartesian Beast-Machine in English Literature (1663–1750)' in: *Journal of the History of Ideas* 29 (2): 279-292.

Simmons, M.B. 1995. *Arnobius of Sicca. Religious Conflict and Competition in the Age of Diocletian.* Clarendon Press, Oxford.

Smith, C.R. 1994. 'Chiliasm and Recapitulation in the Theology of Ireneus' in: *Vigiliae Christianae* 48 (4): 313-331.

Smith Jr, H.B. 2007. 'Cosmic and Universal Death from Adam's Fall: an Exegesis of Romans 8:19-23a' in: *Journal of Creation* 21 (1): 75-85.

Smith, Q. 1991. 'An Atheological Argument from Evil Natural Laws' in: *International Journal for Philosophy of Religion* 29 (3): 159-174.

Snoke, D. 2004. 'Why Were Dangerous Animals Created?' in: *Perspectives on Science and Christian Faith* 56 (2): 117-125.

Sollereder, B.N. 2010. 'The Darwin–Gray Exchange' in: *Theology and Science* 8 (4): 417-432.

Sollereder, B.N. 2019. *God, Evolution, and Animal Suffering. Theodicy without a Fall.* Routledge, London.

Sorabji, R. 1993. *Animal Minds and Human Morals. The Origins of the Western Debate.* Cornell University Press, Ithaca.

Southgate, C. 2002. 'God and Evolutionary Evil: Theodicy in the Light of Darwinism' in: *Zygon* 37 (4): 803-824.

Southgate, C. 2008. *The Groaning of Creation. God, Evolution, and the Problem of Evil.* Westminster John Knox Press, Louisville.

Southgate, C. 2011. 'Re-Reading Genesis, John, and Job: a Christian Response to Darwinism' in: *Zygon* 46 (2): 370-396.

Southgate, C. 2014. 'Divine Glory in a Darwinian World' in: *Zygon* 49 (4): 784-807.

Southgate, C. 2015. 'God's Creation Wild and Violent, and Our Care for Other Animals' in: *Perspectives on Science and Christian Faith* 67 (4): 245-253.

Southgate, C. 2018. 'Response with a Select Bibliography' in: *Zygon* 53 (3): 909-930.

Southgate, C. 2018. *Theology in a Suffering World. Glory and Longing.* Cambridge University Press, Cambridge.

Southgate, C. '"Free-Process" and the "Only Way" Arguments' in: Rosenberg, S.P. (ed.). 2018. *Finding Ourselves After Darwin. Conversations on the Image of God, Original Sin, and the Problem of Evil.* Baker Academic, Grand Rapids: 293-305.

Southgate, C. 'Beyond the Disguised Friend: Immanence, Transcendence and Glory in a Darwinian World' in: Fuller, M., Evers, D. et al. (eds). 2020. *Issues in Science and Theology: Nature—and Beyond. Transcendence and Immanence in Science and Theology.* Springer, Cham: 57-68.

Southgate, C., Robinson, A. 'Varieties of Theodicy: an Exploration of Responses to the Problem of Evil Based on a Typology of Good-Harm Analysis' in: Murphy, N., Russell, R.J. Stoeger, W.R. (eds). 2007. *Physics and Cosmology: Scientific Perspectives on the Problem of Natural Evil.* Vatican Observatory and Center for Theology and the Natural Sciences, Vatican City and Berkeley: 67-90.

Spector, B. 1942. 'Sir Charles Bell and the Bridgewater Treatises' in: *Bulletin of the History of Medicine* 12: 314-322.

Spurr, J. 1988. 'Latitudinarianism' and the Restoration Church' in: *The Historical Journal* 31 (1): 61-82.

Srokosz, M, Kolstoe, S. 2016. 'Animal Suffering, the Hard Problem of Consciousness, and a Reflection on why We Should Treat Animals Well' in: *Science & Christian Belief* 28 (1):3-19.

Stambaugh, J. 'Whence Cometh Death? A Biblical Theology of Physical Death and Natural Evil' in: Mortenson, T., Ury, T.H. (eds). 2008. *Coming to Grips with Genesis. Biblical Authority and the Age of the Earth.* Master Books, Green Forest: 373-397.

Stanley, M. 2015. *Huxley's Church & Maxwell's Demon. From Theistic Science to Naturalistic Science.* The University of Chicago Press, Chicago.

Steenberg, M.C. 2008. *Irenaeus on Creation. The Cosmic Christ and the Saga of Redemption.* Brill, Leiden.

Steiner, G. 2005. *Anthropocentrism and Its Discontents. The Moral Status of Animals in the History of Western Philosophy.* University of Pittsburgh Press, Pittsburgh.

Steintrager, J.A. 2001. 'Monstruous Appearances: Hogarth's "Four Stages of Cruelty" and the Paradox of Inhumanity' in: *The Eighteenth Century* 42 (1): 59-82.

Stephen, L. 'Amory, Thomas (1691?-1788)' in: *Dictionary of National Biography, 1885-1900, Volume 01.*

Stephen, L. 'Balguy, Thomas' in: *Dictionary of National Biography, 1885-1900, Volume 03.*

Stiling, R.L. 'Scriptural Geology in America' in: Livingstone, D.N., Hart, D.G., Noll, M.A. (eds). 1999. *Evangelicals and Science in Historical Perspective.* Oxford University Press, New York: 177-192.

Strickland, L. 2013. 'God's Creatures? Divine Nature and the Status of Animals in the Early Modern Beast-Machine Controversy' in: *International Journal of Philosophy and Theology* 74 (4): 291-309.

Strong, R. 'Series Introduction' in: Milton, A. (ed.). 2017. *The Oxford History of Anglicanism. Volume I. Reformation and Identity, c.1520-1662.* Oxford University Press, Oxford: xvii-xxvi.

Suddendorf, T. 2013. *The Gap. The Science of What Separates Us from Other Animals.* Basic Books, New York.

Swinburne, R. 1998. *Providence and the Problem of Evil.* Oxford University Press, Oxford.

Tague, I.H. 2008. 'Dead Pets: Satire and Sentiment in British Elegies and Epitaphs for Animals' in: *Eighteenth-Century Studies* 41 (3): 289-306.

Tallis, R. 2011. *Aping Mankind. Neuromania, Darwinitis and the Misrepresentation of Humanity.* Acumen, Durham.

Tallis, R. 2014. *In Defence of Wonder and Other Philosophical Reflections.* Routledge, London.

Tallis, R. 'Biological Reasons for Being Cheerful?' in: Tallis, R. 2014. *In Defence of Wonder and Other Philosophical Reflections.* Routledge, London: 95-100.

Tanzella-Nitti, G. 2005. 'The Two Books Prior to the Scientific Revolution' in: *Perspectives on Science and Christian Faith* 57 (3): 235-248.

Taylor, Ch. 2018 [2007]. *A Secular Age.* Harvard University Press, Cambridge (MA).

Thomas, K. 1983. *Man and the Natural World. Changing Attitudes in England 1500-1800.* Penguin Books, Harmondsworth.

Thomson, A. 2008. *Bodies of Thought. Science, Religion, and the Soul in the Early Enlightenment.* Oxford University Press, New York.

Thomson, A. 2010. 'Animals, Humans, Machines and Thinking Matter, 1690-1707' in: *Early Science and Medicine* 15 (1/2): 3-37.

Thomson, K. 2005. *Before Darwin. Reconciling God and Nature.* Yale University Press, New Haven.

Tomasello, M. 2018. 'How We Learned to Put Our Fate in one Another's Hand. The Origins of Morality' in: *Scientific American* September: 70-75.

Topham, J. 1992. 'Science and Popular Education in the 1830s: the Role of the "Bridgewater Treatises"' in: *The British Journal for the History of Science* 25 (4): 397-430.

Topham, J.R. 'Science, Natural Theology and Evangelicalism in Early Nineteenth-Century Scotland' in: Livingstone, D.N., Hart, D.G., Noll, M.A. (eds). 1999. *Evangelicals and Science in Historical Perspective.* Oxford University Press, New York: 142-174.

Topham, J.R. 'Biology in the Service of Natural Theology: Paley, Darwin, and the Bridgewater Treatises' in: Alexander, D.R., Numbers, R.L. (eds). 2010. *Biology and Ideology. From Descartes to Dawkins.* The University of Chicago Press, Chicago: 88-113.

Turner, F.M. 1978. 'The Victorian Conflict between Science and Religion: a Professional Dimension' in: *Isis* 69 (3): 356-376.

Turner, F.M. 'The Victorian Crisis of Faith and the Faith that Was Lost' in: Helmstadter, R.J., Lightman, B. (eds). 1990. *Victorian Faith in Crisis. Essays on Continuity and Change in Nineteenth-Century Religious Belief.* Stanford University Press, Stanford: 9-38.

Turner, J. 1980. *Reckoning with the Beast. Animals, Pain, and Humanity in the Victorian Mind.* The Johns Hopkins University Press, Baltimore.

Tyacke, N. 'Puritan Politicians and King James VI and I, 1587–1604.' in: Cogswell, T., Cust, R., Lake, P. (eds). 2002. *Politics, Religion and Popularity in Early Stuart Britain. Essays in Honour of Conrad Russell.* Cambridge University Press, Cambridge: 21-44.

Tyra, S.W. 2019. 'Christ Has Come to Gather together All the Creatures' in: *Journal of Theological Interpretation* 13 (1): 53-75.

Urquhart, J. 1920. *William Honyman Gillespie of Torbanehill. Scottish Metaphysical Theist. Prepared on Behalf of the Trustees of Mrs. Honyman Gillespie of Torbanehill.* T&T Clark, Edinburgh.

Ury, T.H. 2001. *The Evolving Face of God as Creator: Early Nineteenth-Century Traditionalist and Accommodationist Theological Responses in British Religious Thought to Paleonatural Evil in the Fossil Record.* Dissertations. 158. Andrews University, Berrien Springs.

Ury, T.H. 'Luther, Calvin, and Wesley on the Genesis of Natural Evil: Recovering Lost Rubrics for Defending a *Very Good* Creation' in: Mortenson, T., Ury, T.H. (eds). 2008. *Coming to Grips with Genesis. Biblical Authority and the Age of the Earth.* Master Books, Green Forest: 399-423.

Vanderjagt, A., Berkel, K. van. (eds). 2005. *The Book of Nature in Antiquity and the Middle Ages.* Peeters, Leuven.

VanderMolen, R.J. 1973. 'Anglican against Puritan: Ideological Origins During the Marian Exile' in: *Church History* 42 (1): 45-57.

VanderMolen, R.J. 1978. 'Providence as Mystery, Providence as Revelation: Puritan and Anglican Modifications of John Calvin's Doctrine of Providence' in: *Church History* 47 (1): 27-47.

VanDoodewaard, W. 2015. *The Quest for the Historical Adam. Genesis, Hermeneutics, and Human Origins*. Reformation Heritage Books, Grand Rapids.

Vaughan, C.R. (ed.). 1892. *Discussions by Robert L. Dabney. Vol III. Philosophical*. Presbyterian Committee of Publication, Richmond.

Velde, D. te (ed.). 2015. *Synopsis Purioris Theologia. Synopsis of a Purer Theology. Latin Text and English Translation, Volume 1*. Brill, Leiden.

Ventureyra, S. 2015. 'Dembski's Theodicy in Dialogue with Domning and Hellwig's Original Selfishness: a Potentially Fruitful Approach to Understanding the Intersection of Evolution, Sin, Evil and the Fall' in: *The American Journal of Biblical Theology* 16 (39): 1-22.

Vergata, A. 1988. 'Theodicy and Nature's Economy' in: *Nuncius / Istituto e Museo di Storia della Scienza* 3 (1):139-152.

Vermij, R.H. 'Nature in Defense of Scripture. Physico-Theology and Experimental Philosophy in the Work of Bernard Nieuwentijt' in: Berkel, K. van, Vanderjagt, A. (eds). 2006. *The Book of Nature in Early Modern and Modern History*. Peeters, Leuven: 83-96.

Vessey, M. (ed.). 2012. *A Companion to Augustine*. Blackwell, Chichester.

Vian, A.R. 'Edwards, Thomas (1599-1647)' in: *Dictionary of National Biography, 1885-1900, Volume 17*.

Vulikovsky, A. 2007. 'Creation and Genesis: a Historical Survey' in: *Creation Research Society Quarterly* 43: 206-219.

Waal, F. de. 'The Tower of Morality' in: Macedo, S., Ober, J. (eds). 2006. *Primates and Philosophers. How Morality Evolved*. Princeton University Press, Princeton: 161-181.

Waal, F.B.M. de. 2011. 'What Is an Animal Emotion' in: *Annals of the New York Academy of Sciences* 1224: 191-206.

Waal, F.B.M. de. 2013. *The Bonobo and the Atheist. In Search of Humanism among the Primates*. W.W. Norton & Company, New York.

Waal, F.B.M. de. 2014. 'Natural Normativity: the 'Is' and 'Ought' of Animal Behavior' in: *Behaviour* 151 (2-3): 185-204.

Waal, F.B.M. de. 2019. *Mama's Last Hug. Animal Emotions and What They Tell Us about Ourselves*. W.W. Norton & Company, New York.

Watkins, M.G. 'Franck, Richard' in: *Dictionary of National Biography, 1885-1900, Volume 20*.

Watson, R.N. 2014. 'Protestant Animals: Puritan Sects and English Animal-Protection Sentiment, 1550–1650' in: *English Literary History* 81 (4): 1111-1148.

Waytz, A., Cacioppo, J., Epley, N. 2010. 'Who Sees Human? The Stability and Importance of Individual Differences in Anthropomorphism' in: *Perspectives on Psychological Sciences* (3): 219-232.

Webb, S.H. 2010. *The Dome of Eden. A New Solution to the Problem of Creation and Evolution.* Cascade Books, Oregon.

Webster, C. 1969. 'Henry More and Descartes: Some New Sources' in: *The British Journal for the History of Science* 4 (4): 359-377.

Webster, C. 'Puritanism, Separatism, and Science' in: Lindberg, D.C., Numbers, R.L. (eds). 1986. *God & Nature. Historical Essays on the Encounter between Christianity and Science.* University of California Press, Berkeley: 192-217.

Weinberg, C. 2014. '"Ye Shall Know Them by Their Fruits": Evolution, Eschatology, and the Anticommunist Politics of George McCready Price' in: *Church History* 83 (3): 684-722.

Weiss, K.M. 2010. '"Nature, Red in Tooth and Claw", So What?' in: *Evolutionary Anthropology* 19: 41-45.

Wennberg, R. 1991. 'Animal Suffering and the Problem of Evil' in: *Christian Scholar's Review* 21: 120-140.

Wennberg, R.N. 2003. *God, Humans, and Animals. An Invitation to Enlarge Our Moral Universe.* Wm. B. Eerdmans, Grand Rapids.

White Jr, L. 1967. 'The Historical Roots of Our Ecologic Crisis' in: *Science* 155: 1203-1207.

White, P. 2010. 'Darwin's Church' in: *Studies in Church History* 46: 333-352.

Wiertel, D.J. 2017. 'Classical Theism and the Problem of Animal Suffering' in: *Theological Studies* 78: 659-695.

Wildman, W.J. 'Incongruous Goodness, Perilous Beauty, Disconcerting Truth: Ultimate Reality and Suffering in Nature' in: Murphy, N., Russell, R.J., Stoeger, W.R. (eds). 2007. *Physics and Cosmology: Scientific Perspectives on the Problem of Natural Evil.* Vatican Observatory and Center for Theology and the Natural Sciences, Vatican City and Berkeley: 267-294.

Wilkinson, J.F. 'Willet, Andrew' in: *Dictionary of National Biography, 1885-1900, Volume 61.*

Willey, P., Willey, E. 1998. 'Will Animals Be Redeemed' in: Linzey, A., Yamamoto, D. (eds). 1998. *Animals on the Agenda. Questions about Animals for Theology and Ethics.* University of Illinois Press, Urbana: 190-200.

Williams, G.H. 2015. *Christian Attitudes toward Nature.* Wipf & Stock, Eugene. Previously published by *Christian Scholar's Review* 1970-1971.

Williamson, G. 1935. 'Mutability, Decay, and Seventeenth-Century Melancholy' in: *English Literary History* 2 (2): 121-150.

Wise, J.N. 1973. *Sir Thomas Browne's Religio Medici and Two Seventeenth Century Critics.* University of Missouri Press, Columbia.

Wolloch, N. 2019. *The Enlightenment's Animals. Changing Conceptions of Animals in the Long Eighteenth Century.* Amsterdam University Press, Amsterdam.

Wolpoff, M., Caspari, R. 1997. *Race and Human Evolution.* Simon & Schuster, New York.

Wootton, D. 2015. *The Invention of Science. A New History of the Scientific Revolution.* HarperCollins, New York.

Wright, C. 1941. 'The Religion of Geology' in: *The New England Quarterly* 14 (2): 335-358.

Yale, D.E.C. "Sir Matthew Hale". *Encyclopedia Britannica*, 28 Oct. 2021, https://www.britannica.com/biography/Matthew-Hale. Accessed 14 December 2021.

Yamamoto, D. 'Aquinas and Animals: Patrolling the Boundary' in: Linzey, A., Yamamoto, D. (eds). 1998. *Animals on the Agenda. Questions about Animals for Theology and Ethics.* University of Illinois Press, Urbana: 80-89.

Yang, C. 'Gross Metempsychosis and Eastern Soul' in: Palmeri, F. (ed.). 2006. *Humans and Other Animals in Eighteenth-Century British Culture. Representation, Hybridity, Ethics.* Ashgate, Aldershot: 13-30.

Yang, J. 'John Norris' in: Zalta, E.N. (ed.). 2014. *The Stanford Encyclopedia of Philosophy* (Spring 2014 Edition). https://plato.stanford.edu/entries/john-norris/. Accessed on 07 February 2022.

Yarchin, W. 2004. *History of Biblical Interpretation. A Reader.* Hendrickson Publishers, Peabody.

Yeo, R.R. 1986. 'The Principle of Plenitude and Natural Theology in Nineteenth-Century Britain' in: *The British Journal for the History of Science* 19 (3): 263-282.

Young, D.A. 2007. *John Calvin and the Natural World.* University Press of America. Lanham.

Zijlstra, C.P. 2005. *The Rebirth of Descartes: the Nineteenth-Century Reinstatement of Cartesian Metaphysics in France and Germany.* PhD Thesis, University of Groningen, Groningen.

Zimmer, C. 2004. *Soul Made Flesh. The Discovery of the Brain—and How It Changed the World.* Free Press, New York.

Zirkle, C. 1941. 'Natural Selection before the "Origin of Species"' in: *Proceedings of the American Philosophical Society* 84 (1): 71-123.

Zuiddam, B.A. 2014. 'Early Church Fathers on Creation, Death and Eschatology' in: *Journal of Creation* 28: 77-83.

Index of Names

Agassiz	280n, 326
Ambrose	42, 43, 52, 71, 225
Amory	201, 202, 222, 248
Anderson	146n, 199n, 281-283, 298, 302, 374n, 389n
Aquinas	23, 53-56, 63, 68, 71, 73, 93, 101, 111, 132n, 258, 384, 390n, 401
Arnobius	36-38, 69
Athanasius	35, 36, 52
Aristotle	27n, 28, 53, 68, 73
Augustine	23, 28n, 42, 44-50, 52, 60n, 68, 70, 71, 73, 99, 101, 132n, 133, 148, 217n, 379, 401
Balguy	215, 216, 222, 251n
Barnes	335, 336, 377
Bartas	225
Barth	347, 383
Basil	39-42, 52, 68, 70, 128, 400
Baxter	115, 116, 137, 148-150
Bayle	142, 143
Beach	345, 349
Bell	262, 263, 298, 301, 303
Bentham	156n, 220, 221n, 235, 236n
Bentley	94n, 144, 233n
Berrow	202, 203, 222
Blocher	363, 364n
Bochart	138-140
Bonnet	194n, 199, 200
Bougeant	173, 174n, 175, 176, 188, 190, 202, 207, 222
Bowler	22n, 164n, 199n, 234n, 235n, 237n, 241n, 243n, 244n, 293n, 296n, 309n, 310n, 313n, 332n, 333n, 335n, 341n, 345n, 346n, 347n, 351n, 393n, 394n
Boyd	241, 242n

Boyle	125-128, 131, 136, 137, 144, 150, 157, 161n, 358n, 386n, 394n
Brougham	236n, 290
Browne	104-106, 113, 124n, 128, 129, 137, 140
Bruckner	209-211, 222, 225, 254
Buckland	239n, 259-262, 277, 281, 298, 301, 320
Bugg	270-275, 288, 300
Bushnell	336-338, 342, 375
Bryan	320
Calvin	23, 27, 29n, 59, 63-66, 67n, 68, 70-73, 82, 90, 101n, 148, 149n, 201n, 281n, 362, 365, 374, 390n, 401, 405
Chalmers	256-258, 276, 278, 281, 289, 290n, 298, 302, 303, 304n, 317, 330n, 362, 384
Chambers	243n, 244, 312
Charnock	121-123, 137, 141, 149, 150
Charron	113, 142, 145n
Chrysostom	43, 44, 52, 70, 71
Clarke	44n, 50n, 299
Clough	21n, 55n, 62n, 74n, 85n, 243n, 347n, 366, 368, 370n, 371, 375n, 386, 388n, 389n, 390n
Cohen	68n, 112n, 144, 346, 347, 352, 353, 356n, 366n, 391, 393n
Coleridge	235
Corey	360n, 382
Crombie	254-256, 258, 298, 302
Cudworth	119-121, 126, 128, 131, 137, 147, 148, 180
Cuvier	239, 241, 242, 256, 259
Cyril	36, 52, 71
Dabney	275
Dana	287, 288, 298, 300, 301, 331n, 337, 338n, 375
Darwin, Charles	19, 20, 22n, 25, 31n, 32n, 49, 50n, 51n, 74n, 80n, 81n, 86n, 114n, 118n, 127n, 147n, 156n, 160n, 163n, 166n, 168n, 185, 194, 195n, 199n, 219, 227, 229, 233n, 234, 235n, 237n, 238, 241n, 245, 256n, 258n, 259n, 263, 266, 267n, 270, 275, 276, 278n, 282n, 285n, 293-298, 301, 302, 304, 305, 307-326, 327n, 328,

	329n, 330, 331, 335n, 336, 338, 340-347, 348n, 350-359, 361n, 362, 363, 364n, 365n, 367n, 368, 370, 371, 372n, 373n, 375, 377n, 380, 381, 383-387, 388n, 389n, 390-394, 396n, 397, 399, 400, 404, 407-410
Darwin, Erasmus	25, 227, 245-249, 261, 294, 298, 300, 324, 382
Dawkins	18n, 81n, 160n, 233n, 292n, 308, 353n, 360n, 392, 393
Dawson	316-319, 320n
Dean	204-208, 222, 223, 366, 390n
Deane-Drummond	55n, 62n, 370, 378, 389n
Dembski	288, 375, 380n, 387
Derham	24, 166, 167, 177n, 195, 222
Descartes	75, 81n, 84, 86, 87, 106, 109n, 112, 116, 118n, 120, 127, 131, 132n, 142, 144, 156n, 160n, 169, 171, 173, 176, 181, 193, 223, 233n, 246n, 322n, 358, 402
Digby	106, 107, 137, 144
Doedes	295, 421
Domning	367n, 370, 371, 375n, 379n, 380
Donne	76, 77n
Dougherty	360, 388n
Draxe	94-96, 98, 103, 119, 137, 141, 142, 149, 150
Edgar	364
Edwards, John	128-131, 137, 147
Edwards, Thomas	97, 150
Elton	98, 102, 119, 137, 141, 142, 149, 150
Emberger	71n, 377
Emes	131, 132, 137, 144
Etzelmüller	368
Farrar	349
Farrer	381n, 382, 384
Flavel	78
Flint	338
Franck	124, 125, 137
Fry	322, 323
Galilei	84
Garvey	29n, 51n, 55n, 59n, 71n, 359, 360n, 374, 379n, 390n

Geach	364, 365n
Gibbons	90-93, 137, 141
Gillespie	81n, 125n, 127n, 160n, 233n, 235n, 273, 274, 285, 300, 319, 376n
Gisborne	253, 254, 298, 300
Glanvill	83
Gloag	283-285, 298, 301
Godwin	289, 343
Goodman	95, 96, 99, 100, 137, 141, 149, 150, 307n
Gott	116-118, 137, 138, 287, 375
Granger	206
Gray	18n, 185n, 195n, 294n, 296n, 312n, 324-328, 332, 340n
Gregory of Nyssa	41, 42, 48, 52, 68, 70, 400
Griffith-Jones	333-335, 369, 386
Hakewill	99-101, 104, 129, 135, 137, 138, 225n
Harrison	18n, 22n, 29n, 34n, 40n, 41n, 53, 55n, 58n, 59n, 69n, 76n, 78n, 79n, 80n, 81n, 83, 84n, 85n, 86n, 112n, 124n, 132n, 140n, 142n, 147n, 150n, 160n, 174n, 230n, 359, 360n
Hart	83n, 169n, 233n, 235n, 239n, 240n, 246n, 256n, 270n, 278n, 310n, 312n, 396n, 397n
Hartley	181-184, 222, 254
Hellwig	367n, 371, 375n, 380n
Hick	50n, 71n, 341n, 348n, 360n, 374n, 379n, 382, 388n, 390n
Hildrop	175-177, 195, 204, 207, 208n, 222, 223
Hill	44n, 163n, 184-187, 193, 194, 219, 222, 225
Hitchcock	285-287, 298, 300, 337, 338n, 375
Hodges	118, 119, 137, 142, 150
Hoggard Creegan	367, 368, 377
d'Holbach	289, 290, 329, 343
Hooke	163, 294n
Hugh of St. Victor	23, 53, 54, 66n
Hull	356n, 393n
Hume	226, 227, 234, 390n
Hutton	111n, 238
Huxley	243n, 323n, 330n, 332n, 341, 409
Illingworth	328, 329

Index of Names - 487

Ingersoll	344
Irenaeus	23, 27, 30-32, 35, 38, 40, 41, 44, 50, 51n, 52, 70, 71, 149, 374n, 387, 390n, 400
Iverach	330, 332, 333, 341
Jenyns	188-192, 196n, 202, 222
Kant	384n, 385n, 393n
King, David	278
King, William	171-173, 222, 224, 251, 381
Kingsley	321, 330
Kirby	265-269, 272, 282, 288, 290, 291n, 298, 300, 333, 384n, 386
Lactantius	23, 34, 35, 52, 71
Lamoureux	383, 393n
LeConte	326, 327, 332, 338
LeDoux	360, 361n, 372, 389n
Leibniz	172n, 200, 224, 225n
Lewis	336, 348, 360n, 377, 388n, 395n
Livingstone	22n 83n, 233n, 234n, 235n, 239n, 240n, 246n, 256n, 270n, 275n, 278n, 285n, 293n, 297n, 310n, 312n, 316n, 324n, 327n, 331n, 345, 351n, 396n, 397n
Locke	145, 156, 161
Lloyd	335n, 375n, 377
Luther	23, 27, 29n, 59-63, 70-72, 94, 103, 150, 151n, 201n, 374, 390n, 401
Lyell	241, 243n, 316n
Macaulay	104n
Malebranche	132n, 142-144
Mandeville	169-171, 222, 226, 227, 391
Mantell	268-270
McCosh	255, 331, 363, 396
McDaniel	388
McGrath	22n, 80n, 81n, 86n, 114n, 147n, 160, 166n, 168n, 233, 234n, 235n, 249n, 258n, 259n, 295n, 310n, 336n, 347n, 348n, 353n, 392n
Messer	378
Mill	334n, 343, 344, 347
Miller	28n, 30n, 44n, 192n, 278-283, 302, 317, 320n, 330n, 346n, 362, 363n, 382n, 395n

Milton	24, 77, 78, 81n, 82n, 155n, 170, 218, 225n, 274n, 286
Mivart	322, 369
Monod	353
Montaigne	140, 142
Moore	22n, 235n, 236n, 282n, 293n, 309n, 310n, 311n, 317n, 324n, 326n, 327-331, 338, 340n, 348n, 351n, 359n, 363
More	68, 80n, 109-113, 119, 121, 126, 128, 129, 131, 136n, 137, 144n, 147, 148, 180, 184, 194n, 236, 382
Moritz	21n, 366n, 367, 368
Morris, Francis	317-320, 387n
Morris, Henry	309, 348, 349, 356
Murray	47, 51n, 243n, 260n, 293n, 313n, 321n, 328n, 347n, 350n, 359n, 360, 377n, 379n, 382n, 386, 388
Newman	321, 322, 368
Newton	79n, 84, 111n, 129n, 161n, 191, 230n, 296
Nieuwentijt	167-169, 177n, 195, 222, 249n
Norris	132-134, 137, 144, 150
O'Holloran	377
Origen	28n, 34, 203, 204
Overton	97, 137, 149, 150
Owen	63n, 64n, 149n, 303
Page	112n, 171n, 381, 386
Paley	25, 216, 233n, 234, 235n, 236n, 249-255, 257, 267n, 295, 298, 330, 336-338, 344, 392n, 405
Palgrave	157n, 230n, 235, 360n
Parkinson	164, 165, 238
Pascal	340
Pember	319, 376n
Physiologus	23n, 58
Plotinus	111, 112n, 148, 202, 382
Pope	156n, 162, 168, 169n
Porphyry	28
Pratt, John Henry	285
Pratt, Samuel Jackson	206, 207, 222
Price	344, 345, 349
Priestly	213-215, 222

Index of Names - 489

Primatt	211-213, 214n, 221n, 222
Proba	52, 71
Prout	264, 265, 298, 302, 362
Pye-Smith	31n, 276-278, 281, 285, 298, 301, 320, 348
Ramm	
Ramsay	175, 190, 202-204, 222, 224n
Raven	335, 336, 359n, 386
Ray	81, 105, 127, 128, 131, 136, 137, 147, 160, 163-165, 180, 193, 195, 211, 225
Reade	22, 343, 344, 347
Robinson	24, 128n, 129n, 135, 136, 138, 147, 161, 206n, 289n, 293n, 312n, 343n, 347n, 379n
Roget	263, 264, 298, 382
Rolston	382, 389n, 390n
Romanes	5, 327, 338-343
Rothwell	207-209, 222, 390n
Russell	88n, 147n, 345, 346n, 347, 353, 364n, 379n, 388n, 391, 393n
Saluste	see Bartas
Schneider	51n, 357n, 365, 389n
Schopenhauer	231n, 384n, 385n
Sedgwick	244, 245, 275, 276n, 281, 320
Shields	327, 328, 331
Simpson	332-334, 341, 369, 386
Smellie	24, 216-219, 222, 225
Smith	18n, 51n, 151n, 267n, 370n, 374n, 380
Snoke	363, 364
Sollereder	7, 312n, 325n, 347n, 358n, 374n, 377n, 379n, 386, 388n
Southgate	61n, 147n, 298n, 328n, 347n, 353n, 356n, 366, 370, 371n, 373n, 374n, 377n, 379n, 381n, 383, 384n, 388n, 390n
Spurgeon	313, 314
Stanley	235n, 341n, 352n
Suddendorf	372
Swan	97, 225n, 231n, 301n, 384n
Swinburne	360n, 382, 384
Tallis	74n, 361n, 372
Temple	323, 324, 327, 328, 330, 369
Tennant	341, 342, 367, 369, 380
Tennyson	25, 242

Theophilus	23, 32-34, 38, 50, 52, 70, 71, 205, 366, 374n, 400
Toogood	220, 222
Topsell	24, 88-90, 95, 96, 98, 102, 103, 119, 137, 141, 142, 149, 150
Townsend	90n, 318, 319
Ursinus	70
Ury	29n, 72, 201n, 239n, 246n, 270n, 357n, 374n, 391n
Vogt	311, 312
Waal, de	361n, 372, 373n
Waite	107-109, 137, 141, 149, 150, 388n
Walker	101-103, 119, 137, 142, 149, 150, 322n
Wallace	344
Watts	178-180, 184, 222, 280
Webb, Clement Charles Julian	334, 376n
Webb, Stephen H.	377
Wennberg	74n, 364n, 377387n
Wesley	29n, 72n, 175n, 192-201, 222, 223, 234n, 240n, 248, 261, 270n, 390n
Whewell	236n, 243n, 244n, 245, 269n
Whitcomb	309, 348, 349
Wildman	364
Wilkins	79n, 92n, 105n, 113-115, 126, 128, 129, 131, 136, 137, 225, 299
Willet	92-94, 117, 118n, 137, 138, 287, 375
Williams	22n, 53n, 70n, 74n, 84n, 90n, 99n, 106n, 334, 369, 376n
Wimmer	379n, 380
Witty	134, 135, 138
Wood	329, 330
Wright	157, 358n, 287n, 331, 332n, 396
Young	66n, 71n, 272-274, 282, 288, 300

Index of Terms

Anglicans	81-83, 94, 95, 98, 99, 106, 109n, 113n, 115, 118, 119, 128, 132, 144, 150, 171, 181, 192, 202, 206, 215, 235, 244, 253, 265, 270, 285, 293n, 300, 317, 319, 321, 323, 327, 335, 338, 347, 352n, 405
Anthropocentricity	32, 37, 50, 53, 54, 73, 74, 106, 121, 128n, 140, 149, 151, 155, 189, 216, 221, 336, 386, 396n
Atheism	17, 111, 119, 120, 121, 125, 136, 147, 167, 168, 171, 182, 210, 289, 290, 291, 297, 298, 300, 305, 307, 321, 328, 331, 345, 352, 353, 354, 391-394, 408
Bestiaria	23, 56, 69, 71, 90, 124
Calvinism	79n, 95n, 99, 100, 101, 109n, 128, 252, 281, 302, 363, 365n, 409
Cambridge Platonists	82, 109, 112, 119, 121, 126, 128, 131, 150, 151, 184
Cartesianism	112n, 113, 125, 132, 145, 147, 154, 336, 362
Catastrophism	241, 244, 259
Catholicism	96n, 106, 150, 321
Chain of Being	23, 55, 148, 161-163, 165, 184, 185, 199, 255
Commonwealth	82, 104, 149, 160
Creationism	25, 72, 151, 201, 346n, 348, 349n, 396, 408
Darwinism	19, 32n, 219, 229, 276, 305, 309, 310, 312n, 317, 318, 320, 322, 324, 325, 328, 331, 342, 345, 348n, 351-353, 355, 356n, 357, 359, 385n, 386, 387, 396, 397, 407
Deism	134, 246, 260, 328, 391
Design, argument from	147, 148, 154, 158, 162, 167, 171, 226, 235,
Dualism	223, 224, 335, 337
Eden, Garden of	58, 76, 79, 317, 367 (see also Paradise)

Enlightenment	153
Fall, angelic	173, 202, 203, 224, 275, 300, 319, 376, 377, 404, 406
Fall, cosmic	43, 59, 100, 101, 200, 373, 376
Fall, of Adam	40, 43, 44, 51, 60, 62, 69, 70-73, 92, 93, 98, 99, 114, 117, 122, 136, 138, 140, 141, 150, 151, 189, 192, 209, 257, 270, 282, 287, 319, 329, 349, 373, 401-403, 405, 406
Fossils	39n, 115n, 128, 163, 164n, 211, 225, 233, 237, 240, 242, 243, 254, 288, 316, 376404, 405
Gap theory	256, 257n, 311319n
Gnosticism	28, 30, 38, 44, 381
Ichneumon wasp	17, 185-187, 194, 195, 219, 266, 267n, 294, 323, 356,
Latitudinarians	109n, 113, 128, 150, 157,
Legislation to protect animals	211, 229, 230, 231n, 318, 404
Levellers	97, 150
Manichaeism	28, 44, 45
Metempsychosis	174, 188, 190-192
Morality	120, 154, 169, 232, 367, 369, 371, 372, 384n
Omphalism	240
Pain (in animals)	47, 262, 359, 360, 365, 381, 384
Paradise	41, 51n, 78, 93, 105, 126, 173, 177, 197, 209, 246, 261, 273,
Philosophy,	
Platonic	30, 110
Plotinian	121, 148, 151, 171, 183, 184, 192, 195, 198, 209, 251, 262, 281, 284
Pythagorean	30, 120, 188, 191
Stoic	28, 30, 73, 74, 109n, 113n, 140, 180, 191, 208, 215, 225, 251, 284, 409
Physico-theology	81, 114, 128, 150, 151, 160, 166-169, 235, 260
Presbyterians	254, 256, 258, 272, 275, 278, 300, 302, 312, 316, 317, 319, 324, 331, 332, 338, 363, 405
Protectorate	82, 104, 160

Index of Terms - 493

Providence	65, 82, 87, 95, 109, 111, 112, 126, 130, 135, 148, 151, 179, 202, 206, 209, 218, 244, 255, 266, 267, 277, 279, 289, 290, 330n, 344, 365
Puritans	62n, 81-83, 88, 90, 92n, 94n, 97, 98, 101, 102-104, 107, 109, 113, 115, 119, 121-128, 149, 150, 157, 158, 230
Quakers	322
Reformation	21, 29, 59, 67, 225, 400, 401
Restoration	104, 118n, 127, 149, 160,
Scopes' trial	320n
Secularization	392
Teleology	85, 234, 324, 325, 340n, 384
Theism	246, 329, 338, 341, 394, 395, 397, 408
Theodicy	72, 172n, 342, 358, 378, 386, 390, 397, 402
Transmigration of souls	146, 175, 188, 189, 190, 202, 204, 378, 404
Transmutation	164n, 243, 244
Uniformitarianism	241
Utilitarianism	156, 343
Vegetarianism	117, 184
Vivisection	93n, 156, 157, 231, 232, 303, 304, 317, 318, 385, 386n,

Index of Holy Scripture

Old Testament

Genesis 1:24	63n
Genesis 1:28	44, 72n, 386
Genesis 1:30	45, 105n, 114, 131
Genesis 1:31	118, 195
Genesis 6:6	292n
Genesis 9:3	40n, 72, 73n
Judges 12:5–6	350n
Psalm 8:3	80n,
Psalm 19:1	17n, 151n, 288n,
Psalm 73:22	122n
Psalm 104:21	61
Proverbs 12:10	89n, 119
Isaiah 11:6–8	61, 64n, 215, 261n, 284n, 387n
Isaiah 25:6	387n
Isaiah 65:25	61
Joel 1:18,20	88

New Testament

Matthew 10:29	365n
Luke 16:26	313n
John 11:49–52	187n
John 13:7	397n
Romans 1:20	58, 80n
Romans 5:12	261n, 276, 284n, 286n
Romans 5:17–18	261n
Romans 6:23	97
Romans 8:18–22	44n, 61, 64, 90, 93, 94, 98, 107, 148-151, 196, 215, 261n, 273, 284n, 288, 349, 374n
Romans 9:21	208
1 Corinthians 9:9	364n
1 Corinthians 15:21	261n, 276, 286n
1 Corinthians 15:22	97, 178
1 Corinthians 15:55	248

Hebrews 1:3	391n
1 Peter 1:24	105n
2 Peter 3:4	115n